Portfolio Management Under Stress

Portfolio Management Under Stress offers a novel way to apply the well-established Bayesian-net methodology to the important problem of asset allocation under conditions of market distress or, more generally, when an investor believes that a particular scenario (such as the break-up of the Euro) may occur. Employing a coherent and thorough approach, it provides practical guidance on how best to choose an optimal and stable asset allocation in the presence of user-specified scenarios or 'stress conditions'. The authors place causal explanations, rather than association-based measures such as correlations, at the core of their argument, and insights from the theory of choice under ambiguity aversion are invoked to obtain stable allocations results. Step-by-step design guidelines are included to allow readers to grasp the full implementation of the approach, and case studies provide clarification. This insightful book is a key resource for practitioners and research academics in the post-financial-crisis world.

RICCARDO REBONATO is Global Head of Rates and FX Analytics at PIMCO, and a visiting lecturer in Mathematical Finance at Oxford University (OCIAM). He has previously held positions as Head of Risk Management and Head of Derivatives Trading at several major international financial institutions. Dr Rebonato has been on the Board of ISDA (2002–2011), and still serves on the Board of GARP (2001 to present). He is the author of several books on finance and an editor for several journals (*International Journal of Theoretical and Applied Finance, Journal of Risk, Applied Mathematical Finance, Journal of Risk for Financial Institutions*).

ALEXANDER DENEV is a senior team leader in the Risk Models department at the Royal Bank of Scotland. He is specialized in Credit Risk, Regulations, Asset Allocation and Stress Testing, and has previously worked in management roles at European Investment Bank, Société Générale and National Bank of Greece.

'Standard portfolio theory has been shown by recent events to have two major short-comings: it does not deal well with extreme events and it is often based on mechanical statistical procedures rather than modelling of fundamental causal mechanisms. In this book, Rebonato and Denev put forward an interesting approach for dealing with both of these problems. Their method is flexible enough to accommodate individual views of underlying causal mechanisms, but disciplined enough to ensure that decisions do not ignore the data. Anyone with a serious interest in making good portfolio decisions or measuring risk will benefit from reading this book.'

Ian Cooper, Professor of Finance, London Business School

'This book is self-contained in that it covers a lot of familiar but diverse material from a fresh perspective. Its purpose is to take an ambitious new approach to combining this material into a coherent whole. The result is a new methodology for practical portfolio management based on Bayesian nets, which satisfactorily takes into simultaneous account both normal and extreme market conditions. While readers may themselves be under stress in absorbing the details of the new approach, serious fund managers and finance academics will ignore it at their peril.'

M. A. H. Dempster, Emeritus Professor, Department of Mathematics, University of Cambridge; Cambridge Systems Associates Limited

'Rebonato and Denev have demolished the status quo with their radical extension of best-practice portfolio management. The key is to integrate realistic "extreme" scenarios into risk assessment, and they show how to use Bayesian networks to characterize precisely those scenarios. The book is rigorous yet completely practical, and reading it is a pleasure, with the "Rebonato touch" evident throughout.'

Francis X. Diebold, Paul F. and Warren S. Miller Professor of Economics, Professor of Finance and Statistics, and Co-Director, Wharton Financial Institutions Center, University of Pennsylvania

'Here is a book that combines the soundest of theoretical foundations with the clearest practical mindset. This is a rare achievement, delivered by two renowned masters of the craft, true practitioners with an academic mind. Bayesian nets provide a flexible framework to tackle decision making under uncertainty in a post-crisis world. Modeling observations according to causation links, as opposed to mere association, introduces a structure that allows the user to *understand* risk, as opposed to just measuring it. The ability to define scenarios, incorporate subjective views, model exceptional events, etc., in a rigorous manner is extremely satisfactory. I particularly liked the use of concentration constraints, because history shows that high concentration with low risk can be more devastating than low concentration with high risk. I expect fellow readers to enjoy this work immensely, and monetize on the knowledge it contains.'

Marcos Lopez de Prado, Research Fellow, Harvard University;
Head of Quantitative Trading, Hess Energy Trading Company

'In a recent book of my own I bemoan rampant "confusion" among academics as well as practitioners of modern financial theory and practice. I am delighted to say that the authors of *Portfolio Management Under Stress* are *not* confused. It is heart-warming to find such clarity of thought among those with positions of great influence and responsibility.'

Harry M. Markowitz, Nobel Laureate, Economics 1990

'Rebonato and Denev have ploughed for all of us the vast field of applications of Bayesian nets to quantitative risk and portfolio management, leaving absolutely no stone unturned.'

Attilio Meucci, Chief Risk Officer and Director of
Portfolio Construction at Kepos Capital LP

Portfolio Management Under Stress

A Bayesian-Net Approach to
Coherent Asset Allocation

Riccardo Rebonato

and

Alexander Denev

CAMBRIDGE
UNIVERSITY PRESS

CAMBRIDGE
UNIVERSITY PRESS

University Printing House, Cambridge CB2 8BS, United Kingdom

Cambridge University Press is a part of the University of Cambridge.

It furthers the University's mission by disseminating knowledge in the pursuit of education, learning and research at the highest international levels of excellence.

www.cambridge.org
Information on this title: www.cambridge.org/9781107048119

First published 2013
Reprinted 2014

Printed in the United Kingdom by CPI Group Ltd, Croydon CR0 4YY

A catalogue record for this publication is available from the British Library

Library of Congress Cataloguing in Publication data
Rebonato, Riccardo.
Portfolio management under stress : a Bayesian-net approach to coherent asset allocation / Riccardo Rebonato and Alexander Denev.
    pages   cm
Includes bibliographical references and index.
ISBN 978-1-107-04811-9 (hardback)
1. Portfolio management – Mathematical models.   2. Investments – Mathematical models.   3. Financial risk – Mathematical models.   I. Denev, Alexander.   II. Title.
HG4529.5.R43   2013
332.601'519542 – dc23   2013037705

ISBN 978-1-107-04811-9 Hardback

To my father, my wife and my son.
[RR]

To my mother and brother. What I am today, I owe to them.
[AD]

Contents

Figures

The figures of the Bayesian net were drawn with Netica from Norsys Software Corp. (www.norsys.com).

Tables

Acknowledgements

We would like to thank the many friends, colleagues, academics and professionals who have helped us by providing suggestions and correcting our errors.

In particular, we would like to acknowledge the help received by Professor Didier Sornette for the parts of book on econophyiscs, Sir David Forbes Hendry for his comments on our discussion of predictability in finance, Dr Attilio Meucci for the parts on entropy pooling, Professors Uppal and Garlappi for reviewing our treatment of ambiguity aversion, Professor Stoyan Stoyanov, who gave us useful pointers on the conceptual links between Extreme Value Theory, Pareto distributions and econophysics, Dr Vasant Naik for discussing with us the sections on private valuation, Professor Diebold for his support of the general approach, Dr Marcos Lopez de Prado, Ms Jean Whitmore, Mr Sebastien Page, Dr Vineer Bhansali and Dr Richard Barwell for general discussions and comments on the structure of the book, and two anonymous referees, whose comments have substantively improved both the content of the book and the presentation of the material.

We are very grateful to Cambridge University Press, and Dr Chris Harrison in particular, for the enthusiasm with which they have accepted our proposal, and for the rigour and constructive nature of the reviewing process. We found in Ms Mairi Sutherland an excellent editor, who has managed to navigate successfully the difficulties inherent in dealing with a manuscript which had patently been written *a quattro mani*.

We are, of course, responsible for all the remaining errors.

Part I

Our approach in its context

In the first part of this book we explain why taking 'stress' events into account is so important in portfolio construction. We argue that the possibility of non-normal events should always be taken into account in the construction of the portfolio, and not only in periods of crisis. We also provide a conceptual framework for dealing with exceptional events, based on causation rather than association.

1 How this book came about

[Under uncertainty] there is no scientific basis on which to form any calculable probability whatever. We simply don't know. Nevertheless, the necessity for action and for decision compels us as practical men to do our best to overlook this awkward fact and to behave exactly as we should if we had behind us . . . a series of prospective advantages and disadvantages, each multiplied by its appropriate probability waiting to be summed. *J M Keynes, 1937*

This book deals with asset allocation in the presence of stress events or user-specified scenarios. To arrive at the optimal allocation, we employ a classic optimization procedure – albeit one which is adapted to our needs. The tools employed to deal consistently and coherently with stress events and scenario analysis are Bayesian nets.

The idea of applying the Bayesian-net technology, recently introduced in Rebonato (2010a, b), Rebonato and Denev (2012) and Denev (2013) in the context of stress testing and asset allocation, seems a very straightforward one. So straightforward, indeed, that one may well wonder whether a 500+ page book is truly needed, especially given that two thirty-page articles are already available on the topic.

We decided that this book was indeed needed when we began using this technique in earnest in practical asset-allocation situations. We soon discovered that many slips are possible between the cup of a promising idea and the lips of real-life applications, and that only a thorough understanding of these intermediate steps can turn a promising idea into something really useful and practical.

The steps we refer to are not purely computational or, in a wider sense, 'practical' (although in the book we deal with quite of few of these). We have found that the praxis of actually obtaining asset allocation using the Bayesian-net methodology has also enriched our theoretical understanding of how it works, and has given us a better appreciation of what it can deliver – and of what it can't. It has also shed light on, and enriched our understanding of, broader aspects of asset allocation in general.

In short, we would like in this book to share with the investment community a way of dealing with the problem of choosing an optimal portfolio composition when the probability of occurrence of stress events is non-negligible (that is to say, always). And we like to think that the way we propose to do this is novel, practical, theoretically justifiable, intuitive and, last but not least, rewarding to work with.

We do not consider our offering as *the* solution of the asset-allocation problem, but we hope that it can give a tool to be used alongside, say, the Black–Litterman prescription or the Michaud technique(s). Above all, we feel that the greatest virtue of the approach we propose does not lie in any one formula or numerical 'trick'. Rather, we concur with General Eisenhower that, yes, the best-formulated plans will prove useless in the heat of the battle, but that the preparation itself will turn out to be priceless.[1]

1.1   An outline of our approach

Diversification is at the heart of modern portfolio theory. Before Markowitz, asset allocation was a rather straightforward affair. As late as 1938, the then-standard reference work on financial investments by Williams (1938) implicitly recommended that investors should place all their wealth in the investment with the maximum expected return. This recommendation was not made in the get-rich-quick investment column of an evening paper, but in a book on investing published by no less august an institution than Harvard University Press. So, in the late 1930s, putting all your eggs in the most promising basket was still 'best industry practice'.

The work by Markowitz (e.g. 1991 [1959], 1987) fundamentally changed all that because of his insights about diversification and risk-reward trade-offs. But the reach of his ideas spread further, as the concept of diversifiable and undiversifiable risk was to pave the way to building the Capital Asset Pricing Model (CAPM), and the subsequent developments in asset pricing. Diversification – and, more generally, the idea that to build a desirable portfolio it is essential to understand how asset prices move together, not just in isolation – has transformed finance for good.

Our work takes this for granted. If anything, we put diversification at the very heart of our approach. We are acutely aware of a problem, however. Our concerns are well expressed by the words of Mohamed A. El-Erian, PIMCO's co-CEO, written in the wake of the 2007–9 financial crisis:

[Recent] developments will serve to further highlight the danger of ... being overly committed to an historical policy portfolio whose rigid backward-looking characterization no longer corresponds to the realities of today and tomorrow ...

[W]ith its conventional (or, to be more precise, reduced-form) analytical foundation now subject to some motion, it will become even more difficult to rely just on a traditional portfolio diversification as both necessary and sufficient to deliver high returns and mitigate risks. Diversification will remain necessary, *but a lot more attention will be devoted to the appropriate specification of tail scenarios and tail hedges* ...[2]

These words clearly suggest that the investment community requires something more than a minor tinkering at the edges of the usual statistically based assessment

---

[1] 'In preparing for battle I have always found that plans are useless, but planing is indispensible.' Dwight D. Eisenhower, 34th President of the US.

[2] El-Erian (2010, p. 4, our emphasis).

diversification techniques. It requires something different. And something different is indeed what we offer in this book.

In a nutshell, this is our 'philosophy'.

First, we believe that, at least 'locally', correlations are relatively stable (or, at least, statistically predictable) during normal market conditions.[3] These local and relatively stable correlations (covariances, really) can therefore be profitably extracted using traditional statistical (frequentist) techniques.

Second, we believe that in conditions of market turmoil the codependence among changes in asset prices is radically altered. Along with many econophysicists, we do believe that extreme events are 'in a class of their own'.

Third we have found little empirical support for the belief that extreme events leave a regular, invariant 'signature' in the distribution of joint returns. We believe instead that each crisis unfolds according to its own idiosyncratic dynamics.[4] So, for instance, we do not think that the way asset prices moved together during, say, the Mexican peso crisis of 1994 carries a lot of information about how asset prices moved together in the occasion of the subprime crisis. More generally, we do not believe that what happened during any one particular crisis can *ex ante* be relied upon to tell us much about how prices will move together in the next.[5]

Fourth, we recognize that establishing these crisis-specific codependencies is very difficult. But we also believe that we can go a long way towards building a sound understanding of how asset prices may move in stress conditions by injecting *causal* information about how the world works. This causal information comes from our understanding, imperfect as it may be, of what causes what, and of which events should *today* be at the forefront of our attention. We know that water causes mud, and that mud does not cause water – or, in a financial context, we know that a fall in equity prices would cause equity-implied volatilities to spike, and not the other way around. When we adopt a purely correlation-based description we relinquish this precious information. This cannot be good. We feel that the task faced by asset managers is difficult enough without throwing away any useful piece of information they may have. Every nugget of information, however limited, should be cherished and 'squeezed' as much as possible, exactly *because* the task at hand is so difficult. Bayesian nets will be the tool we employ for the task.

---

[3] What we really mean here is that in normal market conditions correlations can remain stable over periods of time of comparable length to the rebalancing horizon of most asset managers. See the discussion in Chapters 20 and 21.

[4] We stress that, if the reader does not agree with our views on this matter, our approach is still applicable. We discuss this point in Chapter 18.

[5] Of course, we do not deny that one can detect some crisis-specific regularities: asset prices, for instance, move 'more' (their volatilities increase) during crises. And, yes, some common factors of returns such as liquidity, which in normal market conditions are almost latent, take on a much greater role during periods of turmoil, thereby inducing a greater degree of codependence among assets which are normally weakly correlated. But, as we argue in what follows, even mantra-like statements like 'in crises all correlations go to 1' need strong qualifications and, taken at face value, offer little help in tail hedging and robust portfolio construction.

We discuss the regularity or otherwise of crisis patterns in Chapter 4 (see Section 4.2 in particular).

Fifth, we combine the statistical information that pertains to the normal market conditions with the information that we have extracted from our understanding of how the world may work *today*. Once this conditional joint distribution of returns has been obtained, we can move to the traditional asset-allocation procedures based, implicitly or explicitly, on utility maximization. Our approach can be seen as a natural extension of the research programme ushered in by Black and Litterman (1992): Black and Litterman ask the asset manager to provide subjective estimates of the first moments of the return distributions; later developments asked the asset manager for subjective inputs about the covariance matrix (see, e.g., Rebonato and Jaeckel 1999); what *we* require in our approach is for the portfolio manager to add her subjective assessment about the joint tail behaviour of asset prices.[6]

We realize that doing so directly is very difficult. This is why we 'distil' this complex information from simpler building blocks, linked together and made consistent via the Bayesian-net technology. We can summarize our approach by saying that we *elicit* 'simple' probabilities and *construct* 'complex' ones.

Sixth, there are two overriding principles, arguably the most important of all, that inform our work. The first is that we want our results to be intuitively understandable and challengeable by the intelligent-but-not-mathematically-versed professional. We believe that the time of black-boxes is rapidly running out for asset allocation systems – and, for that matter, for risk management in general. Yes, in our approach we employ relatively sophisticated mathematical techniques. However, if an asset manager cannot interrogate the output of her asset-allocation system, if she cannot carry out simple and transparent sensitivity analyses, if she cannot reconstruct in an intuitive way why the suggested allocation turns out to be like this rather than like that, then we really recommend that she should not trust the output of the model she uses. She should move to something simpler – something, that is, that she can *understand* and *trust*.

Our second overriding principle is the robustness of the output. We are ambitious but modest. We know that we are trying something very difficult, and we therefore want our final results to be forgiving, in the sense of not displaying a high sensitivity to small changes in the necessarily approximate inputs. To use a hackneyed expression, we want to be approximately right, not precisely wrong.

If the reader 'buys into' our philosophy, we believe that we can offer such an intuitively understandable, auditable and robust approach to asset allocation. Our method has the added advantage of treating 'normal' and 'exceptional' events on a consistent footing, and of allocating assets in a coherent manner.

Of course, asset managers have always been aware of what 'lurks beneath'. They have typically tried to 'defend' their portfolios with the safety nets and parachutes provided by tail hedges. However, these have typically been added as afterthoughts to the allocation suggested by their stress-naive model. Doing so clearly destroys whatever optimality there was in the original allocation, as the parachutes were not included at

---

[6] We have not defined what we mean by 'tails'. We refer the reader to Chapters 4 and 5, where we deal with exceptional returns in general.

the outset in the universe of allocation assets. We propose instead a *coherent* way to combine all assets (including the protection hedges) in one single allocation framework.

1.2 Portfolio management as a process

This book is mainly about portfolio management and asset allocation. What is needed for the task? Should a manager rely on her intuition, or use a formalized method – of which Markowitz's mean-variance optimization is an early and still prime example, and of which the suggestions in this book are just another and modest variation? Modifying the taxonomy in Markowitz (2010), one can list the following alternatives. The portfolio manager could

1. use the tried-and-tested mean-variance approach pioneered by Markowitz, possibly with some of the many 'improvements' that have been suggested;
2. use other measures of risk or return in a risk-return analysis;
3. determine the investor's utility function explicitly and maximize its expected value;
4. use constraints and guidelines instead of optimizing;
5. proceed intuitively.

From the point of view of logical coherence, the third alternative is arguably the best. However, as Markowitz (2010) points out, it is not without its drawbacks: an inappropriate utility function may be chosen for analytical tractability; assuming time invariance of preferences may have serious drawbacks; the process may end up being too much of a black-box; it may be difficult to model the nexus of agency relationships in a real investment process (think of the interactions between the sponsor, the trustees, and the present and future retirees in the case of a pension fund).[7]

As for the question of whether it is better to use constraints on their own or as part of a risk-return analysis, Markowitz, as usual, makes the case very clearly.

The answer is that rarely, if ever, do the intuitively desired constraints completely specify one and only one portfolio. (If the portfolio analyst tried to do so, he or she would probably overspecify the portfolio and end up with a system with no feasible solution.) So then, how is the analyst to choose among the many portfolios that meet the constraints? . . . If the choice is made using some kind of decision rule (such as, 'Try to get as close to equal weighting as possible, subject to the constraints'), either the procedure employed would be 'closet' risk-return (e.g., equal weighting subject to constraints is the same as mean-variance with all assets having the same means, variances, and covariances), or it is probably a procedure unrelated to the maximization of expected utility. . .

Concerning the [fifth] alternative to proceed intuitively, the behavioral finance literature is full of ways that seat-of-the-pants investing leads to irrational choices. For example, Barber & Odean (2000) show that investors who fancy that they can outperform the market by active trading typically make a lot of money for their brokers and little, if any, for themselves.

So, what is the asset or portfolio manager to do? Judging from our experience, and from the insights we have gathered by talking to professionals who do manage

---

[7] See in this respect the discussion in Part VIII of this book.

investment funds (and who very often do use variations of the Markowitz mean-variance approach) what they need is a framework that allows them to bring their financial understanding into play, but does so in a coherent, organized and 'auditable' manner. What do we mean by this?

Even when these asset managers use mean-variance analysis, or the Black–Litterman approach, or any of the many variants that have been proposed, they don't really 'believe in' mean-variance, or Black–Litterman, or the asset allocation approach of choice in the same way that a physicist 'believes in', say, quantum mechanics. Rather, they have the need for a coherent (as opposed to haphazard) way to organize their intuition, make the result 'inspectable' and to point at a well-defined procedure to go from their 'hunches' to investment actions. They need (and cherish) intuition, but they also need a process. Quoting Markowitz again, '[d]uring a conference discussion session, Peter Bernstein described the haphazard way in which institutional portfolios were formed in the 1950s and earlier. He concluded with the statement, "Now you have a process." [Markowitz's] thought at the time was, "Now I understand what I started."'

This is a simple but powerful insight: the asset management profession needs intuitive tools that can be 'understood' even leaving the maths aside (mean-variance is, in this respect, probably unbeatable); but they also need a logical framework by means of which this intuition can be organized into an auditable process. This is what Markowitz started. Arguably his legacy in this area is probably more important, and may end up being more enduring, than his legacy for the specific contribution to asset allocation – impressive as this is.

The work presented in this book tries (with modesty) to offer a complementary approach. The intellectual origin of the work is still firmly in the Markowitz camp: diversification, trade-off between risk and return, probabilistic (although not necessarily frequentist) approach: all these building blocks are still there. It proposes some (important) variations on the theme, but tries to keep in mind that what the asset or portfolio manager needs is not 'the truth', but a logically sound, intuitively appealing and logically 'inspectable' investment process.

1.3   Plan of the book

The book has been organized in a modular fashion, with each module reasonably autonomous and self-contained. Like every author, we hope that the reader will go through every single page of our book, from the acknowledgements to the last entry of the index. However, we have structured our work in such a way that several shortcuts can be taken. In this section we therefore outline the structure of the book first, and then propose several suggested itineraries, from the scenic historic route to the equivalent of the high-speed option of 'taking the highway'.

The structure of the book is as follows.

Part I spells out our philosophy, and places it in its context. In particular we stress the difference between correlation (which is an association-related concept) and causation. We place casual models at the heart of our approach.

In Part II we review some popular approaches to dealing with extreme events (Extreme Value Theory, econophysics, and others). We highlight similarities and stress differences with our approach.

In Part III we deal with diversification and its problems. This brings us to a brief discussion of Markowitz's results and of the Capital Asset Pricing Model (CAPM). We encounter for the first time the problem of the instability of the optimal allocation weights to small changes in the inputs. We also begin to discuss a few approaches (Michaud's, Black–Litterman's, Doust's and Meucci's) that can be employed to 'tame' this instability.

In Part IV we are finally ready to introduce the theoretical foundations of the technology at the heart of our book, namely Bayesian nets. We present rather than prove most results, with a couple of exceptions.

Part V deals with how to apply Bayesian nets in practice. Needless to say, this is a very important part of the book.

Recall that our overall approach combines the business-as-usual part of the return distribution with the stressed contribution provided by the Bayesian-net construction. Part VI therefore deals with the body of the distribution, and Part VII with how to combine ('splice', in our language) the body and the tails of the distribution.

Part VIII deals with how to adapt expected utility maximization to the problem at hand.

Part IX presents a number of numerical techniques that will prove invaluable in real-life applications.

Finally Part X looks at a reasonably realistic allocation problem in detail, explores the effectiveness of the numerical techniques presented in Part IX, and revisits the problem of the instability of the allocation weights. Most importantly, it proposes our favoured approach to dealing with this problem, and to using Bayesian nets in general.

The extremely hasty reader who is already familiar with portfolio theory and its main variants and with the statistical techniques to fit multivariate distributions to time-varying data could fast forward to Parts IV and V (which deal with Bayesian nets); she could then move to Part VII (which shows how to splice the normal-times and the Bayesian-net-produced parts of the distribution) and to Part IX (which deals with the numerical techniques); and may want to sprint to the finish line with Part X. This would give a limited, but self-contained, view of our approach.

For those readers who would like to get more out of the book than a 'how-to' guide, the following detours can be added.

In Chapter 2 we present our views about association and causation. As these views are central to our approach, we expand on the topic in Chapter 4. Readers interested in 'foundational issues' will also want to read Chapters 5 and 6, where we discuss alternative established ways to deal with extreme events.

Part III should only be skipped by the hastiest of readers, because it places our approach in the broader context of portfolio diversification, and presents the first discussion of the issue of the stability of the allocation weights. As we consider the stability issue very important, we return to it in Part X, and Chapters 28 and 29 in particular.

Implicitly or explicitly, almost all of modern portfolio theory is based on the maximization of some sort of utility (or objective) function. Part VIII has therefore been written with those readers in mind who would like to understand the strengths of, and the problems with, utility theory. The arguments presented in this section are intimately linked with the stability issues mentioned above.

Part VI (which presents the statistical techniques required to identify and fit to the body of the distribution) will be of use for those readers who want step-by-step guidance in implementing all parts of our approach.

Finally, the first part of Chapter 21 will be of help to almost all readers when it comes to choosing the most delicate inputs to any portfolio optimization model, namely the expected returns. The attentive reader (who hasn't taken too many shortcuts) will see direct links between this chapter and our preoccupation with the stability of results.

2 Correlation and causation

We never step in the same river twice. *Heraclitus*

2.1 Statistical versus causal explanations

We stated in the previous chapter that we look at causation as a primary concept and at correlation as a derived one. It is useful to explain in some detail what we mean.[1] Doing so will also help the reader understand why we regard Bayesian nets as more than a tool for factorizing efficiently complex joint probabilities. We think that such a factorization view of Bayesian nets, powerful as it is, is too reductive, and misses their real potential. The ability afforded by Bayesian nets[2] to 'represent' (conditional) independence in a transparent and intuitive way is only one of their strengths. The real power of Bayesian nets stems from their ability to describe causal links[3] among variables in a parsimonious and flexible manner.[4] See Pearl (1986, 2009) for a thorough discussion of these points. To use his terminology, casting our treatment in terms of causation will make our judgements about (conditional) (in)dependence 'robust'; will make them well suited to represent and respond to *changes* in the external environment; will allow us to work with conceptual tools which are more 'stable' than probabilities; will permit extrapolation to situations or combination of events that have not occurred in history.

We will explain what these concepts (robustness, stability, ability to deal with change and to 'extrapolate') mean immediately below, but, before doing so, we want to stress

---

[1] Parts of this section have been adapted from Rebonato (2010a).
[2] Or, more precisely, of directed *acyclical* graphs.
[3] Bayesian nets are also ideally suited to dealing with temporal links. In this book we only cursorily deal with temporal structures. Of course, the concept of temporal ordering plays an important, and complex, part in defining causality. When we say that we deal 'cursorily' with temporal structures, we simply mean that we only require that a 'cause' in our net should occur before its effect. We are not concerned, for instance, with the temporal ordering of different causes, as long as all the correct cause–effect relationships are satisfied.
[4] Bayesian nets need not be given either a causal or a temporal interpretation at all. For the applications at hand, we choose to endow our nets with these interpretations, and to structure the problem accordingly (for instance, in order to facilitate the elicitation process). As we discuss, we think that this is very powerful, but it is not logically necessary. See Sections 12.3 and 12.6. There is more to Bayesian nets than causal links, and there is (far) more to causality than Bayesian nets.

what we perceive to be a fundamental difference between a statistical and a causal description of a phenomenon. To do so, we could no better that quoting Weisberg (2010, p. 4):

[to] the layperson, it must seem odd that statistics has so little to offer for learning about causal effects. To understand this irony, we must understand the primary problem that statistical methods were originally designed to address.

Classical statistical methods were devised primarily to deal with uncertainty that arises from the limited nature of the available data. Intuitively, it was recognized long ago that a small set of observations of some quantity was in general less reliable as a guide to action than a larger sample. . . . Having [more data] would provide much better information than relying on only a few. But better in what sense and by how much? The genius of modern statistical theory lies largely in its conceptual framework for formalizing and answering such questions . . .

Of course, being able to answer these questions can sharpen our predictions. But this is just one aspect, and a rather limited one at that, of prediction-making. Weisberg (2010, p. 5) continues:

Now let us consider the problem of causal inference. Causal inference is also about making predictions. However, causation is not concerned primarily with random variation *under a stable set of circumstances*.[5] Rather, causation pertains to what systematic alteration would occur if the circumstances were to change in a specified manner. . . . The key point . . . is that the stable population assumed by traditional statistical methods can only reveal how various factors are *associated*,[6] but it does not by itself disclose how a change in one factor would produce changes in some other factor of interest.

These quotes only skim the surface of the debate about statistical analysis and causation (see, also, Angrist and Pischke (2009), for a useful discussion) and they make no reference to statistical techniques such as Granger causation (Granger 1969). However, they reflect well our underlying philosophy, and provide one set of justifications for the causal interpretation we give to Bayesian nets in this book.[7]

We can now go back to the properties of causal relationships (robustness, stability and ability to deal with change and interpolation) alluded to above, and we can try to explain what we mean by these terms using a concrete example, presented in Figure 2.1 by way of a simple Bayesian net.

We have not defined what Bayesian nets are yet, but, for the moment, we ask the reader to go with the flow, and simply regard each node in the picture as signifying a random variable (the occurrence of an 'event'), and each arrow as describing a causal link from parent to child, encoded in a set of conditional probabilities. By the way, it is a testament to the intuitive power of Bayesian nets that no further information is needed at this stage to get the gist of the intuitive explanation that we are about to provide.

---

[5] Our emphasis added.   [6] Emphasis in the original.

[7] There are other, less philosophical, but just as important, reasons for building Bayesian nets in a casual manner. In particular, the topology is almost invariably simpler when the links are in the causal direction (see the discussion in Section 12.6), and the elicitation problem is far simpler (see, e.g., Pearl 1986, Section 3 in particular, and references therein).

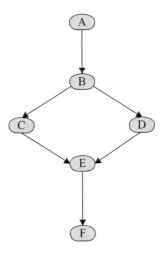

Figure 2.1 The example of Bayesian net discussed in the text: event A is the selling by China of a large portion of its holdings on US Treasuries and Agency paper; event B is a sharp increase in mortgage spreads and Treasury yields caused by event A; event C is the collapse of the price of residential mortgage-backed securities (MBSs), caused by event B; event D is the widening of the credit spread of the US government, also caused by event B; event E is a default of a major international bank caused by the market events in C and D; finally, there is a run on several other banks (event F) caused by default in E.

The 'story' underlying this net could then be the following:

- event A is the sudden and unexpected selling by China of a large portion of its holdings on US Treasuries and Agency paper, due to geopolitical tension about Taiwan;
- event B is a sharp increase in mortgage spreads and Treasury yields caused by event A;[8]
- event C is the collapse of the price of residential mortgage-backed securities (MBSs), caused by event B;
- event D is the widening by 100 basis points (bp) of the credit spread of the US government, also caused by event B;
- event E is a default of a major international bank caused by the market events in C and D;
- finally, there is a run on several other banks (event F) caused by default in E.[9]

With this stylized example in mind, we can go back to the four strengths of causal links pointed out above.

---

[8] We must make clear that when we say that a event X causes event Y we are not referring to *deterministic* causation (see Rebonato 2010a, Ch. 5). We are simply saying that the occurrence of event X makes event Y more likely to occur. Loosely speaking, we use causation in the same sense as in the sentence 'Smoking causes cancer.'

[9] By the way, the reader may disagree with the particular causal links posited in this illustrative example. The possibility of this disagreement is a *positive* feature, as it shows a degree of engagement with the joint scenarios absent from a purely probabilistic description.

Our first claim was that casual links make our judgement about (conditional) (in)dependence 'robust'. This means that we have a way of telling whether observed regularities present in our data are accidental and spurious or can be relied upon to occur regularly. For instance, the widening by 100 bp of the credit spread of the US government debt (event D) and the collapse of the price of residential-backed MBSs (event C) would in general be weakly, if at all, connected. However, they may become strongly linked given the posited dramatic increase in Treasury yields (that cause greater debt servicing costs by the US government) and mortgage rates (that weaken the housing market).

This is just an example of how important causal connections are in determining the relevance of estimated codependencies to today's conditions. The use of exotic fat-tailed probability distributions, of Extreme Value Theory, of copula approaches to the study of tail codependence, and of similar tools, *when used in a frequentist manner*, fails to address one fundamental issue: even if we were able to ascertain with the required statistical confidence the existence of a certain degree of codependence, or the marginal probability of a stand-alone event, without an underlying structural model we have no way of telling whether we should worry *today*. Are today's conditions such that the observed codependence can be expected to recur with high probability? Or do they work *against* the joint occurrence of the events in question? Being able to answer these questions is just what is needed for effective asset allocation (and, not coincidentally, risk management). And they can only be suggested by a structural (causal) model.[10]

The second strength of causal approaches is how well they lend themselves to explaining changes and responding to them. To see what this means in practice consider, for instance, what happened after the default of Lehman. Before the event, central bankers were divided as to whether allowing a bank to fail could be, in some circumstances, a good thing – say, in order to discourage moral hazard. After seeing the mayhem caused by Lehman's demise, very few central bankers still think now that, at least until the institutional and regulatory arrangements that were in place at the time are fundamentally changed, a major bank's default would be a price worth paying to discourage moral hazard. In this respect, before and after the default of Lehman the world has therefore become a different place, with different expected causal links between events. As the world changes, it is very easy to reflect these changes in the structure of a Bayesian net, or in the associated probability tables (which we have not described yet, but which take into account the marginal and conditional probabilities of various events). Furthermore, adjusting a Bayesian net as a consequence of a change in causal links is 'modular': if we look at the portion of the Bayesian net sketched above dealing with the default of a major bank, the only probability table that needs

---

[10] Since we repeatedly mention the word 'structural' we could define what a structural approach is by citing Hoover (2001): 'The structural approach asserts that physical, social and economic structures are real. They exist externally and independently of any (*individual*) human mind. These structures possess causal powers and transmit causal efficacy. They account for the ubiquitous human experience of manipulation and control, as well as for the characteristic asymmetry of causal relations' (emphasis in the original). We too embrace the view that causal structures are fundamental – although, as we are well aware, the inference of causal relationships might be a daunting task.

updating after the post-Lehman policy changes is the one associated with node F (the generalized run on several banks).

Contrast this with a probabilistic (association-based) description of the same 'world change'. Even if such a probabilistic description were possible (and, in the immediate aftermath of the new event, it would only be so in a subjective-probability sense), it would be much more complex, as a number of joint probabilities would change in a very complex, interlinked and opaque manner. It would also be much more difficult to interpret. We show this with a detailed example below. The *modular* causal structure of Bayesian nets allows us to see with great clarity what happens when something changes, and what effect our (or nature's) interventions (at any point in the net) would have.[11]

The third strength of a causal description lies in its 'stability'. This stability comes about because causal descriptions use what Pearl (2009) describes as ontological rather than epistemic relationships. As these are long, or, at least, difficult words, let us explain how we understand them.

Ontological relationship describe objective constraints on and links among variables in the world out there. As such, they are relatively stable.[12] They do change, but only do so when the world changes.

Probabilistic relationships are, on the other hand, epistemic in the sense that they can be influenced by our state of knowledge about a phenomenon, and this state of knowledge continuously changes as new information arrives. As a consequence, epistemic relationships (and probabilistic statements) are by nature dynamic and ever-changing even when the world out there does not change at all (or does not change much). As Black (2010) comments about the volatility of asset prices: 'I have never found this question as interesting as Shiller (1989) has. He looks at current news and finds that prices seem to change even when there's no news. I think about expectations, which are constantly changing as people process old news.' In Pearl's language, Black is emphasizing the epistemic nature of the information conveyed by the volatility of asset prices. *Pace* Heraclitus (whose quote opens this chapter), it is not the world that is in constant flux, but our understanding of it, and hence our probabilistic interpretation of it.

As causal descriptions concern themselves with the structure of the 'world out there', they are intrinsically more stable – and hence easier to work with. To give a concrete example, consider the well-known 'instability' of correlations during periods of financial crises: asset classes which are weakly correlated during normal market

---

[11] Neeldess to say, we are not claiming here that all causal relationships display the feature of modularity that makes the simple Bayesian nets we shall use in this chapter so practical. However, simple modular causal links can be considered as a first approximation to more complex causal descriptions of reality. Since quantitative risk management has so far almost completely eschewed *any* causal description, modularity is a first, but also a significant, step in the right direction.

[12] In our previous example Bayesian nets *do* give us the ability to describe a change in the world (say, pre- and post-Lehman) by altering the appropriate conditional probability tables or the location or direction of arrows, and this is indeed one of their strengths. These major changes in the world, however, should – thankfully – be rare.

conditions suddenly become very strongly (positively or negatively!) correlated as financial turmoil sets in. All the statistical (association-based) relationships we have established during the normal periods break down – and they seem to do so in a complex and unaccountable manner. However, as one of us has discussed in Rebonato (2010), it is possible to build a very simple and parsimonious *causal* toy model with *stable* relationships among its variables that naturally explains the time-varying correlations and their signs. Related ideas are also expressed in Page and Taborski (2011), who make a distinction between asset prices and risk factors (something close to what we would call in our language 'causal transmission mechanisms'): 'correlation across risk factors are lower than across asset classes ... Most importantly, diversification across risk factors is more robust to market turbulence.'

Finally, we mentioned as a strength of Bayesian nets the ability afforded by a causal description to extrapolate beyond what has been observed in the past. Let us provide a concrete example also in this case. Before the events of 2007–9 rates had never been so low for so long in so many countries at the same time. What is the effect of these exceptionally accommodative monetary policies on the demand for credit or on inflation? Just by looking at our data set, we simply do not know, exactly because we have never had such low rates for so long in so many countries.[13] And, of course, as of this writing, nobody knows what past data, if any, are relevant to tell us much about what would happen if the concern *du jour*, the break-up of the Euro, would occur.

For probabilistic and statistical approaches (especially of frequentist bent) these 'out-of-sample' questions are extremely hard to answer. But if a structural model tells us *why and how* something changes as a response to changes in some other variable and provides a structural link between the two variables, then it can suggest what would happen in hitherto unexplored conditions.

Of course, these models of reality can (and in general will) be imperfect and defective. However, disregarding them because of their incompleteness would be a great mistake. We know that quoting Greenspan has recently gone somewhat out of fashion, but his words in this respect are still very apposite:

Policymakers often have to act ... even though [they] may not fully understand the full range of possible outcomes, let alone each possible outcome's likelihood. As a result, ... policymakers have needed to reach to broader, though less mathematically precise, hypotheses about how the world works ... [14]

We note in closing this section that there is a connection between robustness and stability. In fact, the statement that the relationships in a net are stable means that assertions of the type 'switching on a sprinkler does not cause rain' are more stable than some spurious temporary correlations (or the lack of them) like 'the rain and the activation of the sprinkler are dependent', which changes according to the state of our

---

[13] Japan, of course, is an exception. But is Japan 'relevant'? Again the answer can only come from a structural model that suggests whether the lessons for Japan the the 1990s and 2000s are of relevance to the industrialized countries of the 2010s. Incidentally, see Koo (2009) and Wolf (210) for an interesting discussion of this specific point.

[14] Quoted in Frydman and Goldberg (2007).

knowledge about the other variables (whether we know that it rained or not).[15] In the same vein, consider two events like 'Increase of the yield on the US government debt' and 'Fall of the prices of MBSs'. When we say that they are generally weakly connected, but they might become strongly connected if the increase of Treasury yields is very large, we say that a probabilistic statement of weak connection (correlation) becomes strong if some additional conditions become true, i.e., if we know that Treasury yields have increased a lot.

2.2   A concrete example

Abstractions are important, but examples are even better.[16] So, let us give a concrete comparison of a causal and an associative description of the interaction among a very small number of variables. Let's suppose that we have four events (Boolean variables), A, B, C and D, and that we have managed to establish all their marginal probabilities (Table 2.1) and the (event) correlations between them (Table 2.2), conditional on the information available up to time T:

Table 2.1 *The marginal probabilities of the four events at time T*

$$
\begin{bmatrix}
& P(E_i) \\
A & 0.10 \\
B & 0.20 \\
C & 0.75 \\
D & 0.35
\end{bmatrix}
\tag{2.1}
$$

Table 2.2 *The true (event) correlation matrix, $\rho_{ij}(T)$, between events A, B, C, D at time T*

$$
\begin{bmatrix}
\rho_{ij}(T) & A & B & C & D \\
A & 1 & 0 & -48.50\% & 31.45\% \\
B & 0\% & 1 & 9.24\% & 0\% \\
C & -48.50\% & 9.24\% & 1 & -15.25\% \\
D & 31.45\% & 0\% & -15.25\% & 1
\end{bmatrix}
$$

Let's not worry that establishing correlations as precise as those in Table 2.2 must have been quite a statistical feat. Let's just assume that the portfolio manager has struck a Faustian pact with the Prince of Darkness of Frequentist Statistics, and, in exchange for her soul, she has asked not for untold riches or world domination, but for knowledge of the 'true' correlation matrix between the four events.[17]

The portfolio manager comes back some time later (say, at time $T + \tau$), and, as a second instalment of her Faustian bargain, she asks for the new marginal probabilities and the new correlation matrix. She finds that the marginal probabilities have changed very little, or not at all, as shown in Table 2.3:

---

[15] See Pearl (2009, p. 25).
[16] This section has been adapted and modified from Rebonato (2010b).
[17] We stress that we speak here about *event* correlation. This is defined in Section 14.7.

Table 2.3 *The marginal probabilities of the events A, B, C, D at time* $T + \tau$

$$
\begin{bmatrix}
 & P(E_i) \\
A & 0.10 \\
B & 0.20 \\
C & 0.64 \\
D & 0.29
\end{bmatrix}
$$

So far, so good. However, she finds that the correlation matrix, shown in Table 2.4, is now distressingly different.

Table 2.4 *The true correlation matrix,* $\rho_{ij}(T + \tau)$, *between events A, B, C, D, at time* $T + \tau$

$$
\begin{bmatrix}
\rho_{ij}(T + \tau) & A & B & C & D \\
A & 1 & 0\% & -26.22\% & -0.066\% \\
B & 0\% & 1 & 27.28\% & -0\% \\
C & -26.22\% & 27.28\% & 1 & 17.3\% \\
D & -0.066\% & -0\% & 17.3\% & 1
\end{bmatrix}
$$

Again, we can assume that the Prince of Darkness has revealed the new correct values for $\rho_{ij}(T + \tau)$ without any estimation errors. What can a reasonable portfolio manager conclude by comparing these two correlation matrices? Surely, not just that the world has changed while she wasn't looking, but that it must have changed *a lot*! For ease of comparison, all the changes in the correlation matrices are shown in Table 2.5, which clearly shows that, for some entries, the changes are much larger than the correlations we started with.

Table 2.5 *The difference between the correlation matrix at time T,* $\rho_{ij}(T)$ *and the correlation matrix at time* $T + \tau$, $\rho_{ij}(T + \tau)$

$$
\begin{bmatrix}
\rho_{ij}(T + \tau) - \rho_{ij}(T) & A & B & C & D \\
A & 0 & 0\% & -22.28\% & +31.52\% \\
B & 0\% & 0 & -18.04\% & 0 \\
C & -22.28\% & -18.04\% & 0 & -32.55\% \\
D & +31.52\% & 0 & -32.55\% & 0
\end{bmatrix}
$$

Now, the Prince of Darkness may well have truthfully told the portfolio manager the old and the new correlations, but how is she to make sense of what has happened while she wasn't looking? And the poor portfolio manager is only dealing with four assets! How could she make sense of the changes in a, say, 10×10 correlation matrix?

In order to try to *understand* what has happened, consider instead the super-simple Bayesian net shown in Figure 2.2.

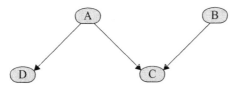

Figure 2.2 The simple Bayesian net used to explain the dramatic changes in correlations discussed in the text.

Again, it does not take a course in Bayesian nets to guess what the graph signifies: event A causes events C and D; event B causes event C; events A and B display no direct causal link; and event B has no causal effect on event D.

Given this simple structure, the reader can at this stage take our word that all that is required in order to understand what has happened to the correlation matrix between time T and time $T + \tau$ is to be told that a single variable (variable A) behaves differently after and before time τ. By 'behaves differently' we mean that it changes the type of influence its exerts on its direct 'children': 'before', its occurrence *decreased* the probability of variable C, and *increased* the probability of variable D; 'after' it had the opposite effect.[18]

This is prima facie surprising: this very simple and very easy-to-understand piece of information (a type of information that directly comes from our structural understanding of a phenomenon) is *all* that is required to account for all the complex changes in the correlation matrices above!

Now, what type of information would you prefer to have – and, more to the point, which type of information would you prefer to have if you had *to intervene in some way* on the new world (say, if you had to devise a robust hedging strategy, or to put together a well-diversified portfolio)? The associative information contained in the marginal probabilities and the two correlation matrices? Or the causal information contained in the marginal and conditional probabilities plus the two Bayesian nets at time T and $T + \tau$? What kind of information would allow you to understand more easily what has happened? What kind of information, the associative or the causal one, 'chimes' cognitively better with your way of understanding the world? If you were just given the changes in correlation matrices, would you find it easy to guess how the world has changed?

And let's keep in mind that we are working with just four variables, and with about as simple a change in the 'world out there' as we can imagine! Of course, if the net were only a bit more complex – with a few more children, or with more 'prolific' parents – and if the world had changed in a slightly more complex way, our ability to 'understand' what is happening would diminish even more, as dependences would quickly trickle from a few localized causes down the whole structure of the net.

---

[18] More precisely, all that has happened is that three conditional probabilities, namely $P(C|AB)$, $P(C|\tilde{A}B)$, $P(D|A)$, have changed.

2.3   Implications for hedging and diversification

It is easy to see what this means for diversification and, in general, for hedging. Suppose, for instance, that we want to explore how our portfolio will perform if something changes in the world out there. Specifically, we may want to see what happens if, as in the case above, the occurrence of event A changes the probability of occurrence of event C. We may do that by changing directly the entry of the correlation matrix between events C and A. For those of us who have been schooled in associative statistical techniques this is probably the most natural line of action. Indeed, almost ten years ago one of us presented (with Peter Jaekel) a procedure to ensure that, after tinkering with a given correlation matrix, we still obtain a bona fide, all-positive-eigenvalues, subjectively perturbed correlation matrix (see Rebonato and Jaeckel 1999, 2004). However, if we pursued a purely correlation-based, associative, non-causal approach the changes in correlation between variables C and D or B and C would be very difficult to guess – more to the point, they would be very difficult to *understand*.

Without a structural model and a causal understanding of what is happening, it would be difficult for the asset manager to express an opinion as to whether the new estimated correlations should be 'trusted' – i.e., if they are sufficiently robust to be trusted over the next investment period.

In sum: we have tried to explain an important part of our philosophy. We believe that providing a causal description of reality (even a crude or a highly imperfect one) is a qualitatively different task than giving a purely probabilistic account. Not only is it different, but it is also richer, more powerful and easier to work with. Of course our models may be crude and even faulty. But a crude model is better than pretending that we know nothing about how the world works – that we do not know, for instance, whether an equity market crash causes equity implied volatility to increase or the other way around.

And as for faulty models, all models are wrong, but, as the saying goes, some are more useful than others. Since Galileo onwards, scientific enquiry has not been hindered, but helped, by such crude models as point masses, harmonic pendulums and frictionless planes. Building 'faulty' models is just part of the process of scientific discovery. The only model which is not faulty is the world itself. Unfortunately, it is not a model.

Why do we feel that we should stress these points? Because, yes, Bayesian nets can be used just as a tool to obtain joint probabilities. However, looking at them purely in this light would mean throwing away some of their more powerful offerings. Bayesian nets can provide us with an intuitive, yet rigorous, way to organize our understanding using powerful causal constructs. This is the way we intend to use them. And we note in closing that, when Bayesian nets are built in a causal manner, they also enjoy very pleasing mathematical properties (for instance, they have the smallest number of directed arcs); and – every bit as important – they allow the easiest, most economical, and most natural elicitation of the attending conditional probabilities.

3   Definitions and notation

This is not going to be an exciting chapter, but a useful one, because it is important to define precisely the quantities we are going to work with, and to get the notation straight.

3.1   Definitions used for analysis of returns

In this book we assume that we have n *assets*. Some of these 'assets' could be tradeable indices which are proxies for the underlying asset class. We denote the set of the assets in our universe by $\{x_i, i = 0, 1, 2, \ldots, n - 1\}$. Almost invariably we shall position ourselves at time t_0 ('today') and consider returns over a single period. The end date of this single period will be denoted by t_1. When it is important to specify the time, the asset prices will be denoted by $\{x_i^j, i = 0, 1, 2, \ldots, n - 1, j = 0, 1\}$. When we use vector notation we will denote it by $\{\mathbf{x}\}$, and it is an $n \times 1$ column vector.

The *payoffs* from these assets are in general stochastic (i.e., they are not known with certainty at time t_0). The one exception is the *riskless asset*, x_0. If at time t_1 the asset x_i pays a *cash flow* (which could be certain or stochastic as seen from time t_0), this *cash flow* is denoted by cf_i^1. In a one-period, two-time setting, the superscript '1' is redundant, because we only consider cash flows at time t_1, but we retain it for clarity.

The *gross arithmetic return*, GR_i, from asset x_i is given by

$$GR_i = \frac{x_i^1 + cf_i^1}{x_i^0}, \quad i = 0, 1, 2, \ldots, n - 1 \tag{3.1}$$

and the *arithmetic return*, R_i, is given by

$$R_i = \frac{x_i^1 + cf_i^1}{x_i^0} - 1, \quad i = 0, 1, 2, \ldots, n - 1 \tag{3.2}$$

So, the gross arithmetic return is a number like 1.05 and the arithmetic return is a number like 0.05 (or 5%). For brevity, whenever we refer to a 'return' we will always imply an arithmetic return. If we mean otherwise, we will say so. In vector notation, we will often denote the returns by $\mathbf{R}$, which is also an $n \times 1$ column vector.

A *portfolio*, Π, is a linear combination of assets with weights $\{w_i, i = 0, 1, 2, \ldots, n - 1\}$. In vector notation we will denote the weights by $\boldsymbol{w}$. It can be compactly denoted as a $n \times 1$ column vector.

From the definitions above it immediately follows that the expected arithmetic return of a portfolio, R_Π (a scalar), is given by

$$R_\Pi = \boldsymbol{w}^\mathrm{T} \boldsymbol{R} \tag{3.3}$$

Thanks to the linearity of the portfolio return, we can calculate returns on any partition of assets, and aggregate as we please using the appropriate weights, as explained in detail in Connor *et al.* (2010).[1] The result is both obvious and profound.

We will not in general assume that we know the distribution of the returns. However, we will denote their expected values by the $n \times 1$ vector $\{\mu_i, i = 0, 1, 2, \ldots, n - 1\}$, or just $\boldsymbol{\mu}$ in vector notation.

How long is the one-period in our analysis? It can be anything we want (hourly, daily, weekly, $\ldots$, yearly), as long as we specify it clearly. In our applications it will typically be equal to the period of time over which we have to, or we choose to, leave our portfolio unchanged. When it is important to specify the length of the investment period, we will write for the return vector $\boldsymbol{R}_{0,T}$. If the investment horizon is $[0, T]$, and we consider sub-intervals within it, $0 = t_0, t_1, \ldots, t_{n-1} = T$, then, with obvious notation, the T-period expected return is linked to the expected returns in the underlying sub-periods by

$$\mu_0^\mathrm{T} = \left[\prod_{k=0}^{n} (1 + \mu_{t_k}^{t_{k+1}}) \right] - 1 \tag{3.4}$$

Needless to say, if we worked with log returns the expression for the T-period expected return would look nicer (with a sum in the argument of the exponent replacing the product, and the awkward factors of '1' disappearing). However, the portfolio linearity coming from Equations (3.2) and (3.3) would be lost, and this is a price we are not happy to pay. As a consequence we will almost invariably deal with arithmetic returns in this book (and we will always say so when we don't).

The *covariance*, Cov, among the n assets is an $n \times n$ matrix and is defined by

$$\mathrm{Cov} = \mathbb{E}^\mathbb{P} \left[(\boldsymbol{R} - \boldsymbol{\mu})(\boldsymbol{R} - \boldsymbol{\mu})^\mathrm{T} \right] \tag{3.5}$$

where the superscript $\mathbb{P}$ indicates that we are working in the physical (objective, 'real-world') measure. Using the additive property of the portfolio weights we can immediately derive for the portfolio expected return and variance, Var_Π, (two scalars)

$$\mu_\Pi = \boldsymbol{w}^\mathrm{T} \boldsymbol{\mu}$$

$$\mathrm{Var}_\Pi = \boldsymbol{w}^\mathrm{T} \mathrm{Cov} \, \boldsymbol{w} \tag{3.6}$$

So far we have said nothing about the distributional property of the returns (apart from implying that the first two moments exist). If the asset returns follow a joint

[1] Connor *et al.* (2010, p. 3).

Gaussian distribution, $\mathcal{N}(\boldsymbol{\mu}, \text{Cov})$, then the portfolio return is just a linear combination of Gaussian variables and, as such, follows a univariate Gaussian distribution as well:

$$R_\Pi \tilde{} \mathcal{N}(\boldsymbol{w}^\mathsf{T}\boldsymbol{R}, \boldsymbol{w}^\mathsf{T}\,\text{Cov}\,\boldsymbol{w}) = \mathcal{N}(\mu_\Pi, \text{Var}_\Pi) \tag{3.7}$$

In general, we will denote the joint distribution of returns by $f(R_0, R_1, \ldots, R_{n-1})$, or $f(R_1, R_2, \ldots, R_n)$ if we do not include the riskless asset in our analysis.

3.2 Definitions and notation for market risk factors

The change in the value of an asset over the holding period will in general depend on the changes in N market risk factors. We denote the ith market risk factor by ξ_i, and the change in the risk factor[2] over the investment horizon by $\Delta\xi_i(t)$:

$$\Delta\xi_i(t) = \xi_i(t+T) - \xi_i(t) \tag{3.8}$$

So, the return for asset i, R_i, will be a deterministic function of the changes in the market risk factors over the investment horizon:

$$R_i = R_i(\Delta\xi_1, \Delta\xi_2, \ldots, \Delta\xi_N) \tag{3.9}$$

where we have dropped the dependence on time.

Changes in market risk factors 'drive' change in market prices. Each market price will, in general, display 'loadings' onto a number of risk factors. In a parsimonious description of the economy there should be many fewer market risk factors than market prices. In this sense, risk factors are fundamental in a way that asset prices are not. To avoid confusion, we tend to avoid talking about *returns* in market risk factors, and prefer to talk of *changes*, defined as in Equation (3.8) above.

Finally, the changes in the market risk factors will be characterized by a joint distribution that we will denote by $\varphi(\Delta\xi_1, \Delta\xi_2, \ldots, \Delta\xi_N)$. Determining the joint distribution of the risk factors in the presence of tail events or user-assigned scenarios is the central task of the book. This is because the allocation weights will be determined by maximizing an objective function of choice (typically a suitably defined utility function) over the distribution $\varphi(\Delta\xi_1, \Delta\xi_2, \ldots, \Delta\xi_N)$.

---

[2] To avoid confusion, we stress that for us an example of a risk factor is, say, the level of an equity index, not the return on the index. Also, we could write more generally, $\Delta f(\xi_i(t)) = f(\xi_i(t+T)) - f(\xi_i(t))$, where the function $f(\cdot)$ could, but need not, be $f(x) = \ln(x)$. See de Guilluame, Rebonato and Pogudin (2012) for alternative possible forms for the function $f(\cdot)$ in the case of interest rates.

Part II

Dealing with extreme events

The approach we propose in this book does not stand in a vacuum, but is related (sometimes, perhaps, in terms of opposition) to well-established ways of looking at asset allocation in general, and at exceptional events in particular. It is therefore useful to explain where we stand with respect to these important topics. This we do in the next two parts of the book.

In Part II we start by positioning our proposed approach in the context of predictability and causation in finance; we specialize the discussion in Chapters 5 and 6 to the treatment of outliers. Then, in Part III, which is dedicated to diversification, we will move to the asset-allocation aspect proper, with a discussion of selected topics in the approaches by Markowitz (Chapters 7 and 8), Black–Litterman and Doust (Chapter 9). We will then conclude Part III by looking in Chapter 10 at a recent approach (by Meucci) which presents interesting similarities with – and differences from – our way of looking at the problem of asset allocation.

4 Predictability and causality

Effect, n. The second of two phenomena which always appear together in the same order. The first, called a Cause, is said to generate the other – which is no more sensible than it would be for one who has never seen a dog except in pursuit of a rabbit to declare the rabbit the cause of the dog. – Ambrose Bierce, *The Devil's Dictionary*

4.1 The purpose of this chapter

Extreme events or, more generally, user-specified scenarios that describe atypical market conditions play a central role in the approach to asset allocation described in this book. As we shall see, our procedure requires the portfolio manager to assign conditional probabilities to the events that connect causes and effects. However, before assigning probabilities, one must identify the potential consequences of a certain conjunction of events. In particular, in order to get the procedure started, the asset manager must be able to specify what the potential consequences of a given extreme or unusual event might be. This brings into play the vexed questions both of predictability and causation, and of what an extreme event is. We briefly look at both questions in this chapter.

Before delving into a discussion of predictability and forecasting, it is important to clarify one aspect of our approach. We believe that the main benefit of employing the causal structural mechanisms that we embed in the Bayesian-net technology is *not* the production of a point forecast of the first or higher moments of a distribution given an assumed structural model. Rather, it is the enforcement of a rigorous logical structure that ensures that the implications of our assumptions are internally consistent. How the conditional probabilities are assigned in the construction of the net will in general depend on the degree of confidence a user will place on causality-driven predictability. If the expert has a strong degree of confidence in a particular structural model, then the conditional probability she will attach to a child will be sharp and tightly centred around the prediction of her model. If she subscribes to a more 'catholic' view of models, then the associated conditional probabilities will be correspondingly more diffuse. Or perhaps her degree of uncertainty may be truly 'Knightian'. Bayesian nets can accommodate all of this – and it is interesting to derive logically what the asset allocation would be under these various degrees of predictability.[1] As we shall see, uncertainty about models, and hence about forecasts, is a central ingredient of our approach, and is directly linked to our use of ambiguity aversion.

4.2   *Is* **this time different?**

A recurrent theme in economic analysis and in economic history is the identification of patterns and regularities in the occurrence of periods of 'boom and bust'. Of course, the idea of cycles in modern economics goes all the way back at least to Schumpeter (1939),[2] with his business cycles of creative destruction. More recently, the Minsky theory (see, e.g., Minsky (1982), and the ideas presented in Minsky's (1975) book on Keynes), with his taxonomy of hedge finance, speculative finance and 'Ponzi' finance,[3] has regained popularity after years of neglect.[4] To the extent that crises display a recurrent pattern, their unfolding, if not the precise timing of their occurrence, becomes to some extent predictable.

In addition to this cyclical view of business and finance in a capitalist system, however, there exists in parallel a stronger version of the predictability school. In this view what is recurrent are not just the broad patterns of crises and recoveries and their causes, but how they unfold. Two excellent examples of this type of analysis are, for instance, the works by Reinhart and Rogoff (2009), and by Kindleberger and Aliber (2011). The account afforded by the latter is predominantly narrative, historically based and qualitative. But Reinhart and Rogoff provide 'hard' statistical analysis,[5] and stress the *quantitative* similarities among crises. And the title of their book (*This Time Is Different*)[6] is, of course, tongue in cheek, as the underlying thesis is that this time is *not* different.

This position seems to be strongly at odds with our view that the unfolding of each crisis is largely idiosyncratic, and that little reliance should be placed on what happened 'last time around'. The differences, in reality, are more apparent than real. We explain in this section why we think this to be the case.

First of all, we agree that certain financial and macroeconomic conditions (such as, for instance, an increase of debt channelled towards speculative activities or an

---

[1] For a precise definition of intrinsic unpredictability see, e.g., Hendry (2011). For a discussion of forecasting from structural econometric models, see Hendry (2012).

[2] See, for instance, Schumpeter (1939, Vol. 1, Ch. 4, p. 161).

[3] According to the Minsky theory, in the hedge-finance phase companies borrow and both service the interest on the debt and engage in progressive repayment of the debt out of operating profits. In the speculative phase, the interest on the outstanding debt is at least in part provided by entering into new debt. Finally, in the Ponzi phase, the firm has to raise new debt to to service both interest and principal.

[4] See, e.g., the sympathetic treatment in Krugman (2012).

[5] See, e.g., their Chapter 5, Section 'The Duration of Default Episodes' (p. 81), Chapter 12, Section 'The Aftermath of High Inflation and Currency Collapse', p. 191 and Chapter 14, Section 'The Downturn after a Crisis: Depth and Duration', p. 226.

[6] See, e.g., their Chapter 13, p. 208, for an argument as to why the this-time-is-different argument was misplaced in the case of the subprime crisis. More generally Reinhart and Rogoff (2012) argue that '[a]lthough no two crises are identical, we have found that there are some recurring features that cut across time and national borders. Common patterns in the nature of the long boom-bust cycles in debt and their relationship to economic activity emerge as a common thread across very diverse institutional settings' (p. 5).

increase in leverage) recur with great regularity before a crisis, and have a convincing explanatory power as to why the crisis itself might have arisen. We also recognize that the asset class that is the object of the credit-fuelled speculative frenzy is often the very asset class that is most likely to experience the bursting of the bubble when plentiful credit ceases to be forthcoming.[7]

We also empirically observe, however, that the destination of the 'hot money' is far from unique. Yes, real estate is one favourite instrument of bubble-creation. This, however, has probably more to do with the existence of large institutions (banks, thrifts, Aufbau Banken, building societies, etc.) whose *raison d'être* is exactly to provide the leverage required to invest in real-estate asset than with any other deeper reason. As long as ways of leveraging are available, many other instruments (say, Greek bonds in the 2000s, which could be repoed at the European Central Bank (ECB) with the same haircut as German Bunds, dot.com stock, which could be pledged as security against further borrowing, and, yes, even tulip bulbs, which could be used as collateral[8] against the purchase of more tulips-to-be) can become vehicles of speculative bubbles.

Now, *at least in the short term* (the several-month cyclical horizons we are interested in), which particular asset class is associated with a bubble certainly matters for how the crisis unfolds, because it can set in motion completely different macroeconomic and financial chains of events. The recent European sovereign-debt crisis is a clear point in case.

The institutional arrangements and the monetary conditions at the time of the crisis also make a big difference: whether an emerging country has pegged its currency to the US\$ or not; whether a central bank can 'print its own money' or not; whether short-term nominal rates are effectively already at zero or not – all these factors by necessity imply different short- and medium-term responses and relative movements of the various asset classes.

So, we agree that the narrative of crises may well rhyme, but, changing metaphor, we observe that the lyrics are certainly not identical. However, the difference between the *this-time-is-the-same* philosophy and our approach is probably not very deep, and has more to do with the time frame and the granularity of the analyses. It may well be the case, as Reinhart and Rogoff point out, that, for instance, deep crises tend to last many years; that this length displays less variability than one may think; that the duration of a crisis may be statistically linked to its depth; etc.[9] However, *while*

---

[7] We are aware that speaking of 'frenzies' and 'bubbles' is far from uncontroversial, and entering the discussion would mire us in the debate about the efficiency of markets and the rationality (literal, or in an *as-if* sense) of investors. We sidestep this topic, and take the view that, much as with pornography, bubbles and frenzies may be difficult to define, but we can recognize them when we see them.

[8] See, e.g., Kindleberger and Aliber (2011, Ch. 3).

[9] We note in passing that even the high-level conclusions by Reinhart and Rogoff have recently been criticized (see Pollin and Ash 2013), both methodologically (were the calculations 'correct'?) and 'philosophically' (does the unconditional approach make sense?). Without entering the specifics of the disagreement (which are irrelevant to our argument) we quote Pollin and Ash's words regarding the degree of regularity of crises: 'We ... found that the relationship between growth and public debt *varies widely over time and between countries.* ... [O]ur corrected evidence shows that a country's growth may be somewhat slower once it moves past the 90 per cent public debt-to-GDP level. *But we cannot count on this being true under all, or even most, circumstances.* Are

the crisis runs its course following patterns that are, from a 30 000-feet perspective, probably rather similar, the portfolio manager still has to negotiate tactically the eddies and undercurrents of *this* particular crisis. We all agree that water flows downward in rivers. But, especially when the going gets turbulent, fluid dynamics indicates that a surprising variety of local patterns can arise – so surprising, that, as canoeists tell us, locally water can even, if briefly, flow upwards.

So, we welcome the analyses, both narrative and quantitative, of the recurrent and regular features of crises carried out by serious scholars such as the ones mentioned above (and, of course, many others). We are very happy to incorporate their insights in our study.[10] We observe, however, that the persistence of theoretical disagreement among different schools of thought about the causes, the modality and the very existence of speculative bubbles suggests that prediction (especially over the turbulent near future) may be more difficult than each school of thought asserts it to be. And, *in the short term*, we therefore prefer to look at the immediate unfolding of each individual crisis as having more idiosyncratic features than partaking of universal and recurrent characteristics. Again, we believe – or hope – that Reinhart and Rogoff would agree, given their focus on '*long* boom-bust cycles'.[11]

4.3   Structural breaks and non-linearities

It is the theory that decides what we can observe. Werner Heisenberg, *Physics and Beyond*

Errors of Nature, Sports and Monsters correct our understanding in regard to ordinary things, and reveal general forms. Francis Bacon, *Novum Organon*

It is common to speak loosely, and almost interchangeably, of 'stress events', 'extreme scenarios', 'outliers', 'regime shifts', 'structural breaks' (or even to try to capture every-thing with the ultimate catch-all term: 'black-swans'). However, there are important distinctions that should inform the treatment of these exceptional events.

When the topic is looked at from the macroeconomic perspective, the literature in this area tends to focus on the interplay between econometric models and the effect of policy actions.[12] Following Hendry (2001), the first distinction to make in this context is between *structural breaks*, ('changes in the parameters of the econometric system'[13]), and *regime shifts* ('change in the behavior of non-modelled, often policy, variables'[14]). The switch of European currencies to the Euro in 1999; the introduction of new types of fiscal policies or regulations; the move from over-the-counter transactions

we considering the US demobilisation after the second world war or New Zealand experiencing a severe one-year recession? Our evidence shows that one needs to ask these and similar questions, including whether slow growth was the cause or consequence of higher public debt, before we can draw meaningful conclusions . . .' (our emphasis). For a fuller account of the criticism levelled at the work by Reinhart and Rogoff in the context of sovereign debt level, see Herndon, Ash and Pollin (2013).

[10] Where else, after all, can we acquire the background factual knowledge that is one essential component to form the subjective beliefs about the conditional probability tables?

[11] Rienhart and Rogoff (2012, p. 5), our emphasis.

[12] See, e.g., Hendry and Mizon (1999, 2001), Clements and Hendry (2008), Hendry (2004, 2005), Hoover (2001).

[13] Hendry (2001, p. 3).   [14] *Ibid.*, p. 3.

and open outcry to electronic exchanges and high-frequency trading[15] – these are all examples of regime shifts.

Of course, the two can be linked: a regime shift can give rise to a structural break.[16] This potential interplay brings in the delicate topic of causation.[17] We quickly move away from this difficult area.

In the macroeconomic treatment of structural breaks the emphasis has been mainly devoted to shifts in the means of the underlying time series.[18] The distinguishing feature of structural breaks is that the shifts in means associated with them are persistent. After a structural break has occurred the world is different, *and it is so in a permanent way.* See Clements and Hendry (2008) for a discussion of this point.[19]

Not surprisingly, when it comes to econometric estimation, structural breaks present the greatest challenge. They can also be the most important 'polluters' of a naive statistical estimate of means and covariances that fails to distinguish between different epochs. From the point of view of diversification – one of the pillars of portfolio theory in general, and of our approach in particular – neglecting switches between structurally different periods can completely invalidate the results.

Assuming that the break can be identified – and this can sometimes be done by supplementing statistical information with political, financial or institutional background knowledge – the simplest procedure is only to use data since the last break. The recent work by Timmermann (2001) is one example of this approach. Needless to say, it is also very wasteful.

Why are structural breaks so important? To understand their relevance, consider the stylized case discussed in Clements and Hendry (2008). They begin by noticing that '[i]n financial data analysis, it is common to allow for distributions with fatter tails than the normal, to take account of outliers'.[20] They then consider the case of a non-fat-tailed distribution of *levels* (not of *differences* in levels) that suddenly changes

---

[15] For a discussion, see, e.g., Lopez de Prado (2011) and references therein.

[16] For example Capielo *et al.* (2003) find evidence of a structural break in the correlations between EU bonds after the introduction of the Euro as common currency. Stock and Watson (1996) reported that the majority of the macroeconomic times series analysed by them displayed evidence of instability.

[17] See, in this respect Hoover (2001) for a thoughtful discussion.

[18] As Haldane (2012) suggests, however, also *micro*structural changes can bring about profound transformations of the trading dynamics, and, as a consequence, of the full distributional properties of the time series affected. See also Easley, Lopez de Prado and O'Hara (2011).

[19] As for non-linearities, these are associated with *periodic*, as opposed to permanent, changes in economic conditions, such as those associated with business cycles. (The term 'periodic' does not imply that certain economic conditions will recur at regular intervals – this case is referred to as 'seasonality'.) Focusing again on the means, the most salient characteristic of non-linearities is that the shifts in means, unlike those assumed for structural breaks, are only transient. The world is different today from yesterday, but it looks like a 'season' ago, *and tomorrow, or the day after tomorrow, it may look like yesterday again.* Regime switching and Threshold Auto Regressive (TAR) techniques are some of the tools of choice to deal with these phenomena.

We must remember, of course, that the definitions presented above are clear and neat, but in practice exceptional events do not come with a convenient label attached to them, and that in real-world empirical analysis the classification can often be messy. Is for instance the Great Recession of 2007–9 a non-linearity (a severe variation on the recurrent theme of recessions that do periodically occur), or a structural break (the harbinger of persistent changes in monetary policies, regulation and market infrastructure)? So, the neat definitions above are often blurred, and, as noted for instance by Diebold and Nason (1990), apparent non-linearities can be due to the presence of a structural breaks and/or outliers.

[20] Clements and Hendry (2008, p. 7).

its mean by an amount, $\Delta\mu$, much larger than its standard deviation. If one were to neglect the possibility of the change in mean, an unexceptional draw from the new shifted distribution may well now be interpreted as a '10-standard-deviation event'.[21] And the same 'exceptional' interpretation would be given to all the subsequent events as well. As Clements and Hendry (2008) point out, even GARCH-like models, which allow for 'a large draw in one period [to induce] a large shock in the next period',[22] do not fix the problem, because they make large draws *of either sign* more likely. This does not help, because if the shift in mean of the otherwise identical 'benign' distribution has been say, upwards, a GARCH model can give high probability to 'a [large] negative value, whereas the location shift has essentially no probability of such an outcome'.[23]

Clearly, as one observes one near-impossible event after the other, one soon draws the conclusion that the model needs revising. However, owing to the non-stationarity of most financial level time series, data are usually differenced prior to statistical analysis. When this is done, the shift in mean produces one single 'outlier', all subsequent realizations fall neatly on the body of the previous (pre-shift) distribution, and the original data-generating model *for the first-differenced variable* may appear to need revision in the variance (and in its higher moments), but not necessarily in the mean.

This goes some way towards explaining why many statisticians who examine time series of first differences in financial prices seem to find almost by default a suitably leptokurtic distribution. Econometricians, especially when engaged in testing macroeconomic theories, tend to look instead at shifts in the means of the level variables as their first port of call. (Needless to say, the second approach invites a more thoughtful approach to model-making, as questions about the reason, timing and plausibility of the shift in means naturally arise.)

Faced with these two different possible pictures of how the world changes, it often appears that which modelling route is chosen depends more on which graduate school one researcher has attended, which journals she publishes in, and with which of her colleagues she sits at the university cafeteria, than on a dispassionate analysis of the problem at hand. These sociological preferences notwithstanding, the fact remains that, depending on whether we allow for the possibility of a change in mean or not, we are drawn to two radically different views of the world: in one case we have a 'tame' and non-leptokurtic distribution for the levels which occasionally undergoes shifts in mean; in the other we look for an invariant distribution of the first differences, with significantly fat tails.[24]

Not surprisingly, the statistical techniques to deal with these different views of the world are very different. More insidiously, if we associate special and deep meanings

---

[21] As practitioners used to quip in the weeks immediately before and after the 2008 Lehman events once-in-the-lifetime-of-the-universe events used to occur almost every other day.

[22] *Ibid.*, p. 7. GARCH: Generalized Auto-Regressive Conditional Heteroskedasticity.   [23] *Ibid.*, p. 7.

[24] One might object that the shift-in-means explanation produces a single outlier in the time series of the first differences, while higher volatility appears to be clustered. This is true, but it is not implausible to suppose that, in the immediate aftermath of a structural change, uncertainty may increase *exactly as a result of the shift in means.*

to the observation of outliers, we are drawn to building complex models, where much simpler, although less 'sexy', explanations are possible.

Apart from a ruthless application of Occam's principle (*Entia non sunt multiplicanda* can be effectively if not accurately translated as 'Go for the simpler model'), what can guide our choice of the modelling approach? Indeed, one could well argue that, whatever the generating mechanism, an outlier is an outlier is an outlier, and that if one wants to throw late-Latin quotes around one could counterpoint Occam's dictum with Newton's *Hypotheses non fingo*: we do not need to speculate what the 'true origin' of an outlier is, one might say, and simply study its statistical properties in a non-theory-laden manner. If the observable effect of repeated changes in means is indistinguishable from periodic bursts of volatility, why should we bother distinguishing between the two?

In line with the philosophy of this book, we believe that there is a profound difference between describing and trying to understand, and that the latter approach is both more cognitively 'natural' and more fruitful. It is for this reason that we advocate in this respect the use of structural models endowed with a causal explanatory structure. Data, we believe, do *not* speak by themselves, and their interpretation only becomes meaningful – indeed, possible – when they are integrated with a theoretical model.[25] For the reasons presented in the previous chapters, and further expanded upon in Chapter 11, we also believe that the most powerful models are causal ones. As the quote that opens this chapter indicates, we do not quite know what causation is, but we nonetheless believe that thinking causally is very powerful. So, faced with an 'outlier', we like to think about what might have 'caused' its occurrence, and to choose between the shift-in-the-mean or the increase-in-uncertainty views of the changing world on the basis of each specific problem at hand.

4.4   The bridge with our approach

How do these theoretical (and, admittedly, somewhat vague) considerations affect our modelling approach?

The most important feature of our approach is that we place causation, rather than association, firmly at centre stage. We are well aware that the concept of causation is difficult, and, given the philosophical heavyweights that have engaged with the subject in the last two thousand years or so, we are understandably reluctant to enter the fray. We simply point to the fact that, whatever its epistemic status, causation does seem to be one of the recurrent and most familiar modes of reasoning for the human species. We simply acknowledge this cognitive fact, and exploit it for our means.

---

[25] Even in the physical sciences what is observable (a 'datum') is not given *a priori*: so, for instance, even a positivist like Heisenberg admitted in his exchange with Einstein that '[i]t is the theory that decides what we can observe' (Heisenberg, 1971, quoted in Camilleri 2009). Lest the reader be tempted to think that this statement only applies to the more exoteric areas of physics (like observability in quantum mechanics), she may want to ponder about the 'observability' status of epicycles in pre- and post-Copernican astronomy: in one theory they were observable quantities worthy of precise investigation; in the other, they simply did not exist.

We therefore wholeheartedly agree with Clements and Hendry (2008) that no-one can predict the unpredictable, and we certainly do not posses the crystal ball mentioned in Hendry (2005).[26] However, we do not take this to be an indictment of a causality-based approach. We do not try to use deterministic causality (of the type 'If A then certainly B') in order to carry out sharp point forecasts. We simply invoke causality to assist our reasoning in assigning subjective conditional probabilities.

There is something deep here. We are well aware that Bayesian nets need not be endowed with a causal and/or temporal interpretation. However, we find it at last intriguing that when such an interpretation is possible *and used*, the resulting directed graph turns out almost invariably to be the most parsimonious (in the sense of having the smallest number of arcs) of all the graphs that can be built among the same variables *and that give rise to exactly the same joint probability*; and that the assignment of the *subjective* conditional probabilities becomes easy to the point of becoming almost 'spontaneous' in the causal mode, and well-nigh impossible in the non-causal set-ups. As former physicists, we believe that simplicity, parsimony and elegance are a powerful indication that 'we are on the right track'.

Given our approach to causation, how exactly do we propose to deal with non-linearities, structural breaks and outliers?

Starting from structural breaks, let's consider a real-world example. At the time of writing we are facing the possibility of the demise of the Euro and the default of one or more European sovereigns. This would certainly qualify as a structural break. In our approach we cannot predict (in the sharp sense that Clements and Hendry (2008) seem to attribute to the word) if and when such an event will happen. Neither can we predict how exactly such a crisis will unfold. However, we can express via the logical constructs we employ in this book (the Bayesian nets) our assessment of the changing probabilities of the consequences of such a structural break.

When it comes to structural breaks, we have little, if any, confidence in our ability to read precursor signs in the tea-leaves of past data. We also think that, *if we fear that a structural break may be about to happen*, making use of more recent data in order to predict how the event we are most interested in is going to unfold is often of little use.[27] We look instead to structural models to guide us as to what might happen if the break does materialize.

---

[26] The following quotation from Hendry (2005) illustrates his position about predictability:

'[The forecaster] essentially requires a crystal ball that can foresee looming changes. In some cases, however, this may be possible. For example, related situations may have occurred previously, allowing a model to be built of the change process itself (though that too could change): regime-switching models are one attempt to do so for states that often change and are partly predictable as the conditional probability of the state differs from the unconditional. To date, their forecasting performance has not proved spectacular, even against univariate predictors, partly because the timing of the switch remains somewhat elusive albeit crucial to their accuracy. Another possibility is that although breaks are relatively rare, they have discernible precursors, either leading indicators or causal, as is being discovered in volcanology. Here, more detailed studies of evolving breaks are merited . . .'

[27] Of course, if we are at the very beginning of a new structural phase, sensitive and responsive statistical techniques based on extremely recent data can be very useful. The use of high-frequency data can be of help here.

In almost every financial or economics-related domain we can think of, we do not believe that any one model should warrant our exclusive attention.[28] We think instead that the unavoidable – and healthy – uncertainty about reasonable structural descriptions of reality can be accounted for in an approximate way using a probabilistic language. In particular, we take seriously the link between the plurality of possible models and investors' aversion to ambiguity (as opposed to risk). See the discussion of this important topic in Chapters 23 and 29.

Finally, we acknowledge that, even if one made a brave attempt to account as best one could for non-linearities and structural breaks, outliers – in the sense of realizations that, given the distributional assumptions made, should not exist – would still appear. Together with Hamlet, we are aware that there is more in Heaven and Earth that is dreamt of in our philosophy.[29] As we explain in Chapters 11 and 20, we therefore deal with the possibility of occurrence of what Sornette calls 'monsters of nature' by allowing the expert to carry out draws in the excited state from a distribution centred around as extreme a value as she may like – and we invite her to test the robustness and sensitivity of the results to these extreme assignments. The possibility of incorporating outliers is therefore naturally built into our approach.

So, in short, this is where we stand with respect to non-linearities, structural breaks and outliers. Where does this place us with respect to other, better known and more firmly established modelling approaches to tail, extreme, and variously exceptional events? To answer these questions we look in some detail in the following chapter at some of the best known approaches, starting from econophysics and moving then to Extreme Value Theory.

---

[28] As we write there is a lively debate about the possible Nipponization of the Western economies (see, e.g., Koo 2009). We do not know for sure whether this view is correct. However, it would be negligent not to include scenarios based on the possibility of this occurrence.

[29] 'There are more things in heaven and earth, Horatio, than are dreamt of in your philosophy.' *Hamlet* (Act I, Scene V, 166–167).

5 Econophysics

For the reasons we discussed in the previous chapter, exceptional events and disconti-
nuities play a central role in our book. At least two well-known approaches are often
thought of as the solution of choice when one deals with exceptional events, namely
econophysics and Extreme Value Theory. It is important to position our approach in
relation to these well-established disciplines, and to explain why we borrow little from
their tool-kit. This we do in the next two chapters.

5.1 Econophysics, tails and exceptional events

In this and the following sections we look at econophysics from the rather reductive
prism of its treatment of extreme events in general. The econophysicists' programme
is far broader (and methodologically very interesting), but doing justice to it would
entail too long a detour – hence our narrow focus.

In order to appreciate how extreme events fit in the broader philosophy of the
econophysicists, we look at two distinct aspects of their research progamme – namely,
the quest for 'more realistic assumptions', and the belief that valuable insight into
economic and financial phenomena can be obtained using the techniques and the
conceptual framework offered by the physical sciences. We start our discussion by
giving a brief definition of what econophysics is.

5.2 The scope and methods of econophysics

Econophysics is a proteiform beast, and no single definition will be found satisfactory
by all of its practitioners. Since we have to start somewhere, we choose to begin with
Mantegna and Stanley (2000), arguably two of the founding fathers of the discipline,
who provide the following definition of econophysics:

the multidisciplinary field of econophysics . . . [is] a neologism that denotes the activities of physicists
who are working on economics problems to test a variety of new conceptual approaches deriving
from the physical sciences[1]

---

[1] Mantegna and Stanley (2000, pp. viii–ix).

As we shall see,[2] this focus on the physicists' way of looking at certain problems, and on their methods, has a profound influence on the conceptual foundations of econophysics, and on the scope of its field of interest.

Since a (set of) method(s) rather than a (set of) problem(s) is the main distinguishing feature of the discipline, a variety of apparently disparate topics have been tackled by econophysicists, such as 'the distributions of returns in financial markets [Mirowski 1989; Mantegna 1991; Bouchaud and Cont 2002; Gopakrishnan *et al.* 1999; Farmer and Joshi 2002; Sornette 2003], the distribution of income and wealth . . . , the distribution of economic shocks and growth rate variations . . . , the distribution of firm sizes and growth rates . . . , the distribution of city sizes . . . , and the distribution of scientific discoveries'.[3]

As the quote above indicates,[4] one of the areas of research for which econophysicists are better known is the study of the distribution of asset returns. This focus is not a gratuitous obsession, but underlies the conviction that, to make progress in finance and economics, one must look in detail at the phenomenology of prices and returns, and take these empirical results as the foundations upon which financial theories can be built.

There is more, though, in the strong focus given by econophysicists on the distributional features of returns – and on power laws in particular – than a simple attention to the empirical details of the phenomenon at hand. The reason why scaling and power laws play such an important part in the econophysicists' programme is threefold: first, there is a desire to move away from 'stylized' models of financial reality and to provide a solid phenomenological and empirical grounding to theoretical work. Second, these laws are supposed to underlie a variety of physical, social and economics-related phenomena, to appear as manifestations of deep underlying similarities in the generative mechanisms, and naturally to display the signature of common high-level underlying regularities.[5] Third, and arguably most important,

---

[2] As Rosser (2006) correctly points out '[w]hat is most striking about this definition is that it is not an intellectual one primarily, but rather a sociological one. It is based on who is doing the working on economics problems, physicists, not specifically on what those problems are or what the specific methods or theories are that they are using from physics to study or solve these problems.' While this is true, the emphasis is, of course, not on the physicists as individuals, but on the methods they employ, such as statistical physics, renormalization group theory, self-organized criticality, or random matrix theory, to cite only a few.

[3] Rosser (2006, p. 4), some of the citations omitted.

[4] Another indication of the supposedly near-universal applicability range of the econphysicists' interests can be gleaned from the following quote from Sornette (2004) (book that is addressed to 'researchers . . . in physics, econophysics, geophysics and metereology'), about the range of applicability of the stretched exponential distribution: 'distribution of radio and light emissions from galaxies, of US GOM OCS oilfield reserve sizes, of World, US and France agglomeration sizes, of the United Nations 1996 country sizes, of daily Forex US-Mark and Franc-Mark price variations, and of the Raup-Sepkoskis kill curve in evolution.'

[5] For a statistical-mechanics treatment of phase transitions, order parameters and complexity see, e.g., Sethna (2006), Kadanoff (2000). A gentle but quantitative introduction to renormalization-group techniques is provided in McComb (2004). For readers who actually may want to carry out 'real' calculations, critical phenomena in physical systems and renormalization-group techniques are well described from a quantitative perspective in Ma (2000). For a simple but precise treatment of non-linear dynamics and chaos, see, e.g., Thomson and Stewart (1986), or, at a more introductory level, Addison (1997).

[p]ower laws have a particular meaning and appeal to physicists. . . . [T]he irrelevance of the collective behaviour on microscopic detail becomes extreme when the system is close to a phase transition. At the phase transition point, called critical point, the system exhibits scale invariance properties . . . which manifest in power laws. . . . [T]heoretical models . . . reproduce the exact values of the exponents of the power laws. These *critical* exponents . . . are *universal* because their values do not depend on microscopic details but only on the qualitative nature of the interaction (which in physics is embodied in symmetries, conservation laws, and in the space dimensionality). . . . This is remarkable because it allows us to classify the (critical) behaviour of different systems into so-called universality classes. Then it is sufficient to understand the behaviour of one member of a universality class to know that of all the others. Conversely, showing that a model belongs to a known universality class (e.g. by measuring its critical exponent) implies that all the known results about the latter also apply to the model . . .[6]

Let's look to the first justification for paying special attention to the distribution of returns, i.e., to the 'empirical-grounding' justification. Of course, 'traditional' economists are well aware that, say, the Gaussian distribution does not afford a 'perfect' description of the phenomena under study and when they do employ it, they do so on tractability grounds, or to focus on the essence, rather than the fine details, of a problem. In the eyes of the econophysicists, however, the price to pay for using such simpler and more tractable distributions is too high, because by doing so one misses *essential* features of the problem at hand. As Potters states in a debate about predictability in finance,[7] 'influential pricing models have typically relied on assumptions too simple to have *any* relation to the reality they seek to predict'.[8] As a result, econophysicists believe that better models can only be formulated by paying close empirical attention to the phenomena at hand. They believe that this 'Baconian' practice is at the heart of research in the physical sciences, and therefore present themselves as the students of the physics of the economic world – hence their name.

This approach should be contrasted with what we will call the 'axiomatic' view. In this modelling approach certain properties are posited for, say, time series (e.g., normality) or economic actors (e.g., rationality), and the logical consequences of these assumptions are then obtained.[9] In the axiomatic approach, it is the consequences, not the assumptions, that are confronted with the empirical evidence.

---

[6] Challet, Marsili and Zhang (2005, pp. 75–76).   [7] In Davidson (2010, p. 3).

[8] Emphasis added. Coming from physicists, this comment is puzzling: some of the most fascinating and insight-providing models in physics – such as the Ising model, the perfect-gas model or the spring-and-ball model of a solid – are outrageously simplified, yet they have been extremely useful in helping our understanding properties of the real world. The 'trick', in physics much as in finance, is to understand when a model should be abandoned, not to strive for a more and more 'realistic' set of assumptions.

[9] There is a deep, but seldom recognized, parallel between econophysicists and behavioural economists. Both reject the 'axiomatic' method (in the sense above), and try to ground the proper study of the financial world on the painstaking observation of how prices in one case, or human beings in the other, actually behave.

    Both schools of thought show impatience with stylized (and parsimonious) models, both implicitly or explictly reject *as-if* approaches to model building, and both have had their share of running-ins and misunderstandings with the 'neoclassical' school.

    Both have been depicted in the popular – and, sometimes, not-so-popular – press as 'thought martyrs' fighting against a reactionary academic establishment.

    This engaging story of 'insurgency against the establishment' would be even more convincing if some of the proponents of at least one of the two schools had not been awarded Nobel prizes, and did not teach at institutions such as the University of Chicago.

This is not the place to enter the debate as to which approach is more reasonable, or even as to which more closely resembles the practices actually found in the natural sciences.[10] (See, however, MacKenzie (2008) for a thoughtful discussion of the subtle interactions in finance between reality and models, which act as 'engines', not 'cameras'.) The pertinent comment for our purpose is that it is only when the axiomatic method is caricatured, or is poorly understood, that it seems 'absurd', and its proponents become either reactionaries or actors in a conspiracy of thought repression. We (reluctantly) leave this discussion to one side.

The more interesting and original reasons for paying great attention to distributional features alluded to above are, however, the supposedly extremely wide range of phenomena that can be described by similar distributions; and the alleged universalities that underlie these regularities. We look at these in some detail below.

5.3 'Deep analogies'

Important as they may be in the econophysicists' programme, return distributions are only a part of their research field, and, as mentioned above, if one looks for the ultimate cornerstones of their approach, one must look elsewhere. As we said, this 'ultimate core' is to be found in the belief that finance and economics can be profitably studied using the conceptual framework and the analytical techniques that have proven so successful in the physical sciences, and in statistical mechanics in particular.[11]

It is important to stress that the tool-kit of the physicist is often not offered as a complementary tool to be used alongside more traditional approaches to understand financial and economic matters. Instead, it is presented as a fundamental and essential methodological development. Malevergne and Sornette (2006), for instance, first point to those situations in statistical physics where there is a spontaneous breaking of symmetry. Then they state that 'the sudden macroscopic changes of organization due to small variations of control parameters has led to powerful concepts such as "emergence": the macroscopic organization has many properties not shared by its constituents'.[12] And from this they conclude that '[f]or the market, . . . its overall properties can *only* be understood through the study of the transformation from the microscopic level of individual agents to the macroscopic level of the global market. In statistical physics, this can often be performed by the very powerful tool called "renormalization group".'[13]

Along similar lines, in a recent review article Chakraborti *et al.* (2011a) make a case for deep analogies between physics and economics by claiming that

---

[10] One could argue, for instance, that much of the work by Einstein in relativity was conducted more in the axiomatic rather than in the empirical mould. Einstein himself even later professed ignorance of the Michelson–Morley experiment at the time when he was obtaining the results of special relativity (see, e.g., Pais 1982, pp. 111–119, esp. p. 115). More generally, in physics outrageously simple models abound (think of the Ising model, of 'cloacked' particles in quantum field theory, or of the pseudopotential approach to band structure calculations), whose validity is posited as a working assumption, and whose *consequences* are tested against reality. Testing the 'realism' of, say, the Ising model is a close-to-meaningless endeavour.

[11] For a wide-ranging review of topics dealt with in the econophysics literature see, e.g., Mandelbrot (2001a, b, c, d, e).

[12] Malevergne and Sornette (2006, p. 22).   [13] *Ibid.*, p. 22, our emphasis added.

[o]n a general level, both economics and physics deal with 'everything around us', but from different perspectives. On a practical level, the goals of both disciplines can be either purely theoretical in nature or strongly oriented towards the improvement of the quality of life. On a more technical side, analogies often become equivalences . . .

When it comes to the analogies that 'often become equivalences' Chakraborti *et al.* (2011b) defend the use in economics of statistical mechanical tools by pointing out that 'it is difficult or almost impossible to write down the "microscopic equations of motion" for an economic system with all the interacting entities'. These authors then go on to claim that 'since economic systems may be investigated on various scale sizes', 'an understanding of the global behaviour of economic systems seems to need concepts such as stochastic dynamics, correlation effects, self-organization, self-similarity and scaling, and for their application we do not have to go into the detailed "microscopic" description of economic systems'.

Appealing as the argument may be, we would like to point out that while *'self-organization, self-similarity and scaling'* may well call for a macroview account of the system at hand, the latter can be invoked without reference to these statistical-mechanics-inspired concepts. For instance, the same macro-level description is commonly found in traditional economics (see, e.g., representative agents, single-good economies, etc.) without any reference to self-organization, self-similarity or scaling. Ironically, when traditional economics employs these high-level aggregate description, it is often criticized by econophysicists for its 'unrealistic assumptions'.

As for the phenomenological evidence, there are skeptics who doubt that it may be as compelling as econophysicists claim, as this extended quotation from Gallegati *et al.* (2006) makes clear,

[i]t must be . . . emphasized that there is no reason to believe that one *should* find simple power laws in *all* types of socioeconomic data that are universal over countries and time horizons. Although [the econophysicists'] interpretations of power laws as signatures of complex, possibly self-organizing systems makes them a much wanted object, one should be careful in not seeing a power-law decline in each and every collection of data points with a negative slope. In fact, the ubiquitous declarations of studied objects as fractals or self-similar has been criticized also in a paper [Avnir (1998)] that surveyed all 96 papers in *Physical Review* journals over the period 1990-1996 which contain an empirical scaling analysis of some natural or experimental time series. They find that 'the scaling range of experimentally declared fractality is extremely limited, centred around 1.3 orders of magnitude.' . . . They find it doubtful to claim that all these studies show that 'the geometry of nature is fractal' . . .

We would also like to add (echoing in this respect Bouchaud (2001)) that, while critical phenomena give rise to power laws, power laws need not be associated with critical phenomena, and that 'they can arise from much more simple mechanisms . . . In these cases power laws . . . do not carry much information on the specific interaction mechanism'.[14]

As this statement, which comes after all from a respected econophysicist, is clearly correct, it pays to ask the question as to why many econophysicists are so wedded

---

[14] Challet, Marsili and Zhang (2005, p. 76).

to linking power laws (whose applicability or otherwise to a specific phenomenon is a rather 'dry' empirical issue) to statistical mechanics and phase transitions (a methodological and modelling position). We offer a possible explanation in the next section.

5.4   The invariance of physical and financial 'laws'

One of the consequences of treating matters in finance and economics on the same footing as phenomena in physics is the implicit requirement that the laws governing the subject matter should, at some level, be invariant – in the same way as the laws of physics are. Invariance of a physical mechanism, however, does not require that the observable phenomenon should look 'always the same'. Consider, for instance, the case of phase transitions. Water looks and behaves very differently from ice or vapour, but still remains an aggregation of molecules of H_2O that always obey the same laws. Faced with very different regimes in finance and economics (booms and busts, market euphoria and market crashes, etc.), econophysicists pursue this analogy and suggest that phenomena such as market crashes can be regarded as a different 'phase' of the same underlying phenomenon.

As a consequence, one of the econophysicists' responses to the patent non-stationarity of financial time series is to neglect, or downplay, the possibility of structural breaks (there are no structural breaks in the laws of physics), and to assert instead that beyond certain 'critical points', long-rate fluctuations (precursors) begin to appear,[15] and the macroscopic behaviour of a given phenomenon qualitatively changes. In this picture, the outliers identified in the empirical phase of the econophysicists' analysis often become the realizations of the returns that obtain immediately before or after a phase transition.

So, because of this phase-transition-like view of non-stationarity, in the views of some econophysicists the abrupt changes observed in empirical analysis (the 'outliers') are due neither to structural breaks, nor to the periodic non-linearities (business-cycles-like) of traditional econometric analysis, but to the manifestation across phase changes of an invariant reality.

More generally, power laws play a particularly important role in the view of econophysicist because they are interpreted as the 'signature' of a number of interesting and 'rich' mechanisms where self-organization, tipping points, scale-free networks[16] and other 'non-classical' interactions are at play. Yes, indeed, power laws are found almost ubiquitously in social and natural phenomena.[17] However, one should always keep in mind that there is no such thing as *a* 'power-law-generating' mechanism. As Mitchell

---

[15] Sornette (2003).   [16] For a discussion, see, e.g., Mitchell (2009, p. 250).

[17] Perhaps *too* ubiquitously? The data that support some power-law analyses lend themselves to complex statistical interpretations, and sometimes the precise exponent, or even the very power-law nature, of the dependence become the topic of heated dispute. (See, e.g., the Kleiber–Rubner debate about metabolic scaling rate, as discussed in Mitchell (2009).) So, Keller (2005) states that '[c]urrent assessments of the commonality of power laws are probably an overestimate'. Less diplomatically, Shalizi (2005) claims that '[o]ur tendency to hallucinate power laws is a disgrace' (quoted in Mitchell 2009).

(2009) reports, 'when [she] was at the Santa Fe Institute, it seemed that there was a lecture every other day on a new hypothesized mechanism that resulted in power law distributions':[18] the problem, therefore, is that 'there turn out to be nine and sixty ways of constructing power laws, *and every single one of them is right*'.[19]

5.5   Where we differ

In sum: we believe that a lot can be learned from the accurate analysis of how market prices really behave in 'usual' and 'unusual' market conditions (and we do not see why this type of analysis cannot complement what we have dubbed above the 'axiomatic' approach).

We do find the methodological emphasis on the invariance of the underlying 'physical laws' and the explanation of instances of non-stationarity as 'phase transitions' intriguing. However, we do not find this way of modelling the financial world as widely applicable as many econophysicists, in their quest for universality, maintain. Generalizing perhaps too broadly, we also find the theoretical justifications offered by econophysicists for their approach to be at times more 'analogical' than cogent.[20]

We are intrigued by the apparent ubiquity of power-law behaviour, non-linear dynamics and self-organized criticality, instances of which are claimed to have been found literally almost everywhere: from weather systems (Lorentz 1963), to forest fires (Miller and Page 2007), sand piles (quoted in Haldane and Nelson 2012), the flow of traffic flow, the behaviour of equity prices (Mandelbrot 1963), fluctuations in business inventory (Sterman 1989a, b), to the floods of the river Nile (Mandelbrot and Hudson 2005).[21] The high-level conceptual insights offered by these ideas are certainly dazzling. When we leave the 30 000-feet perspective, we are nor sure, however, to what extent this taxonomization can help action-level understanding and intervention (say, in creating diversified portfolios, or in designing effective financial regulation). To explain better what we mean, consider a similarly wide-ranging, high-level idea, such as the concept of linearity in physics. It is certainly a very deep and profound one, and is found, exactly or as an approximation, in apparently unrelated fields (from electromagnetism to quantum mechanics). Much as it may afford deep insights and it allows similarities to be appreciated among apparently unrelated phenomena, *in itself* it does not take one very far. And, at least in the case of linear systems, taking the 'deep analogies' too far would make one overstate the similarities between, say, the electromagnetic field and

---

[18]   Mitchell (2009, p. 254).

[19]   Shalizi (2005), quoted in Mitchell (2009). In this context it is entertaining to report the controversy among Zipf, Mandelbrot and Simon about the 'cause' for the occurrence of Zipf's law in human language (according to which, given an almost arbitrary text of some length, the frequency of a word is approximately proportional to the inverse of its rank – a power law with exponent −1). Zipf (1932) defended a 'principle of least effort', Mandelbrot (1953) put forth an explanation using information theory and Herbert Simon (he of 'satisficing' fame) advocated preferential attachment. Some cold water was poured on the heated debate when Miller (1957) showed that 'the text generated by monkeys typing randomly on a keyboard, ending a word every time they (randomly) hit the space bar, will follow Zipf's law as well.' (Mitchell, 2009, p. 272).

[20]   See, e.g., Chakraborti *et al.* (2011a) discussed above.

[21]   See Haldane and Nelson (2012) for a discursive account of these phenomena.

the behaviour of quantum mechanical objects. When it comes to 'interventions' (say, creating a robustly diversified portfolio), the problem is not that we have no potential high-level mechanisms to generate power laws or 'phase transitions': as discussed above, the real problem is that we have too many.

In our modelling of exceptional events we therefore prefer to start from a more agnostic position, namely the view that each crisis might be potentially *intrinsically* different. As a consequence, we keep a methodologically open mind, and we believe that information about the next crisis (the one of greatest concern to the portfolio manager) can be gleaned from a variety of sources. Some of these sources are intrinsically forward-looking (say, 'implied' volatilities or spreads, or the domain knowledge of economists or political observers); some rely on structural models; and some, of course, benefit from an enlightened and phenomenologically aware analysis of past data – and if the econophysicists can make us better aware of power-law features of return distributions, we are grateful for this empirical assistance.

There is another reason why we should pay attention to econophysics. As we shall argue in the last parts of this book, uncertainty about models is one of the problems faced by the portfolio manager. Indeed, we give ambiguity aversion (which is closely linked to model uncertainty) an important role in our final approach. At least in this respect, econophysics should therefore be taken into account – if for no other reason that many academics and practitioners take it seriously, and can therefore influence via reflexivity financial observables (see, e.g., Mackenzie 2008; Soros 2003, 2008). However, we do not believe that econophysics contains all the answers (or the most compelling and universally applicable answers) to the question of how to deal with tail events, and we make scant use of its methodological (as opposed to phenomenological) teachings.

We do this with some regret: as one-time physicists,[22] we find the parallels with phase transitions and similar physics-inspired explanations fascinating. In a sense, we would therefore 'like' these explanations to be true. However, we find the leap of faith required for the bolder methodological generalizations of econophysics too audacious for our timorous hearts, and we prefer to remain closer to shore.

---

[22] As it happens, in a previous life one of us (RR) was actively involved in phase-transition studies in condensed-matter physics.

6 Extreme Value Theory

6.1 A brief description

The second mainstream approach that has often been invoked as a, or sometimes *the*, solution to the problem of estimating the probability of extreme events is Extreme Value Theory (EVT). There are many good treatments of Extreme Value Theory, of different levels of sophistication.[1] We limit our discussion here to those conceptual aspects of the theory that are of relevance to the topic of this chapter. We follow closely the treatment in McNeil, Frey and Embrechts (2005).

Our first observation[2] is that there is a close parallel between the central limit theorem for the sum of *identical and independently distributed* and normal (or, more generally, stable) distributions on the one hand, and on the other the limiting distribution of normalized maxima of distributions also with *identical and independently distributed* random variables. More precisely, given a random variable X, with cumulative distribution F, define as block maximum the maximum realization of this random variable out of n realizations:

$$M_n = \max\{x_1, x_2, \ldots, x_n\} \tag{6.1}$$

Call $F^n(x)$ the probability that the maximum of a given n-block should be less than the value x:

$$P(M_n < x) = P(x_1 < x, x_2 < x, \ldots, x_n < x) \tag{6.2}$$

$$= P(x_1 < x)P(x_2 < x) \ldots P(x_n < x) = F^n(x) \tag{6.3}$$

Let's now make the size, n, of the block larger and larger. If there exist sequences of constants, $\{c_n\}$ and $\{d_n\}$, with $\{c_n\} \in \mathbb{R}^+$ and $\{d_n\} \in \mathbb{R}$, such that the following limit exists:

$$\lim_{n \to \infty} P\left(\frac{M_n - d_n}{c_n} \le x\right) = \lim_{n \to \infty} F^n(c_n x + d_n) = H(x) \tag{6.4}$$

---

[1] See, e.g., de Haan and Ferreira (2006), Kotz and Nadarajaham (2000), Reiss and Thomas (2007).
[2] In our presentation we draw on McNeil, Frey and Embrechts (2005, esp. p. 265).

then (assuming that some regularity conditions are satisfied) the distribution F is said to be in the maximum domain of attraction, $MDA(H)$, of H: $F \in MDA(H)$.

As a next step we can define the distribution function of the (standard) Generalized Extreme Value Distribution, H_ξ, to be given by

$$H_\xi = \exp[-(1+\xi x)^{-\frac{1}{\xi}}] \quad \text{for } \xi \neq 0 \tag{6.5}$$

$$H_\xi = \exp[-\exp(-x)] \quad \text{for } \xi = 0 \tag{6.6}$$

As is well known, the distribution above nests the popular Frechet, Gumbel and Weibull distributions for values of $\xi > 0$, $\xi = 0$ and $\xi < 0$, respectively.

The link between Generalized Extreme Value Distributions and the limit H defined above is then established by the Fisher–Tippet (or Gnedenko) theorem, which states that if a distribution F belongs to the maximum domain of attraction of H ($F \in MDA(H)$), then H must belong to the family H_ξ, i.e., must be a Generalized Extreme Value Distribution and therefore have the form (6.5) or (6.6).

6.2 Applications to finance and risk management

The theorem above has been used (and misused) in finance to claim that, loosely speaking, exceptional returns must belong to an identifiable class of Extreme Value Distributions, and that the task for the portfolio or risk manager worried about tail events should be the estimation of the (location, shape and family) parameters of a suitable distribution.

The block maximum approach presented above for simplicity of exposition is certainly not the numerically the most effective one – it is actually very wasteful (because to perform the analysis one only retains the maximum realization of the variable X in a rather large block). We are therefore happy to concede that other methods – such as, for instance, the threshold exceedance method[3] – can be much more powerful for practical applications. Whatever the estimation approach, however, the conceptual requirement remains that the realizations of the underlying random variable should be *independently* drawn from an *identical* distribution. In the presence of structural breaks and non-linearities, we believe that this assumption is not warranted for the distribution of returns. And studies one of us has carried out for interest rates (Rebonato and Gaspari 2006) also make us believe that, when it comes to exceptionally large drawdowns, also the assumption of independence is not satisfied. Therefore both *i*s in the iid requirement seem to be violated.

Our reservations are not limited to these rather 'technical' objections (lack of independence and lack of homoskedasticity), but go to the methodological core of the approach. Extreme Value Theory has traditionally been applied to phenomena such as meteorology (strength of hurricanes), fires, various disasters of relevance for the insurance industry, and the like. Its applied roots are firmly actuarial. In all these phenomena, it is reasonable to assume that neither structural breaks nor non-linearities

---

[3] See, e.g., McNeil, Frey and Embrechts (2005, Section 7.2).

in the sense described above should be prevalent (at least over the next observation period). Therefore, given that the 'technical' conditions for its application are met, we think that EVT can provide a powerful investigative tool for these phenomena.

For our applications, the question then arises as to whether the EVT methodology can be successfully applied to the types of 'discontinuity' encountered in finance and economics. We do not see how it can used in the presence of structural breaks. In the case of periodic changes, EVT analysis may be able to give us *unconditional* estimates about the probability of extreme events. However, for a conditional estimate of relevance to the here and now, we are skeptical that sufficient data are available for a meaningful estimation (with the possible exception of high-frequency data) – we should not forget, after all, that the EVT methodology can be very data-hungry.

We hasten to add that we have nothing against the 'proper' application of EVT (both a mathematically rigorous and an intriguing subject) to those domains where the generating mechanisms of the exceptional data are time-invariant. We qualify our statement, however, by pointing out that whether a certain phenomenon is time-invariant or not strongly depends on the projection horizon of our prediction. And the more one looks carefully, the more one realizes that very few, if any, phenomena can be safely considered time-invariant *over all time scales*: life expectancy has changed significantly over a period of decades; the Earth's climate has certainly changed dramatically during its history (and it may be doing so now anthropogenetically at unprecedented speed); the rate of arrival of meteorites on any given planet depends on the astronomical age of the 'solar' system in question; and, well, even the laws of physics may have been *in fieri* in the immediate aftermath of the Big Bang.

Luckily, asset managers need not concern themselves with such ultimate limits of time-homogeneity, as they are bound to encounter time-changing phenomena much, much closer to home.

Part III

Diversification and subjective views

In the previous parts of this book we have argued the merits of causal over an association-based way of dealing with stress events, and we have tried to put our proposed approach in the context of some well-known ways to look at extreme events and outliers. In this part we look at the similarities and differences between what we propose and some better established ways to deal with diversification and to assign subjective scenarii. Not surprisingly, Modern Portfolio Theory, pioneered by Markowitz half a century ago, is the best place to start. We also look, however, at the approaches by Black–Litterman, Meucci and Doust, because of their relevance to the assignment of subjective views.

In Part III we also introduce for the first time the topic of stability (of the allocation weights). Achieving stability will be one of the underlying themes of our book, and we shall therefore return to the topic in the later parts.

7 Diversification in Modern Portfolio Theory

The approach to asset allocation pioneered by Markowitz in the late 1950s and developed over the next five decades truly changed the investment landscape. As we mentioned in our Introduction, it was not much earlier that asset allocation and stock-picking were fundamentally equivalent with identifying the investment opportunity with the highest expected return (see, e.g., Williams 1938).

There are two distinct insights in the Markowitz's approach: the first is that, for most plausible 'utility functions' (i.e., behavioural responses to certain and uncertain changes in consumptions), risk and return are inextricably linked.[1] The second insight points to the importance of diversification in appraising a given investment opportunity given the available universe of investable assets.

One may disagree with the particular statistic used by Markowitz to describe 'risk' (variance); one may argue that correlation is too crude a tool to describe diversification – but these objections simply point to refinements of Markowitz's original insight. Some modern philosophers have argued that all of Western philosophy is a series of footnotes to the work of Plato. We do not know whether this is tenable, but we certainly believe that most of modern investment theory is a series of footnotes to Markowitz's work.

These observations are simply meant to stress that, for all the apparent differences our approach presents with respect to a classic mean-variance optimization problem, we work fully in the conceptual furrow first ploughed by Markowitz. And, as the final chapters of this book show, for most applications it is possible to rewrite with little loss of accuracy the results of our Bayesian-net approach in an 'equivalent' mean-variance language. We too, then, are writing footnotes, and, whenever we criticize some aspect of mean-variance theory, as we do immediately below, we are fully conscious that we are not proposing anything truly revolutionary.

In order to understand which aspects of the classic approach need fixing in what follows we briefly review Markowitz's theory. We do so in a rather idiosyncratic manner – there are, after all, literally dozens of introductions to the topic ranging in quality from the indifferent to the excellent. We, rather ungraciously given the remarks above, present the theory in such a way as to highlight why it needs fixing, and how such a fixing can be accomplished.

---

[1] See also the discussion in Section 26.2.

7.1   Basic results

We assume that our readers are already familiar with the derivation of the 'plain-vanilla' Markowitz allocation formula, and we therefore move at a (very) brisk pace over this well-trodden ground. We spend, however, a couple of introductory words on its logical underpinnings.

There are two distinct ways to look at Markowitz's approach. The first does not depend on the maximization of an expected utility function, and simply solves the problem of finding an optimal trade-off between risk and return, when risk is perceived by the investor to be given by the variance of her returns. In this interpretation, the theory does not explain why this should be the case, but, at least as a starting point, the Ansatz is certainly plausible. Furthermore, if returns were normal, then even if the investors cared about all manner of higher moments, these exotic moments would still be expressible as a function of the variance, and so nothing would be lost in generality. We do not have to spend too much time in alerting the reader to the fact that the assumption of normality should be handled with care.[2]

In the second interpretation of the Markowitz approach we place ourselves in a discounted-expected-utility framework (possibly under constraints) and carry out a maximization of the target function (the discounted expected utility). As for the choice of the utility, we can either assume that it is a quadratic function of wealth[3] (over a useful range), or we expand to second order a more palatable utility function. Markowitz (1991 [1959]),[4] Levy and Markowitz (1979), Pulley (1981), and Kroll, Levy and Markowitz (1984) convincingly argue that, over reasonable ranges of changes in wealth, this can be a surprisingly good approximation.[5] So, for instance, Kroll, Levy and Markowitz (1984) state that

[i]t is frequently asserted that mean-variance analysis applies exactly only when distributions are normal or utility functions quadratic, suggesting that it gives almost optimal results only when distributions are approximately normal or utility functions look almost like a parabola. On the other hand ... Levy and Markowitz showed empirically that the ordering of portfolios by the mean-variance route was almost identical to the ordering obtained by using expected utility for various utility functions and historical distributions of returns ...

We wholeheartedly agree, and discuss this point at length in the final chapters.

---

[2] We point out, however, that a mean-variance utility is appropriate for a wider class of distributions than the Gaussian one. See, e.g., Chamberlain (1983), and his discussion of elliptical distributions.

[3] In our approach we take wealth as a proxy for consumption. We agree with Cochrane (2001) that all utility theories that are not (ultimately) rooted in consumption are 'vacuous' (to use his term). Under the usual assumption that, modulo any initial endowment, all of the investor's consumption purely derives from her investment (see, again, Cochrane 2000), equating investment-generated wealth and consumption is reasonable.

[4] For a discussion of the quality of the quadratic approximation in the case of a logarithmic utility function see Markowitz (1991 [1959]), pp. 121–125, and for a general discussion pp. 282–285.

[5] In this book we are looking at stress (tail) events. When these happen, changes in the risk factors (and hence in wealth) are expected to be large. In this case the use of a quadratic utility function (either 'literally interpreted', or seen as a second-order expansion of a different utility function) could be particularly problematic. Surprisingly, we find that in practical and realistic stress applications this is rarely, if ever, the case.

Why is it important to distinguish between these two possible interpretations of the mean-variance approach? Because, in order to overcome some of the problems of the naive Markowitz approach (namely, the instability of its allocations – about which more below) some fixes have been proposed (e.g., Michaud's resampling) based on the averaging of different Markowitz solutions (see Section 8.3). This approach makes sense if one looks at mean-variance as a prime driver of choice, but cannot be easily justified in the context of a 'proper' expected-utility-maximization framework. Whether this is good or bad will be discussed in Part VIII of this book and in the last chapter. Resampling of the efficient frontier (which we have not defined yet, but with which the reader has no doubt at least a passing acquaintance) is equivalent to averaging in some clever manner the results obtained with successive applications of the mean-variance formula, once we allow for the inputs to be imperfectly known. This is all good and well if we take mean-variance optimization as a self-evident truism that does not require a higher (e.g., utility-based) justification. However, if we look at mean-variance as obtained from the maximization of a quadratic utility function, then we are no longer at liberty to average *over solutions*. We can, of course, still incorporate uncertainty about the inputs (this, indeed, has been one of the many footnotes to Markowitz's work alluded to in the introduction to this chapter). But this uncertainty simply 'widens' and stretches the distribution of returns over which the optimization is carried out.[6] There is no justification in the utility-based approach for averaging over utility-optimized solutions obtained with different but (for each optimization, certain!) parameters.[7] Since stability of allocations is one of the recurrent problems with which we are faced, and since Michaud's resampling method is touted as a possible fix to this problem, it is important for future discussions to keep the distinction between these two interpretations of the mean-variance approach clearly in mind.

With these conceptual caveats out of the way we can present the derivation of the Markowitz results in the 'purest' and cleanest (although, arguably, least practically useful) case: no short-selling constraints (i.e., no positivity constraint on the weights), no budget constraints, no riskless asset. There are three equivalent possible approaches: determining the maximum expected portfolio return given a fixed portfolio variance; determining the minimum portfolio variance for a given portfolio expected return; or by assuming that the expected discounted utility is a smooth concave function, and proceeding by direct differentiation. We will switch between these equivalent approaches.

---

[6] Whether reasonable uncertainty in the inputs generates enough of a stretching and widening as to make an appreciable difference in terms of stability of solution is an important question, which we address in Chapter 28.

[7] Furthermore, averaging over utility-optimized solutions can lead to violation of investment constraints. Meucci (2009), for instance, considers the constraint of having allocations to M out of N assets. Although each optimization can be made to satisfy this constraint, the average of the solutions will, in general, no longer satisfy it.

Starting from the last (the direct derivation from a utility function), given an exogenously assigned $(n \times 1)$ vector of expected returns, $\boldsymbol{\mu}$, and an $(n \times n)$ covariance matrix, $\boldsymbol{\Sigma}$, one has to maximize the utility, U, given by

$$U = \sum_i w_i \mu_i - \frac{1}{2\lambda} \sum_{ij} w_i \sigma_{ij} w_j \tag{7.1}$$

or, in matrix form,

$$U = \boldsymbol{w}'\boldsymbol{\mu} - \frac{1}{2\lambda} \boldsymbol{w}'\boldsymbol{\Sigma}\boldsymbol{w} \tag{7.2}$$

In the two equations above, the quantity w_i is the weight in the portfolio assigned to the ith asset, μ_i is the expected return from the same asset, σ_{ij} is the i, jth element of the covariance matrix for the assets, and λ is (linked to) the coefficient of risk aversion. Differentiation with respect to the weights and setting the derivative to zero to obtain the condition of extremum yields

$$\left. \frac{\partial U}{\partial \boldsymbol{w}} \right|_{\boldsymbol{w}=\boldsymbol{w}^*} = \boldsymbol{\mu} - \frac{1}{\lambda}\boldsymbol{\Sigma}\boldsymbol{w}^* = 0 \tag{7.3}$$

and

$$\boldsymbol{w}^* = \lambda^{-1}\boldsymbol{\Sigma}^{-1}\boldsymbol{\mu} \tag{7.4}$$

As we said, the same result can be equivalently obtained by casting the problem in term of minimization of the variance of the portfolio, Σ_Π,

$$\Sigma_\Pi = \boldsymbol{w}'\boldsymbol{\Sigma}\boldsymbol{w}$$

subject to a given portfolio return, μ_Π,

$$\mu_\Pi = \boldsymbol{w}'\boldsymbol{\mu}$$

or, equivalently, in terms of a maximization of the expected portfolio return for a fixed portfolio variance.

7.2   Important special cases

While theoretically 'clean', the solution just obtained is not very useful in practice. To begin with, it reflects no budget constraint. In theory, one could always adjust this constraint ex post by riskless lending or borrowing (which has zero excess return and does not contribute to the portfolio variance). Needless to say, this is not a realistic option for a variety of reasons. The budget constraint is readily dealt with by means of Lagrange multipliers, while retaining a linear-algebra solution. We present the solution in the case of more general linear constraints on the weights, and we then specialize to the case of the unit budget constraint. (For a discussion of the desirability and the implicit economic interpretation of linear constraints, see Chapter 23.)

More significantly, portfolio managers are often faced with institutional constraints that prevent them from being short. Positivity constraints are therefore very important.

Unfortunately, this type of constraint no longer allows for a simple linear-algebra solution. We show how this problem can be solved in the following section.

7.2.1   Optimal weights with linear constraints

Linear constraints on the weights can be used to specify that the total weights given to particular sub-portfolios should satisfy certain binding constraints. So, for instance, we may have six distinct equity markets, USD, EUR, GBP, YEN, RMB and RUB. We may want to specify that the sum of the investment for the 'emerging markets' (RMB and RUB) should be equal to $X; and that the allocations to USD and EUR should add up to $Y. We then have six assets ($n = 6$) and two constraints ($m = 2$).

$$\begin{bmatrix} 0 & 0 & 0 & 0 & 1 & 1 \\ 1 & 1 & 0 & 0 & 0 & 0 \end{bmatrix} \begin{bmatrix} w_1 \\ w_2 \\ w_3 \\ w_4 \\ w_5 \\ w_6 \end{bmatrix} = \begin{bmatrix} X \\ Y \end{bmatrix} \tag{7.5}$$

Recall that we obtained above Markowitz's optimal weights, w^*, in the case when there are no constraints by maximizing a quadratic utility function:

$$w^* = \lambda \Sigma^{-1} \mu \tag{7.6}$$

Let's see how these change when we impose *linear* constraints on the weights.

Let the utility function be again

$$U = \sum_i w_i \mu_i - \frac{1}{2\lambda} \sum_{ij} w_i \sigma_{ij} w_j \tag{7.7}$$

$$U = w' \mu - \frac{1}{2\lambda} w' \Sigma w \tag{7.8}$$

and let's maximize this utility subject to m linear constraints on the weights of the form

$$\sum_j a_{ij} w_j = b_i \tag{7.9}$$

or, in matrix form,

$$A w = b \tag{7.10}$$

(the matrix A has m rows and n columns). To carry out the constrained optimization, we have to introduce a vector of Lagrangian multipliers, $\gamma_k, k = 1, \ldots, m$, and to create a Lagrangian function, $\mathcal{L}$, given by

$$\mathcal{L} = U - \sum_k \gamma_k \left[\left(\sum_j a_{kj} w_j \right) - b_k \right] \tag{7.11}$$

$$\Longrightarrow \mathcal{L} = U - \gamma'(A w - b) \tag{7.12}$$

In order to find the extremum we have to evaluate $\frac{\partial \mathcal{L}}{\partial w}$ and $\frac{\partial \mathcal{L}}{\partial \gamma}$. We present the derivation in Appendix 7.A. The result for the optimal weights, w^*, is given by:

$$w^* = \lambda \Sigma^{-1}(\mu - A'\gamma) = \lambda \Sigma^{-1}\mu - \lambda \Sigma^{-1}A'\gamma$$

$$= \lambda \Sigma^{-1}\mu - \lambda \Sigma^{-1}A'C^{-1}\left(A\Sigma^{-1}\mu - \frac{1}{\lambda}b\right) \tag{7.13}$$

We specialize this result to the important case of budget constraint below.

    An important special case: budget constraint   There is a very special and important special case of the linear constraints above: it is the so-called budget constraint, which forces the total amount invested to be equal to a given amount – often normalized to \$1. The budget constraint in this case can be expressed as follows:

$$\begin{bmatrix} 1 & 1 & 1 & 1 & 1 & 1 \end{bmatrix} \begin{bmatrix} w_1 \\ w_2 \\ w_3 \\ w_4 \\ w_5 \\ w_6 \end{bmatrix} = 1 \tag{7.14}$$

In this particular important case the vectors γ and b become scalars (γ and b), and the equations above simplify accordingly. It is simplest to re-derive them starting from

$$U = \sum_i w_i \mu_i - \frac{1}{2\lambda} \sum_{ij} w_i \sigma_{ij} w_j \tag{7.15}$$

$$U = w'\mu - \frac{1}{2\lambda} w'\Sigma w \tag{7.16}$$

$$\sum_i w_i = 1 \implies w'\mathbf{1} = 1 \tag{7.17}$$

with $\mathbf{1}$ an $n \times 1$ vector of 1s:

$$\mathbf{1} = \begin{bmatrix} 1 \\ 1 \\ 1 \\ \vdots \\ 1 \end{bmatrix} \tag{7.18}$$

The Lagrangian is now:

$$\mathcal{L} = \sum_i w_i \mu_i - \frac{1}{2\lambda} \sum_{ij} w_i \sigma_{ij} w_j - \gamma \left(1 - \sum_i w_i\right) \tag{7.19}$$

$$\mathcal{L} = w'\mu - \frac{1}{2\lambda} w'\Sigma w - \gamma(1 - w'\mathbf{1}) \tag{7.20}$$

Note that in the vector above γ is just a constant (not a vector) because we have a single binding constraint. Proceeding as above we now have:

$$\frac{\partial \mathcal{L}}{\partial w} = \mu - \frac{1}{\lambda}\Sigma w - 1\gamma = 0 \tag{7.21}$$

$$\frac{\partial \mathcal{L}}{\partial \gamma} = (1 - w'1) \Longrightarrow w'1 = 1 \Longrightarrow 1'w = 1 \tag{7.22}$$

From Equation (7.21) we obtain:

$$w^* = \lambda^{-1}\Sigma^{-1}\mu - \lambda^{-1}\gamma\Sigma^{-1}1 \tag{7.23}$$

Substituting (7.23) into (7.22) we get:

$$\lambda^{-1}1'\Sigma^{-1}\mu - \lambda^{-1}\gamma 1'\Sigma^{-1}1 = 1 \tag{7.24}$$

Note now that both $1'\Sigma^{-1}\mu$ and $1'\Sigma^{-1}1$ are just numbers. Let's call them a and b:

$$a = 1'\Sigma^{-1}\mu = \sum_{ij}\sigma_{ij}^{-1}\mu_j \tag{7.25}$$

$$b = 1'\Sigma^{-1}1 = \sum_{ij}\sigma_{ij}^{-1} \tag{7.26}$$

Then

$$\lambda^{-1}a - \lambda^{-1}\gamma b = 1 \Longrightarrow \gamma = \frac{a}{b} - \frac{\lambda}{b} \tag{7.27}$$

The ratio a/b can be seen as an average weighted excess return (where the weights are the normalized elements of the inverse of the covariance matrix):

$$\frac{a}{b} = \sum_{j}\omega_j\mu_j = \langle\mu\rangle \tag{7.28}$$

with

$$\omega_j = \frac{\sum_i \sigma_{ij}^{-1}}{\sum_{ij}\sigma_{ij}^{-1}} \tag{7.29}$$

Looking at the expression for b, and remembering that the elements of the summation are the *inverse* of the covariance matrix, we can intuitively interpret the term $\frac{\lambda}{b}$ as an average variance risk (that we can denote by $\langle\sigma^2\rangle$) scaled by the risk aversion λ. The two terms $\frac{a}{b} - \frac{\lambda}{b}$ together therefore suggestively express the multiplier γ as an average utility:

$$\gamma = \langle U\rangle = \langle\mu\rangle - \lambda\langle\sigma^2\rangle \tag{7.30}$$

Now we only have to substitute the expression for γ back into Equation (7.23) to obtain:

$$w^* = \lambda^{-1}\Sigma^{-1}\mu - \lambda^{-1}\left(\frac{a}{b} - \frac{\lambda}{b}\right)\Sigma^{-1}1 \tag{7.31}$$

7.2.2   *Optimization when a riskless asset is available*

So far we have not considered the existence of a riskless asset, an asset for which, that is, the return is certain (let's call it R_f). Let's now allow for the possibility of lending or borrowing at this riskless rate. Let the weight invested in the riskless asset be denoted by w_0.

The budget constraint can now be written as

$$w'1 + w_0 = 1 \Rightarrow w_0 = 1 - w'1 \tag{7.32}$$

The optimization programme becomes

$$\min_w [w'\Sigma w] \text{ such that } w'\mu + (1 - w'1)R_f = \mu_\Pi \tag{7.33}$$

where μ_Π is a pre-assigned portfolio return.

Using Lagrange multipliers as above gives for the optimal weights

$$w^* = \Sigma^{-1}(\mu - 1R_f)\frac{\mu_\Pi - R_f}{(\mu - 1R_f)'\Sigma^{-1}(\mu - 1R_f)} \tag{7.34}$$

and the resulting portfolio variance, Σ_Π, is given by

$$\Sigma_\Pi = \frac{(\mu_\Pi - R_f)^2}{J} \tag{7.35}$$

with

$$J = B - 2AR_f + CR_f^2 \tag{7.36}$$

and

$$A = 1\Sigma^{-1}\mu \tag{7.37}$$

$$B = \mu'\Sigma^{-1}\mu \tag{7.38}$$

$$C = 1'\Sigma^{-1} \tag{7.39}$$

$$D = BC - A^2 \tag{7.40}$$

The couple of values $\{\mu_\Pi, \Sigma_\Pi\}$ thus determined trace the efficient frontier in the $[\mu_\Pi, \Sigma_\Pi]$ plane.

This setting is important, because, in the presence of the riskless asset the two-fund theorem (see, e.g., Markowitz 1987) applies in its simplest form. The theorem states that the optimal portfolio is a combination of a position in the riskless rate (lending – deleveraged position – or borrowing – leveraged position) and the tangent portfolio, Π_m.[8] The expected return is therefore given by:

$$\mu_\Pi = xR_f + (1 - x)\mu_{\Pi_m} \tag{7.41}$$

See Figure 7.1. The solution lies on this line for any degree of risk aversion: the conservative investor will lend more at the riskless rate and invest little in the market

---

[8] As is well known, the tangent portfolio is the market portfolio (hence the subscript 'm').

Markowitz efficient frontier

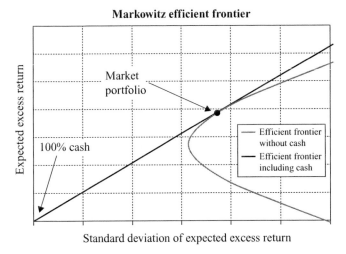

Standard deviation of expected excess return

Figure 7.1 The efficient frontier. In the presence of a riskless asset ('cash' in the figure), for any degree of risk aversion the optimal portfolio lies on the tangent line to the efficient frontier: the conservative investor will lend more at the riskless rate and invest little in the market portfolio; the 'aggressive' investor will leverage her position by borrowing at the riskless rate and invest the proceeds in the market portfolio. The infinitely risk-averse investor will simply put all of her wealth in the riskless asset. In the absence of a riskless asset, the infinitely risk-averse investor will invest all of her wealth in the minimum-variance portfolio.

portfolio; the 'aggressive' investor will leverage her position by borrowing at the riskless rate (assuming that she is allowed to do so) and will invest the proceeds in the market portfolio. The infinitely-risk-averse investor will simply put all of her wealth in the riskless asset. However, apart from this degenerate case, all investors will hold (some fraction of) the same portfolio.

7.3 The link with the CAPM – a simple derivation

As we shall see in Chapter 21, the CAPM model plays an important benchmarking role in our approach. We therefore state in this section the main results derived from the CAPM approach, with an eye to the specific applications that we present in Part VII of this book. We also sketch a derivation of the CAPM that highlights the links with the Markowitz mean-variance optimization problem. For a self-consistent treatment see, for example, Cochrane (2001)[9] or for a brief, correct, yet mathematically friendly treatment Litterman (2003).[10]

Before sketching the derivation, let's state the main result first. According to the CAPM the expected return on the ith asset, $\mu_i \equiv \mathbb{E}[R_i]$, is given by

$$\mathbb{E}[R_i] = R_{\mathrm{f}} + \beta_i(\mathbb{E}[R_{\mathrm{m}}] - R_{\mathrm{f}}) \tag{7.42}$$

$$\beta_i = \rho_{i,\mathrm{m}}\frac{\sigma_i}{\sigma_{\mathrm{m}}}$$

[9] See Ch. 9, Sections 9.1 to 9.3 in particular.   [10] See Ch. 4 in particular.

where R_f is the riskless rate, R_m is the return from the market portfolio, σ_i and σ_m are the standard deviations of the ith asset and of the market portfolio, respectively, and $\rho_{i,m}$ is the correlation between the returns from the ith asset and the market portfolio.

The first observation is that, according to the CAPM, only the first two moments of the joint distribution of asset and market returns matter. So, it is intuitively clear that there must be a fundamental link between Markowitz's mean-variance approach and the CAPM, and it must be the case that the CAPM can be derived from, and is consistent with, the maximization of a quadratic utility function.[11] We deal with this immediately below, but we can already see that, in a world with a fixed outstanding supply of assets, two conditions will have to be satisfied at equilibrium (see Litterman 1983): first, the equilibrium weights must be such that every asset should have the same ratio for its marginal contribution to portfolio risk; second, the marginal change in portfolio weights must create a change in expected return proportional through the coefficient of risk aversion to the marginal change in portfolio variance.

7.3.1 Derivation of the links between Markowitz and CAPM

In order to see more precisely the links between Equation (7.42) and the mean-variance framework we can proceed as follows. We follow Zimmermann (2011).

Denote by $\overline{\mu}$ the vector of excess expected returns, and start from the optimal asset allocation per unit wealth for the jth investor, who has relative risk aversion λ_j. This allocation is given by

$$w_j = \frac{1}{\lambda_j} \Sigma^{-1}\overline{\mu} = t_j \Sigma^{-1}\overline{\mu} \tag{7.43}$$

where we have defined by t_j the risk tolerance of the jth investor. We stress that this is the result for the jth investor, obtained by maximizing *her* quadratic utility function.

Let W_M be the vector containing the fraction of the total wealth invested in the available assets, and let W_j be the vector of the wealth invested by the jth investor in the available assets. We have

$$W_M = \sum_j W_j w_j \tag{7.44}$$

We assume that all investors share the same expectations about returns, and know exactly the covariance matrix. They differ only in their risk aversion.

Therefore combining the individual allocation in Equation (7.43), we have for the vector of the total wealth invested in the available assets

$$W_M = \sum_j [t_j W_j][\Sigma^{-1}\overline{\mu}] \tag{7.45}$$

---

[11] This is indeed the treatment in Litterman (2003), who highlights very clearly the links with, and the conceptual differences from, Markowitz's mean-variance approach as follows: 'The analysis [of the CAPM] model up to this point follows the original mean-variance optimization developed by Harry Markowitz in his work. What makes the CAPM interesting, however, is that it goes beyond this individual investor optimization problem. ... Rather than take [the expected returns] as given, ... CAPM asks for what values of these mean returns will the demand for asset be equal to outstanding supply.' (p. 40)

Note that the second term in square brackets is investor-independent. The first term gives the aggregate risk aversion, weighted by the wealth of each investor. Clearly, W_M is the market portfolio. So, if we define the risk tolerance of the representative investor, t_M, to be given by the wealth-weighted risk tolerance of the individual investors

$$\sum_j [t_j W_j] \equiv t_M \tag{7.46}$$

the market portfolio per unit wealth is given by

$$w_M = t_M \Sigma^{-1} \overline{\mu} \tag{7.47}$$

This is the overall market allocation of the total wealth normalized to 1 to all the assets in positive net supply.

Equation (7.47) allows us to 'solve for' the equilibrium excess expected return, and we can finally write for the vector of expected returns, μ,

$$\mu = r_f + \lambda_M \Sigma w_M \tag{7.48}$$

with

$$\lambda_M \equiv \frac{1}{\sum_j \left[\frac{1}{\lambda_j} W_j\right]} \tag{7.49}$$

This is, *in nuce*, the CAPM, i.e., an equilibrium relationship between risk (Σ), aggregate risk aversion (λ_M), the structure of the market portfolio, w_M, and risk premia ($\mu - r_f$). It is not, however, in the familiar 'beta formulation' investors are familiar with. This we obtain as follows.

7.3.2   Obtaining the familiar β-formulation
To see how to get from Equation (7.48) to the form (7.42) consider the kth security, for which Equation (7.48) can be written as

$$\mu_k = r_f + \lambda_M \sum_l \Sigma_{kl} w_M^l = r_f + \lambda_M \sum_l \text{Cov}(R_k, R_l) w_M^l \tag{7.50}$$

Equation (7.48) and (7.50) contain the market risk aversion, which is normally 'hidden' in the usual (beta) formulation of the CAPM model. Its 'disappearance' comes about as follows. For the kth security Equation (7.48) can be written as

$$\mu_k = r_f + \lambda_M \sum_l \Sigma_{kl} w_M^l = r_f + \lambda_M \sum_l \text{Cov}(R_k, R_l) w_M^l \tag{7.51}$$

$$= r_f + \lambda_M \sum_l \text{Cov}(R_k, w_M^l R_l) = r_f + \lambda_M \text{Cov}(R_k, R_M) \tag{7.52}$$

because

$$\sum_l w_M^l R_l = R_M \tag{7.53}$$

This says that the expected excess return for the kth security is given by the aggregate risk aversion and the covariance of the same security with the market. This relationship must be true for any (portfolio of) securities. In particular, it must hold for the market portfolio, in which case Equation (7.51) becomes

$$\mu_M = r_f + \lambda_M \sigma_M^2 \qquad (7.54)$$

and therefore the 'unobservable' aggregate risk aversion can be solved to be

$$\lambda_M = \frac{\mu_M - r_f}{\sigma_M^2} \qquad (7.55)$$

This quantity can now be substituted back into Equation (7.51) to give

$$\mu_k = r_f + \lambda_M \sum_l \text{Cov}(R_k, R_M) = r_f + (\mu_M - r_f)\frac{\text{Cov}(R_k, R_M)}{\sigma_M^2}$$

$$\equiv r_f + \beta_k^M (\mu_M - r_f)$$

This is the usual formulation for the CAPM.

Finally, we recall that, in a CAPM world, the stochastic discount factor, m_{t+1}, given by

$$m_{t+1} = \beta \frac{u'(c_{t+1})}{u'(c_t)} \qquad (7.56)$$

is a linear function of the gross return from the market portfolio:

$$m_{t+1} = a - bGR^{\text{MKT}} \qquad (7.57)$$

We sketch a derivation of this result in Appendix 21.A. As for expression (7.56) for the stochastic discount factor, a skeleton of the derivation is provided in Appendix 7.B.

7.4   Reverse-engineering the CAPM

These observations were obtained in a CAPM-like universe. They were meant to show that if we believe in a CAPM world there are constraints that any exogenous assignment of returns and covariances must obey. As the Bayesian-net procedure obviously builds an implicit joint distribution of risk factors, having this guidance is very important.

In practice we may believe that the CAPM is not perfect, but to the extent that we also believe that it is not too bad an approximation to the real world, we should make sure that the expected returns we assign should be, in some sense, 'CAPM-compatible'. So, for instance, we should not assign excess returns that are not even compatible with the very *existence* of the assets actually traded in the market – i.e., excess returns that imply negative weights for some assets in the market portfolio.

Of course, we can push the reasoning further and say that the real world *exactly* behaves as the CAPM prescribes. Then the vector of excess returns would in this case be uniquely determined from the observed 'market weights' (the market capitalization) through the inverse of Equation (7.6):[12]

$$\boldsymbol{\mu}_{\mathbf{m}} = \frac{1}{\lambda} \boldsymbol{\Sigma} \boldsymbol{w}_{\mathbf{m}} \tag{7.58}$$

However, the important point here is that between full specification of the optimal weights (Equation (7.6)) and no constraints whatsoever there exist mildly model-dependent results that can guide us in our understanding of the relationships between present and expected market prices. This is particularly important when the asset manager is requested to give her 'views' about future returns, as she is in the Black–Litterman approach (which we cover in Chapter 9), and, of course, with our model.

Now, recall that our approach requires the subjective assignment of quantities that will ultimately determine the expected returns of, and the covariance matrix for, the various assets of interest (and the market portfolio). As we shall see, however, plausible but 'naive' assignments can turn out to be incompatible with what a reasonable (although not perfect) model like the CAPM indicates, when understood in a prescriptive sense. As a safeguard against insidious asset-pricing 'absurdities', we will therefore make use of this type of consideration, and of the intuition it facilitates, in Chapter 21.

Appendix 7.A: Asset allocation in the presence of linear equality constraints

In order to solve the weight allocation problem in the presence of linear equality constraints, we want to determine the optimal weights given the Lagrangian

$$\mathcal{L} = U - \sum_i \gamma_i \left[\left(\sum_j a_{ij} w_j \right) - b_i \right] \tag{7.59}$$

$$\Longrightarrow \mathcal{L} = U - \boldsymbol{\gamma}'(\boldsymbol{A}\boldsymbol{w} - \boldsymbol{b}) \tag{7.60}$$

To this effect, we need to evaluate the derivatives $\frac{\partial \mathcal{L}}{\partial \boldsymbol{w}}$ and $\frac{\partial \mathcal{L}}{\partial \boldsymbol{\gamma}}$ and set them both to zero.

Let's begin by looking at the first derivative, whose kth component is $\frac{d\mathcal{L}}{dw_k}$.

$$\frac{\partial \mathcal{L}}{\partial w_k} = \frac{\partial}{\partial w_k} \left(\sum_i w_i \mu_i - \frac{1}{2\lambda} \sum_{ij} w_i w_j \sigma_{ij} - \sum_i \gamma_i \left(\left(\sum_j a_{ij} w_j \right) - b_i \right) \right)$$

Let's consider the terms in the square bracket in turn:

$$\frac{\partial}{\partial w_k} \sum_i w_i \mu_i = \mu_k \Longrightarrow \frac{\partial \mathcal{L}}{\partial \boldsymbol{w}} = \boldsymbol{\mu} \tag{7.61}$$

$$\frac{\partial}{\partial w_k} \left(\sum_{ij} w_i \sigma_{ij} w_j \right) = \sum_i \sigma_{ki} w_i + \sum_i w_i \sigma_{ik} = \boldsymbol{\Sigma} \boldsymbol{w} + \boldsymbol{\Sigma}' \boldsymbol{w} \tag{7.62}$$

---

[12] This, of course, sweeps under the carpet the question of how easy it is to determine the 'market weights' (or indeed if it is possible at all). See Litterman (2003) for a discussion.

Since the matrix Σ is symmetric $\sigma_{ki} = \sigma_{ik}$. It follows that

$$\sum_i \sigma_{ki} w_i + \sum_i w_i \sigma_{ik} = 2 \sum_i \sigma_{ki} w_i = 2\Sigma w \tag{7.63}$$

and

$$\frac{\partial}{\partial w_k} \left(-\frac{1}{2\lambda} \sum_{ij} w_i w_j \sigma_{ij} \right) = -\frac{1}{\lambda} \sum_i \sigma_{ki} w_i = -\frac{1}{\lambda} \Sigma w \tag{7.64}$$

As for the third term we get:

$$\frac{\partial}{\partial w_k} \left(-\sum_i \gamma_i \left(\sum_j a_{ij} w_j \right) \right) = -\sum_i a_{ik} \gamma_i = -A'\gamma \tag{7.65}$$

Putting the pieces together gives:

$$\frac{\partial \mathcal{L}}{\partial w_k} \bigg|_{w=w^*} = \mu_k - \frac{1}{\lambda} \sum_i \sigma_{ki} w_i - \sum_i a_{ik} \gamma_i = 0 \tag{7.66}$$

or, in matrix form,

$$\frac{\partial \mathcal{L}}{\partial w} \bigg|_{w=w^*} = \mu - \frac{1}{\lambda} \Sigma w^* - A'\gamma = 0 \tag{7.67}$$

Let's now move to the second Lagrangian equation, $\frac{d\mathcal{L}}{d\gamma}$. For its kth component we have

$$\frac{\partial \mathcal{L}}{\partial \gamma_k} = \frac{\partial}{\partial \gamma_k} \left(-\sum_i \gamma_i \left(\left(\sum_j a_{ij} w_j \right) - b_i \right) \right)$$

$$= \frac{\partial}{\partial \gamma_k} \sum_i \left(-\gamma_i \left(\sum_j a_{ij} w_j \right) \right) + \frac{\partial}{\partial \gamma_k} \sum_i \gamma_i b_i$$

$$= -\sum_j a_{kj} w_j + b_k = 0 \implies \sum_j a_{kj} w_j = b_k \tag{7.68}$$

or, in matrix notation,

$$\frac{\partial \mathcal{L}}{\partial \gamma} \bigg|_{w=w^*} = -Aw + b = 0 \implies Aw = b \tag{7.69}$$

which is our constraint equation again.

From Equation (7.67) one obtains:

$$\mu - \frac{1}{\lambda} \Sigma w^* - A'\gamma = 0 \tag{7.70}$$

Solving for the optimal weights w^* in Equation (7.70) gives:

$$w^* = \lambda \Sigma^{-1} (\mu - A'\gamma)$$

Substituting this expression into Equation (7.69) one gets:

$$Aw^* = b \Longrightarrow A\Sigma^{-1}\mu - \frac{1}{\lambda}b = A\Sigma^{-1}A'\gamma \tag{7.71}$$

Note now that the matrix $A\Sigma^{-1}A'$ is a square invertible matrix (let's call it C). Then

$$\gamma = C^{-1}\left(A\Sigma^{-1}\mu - \frac{1}{\lambda}b\right) \tag{7.72}$$

This finally gives for w^*:

$$w^* = \lambda\Sigma^{-1}(\mu - A'\gamma) = \lambda\Sigma^{-1}\mu - \lambda\Sigma^{-1}A'\gamma$$

$$= \lambda\Sigma^{-1}\mu - \lambda\Sigma^{-1}A'C^{-1}\left(A\Sigma^{-1}\mu - \frac{1}{\lambda}b\right) \tag{7.73}$$

Appendix 7.B: Derivation of the stochastic discount factor

This derivation is adapted from Cochrane (2001).

The investor has one investment opportunity (a stock), of price p_0, and lives in a two-period economy. She has a time-separable utility over consumption at time t and time $t + 1$. One unit of stock pays a stochastic payoff, x_{t+1}, at time t_1. The investor has an impatience of consumption, β. She wants to maximize her utility over consumption at time t and time $t + 1$:

$$u(c_t, c_{t+1}) = u(c_t) + \beta E_t[c_{t+1}]$$

She can consume at time t and time $t + 1$.

Suppose that she invests a part of her initial wealth at time t in order to invest a units of stock, which costs p_t. So, her utility at time t is

$$u(c_t) = u(W - ap_t) \tag{7.74}$$

Her discounted expected utility from consumption at time $t + 1$ is:

$$\beta E_t[u(ax_{t+1})] \tag{7.75}$$

So, we have

$$u(c_t, c_{t+1}) = u(W - ap_t) + \beta E_t[u(ax_{t+1})] \tag{7.76}$$

The distribution of the return x_{t+1} is assumed to be known.

The investor wants to determine how much she should invest today (i.e., forfeit current consumption) in order to get a fraction of this expected payoff. Remembering that

$$c_t = W - ap_t$$

$$c_{t+1} = ap_t x_{t+1}$$

taking the derivative with respect to a, and setting it to zero gives

$$-u'(c_t)p_t + \beta E_t[u'(c_{t+1})x_{t+1}] = 0 \tag{7.77}$$

$$p_t = \frac{\beta E_t[u'(c_{t+1})x_{t+1}]}{u'(c_t)} = \beta E_t\left[\frac{u'(c_{t+1})}{u'(c_t)}x_{t+1}\right]$$

$$= \beta E_t[m_{t+1}x_{t+1}] \tag{7.78}$$

with the stochastic discount factor defined by

$$m_{t+1} = \frac{u'(c_{t+1})}{u'(c_t)} \tag{7.79}$$

The stochastic discount factor reflects the trade-off between the marginal utility of consuming today when the investor's wealth level is $W - a \times p_t$, and the expected marginal utility of the consumption that the stochastic payoff may provide at time $t + 1$. It is stochastic because the investor does not know how much she will be able to consume at time $t + 1$. Expression (7.77) recovers Eqn 1.3 in Cochrane (2001).

Equation (7.77) nicely factorizes the price as made up of the expectation of a security-dependent component (the payoff x_{t+1}), and an investor-dependent part (βm_{t+1}).

8 Stability: a first look

8.1 Problems with the stability of the optimal weights

There are two main problems with the Markowitz approach. The first is that, unless positivity constraints are assigned, the Markowitz solution can easily find highly leveraged portfolios (large long positions in a subset of assets financed by large short positions in another subset of assets). Needless to say, given their leveraged nature the returns from these portfolios are extremely sensitive to small changes in the returns of the constituent assets. These leveraged portfolios can therefore be extremely 'dangerous'.

Positivity constraints are easy to enforce, and fix this problem. However, if the user wants to 'believe' in the robustness of the Markowitz approach, it would be nice if better-behaved solutions (at the very least, *positive* weights) were obtained in an unconstrained manner when the set of investment assets is close to the available investment opportunities (the market portfolio).[1] This is often not the case.[2]

The second, closely related (and practically more vexing) problem is the instability of the Markowitz solution: small changes in inputs can give rise to large changes in the portfolio. Somewhat unkindly, mean-variance optimization has been dubbed an 'error maximization' device (Scherer 2002): 'an algorithm that takes point estimates (of returns and covariances) as inputs and treats them as if they were known with certainty will react to tiny return differences that are well within measurement error'. In the real world, this degree of instability will lead, to begin with, to large transaction costs. More important, the magnitude of these changes is also likely to shake the confidence of the portfolio manager in the model. The topic is well known, and we refer the reader to Jobson and Korki (1983), Michaud (1989), Best and Grauer (1991), Chopra and Ziemba (1993) and Nawrocki (1996) for a discussion.

Despite the fact that much has been written on the subject, we would like to present it from an angle that we have not seen emphasized in the literature, but which we think greatly helps the reader to see 'where the problem lies'.[3]

---

[1] As Equation (8.12) shows, the vector of expected returns of the market portfolio can be obtained as the solution to an unconstrained Markowitz allocation problem.

[2] However, we discuss in Section 21.1 that small changes in the imperfectly known inputs (especially expected returns) can often produce positive and plausible allocations. See in his respect Ni *et al.* (2011).

[3] Helpful discussions with Dr Vasant Naik are gratefully acknowledged.

8.2   Where the instability comes from

In order to help the intuition we deal with the simplest and clearest case of unconstrained optimization. As a first step we derive the sensitivity of the allocation weights to changes in the expected returns. Recall that in this setting the optimal weights, w^*, are given by[4]

$$w^* = \lambda^{-1}\Sigma^{-1}\mu \tag{8.1}$$

From this it is straightforward to obtain the sensitivity of the weights to the returns, by differentiating with respect to the return vector, μ.[5] One immediately obtains

$$\frac{\partial w^*}{\partial \mu} = \lambda^{-1}\Sigma^{-1} \tag{8.2}$$

It is clear from this expression that the sensitivity of the weights to the returns is inversely related to the coefficient of risk aversion (which is proportional to $1/\lambda$), and directly related to the magnitude of the inverse of the covariance matrix, Σ^{-1}.

Before proceeding, it is important to pause to comment on the coefficients of absolute, $A(w)$, or relative, $R(w)$, risk aversion for the quadratic or power (logarithmic) utility functions, because these will be central to the arguments we shall develop in the latter parts of the book:

$$A(w) = -\frac{u''(w)}{u'(w)} \tag{8.3}$$

$$R(w) = -w\frac{u''(w)}{u'(w)} \tag{8.4}$$

Now, Equation (8.2) can be arrived at from the maximization of a quadratic utility function (see Equation (7.2)), in which case the parameter λ is the coefficient of the second power of wealth:

$$u_{\text{quad}}(w) = a + bw + \lambda w^2 \tag{8.5}$$

As we show in Appendix 8.A, for a quadratic utility function the coefficient λ is related, but not equal, to the (absolute or relative) coefficient of risk aversion. More generally, the match of the coefficients of risk aversion of a quadratic and a power utility function can only be achieved locally (i.e., in the neighbourhood of a given level of wealth).[6] We would, however, like to compare (even if only locally) coefficients of risk aversion across the two utility functions. We can do so if we assume that the initial level of wealth is normalized to 1, in which case the parameter $-\lambda$ becomes (locally) the coefficient of risk aversion for the quadratic utility function; see Equation (8.5). Unless we say otherwise, in the following we will therefore always assume that we work with this

---

[4] For simplicity we look here at the unconstrained optimization case. Qualitatively similar considerations hold for the more realistic cases of unit sum for the weights ($w^{\text{T}}1 = 1$) or of non-negative holdings.

[5] We are grateful to Dr Vasant Naik for useful discussions of this point.

[6] As Markowitz (1991 [1959]) points out (pages 283 and *passim*) this match is valid over a surprisingly large range of values of wealth.

normalized level of the initial wealth, and we will therefore be allowed loosely to refer to $-\lambda$ as 'the' coefficient of risk aversion.

Going back to Equation (8.2) after this important observation, we note that the elements of the covariance matrix (which are given by the square of volatilities time correlations) are 'small' numbers (compared to unity), and the elements of the inverse of the covariance matrix are therefore 'large' numbers. This implies that the sensitivity of the optimal weights to changes in the expected return is also high. To some extent this high sensitivity can be tempered by a high degree of risk aversion, but, for 'reasonable' values of λ (say, between 0.5 and 2),[7] the stabilization effect brought about by the risk aversion coefficient is limited.[8]

This simple result has profound consequences, which we discuss more fully in Chapter 22. For the moment, let's get a feel for the results by looking in some detail at the simplest possible setting: a two-assets universe. The risk aversion coefficient, λ, was set to 1 for this simple example (which corresponds to the logarithmic utility case).

For volatilities of the two assets of, say, 14% and 16%, and for zero correlation, we find for the four sensitivities $\frac{\partial w_i}{\partial \mu_j}$, with $i, j = 1, 2$, $\frac{\partial w_1}{\partial \mu_1} = 51.02$, $\frac{\partial w_1}{\partial \mu_2} = \frac{\partial w_2}{\partial \mu_1} = 0$ and $\frac{\partial w_2}{\partial \mu_2} = 39.06$. Finding uncorrelated assets, however, is not easy. If we have a non-zero correlation (say, $\rho = 0.4$), the sensitivities increase and we get $\frac{\partial w_1}{\partial \mu_1} = 60.73$, $\frac{\partial w_1}{\partial \mu_2} = \frac{\partial w_2}{\partial \mu_1} = -21.25$ and $\frac{\partial w_2}{\partial \mu_2} = 46.50$. If the correlation were, say, $\rho = 0.75$, then the sensitivity of the first weight to a change in the expected return of the first asset becomes 116.62: this means that for a minuscule ten-basis-point change in this difficult-to-estimate expected return, the associated weight changes by 11.6%. A 1% upward change in expected return increases the weight by 116%.[9]

One should not think, however, that uncertainty in the expected returns is always 'the main culprit of the instability of portfolio weights'.[10] Indeed, Palczewski and Palczewski (2010) challenge the commonly held notion that most of the uncertainty in the weights always stems from uncertainty in the returns, as argued, for instance, as early as 1980 by Merton (1980) and then by Chopra and Ziemba (1993), Best and Grauer, (1991), Jagannathan and Ma (2003) and others. Palczewski and Palczewski (2010) show that portfolio estimation errors can be decomposed into three parts: a component related to uncertainty in the expected returns; a component associated with uncertainty in the covariance matrix; and a third non-linear component due to the superposition of errors in the two estimates. They reach the following conclusions:

- 'the impact of the estimation errors of the covariance matrix can be of the same magnitude as the impact of the estimation error of the mean';

---

[7] See, however, the discussion in Chapter 22 about the 'reasonableness' of this value.
[8] See Section 22.4 for generally accepted values of the coefficient of risk aversion, when this is elicited from risky settings ('lotteries') with perfectly known risk. See Section 23.5 about the possible values it can assume when ambiguity aversion is taken into account.
[9] Weights do not have to be smaller than or equal to 1, as we are looking at unconstrained optimization.
[10] Palczewski and Palczweski (2010, p. 1).

- 'the precision of the optimal portfolio weights estimator computed with the true mean depends on the ratio of the variances and covariances of assets rather than their absolute values';
- 'the stability of optimal portfolio weights computed with the estimated mean deteriorates with the decrease of the eigenvalues of the covariance matrix'.[11]

The upshot of this discussion is that it is difficult to make universal statements about the origin of the instability without looking at the precise combination of expected returns and covariance elements. In keeping with the 'received wisdom', in the rest of the book we mainly refer to instability due to uncertainty in expected return, but the results by Palczewski and Palczewski (2010) should be kept in mind.

These observations, preliminary as they are, already have a direct bearing on our project. We show in fact in the last chapters that a 'naive' expected-utility-maximization approach suffers from the same instability problems highlighted above in the case of mean-variance optimization. Disappointingly, if we apply Bayesian nets in a similarly 'naive' expected-utility-maximization framework, we find that these stability problems do not go away. We shall argue (and the discussion in this section already gives a taste of our argument) that the main reason for this is to be found the too-small role played by risk aversion in the selection of weights. One way to understand what we mean by 'too-small role played by risk aversion' is to observe that, for a behaviourally plausible utility function such as the logarithmic one,[12] even relatively large variations in wealth (say, of the order of 10%) cause little more than a linear variation in the utility (see Figure 29.1). But if the curvature is so shallow, the investor behaves (makes her choices) as if she were almost risk-neutral. If she is almost risk-neutral, she will chase small differences in expected return, with little regard for the variance of portfolio returns. Diversification matters little. And if the variations in expected returns are 'fickle', wild changes in weight allocations will result. This, we believe, is one important reason for the allocation-instability problem. We also believe that, unless these stability issues are satisfactorily addressed, the allocations suggested by approaches based on the maximization of expected utility lack credibility.

There is no 'magic formula' to fix to this problem, and many solutions have been proposed (see, e.g., Black and Litterman 1990, 1991, 1992; Michaud 1989; Doust 2005; Meucci 2008).[13] In the last chapters of this book we will offer our own 'remedy'. In order better to put our suggestions in context, however, we first review in the following sections some of the other popular 'fixes' that have been suggested.

---

[11] *Ibid.*, Statements A, B, C, pp. 8–9. See, in particular, their Figures 1.a to 1.c.

[12] The reader may well ask: 'How can it be that a properly calibrated utility function does not account for risk aversion properly. Isn't this what the calibration is supposed to account for?' We discuss this point in Chapters 22 and 23.

[13] The Black–Litterman's and Doust's Geometric Mean-Variance approaches were not designed with the prime goal in mind to regularize the naive Markowitz solution, but that can do so as a welcome by-product. We review Doust's approach in the next section, and the Black–Litterman model in the next chapter.

8.3 The resampling (Michaud) approach

Resampling, first introduced in a financial context by Michaud (1989), is one of the better-known proposed solutions to the instability problem. In this section we briefly illustrate the ideas behind the approach.

The procedure starts by estimating the sample vector of expected returns, $\overline{\mu}$, and the sample covariance matrix, $\overline{\Sigma}$. Then two reference portfolios are determined: the minimum-variance and the maximum-return portfolios. Let μ_{MV} and μ_{MR} denote the returns associated with the minimum-variance and the maximum-return portfolios, respectively. As a first step, let us partition the interval $\mu_{MR} - \mu_{MV}$ into N sub-intervals: $\mu_{MR} = \mu_1, \mu_2, \ldots \mu_i, \ldots = \mu_N = \mu_{MR}$. We then evaluate the weights, $w_i, i = 1, 2, \ldots, N$, corresponding to each vector μ_i by finding the minimum-variance portfolio corresponding to each vector of expected returns, subject to whatever other constraint – say, positivity – we may want to impose. (We stress that the subscript i in the expression w_i refers to the ith vector of expected returns.) These weights correspond to the discretely sampled efficient frontier.

Now, consider a multivariate Gaussian distribution, $\mathcal{N}(\mu, \Sigma)$, with mean equal to the sample vector of expected returns, $\overline{\mu}$, and covariance matrix equal to the sample covariance matrix, $\overline{\Sigma}$: $\mathcal{N}(\overline{\mu}, \overline{\Sigma})$. Using this distribution we can create as many synthetic sets of data (returns) as we please. enote by j the jth simulation of data, $j = 1, 2, \ldots, N_{sim}$. Then, for each realization of returns, we can calculate the simulated-sample vector of expected returns, $\overline{\mu}_j$, and the simulated-sample covariance matrix, $\overline{\Sigma}_j$. These estimates are 'statistically equivalent' to $\overline{\mu}$ and $\overline{\Sigma}$, in the sense that, given the information at our disposal, they are just as likely to be drawn as the actual sample vector of expected returns, $\overline{\mu}$, and sample covariance matrix, $\overline{\Sigma}$, that we happen to have observed.

Proceeding as above, for each of these possible 'parallel but equivalent' universes, we can determine the returns associated with the minimum-variance and the maximum-return portfolio, partition this interval into N sub-intervals: $\mu_{MV}^j = \mu_1^j, \mu_2^j, \ldots = \mu_M^j = \mu_{MR}^j$, and calculate the associated weights w_i^j. Note that the superscript j refers to the simulation (the 'universe'), and the subscript i to the partition of the range of expected returns between the minimum variance and the maximum-return portfolios.

Finally, we can average the weights obtained in the N_{sim} simulations to obtain for the 'resampled' weight, $w_{i,k}^{Resampled}$, associated with asset k for return μ_i:

$$w_{i,k}^{Resampled} = \frac{1}{N_{sim}} \sum_{j=1, N_{sim}} w_{i,k}^j \tag{8.6}$$

The optimal portfolios are therefore given by a suitable average of the statistically equivalent weights obtained in the various simulations. We take, in other words, an expectation of weights (each set of weights having been obtained under conditions of parameters certainty), not an expectation of utility over uncertain weights.

Now, if one takes expected utility maximization seriously, the theoretical justification for the procedure is dubious. However, one can take a different view. In a more ad hoc, but less theory-laden, fashion one can leave to one side expected utility maximization, and take a 'like' for greater returns and a 'dislike' for variance of returns as primitives – empirical observations of what investors seem to like and dislike. If one takes this approach, then the prescription of averaging over allocation weights in the presence of statistical noise (or, as we shall see, of uncertainty of any nature in the inputs) becomes much easier to justify. Suppose, in fact, that, *ceteris paribus*, we prefer greater to smaller returns and smaller to greater variance of returns. Let's also accept that we think that our input parameters are *for any reason*[14] imperfectly known. Finally, let's place ourselves in a setting where the results we are after (the allocations) depend strongly on small variations in the imperfectly known inputs. Then averaging the allocation weights over their distribution can be seen as a plausible way to 'stabilize' the results. We used the word 'plausible' because, as we discuss in Appendix 29.A, the actual effectiveness of the averaging procedure depends on the details of what is averaged and in which way. As we shall see, some plausible and appealing averaging procedures fail to bring about any stabilization.

How do Michaud's portfolios behave? Pragmatically, the resampled portfolios tend to be more diversified, to be less sensitive to small changes to the input parameters, to incur smaller transaction costs than naive Markowitz portfolios. They have at times also provided better out-of-sample performance. See Scherer (2002) for a discussion of those situations when Michaud's resampling works better.[15] In a similar vein, Markowitz and Usmen (2003) present a 'horse race' between frontier resampling and Bayesian smoothing and, to their surprise, the resampling technique is a clear winner.

Michaud's approach is one way to grapple with the instability problem. The Black–Litterman and the Doust methodologies discussed below are – or can be interpreted as – two other ways of tackling this problem, and we therefore look at them in the following.

8.4   Geometric asset allocation

Doust (2008) suggests an interesting 'geometric' version of mean-variance optimization that offers one possible way to deal with the stability issue. At the same time, it will also be helpful in our discussion of the Black–Litterman approach. Doust's Geometric Mean-Variance approach is also related to the discussion of exogenous linear constraints that we present in Section 22.6.

In the simplest (unconstrained) case we have seen that the Markowitz allocation formula gives for the optimal weights

$$w^* = \lambda^{-1} \Sigma^{-1} \mu \tag{8.7}$$

---

[14] The reasons for our imperfect knowledge could be mundane statistical noise, but could also be rooted in deeper epistemic limitations about the knowability and stability of the statistical properties of returns.

[15] It is of course difficult to say to what extent this better performance stems from the specific construction suggested by Michaud, because many 'regularizations' (including the drastic $1/n$ allocation) display attractive out-of-sample properties (see, e.g., de Miguel, Garlappi and Uppal 2009).

Equivalently one can write

$$\mu = \frac{1}{\lambda} \Sigma w^* \qquad (8.8)$$

In Equation (8.8) the term Σ/λ defines a linear mapping between return space (μ-space) and weight space (w-space).

Typically we want to go from a set of expected returns (which we assume to be known) to a set of weights. But we can think of moving in the opposite direction, i.e., we can ask ourselves the question: which returns are compatible with a given set of weights? More precisely, first we can specify a set of weights, w, in w-space, that we find acceptable. Then we can associate to this set of acceptable weights, w, the vectors μ_w in (μ-space) obtained by applying the mapping Σ/λ from w-space to μ-space:

$$\mu_w = \frac{1}{\lambda} \Sigma w \qquad (8.9)$$

Of course, a *region* of acceptability (a set of vectors) in weights space is associated to a whole *region* (a set of vectors) of expected returns.

Within this set of expected-returns vectors, there exists then one optimal vector. Indeed, as Doust (2008) shows, by direct substitution one readily obtains that the quadratic utility that one maximizes in the classic Markowitz setting can be written as[16]

$$U(\mu_w) = -\frac{\lambda}{2}(\mu_w - \mu)' \Sigma^{-1}(\mu_w - \mu) + K \qquad (8.10)$$

with the constant, K, given by

$$K = \frac{\lambda}{2}\mu' \Sigma^{-1}\mu \qquad (8.11)$$

Maximization of the utility expressed as in Equation (8.10) therefore produces the optimal vector of expected returns (and, thanks to the mapping (8.7), of weights) consistent with the weights admissibility criteria that we have specified.[17]

This affords a nice intuitive interpretation of the procedure: maximization of the utility subject to the weight constraints that we have exogenously assigned is equivalent to minimization (because of the minus sign) of the distance in μ-space between the returns of the unconstrained optimal portfolio, μ, and the achievable portfolio returns,

---

[16] We note that Doust's results differ from the expression above by a term $\frac{\lambda}{\lambda_m}$:

$$U(\mu_w) = -\frac{\lambda}{2}\left(\frac{\lambda}{\lambda_m}\mu_w - \mu\right)' \Sigma^{-1}(\mu_w - \mu) + K$$

See, e.g., Doust (2008, p. 91). The difference stems from when in the derivation one switches from the individual investor to the representative investor, and on whether one thinks that modelling a possibly-different degree of risk aversion for the market and the individual investor is essential. For the reasons we explain in Chapter 21, we prefer to focus on differences in views (or, in this case, constraints), rather than in impatience or degrees of risk aversion.

[17] Note that, as explained in Section 17.5, the quantity $(\mu_w - \mu)' \Sigma^{-1}(\mu_w - \mu)$ is just the square of the Mahalanobis distance between μ_w and μ, induced by the metric Σ.

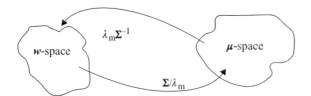

Figure 8.1 Traditional unconstrained mean-variance. With traditional unconstrained mean-variance, for any optimal weight vector $\boldsymbol{w}$ there is a corresponding excess return vector $\boldsymbol{\mu}$. The transformation from the input expected returns to the optimal weights can be seen as a (linear) mapping from $\boldsymbol{\mu}$-space to $\boldsymbol{w}$-space.

$\boldsymbol{\mu}_w$, given the constraint we have assigned. Of course, as a sanity check, one can see immediately that the unconstrained solution gives $\boldsymbol{\mu}_w = \boldsymbol{\mu}$, as it should (see Figure 8.1).

Let us now place ourselves in a CAPM world, and let us denote the market portfolio vector of excess returns by $\boldsymbol{\mu_0}$

$$\boldsymbol{\mu_0} = \frac{1}{\lambda_m} \Sigma \boldsymbol{w_m} \tag{8.12}$$

In Equation (8.12) $\boldsymbol{w_m}$ are the weights of the assets the market portfolio and

$$\lambda_m = \frac{\sigma_m^2}{\mu_0} \tag{8.13}$$

where σ_m^2 denotes the variance of the market portfolio. Writing the CAPM this way shows immediately that its associated vector of expected returns can be obtained as the solution to an unconstrained Markowitz allocation problem.

Now, if we use as input to the Markowitz allocation problem the market portfolio vector of excess returns, $\boldsymbol{\mu} = \boldsymbol{\mu_0}$, we will certainly obtain a well-behaved solution with positive weights (namely $\boldsymbol{w} = \boldsymbol{w_m}$). Let's consider then an 'acceptable region of allocation weights' around this solution, i.e., a region in $\boldsymbol{w}$-space where we, as asset managers with our beliefs, prejudices and constraints, would find the solution unobjectionable. For instance, we could simply require that the positivity of weight of the market portfolio should be retained and therefore choose the region Θ_w

$$\Theta_w = \{\boldsymbol{w} : \boldsymbol{1}'\boldsymbol{w} = 1, \boldsymbol{w} \geq 0\} \tag{8.14}$$

Of course, the weight constraints around the market portfolio could be more binding – we could require, for instance that the weights should lie in a sphere of radius ε centred on the weights of the market portfolio – but the idea does not change.

Using again the matrix Σ/λ_m to define a mapping between return space ($\boldsymbol{\mu}$-space) and weight space ($\boldsymbol{w}$-space), this acceptability region can then be mapped into a region in $\boldsymbol{\mu}$-space, Θ_μ (see Figure 8.2).

This is the set of returns compatible with the conditions we have chosen to impose.

Now, assume that, in a Black–Litterman fashion, or following the Bayesian-net procedure described in this book, we had assigned, exogenously and independently,

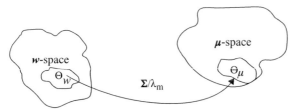

Figure 8.2 A region of acceptability in w-space ($w \in \Theta_w$) is transformed by the linear mapping into a region of acceptability in μ-space ($\mu \in \Theta_\mu$).

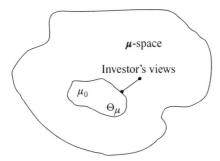

Figure 8.3 The distance between the investor's views and the acceptability region in μ-space.

our vector of 'return views', $\widehat{\mu}$. This vector may, but most of the times will not, lie inside the acceptability region, Θ_μ. What are we to do?

A reasonable approach could be to find the vector $\widetilde{\mu}$ inside the acceptability region Θ_μ, as close as possible to our view vector, $\widehat{\mu}$. Of course, saying 'as close as possible' means introducing a metric. The natural metric for the problem at hand is the Mahalanobis distance defined in Equation (17.1). We should therefore try to find the vector $\widetilde{\mu}^*$ such that its (Mahalanobis) distance, $\| \cdot \|_M$, from $\widehat{\mu}$ is minimum:

$$\widetilde{\mu}^* = \min\{\|\widetilde{\mu} - \widehat{\mu}\|_M\}$$

See Figure 8.3.

By doing so we have found the solution that lies within the acceptability region, and that is closest to the subjective views we have exogenously assigned. This geometric interpretation will help us understand better, and, as shown by Doust (2008), improve upon, the Black–Litterman allocation procedure. It is to this important topic that we therefore turn in the next chapter.

Appendix 8.A: Absolute and relative coefficients of risk aversion for power and quadratic utility functions

Let

$$u(w) = \frac{w^{1-\beta} - 1}{1 - \beta} \tag{8.15}$$

or

$$u(w) = \log(w) \quad \text{for } \beta = 1 \tag{8.16}$$

Define the Absolute, $A(w)$, and Relative, $R(w)$, coefficients of risk aversion as

$$A(w) = -\frac{u''(w)}{u'(w)} \tag{8.17}$$

$$R(w) = -w\frac{u''(w)}{u'(w)} \tag{8.18}$$

Then we have for the power utility function

$$A^{\text{power}}(w) = \frac{\beta}{w} \tag{8.19}$$

$$R^{\text{power}}(w) = \beta \tag{8.20}$$

So, for a power utility function (and, of course, for the logarithmic utility function) the coefficient of relative risk aversion is independent of the level of wealth.

Consider now a quadratic utility function

$$u(w) = w - cw^2 \tag{8.21}$$

The bliss point, $\widehat{w}$ (i.e., the point above which the utility begins to decrease), is

$$\widehat{w} = \frac{1}{2c} \tag{8.22}$$

So, we will consider levels of w smaller than $\widehat{w}$. We get

$$A^{\text{quad}}(w) = \frac{2c}{1 - 2cw} \tag{8.23}$$

$$R^{\text{quad}}(w) = \frac{2cw}{1 - 2cw} \tag{8.24}$$

We see that for a quadratic utility function both the absolute and the relative coefficients of risk aversion depend on the level of wealth.

8.A.1   *Local derivatives matching*

We want to see to what extent the coefficients of risk aversion of a quadratic and a power utility function can be matched. As we shall see, the match can only be local. Fortunately for future approximations, the range of values of wealth over which the match remains close is surprisingly wide. This is the point insightfully made by Markowitz almost half a century ago, and reprised in Markowitz (1959, 1991). See Figure 8.4.

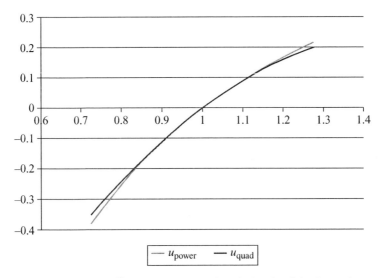

Figure 8.4 A quadratic and a power utility function, when the level and the first and second derivatives have been matched in the neighbourhood of $w = 1$, for a coefficient of risk aversion for the power utility function of $\lambda = 1$. Note how closely the two curves track each other over a wide range of changes in wealth.

Consider first the case of a power utility function

$$u_{\text{power}}(w) = \frac{w^{1-\lambda} - \beta}{1-\beta} = \frac{w^{1-\lambda}}{1-\beta} - \frac{\beta}{1-\beta} \qquad (8.25)$$

$$u'_{\text{power}}(w) = w^{-\beta} \qquad (8.26)$$

$$u''_{\text{power}}(w) = -\beta w^{-(\beta+1)} \qquad (8.27)$$

Then for a quadratic utility function we have

$$u_{\text{quad}}(w) = a + bw + cw^2 \qquad (8.28)$$

$$u'_{\text{quad}}(w) = b + 2cw \qquad (8.29)$$

$$u''_{\text{quad}}(w) = 2c \qquad (8.30)$$

Matching the value of the function and of the first two derivatives at a particular value of $\tilde{w}$ gives

$$2c = -\beta \tilde{w}^{-(\beta+1)}$$

$$c = -\frac{1}{2}\beta \tilde{w}^{-(\beta+1)} \qquad (8.31)$$

$$\tilde{w}^{-\beta} = b + 2c\tilde{w} = b - \beta \tilde{w}^{-\beta}$$

$$b = \tilde{w}^{-\beta}(1 + \beta) \qquad (8.32)$$

and finally

$$a + b\tilde{w} + c\tilde{w}^2 = \frac{\tilde{w}^{1-\beta}}{1-\beta} - \frac{1}{1-\beta}$$

$$= a + \tilde{w}^{-\beta}(1+\beta)\tilde{w} - \frac{1}{2}\lambda\tilde{w}^{-(\beta+1)}\tilde{w}^2$$

$$= a + \tilde{w}^{1-\beta}(1+\beta) - \frac{1}{2}\beta\tilde{w}^{1-\beta} = \frac{\tilde{w}^{1-\beta}}{1-\beta} - \frac{1}{1-\beta}$$

$$a = \tilde{w}^{1-\beta}\left(\frac{1}{1-\beta} - 1 - \beta + \frac{1}{2}\beta\right) - \frac{1}{1-\beta} \qquad (8.33)$$

Figure 8.4 shows how close the match is between the two utility functions over a wide range of changes in wealth (from the initial value of 1). Note also that, for $\tilde{w} = 1$, and only for this value, $\lambda = -\frac{1}{2}\beta$. For this level of wealth we can therefore refer to -2λ as the (local) coefficient of risk aversion.

8.A.2   The coefficient of relative risk aversion

Let's now calculate the coefficient of relative risk aversion, R_{quad}, for this derivatives-matched quadratic utility function. We get

$$R_{quad} = -w\frac{u''(w)|_{w=\tilde{w}}}{u'(w)|_{w=\tilde{w}}} = -\tilde{w}\frac{2c}{b+2c\tilde{w}} \qquad (8.34)$$

Substituting the values for b and c obtained above we get:

$$R_{quad} = \tilde{w}\frac{\beta\tilde{w}^{-(\beta+1)}}{\tilde{w}^{-\beta}(1+\beta) - \beta\tilde{w}^{-(\beta+1)}\tilde{w}}$$

$$= \tilde{w}\frac{\beta\tilde{w}^{-\beta}\tilde{w}^{-1}}{\tilde{w}^{-\beta}(1+\beta-\beta)} = \beta \qquad (8.35)$$

It then follows that, if we choose the coefficients of a quadratic utility function to match the level and the first and second derivative of a power utility function at a given level of wealth, $\tilde{w}$, then the coefficient of relative risk aversion implied by the quadratic utility will automatically match the coefficient of relative risk aversion implied by the power utility – as it must, since we have matched the derivatives.

However, we stress that the match is only local, i.e., in the neighbourhood of $\tilde{w}$.

9 Diversification and stability in the Black–Litterman model

9.1 What the Black–Litterman approach tries to achieve

The methodology we present in this book has obvious links with the Black–Litterman framework:[1] in a nutshell, Black and Litterman suggest how to construct an optimal portfolio once the investor's subjective views about expected returns are supplied. The portfolio we construct is a function of the subjective views about asset returns *and codependencies*. Black and Litterman elicit subjective information about where the distributions of returns are centred. We also require subjective information about what will happen in the tails. Since in our approach the input subjective views are more complex, it is essential to work through their logical consequences in a self-consistent and structured manner. This we do using Bayesian nets.

In order to move beyond the soundbites, and to appreciate more clearly what the links (and the differences) between their approach and our approach are, we provide in this chapter a concise presentation of the Black–Litterman model. As in the case of the Markowitz model, our treatment is not meant to be a balanced introduction to the Black–Litterman approach, but a rather idiosyncratic presentation focused on its subjective aspects, and on the stability of the asset allocations that it produces.[2]

We saw in the previous chapter that one of the problems associated with the Markowitz approach is the instability of the solutions (allocations) it can produce.[3] Now, one way to look at the Black–Litterman approach is to regard it as a blend of the 'market's views' and the expert's views, with the proximity of the solution to the market portfolio determined by a confidence coefficient. If the confidence is low, the result will be close to market portfolio, and therefore the weights will, by construction, be stable and well-behaved.

---

[1] See Black and Litterman (1990, 1991), expanded in (1992).

[2] The Black–Litterman model is discussed in Bevan and Winkelmann (1998) and Litterman (2003). For a Bayesian interpretation of the Black–Litterman model see Satchell and Scowcroft (2000). For a discussion of the intuition behind the model, and of the greater stability it affords with respect to traditional mean-variance optimization, see He and Litterman (1999). For a step-by-step guide to the implementation of the approach see, e.g., Idzorek (2005). This paper also contains a good discussion of the 'confidence parameter', τ, which has been interpreted in very different ways in the literature. Finally, see Doust (2008) for a critical reappraisal of the Black–Litterman model – a critique we discuss in Section 9.3.

[3] See on this point, Lee (2000) and Michaud (1989) among many.

There is, however, a price to pay for this stability: if the investor has little confidence in her views, the procedure will only produce a modest tilt away from the market allocation. As a consequence, her views will have had little impact. If, instead, the investor's confidence in her views is high the solution will be strongly tilted away from the market solution, but the weights will likely be badly behaved. This is the intrinsic tension at the heart of the Black–Litterman approach.

In this chapter we will give a presentation that tries to find an inspired compromise between these two requirements: stability on the one hand and responsiveness to our views on the other. This will be achieved following the approach pioneered by Doust (2008). We will start, however, from a more conventional angle, as presented by Satchell and Scowcroft (2000).

9.2   Views as prior: the Satchell and Scowcroft interpretation

The Black–Litterman approach has become inextricably linked with a Bayesian interpretation of the asset-allocation process. This Bayesian veneer, however, has been very much a 'reconstruction of history' or an afterthought – so much so that many modern readers are surprised to discover that the words 'Bayes' or 'Bayesian' never appear in Black and Litterman's original paper. What Black and Litterman *do* say is the following:

The expected excess return, $E[R]$, is unobservable. It is assumed to have a probability distribution that is proportional to the product of two normal distributions. The first distribution represents equilibrium and is centred at Π^4, with a covariance matrix $\tau\Sigma$, where τ is a constant. The second distribution represents the investor's views about k linear combinations of the elements of $\mathbb{E}[r]$.

Now, for any reader with a passing acquaintance with Bayesian analysis the 'product of two normal distributions' mentioned above screams of prior beliefs, likelihood functions and conjugate priors, and immediately suggests that a Bayesian interpretation can be given to the procedure. This has been done with gusto, and, indeed, with insightful results. It must be stressed, however, that, given the reconstructive nature of the enterprise, there is no general agreement about some rather fundamental elements of the Bayesian translation: for instance, different interpretative schools hold different views regarding what should be regarded as a prior distribution (the investor's views, or the market equilibrium distribution), or about the role of the constant τ ('very small' for some commentators, 'close to one' for others).[5]

So, as we endorse one of these two interpretations (Satchell and Scowcroft's), we do so simply because it allows a simpler reconciliation with our approach, not because we

---

[4] We stress that in Black–Litterman's notation Π is the vector of equilibrium returns.

[5] So, for instance, 'Black and Litterman (1992) and Lee (2000) [argue that] since the uncertainty in the mean is less than the uncertainty in the returns, the scalar (τ) is close to zero. [...] Lee [...] typically sets the value of the scalar (τ) between 0.01 and 0.05. Conversely, Satchell and Scowcroft (2000) say the value of the scalar (τ) is often set to 1. Finally Blamont and Firoozye (2003) interpret $\tau\Sigma$ as the standard error of estimate of the Implied Equilibrium Vector; thus the scalar (τ) is approximately 1 divided by the number of observations' (Idzorek 2005, p. 14).

think that it is the 'right' one. Also, to make references to the existing literature easier, we modify our notation slightly in this chapter.

We denote the investor's views about returns by r the $n \times 1$ vector of asset (excess) returns.[6] The time-t mean expected forecast returns are denoted by $\mathbb{E}[r_t]$, which is a shorthand notation for $\mathbb{E}[r_t|\mathcal{F}_{t-1}]$, where $\mathcal{F}_{t-1}$, as usual, denotes all the 'information' (filtration) up to time t.

We then denote by π the $n \times 1$ vector of (excess) equilibrium returns. When we say 'equilibrium' we imply an underlying equilibrium asset-pricing model. For simplicity we assume this to be given by the CAPM.

In a CAPM world we have shown in the previous chapters that one can write

$$\pi = \beta \left(\mu_{\mathrm{m}} - r_{\mathrm{f}} \right) \tag{9.1}$$

where μ_{m} is the global market return (in the domestic currency) and r_{f} is the riskless rate. As for β, it is the $n \times 1$ vector of asset covariances divided by the variance of the market portfolio (asset 'betas') given by

$$\beta = \frac{\mathrm{Cov}\left(r, r^{\mathrm{T}} w_{\mathrm{m}} \right)}{\sigma_{\mathrm{m}}^2} \tag{9.2}$$

In this expression w_{m} are the weights of the global market portfolio, the quantity $r^{\mathrm{T}} w_{\mathrm{m}}$ is the return on the global market portfolio, and σ_{m}^2 is the variance of the return on the global market portfolio. (Superscript T denotes transposition.)

We can substitute Equation (9.2) into Equation (9.1), to obtain

$$\pi = \beta \left(\mu_{\mathrm{m}} - r_{\mathrm{f}} \right) = \frac{\mathrm{Cov}\left(r, r^{\mathrm{T}} w_{\mathrm{m}} \right)}{\sigma_{\mathrm{m}}^2} \left(\mu_{\mathrm{m}} - r_{\mathrm{f}} \right) = \delta \Sigma w_{\mathrm{m}} \tag{9.3}$$

with

$$\delta = \frac{\left(\mu_{\mathrm{m}} - r_{\mathrm{f}} \right)}{\sigma_{\mathrm{m}}^2} \tag{9.4}$$

and

$$\Sigma = \mathrm{Cov}\left(r, r^{\mathrm{T}} w_{\mathrm{m}} \right)$$

So, in this interpretation, the $n \times 1$ vector π is the vector of excess returns implied by our chosen asset-pricing model (in this case the CAPM), given (i) the observed market weights, (ii) the estimated return, μ_{m}, and (iii) the estimated variance, σ_{m}^2, of the market portfolio.

Now that we have an expression for the market-implied expected returns, as captured by the vector π, we have to combine it with the investor's views. This is where Satchell and Scowcroft (2000) bring in their Bayesian version of the Black–Litterman model, and write

$$\phi \left(\mathbb{E}[r] | \pi \right) = \frac{\phi \left(\pi | \mathbb{E}[r] \right) \phi \left(\mathbb{E}[r] \right)}{\phi \left(\pi \right)} \tag{9.5}$$

where, with clear overloading of notation, we have denoted by $\phi(\cdot)$ different probability density functions. More precisely

---

[6] As the cash return is not included in this vector, the associated covariance matrix, Σ, is non-singular.

- $\phi(\mathbb{E}[r])$ represents the prior views of the investor;
- $\phi(\pi)$ is the distribution of equilibrium asset returns;
- $\phi(\pi|\mathbb{E}[r])$ is the 'likelihood function', i.e., in this case, the probability of the equilibrium returns, given the views held by the investor;
- $\phi(\mathbb{E}[r]|\pi)$ is the posterior we are after, i.e., the combined distribution that reflects both the investor's views, as expressed in the distribution $\phi(\mathbb{E}[r])$, and the wisdom of the market, as embedded in the equilibrium return distribution, $\phi(\pi)$.

Given this interpretation, it is then natural to make this abstract blueprint more specific as follows. The likelihood function, $\phi(\pi|\mathbb{E}[r])$, is assumed to be a Gaussian distribution:[7]

$$\phi(\pi|\mathbb{E}[r]) = \mathcal{N}(\mathbb{E}[r], \tau\Sigma) \tag{9.6}$$

As for the prior $\phi(\mathbb{E}[r])$, it is represented as follows. Let n denote the number of assets. The investor has k beliefs. Each belief refers to one or more of the n assets. The beliefs are expressed by means of a $k \times n$ matrix P, and a $k \times 1$ vector Q, where the ith row of P contains the weights of the linear combinations of the various assets in the ith view, and the ith element of Q is the investor's view of the return associated with the ith view. See Tables 9.1 and 9.2 for an example of the matrix P and the vector Q in the case of five assets (x_i, $i = 1, 2, \ldots, 5$) and three views.

Table 9.1 *The matrix P to represent absolute and relative views. Each column corresponds to one asset. The first view relates to asset 2 only; the second view refers to the relative performance of assets 3 and 4; and the third view refers to the market as a whole*

P matrix (3×5)	x_1	x_2	x_3	x_4	x_5
View 1	0	100%	0	0	0
View 2	0	0	−100%	100%	0
View 3	20%	20%	20%	20%	20%

Table 9.2 *The vector Q to represent the excess returns associated with the views in Table 9.1. The first entry means that the expected return of asset 2 is 2.5%; the second entry means that asset 4 is expected to outperform asset 3 by 0.5%; and the last entry implies that the investor expects the (excess) return for the market as a whole to be 1.75%*

Q vector	Expected return
View 1	2.5%
View 2	0.5%
View 3	1.75%

[7] As mentioned in the previous footnote, there is a small cottage industry around the interpretation of the constant τ. Satchell and Scowcroft set it close to 1, and we leave at that. However, see the references in footnote 4 and Walters (2011), for all, and more than, you ever wanted to know about τ.

So, the first view expresses the belief that the excess expected return of asset 2 will be 2.5%; the second view that a short position in asset 3 and a long position in asset 4 will produce an excess return of 0.5%; and the last view simply says that an equally weighted combination of assets is expected to yield an excess return of 1.75%.

With these definitions

$$y = P\mathbb{E}[r]$$

is a $k \times 1$ vector, which is assumed to be normally distributed with covariance matrix, Ω, as in

$$y \tilde{} \mathcal{N}(Q, \Omega) \tag{9.7}$$

In Satchell and Scowcroft's interpretation, Equation (9.7), Ω is a diagonal matrix whose elements represent the degree of confidence in the ith view. (A large Ω_{ii} element means little confidence, and $\Omega_{ii} = 0$ means absolute confidence.[8]) In practice the matrix Ω is often taken to be proportional to the matrix Σ:

$$\Omega \propto P\Sigma P' \tag{9.8}$$

Readers familiar with Bayesian analysis will recognize Q and Ω as model hyper-parameters that parametrize the prior distribution and are known to the investor – for instance, the investor knows how confident she is about each of her views.

Some simple but tedious matrix algebra[9] then gives the final result (that recovers the Black–Litterman prescription):

$$\phi(E[r]|\pi) = \mathcal{N}(a, b) \tag{9.9}$$

with

$$a = \left[(\tau\Sigma)^{-1} + P'\Omega^{-1}P\right]^{-1} \left[(\tau\Sigma)^{-1}\pi + P'\Omega^{-1}q\right] \tag{9.10}$$

$$b = \left[(\tau\Sigma)^{-1} + P'\Omega^{-1}P\right]^{-1} \tag{9.11}$$

The quantities a and b are now the new parameters to feed into an optimization engine in order to to obtain the new allocation.

It is clear that the less the investor is confident about her views, the larger the elements Ω_{ii}, the lower the weight of the prior distribution, the closer the posterior will be to the market equilibrium distribution, and the more likely that the final weights will be 'well-behaved'. We pursue this line of thought in the next section.

9.3 Doust's geometric interpretation again

Recall from the previous chapter that, following Doust's (2008) idea, we used the matrix Σ/λ_m to define a mapping between return space (μ-space) and weight space

---

[8] For a discussion of the matrix Ω see, e.g., Idzorek (2005, pp. 10–11).
[9] See, e.g., Appendix 1 in Satchell and Scowcroft (2000).

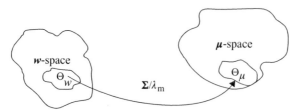

Figure 9.1 An example of mapping from an acceptable allocation to an acceptable set of expected returns. Any point in the acceptable region in w-space ($w \in \Theta_w$) is mapped to an acceptable point in μ-space ($\mu \in \Theta_\mu$).

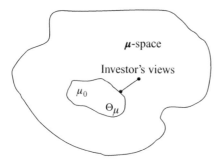

Figure 9.2 The distance between the investors' views and the acceptability region in μ-space.

(w-space). As a next step, we chose an 'acceptable' region in weight space (weights that we would not find objectionable, or that satisfy constraints such as positivity). This acceptability region was then mapped into a region in μ-space, Θ_μ, as shown in Figure 9.1.

This is the set of returns compatible with the conditions we have chosen to impose. If we had assigned, exogenously and independently, our vector of 'return views', $\widehat{\mu}$, this might, but most of the time will not, be inside the acceptability region, Θ_μ. We were left with the question of how to proceed.

Following Doust (2008), we suggested that a reasonable approach could be to find the vector $\widetilde{\mu}$ inside the acceptability region Θ_μ, as close as possible to our view vector, $\widehat{\mu}$. This means that we should try to find the vector $\widetilde{\mu}$ such that its (Mahalanobis) distance from $\widehat{\mu}$ is minimum. More precisely, the covariance matrix defines a metric, and the utility maximization can be reduced to the minimization of the distance, d_M, induced by this metric

$$d_\text{M} = (\mu_w - \mu)' \Sigma^{-1} (\mu_w - \mu)$$

We can now revisit the Black–Litterman solution in the light of this geometric interpretation (see Figure 9.2). To do so, let's briefly backstep, an ask ourselves under what conditions a Bayesian approach works well in the physical sciences. Following

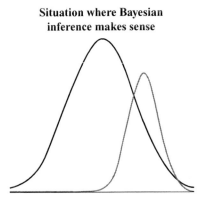

Figure 9.3 The prior distribution and the likelihood function in the case of a reasonable overlap between the two. In this situation applying the Bayesian procedure makes perfect sense.

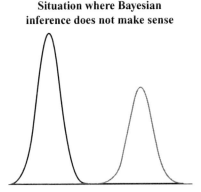

Figure 9.4 Same as Figure 9.4, but now with negligible overlap.

the argument presented in Doust (2008), consider the two stylized situations depicted in Figures 9.3 and 9.4.

Using the Bayesian procedure in a situation such as the one depicted in Figure 9.4 is technically still possible, but raises questions about the lack of congruence between the prior and the 'evidence'. The thoughtful user would be well advised to ask herself why such discordant results occurred (Was the evidence unreliable? Was the prior theory faulty?), rather than ploughing ahead with a mechanical application of the Bayesian recipe. If there is a reasonable overlap between the two distributions (the prior and the likelihood function) that have to be 'blended', then a Bayesian approach works well and makes sense. But if the overlap is minimal, then we are really saying that what we believe and what the evidence suggests are fundamentally at loggerheads. Rather than blindly applying the Bayesian recipe, we would be much better off asking ourselves why there is such a profound disagreement between our 'model' and our 'data'.

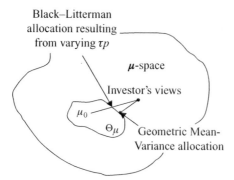

Figure 9.5 A comparison of the Black–Litterman and the Geometric Mean-Variance allocation: with Black–Litterman, the optimal allocation corresponds to the upper straight line emanating from the investors' views, and approaches the market portfolio as the confidence in her views (linked to the parameter τ) decreases.

This has clear implications in the asset-allocation setting. Simplifying greatly, in the physical sciences (usually) there are no 'fudge factors' such as the confidence parameter τ, or the matrix Ω. Either model and data are roughly compatible – and the two distributions have a significant overlap – or they are not. We can therefore inspect the two distributions and carry out an *a priori* sanity check.

Such a sanity check is, however, close-to-impossible in the Black–Litterman framework, because the investor can always choose a sufficiently low degree of confidence to ensure that the two distributions overlap as much as she wants (even perfectly, if she were particularly fainthearted).

Let's revisit our geometric construction in the light of these observations.

The allocation corresponding to Geometric Mean-Variance allocation is shown in Figure 9.5 to be given by the intersection of the lower straight line with the region of acceptability. With Geometric Mean-Variance all the effort goes into defining Θ_w (and hence Θ_μ) rather than Ω and τ. Once Θ_w (and hence Θ_μ) are chosen, the optimal allocation is given by a singe intersection point. If Ω is chosen so that

$$\Omega \propto P \Sigma P' \tag{9.12}$$

it is straightforward to show that varying τ results in a simple linear interpolation in μ-space between μ_0 and the investor's views (see Figure 9.5). Therefore the Geometric Mean-Variance allocation provides a solution within the μ-space region of admissibility that is closer to the investor's views than the Black–Litterman solution resulting from varying τ until the μ-space region of admissibility is touched.

9.4   The link with our approach

We will present in Appendix I the conceptual links between this way of looking at the Black–Litterman model and our way of specifying the expected returns of our 'spliced' distribution. Beyond these similarities, however, there are deeper points of contact with the Doust approach. We shall see that two themes that loom large in our approach are (i) constraining the allocation solutions to an area to admissibility, and (ii) avoiding small changes in the expected-return inputs producing large changes in the allocations. We will deal with these topics in Chapters 26 to 29.

10 Specifying scenarios: the Meucci approach

The approach by Meucci (2008, 2010a, b) tries to answer some of the questions we address with our model. We briefly review it in this chapter to highlight similarities and differences between his approach and our approach.[1]

Let there be N market risk factors, $\{\xi^1, \xi^2, \ldots, \xi^N\}$. Each joint realization at time t of the changes, $\Delta\xi_t^i$, in these risk factors is called a scenario:

$$\Delta\boldsymbol{\xi}_t = \left\{\Delta\xi_t^1, \Delta\xi_t^2, \ldots, \Delta\xi_t^N\right\} \tag{10.1}$$

We assume that we have T scenarios, i.e., one scenario for each of the T sampling points. Each scenario, $\Delta\boldsymbol{\xi}_t$, is supposed to be an independent realization from a joint probability, $\varphi(\Delta\boldsymbol{\xi})$. We also assume that each scenario occurs with equal probability, p_t:

$$p_t = \frac{1}{T} \tag{10.2}$$

The panel therefore has dimensions $T \times N$.

A scenario can be obtained from a historical record (in which case the independence of the draw is an assumption whose validity should be carefully checked); or it can be obtained by Monte-Carlo simulation, in which case independence can be directly built into the generation of the scenarios. With Meucci we will concentrate on the case where the scenarios are historically obtained.

As a next step the unknown distribution $\varphi(\Delta\boldsymbol{\xi})$ is represented by the generalized empirical distribution

$$\varphi(\Delta\boldsymbol{\xi}) = \sum_{t=1}^{T} p_t \delta(\Delta\boldsymbol{\xi} - \Delta\boldsymbol{\xi}_t) \tag{10.3}$$

where $\delta(\cdot)$ denotes the N-dimensional Dirac distribution.

---

[1] A methodological observation may be useful here. Perhaps more for historical than for fundamental reasons, the related disciplines of risk management and portfolio allocation tend to employ different approaches to describe the marginal distribution of market risk factors. (The two disciplines are, of course, related because diversification is at the heart of both.) By and large, the asset-allocation community has followed a parametric approach, while risk management professionals have tended to rely on historical or Monte-Carlo-produced joint realizations of changes in risk factors (i.e., on a panel representation). Meucci's approach is more easily presented using the panel language, and in this chapter we will therefore adopt this perspective, but nothing fundamental hinges on this.

We assume that there exists a mapping from the changes in risk factors to the profit and loss (ΔW) of a given portfolio. We can then associate to each scenario a profit and loss:

$$\Delta\boldsymbol{\xi}_t \rightarrow \Delta W_t \tag{10.4}$$

As the scenarios $\{\Delta\boldsymbol{\xi}_t\}$ are fixed, it is clear that the crucial part of the representation (10.3) are the probabilities, $\{p_t\}$. When it comes to these probabilities, can we do anything better than assuming that each scenario is equally relevant today? Should we necessarily assume, that is, that $p_t = \frac{1}{T}$?

Before answering the question, we can pause to reflect on the implication of Equation (10.2). When the choice $p_t = \frac{1}{T}$ is made, the length of the panel is often set equal to all the available data points. The researcher, that is, tries not to throw away any information and does so by using as many points as possible. By so doing she is implicitly making the assumption that any past datum is as relevant today as any other.

What alternatives are there? The simplest and crudest one is the rolling-window choice. In the attempt to give more weight to more recent (and hence, presumably, more relevant) information, the whole data set is truncated to $\tau < T$ scenarios before the most recent one. Everything proceeds as before, after an obvious renormalization of the probabilities. The crudeness of the approach is evident: by doing so, the statistician is saying that what occurred τ days before 'today' is every bit as relevant as what happened yesterday, but that what happened $\tau + 1$ days before is totally irrelevant.

The next choice in sophistication is exponential smoothing, where each past date is given a progressively (exponentially) lower weight.[2] The simplest way to calculate the expected values of the portfolio profit and loss, $E(\Delta W)$, the expectation of the changes in the risk factors, $E(\Delta\boldsymbol{\xi}_t)$, and covariances among the same risk factors is to set the probabilities equal to

$$p_t \propto \exp[-\lambda(T - t)] \tag{10.5}$$

and to renormalize to 1 as required. Of course, once the probabilities $\{p_t, t = 1, 2, \ldots, T\}$ are chosen, any function, Y, of the changes in the market risk factors can be easily obtained thanks to the useful and general result (see Meucci 2010)

$$\varphi_Y(y) = \sum_{t=1}^{T} p_t \delta(y - y_t) \tag{10.6}$$

where y_t is the realization at time t of an arbitrary function of the changes in market risk factors at time t, and $\varphi_Y(y)$ is the distribution of this function.

Both the rolling-window and the exponential smoothing techniques constitute rather crude ways of conditioning, i.e., of making the distribution of interest relevant to the present market conditions: the only variable of relevance in determining the weight

---

[2] Also with exponential smoothing at some point the statistician will probably introduce a truncation, but the sharpness of the 'cliff' (full information / no information) is now much smaller.

of a given observation is its distance from today. They are also, of course, extremely informationally wasteful. Can we do any better?

Indeed we can, as we often have non-data-driven information (model information or expert knowledge), which may suggest that time distance of some data from today is not necessarily the most relevant criterion of their relevance for the present conditions. Perhaps today we are in a recession, and we may believe that past data gathered during recessionary periods bear more relevance to what is happening today than chronologically closer data gathered in expansionary periods. Or we may be in a period of market turmoil, and we may believe that all periods of market excitation have some important common features. (These writers have reservations about such statements, but we are not talking about us, for the moment.) How can we incorporate this information in our specification of the probabilities, p_t?

Following Meucci (2008) we focus on the case where the variable we want to condition on is a macroeconomic variable, say, Y, that occurred, or was 'strong', in certain regions $\mathcal{Y}$ of our data set. We can easily modify the probabilities, p_t, either in a binary way (Meucci uses the term 'crisp') or in a smooth manner (Meucci refers to a 'smooth kernel'). We can posit, that is, either

$$p_t \propto 1 \quad \text{if } y_t \in \mathcal{Y}$$

$$p_t = 0 \quad \text{otherwise}$$

or

$$p_t \propto \exp\left[-\frac{1}{2}\frac{(y_t - \bar{y})^2}{s^2}\right]$$

where $\bar{y}$ is the reference value of the macroeconomic variable we believe is relevant, and s is normally referred to as the bandwidth.[3] As usual, the smoothly or crisply manipulated probabilities will have to be renormalized at the end.

The generalization to several conditional macroeconomic variables is straightforward. We note in passing that, if a smooth multivariate kernel is used, the probabilities become weighted by a variation of the Mahalanobis distance (see Section 17.5 and Doust's Geometric Allocation approach discussed in Sections 8.4 and 9.3).

The idea of assigning weights to the probabilities in order to determine distributions conditional on the current market conditions is very appealing, and, as we have shown, dear to our hearts. However, by changing the bandwidth, s, from 0 to ∞, one can move from a totally crisp specification to a weighting scheme virtually indistinguishable from the totally uninformative one, $p_t = \frac{1}{T}$. How can this arbitrariness be handled?

Again, Meucci follows a conceptual path that shares many similarities with our overall philosophy (and, in a sense, with the Black–Litterman approach). This is how it is done.

---

[3] It is easy to see why the term 'bandwidth' is used by considering the limiting cases of $s \to 0$ and $s \to \infty$: if $s = \infty$ 'anything goes' (the bandwidth is infinitely wide), and if $s = 0$ only exact matching will do (and the bandwidth is infinitely narrow).

Suppose that the expert wants to specify that the macroeconomic variable (or vector of macroeconomic variables) of interest should have a certain expectation (vector). Focusing on the one-dimensional case for simplicity, we want to impose that

$$\overline{y} = \sum_{t=1}^{T} p_t y_t \tag{10.7}$$

There exist an infinity of probabilities, $\{p_t\}$, such that Equation (10.7) is satisfied. Which set shall we choose? Meucci (2008) recommends choosing the probabilities that fully satisfy the constraint (10.7), while at the same time minimizing the distance from the historical distribution (i.e., the distribution that corresponds to the choice $p_t = \frac{1}{T}$). As a measure of distance from the 'historical prior', Meucci chooses the cross-entropy (or Kullback–Leibler distance between two distributions p and q), defined by

$$d_{KL}(p, q) = \sum_{t=1}^{T} p_t \ln \frac{p_t}{q_t} \tag{10.8}$$

As is well known, the Kullback–Leibler distance is not truly a distance (because of the lack of symmetry: $d_{KL}(p, q) \neq d_{KL}(q, p)$). However, its information-theoretical properties[4] make it very attractive, and have justified its use in a variety of contexts.

We note in passing the similarity of this approach with the variance-reducing technique by Avellaneda et al. (2000) – a technique that we shall adapt for our implementation of Monte-Carlo sampling on Bayesian nets. See Section 15.2.2.

10.1 Generalizing: entropy pooling

How to weight a panel of data is one of the interesting ideas put forth by Meucci. His more original and interesting idea, however (see Meucci 2008), goes under the name of entropy pooling. This is how the approach works.

Meucci proposes a recipe to blend a reference model (prior) for the market[5] with subjective views in order to obtain a posterior distribution. As in the Black–Litterman model, views are opinions that distort the market model. In the entropy-pooling approach, however, the attempt is made to effect this distortion without imposing extra spurious structure. Since a natural measure of 'structure' is entropy, the posterior distribution is defined then as the one that minimizes the entropy relative to the prior given the constraints. The spectrum of views can be wide and cover views on non-linear combinations of risk factors, correlations, ranking, etc. Step by step, the procedure suggested in Meucci (2008) is the following:

---

[4] See, e.g., Ash (1990 [1965]), Caticha (2008), Cover and Thomas (2006) and Williamson (2005) for foundational aspects and, e.g., Avellaneda (1998), Avellaneda et al. (1997) and Avellaneda et al. (2000) for financial applications.

[5] In order to carry out a comparison with the Black–Litterman approach in what follows we must reason using the interpretation that views the market distribution as a prior, i.e., opposite to the interpretation of Satchell.

- First one specifies the reference model. The market factors X are assumed to be distributed like $X \sim f_X$, where the distribution f_X is not necessarily normal.
- Then one specifies the views, V. The views are represented as:

$$V \equiv g(X) \tag{10.9}$$

where the g_i are not necessarily linear.

- As a next step, one calculates the posterior. The posterior distribution is the one that satisfies the constraints and is the closest in entropy to the reference distribution f_X. The relative entropy between the reference model and a generic distribution $\tilde{f}_X$ is defined as

$$d_{KL}(f_X, \tilde{f}_X) = \int \tilde{f}_X(x)[\ln \tilde{f}_X(x) - \ln f_X(x)]dx \tag{10.10}$$

The posterior is then defined as

$$\tilde{f}_X = \arg\min_{f \in V} d_{KL}(f_X, \tilde{f}_X) \tag{10.11}$$

where $\arg\min_{f \in V}$ means minimization with respect to all the distributions compatible with the set of constraints V.

- Finally, the investor must specify her degree of confidence. If the investor accepts $\tilde{f}_X$ as posterior this means that she has full confidence in the model. If her confidence is less than full, $\tilde{f}_X$ can be shrunk to the market model f_X by opinion pooling, i.e.,

$$f_X^c = (1 - c)f_X + c\tilde{f}_X \tag{10.12}$$

where the pooling parameter c lies in $[0\ 1]$. If the confidence is full ($c = 1$), we will have as posterior $f_X^c = \tilde{f}_X$. On the other hand if $c = 0$ we are led back to the market model: $f_X^c = f_X$.

Only in particular cases can analytical solutions be obtained. A numerical implementation is, however, always viable.

Now, the above approach can be cast in panel terminology, and the weighting schemes alluded to in the opening sections of this chapter become particular cases of what we have just described. More precisely, the reference market distribution is represented as a $J \times N$ panel of χ simulations. We can associate a vector of probabilities p with these scenarios, where each probability could be set equal to $1/J$ (as discussed above, other choices are possible). The views are represented as a $J \times N$ panel:

$$V_{jk} = g_k(\chi_{j,1}, \ldots, \chi_{j,N}) \tag{10.13}$$

For example, a view on the mean of a risk factor k can be represented as:

$$m_k = \sum_{j=1}^{J} p_j V_{jk} = \sum_{j=1}^{J} p_j \chi_{jk} \tag{10.14}$$

Then, instead of generating new Monte-Carlo simulations, the posterior distribution of the market can be inferred from the scenarios that have already been generated, but with a modified set of probabilities $\widetilde{p}$.

All the constraints discussed in Meucci (2008) can be written in the following form:

$$a_1 \leq A\widetilde{p} \leq a_2 \tag{10.15}$$

where A, a_1 and a_2 are expressions of the panel on the views. Then relative entropy is

$$d_{\mathrm{KL}}(\widetilde{p}, p) = \sum_{j=1}^{J} \widetilde{p}_j[\ln \widetilde{p}_j - \ln p_j] \tag{10.16}$$

The posterior is:

$$\widetilde{p} = \arg \min_{a_1 \leq Af \leq a_2} d_{\mathrm{KL}}(f, p) \tag{10.17}$$

and the entropy-pooling probabilities are given by:

$$p_c = (1 - c)p + c\widetilde{p} \tag{10.18}$$

10.2   The link with Bayesian nets (and Black–Litterman)

The conceptual similarity with the Black–Litterman approach is evident: in that context the asset manager has the freedom to give more or less weight to her views. As her confidence becomes weaker and weaker, the distribution approaches more and more closely the market portfolio.

Getting a bit ahead of ourselves, we can already say that in our approach we will obtain the full distribution of the market risk factors by splicing together a 'normal' and an 'excited' component. The excited distribution will be obtained as a by-product of the Bayesian-net construction. As we shall see, it will often be the case that the asset manager may want to vary 'by hand' the probability mass concentrated in the normal-times part of the spliced distribution. (We call this procedure 'varying the normalization factor'.) The joint excited distribution is then underspecified: many possible sets of probabilities will be compatible with the incomplete inputs that the asset manager has provided. We therefore also face Meucci's dilemma: which of these infinite number of possible distributions shall we choose?

In Sections 24.4 and 27.3 we also offer an answer based on Maximum Entropy: if we do not know enough, then we should choose the least 'committal' (least informative, prejudicial) distribution. There is another, Meucci-inspired possibility, though: we could choose those values of the input conditional probabilities that minimize the distance between the spliced (normal + excited) distribution and the historical distribution. Note that this will not be obtained by setting the 'normalization factor' of the excited portion to zero, because in our approach the 'normal' component has been culled of the historical outliers, and will therefore be different from the historical full distribution (which does contain the historical exceptional events).

If this does not make too much sense now, the reader should come back to this section after reading Sections 24.4 and 27.3. In any case, for the reasons explained in Chapter 4, we are reluctant to place a strong unconditional reliance on historical occurrences of past stresses events. Therefore we do not pursue this otherwise interesting avenue in our approach.

10.3   Extending the entropy-pooling technique[6]

The entropy-pooling approach described above has also been extended by Meucci (2010) to an earlier version (Rebonato 2010) of the model we propose in this book. As we have not introduced our Bayesian network methodology yet, the following remarks may not be very clear at this stage, but the reader may want to revisit these comments after reading Parts IV and V of this book.

Meucci's extension of the Rebonato (2010a) approach is based on the procedure described above.

Beginning with the prior, Meucci (2010b) starts from a set of risk drivers X and discretizes them. He then forms a joint probability table by assigning a probability to each combination of risk factors. The probability assignment can be done either using a Bayesian net, or by employing traditional frequentist means.

Then the 'stress views' are introduced. The investor is required to express her views about probabilities. As we shall see, Bayesian nets are characterized by assigning conditional probabilities of events. Consider two such events, say E_1 and E_3. For example, the portfolio manager may assign $P(E_1|E_3) > 0.7$. Suppose now that the probability $P(E_1|E_3)$ does not enter into the Master Equation associated with the Bayesian net, perhaps because the two nodes, E_1 and E_3, may not be directly connected by an arc. Whatever the reason, the 'non-canonical' probability $P(E_1|E_3)$ can be regarded as a stress view. Each stress view can be represented as before as a set of constraints on the new set of probabilities $\widetilde{p}$ to be associated with each scenario:

$$A\widetilde{p} \leq b \tag{10.19}$$

Meucci (2010b) shows that 'stress views' on correlations, volatilities, etc. can also be expressed in the same manner, because the constraints on these can also be expressed in the form of Equation (10.19).

As a next step a consistency check is carried out by modifying the quantities b

$$b \longrightarrow b + \delta b \tag{10.20}$$

This is done using an algorithm that searches for the values of δb that ensure consistency with the constraints. (If the views were already consistent, then, of course, $\delta b = 0$.)

---

[6] This section can be skipped on a first reading.

Finally, the posterior is calculated as

$$\tilde{p} = \arg \min_{Aq \leq b+\delta b} d_{KL}(q, p) \tag{10.21}$$

As we said, all of this will be clearer after Parts IV and V. In particular, we direct the reader to Section 14.4, where we explain our way of dealing with non-canonical information.

Part IV

How we deal with exceptional events

Having laid the groundwork for our approach, we finally reach the core of the book: Bayesian nets. In this part we present as simply as possible the theoretical foundations of the subject, with a focus on the problem at hand. In particular, given our emphasis on a causal approach, we present *causal* Bayesian nets, and we show that they afford very 'pleasant' mathematical and cognitive features. In this part the reader will begin to understand why structuring our Bayesian nets in a causal manner will be one of the cornerstones of the approach we propose.

11 Bayesian nets

If people do not believe that mathematics is simple, it is only because they do not realize how complicated life is. John von Neumann

One of the core ideas at the heart of our approach is to treat separately 'normal' and 'exceptional' events. We begin with the latter, because herein lies the more original part of our work, and both we and reader are therefore understandably eager to start in earnest.

There is, however, another reason for starting from the 'excited' component. Paradoxically, defining and handling the 'normal' part of the problem (and, quantitatively, the joint distribution of returns) is surprisingly subtle and far from unambiguous. So, starting from the tails can be conceptually, if perhaps not technically, easier. We address the 'subtle' issues we have just referred to in the opening pages of Section 17.1. We invite the reader to ponder those pages carefully.

In this chapter we introduce Bayesian nets. As we shall see, in the narrowest sense Bayesian nets are a tool to obtain (factorize) the joint probabilities between a number of (discrete) variables. In general, Bayesian nets need not be endowed with a temporal or causal interpretation. However, when such an interpretation is adopted (and warranted!) Bayesian nets become particularly powerful tools – tools, that is, that can aid and enhance our understanding of a problem; that, when used subjectively, we can implement with confidence; that can help us avoid logical mistakes; and that, by pushing any assumptions we make to their ultimate logical consequences, tell us if we are 'thinking straight'.

Causal Bayesian nets are also 'economical': if the set of dependencies between the variables at hand are expressed by means of a *causal* Bayesian net, then we need the smallest number of arcs in the graph for the task at hand. We also need to specify conditional probabilities of the lowest order (say, singly- rather than doubly-conditioned). If the precise meaning of this statement is not clear at this stage (and, unless the reader is already familiar with graphs, it probably isn't) we explain more precisely in Section 11.6 what we mean.

11.1   Displaying the joint probabilities for Boolean variables

To see how Bayesian nets can help in analysing a problem of choice under stress, let's begin to understand where the problem lies. To focus on the essence of the discussion, in what follows we deal with Boolean variables, i.e., variables that can only assume the logical value *TRUE* or *FALSE* (often denoted as *T* or *F*). We stress that extending the analysis to variables that can assume several, instead of just two, possible values, is usually straightforward. It is only for the sake of simplicity that we deal mainly with the two-valued case.[1]

Suppose that we have n Boolean variables. One can immediately see that there are 2^n possible combinations of *TRUE* and *FALSE* values for these n variables. Each of these combinations is called a joint event. To each joint event, i.e., to each combination, one can associate a joint probability, $p(i), i = 1, 2, \ldots, 2^n$.

A common tabular representation of the various combinations of *TRUE* and *FALSE* values for the n Boolean variables (i.e., of the various possible events) and of the associated joint probabilities is achieved by means of a truth table. This is made up of n columns, each of length 2^n. The entry in the jth column and ith row contains a 1 or a 0 to indicate whether the variable associated with the jth column is *TRUE* or *FALSE*, respectively, for the ith joint event (i.e., for the joint event that one can read along a row).

So, for the case of three variables depicted in Table 11.1, the symbol '0' written in the fourth position of the column associated with variable E_1 means that for the fourth combination of realizations (joint event J_4) the first variable was *FALSE* (the second was also *FALSE* and the third *TRUE*).

The 1s and 0s must be arranged in the various columns in such a way that each row will have a different combination of *TRUE* and *FALSE* realizations. Since there are 2^n such realizations, and n columns, there will always be one, and only one, such representation. (Two representations with two or more rows switched around are deemed to be equivalent.)

For $n = 3$ the truth table for Boolean variables described above has the following representation:

Table 11.1 *The truth table for the case of three Boolean variables*

	E_1	E_2	E_3	
J_1	1	1	1	$p(1)$
J_2	0	1	1	$p(2)$
J_3	1	0	1	$p(3)$
J_4	0	0	1	$p(4)$
J_5	1	1	0	$p(5)$
J_6	0	1	0	$p(6)$
J_7	1	0	0	$p(7)$
J_8	0	0	0	$p(8)$

(11.1)

[1] In our applications we will always assume that the variables can only take on a finite number of possible values. Whenever conceptual subtleties arise we have taken care to highlight them. See Section 12.11 for the extension of the formalism to the multi-valued setting.

The quantities labelled $J_i, i = 1, 2, \ldots, 8$, in the first column denote the joint events. To each joint event we then associate the probability in the last column.

Once we have the joint probabilities we have (statistically) everything. In particular, we can do diagnostic and predictive inference, and we can look at the effect of combining evidence.

We do diagnostic inference when we try to work our way back from effect to causes (i.e., by calculating $P(Cause(s)|Effect(s))$:[2] we know that a patient has a fever and red spots, and we want estimate the probability that she may have chicken-pox).

We do predictive inference when we go the other way round, i.e., when we know the causes and we try to establish the probability of the effects: $P(Effect(s)|Cause(s))$: we know that the patient has chicken-pox and we want to estimate the probabilities that she will be running a fever and/or displaying red spots.

As for combining evidence, with the joint probabilities we can calculate $P(Cause(s)|Effect_1, Effect_2, \ldots, Effect_k)$. In all these cases, we are always led to evaluating conditional probabilities of the following type (for, say, four variables w, x, y and z)

$$p(w|z) = \frac{P(w, z)}{P(z)} = \frac{\sum_{x,y} p(w, x, y, z)}{\sum_{w,x,y} p(w, x, y, z)} \tag{11.2}$$

If we denote by $e_i, i = 1, 2, \ldots, n$, the $n \times 1$ column vectors of 0s and 1s associated with the n variables, it is straightforward to prove that for Boolean variables the conditional probability above can be computed as[3]

$$p(w|z) = \frac{\sum_{i=1,n} e_w(i)e_z(i)p(i)}{\sum_{i=1,n} e_z(i)p(i)} \tag{11.3}$$

If one wanted to calculate, say, $p(w|\tilde{z})$, one can make use of an auxiliary $n \times 1$ column vector 1_n, whose elements are all 1s. Then

$$p(w|\tilde{z}) = \frac{\sum_{i=1,n} e_w(i)[1_n(i) - e_z(i)]p(i)}{\sum_{i=1,n} [1_n(i) - e_z(i)]p(i)} \tag{11.4}$$

The joint-probability approach (and the representation that goes with it) is very general – indeed, for two-valued random variables, it is *the most general* representation of their joint probabilities. However, it is very 'expensive': for 10 variables we have to

---

[2] The diagnostic mode used to be called in statistics the estimation of inverse probabilities. For an interesting historical account of the troubled history of the concept of inverse probabilities from Reverend Bayes to modern Bayesian theory through Price and Laplace see McGrayne (2011, esp. Chs 1–5).

[3] We are not saying that this is the numerically most efficient way to do so. Conceptually, however, it is the most transparent.

specify $2^n - 1 = 2^{10} - 1 = 1024 - 1$ joint probabilities (where the -1 term of course comes from the normalization constraint $\sum_{i=1,2^n} p(i) = 1$).

For 20 variables we already have to deal with 1 048 575 joint probabilities. And with 30 variables we are faced with approximately 10^9 joint probabilities. As if this were not bad enough, we would also be faced with the problem that the conditional probabilities that allow us to draw inferences soon become non-computable in practice, because summing out (marginalizing out) a variable from a joint distribution requires an exponential number of operations (exponential in the number of variables).

Note that, as the number of variables grows, we are soon faced with two distinct sources of problem: a computational and a cognitive one. When it comes to computational problems there is always the hope that some clever algorithm will be found, or that Moore's law will continue to work its magic. But the cognitive barrier is much harder to overcome if we want to assign our probabilities in a subjective manner – for instance, if we want to elicit the probabilities from a panel of experts, it is neither reasonable nor feasible to ask a panel of experts for 10^6 or 10^9 subjective inputs.

There is another (and, for our applications, more serious) problem, of a cognitive nature: even when the total number of joint probabilities is rather small (as in the four-variable case above), the human mind is not well suited to assigning directly subjective probabilities to joint events such as, say, 'A happening, B not happening, C not happening and D happening'. If joint probabilities are directly elicited, even for as few as three or four variables we immediately begin to find ourselves at a cognitive loss. We must stress that, for the type of problems we deal with in this book, *the cognitive barrier kicks in much sooner than the computational one*. Indeed, for our relatively-small-size problems, we will still be able to use Equations (11.2) to (11.4) to calculate conditional probabilities. However, the task of assigning the joint probabilities directly would be impossible, even for far fewer variables than we will work with.

What are we to do then? A table such as the one in (11.1) conveys all the probabilistic information we may want, but (subjectively) we do not know how to fill it in. And, for events of financial or economic nature, there is virtually no hope that the joint probabilities can be directly estimated using frequentist methods. We seem to be at a dead end. This is where Bayesian nets come to the rescue.

11.2   Graphical representation of dependence: Bayesian nets

We leave joint probabilities to one side for the moment and we look at ways to express graphically the dependence between variables. More specifically, we are going to work with variables linked by *causal* relationships. As we said, Bayesian nets do not have to reflect causal links, but we will restrict our treatment to this (important) special case. Then Bayesian nets can be seen as '[a] way of structuring a situation for reasoning under uncertainty [when there is a] causal relations between events'.[4] Pearl (2009),

---

[4] Pearl (2009, p. 24).

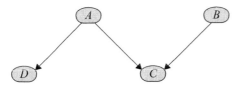

Figure 11.1 The Bayesian net associated with four variables, A, B, C and D. The net conveys the information that A influences C and D, B influences C, and A and B do not influence each other. Strictly speaking, no direction is required in the arc connecting two variables which influence each other. In causal Bayesian nets, however, 'influencing' is synonymous with 'causing', and the direction of the arrow indicates the flow of causation. See the discussion in Section 11.3.

among others, explains clearly the advantages of a causal interpretation of Bayesian nets:

The interpretation of direct acyclical graphs [DAGs] as carriers of independence does not necessarily imply causation. . . . However, the ubiquity of DAG models in statistical and AI applications stems (often unwittingly) primarily from their causal interpretation – that is, a system of processes . . . that could account for the generation of the observed data. It is this casual interpretation that explains why DAG models are rarely used in any variable ordering *other than those which respect the direction of time and causation.*[5]

We return to the causal interpretation of Bayesian nets in Section 11.6 (where further important advantages in terms of parsimony of description and simplicity of child/parent structure are discussed). In the meantime we proceed to the description of how these (causal) Bayesian nets can be built in practice. Again, for the sake of simplicity we deal with Boolean variables.

Each logical variable in the problem at hand is associated with a node. Since we have for the moment decided to work with Boolean variables, following Jensen and Nielsen (2007), it is useful to think of the logical variables associated with a node as propositions (such as 'Sovereign X will default within one month') that can be *TRUE* or *FALSE*.

Nodes that can 'influence each other' are connected by an arrow. The direction of the arrow indicates the direction of causality. We can show this graphically as in Figure 11.1.

Two nodes connected by an arrow stand in a parent/child relationship. Changing metaphors, nodes with no parents (A and B in Figure 11.1) are called roots, and nodes with no children (C and D in the same figure) are called leaves (or sinks). All the nodes and the arrows (arcs) together make up a graph.

Each node has a conditional probability table associated with it. What the conditional probability table contains depends on whether the node is a root or not. If it is a root, it will contain only the marginal probability of that node. If it is not a root it will contain

---

[5] *Ibid.*, p. 21, emphasis added.

the conditional probabilities of that node,[6] conditioned on all the possible combinations of *TRUE* or *FALSE* for its parents.

So, making reference again to Figure 11.1, the conditional tables for variables A and B just contain the marginal probability of A and B assuming the value *TRUE* or *FALSE*:

Conditional probability table for variable A

$$\begin{bmatrix} P(A) \\ P(\widetilde{A}) \end{bmatrix}$$

Conditional probability table for variable B

$$\begin{bmatrix} P(B) \\ P(\widetilde{B}) \end{bmatrix}$$

Of course, since, for any Boolean-variable event E_j, $P(E_j) + P(\widetilde{E}_j) = 1$, only one probability has to be elicited per root node.

The conditional probability table for variable D is as follows:

Conditional probability table for variable D

$$\begin{bmatrix} P(D|A) \\ P(D|\widetilde{A}) \\ P(\widetilde{D}|A) \\ P(\widetilde{D}|\widetilde{A}) \end{bmatrix}$$

For Boolean variables, it is always true that

$$P(D|A = a) + P(\widetilde{D}|A = a) = 1 \qquad (11.5)$$

for $a = T, F$. Therefore, in order to fill in the conditional probability table associated with variable D the expert has to provide only two independent conditional probabilities, say, $P(D|A)$ and $P(D|\widetilde{A})$.

Finally the conditional probability table for variable C is as follows:

Conditional probability table for variable C

$$\begin{bmatrix} P(C|A, B) \\ P(C|\widetilde{A}, B) \\ P(C|A, \widetilde{B}) \\ P(C|\widetilde{A}, \widetilde{B}) \\ P(\widetilde{C}|A, B) \\ P(\widetilde{C}|\widetilde{A}, B) \\ P(\widetilde{C}|A, \widetilde{B}) \\ P(\widetilde{C}|\widetilde{A}, \widetilde{B}) \end{bmatrix}$$

---

[6] And, for Boolean variables, of its negation. For Boolean variables, the negated conditional probabilities are trivial, because, for any event $\mathcal{E}$, and for any Boolean variables, BV, it is always true that $P(BV|\mathcal{E}) = 1 - P(\widetilde{BV}|\mathcal{E})$.

Again,

$$P(C|A = a, B = b) + P(\widetilde{C}|A = a, B = b) = 1 \qquad (11.6)$$

for $a, b = T, F$. Therefore the expert has to provide only four independent conditional probabilities to fill in the table associated with node C.

Generalizing from this example, it is clear that, for a node with m parents, the expert has to provide 2^m conditional probabilities.[7]

Now, consider the case of four variables. Any joint probability, $P(A = a, B = b, C = c, D = d)$, for $a, b, c, d = T, F$, can be written as a product of lower- and lower-order conditional probabilities. So, for instance

$$P(A = a, B = b, C = c, D = d) \qquad (11.7)$$
$$= P(A = a|B = b, C = c, D = d)$$
$$\times P(B = b|C = c, D = d)$$
$$\times P(C = c|D = d)$$
$$\times P(D = d)$$

In full generality, providing all the conditional probabilities corresponding to the possible values for $a, b, c, d = T, F$ in Equation (11.7) is equivalent to providing the full set of joint probabilities. A simple counting exercise will show that the equivalence is not just conceptual, but also 'computational': we need $2^n - 1$ numbers in one representation, and $2^n - 1$ numbers in the other.

Note, however, that the conditional probability tables that make up a Bayesian net do not contain all the possible conditional probabilities associated with a given node. For instance, the conditional probability table for node A only contains $P(A)$ and $P(\widetilde{A})$. How can the full joint distribution can be recovered with such limited information?

The power of Bayesian nets comes from the observation that, thanks to the Master Equation presented in Section 11.5.2, if the links between variables embedded in our net have indeed been correctly specified, then the many fewer and much-easier-to-specify entries of the conditional probability tables are all that is needed to fully identify the joint probabilities. For the simple example in Figure 11.1 this means that we only have to provide $2^0 + 2^0 + 2^1 + 2^2 = 8$ conditional (or marginal) probabilities instead of $16 - 1 = 15$. And, just as relevantly, for the Bayesian net in the example above we only have to supply at most doubly-conditioned probabilities, instead of trebly-conditioned ones. For this trivial example with only four variables the gain may seem rather underwhelming. Not so, as soon as we deal with ten or more variables.

And, as we shall see, using a causally constructed Bayesian net also means that the conditional probabilities to be specified are cognitively simpler to assign.

---

[7] If a node has no parents, then there will be $2^0 = 1$ (conditional) probabilities. In this case the conditioned probability is degenerate (is conditioned on 0 parents) and therefore corresponds to a marginal. In what follows we will assume that conditional probability tables always contain conditional probabilities, with the understanding that if the table refers to a root, then the conditional is actually a marginal.

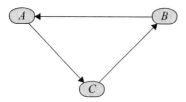

Figure 11.2 A Bayesian net depicting a feedback loop (or, more precisely, a directed cyclical graph: starting from one node it is possible (in this case trivial) to get back to the same node following the arrows in the graph.

11.3   Influencing and 'causing'

For the purpose of our discussion we shall say that two variables (say, A and B) affect or influence each other if knowledge of occurrence of A changes our estimate of the probability of occurrence of B: $P(B|A) \neq P(B)$, and, vice versa, if knowledge of occurrence of B changes our estimate of the probability of occurrence of A: $P(A|B) \neq P(A)$.

Note that specifying an influence between two variables says nothing about the direction of causality. Indeed, conditional probabilities do not specify, or imply, causality. Causality is an extremely subtle and complex concept, and philosophers have had a go at coming to grips with this concept for over 2000 years. Understandably, we are reluctant to enter the fray, and we shall simply assume that 'we know' what causes what (because of our understanding of how the world works), and we will translate this knowledge in the direction of the arrow.

Note also that when, in the context of Bayesian nets, we say that variable A 'causes' variable B, we do not have in mind deterministic causation, in the sense that, if A happens, then B will certainly happen. Rather, we use the term 'cause' in the same sense as when we say that, say, smoking causes lung cancer. When we use this shorthand expression, in reality we are really implicitly making two statements: first we say that knowledge of occurrence of, say, $A = Smoking$ changes our estimate of the probability of occurrence of $B = Lung\ Cancer$: $P(B|A) \neq P(B)$; and then we say that we know what causes what (i.e., that smoking causes lung cancer, but lung cancer does not causes smoking).

Now, it could very well be that variable A 'causes' (in the sense above) variable C, which 'causes' variable B, which in turn 'causes' variable A. This would be depicted by a graph such as the one shown in Figure 11.2.

Logically there is nothing impossible about this (in real life, such feedback loops are actually more common than is often recognized). More generally, the causal dependence between the variables at hand may be such that one may want to draw a graph such that a path (as indicated by edges and arrows) may lead after many steps out of one node and back to the same node. When this happens the graph is said to be *cyclical*. Computationally and conceptually it is much more difficult to deal with cyclical graphs, and we will therefore restrict our attentions to graphs in which no node can be reached back by any path inside the graph itself.[8] Not surprisingly, these well-behaved graphs are called *directed acyclical graphs* (DAGs).

As we shall see, the characterization of a Bayesian net by means of directed edges helps the intuition enormously, but does not lend itself very well to performing computer calculations. If we want to describe the topological structure of a Bayesian net in a way that can be readily understood by a computer programme we can use the g-matrix (see, e.g., Jackson 2008).[9] For a directed Bayesian network that links n Boolean random variables this is an $n \times n$ matrix that contains 1s and 0s. The entries with 1s are those corresponding to causation links. Those with 0s signify that there is no edge connecting the two variables. By convention, the diagonal is filled with 1s. So, for instance, for the Bayesian net in Figure 11.1, the g-matrix has the form shown in Table 11.2.

Table 11.2 *The g-matrix for the Bayesian net depicted in Figure 11.1, where we have arbitrarily adopted the convention that the causal link goes from the row entries to the column entries*

$$g = \begin{array}{c} \\ A \\ B \\ C \\ D \end{array} \begin{bmatrix} A & B & C & D \\ 1 & 0 & 1 & 1 \\ 0 & 1 & 1 & 0 \\ 0 & 0 & 1 & 0 \\ 0 & 0 & 0 & 1 \end{bmatrix} \qquad (11.8)$$

For undirected graphs the g-matrix is, of course, symmetric. For directed graphs we have to choose whether the row or the column variables are the parents. In Table 11.2 we have arbitrarily adopted the convention that the causal link goes from the row entries to the column entries. So a 1 in the cell (row = A, column = C) means that A 'influences' C – or, more precisely, that there is a directed edge (arrow) *from A to C*.

11.4   Independence and conditional independence

Tout se tient. (This is the quote we fear most)

We have mentioned that, thanks to the Master Equation presented below, many fewer and much simpler conditional probabilities than the full set are enough to specify fully all the joint probabilities. But where does this saving 'come from'? In this subsection we try to gain an intuitive understanding of why Bayesian nets are so powerful – and, indirectly, of their limitations.

---

[8] As late as 1994, it was still the case that 'almost nothing is known about how directed cyclical graphs (DCGs) represent conditional independence constraints, or about their equivalence or identifiability properties, or about characterizing classes of DCGs from conditional independence relations or other statistical constraints' (Spirtes 1994, p. 1). Spirtes' contribution was to propose a solution to the first of these problems, 'which is a prerequisite for the others' (p. 1). The results, however, were not heart-warming: 'the equivalence of the fundamental global and local Markov conditions characteristic of DAGs [Directed Acyclical Graphs] no longer holds, even in linear systems ...' (p. 1).

[9] Page 23 and *passim*.

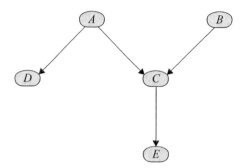

Figure 11.3 A Bayesian net showing a case of conditional independence: variable C 'screens' variable E from variables A and B; as a consequence, $P(E|C, A, B) = P(E|C)$.

The reader is certainly familiar with the concept of independence between two variables, A and B. Formally this is expressed as follows:

$$P(A|B) = P(A) \quad \text{(independence)} \tag{11.9}$$

from which one immediately obtains

$$P(A, B) = P(A)P(B) \quad \text{(independence)} \tag{11.10}$$

and, of course,

$$P(B|A) = P(B) \quad \text{(independence)} \tag{11.11}$$

What Equations (11.9) to (11.11) say is that information about the occurrence of B does not change our estimate of the probability of event A – and that, when this is true, information about the occurrence of A does not change our estimate of the probability of event B. When this is true, the joint probability of the two variables then neatly factorizes as in Equation (11.10).

Independence between variables is very powerful, but also relatively rare. A more common, somewhat weaker, but still very powerful, condition is *conditional independence*. Formally A is said to be conditionally independent of B if

$$P(A|BC) = P(A|C) \quad \text{(conditional independence)} \tag{11.12}$$

In words, knowledge that B and C have happened does not help us in assessing the probability of A happening more than just knowledge that C has happened does; or, equivalently, knowledge that B has occurred does not change our estimate of the conditional probability $P(A|C)$.

Let's see how this condition is reflected in a Bayesian net. If $P(E|BC) = P(E|C)$, we will suggestively say that variable C *screens off* variable E from variable B. To understand why this is the case consider the net in Figure 11.3.

Let us give the following interpretation to the five variables: let

- A represent an unexpectedly strong release for GDP growth;
- B represent an unexpectedly strong release for non-farm payroll;

- C represent an increase in inflation expectations;
- D represent a decline by 10% or more in the Standard and Poor's (S&P);
- E represent a rally in Treasury Inflation Protected products (TIPs).

Now, the rally in TIPs is certainly not independent of the GDP growth, or of the non-farm payroll. However, what the Bayesian net is expressing is *conditional* independence between the rally in TIPs on the one hand and the GDP growth and the non-farm payroll releases on the other *once the change in inflation expectations is known*. We only need to know whether the inflation expectations have changed in order to change our assessment of how the TIPs will respond, not where the change in inflation expectation came from. Formally

$$P(E|C, A, B) = P(E|C) \quad \text{(conditional independence)}$$

The variable C 'screens' the variable E from variables A and B, and destroys any path-dependence from the roots to variable E.

It is thanks to this 'screening' effect (defined more precisely below) that we can build joint probabilities without having to use conditional probabilities such as $P(E|C, A, B)$. This is what makes Bayesian nets so 'economical' and so powerful. In general, the simpler the net (i.e., the smaller the average number of parents per node), the stronger the screening, the greater the computational and cognitive saving.

This beautiful property should not, however, blind us to the fact that, yes, once the Bayesian net has been laid down, the mathematical results associated with conditional independence flow with absolute certainty. The justification for a given layout for our Bayesian net lies in our understanding of how the world works, not in mathematics. It is for this reason that the example we have chosen for Figure 11.3 does not deal with canonical sprinklers and burglar alarms, but is deliberately somewhat 'controversial': the reader may not agree, for instance, that the probability of a rally in TIPs depends *only* on the change in inflation expectations, irrespective of whether this change was due to an overtight labour market, or a surge in GDP growth. If the reader disagreed with this 'path-independence' assumption, then she would have to redraw the net, adding greater realism (and complexity) by introducing additional arrows, or auxiliary variables (see below).

In general, if one looks deep enough, absolute independence (conditional or otherwise) is extremely difficult to justify in principle. Invoking independence is almost invariably an approximation, which the builder of the net should make with a keen eye to the realism of the description on the one hand, and the computational and conceptual saving on the other.

The informal discussion of 'screening' presented above naturally leads to the concept of d-separation, which makes the intuition more precise, and offers a powerful tool for joining different Bayesian nets and for Maximum-Entropy applications. We will look at d-separation in some detail below. Before that, we have to make the links between probability distributions and Bayesian nets more precise.

11.5   The link between Bayesian nets and probability distributions

11.5.1   Screening and Markov parents

All factorizations are equal, but some factorizations are more equal than others. Paraphrased from George Orwell, *Animal Farm*

We start from a joint distribution p on a set V of n discrete-valued (in most of our applications, Boolean) variables, $\{X\}$, that we choose to order as $V = \{X_1, X_2, \ldots, X_n\}$.[10] For the moment the ordering is arbitrary and, obviously, not unique. We shall see that choosing a 'good' criterion to order our variables will be very important, and will be linked to our causal interpretation of the Bayesian net. For the moment, however, we keep the treatment general.

Given these variables and this ordering, we know that, thanks to the chain-decomposition rule, we can always write:

$$p(x_1, x_2, \ldots, x_n) = \prod_{j=1,n} P(x_j | x_1, x_2, \ldots, x_{j-1}) \tag{11.13}$$

Note that in the various terms that appear in the product, the conditioning is carried out only on those variables that have been given a label smaller than j: $P(x_j | x_1, x_2, \ldots, x_{j-1})$. Therefore the conditional probabilities that are used to factorize the joint probability depend on the arbitrary ordering that we have chosen. There are many ways in which the variables could have been ordered, and there are therefore just as many ways in which the joint probabilities can be factorized. They are all mathematically equivalent, but, as we shall see, some orderings (and hence some factorizations) are (much) more useful than others.

Now, let's focus on variable X_j. It may be the case that this variable does not depend on (is not influenced by) the full set of its arbitrarily chosen predecessor variables $\{X_1, X_2, \ldots, X_{j-1}\}$, but only on some subset of its predecessors. (We stress that, since we are not looking at Bayesian nets yet, but only at probability distributions, the term 'predecessor' only indicates variables that we have indexed with labels $k < j$ in the arbitrarily chosen ordering.) With some foresight we call this set of predecessors, denoted by PA_j, the *Markov parents* of X_j (or, for short, just the *parents* of X_j). More precisely we have the following definition, taken from Pearl (2009, p. 14).

DEFINITION 1 (MARKOV PARENTS)   *Let* $V = \{X_1, X_2, \ldots, X_n\}$ *be an arbitrarily-ordered set of variables, and let* $p(v)$ *be the joint probability distribution on these variables. A subset of variables,* $PA_j \subset V$, *is said to constitute the Markov parents of variable* X_j *if* PA_j *is a minimal set of predecessors of* X_j *that renders* X_j *independent of all its other predecessors. In other words, the set,* PA_j, *of parents of node* X_j *is any subset of* $\{X_1, X_2, \ldots, X_{j-1}\}$ *satisfying*

$$P(x_j | pa_j) = P(x_j | x_1, x_2, \ldots, x_{j-1}) \tag{11.14}$$

and such that no proper subset of PA_j *satisfies Equation (11.14).*

---

[10]   The treatment in this section draws heavily on Pearl (2009, Ch. 1).

With Equation (11.14) we are therefore saying that conditioning on the (Markov) parents of variable X_j has the same effect as conditioning on all its predecessors – or, conversely, that the Markov parents are the minimal set of predecessors that carry the same conditioning information as all the predecessors: these are the *preceding* variables that are sufficient to determine the probability of X_j.

It is important to stress that we are not saying that variable X_j is conditionally independent of variables X_k, $k > j$, i.e., on 'later' variables in the arbitrary ordering. We are only saying that in the factorization (11.13) we only need to condition variable X_j on its Markov parents' predecessors in order to obtain the fully conditioned probabilities, and hence, as the Master Equation(11.15) below shows, the joint probability $p(x_1, x_2, \ldots, x_n)$.

We are now in a position to give a precise meaning to the concept of screening that we have intuitively introduced above.

DEFINITION 2 (SCREENING)   *Given a set PA_j of parents for variable X_j we say that the set of Markov parents PA_j screens off variable X_j from all the variables X_k, $k < j$, such that $X_k \notin PA_j$.*

Now we can introduce the link between joint distributions and Bayesian nets. More precisely, given these definitions, given the chosen ordering, given the ordered set $V = \{X_1, X_2, \ldots, X_n\}$ and given the Markov parents of each node, PA_j, *we can associate to each joint distribution a directed acyclical graph*. We can do so by construction, with the construction following recursively from the definitions above. This is how to do it.

As a first step we associate variables with nodes. Then we number (at this stage arbitrarily) the variables and go in order through all the variables. At step j in the construction of the net we are therefore focussing on variable X_j. At the jth step in the construction, we look at the minimal set of predecessors that screen off X_j from its other predecessors (i.e., at its Markov parents, PA_j), as in Equation (11.14), and draw an arrow from each variable in PA_j to X_j.

How do we know which variables belong to the minimal set of predecessors? This is where our understanding of how the world works comes to the fore, in allowing us to establish which variables render variable X_j independent of all its other predecessors – the reader can think back to our TIPs-and-inflation example, and see whether she agrees with our understanding of the world, and hence with our choice of Markov parents.

We do not prove, but it is intuitively plausible, that this procedure of associating variables with nodes and drawing arrows from each node in the parent set PA_j to the child X_j will always produce a directed acyclical graph, i.e., in our terminology, a Bayesian net. We direct those readers who feel they need a proof to Pearl (2009, p. 14).

11.5.2   *The Master Equation*
We stress that, up to this point, we have not built a *causal* Bayesian net (because our ordering is still arbitrary). The Bayesian net built using definition (11.14) is simply a carrier of conditional independence relationships following the so-far-arbitrary order of construction.

Clearly, given definition (11.14), by direct substitution, one can write

$$p(x_1, x_2, \ldots, x_n) = \prod_j P(x_j | x_1, x_2, \ldots, x_{j-1}) = \prod_j P(x_j | pa_j) \qquad (11.15)$$

This is the *Master Equation*. It states that any probability distribution such that Equation (11.14) is true must factorize according to Equation (11.15). The slightly subtle, but very important, point is that the joint distribution obtained trough the factorization (11.15) no longer depends on the ordering. Indeed, given a distribution p and a directed acyclical graph G we can always check whether the distribution p actually factorizes as prescribed by Equation (11.15) without making any reference to the ordering of the variables.

Therefore a characterization of the set of distributions compatible with a given directed acyclical graph, G, can be simply obtained by listing the conditional independencies that these distributions must satisfy. These conditional independencies can be directly read off a directed acyclical graph using the criterion of d-separation, to which we will turn shortly. First, however, we must discuss the choice of ordering for the variables.

11.6   Ordering and causation – causal Bayesian nets

The structure (topology) of a Bayesian net will depend on the arbitrary choice of ordering for the variables in the problem (even if the resulting joint probabilities do not). As Hackerman and Breese (1995) point out, 'if this ordering is chosen carelessly, the resulting network may fail to reflect many conditional independencies in the domain'. What this terse expression means is that, unless we give a 'good' ordering to the variables, in order to obtain a mathematically complete specification, we have to assign more conditional dependencies than strictly necessary. How are we then to choose the 'best' ordering?

In order to answer this question, let us introduce the 'burglar alarm' example, which has found its way into almost all the books (and many articles) on Bayesian nets we are aware of. The story is as follows.

An anxious home owner has installed a burglar alarm. This alarm is not perfect: it may be activated by a fault, or by some event (say, an earthquake) other than the intrusion of a burglar. Also, it may fail to send a message even if a burglar has entered the house. If the alarm *is* activated, it will place a call to two friends (of the home owner, not of the burglar), John and Mary, who are then supposed to call the home owner. If we call A, B, E, J and M the variables associated with the propositions

- A: the alarm is activated
- B: a burglar has entered the house
- E: an earthquake has occurred
- J: friend John calls the home owner
- M: friend Mary calls the home owner

then we can order the five variables in several different ways. Let's start from the following ordering: $\{B, E, A, J, M\}$.[11] Let's follow the procedure described above to create a Bayesian net.

We start from the first variable $\{B\}$, the proposition 'A burglar has entered the house'. As it is the first variable in our ordering, it has no parents, so $PA\{B\} = \{0\}$. Therefore we place a square on the graph, but at this stage we have no arrows to draw.

We move to the second variable, E, associated with the occurrence of an earthquake. There are no links between the occurrence of the earthquake and its only predecessor, B (given the ordering we have chosen). So $PA\{E\} = \{0\}$. We place another square in the graph, but, again, we have no arrows to draw.

Let's look at the third variable, A (the alarm is activated). Now $PA\{A\} = \{B, E\}$. We therefore draw the variable on the graph, and we also draw two arrows: both the entry of a burglar and the occurrence of the earthquake are in the set of the minimal set predecessors of A needed to make A independent of all its other predecessors (see Definition 1, Equation (11.14)). Following the procedure outlined above we draw the arrows *from* B and E *towards* A because B and E are predecessors of A, not because we know what causes what (i.e., not because we know that burglar alarms do not cause earthquakes).

Let's move to the fourth variable, J (friend John calls the home owner) Its predecessors are $\{B, E, A\}$. Among these variables $\{B, E, A\}$ the activation of the alarm (A) is the minimal set of predecessors that makes J independent of all its other predecessors. Therefore $PA\{J\} = \{A\}$. We therefore draw an arrow from A to J – again, the direction of the arrow is simply dictated by our arbitrary ordering.

Finally we have variable M (friend Mary calls the home owner) Its predecessors are $\{B, E, A, J\}$, and its parents are $PA\{M\} = \{A\}$. Following the same reasoning we draw a cell for the variable, and an arrow from A to M.

The step-by-step procedure is shown in Figure 11.4.

The construction looks easy and 'natural'. But what if we had chosen a different ordering? The reader can follow the same procedure and verify that ordering $\{M, J, A, B, E\}$ gives rise to the graph in Figure 11.5.

The parents of the various variables are

- $PA\{M\} = \{0\}$
- $PA\{J\} = \{M\}$
- $PA\{A\} = \{M, J\}$
- $PA\{B\} = \{A\}$
- $PA\{E\} = \{A, B\}$

A couple of observations are in order. First, the direction of the arrows does not reflect causal relationships, but is simply a function of which variable was arbitrarily chosen to be a predecessor of which (that's why at stage 2 in the procedure there is an arrow from M to J, despite the 'symmetry' between the two friends). Second, there

---

[11] The following example has been adapted from Zhang (2008).

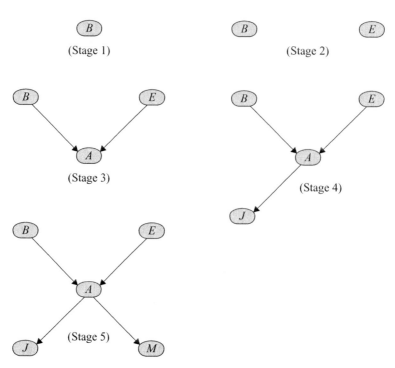

Figure 11.4 The step-by-step construction of the arcs for the Bayesian net associated with the burglar story discussed in the text, and the ordering of variables $\{B, E, A, J, M\}$.

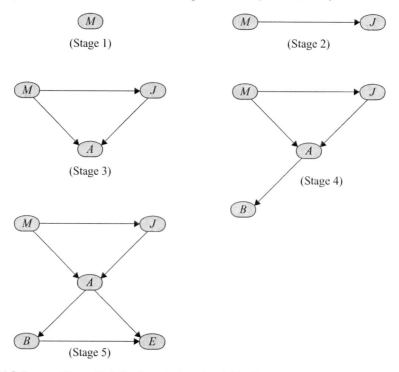

Figure 11.5 Same as Figure 11.4, for the ordering of variables $\{M, J, A, B, E\}$.

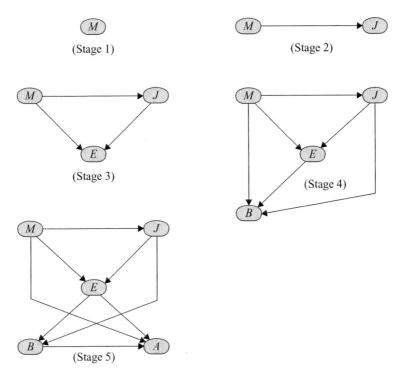

Figure 11.6 Same as Figure 11.4, for the ordering of variables $\{M, J, E, B, A\}$.

is an arrow from B to E at the last stage not because burglars cause earthquakes, but because knowledge that there has been no burglar ($B = F$) and yet the alarm has been activated ($A = T$) changes our estimate of the probability of an earthquake having occurred ($E = T$). (We shall see more precisely in the following section how information is transmitted through Bayesian nets.)

Finally, consider the ordering $\{M, J, E, B, A\}$. The (patient) reader can verify that the associated Bayesian net can be drawn as in Figure 11.6.

Now, all these Bayesian nets are produced by different (and so far arbitrary) ordering of the variables, which give rise to different factorizations, and which in turn produce the same joint probabilities. So, the various nets may well be, in some sense, equivalent, but their relative topological simplicity (e.g., number of arcs) and transparency ('naturalness' of influencing dependencies) are very different. We can probably all agree that we would prefer to work with the Bayesian net in Figure 11.4 than with the net in Figure 11.6. How can we systematically choose an ordering that gives rise to 'nice' nets?

One powerful criterion is to make use of our expert knowledge (often referred to as 'domain knowledge') to choose an ordering in which causes come before their (direct) effects. So, the order $\{M, J, E, B, A\}$ is not a good order because M and J (friends Mary and John calling the home owner) are effects of A (the alarm being activated), but come before A. Instead, ordering $\{B, E, A, J, M\}$ is good because causes come before their immediate effects.

There is another important and positive consequence of the 'causal ordering': as Zhang (2008) points out, the probabilities that have to be provided to populate the conditional probability tables in causal Bayesian nets are 'natural' to assess: we need two marginals, $P(B)$ and $P(E)$ (the frequency of earthquakes and of burglar break-ins); one set of doubly conditioned probabilities, $P(A|B, E)$, that depend on properties of the alarm system (its reliability, its robustness to spurious causes, its sensitivity); and two singly conditioned probabilities, $P(J|A)$ and $P(M|A)$, that depend on our knowledge of how reliable and conscientious friends John and Mary are. Compare this with a conditional probability such as $P(A|B, M, E, J)$, which is called for by ordering 3 (and by the associated Bayesian net): most readers, and certainly these writers, are unlikely even to know where to begin to estimate such a difficult set of conditional probabilities (recall that we have to provide $P(A = a|B = b, M = m, E = e, J = j)$, for $a, b, m, e, j = T, F$).

There is more: it also turns out that, in most cases, a causal ordering of variables gives rise to the minimum number of arcs between a given set of variables, and the lowest order of conditioning in the conditional probability sets. See, e.g., the discussion in Jensen and Nielsen (2007, pp. 72–73). This is a great computational and cognitive advantage.

The naturalness of employing a causal ordering is such that very often (as Heckerman (1993) recommends) we can use domain knowledge about causality to construct directly the Bayesian net without pre-ordering the variables: we do so by drawing directed arcs from each cause to its immediate effect. 'In almost all cases this results in Bayesian networks whose conditional-independence implications are accurate' (Heckerman 1993, p. 3).

Bayesian nets built from (an ordering that respects) causal dependencies are called *causal Bayesian nets. We shall work only with causal nets in the following.*[12]

In the discussion of the second ordering, we mentioned flow of information from the variables B and A (the burglar break-in and the alarm setting off) to the variable E (the occurrence of an earthquake). We gave a common-sense explanation of why knowledge of the occurrence or otherwise of B and A should change our estimate of E, but we would like to make these considerations more precise and systematic. This can be achieved by means of the concept of d-separation, to which we now turn.

11.7 d-separation

11.7.1   Definition

In order to gain an intuitive understanding of d-separation,[13] it pays to look at the way nodes can be connected in a Bayesian net. There are three ways in which nodes can be linked:

---

[12] See Heckerman (1993, p. 3) for additional references.

[13] What does the d in d-separation stand for? There is no universal agreement in the literature, but Pearl (2009), who is one of the doyens of Bayesian nets, states that it stands for 'direction'. We note, however, that other authors prefer to think that it stands for 'distance'. Neither term, it has to be said, is extremely felicitous.

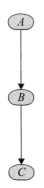

Figure 11.7 An example of serial connection (chain).

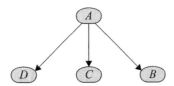

Figure 11.8 An example of diverging connection (fork).

1. via a serial connection (also known as a chain);
2. via a diverging connection (also known as a fork);
3. via a converging connection (also known as an inverted fork or a collider).

The first two modes of connection are very straightforward, but the third requires slightly more careful handling. Let's begin with serial connections, shown in Figure 11.7.

In this simple net, A influences B and B influences C. So, in general, evidence about C will influence our assessment of A being *TRUE* or *FALSE*, and vice versa. However, if the state of B is known (*TRUE* or *FALSE*), then there is nothing else that knowledge of A can tell us about the state of C. Using Jensen's terminology, 'B blocks the flow of information' between A and C. When this happens, we say that A and C are d-separated.

The second 'easy' case is shown in Figure 11.8.

Here information can flow between the three children B, C and D as long as the state of A is not known. Node A d-separates C from D, C from B and D from B. Let's understand the intuition behind this with a simple example.

Suppose that

- node A is associated to the proposition 'A strong earthquake has occurred';
- node B is associated to the proposition 'Several buildings are seriously damaged';
- node C is associated to the proposition 'Telephone landlines are down';
- node D is associated to the proposition 'There are cracks in major roads'.

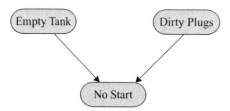

Figure 11.9 An example of converging connection (inverted fork, or collider).

Now, if we don't know whether the earthquake has happened or not, knowing that there are cracks in major roads changes the probability that several buildings are seriously damaged. However, once we know that a strong earthquake has happened, observation of the cracks in the road no longer alters our assessment of the probability that several buildings have been damaged. The instantiation of *A* (i.e., knowing whether *A* has occurred or not) blocks the flow of information between *C* and *B*. Node *A* *d*-separates *C* and *B*. *Diverging connections (also called 'forks') represent the situation of one cause producing many effects.*

Finally, let's look at the third case, i.e. converging connections. See Figure 11.9.

Also in this case, a simple example, which we adapt from Jensen and Nielsen (2007), will help the intuition. The example goes as follows. We have a car that may or may not start properly. The most likely causes for its failing to start are either dirty spark plugs or an empty fuel tank. Now, if we don't know whether the car has started or not, knowledge that the tank is either full or empty does not help us in assessing the probability of the plugs being clean or dirty. But suppose that we know that the realization of the variable $\boxed{No\ Start}$ is, say, *TRUE*. Then knowledge that the plugs are clean makes us increase significantly the probability that the tank is empty (otherwise, why wouldn't the car start properly?).

So, in the case of converging connections (inverted forks) – which describes the case of multiple causes influencing the same effect – instantiation of the effect *allows* flow of information between the two possible causes. For the effect variable ($\boxed{No\ Start}$) to block off the flow of information (i.e., for variable $\boxed{No\ Start}$ to *d*-separate variables $\boxed{Empty\ Tank}$ and $\boxed{Dirty\ Plugs}$), *it must not be instantiated. Converging connections describe situations where several causes can be responsible for the same effect.*

This intuitive discussion allows us to understand the following formal definition of *d*-separation, which comes in two steps: by defining a *d*-separating path first, and a *d*-separating set of variables next.[14]

Consider three disjointed sets of variables *X*, *Y* and *Z*. Each set contains nodes in the same directed acyclical graph.

DEFINITION 3 *A path, p, is a sequence of consecutive edges of any directionality*

The idea of path is natural enough. The only important thing to note in this definition is that the edges that make up the path can point in either direction (can have any directionality): a path can flow 'against the arrows'.

---

[14] We follow Pearl (2009, Section 1.2.3).

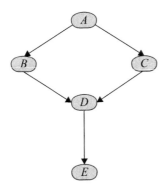

Figure 11.10 The sprinkler example, revisited to illustrate the concept of *d*-separation.

DEFINITION 4 *A path connecting variable X to variable Y is a sequence of consecutive edges of any directionality starting at X and ending at Y.*

DEFINITION 5 *A path p connecting the set of variables X with the set of variables Y is said to be d-separated (or blocked) by a set of nodes Z if and only if*

1. *the path p contains a serial connection (chain) ($i \rightarrow m \rightarrow j$) or a diverging connection (fork) ($i \leftarrow m \rightarrow j$) such that the middle node m is in Z; or*
2. *the path p contains a converging connection (collider, inverted fork) ($i \rightarrow m \leftarrow j$) such that the middle node m is not in Z and such that no descendant of m is in Z.*

These two conditions specify what is required for a particular path to be *d*-separated by a set *Z* of nodes. From the *d*-separation of paths we can then build the concept of *d*-separation for a set with the following definition.

DEFINITION 6 *A set Z d-separates set X from set Y if and only if Z blocks every path from a node in X to a node in Y.*

11.7.2   A worked example

Since the concept of *d*-separation is important but rather subtle, let's look at the canonical 'sprinkler' example in Figure 11.10 (see, e.g., Pearl 2009, Section 1.2).

The sprinkler 'story' goes as follows. Variable *A* stands for the season of the year, variable *B* corresponds to the statement 'The sprinkler is on', variable *C* to the statement 'It has rained', variable *D* to the statement 'The pavement is wet' and variable *E* to the statement 'The pavement is slippery'.

Let's analyse whether variables *B* and *C* are *d*-separated by variable *A*. Using our previous notation we have $X = \{B\}$, $Y = \{C\}$ and $Z = \{A\}$.

As a first step we have to identify all the paths connecting *X* and *Y*: these are $B - A - C$ and $B - D - C$. Note that in identifying these paths we are disregarding the directionality of the arrows – and for this reason we have connected the nodes with a '—' symbol instead of an arrow.

Let's start from the first path, $B - A - C$. Along this path we encounter a diverging connection ($B \leftarrow A \rightarrow C$), such that the middle node (A) is in Z. So, Z blocks X from Y along this path.

Let's move to the second path, $B - D - C$. Along this path we encounter a converging connection ($B \rightarrow D \leftarrow C$). The middle node of this connection is *not* in Z, and neither are its descendants. Therefore, according to the second part of the definition, also for this path Z blocks X from Y.

There were only two paths connecting X and Y, $B - A - C$ and $B - D - C$. For both paths Z blocks X from Y. Therefore Z d-separates X from Y.

This analysis confirms that, in the case of converging connections, if neither the child nor its descendants are observed, the parents are independent – information cannot be transmitted via the child from one parent back to another parent; instead it 'leaks' down through the child to its descendants. Conversely, if either the child or any of its descendants are instantiated, the parents become dependent, and information can be transmitted between parents through the child – the information path is opened by the instantiation of the child or of its descendants.

11.7.3   Hard and soft evidence

The discussion above naturally brings to the fore the distinction between *hard* and *soft* evidence about a variable:

- we have *hard evidence* about a variable if its value is directly observed;
- we have *soft evidence* about a variable if it is *not* directly observed, but the value of a descendant is observed.

The concepts of hard and soft evidence can help our intuition because we can restate the observations above about the flow of information as follows.

- Only hard evidence *blocks* an information path in the case of serial or diverging connections.
- Both hard and soft evidence *open* an information path in the case of converging connections.
- A path between a set of nodes X and a set of nodes Y is blocked by a set of nodes Z if
    1. either the path contains a node belonging to the set Z and the connection at that node is serial or diverging;
    2. or the path contains a node (say node W) such that neither W nor its descendants belong to Z, and the connection at W is converging.
- If all the variables in Z are observed, then the path being blocked means
    1. either that information cannot flow through Z because observing Z blocks the paths;
    2. or information cannot be transmitted through W because it 'leaks'.
- If a path is not blocked, then information can flow between X and Y.

This gives us again the definition of d-separation we provided above.

DEFINITION 7 *Two (sets of) nodes X and Y are d-separated by Z if all paths between X and Y are blocked by Z.*

11.7.4   The link between d-separation and conditional independence
From this the Conditional Independence Theorem immediately follows.

THEOREM 1 (CONDITIONAL INDEPENDENCE THEOREM)   *Given a directed acyclical graph, if X and Y are d-separated by Z, then X and Y are conditionally independent given Z ($X \perp Y|Z$).*

We stress that what we have given is just an intuitive justification as to why the theorem should hold true. For a clear proof, see Zhang (2005), whose approach we have closely followed.

11.8   Are d-separation and conditional independence the same?

The Conditional Independence Theorem goes from d-separation to conditional independence. What about the converse? If two variables are conditionally independent are they necessarily d-separated by some set Z? Not necessarily. The two concepts are not equivalent because there could be 'fine tuning' of the parameters (the conditional probabilities) that describe a Bayesian net such that two variables end up 'by accident' being conditionally independent, even if they are not d-separated. However, in this case the conditional independence is 'fragile': it is enough to move some of the conditional probabilities by a small amount for the conditional independence to disappear. So the conditional Independence Theorem can be extended as follows.[15]

THEOREM 2 (EXTENDED CONDITIONAL INDEPENDENCE THEOREM)   *Given a directed acyclical graph, if X and Y are d-separated by Z, then X and Y are conditionally independent given Z ($X \perp Y|Z$). Conversely, if X and Y are not d-separated by Z, then X and Y are conditionally dependent on Z in at least one distribution compatible with the directed acyclical graph in question.*

Note that the theorem makes reference to 'at least one' distribution, but it is in practice much stronger, because 'accidental' conditional independence can only be produced by very specific fine tuning of the graph parameters.

If one needs to distinguish between probabilistic (specific-probabilities-driven) and structural (graph-driven) conditional independence, the notation $(X \perp Y|Z)_P$ and $(X \perp Y|Z)_G$ can be used (where the subscripts P and G stand for 'probability' and 'graph', respectively). We will rarely, if ever, need to make this distinction.

---

[15] See Pearl (2009, Theorem 1.2.4).

We have introduced the concept of d-separation in order to be able to state the Conditional Independence Theorem. In turn, we will need the Conditional Independence Theorem in order to handle complex nets – more specifically, in order to join nets. Before looking into that, however, we move to the simplest, but also the practically most useful, theorem that we make use of in our applications, the No-Constraints Theorem.

11.9   The No-Constraints Theorem

In this section we present an extremely simple, yet extremely useful, theorem about the constraints on the quantities we provide as inputs to the conditional probability tables. We sketch the proof for the case of Boolean variables. The extensions to multi-valued variables is straightforward.[16]

To prove the theorem, we consider the Master Equation as an algorithm that takes a set of numbers as inputs (appropriate conditional probabilities) and produces another set of numbers (the joint probabilities) as output. Given M parents, we know that the conditional probability tables will contain 2^{M+1} conditional probabilities, where we have included in the count the conditional probabilities that negate the truth variable that is conditioned. In other words, if we denote by $\{Par\}$ a conditioning set of parents with an arbitrary combination of truth values, we count $P(Child|\{Par\})$ and $P(\widetilde{Child}|\{Par\})$ as two distinct probabilities. Of course, for Boolean variables,[17]

$$P(Child|\{Par\}) + P(\widetilde{Child}|\{Par\}) = 1, \quad \forall Child, \{Par\} \qquad (11.16)$$

Therefore it is only truly necessary to assign 2^M conditional probabilities. These 2^M conditional probabilities can contain any combination of truth values for the conditioned child, as long as we do not assign more than one conditional probability with the a given combination of truth values for the conditioning parents. So, if we want to assign only 2^M conditional probabilities, we are at liberty to assign, say, $P(Child|Par_1, Par_2)$ and $P(\widetilde{Child}|Par_1, \widetilde{Par_2})$, but not, say, $P(Child|Par_1, \widetilde{Par_2})$ and $P(\widetilde{Child}|Par_1, \widetilde{Par_2})$. With inelegant terminology we call the 2^M conditional probabilities assigned according to this criterion a set of *concise conditional probabilities*. More precisely we give the following definition.

DEFINITION 8 (CONCISE SET) *Given a child with M parents, 2^M conditional probabilities constitute a **concise set** if no two conditional probabilities contain the same combination of truth values for the parents.*

So, for instance, the set $P(Child|Par_1, Par_2)$, $P(Child|Par_1, \widetilde{Par_2})$, $P(Child|\widetilde{Par_1}, Par_2)$ and $P(Child|\widetilde{Par_1}, \widetilde{Par_2})$ constitutes a concise set, but, say, the set $P(Child|Par_1, Par_2)$, $P(\widetilde{Child}|Par_1, Par_2)$, $P(Child|\widetilde{Par_1}, Par_2)$ and $P(Child|\widetilde{Par_1}, \widetilde{Par_2})$ does not,

---

[16] For a more general, and far more elegant (but less transparent) proof, see, e.g. Pearl (1986, p. 244).
[17] If the variable *Child* could assume k instead of two possible values (which we denote as $child(1), child(2), \ldots,$ $child(k)$) we would have $\sum_{m=1,k} P(Child = child(m)|\{Par\}) = 1, m = 1, 2, \ldots, k$.

because two members of the set ($P(Child|Par_1, Par_2)$ and $P(\widetilde{Child}|Par_1, Par_2)$) contain the same combination of truth values for the parents.

We then provide a proof for the following statement.

PROPOSITION 1 (NO-CONSTRAINTS THEOREM) *A necessary and sufficient condition for the output of the Master Equation to be a set of bona fide joint probabilities is that the inputs to the conditional probability tables should be built from Equations (11.15) and (11.16) using a concise set of conditional probabilities, where each element of the concise set is non-negative and smaller than or equal to 1.*

The necessary part of the proposition above does not require much work to prove: if the inputs to the conditional probability tables did not lie between zero and 1 (included), they could not be probabilities to begin with (conditional or otherwise).

The interesting part of the statement is the sufficient clause: as long as we provide concise inputs to the conditional probability tables between zero and 1, we do not have to worry (mathematically) about anything else, and the outputs of the Master Equation will indeed be joint probabilities, i.e., non-negative numbers, each less than or equal to 1, *and with the property that they add up to 1*.

Note that the Master Equation tells us how to construct a set of joint probabilities given all the required conditional probabilities, but does not tell us if there are any constraints that its concise inputs of conditional probabilities have to satisfy. As it happens, the answer is 'no', and this mathematical fact will be a cornerstone of our approach to filling in the conditional probability tables, to sensitivity analysis, to entropy maximization, etc.

Proving this is very simple, but the result should not be considered obvious. We could supply information equivalent to the required conditional probabilities – perhaps some combinations of marginal and lower-order conditional probabilities from which all the required inputs for the conditional probability tables could be derived. However, if we decided to proceed this way – and sometimes one may well be tempted to do so for cognitive reasons – we would soon find ourselves dealing with a thicket of self-consistency conditions: for instance, it is emphatically *not* the case that simply assigning a non-negative marginal probability for a non-root parent will produce non-negative joint probabilities.

In this book we generally do not provide proofs for the theorems that we report, as there are excellent references that do this job better than we could. We make an exception in this case because the simplest (although not the most elegant) proof of the statement above is a *constructive* proof, i.e., a proof that teaches directly how to build efficiently the joint probabilities that we require. By this we mean that a simple but relatively efficient computer algorithm can be constructed using the proof as a blueprint. So, here it goes.

We place ourselves in a Boolean setting, and proceed inductively, by assuming that we have already built the 2^n joint probabilities for n variables. Our task is to build the 2^{n+1} joint probabilities for $n + 1$ variables obtained by adding a child. Without loss of

Table 11.3 *The truth table and the joint*
probabilities for variables A, B and C in
Figure 11.11

A	B	C	p(ABC)
1	1	1	0.0020
0	1	1	0.0005
1	0	1	0.0030
0	0	1	0.0048
1	1	0	0.0030
0	1	0	0.0093
1	0	0	0.0170
0	0	0	0.9604

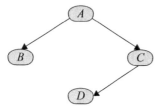

Figure 11.11 The Bayesian net for which the joint probabilities used in the discussion of the No-Constraints theorem are built. See the text for details.

generality we shall assume that in the concise set of conditional probabilities the truth value of the child is always *Child = T*. The reasoning is exactly the same for any other concise set of conditional probabilities. Let's again call M the number of parents for the new-born child. We know that the new child is connected to the rest of the net only via its parents. Suggestively we could say that the parents 'screen off' the rest of the net, but we prefer not to use this term as it has a technical meaning. Whatever the term used, the point is that the child only 'sees' the net through the M parents. 'Behind' these parents, there will be many (2^{n-M}) combinations of truth values for the ancestors and all the other nodes. When these combinations are linked with the 2^M combinations of truth values for each parent, one gets the 2^n joint probabilities we are assumed to have already built. See Table 11.3.

Let us now double this list of joint probabilities, turning a $2^n \times 1$ vector into a $2^{n+1} \times 1$ vector. The $(2^n + j)$th entry of the list will be identical to the jth original joint probability (with $1 \leq j \leq 2^n$). Let's call each copied joint probability the 'mirror image'. Obviously, since we have 'pasted together' two sets of joint probabilities (each of which adds up to 1) the sum of all the entries of this $2^{n+1} \times 1$ vector will be equal to 2.

To construct the joint probabilities for the variables A, B, C and D we begin by creating a double of the truth table and the joint probabilities for variables A, B and

Table 11.4 *The construction to prove the*
No-Constraints Theorem. See the text for details

A	B	C	D
1	1	1	0.0020
0	1	1	**0.0005**
1	0	1	0.0030
0	0	1	0.0048
1	1	0	0.0030
0	1	0	0.0093
1	0	0	0.0170
0	0	0	0.9604
1	1	1	0.0020
0	1	1	**0.0005**
1	0	1	0.0030
0	0	1	0.0048
1	1	0	0.0030
0	1	0	0.0093
1	0	0	0.0170
0	0	0	0.9604

C (see Table 11.4). We have linked and shown in bold two linked probabilities (in this case, the second and the $(2^3 + 2)$th). Because of the Master Equation, the two new joint probabilities corresponding to these entries, $(p(\widetilde{A}, B, C, D)$ and $p(\widetilde{A}, B, C, \widetilde{D}))$, will just be equal to these linked (and identical) values (the 'old' joint probabilities $p(\widetilde{A}, B, C)$) times the conditional probabilities of the new variable being *TRUE* or *FALSE*, conditioned on the particular combination of the old variables at hand (i.e., $p(D|\widetilde{A}, B, C)$ and $p(\widetilde{D}|\widetilde{A}, B, C)$, which must add up to 1).

Let us now consider the jth original joint probability. We know from the Master Equation that this could have been constructed by multiplying in an appropriate manner the required conditional probabilities. We may have obtained these joint probabilities using some other root – perhaps by direct assignment (good luck!) – but we *could* always have obtained them using the Master Equation. That's all we need.

Let's now multiply this jth entry by the *arbitrary* non-negative, smaller-or-equal-to-1 number that we have chosen for the conditional probability of the concise set corresponding to the jth combination of truth values *of the parent(s)*. Call this number cp_j.

Let's now jump to the $(2^n + j)$th entry of the list and let's multiply this entry by the complement to 1 of the conditional probability number used for the jth entry. This complement will also be between 0 and 1, inclusive. See Table 11.4. Call this complement cp_{2^n+j}. By definition of complement, therefore,

$$p_j cp_j + p_{2^n+j} cp_{2^n+j} = p_j(cp_j + cp_{2^n+j}) = p_j \qquad (11.17)$$

Table 11.5 *The full construction to prove the No-Constraints Theorem.*
Note how each pair of conditional probabilities corresponding to the
TRUE and FALSE values for variable D (such as the two conditional
probabilities in bold in Table 11.4), add up to 1

A	B	C	D		CondProb	$p(ABCD)$
1	1	1	0.0020	$P(D\|C)$	0.2	0.0004
0	1	1	**0.0005**	$P(D\|C)$	**0.2**	**0.0001**
1	0	1	0.0030	$P(D\|C)$	0.2	0.0006
0	0	1	0.0048	$P(D\|C)$	0.2	0.00096
1	1	0	0.0030	$P(D\|\sim C)$	0.7	0.0021
0	1	0	0.0093	$P(D\|\sim C)$	0.7	0.00651
1	0	0	0.0170	$P(D\|\sim C)$	0.7	0.0119
0	0	0	0.9604	$P(D\|\sim C)$	0.7	0.67228
1	1	1	0.0020	$P(\sim D\|C)$	0.8	0.0016
0	1	1	**0.0005**	$P(\sim D\|C)$	**0.8**	**0.0004**
1	0	1	0.0030	$P(\sim D\|C)$	0.8	0.0024
0	0	1	0.0048	$P(\sim D\|C)$	0.8	0.00384
1	1	0	0.0030	$P(\sim D\|\sim C)$	0.3	0.0009
0	1	0	0.0093	$P(\sim D\|\sim C)$	0.3	0.00279
1	0	0	0.0170	$P(\sim D\|\sim C)$	0.3	0.0051
0	0	0	0.9604	$P(\sim D\|\sim C)$	0.3	0.28812

But, by Equation (11.16) the complement to 1 of the arbitrarily chosen number is just
the conditional probability for the same combination of truth values for conditioning
parents, and the opposite truth value for the child. So, cp_j and cp_{2^n+j} are the conditional probability needed to build the corresponding new joint probabilities according
to the Master Equation. Call these joint probabilities π_j and π_{2^n+j}. We have by
Equation (11.17)

$$\pi_j + \pi_{2^n+j} = p_j$$

We repeat this operation for $1 \leq j \leq 2^n$. By Equation (11.17) we shall construct by
doing so 2^n two-element sums like the one in Equation (11.17), of values p_1, p_2, ...,
p_{2^n}. These two-element sums will be made up of 2^{n+1} joint probabilities π_j. But, since
by hypothesis we started with a set of bona fide joint probabilities, $\{p_j\}$, the sum of all
these pairs of new joint probabilities $\{\pi_j\}$ must be equal to 1. And, of course, they are
all non-negative by construction. The result is shown in Table 11.5.

11.10   Why is this so important?

The No-Constraints Theorem makes our life extremely easy. Of course, we find it
extremely convenient when we are building Bayesian nets: we can choose any non-
negative, smaller-than-or-equal-to-1 number for our conditional probabilities of any
order, and we can rest assured that what we produce using the Master Equation will be

a set of (mathematically) good joint probabilities. But we will appreciate even more the convenience of this result when we engage in two extremely important exercises: sensitivity analysis and Maximum-Entropy-based filling-in of an incomplete set of conditional probability tables. We shall look at both these procedures in detail below, but it is easy to explain how easy our life is made by the result above.

Let's start from sensitivity analysis. As we shall see, we will often assign, rather than 'sharp'[18] inputs, subjective confidence intervals for our input conditional probabilities: i.e., input values that we would not find incompatible with our understanding of the financial 'story' behind our stress scenario. Then, in order to compute the sensitivity of our output to our uncertain inputs, we can simply vary the inputs over our uncertainty range without having to worry about some of the joint probabilities becoming negative, or not adding up to 1.

In a similar vein, we shall show in Section 14.2 that when we try to fill in the missing elements of an incomplete set of input conditional probabilities using the Maximum-Entropy principle we will vary the missing inputs in such a way as to maximize the entropy of the resulting joint distribution. Once again, it will be immensely convenient to be able to do so without having to worry about non-trivial (i.e., deeply hidden) constraints on the optimization variables (the missing conditional probabilities). We just have to make sure that the trial values are non-negative and smaller than or equal to 1,[19] and we let the Master Equation work its magic without any other worry.

11.11 From Boolean to multi-valued variables

Most of the treatment in this book is devoted to the case where the variables associated with the various nodes are Boolean, i.e., can only assume two values, *TRUE* or *FALSE*. We have always reassured the reader that the extension from the Boolean to the multi-variable case is trivial, and that we have simply chosen to base the presentation on the two-value case to keep notation light. In this section we show that we have not lied, and that the generalization is simple indeed.

First of all, why should we consider more than two values? Consider a large company that is going through a rough patch. An obvious variable would have two states: 'Pulls through' or 'Fails'. But what if a white knight appears? Then the share price may considerably increase. Limiting the possible states of the world to 'business-as-usual' and 'serious-trouble' can be very limiting.

Similar considerations apply to a number to variables: think of 'State of the US economy'; 'Political intervention in the Euro crisis' ('game over', 'muddle through', but also 'decisive and convincing political action'); 'State of the Euro' ('stays as is'; 'some peripheral countries leave the Euro'; 'total break-up'); etc.

---

[18] Meucci (2010c) would say 'crisp'.
[19] This can be easily obtained, for instance, by ensuring that each missing conditional probability be mapped to an 'angle' θ and the optimization be carried over $\sin^2 \theta$.

Table 11.6 *Multi-state joint truth table*

A	B	C	P(AB)		P(ABC)
a_1	b_1	c_1	0.1852	0.5568	0.1031
a_2	b_1	c_1	0.0552	0.5568	0.0308
a_3	b_1	c_1	0.0088	0.5568	0.0049
a_1	b_2	c_1	0.0234	0.5568	0.0130
a_2	b_2	c_1	0.0310	0.5568	0.0172
a_3	b_2	c_1	0.0911	0.5568	0.0507
a_1	b_3	c_1	0.0319	0.5568	0.0177
a_2	b_3	c_1	0.0631	0.5568	0.0351
a_3	b_3	c_1	0.2109	0.5568	0.1174
a_1	b_4	c_1	0.0326	0.5568	0.0181
a_2	b_4	c_1	0.0146	0.5568	0.0081
a_3	b_4	c_1	0.2523	0.5568	0.1405
a_1	b_1	c_2	0.1852	0.4432	0.0821
a_2	b_1	c_2	0.0552	0.4432	0.0245
a_3	b_1	c_2	0.0088	0.4432	0.0039
a_1	b_2	c_2	0.0234	0.4432	0.0104
a_2	b_2	c_2	0.0310	0.4432	0.0137
a_3	b_2	c_2	0.0911	0.4432	0.0404
a_1	b_3	c_2	0.0319	0.4432	0.0141
a_2	b_3	c_2	0.0631	0.4432	0.0280
a_3	b_3	c_2	0.2109	0.4432	0.0935
a_1	b_4	c_2	0.0326	0.4432	0.0144
a_2	b_4	c_2	0.0146	0.4432	0.0065
a_3	b_4	c_2	0.2523	0.4432	0.1119

So, there is an obvious rationale for endowing variables with more than two states. And, as we discuss in the next chapter, turning two Boolean variables into a single three-valued variable can sometimes considerably simplify the cognitive task of assigning conditional probabilities. The next question then is: what changes are required to the set-up presented so far?

All the main concepts, such as conditional independence, *d*-separation, flow and 'blockage' of information, etc. are unchanged. So is the Master Equation. The truth table has to be modified in an obvious way. Table 11.6, for instance, displays the truth table for the case of three variables, imaginatively called *A*, *B* and *C*, where variable *A* can assume three possible values (a_1, a_2 and a_3), *B* four (b_1, b_2, b_3 and b_4), and *C* two (c_1 and c_2).

It is only the No-Constraints Theorem that requires a small modification. To understand what this entails, let's clarify a few concepts.

First of all, how does the assignment of *TRUE* or *FALSE* generalize to the multi-valued case? If we say that variable *Colour* can have values *Red*, *Green* and *Blue*, we are saying

1. that it can only have three values (*Black* is not possible);
2. that, once the variable is instantiated, one of these colours will turn out to be *TRUE*;
3. that, once the variable is instantiated, no two colours will be *TRUE* at the same time.

Conditioning a child of *Colour* on, say, *Red = TRUE* then means that we want the probability of that child being in a particular state given that the parent is in state *Red* and *in no other state*.

Now, consider then a Boolean variable, say, A, conditioned on variables, B, C, ..., Z that can assume values b_i, $i = 1, 2, \ldots, n_b$, c_j, $j = 1, 2, \ldots, n_c$, ..., z_k, $j = 1, 2, \ldots, n_z$, where $n_a, n_b, \ldots, n_z$ are the number of values the conditioning variables can assume. Then we know that

$$P(A|B = b_i, C = c_j, \ldots, Z = z_k) + P(\widetilde{A}|B = b_i, C = c_j, \ldots, Z = z_k) = 1$$

(11.18)

for any combination of conditioning variables. If the variable A can assume n_a values with $n_a > 2$, Equation (11.18) obviously generalizes to

$$\sum_{m=1, n_a} P(A_m|B = b_i, C = c_j, \ldots, Z = z_k) = 1 \qquad (11.19)$$

So, for a variable X that can assume n_x states, the No-Constraints Theorem has to be modified by requiring that any combination of $n_x - 1$ non-negative, smaller-than-1 numbers can be assigned to any group of $n_x - 1$ conditional probabilities $P(X_m|B = b_i, C = c_j, \ldots, Z = z_k)$, as long as all their partial sums are smaller than 1. This means that, if we have $n_x = 3$, we must, for instance, ensure that

$$P(X_1|B = b_i, C = c_j, \ldots, Z = z_k) + P(X_2|B = b_i, C = c_j, \ldots, Z = z_k) \leq 1$$
$$P(X_1|B = b_i, C = c_j, \ldots, Z = z_k) + P(X_3|B = b_i, C = c_j, \ldots, Z = z_k) \leq 1$$
$$P(X_2|B = b_i, C = c_j, \ldots, Z = z_k) + P(X_3|B = b_i, C = c_j, \ldots, Z = z_k) \leq 1$$
$$P(X_1|B = b_i, C = c_j, \ldots, Z = z_k) + P(X_2|B = b_i, C = c_j, \ldots, Z = z_k)$$
$$+ P(X_3|B = b_i, C = c_j, \ldots, Z = z_k) \leq 1$$

(11.20)

This condition can be easily satisfied in a number of ways, of different degrees of complexity and elegance. For instance, we can simply require that the n probabilities should be given by the polar coordinates of a hypersphere of unit radius. (This is the obvious multi-dimensional generalization of the observation that, for any angle θ, $\sin^2 \theta + \cos^2 \theta = 1$.) Then all the associated 'angles' are totally unconstrained, and the No-Constraints Theorem truly remains a *No-Constraints* theorem.

12 Building scenarios for causal Bayesian nets

The treatment presented in the previous chapter makes extensive use of the notion of 'events'. Where do 'events' come from? How are we choose them? How can we relate them to the positions in our portfolios?

In this chapter we answer these questions. In a nutshell, we find that, when it comes to building a causal Bayesian net for portfolio management purposes, a useful way to organize our thinking is to make use of four clearly distinct components:

1. root event(s);
2. transmission channels;
3. changes in the market risk factors that affect the value of a given portfolio;
4. deterministic mappings to portfolio profits and losses.

The task faced by the expert is how to connect the root events with the changes in the market risk factors that affect a given portfolio. The connection is mediated by causal transmission channels, i.e., specific events triggered by the root event(s).

Of course, there could in principle be a variety (and perhaps an infinity) of transmission channels whereby a given root event may affect a set of market risk factors. The skill of the expert lies in her ability to identify the most plausible linkages given the specific context attaching to the chosen root event. 'Most plausible' is clearly an imprecise term, and good results tend to be the outcome of vivid, yet restrained, imaginations. For reasons that we explain later in the chapter, we like to call these connecting transmission channels 'paths of low resistance'.

Once the expert has traced the pertinent 'low-resistance' paths from the root event(s) to the changes in the market risk factors, a (deterministic) mapping from these changes to portfolio profits and losses must be applied. This is the simplest and most mechanical part of the process, as any financial organization must already have at its disposal a tool (say, a VaR (Value at Risk) engine, a simple sensitivity calculator or perhaps a more complex factor model) devoted to the task.

The purpose of this chapter is to flesh out in some detail the sketchy blueprint provided in these introductory paragraphs.

12.1   What constitutes a root event?

The first component of our process was a 'root event'. What do we mean by this?

The root events we deal with in our treatment are those *major, specific* occurrences that may have a profound impact on a particular portfolio *given the present economic, financial and geopolitical conditions*. Note how we stressed the words 'major', 'specific' and 'given the present economic, financial and geopolitical conditions'. Let us explain what we mean by this.

There are generic events − like, say, earthquakes, terrorist acts, assassinations of presidents or political figures, natural disasters, etc − whose occurrence can certainly have a profound impact on market sentiment in general, and on specific asset classes in particular. However, this type of event constitutes a sort of 'background danger' in the overall appreciation by the market of possible positive and negative outcomes. One can therefore expect these background events (severe as they may be) to be incorporated or 'impounded' in the prices of assets traded in a reasonably efficient market. Equity volatility smiles, for instance, tend to display some degree of negative skew even in the quietest periods. One of the possible explanations for this shape of the implied volatility surface is the pricing in of the possibility of unspecified negative events.

In a similar vein, emerging markets are often perceived as susceptible to sudden corrections under a variety of non-emerging-market-specific stress conditions. This is a plausible explanation of the risk premium they command even in quiet periods. Conversely, investors tend to associate 'safe-haven' value to assets such as Treasuries and German-government-issued bonds, and some degree of 'insurance premium' is present even in the absence of any market turmoil. In short, even in the quietest periods the market never forgets that things can change abruptly.

This discussion does not suggest that one should only incorporate in the Bayesian nets events the market is not aware of, or for which it underestimates the probability of occurrence. The portfolio manager who thought she could do that on a regular basis would be either extremely courageous, or foolhardy, or, probably, both. Rather, an event that lends itself to the Bayesian-net treatment would typically be an event the possibility of which the market is very well aware *today*, but whose ramifications and consequences have not been encountered in the past, and cannot therefore be ascertained using frequentist techniques. At the time of writing, the possibility of the sovereign default of a weaker European country that may trigger the break-up of the Euro is one such event: it is on everybody's minds, but not in our data series. The market is not 'asleep at the wheel' and certainly assigns some probability to this event, and has in 'its mind' some causal links connecting the uncertain event to the asset prices. So does the portfolio manager. Now we, the portfolio managers, see the same 'clear and present danger' as the market, but we do not know whether our expectations are the same as those of the market. What we would like is to obtain our 'private valuation' (the price of assets, given our views) and to compare it with the publicly available valuations (the market prices). This will give us an indication of what we think is 'cheap' or 'dear'. We show how to do this in Chapter 21.

One last word about what constitutes an event. A proposition such as 'the short rate is raised by 75 basis points or more' logically and mathematically lends itself to a Bayesian-net treatment. But it is not a good 'event'. We do not know, in fact, from the statement in itself why the Fed (or the Bank of England, or the ECB) raised rates by that amount. Was it because of an unexpected surge in inflation? Was it because the economy was suddenly and unexpectedly found to be firing on all cylinders? Was it because the domestic currency had come under attack? And if so, why? Unless we know the answers to these questions, it will be well-nigh impossible for the expert to fill in the conditional probability tables in a meaningful way. And the very construction of a *causal* Bayesian net may prove very difficult – how are we to assign the causal dependencies if we do not know what is happening?

One possible way to organize our thinking, and to structure our Bayesian net, is to start from one (or, sometimes, a couple) of 'root events'. A root event must be embedded in a 'story', where by 'story' we mean an economic and financial context, and a reasonably detailed description of the causes that trigger the root event. At the time of writing, a root event could be, say, the break-up of the European Monetary Union. If we choose this as a root it is essential to specify why such a momentous event might take place, and how it may unfold. For instance, it may be triggered by the decision of a heavily indebted southern European government not to accept the austerity measures attached to a bail-out plan. The expert should also specify whether in the chosen scenario the Euro survives almost unchanged but with fewer participating countries; or whether there is a reversion to many currencies, of different strengths and degrees of credibility, probably with a new Deutsche Mark. If both scenarios (total fragmentation or 'trimmed-down' Euro) are considered plausible, it may be advisable to work for three-state variables, rather than trying to deal with a poorly specified root event. Or, perhaps, one could have an Ur-root (say, *Major disruptive event in the Euro area*) with two children (*Total fragmentation* and *Trimmed-down Euro*). The reason, again, is that causal links and conditional probabilities can only be specified (if at all) once the precise context is made clear.

The last chapter of a recent book by US economist Barry Eichengreen (2011) devoted to the scenario of a fall in the dollar provides a clear example of how a stress event should be constructed, and of what it means to embed a root event in a 'story'. The chapter is appositely named 'Dollar Crash', and in the opening sentences one reads:

But what if the dollar does crash? What if foreigners dump their holdings and abandon the currency? What, if anything, could U.S. policymakers do about it?...

[If scenario planning were] undertaken, *it would have to start with what precipitated the crash and caused foreigners to abandon the dollar*...[1]

The author then carefully analyses several possible scenarios that may give rise to the event in question (the run on the dollar); assesses under what circumstances they might happen; draws historical parallels (e.g., with the Suez Canal debacle for the UK

---

[1] Eichengreen (2011, p. 15), our emphasis.

in the 1950s); highlights the differences; and specifies what the 'boundary conditions' would have to be for each of these scenarios to materialize.

In general, the importance of contextualizing stress events is well recognized in scenario planning conducted for geopolitical and military purposes. See Rebonato (2010a) and Davis and Sweeney (1999) for a detailed discussion of this important point. The experience accumulated over decades in this field becomes particularly relevant in the construction of causal Bayesian nets.

12.2   The leaves: changes in market risk factors

Even if transmission channels are logically the second component of the process we suggest, they can only be identified once we know 'in which direction we are heading'. Where we are heading are the changes in market risk factors that will affect the specific portfolio under consideration. We should therefore look at these changes first.

One of the adjectives we used to describe a root event was 'major'. An event of such magnitude will typically affect a multitude of market risk factors. Trying to model the possible links (the transmission channels) between the root event and this multitude of risk factors would require an extremely complex Bayesian net. Luckily, the portfolio of interest to the manager will typically be exposed to a subset of the possible risk factors. In the example in Chapter 16, for instance, we assume that the portfolio under the watch of the manager is made up of UK Gilts, of UK equities and of UK corporate bonds. In this case, the expert must find the transmission channels between the chosen root event (which may well originate in the United States, or in continental Europe) and, say, changes in the level and slope of the UK Gilt curve, changes in a major UK equity index (say, the FTSE 250) and changes in UK corporate spreads.

How detailed should the description of the market risk factors be? For instance, is the level of the UK Gilt curve enough, or do we have to model the slope as well? Is looking at a move in an index such as the FTSE 250 sufficient, or should we look at the behaviour of specific sectors? The answer largely depends on the specific positions in the portfolio at hand, and on the mandate of the manager. If the mandate of the portfolio manager, for instance, is to express a relative-value view between growth and value stocks, just looking at the overall level of equities will not be adequate. Or, if the portfolio contains a large position in long-dated Gilts, then the average level of the yield curve may be less relevant than the behaviour of the long-dated bonds.

In this sense our process is both top-down and bottom-up. It is top-down, because we start from a well-identified root event, and work through its consequences via the transmission channels. It is bottom-up because it is the specific composition of the portfolio at hand that will determine which market risk factors we have to reach. We need the top-down component (the root event) if we want to know in which direction to begin to move; we need the bottom-up component (the market risk changes) to know where to direct the information that flows through the Bayesian net. As we suggested in the opening section, we make this connection via low-resistance transmission channels. Our next task is to explain what this means.

12.3   The causal links: low-resistance transmission channels

As we have seen, we have to connect one or more root events with the important changes in the market risk factors that we have identified in the previous section. Clearly, there will be in general a multitude of possible transmission channels. We would like to choose for our Bayesian nets the most plausible links, with the obvious caveat that there is no well-defined procedure that can enable the expert to verify that she has indeed identified the most plausible connections – and a moment's thought makes us doubt whether it is indeed possible to define precisely what 'most plausible' or 'most likely' could mean in this context.

All these qualifications notwithstanding, the commonsensical point remains true that we do *not* want to describe via our causal Bayesian net a series of theoretically possible, but intuitively improbable, causes and events. It would be very wasteful to do so; and we would probably not be able to assign in a meaningful manner the conditional probabilities required to use the Master Equation. Most importantly, if we want to make sure that our Bayesian nets will be 'taken seriously' by the ultimate decision makers, we must make sure that the links proposed are plausible and cognitively resonant.

In order to explain what we mean by 'most plausible', we are tempted to provide a suggestive analogy with the least-action principle found in many areas of physics: i.e., we would like to find the path connecting point A (the root event) to point B (the market consequence) such that a functional of this path will be an extremum. In physics, the functional is the action; for our application it may be the overall probability of the path between A and B.

This path of least 'action' may not be the most direct path (just as light does not go from A to B through air and water by following a straight line). Rather, it should be the path that, despite possibly going through the activation of a relatively high number of transmission nodes, will end up with the highest overall probability.

We like the analogy, but we do not want to push it too much – above all, we do not want to convey any sense of scientificity or precision. First of all, if we truly wanted to speak of a maximization, the extremum should be sought over all the possible paths connecting A to B, and we clearly have no way of doing so. Second, the least-action principle identifies *one* extremum path, while in our net we will typically obtain several transmission channels that can plausibly lead from a root event to a change in a market risk factor. To remain with the spirit of the metaphor, we should perhaps speak of 'paths of low resistance' in an electrical circuit: electrons will flow mainly, but not exclusively, down the least-resistance paths. We leave it up to the reader to decide whether either analogy is helpful or confusing.

12.4   Binary, discrete-valued or continuous?

We have described root events, transmission channels and changes in market risk factors. All these building blocks of our Bayesian net are made up of nodes. Nodes can, but need not, be associated with Boolean variables. Nodes can also be associated with multi-valued (but discrete) variables, or even continuous variables. Clearly, multi-valued discrete variables or continuous variables afford greater modelling flexibility, but this comes at a cost: the computational burden can grow quickly, the conditional probability tables require that more complex conditional probabilities be assigned, and the cognitive burden increases significantly. We offer in this section some suggestions as to how good trade-offs can be made.

Boolean variables are, of course, well suited to events that can either happen or not happen (a country defaults or does not default, a currency is depegged or is not depegged, etc.). Root events therefore often lend themselves to a description of this type.

Variables associated with transmission channels are sometimes overly stylized if only two logical values are allowed. Also, if a crisis situation occurs (say, an increase in risk aversion as measured by the Volatility Index, VIX) it is important to specify if the crisis is of relatively 'garden-variety' type, or if it is truly exceptional: different responses (by the markets, by regulators, by politicians) can be expected in the two cases. So, a three-valued variable may at times be useful: business as usual, upset, major crisis.

It is also important not to forget that events can surprise us in a positive manner, and this can have a profound impact on market prices. Perhaps Greece will become an example of fiscal rectitude and the tax receipts will be much higher than anticipated, making its default much less likely, and probability of help forthcoming from Northern European countries much higher.

What really matters is that the expert should be able to fill in the conditional probability tables for a child given the complexity she has chosen for its parents. She must be able to distinguish, for instance, between the probability of the child being true given that, say, parent 1 was in a mildly severe crisis situation, and parent 2 in a very severe one. Specifying several possible values for a variable, and then being unable to fill in a meaningful way the attaching conditional probability tables, defies the purpose of the complication, and increases the computational burden with little benefit.

The terminal nodes associated with changes in the market risk factors ('leaves') often lend themselves to a richer treatment, that remains nonetheless cognitively simple. Consider the case discussed above of a portfolio manager who looks at the possible changes in the market risk factors affecting a UK equity portfolio. An apparently plausible variable might be: 'The FTSE 250 index falls by 20%'. If taken literally, a fall by 19.99% or by 20.01% would make the statement false. What the expert was trying to convey, however, was the magnitude of a very severe equity market fall – a fall of the order of, but not necessarily equal to, 20%. An appealing way to translate this intuition into a mathematically precise statement is to define a 'normal' state for the FTSE 250 one in which returns are centred around, say, +4%, with a variance of, say, 0.0025, and a 'stress state' as one in which returns are centred around −20% with a variance again of 0.0025. If we then stipulate that the system can only be in either of these two states, then we can rephrase the true/false question as: 'Is the world in the normal state?'

12.5   The deterministic mapping

The last stage of the process from the root cause(s) to the changes in value of the target portfolio(s) is the deterministic mapping from the market risk factor to the asset prices. So, for instance, a terminal leaf may be associated with the behaviour of the level of the 10-year US$ Treasury yield. The portfolio of interest may not (and, in general, *will* not) just be made up of 10-year US$ Treasuries. However, we will have worked-out beforehand a mapping from the reference risk factor (in this case the 10-year US$ Treasury yield) to the actual assets in the portfolio of interest.

How direct the link between the market risk factor and the asset price will be will vary greatly on a case-by-case basis. If the portfolio manager has a position exactly in the S&P 500, then market risk factor and asset will be one and the same, and the mapping is trivial. If, on the other hand, the asset manager's portfolio is made up of a large number of south-east Asian, non-Japanese, bonds of varying maturities then a generic risk factor as an emerging-market bond index may give rise to a more imprecise mapping.

Sometimes, of course, the nature and complexity of a portfolio (especially if it contains relative-value position) may call for the introduction of additional leaves in the Bayesian net. So for instance, we may want a leaf associated with the level of the US$ yield curve, and one with its steepness.

Perhaps the asset manager may want to think in terms of principal components, and associate these quantities with some of the terminal leaves. This facilitates greatly (by definition) the mapping stage of the process (because the eigenvectors will provide exactly the loadings from the principal components onto the various assets). However, it can make the link with a transmission mechanism 'upstream' in the net more difficult: we are likely to have a better-developed intuitive understanding of how, say, a round of quantitative easing in the UK would impact the overall level of Gilts, but we may be hard-pressed to specify how the same parent would affect, say, the second principal component extracted from changes in UK government yields.

Notwithstanding the need to handle this last part of the process with some care, and to strike a balance between the granularity of the description on the one hand, and the computational and cognitive complexity on the other, there are rarely insurmountable problems. Once we get to the final leaves, we are (almost) safely home.

Part V

Building Bayesian nets in practice

> In theory, there is no difference between theory and practice. In practice, there is.
>
> *Yogi Berra*

In a very abstract way, the account we have given in the previous chapters of causal Bayesian nets is all that is needed to use them effectively for the applications at hand. But this is true in the same sense that all that there is to classical electrodynamics is contained in Maxwell's four equations: a true statement that ill explains why books on the topic tend to be considerably longer than one half page.

In the same spirit the next three chapters are meant to help the reader use effectively the Bayesian-net technology. Aware of Yogi Berra's wisdom, we intend with these chapters to bridge as much as possible the gap between theory and practice. We do so by teasing out implied results, by providing 'how-to' suggestions, and by offering somewhat more advanced techniques for handling the practical problems that invariably arise.

In this part of the book we also present in detail the construction of a Bayesian net in a realistic case. The net thus constructed will then be used in the later parts of the book to derive the optimal portfolio allocations and to study the stability of the results.

13 Applied tools

13.1 A word of caution

Bayesian nets are a mature technology and many numerical techniques have been developed to handle them effectively. There are literally dozens of papers to deal with virtually any of the problems that one finds when one begins to use large Bayesian nets in earnest – say, the NP-hardness of the computational burden,[1] the exponential explosion (in the number of parents) of the entries of the conditional probability tables, what to do with underspecified nets, etc.[2] Some of the solutions are frankly quite complex. For reasons we explain below, we are lucky, because most of this sophistication is not required for our applications. So, a few simple tricks can be profitably adopted for our applications. These 'tricks' tend to be the simpler ones and they will make our life easier. And these simple, entry-level, techniques have the largest marginal benefit with respect to a totally naive approach to constructing Bayesian nets.

This is great, and reassuring. However, it is very important not to get carried away even by this rather limited toolkit. The reason is that, if one becomes overenthusiastic, one risks losing one of the most positive features of our approach: its intuitional appeal, its transparency, and what we call its auditability (by which we mean the ability of a non-technical intelligent person to question its inputs, its outputs and everything in between).

So, we love the techniques we present in this part of the book, we think that they are really useful (and we extensively use them ourselves); however, we would recommend using them parsimoniously. The words of his thesis advisor still ring in the ears of one of these writers (RR): 'If you have to use too much statistics, you have a problem with

---

[1] The complexity class P consists of all the decision problems that can be solved in polynomial time by a deterministic computer (where 'polynomial' refers to the size of the input). The class NP is widened by relaxing the requirement that the machine should be determinstic.

  A deterministic (Turing) machine is one whose rules prescribe at most one action for any given input configuration. (Non-determininistic Turing machines are equivalent to Turing machines in respect to what can be computed, not the speed with which the task can be performed.)

  NP-hard problems are problems that are at least as hard as the hardest problem in NP. The seminal work that introduced the concept of NP-hardness in computation theory is Garey and Johnson (1979). Despite being older than most of its present-day readers, it remains one of the best books on the subject.
[2] See, e.g., Williamson (2005).

your data.' Perhaps one could paraphrase and say: 'If we have to use too many clever tricks, perhaps we are not using the right tool for the job at hand.'

13.2   Why our life is easy (and why it can also be hard)

We stated that we are in some respects luckier (although in others unluckier), than most other users of Bayesian nets. Here is why.

Starting from the bright side, the scientists and engineers who make regular use of Bayesian nets (in the medical sciences, in artificial intelligence, in computer science, etc.) tend to work with a vastly greater number of variables than we do. Most applications have hundreds, and some thousands, of variables to contend with. As the number of joint probabilities grows exponentially with the number of nodes, this makes brute-force solutions totally inapplicable: for 1000 variables, for instance, there are not enough particles in the universe to store the resulting joint probabilities. Also the number of conditional probabilities that must be assigned grows exponentially with the number of parents. If these conditional probabilities are obtained from data, the number of possible permutations quickly makes even plentiful data far too sparse. (See for instance the discussion in Jensen and Nielsen (2007, p. 75).)

For our applications we are going to work with 10–20 well-chosen variables. For 10 variables everything can be easily accommodated and visually inspected on an Excel spreadsheet, and the calculation of the 2^{10} joint probabilities is virtually instantaneous. For about 15 variables we may not be able to fit everything on a spreadsheet, but with a reasonably efficient code our computer can still handle all the required variables 'internally'. Twenty variables tends to be the boundary where brute-force approaches cease to work well, and approximate techniques come to the fore. The techniques required to handle up to a couple of dozens of variables, however, are still very simple.

This is why our life is easy. As one reads the literature on, say, Maximum Entropy applied to Bayesian nets (we deal with the topic in Section 14.2), one can be bewildered by the complexity of the treatment, and by how special the cases are for which efficient *general* solutions are provided. But this is purely a function of the very high number of variables these solutions are provided for. To remain with the example of the maximization of entropy for Bayesian nets, with the number of variables typical of our applications we can just compute the entropy of the joint distribution, and vary our degrees of freedom (typically, unspecified conditional probabilities) so as to maximize it. Even the ubiquitous Excel-embedded Solver will do the job perfectly well in a few seconds. If we are working with, say, more than 10 but less than 20 variables, we may want to boil the kettle for a cup of tea rather than waiting for the answer in front of the screen, but that's about it.

This is also why our life is not so easy. We work with as few variables as we do because we have to provide the information behind the net 'by hand', i.e., by elicitation of expert knowledge. We probably would not know how to build 'by hand' much more complex nets; even if we did, we certainly would be at a loss when it comes to populating the conditional probability tables. The use of the Bayesian-net technology for the applications dealt with in this book is therefore an exercise in careful and parsimonious model building: it requires an understanding of which features are essentials, which may be important, which are nice-to-haves, and which definitely belong to the icing-on-the-cake category. Our approach requires some skill and experience on how to make these choices in an effective and 'economical' way. Our approach is CPU-time light, and thinking-time heavy.

Nothing is more important in our methodology than a good construction of the Bayesian net – where 'good' means parsimonious, insightful, transparent, cognitively resonant and computationally feasible. The chapters in this part of the book try to ease the thinking task of the portfolio manager who wants to use Bayesian nets, by providing some simple tools that can turn a neat theory into a working technology.

13.3 Sensitivity analysis

As the reader should by now be fully aware, we are not shy about the subjective nature of our approach. This does not mean, however, that we are not conscious of the potential impact on our results of the unavoidable uncertainty in our inputs. One way to quantify how robust our results are, we believe, resides in thoughtful and comprehensive sensitivity analysis – in exploring, that is, to what extent our results depend on the precise inputs we supply.

Sensitivity analysis can, and should, be carried out at almost any stage of our procedure, from the selection of the events to the choice of sampling distributions for the market risk factors all the way to the choice of utility function used for the optimization. Indeed, we devote a whole chapter to a detailed analysis of the sensitivity to *all* the inputs of a simple case-study Bayesian net. One of the areas where this sensitivity analysis is most important, however, is the choice of the subjective conditional probabilities that build the eponymous tables. This task is greatly facilitated by the No-Constraints Theorem we obtained in Section 11.9. Recall that the theorem simply tells us that, as long as the conditional probabilities we assign are non-negative and smaller than or equal to 1,[3] no mathematical inconsistencies will appear anywhere in the Bayesian net, and the resulting joint probabilities will indeed be bona fide joint probabilities (i.e., non-negative quantities smaller than or equal to 1, that all sum up exactly to 1).

This elementary but powerful result gives us a simple way to carry out sensitivity analysis of the input conditional probabilities. Indeed, we can proceed as follows:

- We go in turn, one at a time, over all the K input conditional probabilities.
- We establish a range over which we would not be too surprised to find the 'true value' of the jth input conditional probability – and, as we write this, we put to one side the philosophical complexity attaching to the precise meaning in probability theory of this statement.
- We choose a distribution (perhaps the uniform one) defined over the chosen range.

---

[3] For variables with more than two possible values, the statement should be replaced by: '... as long as the conditional probabilities we assign are non-negative and add up to 1 ...'

- Once a range and a distribution has been chosen for all the input conditional probabilities, we draw (independently) in turn from these distributions. A set of K draws
  will constitute one 'simulation'.
- We perform a number of simulations, each of which corresponds to one particular
  set of K conditional probabilities. (For simplicity we prefer to assume that all the
  draws in a given set are independent.)
- We create distributions for a number of output quantities: e.g., for the individual
  joint probabilities (and, in particular, for p_0, the probability that 'nothing happens'),
  for the asset allocations, for the event correlations, for the moments of the profit and
  loss (P&L) distribution, and, of course for the profits and losses associated with the
  terminal leaves.

Of course, we can proceed similarly when we reach the deterministic connections
that attach to each of the leaves, and which determine the sampling distributions for the
market risk factors. Namely, we can assign ranges and distributions for the parameters
that characterize the sampling distribution of the market risk factor in the 'non-normal'
case.

Which distribution should we choose for each conditional probability? A truncated
Gaussian has obvious appeal, but, in consideration of its simplicity, the uniform distribution should not be discarded. If this simple choice is made, the sampling procedure
is particularly simple: call B_L^k and B_U^k the lower and upper bounds, respectively, for the
kth input conditional probability. Then the new kth conditional probability, cp_k, can be
constructed as

$$cp_k = B_L^k + \left(B_U^k - B_L^k\right)\mathcal{U}(0, 1)$$

where $\mathcal{U}(0, 1)$ denotes the uniform [0 1] distribution.

Needless to say, the price we pay for the simplicity of the choice of the uniform
distribution is the implicit assumption that any value in the allowed range is equally
probable, but a value an ϵ outside this range is impossible. More realistic, although
slightly more complex, choices are truncated Gaussians or truncated exponentials.
Truncated exponentials may be appropriate when we think that the most likely value
of a conditional distribution should be very close to 0 or 1. Truncated Gaussians are
otherwise more natural to use. See Appendix 14.A for some results about truncated
Gaussian distributions and their moments.

13.4   Assigning the desired dependence among variables

We stress throughout this book the causal interpretation we like to give to Bayesian
nets. (See, in particular, Sections 2.1 and 11.6.) This causal interpretation is directly
linked to the structure of the net, and to the conditional probabilities we assign. It
is essential to realize that each net is, by necessity, an approximation to the causal
links we would like to assign to the underlying variables. On the one hand these
limitations are imposed by the need for parsimony (not making a net too complex),

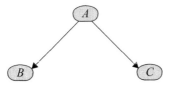

Figure 13.1 A simple Bayesian net describing the effect of a terrorist attack (node *A*) on two equity indices (the FTSE and the S&P 500, nodes *B* and *C*).

and by our cognitive limitations; on the other, they come from the difficulties inherent in expressing our causal understanding using the flexible but limited building blocks of the Bayesian nets. Extremely complex structures can in principle be built out of very simple components, but doing so explicitly is rarely easy (indeed, 'evolutionary' processes, which are often the mechanisms best suited to creating complexity out of simplicity, do not readily lend themselves to *ex-post* intuition-based reconstruction and understanding – witness genetic algorithms and neural networks).[4]

What we are doing here is more akin to (hopefully intelligent) design than to evolution. We must therefore pay special attention to this part of the process. The discussion in Chapter 16 will show how the combined distribution of returns that is at the heart of our approach crucially depends on a thoughtful specification of the causal links among the variables at hand. We therefore look at this topic in some detail, starting from a very simple (and stylized) example.

13.4.1 A worked example: a terrorist attack

What I don't understand is why banks had to invent new ways of losing money, when the old ones were working so well. Warren Buffet, commenting on the bank losses in the aftermath of the sub-prime crisis

Suppose that we look at the following mini-scenario: a serious terrorist attack that may cause a fall in equity prices in the two equity markets that the portfolio manager is exposed to, say the S&P and the FTSE. A very simple way to depict this situation is shown in Figure 13.1.

Here event *A* is the terrorist attack, *B* is associated with a fall in the S&P 500 and *C* with a fall in the FTSE. The Bayesian net looks simple enough, and it would appear that nothing more is required. Let's look, however, in some detail at the joint probabilities and at the implied (event) correlations, in order to see whether what we have built is truly 'what we meant'.

How can we populate the conditional probability tables? First we have to assign $P(A)$, the probability of a serious terrorist attack. This quantity should, we hope, be low. The exact value will depend, of course, on the projection horizon, and on the particular point in time when the subjective estimate is made. Let's choose a period

---

[4] For a discussion, see, e.g., Mitchell (2009), who also shows how, in some cases, an intuitive understanding *can*, with considerable effort, be extracted from the solutions produced by genetic algorithms.

Table 13.1 *The event correlation between the three variables in the net in Figure 13.1 for the base probabilities discussed in the text*

	Terrorist	S&P	FTSE
Terrorist	1	0.231028	0.231028
S&P	0.231028	1	**0.053374**
FTSE	0.231028	**0.053374**	1

of, say, six months for the projection horizon. As for the point-in-time probability of occurrence of the attack over this period, since we are treating a terrorist attack as 'clear and present', rather than 'background' danger (to use the terminology of Section 12.1), we are likely to want to assign to its occurrence a 'low' but 'not-too-low' probability. Therefore the range $0.05 \leq P(A) \leq 0.1$ could be chosen as a reasonable starting point.

To simplify the problem we can assume that the S&P and the FTSE will respond identically to the terrorist attack. We do not know for sure the exact conditional probability of a fall in either index given the serious terrorist attack ($P(B|A)$ and $P(C|A)$), but we certainly want to give a high value, bordering on absolute certainty. Let's assign as a possible range

$$0.85 \leq P(B|A), P(C|A) \leq 0.9999$$

What about the conditional probabilities of a fall in either index given that the terrorist attack has not occurred? Now, major falls in equity indices occur for reasons other than terrorist attacks, so these probabilities should be small (we are talking about *major* falls), but not too small. We assign as a plausible range

$$0.05 \leq P(B|\tilde{A}), P(C|\tilde{A}) \leq 0.15$$

All this looks quite reasonable, but does it truly reflect our understanding of what might happen? Let's look (see Table 13.1) at the event correlation[5] implied by choosing the midpoint for all the probabilities we have assigned.

We have obtained a very low correlation (little more than 5%) between a fall in the S&P and a fall in the FTSE. This comes about because, yes, the net we have built 'knows' that if the terrorist attack occurs, then the two equity falls are very likely to occur together. However, there is no way for us to express our knowledge that *most* factors other than a terrorist attack that would cause a fall in one index would also cause a fall in the other. Without this piece of information, the low probability of occurrence of the terrorist attack is at the root of the low event correlation: we have modelled well the dependence between two variables when a rare event happens, but we have neglected the very high 'background' correlation.

Perhaps we could vary the input conditional probabilities so as to increase the event correlation between a fall in the S&P and a fall in the FTSE. By 'pushing' the

---

[5] See Section 14.7 for a definition of event correlation.

Table 13.2 *The event correlation between the three*
variables in the net in Figure 13.1 for the 'stretched'
probabilities discussed in the text

	Terrorist	S&P	FTSE
Terrorist	1	0.399541	0.399541
S&P	0.399541	1	**0.159633**
FTSE	0.399541	**0.159633**	1

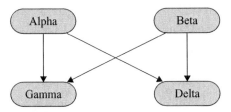

Figure 13.2 A possible modification of the Bayesian net in Figure 13.1 to describe a more realistic correlation between a fall in the FTSE and in the S&P 500.

conditional and marginal probabilities towards the boundaries of our plausibility ranges we can to some extent increase the event correlation. See Table 13.2.

However, the event correlation, despite having increased from about 5% to approximately 26%, is still much lower than we would reasonably expect.

Sure enough, there are a few ways to increase the event correlation we are focusing on. For instance, we could substantially increase $P(A)$. For $P(A) = 0.30$ (and keeping the other input probabilities at the boundaries we had assigned) $\rho_{\mathrm{FTSE,S\&P}}$ becomes 85%. And if we also force $P(B|\tilde{A}) = P(C|\tilde{A}) = 0.001$ (i.e., if we say that a major fall in the index without a terrorist attack is virtually impossible) then $\rho_{\mathrm{FTSE,S\&P}}$ becomes as high as 99.6%. But are we happy with the 'story' we are implying? First of all, to obtain this high correlation, we are forced to say that the probability of a serious terrorist attack is as high as 30%. Of course, if the probability of a terrorist attack is *that* high, and since we have assigned such a high conditional probability of a fall in either index given the terrorist attack ($P(B|A) = P(C|A) = 0.9999$), it is hardly surprising that the correlation increases significantly. Furthermore, by imposing that $P(B|\tilde{A}) = P(C|\tilde{A}) = 0.001$ we are also saying that under virtually no other circumstances can an equity fall take place. It is no surprise, then, that we obtain an event correlation $\rho_{\mathrm{FTSE,S\&P}}$ of 99.6%. But, in order to obtain this one result correctly, we have done serious violence to our 'story', and many undesirable logical consequences flow from this.

On the other hand, we seem to have used all of our degrees of freedom. What could we have done instead?

What is missing from the previous specification of the Bayesian net is a node (a variable, really) associated with a cause *other than a terrorist attack* that can drive a fall in the two equity markets. Consider for instance the simple net depicted in Figure 13.2.

The events *Alpha*, *Delta* and *Gamma* are still the terrorist attack, the fall in the S&P and the fall in the FTSE, respectively. However, we have now added a new variable (*Beta*), independent of the terrorist attack, that can represent any other cause for a fall in the two equity markets. This is purely an auxiliary variable, which has little direct link with the terrorist-attack story, but which is useful to allow us to obtain a more plausible set of correlations among the variables. Let's see how this can happen.

What conditional probabilities should we assign? Let's start from the two roots, *Alpha* and *Beta*. They should both be fairly low probability events. As *Beta* represents all causes other than a terrorist attack for an equity market swoon, it is plausible to assign a higher unconditional probability to *Beta* than to *Alpha*. Therefore we can propose

$$0.001 \leq P(Alpha) \leq 0.01 \tag{13.1}$$

$$0.01 \leq P(Beta) \leq 0.02 \tag{13.2}$$

Let's move to the conditional probabilities. Occurrence of both *Alpha* and *Beta* would raise the probability of an equity market fall close to certainty. On the other hand, since we have defined *Beta* to cover for all the causes for an equity fall other than a terrorist attack, the occurrence of a fall in the FTSE or in the S&P if neither *Alpha* nor *Beta* occurs should be close to zero. Therefore we can suggest

$$0.99 \leq P(Gamma|Alpha, Beta) \leq 0.999 \tag{13.3}$$

$$0.001 \leq P(Gamma|\widetilde{Alpha}, \widetilde{Beta}) \leq 0.0000001 \tag{13.4}$$

As for the probability of a fall in the equity market given that one cause occurs and the other does not, we can propose

$$0.85 \leq P(Gamma|Alpha, \widetilde{Beta}) \leq 0.99 \tag{13.5}$$

$$0.60 \leq P(Gamma|\widetilde{Alpha}, Beta) \leq 0.90 \tag{13.6}$$

As in the previous case, for the sake of simplicity we can treat the two equity markets, *Gamma* and *Delta*, symmetrically. Let us now vary the marginal and conditional probabilities within the assigned ranges in such a way as to maximize the value for the event correlation, $\rho_{FTSE,S\&P}$. The resulting correlation matrix is shown in Table 13.3.

The solution vector of probabilities is

$$P(Alpha) = 0.01 \tag{13.7}$$

$$P(Beta) = 0.01 \tag{13.8}$$

$$P(Gamma|Alpha, Beta) = 0.99 \tag{13.9}$$

$$P(Gamma|\widetilde{Alpha}, \widetilde{Beta}) = 0.0000001 \tag{13.10}$$

$$P(Gamma|Alpha, \widetilde{Beta}) = 0.99 \tag{13.11}$$

$$P(Gamma|\widetilde{Alpha}, Beta) = 0.90 \tag{13.12}$$

Table 13.3 *The event correlation associated with the four variables in Figure 13.2. Note the much higher correlation (shown in bold characters) between a fall in the S&P 500 and in the FTSE*

	Terrorist	Shock	S&P	FTSE
Terrorist	1.0000	−0.0000	0.7185	0.7185
Shock	−0.0000	1.0000	0.6526	0.6526
S&P	0.7185	0.6526	1.0000	**0.9464**
FTSE	0.7185	0.6526	**0.9464**	1.0000

Note how we have now naturally obtained the desired high value for the correlation $\rho_{FTSE,S\&P}$ (0.9464), and we have also built an overall plausible and coherent 'story': *Alpha* and *Beta* are uncorrelated, as they should be, and both the terrorist attack on the one hand and 'all the other causes for a fall' on the other are positively and strongly correlated with a fall in the S&P or in the FTSE. We may want to improve the details of our solutions, but now we are clearly on the right path.

The reason for dwelling on this example at some length is to give an indication of how it can sometimes be worthwhile introducing extra variables in order to embed in the Bayesian net as much of our understanding of the 'world out there' as we can.

Another important reason for analysing this example carefully is that it is representative of the 'tunnel vision' that we can develop when we focus too obsessively on one particular root event (say, the default of a sovereign state on its debt). When we look at the possible effects of this event (say, the failure of a bank) we can sometimes forget that a lot of other causes can conspire to make the effect *TRUE* (i.e., we may forget that banks have a tendency to fail for reasons other than the ones we focus on before the crisis[6]). Adding auxiliary variables to account for these background activation mechanisms can therefore be very useful, and important.

More generally, we will show in Chapter 20 how important this is in order to arrive at a realistic joint distribution for the market risk factors. This distribution is at the heart of the optimization procedure, and all possible care should therefore be placed in constructing it as realistically as possible. The structure and the inputs of our Bayesian net are the tools at our disposal to do so.

13.5 Dealing with almost-impossible combinations of events

Consider the following stylized example. Node A represents the onset of a serious solvency crisis of a European peripheral state, which manifests itself through the dramatic widening of its credit spreads. Let node B (a child of node A) be 'The European Central Bank (ECB) intervenes by massive buying of the government debt of the embattled country in the secondary market'. The conditional probability table

---

[6] Hence the quote that opens this section.

associated with node B will require the specification of $P(B|A)$ and $P(B|\widetilde{A})$. Finally, node C is associated with the variable 'Contagion spreads to a core Euro country'. The question then arises, 'Which should be the parents of C?'

If we were to link C only to B, assigning the conditional probability $P(C|\widetilde{B})$ would be extremely difficult: we are conditioning on the event that the ECB did not intervene. But did it fail to do so *despite* the peripheral state being in trouble (perhaps because the 'fiscal purists' at the ECB prevailed)? Or did it refrain from intervening because there was no reason to intervene in the first place? If we assigned B (the ECB intervention) as the single parent of C (the spread below 200 basis points) we are saying that we do not need to know anything else in order to assign the probabilities conditioned on the occurrence or non-occurrence of the intervention (B). But, as we have just seen in our discussion of $P(C|\widetilde{B})$, this is patently a very poor assumption.[7] Therefore it is far more reasonable to make the variable C depend on both A and B. By so doing we will be able to distinguish between conditioning on no-intervention-because-no-trouble (with associated conditional probability $P(C|\widetilde{A}, \widetilde{B})$) and conditioning on no-intervention-because-purists-prevail (with associated conditional probability $P(C|A, \widetilde{B})$).

This is much better. We are now, however, faced with a difficult assignment: what are we to do about the probability of C given no distress in the peripheral country and the massive purchase by the ECB of its national debt, $P(C|\widetilde{A}, B)$? Why would the ECB enlarge its balance sheet using such non-standard (for the ECB) market operations if there had been no serious trouble in the first place? Recall that in our approach we heavily rely on our understanding of the causal mechanisms at play in the problem at hand in order to populate the conditional probability tables. But the 'unnatural' conjunction of conditioning events taxes our causal sense, and we are likely to feel at a loss when asked to provide a subjective assessment of $P(C|\widetilde{A}, B)$.

We argue elsewhere that, whatever conditional probability we assign, it will matter very little because the joint probability with which it 'works' in conjunction with ($P(\widetilde{A}, B)$) will be very small in any case, if we have constructed our Bayesian net reasonably. This is true, but it is neither elegant nor terribly satisfactory, and we are left with the feeling of something 'dangling'.

There *is* a far better solution. We should collapse two nodes with two-valued variables into a single node with a three-valued variable. So, variables A and B change, and become a new variable (say, D) whose three possible states are:

1. D_1 = There is the onset of a serious solvency crisis of a European peripheral state, with dramatic widening of its credit spreads & the ECB intervenes by massive buying of its government debt.
2. D_2 = There is the onset of a serious solvency crisis of a European peripheral state, with dramatic widening of its credit spreads & the ECB does not intervene by massive buying its Government debt.

---

[7] Note that we are reluctant to say that it is 'wrong'. Whenever we say that a variable only depends on its immediate parent, and not on its ancestors, we are invariably making an approximation. The question is whether this approximation is acceptable or not.

3. $D_3 =$ There is no serious solvency crisis of a European peripheral state, & (as a consequence) the ECB does not purchase its Government debt.

Node C (the contagion to a core Euro state) now has the new, three-state variable D as a single parent, and the conditional probabilities to be assigned are all 'natural': we have to specify the conditional probability of contagion given

1. solvency crisis and no ECB intervention ($P(C|D = D_2)$, arguably a 'high' probability);
2. no solvency crisis and (hence) no ECB intervention ($P(C|D = D_3)$, arguably a 'very low' probability);
3. solvency crisis but ECB intervention ($P(C|D = D_1)$, arguably a 'medium–low' probability).

Overall, we have to assign fewer conditional probabilities. More importantly, we are no longer asked to assign a 'causally unnatural' conditional probability. The advantage we have reaped also reveals the price we have to pay: we have eliminated altogether one combination of state of affairs – an operation that in this case seems reasonable and useful, but that, in general, should not to be undertaken lightly.

13.6   Biting the bullet: providing the full set of master conditional probabilities

In the next chapter we show that, when applicable, the concept of causal independence provides a systematic way to simplify the assignment of the conditional probabilities in the case of several parents. Here we just want to provide some commonsensical suggestions to show that, in some cases, even conditional probability tables that at first sight look intimidating can be tackled by direct assignment in a satisfactorily realistic manner. The reasoning we are going to employ for the task will also serve as a useful limbering-up exercise of the mind for the treatment of causal independence.

We also declare our strong preference (or prejudice) here: having worked extensively with causal Bayesian nets for applications such as those described in this book, we have reached the conclusion that assigning conditional probabilities in the canonical form (i.e., as requested for direct input into the Master Equation) is far less daunting a task than it may at first appear. So, we have rather grimly called this section 'Biting the bullet', but perhaps we should have more positively called it 'Following the main road'.

In a relatively common case several 'causes' (parents) all influence a common effect (the child) in the same 'direction'. For instance, they may all increase or decrease the probability of the same effect happening. Consider, for the sake of concreteness, that we are dealing with four parents who all increase the probability of occurrence of their child. As we know, this requires the assignment of $2^4 = 16$ conditional probabilities.[8] Now, we often have an idea of which of the parents has the strongest effect and which

---

[8] To simplify the exposition we deal with Boolean variables. In this case also the extension to many-valued variables is straightforward.

the weakest. As for the two other parents, either we want to say that they have a similar degree of influence on the child (a 'draw'), or we have complete ordering. For simplicity of exposition, let's number the parents from 1 to 4 (P_1, P_2, P_3 and P_4), with the subscript 1 for the strongest effect.

Given this ranking, we can begin by looking at the probabilities when only one of the parents is *TRUE*. By definition we must have

$$P(C|P_1, \tilde{P}_2, \tilde{P}_3, \tilde{P}_4) > P(C|\tilde{P}_1, P_2, \tilde{P}_3, \tilde{P}_4) \tag{13.13}$$

$$> P(C|\tilde{P}_1, \tilde{P}_2, P_3, \tilde{P}_4) \tag{13.14}$$

$$> P(C|\tilde{P}_1, \tilde{P}_2, \tilde{P}_3, P_4) \tag{13.15}$$

Let's move to the case when two of the parents are *TRUE*. We have to assign

$$P(C|P_1, P_2, \tilde{P}_3, \tilde{P}_4)$$

$$P(C|P_1, \tilde{P}_2, P_3, \tilde{P}_4)$$

$$P(C|P_1, \tilde{P}_2, \tilde{P}_3, P_4)$$

$$P(C|\tilde{P}_1, P_2, P_3, \tilde{P}_4)$$

$$P(C|\tilde{P}_1, P_2, \tilde{P}_3, P_4)$$

$$P(C|\tilde{P}_1, \tilde{P}_2, P_3, P_4)$$

Now, recall that we are dealing with a situation when all of the parents act 'in the same direction'. Consider first the case when the strongest parent, P_1, is *TRUE*. Then it is reasonable to impose the following ordering

$$P(C|P_1, P_2, \tilde{P}_3, \tilde{P}_4) > P(C|P_1, \tilde{P}_2, P_3, \tilde{P}_4) \tag{13.16}$$

$$> P(C|P_1, \tilde{P}_2, \tilde{P}_3, P_4) \tag{13.17}$$

If P_1 is not *TRUE*, then P_2 becomes the strongest active parent. Therefore we can plausibly write

$$P(C|\tilde{P}_1, P_2, P_3, \tilde{P}_4) > P(C|\tilde{P}_1, P_2, \tilde{P}_3, P_4) \tag{13.18}$$

If two parents are *TRUE*, but neither P_1 nor P_2 is *TRUE*, it is reasonable to stipulate that $P(C|\tilde{P}_1, \tilde{P}_2, P_3, P_4)$ should the the smallest of the two-parents *TRUE* case.

Let's move to the case of three *TRUE* parents. We assign the associated conditional probabilities

$$P(C|P_1, P_2, P_3, \tilde{P}_4)$$

$$P(C|P_1, P_2, \tilde{P}_3, P_4)$$

$$P(C|P_1, \tilde{P}_2, P_3, \tilde{P}_4)$$

$$P(C|\tilde{P}_1, P_2, P_3, P_4)$$

Given the assumptions we have made about the relative strengths of the four parents we could then assign

$$P(C|P_1, P_2, P_3, \widetilde{P}_4) > P(C|P_1, P_2, \widetilde{P}_3, P_4) \tag{13.19}$$

$$> P(C|P_1, \widetilde{P}_2, P_3, P_4) \tag{13.20}$$

$$> P(C|\widetilde{P}_1, P_2, P_3, P_4) \tag{13.21}$$

Finally, given our assumptions it must be the case that the greatest conditional probability is $P(C|P_1, P_2, P_3, P_4)$ and the smallest $P(C|\widetilde{P}_1, \widetilde{P}_2, \widetilde{P}_3, \widetilde{P}_4)$. These are also two relatively easy-to-assign anchor points: the former relates to all the 'synergistic causes' occurring together;[9] the latter corresponds to the case when none of the causes occurred. Let's call the two values we want to assign to these reference conditional probabilities A and B, respectively. These anchor points, coupled with the inequalities above, can already help considerably. However, we can often do better by asking ourselves the following questions:

1. Do the two weakest parents together (i.e., when both *TRUE* with the other parents *FALSE*) have a greater effect than the strongest parent by itself? (With our notation, is $P(C|\widetilde{P}_1, \widetilde{P}_2, P_3, P_4) > P(C|P_1, \widetilde{P}_2, \widetilde{P}_3, \widetilde{P}_4)$?)
2. Do the three weakest parents together (i.e., when they are all *TRUE* with the other parent *FALSE*) have a greater effect than the two strongest parents by themselves? (With our notation, is $P(C|\widetilde{P}_1, P_2, P_3, P_4) > P(C|P_1, P_2, \widetilde{P}_3, \widetilde{P}_4)$?)

If the answer to both question is 'yes', then our task is really simple: we have in fact the following ordering:

$$A = P(C|P_1, P_2, P_3, P_4) \tag{13.22}$$

$$> P(C|P_1, P_2, P_3, \widetilde{P}_4)$$

$$> P(C|P_1, P_2, \widetilde{P}_3, P_4) > P(C|P_1, \widetilde{P}_2, P_3, P_4) \tag{13.23}$$

$$> P(C|\widetilde{P}_1, P_2, P_3, P_4) \tag{13.24}$$

$$> P(C|P_1, P_2, \widetilde{P}_3, \widetilde{P}_4) > P(C|P_1, \widetilde{P}_2, P_3, \widetilde{P}_4)$$

$$> P(C|P_1, \widetilde{P}_2, \widetilde{P}_3, P_4) \tag{13.25}$$

$$> P(C|\widetilde{P}_1, P_2, P_3, \widetilde{P}_4) > P(C|\widetilde{P}_1, P_2, \widetilde{P}_3, P_4)$$

$$> P(C|\widetilde{P}_1, \widetilde{P}_2, P_3, P_4) \tag{13.26}$$

$$> P(C|P_1, \widetilde{P}_2, \widetilde{P}_3, \widetilde{P}_4) > P(C|\widetilde{P}_1, P_2, \widetilde{P}_3, \widetilde{P}_4)$$

$$> P(C|\widetilde{P}_1, \widetilde{P}_2, P_3, \widetilde{P}_4) > P(C|\widetilde{P}_1, \widetilde{P}_2, \widetilde{P}_3, P_4) \tag{13.27}$$

$$> P(C|\widetilde{P}_1, \widetilde{P}_2, \widetilde{P}_3, \widetilde{P}_4) = B$$

---

[9] Given the nature of our applications, we often find that this probability is very close to 1 or 0.

We have 16 numbers in the interval $[A \ B]$. If we really do not have any further information, a reasonable assignment[10] would be to space them evenly between A and B. If we thought we could do better than this, then this means that, after all, we did have some useful domain knowledge (understanding of how the world works) – domain knowledge that we should definitely put to use.

Admittedly, we were helped in the assignment by our ability to answer in the affirmative both of the questions above. However, even if this were not the case, articulating why we did not feel that either (or both) can be answered with a 'yes' clarifies our thinking, and gives us guidance in the relative ranking of the probabilities.

As a last remark, the exercise above should not be taken as a fixed how-to guide, but as a generic blueprint as to how one can organize one's thinking. It is not difficult to generalize the treatment above, for instance, to the case when one of the causes works 'against the grain' of the other. It is unlikely that we will be able to arrive at such a neat ordering as the one in (13.22) to (13.27), but any partial ordering of conditional probabilities with simple inequalities within each group can be of great help – for instance, as a way to use the Maximum-Entropy approach, which we introduce in the next chapter, in a less mechanical and more insightful manner than a brute-force approach would entail.

In closing this section we would like to stress again that we present in the next chapter more systematic techniques to deal with this and other elicitation-related problems. The technique to assist in the assignment of conditional probabilities in the case of several causes contributing 'in the same direction', for instance, is making use of causal independence. Powerful, elegant and useful as they are, these techniques bring along with them two twin dangers: mental laziness and potential opaqueness of the results. Overreliance on 'clever tricks' has an added potential drawback: if the thinking process behind the constructions of the Bayesian nets is one of the most valuable by-products of the exercise – and we definitely believe that it is – then any mental shortcut comes at a cost in terms of true understanding of the ramifications and implications of a scenario. Again, we like to think of our approach as CPU-time light, and thinking-time heavy. From experience, we believe that this 'heaviness' is a pro and not a con.

13.7   Event correlation

We have mentioned in this chapter the concept of event correlation.[11] Since we have all been schooled in correlation-inspired thinking, this can be a useful diagnostic tool in the construction phase of a Bayesian net. However, in the case of Boolean variables correlation is somewhat different from the usual correlation encountered in the case of continuous-valued variables. It therefore pays to present briefly its definition and to provide some intuition as to its meaning.

---

[10] Indeed, the least-prejudicial, Maximum-Entropy assignment.
[11] This section has been modified with permission from Rebonato (2010a).

13.7.1   Evaluation

Let us associate with each event E_i a random variable, 1_i, i.e., the indicator function that assumes value 1 if E_i is true, and 0 otherwise:

$$1_i = 1 \quad \text{if } E_i = T$$

$$1_i = 0 \quad \text{if } E_i = F \tag{13.28}$$

Then a natural definition of correlation ρ_{ij} is:

$$\rho_{ij} = \frac{\mathbb{E}[(1_i - \overline{1_i})(1_j - \overline{1_j})]}{\sqrt{\mathrm{Var}(1_i)\mathrm{Var}(1_j)}} \tag{13.29}$$

where the symbols $\mathbb{E}[\cdot]$, $\mathrm{Var}(\cdot)$ and $\overline{1_i}$ denote the expectation operator,[12] the variance operator and the expected value of the indicator function 1_i, respectively. So,

$$\overline{1_i} = \mathbb{E}[1_i] \tag{13.30}$$

For concreteness, let us consider the case of three events. Then the truth table can be written as follows.

	E_1	E_2	E_3	
J_1	1	0	0	$p(1)$
J_2	0	1	0	$p(2)$
J_3	0	0	1	$p(3)$
J_4	1	1	0	$p(4)$
J_5	1	0	1	$p(5)$
J_6	0	1	1	$p(6)$
J_7	1	1	1	$p(7)$
J_8	0	0	0	$p(8)$

$$\tag{13.31}$$

The symbols J_i, $i = 1, 2, \ldots, 8$, denote the joint events (i.e., the eight different possible combinations of TRUE and FALSE values for the three variables). Making reference to this table it is easy to calculate the expected value of 1_i. Take, for instance, the first event, E_1. Then the expectation will be equal to the sum of the products of the value of the indicator function 1_1 for variable 1 for each joint event J_k, times the probability of the joint event, $p(k)$. For $i = 1$ this gives

$$\overline{1_1} = 1 * p(1) + 0 * p(2) + 0 * p(3) + 1 * p(4)$$
$$+ 1 * p(5) + 0 * p(6) + 1 * p(7) + 0 * p(8)$$
$$= 1 * p(1) + 1 * p(4) + 1 * p(5) + 1 * p(7)$$
$$= p(1) + p(4) + p(5) + p(7) = P(E_1) \tag{13.32}$$

---

[12] The expectation is taken, of course, over the joint probabilities $[p(i)]$.

Therefore

$$\overline{\mathbf{1}_i} = \mathbb{E}[(\mathbf{1}_i)] = P(E_i) \quad \text{for any } i \tag{13.33}$$

We can therefore rewrite Equation (13.29) as

$$\rho_{ij} = \frac{\mathbb{E}[(\mathbf{1}_i - P(E_i))(\mathbf{1}_j - P(E_j))]}{\sqrt{\text{Var}(\mathbf{1}_i)\text{Var}(\mathbf{1}_j)}} \tag{13.34}$$

Let's see how we can get a better understanding of this quantity, by analysing the numerator and the denominator in turn.

To calculate the numerator one can construct a table as follows:

$$
\begin{array}{cccccc}
 & E_1 & E_2 & E_3 & \\
J_1 & 1 - P(E_1) & 0 - P(E_2) & 0 - P(E_3) & p(1) \\
J_2 & 0 - P(E_1) & 1 - P(E_2) & 0 - P(E_3) & p(2) \\
J_3 & 0 - P(E_1) & 0 - P(E_2) & 1 - P(E_3) & p(3) \\
J_4 & 1 - P(E_1) & 1 - P(E_2) & 0 - P(E_3) & p(4) \\
J_5 & 1 - P(E_1) & 0 - P(E_2) & 1 - P(E_3) & p(5) \\
J_6 & 0 - P(E_1) & 1 - P(E_2) & 1 - P(E_3) & p(6) \\
J_7 & 1 - P(E_1) & 1 - P(E_2) & 1 - P(E_3) & p(7) \\
J_8 & 0 - P(E_1) & 0 - P(E_2) & 0 - P(E_3) & p(8)
\end{array} \tag{13.35}
$$

Each entry of the table has been constructed in such a way that it can be directly used in Equation (13.34). Indeed, suppose, for instance, that one wanted to calculate the term $\mathbb{E}[(\mathbf{1}_1 - P(E_1))(\mathbf{1}_2 - P(E_2))]$. From the the first two columns of table (13.35) one obtains:

$$
\begin{aligned}
&[(1 - P(E_1))(0 - P(E_2))]p(1) \\
&+ [(0 - P(E_1))(1 - P(E_2))]p(2) \\
&+ [(0 - P(E_1))(0 - P(E_2))]p(3) \\
&+ [(1 - P(E_1))(1 - P(E_2))]p(4) \\
&+ [(1 - P(E_1))(0 - P(E_2))]p(5) \\
&+ [(0 - P(E_1))(1 - P(E_2))]p(6) \\
&+ [(1 - P(E_1))(1 - P(E_2))]p(7) \\
&+ [(0 - P(E_1))(0 - P(E_2))]p(8)
\end{aligned} \tag{13.36}
$$

where $P(E_1)$ and $P(E_2)$ have been derived as above. Every term in the numerator can be evaluated in this way.

Let's move now to the denominator. In evaluating this term we have to calculate the variance of the indicator function $\mathbf{1}_i$. This is given by:

$$\text{Var}[\mathbf{1}_i] = \mathbb{E}[(\mathbf{1}_i)^2] - \mathbb{E}[(\mathbf{1}_i)]^2 \tag{13.37}$$

Now,

$$\mathbb{E}[(\mathbf{1}_i)]^2 = P(E_i)^2 \tag{13.38}$$

But, since the indicator function can only take values 1 or 0, it immediately follows that

$$(\mathbf{1}_i)^2 = (\mathbf{1}_i) \tag{13.39}$$

Therefore

$$\mathbb{E}[(\mathbf{1}_i)^2] = \mathbb{E}[(\mathbf{1}_i)] = P(E_i) \tag{13.40}$$

So, we obtain

$$\mathrm{Var}[\mathbf{1}_i] = P(E_i) - P(E_i)^2 \tag{13.41}$$

As $P(E_i)$ is always less than or equal to 1, Equation (25.8) shows that the variance will always be positive.

Finally, one can rewrite Equation (13.34) as:

$$\rho_{ij} = \frac{\mathbb{E}[(\mathbf{1}_i - \overline{\mathbf{1}_i})(\mathbf{1}_j - \overline{\mathbf{1}_j})]}{\sqrt{[P(E_i) - P(E_i)^2][P(E_j) - P(E_j)^2]}} \tag{13.42}$$

$$= \frac{\mathbb{E}[(\mathbf{1}_i - P(E_i))(\mathbf{1}_j - P(E_j))]}{\sqrt{[P(E_i) - P(E_i)^2][P(E_j) - P(E_j)^2]}} \tag{13.43}$$

with the numerator given by Equation (13.36). The joint probabilities enter expression (13.42) via the expectation operator, $\mathbb{E}[\cdot]$.

13.7.2   Intuitive interpretation

What intuitive meaning can we ascribe to the event correlation thus calculated?

Consider a joint event, say, J_6. If in the joint event J_6 the elementary event E_i is *TRUE* (occurs), then the indicator function will have value 1 and the quantity $\mathbf{1}_i - P(E_i)$ will be greater than or equal to 0. Conversely, if the elementary event E_i does *not* occur the same quantity $\mathbf{1}_i - P(E_i)$ will be less than or equal to 0. The same reasoning applies to the elementary event E_j. So, if both event E_i and event E_j occur in joint event J_6, then the numerator will be positive (positive number times positive number). The numerator will also be positive if neither event occurs (negative number times negative number). The numerator will instead be negative when one event occurs and the other does not occur in joint event J_6. This positive or negative number will then be weighted by the probability of joint event J_6, $p(6)$.

So, the event correlation coefficient tells us the following: when the indicator function for one event is greater than its expected value (i.e., than the marginal probability for that event, $P(E_i)$) and the indicator function for the other event is greater than its expected value (the probability for that event, $P(E_j)$), we have a positive contribution to the correlation coefficient (weighted by $p(6)$). The opposite occurs when the indicator function for one event is greater than its expected value but the indicator function for the other event is smaller than its expected value. The correlation coefficient therefore gives a measure of the concordance of occurrence of two events. It gives a quantitative answer to the question: 'Are the two events likely or unlikely to happen together, after taking into account their stand-alone probability of occurrence?'

14 More advanced topics: elicitation

Il piu' certo modo di celare agli altri i confini del proprio sapere, é di non trapassarli.[1] Giacomo Leopardi, *Pensieri*, LXXXVI

In this and in the following chapter we present some relatively more-advanced techniques that can help in the construction of the Bayesian nets. We focus on the elicitation problem in this chapter, and on a miscellany of additional tools in the next, which can broadly be grouped under the rubric of facilitating the analysis of the quantities of interest (e.g., obtaining joint probabilities for a subset of variables, deriving implied rather than assigned conditional probabilities, etc.), or of enabling the handling of large Bayesian nets.

We said 'relatively more advanced' because, by the standards of sophistication required to deal with hundreds or thousands of variables (see the discussion at the beginning of Chapter 13), these remain entry-level techniques. Since, however, we want to keep our approach as transparent and non-black-box as possible, this is about as far as we are comfortable to go in terms of algorithmic complexity.

The underlying issues are deep and fascinating, pertaining as they do to the topics of causation and inference, and we therefore provide throughout this chapter some bibliographic pointers for the interested reader. We are aware that, once causation is brought into play, matters can quickly become very complex, from both the mathematical and philosophical point of view. Hence the quote that opens this chapter.

14.1 The nature of the elicitation problem: what are the problems?

If you don't like my opinions, I have many others. Groucho Marx

In this chapter we are going to deal with two problems:

1. what to do when the asset manager does not feel confident enough to assign all the canonical probabilities required to fill in a conditional probability table, or when she prefers to assign probabilities other than the conditional probabilities of the correct

---

[1] The safest way to hide from others the limits of one's knowledge is not to exceed them.

order required for the Bayesian net – we refer to these problems as the 'elicitation' problems;

2. what to do when the number of nodes or parents is so high as to make direct computation or elicitation, respectively, too burdensome or even impossible.

Both problems refer to the elicitation stage in the construction of the Bayesian net, the phase which is arguably the most delicate in the whole procedure. If the conditional probabilities are not thoughtfully assigned, and, above all, if the user is not helped during the provision of these all-important probabilities, the outcome is unlikely to be of much value. It is for this reason that we devote a full chapter to the topic.[2]

One of the most delicate parts of the Bayesian-net technology is the provision of the conditional probability tables. For a given node the number of entries is in fact exponential in the number of parents. This certainly creates a problem in diagnostics or artificial-intelligence applications (where a node can have dozens of parents). In these cases no expert can reasonably assign the probabilities pertaining to all the required permutations of *TRUE* and *FALSE* for the parents. And it is most unlikely that sufficient data can be available to provide a frequentist answer to all thee different configurations. (At the *very* least we would need in our data set one realization for each combination of *TRUE* and *FALSE* for the parents.) But, even for our mundane applications, where we can expect to have at most a handful of parents, the knowledge of the expert can be pushed to its limits by the requirement to fill in, say, the eight conditional probabilities that describe the non-trivial dependencies of a child on its three parents. This is the problem dealt with in the rest of the chapter.

We stress that the essence of the problems we deal with in this chapter has mainly to do with the cognitive, not computational, nature of the task at hand. So, for instance, the naive and brute-force Maximum-Entropy solution that we propose below would be totally unusable with hundreds or thousands of variables, but performs perfectly well with the 10–20 variables we will typically deal with.

14.2   Dealing with elicitation: the Maximum-Entropy approach

If you can find something everyone agrees on, it's wrong. Mo Udal

The concept of Maximum Entropy is very general and deep (and, we think, beautiful). It is linked to Occam's razor, and to one of the most fruitful guidelines for successful research in the physical sciences: the quest for simplicity.[3] In simple terms, invoking the principle of Maximum Entropy is equivalent to requiring that, when we only have some information about a phenomenon, in our modelling we should make 'as

---

[2] Our treatment of elicitation does not deal with the 'psychological' aspects of the process (i.e., the various cognitive biases), with the ways to overcome them, or with the techniques to facilitate the communication of expert views. For a recent treatment of these aspects, see, e.g., Gigerenzer and Edwards (2003) and Oakley (2010) and references therein.

[3] For an information-theory-based introduction to the principle of Maximum Entropy see, e.g., Ash (1990 [1965]) and Cover and Thomas (2006). For a clear and simple treatment with an eye to applications in the natural sciences, see, e.g., Gregory (2005).

few' assumptions as possible (we should be as non-committal as possible) about the information that we do *not* have. The principle is certainly reasonable. Why it should be so successful is, in the view of these writers, one of the deepest observations about the links between the human mind and 'the world out there'.[4]

Without getting too philosophical, we take the following extended quote from Gregory (2005), who is in turn heavily influenced by Jaynes (2003), as our operative justification for using the principle of Maximum Entropy:

Principle: Out of all the possible probability distributions which agree with the given constraint information, select the one that is maximally non-committal with regard to missing information.

Question: How do we accomplish the goal of being maximally non-committal about missing information?

Answer: The greater the missing information, the more uncertain the estimate. Therefore, make estimates that maximize the uncertainty in the probability distribution, while still being maximally constrained by the given information.

What is uncertainty and how do we measure it? Jaynes argued that the best measure of uncertainty is the entropy of the probability distribution, an idea that was first introduced by Claude Shannon in his pioneering work on information theory.[5]

This is our interpretation and justification for the use of the Maximum-Entropy principle.

The approach that we present to determine the Maximum-Entropy distributions appropriate to our degree of knowledge is general, and always follows the same blueprint, but the results differ because they depend on the amount and type of knowledge the expert assumes to have. More precisely, we assume that the expert has information about some features of a distribution density (say, its support, or its expected value), and wants to determine the member of the class of distributions which is compatible with her information and which is least prejudicial (in the sense described above). We derive in Appendix 14.A a few important well-known Maximum-Entropy distributions, which depend on the degree and type of the information the expert feels confident to assign. We apply this principle in the next sections to tackle a number of elicitation-related problems. First we look at the case where the expert only feels able

---

[4] One should distinguish between Maximum Entropy (often abbreviated as MaxEnt) and Maximum Relative Entropy (commonly, if elliptically, abbreviated as ME). Roughly speaking, Maximum Entropy is used to obtain ('update') probabilities from a uniform prior. For instance, as we show in Appendix 14.A, if the only thing we know about a distribution is its (bounded) range, or its mean, or its mean and variance, then the diffuse uniform prior is 'updated' to the bounded uniform distribution, the exponential distribution or the Gaussian distribution, respectively. We use Maximum Entropy in Sections 14.2, 16.4, 20.7, 24.4 and 27.3. Maximum Relative Entropy (which we use in Section 15.2.2) minimizes the probability-weighted log-distance (*pseudo* distance, really) between two arbitrary distributions, and therefore has much wider applicability, as it can be applied to updating probabilities from arbitrary priors. The approach by Meucci that we discussed in Chapter 10 is also linked to Maximum Relative Entropy. If one looks at Maximum (Relative) Entropy as a tool to update prior distributions, the deep links with Bayesian updating becomes clear – or, at this stage, at least plausible. For a discussion see, Giffin and Caticha (2007) and Caticha (2008) for an excellent, almost-book-length discussion of the links between probability, entropy and statistical physics from a physics (not *econo*physics) perspective.

[5] Gregory (2005, p. 185).

to provide a range for a canonical. Then we tackle the situation when the expert feels she can only assign lower-order conditional probabilities than required by the Master Equation.

A word of caution before we begin. We find the Maximum-Entropy approach philosophically very appealing, as it provides the least-committal (least-prejudicial) distribution compatible with the information the expert *can* provide. Much as we like this approach, we have already argued that we find that its reach and generality can induce some 'laziness' in the expert, who often tends to throw up her hands in despair far too early. We have therefore offered our recommendation to embrace the Maximum-Entropy approach, but to do so after all the available (partial) information has been made use of. The problem here is that very often this extra information cannot be easily provided neatly 'pre-packaged' in the canonical conditional-probability form required as input to the Bayesian net. The next sections deal with a few such common cases.

14.3   Range-only information for canonical probabilities

We deal in this section with the case when the expert can only specify that a given canonical conditional probability should lie between a lower and upper value. The treatment can be easily generalized to the richer information sets dealt with in Appendix 14.A. Assigning a plausible range operationally can mean choosing a range of possible values over which the expert is 90% confident that the 'correct' answer should lie. Let L_j and U_j be the lower and upper probability values for the jth conditional probability, cp_j, within which the expert is 90% confident that the 'true' conditional probability should lie. Issues of overconfidence in assigning confidence bounds are well documented in cognitive psychology;[6] however, there are also well-established, if imperfect, ways to try to fix them (see, e.g., Speirs-Bridge *et al.* (2009) and references therein).[7]

Let's focus on the elicitation of a range for one conditional probability. To each possible value within the assigned range there corresponds a conditional probability. We know that, via the Master Equation, a number of joint probabilities are affected by this conditional probability. And thanks to the No-Constraints Theorem, we also know that any value within the range (which is, of course, a subset of [0, 1]) will give rise to a set of bona fide joint probabilities.

Then we could ask about the least-prejudiced (least-committal) joint distribution associated with the degree of confidence that we have. This will be given by the Maximum-Entropy distribution consistent with the expert's degree of uncertainty. The

---

[6] See, e.g., Oskamp (1965) and Tsai *et al.* (2008) on overconfidence due to availability of information; Lichtenstein *et al.* (1982) on overconfidence due to the complexity of the question; Lichtenstein *et al.* (1982) and Lichtenstein and Fishhoff (1977) on overconfidence due to the absence of regular feedback; and Tetlock (2005) on overconfidence due to what Speirs-Bridge *et al.* (2009) term the 'cognitive style' of the expert and what Tetlock calls the 'hedgehog' or 'fox' expert.

[7] So, for instance, Speirs-Bridge *et al.* (2009, p. 11) state that '[a]lthough cognitive heuristics and biases can prove challenging to correct ..., refinement in elicitation procedure and question format can be easily implemented'.

entropy, H, is defined as

$$H_p = -\sum_{i=1,2^n} p(i)\log_2 p(i) \tag{14.1}$$

Following the suggestion in Section 13.3, we carry out an unconstrained maximization search, using L_j and U_j as the lower and upper bound, respectively, for the search over the jth conditional probability, cp_j. If we set

$$cp_j(\theta) = L_j + (U_j - L_j)\sin^2\theta_j \tag{14.2}$$

the search can be carried out in an unconstrained manner over the auxiliary variable, θ_j.

We can set similar bounds for as many conditional probabilities as required, and carry out a joint optimization.

We have made extensive use of this technique in real-life applications. Very often, once the expert was presented with the conditional probabilities that maximized the entropy of the distribution, her reply was that it was 'clearly wrong' or 'did not make sense' or 'it jarred with her intuition'. Upon hearing these words, we could not have been happier. If the expert really believed that the conditional probability produced by the Maximum-Entropy technique – a probability about which the expert supposedly had no more information than what was reflected in her 90% confidence bounds – produced 'wrong' or counterintuitive results, then she must have withdrawn some useful information when the problem was first set up. The correct procedure is simply to incorporate this now-so-obvious piece of expert knowledge in the information set, and, if necessary, to repeat the entropy maximization procedure.

14.4   Dealing with elicitation: Non-canonical-information

In this section we deal with the case when the expert feels she can provide conditional probabilities, but not in the form required for direct input into the Master Equation. Most commonly, the expert may find it cognitively easier to provide lower-order probabilities (say, singly rather than doubly conditioned probabilities).

Consider the case when a given child (an 'effect') has n parents (n 'causes'). As we know, in the case of Boolean variables in order to fill in the associated conditional probability table we have to assign 2^n conditional probabilities. Suppose then that the expert may not feel able to assign the probability of an effect conditioned on all the possible permutations for the parents (the 'canonical' conditional probabilities), but may think that lower-order conditional probabilities are easier to assign. So, for instance, the canonical conditional probability $P(E|C_1, C_2, C_3, C_4)$ may be required, but the expert may only feel able to supply $P(E|C_1)$, $P(E|C_2)$, $P(E|C_3)$ and $P(E|C_4)$. This information is, of course, much less rich than what is canonically required, but still very useful. The problem is that there is no analogue of the No-Constraints Theorem for non-canonical conditional probabilities: if the lower-order conditional probabilities are subjectively assigned, just requiring that they should lie between 0 and 1 does not ensure that there exists a set of bona fide joint probabilities from which they could be derived. In practice, directly assigning a large number of lower-order conditional probabilities almost invariably gives rise to inconsistencies (i.e., negative joint probabilities). What is the expert then to do?

14.4.1   Definitions

All the problems dealt with in this section have a common structure, and a similar solution. To present this solution without getting in a terminology tangle, some definitions are first required. We will call *Master Conditional Probabilities* the conditional probabilities of the correct type, number and order required to fill in the conditional probability tables that we are supposed to provide for the Master Equation. We will then call *Non-Standard Conditional Probabilities* the set of conditional probabilities that we are instead able to provide. These could, but need not, be the right number (we may only feel able to give fewer inputs than required); if we have provided the correct number of inputs, at least some of the probabilities in the Non-Standard Conditional Probabilities set will be of lower order[8] than the Master Conditional Probabilities; they may or may not be linearly independent; and they may or may not be of sufficiently high order[9] to determine uniquely the Master Conditional Probabilities.

So, our problem can be stated as follows: we need to provide one type of information (the Master Conditional Probabilities), but we feel unable to do so, and we can only provide a different type of information (Non-Standard Conditional Probabilities).

Two cases then arise: either the Non-Standard Conditional Probabilities provide enough information to pin down uniquely (using the relationships between Non-Standard Conditional Probabilities and Master Conditional Probabilities) as many numbers as elements in the Master Conditional Probabilities as required; or the problem is left undetermined. If the Non-Standard Conditional Probabilities uniquely determine as many numbers as Master Conditional Probabilities, we will call our input set *uniquely invertible*.

Note, however, that unique invertibility does not guarantee that the unique set of numbers obtained from our inputs using the relationships between Non-Standard Conditional Probabilities and Master Conditional Probabilities will represent probabilities, because the unique mapping may not produce numbers in the interval $[0, 1]$. If the input set is uniquely invertible *and* the transformation indeed produces numbers in the interval $[0, 1]$, then we will have obtained a proper set of Master Conditional Probabilities, and we will call our input set of Non-Standard Conditional Probabilities *equivalent*.

We state without proof the following necessary condition for equivalence (see Coca (2011) for a proof):

---

[8] We include marginal probabilities in the set of lower-order conditional probabilities.

[9] By 'order of conditioning' we refer to the number of variables in the conditioning set. So, for instance, $P(A|B, C, D)$ is a conditional probability of the third order.

CONDITION 1 *A necessary condition for a set of Non-Standard Conditional Probabilities to be equivalent is that at least one of the Non-Standard Conditional Probabilities must be of the correct order.*

The need to distinguish between unique invertibility and equivalence is clear: we know from the No-Constraints Theorem (Section 7.8) that we can freely assign Master Conditional Probabilities without any constraints other than non-negativity and that each probability should be smaller than or equal to 1. However, even if all the Non-Standard Conditional Probabilities belong to [0, 1], once we invert them we may get as a result Master Conditional Probabilities that do not lie in [0, 1]. If they don't, there is certainly no underlying supporting joint distribution. If they do, there certainly is.

So much for unique invertibility. What about the case when our input is not *uniquely* invertible? If all the candidate Master Conditional Probabilities produced by the non-uniquely invertible set of Non-Standard Conditional Probabilities belong to [0, 1] we will call the latter *admissible*. Otherwise we will call them *non-admissible*.

Of course, we would love to work with at least admissible, and preferably equivalent, Non-Standard Conditional Probabilities. We may sometimes have to settle for admissible, but we can never work with non-admissible sets.

14.4.2 An example
A simple example can clarify the terminology. Suppose that we have a convergent node with two parents: $P_1 \rightarrow C \leftarrow P_2$ (where C stands for Child, and P_1 and P_2 for Parent 1 and Parent 2, respectively). We will assume that the net has already been built up to the parents. We therefore know everything about the parents – i.e., we know their joint distribution, from which we can derive $P(P_1)$ and $P(P_2)$. Let's assume that the values determined by the net built up to this point are $P(P_1) = X$ and $P(P_2) = Y$. We also know that four Master Conditional Probabilities are called for to fill in the conditional probability table for the child, C, and that they are given by

1. $P(C|P_1, P_2)$
2. $P(C|\tilde{P}_1, P_2)$
3. $P(C|P_1, \tilde{P}_2)$
4. $P(C|\tilde{P}_1, \tilde{P}_2)$

Consider now the following possible sets of Non-Standard Conditional Probabilities. Let's begin with

1. $P(C|P_1) = x$
2. $P(C|\tilde{P}_1) = y$
3. $P(C|P_2) = z$

Since this set of Non-Standard Conditional Probabilities only contains three elements, there is no hope that we may be able to recover uniquely the set of Master Conditional Probabilities. So this first set cannot be uniquely invertible. Furthermore, none of the Non-Standard Conditional Probabilities is of the second order. This is another reason why they cannot uniquely recover the Master Conditional Probabilities.

Depending on the values we assigned it may or may not be admissible. Indeed, we know for instance that

$$P(C|P_1)P(P_1) + P(C|\widetilde{P_1})P(\widetilde{P_1}) = P(C)$$

$$xX + y(1 - X) = P(C) \tag{14.3}$$

Now, if it so happens that $xX + y(1 - X) > 1$, then the Non-Standard Conditional Probabilities we have provided as input cannot be admissible.

Consider now

1. $P(C|P_1, P_2) = a$
2. $P(C|P_2) = b$
3. $P(C|P_1) = c$
4. $P(C) = d$

This may look like a more promising candidate for invertibility: at least we have as many equations as unknowns, and one of the inputs, $P(C|P_1, P_2) = a$, is of the correct order. However, a moment's reflection shows that one equation is not linearly independent of the others, because

$$P(C|P_2)P(P_2) + P(C|P_1)P(P_1) = P(C)$$

(Recall that $P(P_2)$ and $P(P_2)$ are already implicitly assigned by the net we have built up to and including the parents.) So, also in this case we cannot have an uniquely invertible set. As for admissibility, it will depend on the specific values of a, b, c and d.

Finally, consider the following input:

1. $P(C|P_1, P_2) = \alpha$
2. $P(C|P_2) = \beta$
3. $P(C|P_1) = \gamma$
4. $P(C|\widetilde{P_1}) = \delta$

It is easy to prove that these inputs are all independent, and one of the conditional probabilities is of the right order. We are therefore assured of unique invertibility. Whether the mapping from the Non-Standard Conditional Probabilities to the Master Conditional Probabilities will give rise to four numbers in the interval $[0, 1]$ will depend on the numerical values that have been assigned to α, β, γ and δ. So we may or may not have equivalence.

These examples give us a flavour of the scope of the definitions provided above, and of the subtlety of the problem. We present in the following some rather inelegant tools to check whether a given set of Non-Standard Conditional Probabilities allows unique invertibility and equivalence. Again, a more elegant analytical treatment can be found in Coca (2011).

14.4.3   Unique invertibility, uncertain equivalence

Lets's start from the case when we know that our Non-Standard Conditional Probabilities inputs are uniquely invertible, but we are not sure whether they are equivalent. Note that, since we have assumed unique invertibility, as a bare minimum we have provided as many Non-Standard Conditional Probabilities as Master Conditional Probabilities. In general, we can then proceed as follows.

1. We start from an arbitrary guess for the Master Conditional Probabilities. As we know, these just have to lie in the interval [0, 1], so this bit is easy.
2. By feeding our arbitrary guess for the Master Conditional Probabilities into the Master Equation, we build the associated joint probabilities.
3. Given our arbitrary guess for the Master Conditional Probabilities and the associated joint probabilities, we construct the implied Non-Standard Conditional Probabilities. These implied values will in general be different from what we subjectively assigned.
4. We calculate a distance between the implied and the assigned input probabilities.
5. We vary our initial guess for the Master Conditional Probabilities and we repeat steps 2 to 4 until this distance is minimized.

If our Non-Standard Conditional Probabilities inputs were equivalent in the first place, then at the end of the procedure the distance will be zero: we will have found the unique set of Master Conditional Probabilities that exactly recover our input Non-Standard Conditional Probabilities. If the inputs were not equivalent, given the metric we have chosen we will have found the closest equivalent set of Non-Standard Conditional Probabilities.

14.4.4   Non-unique invertibility, uncertain equivalence

Consider now the case when the conditional probabilities provided are certainly non-uniquely invertible (for instance, because they are fewer in number than the required inputs to the conditional probability table), and we are unsure whether they are admissible. We proceed in a similar manner.

1. As above we start from an arbitrary guess for the Master Conditional Probabilities.
2. We feed again these arbitrary Master Conditional Probabilities into the Master Equation, and obtain the associated joint probabilities.
3. Given this guess and the associated joint probabilities, we construct the implied Non-Standard Conditional Probabilities.
4. We define a distance functional, $d(cp)$, between the implied and the supplied Non-Standard Conditional Probabilities.
5. Using the joint probabilities associated with our guess for the Master Conditional Probabilities, we also calculate the functional negative entropy (negentropy), $NH(p)$, as

$$NH(p) = \sum_{i=1,2^N} p(i) \ln[p(i)]$$

where the $p(i)$ denote the joint probabilities.

6. We build a target functional, $T(p, cp)$, given by a weighted sum of the distance and the negative entropy:

$$T(p, cp) = \omega_1 N H(p) + (1 - \omega_1) d(cp)$$

7. We vary our initial guess for the conditional probabilities of the correct order and we repeat steps 2 to 6 until the target functional, $T(p)$, is minimized.

By so doing we will have found the Master Conditional Probabilities that produce Non-Standard Conditional Probabilities which minimize a combination of the distance from our inputs and the negative entropy of the joint distribution. If the Non-Standard Conditional Probabilities we assigned were admissible, we may recover them exactly.[10]

Summarizing: for both approaches we have to define a distance functional, $d(cp)$. A natural choice for this functional is

$$\chi^2(cp) = \sum_{i=1.m} \left| cp_i^{\text{input}} - cp_i^{\text{implied}} \right|^2 \tag{14.4}$$

Then the target functional becomes, in the two cases explored so far,

$$T(cp) = \chi^2(cp) = \sum_{i=1.m} \left| cp_i^{\text{input}} - cp_i^{\text{implied}} \right|^2 \tag{14.5}$$

or

$$T(p, cp) = \sum_{i=1.m} \left| cp_i^{\text{input}} - cp_i^{\text{implied}} \right|^2 + N H(p) \tag{14.6}$$

In the expressions above, cp_i^{input} and cp_i^{implied} denote the input and implied Non-Standard Conditional Probabilities.

All of this can be illustrated with a simple example.

14.4.5 A simple example

Consider again the very simple tree with convergent nodes: $A \rightarrow C \leftarrow B$. Assume for the moment that A and B are the roots.[11] The master set of conditional probabilities is given by:

- $P(A) = y_1$
- $P(B) = y_2$
- $P(C|AB) = y_3$
- $P(C|\tilde{A}B) = y_4$
- $P(C|A\tilde{B}) = y_5$
- $P(C|\tilde{A}\tilde{B}) = y_6$

---

[10] Whether we recover them exactly or not will depend on the weight given by the negative entropy. If the weight given to the negative entropy is high, the 'exact' solution may be penalized, even if possible, because it is very 'committal'.

[11] See the next subsection for a generalization to the case where the parents are not roots.

Suppose the expert wants to assign instead

- $P(A) = \widehat{x}_1$
- $P(B) = \widehat{x}_2$
- $P(C|AB) = \widehat{x}_3$
- $P(C) = \widehat{x}_4$
- $P(C|A) = \widehat{x}_5$
- $P(C|B) = \widehat{x}_6$

So, $\{y_i\}$ denote the Master Conditional Probabilities, and $\{x_i\}$ the Non-Standard Conditional Probabilities. Consider the joint probabilities

$$
\begin{array}{cccll}
A & B & C & p & \\
1 & 1 & 1 & p_1 & y_1 y_2 y_3 \\
0 & 1 & 1 & p_2 & [1 - y_1]y_2 y_4 \\
1 & 0 & 1 & p_3 & y_1[1 - y_2]y_5 \\
0 & 0 & 1 & p_4 & [1 - y_1][1 - y_2]y_6 \\
1 & 1 & 0 & p_5 & \cdots \\
0 & 1 & 0 & p_6 & \cdots \\
1 & 0 & 0 & p_7 & y_1[1 - y_2][1 - y_6] \\
0 & 0 & 0 & p_8 & \cdots
\end{array}
\tag{14.7}
$$

Now, take one of the user-assigned probabilities, say, $P(C) = \widehat{x}_4$. Given the symbolic expressions for the joint probabilities in (14.7), we can always find an expression for any of the assigned probabilities, and, therefore, in particular, for $\widehat{x}_4$, as a function of the $\{y_i\}$. One gets, for instance,

$$
P(C) = x_4 = p_1 + p_2 + p_3 + p_4
$$

$$
= y_1 y_2 y_3
$$

$$
+ [1 - y_1]y_2 y_4
$$

$$
+ y_1[1 - y_2]y_5
$$

$$
+ [1 - y_1][1 - y_2]y_6
\tag{14.8}
$$

and similarly for the other user-assigned input probabilities. We know that each of the $\{y_i\}$ can assume any value in the interval $[0, 1]$. Therefore any attainable value for the $\{x_i\}$, and for x_4 in particular for the specific input we are looking at, can be obtained by sweeping over the interval $[0, 1]^6$.

Define now the distance, $d[\widehat{x}_i, x_i(y_i)]$,

$$
d[\widehat{x}_i, x_i(y_i)] \equiv \sum_{i=1,6} (\widehat{x}_i - x_i(\overline{y}_i))^2
\tag{14.9}
$$

where $\overline{y}$ denotes an arbitrary point in $[0\ 1]^6$, and $x_i(\overline{y}_i)$ are the values of the expert-assigned conditional probabilities as a function of the point $\overline{y}$. Now, vary the point y

(i.e., its six coordinates $\{y_i\}$) in an unconstrained manner (e.g., by setting $y_i = \sin^2 \theta_i$) until the distance is minimized.

Note that we do not even have to invert from the optimal $\{x_i\}$ to the $\{y_i\}$, because we can directly read the values $\{y_i\}$ at the end of the optimization that solve for the minimum distance, and use these in the Master Equation.

14.4.6 *Generalization*

The assumption that A and C were roots was only used in order to create by inspection the joint probability for the parent variables. In general, we can always assume that a Bayesian net has been built up to n variables, that the attending 2^n joint probabilities have been built, and that we want to add one child. Then all the previously built probabilities are just known numbers ($p_k, k = 1, 2, \ldots, 2^n$), and we have a set of master conditional probabilities $\{y_i\}$, and a set of user-assigned Non-Standard Conditional Probabilities, $\{x_i\}$. The range of the index i depends on the number of parents. Everything proceeds as above.

14.5 Dealing with elicitation: exploiting causal independence

We are still dealing here with the case when a given child (an 'effect') has a large number, $n \gg 1$, parents (n 'causes'), and we are still looking for ways to simplify the cognitive task.

We can, of course, always fall back on the principle of Maximum Entropy described in the previous sections, but often with a bit of effort we can do significantly better. In Section 13.6 we have already discussed in an informal and intuitive way how to tackle this problem in a special and particularly simple setting. In this section we look at a more precise and systematic approach to providing the required conditional probability table. This approach – which exploits the concept of conditional independence – also enjoys wider applicability. It is not a panacea, in the sense that it cannot be used to 'decompose' an arbitrary set of dependencies. However, the range of practical situations where the conditions of validity are met is sufficiently wide to make the idea very appealing. The treatment that follows is largely based on Heckerman and Breese (1995, 1998) and adapted from Coca (2011), but see also Jurgelanaite and Lucas (2005) and Zagorecki, Voortman and Druzdzel (2006) for a treatment of more general dependencies among causes and effects than we deal with here, Henrion (1987) for how to deal with leaking causes, Pearl (1986) for an early but still very useful review of some 'foundational' issues, and Jensen and Nielsen (2007) for a recent, and slightly different, approach.

We note in passing that different authors have presented very similar ideas, but there seems to be no universal agreement about the methodology (let alone the notation). We therefore sacrifice generality, and present an approach that is particularly suited to dealing with the two situations (noisy AND, and, especially, noisy OR) that are most likely to be encountered in practical applications.

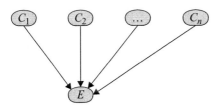

Figure 14.1 Bayesian net with several parents ($C_1, C_2, \ldots, C_n$, causes) and one child (E, effect).

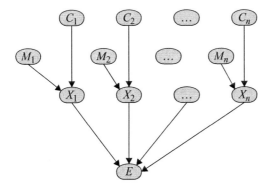

Figure 14.2 Bayesian net with several parents (causes) and one child (effect) after introducing the inhibitors ($M_1, M_2, \ldots, M_n$) and the deterministic functions of the causes and of the inhibitors, ($X_1, X_2, \ldots, X_n$).

To make our presentation concrete, it is useful to start from the net depicted in Figure 14.1. We assume for simplicity of exposition that we are dealing with Boolean (binary) variables. In this picture we have n causes (parent nodes variables). Therefore the associated conditional probability table would in general require 2^n non-trivial entries, each one reflecting the probability of the effect being, say, true ($E = TRUE$), given all the possible configurations of $TRUE$ and $FALSE$ for the causing parents. The nature of the dependence between the causes is, up to this point, quite general.

14.5.1   Local restructuring of the net
Reculer pour mieux avancer[12]

On the way to simplifying the assignment problem, let's introduce some complications. Let's enrich the original parent–child section of our Bayesian net as shown in Figure 14.2: we have added a set of new 'roots' (*inhibitors*), $i = 1, 2, \ldots, n$.[13]

Now, consider for a moment the special but important case where the contribution of cause C_i to effect E is independent of whether cause C_j contributes or not. We will make this statement more precise immediately below (see Equation (14.26)), but for

---

[12] 'To retreat better to advance.'
[13] In the treatment below we follow Heckerman and Breese (1998).

the moment we characterize this state of affairs by saying that all the causes contribute in an independent manner.[14]

A moment's thought shows that the sub-net in Figure 14.2 is a possible way to describe this state of affairs. Indeed, let's first make the variables X_i a *deterministic* function of C_i and M_i. More precisely, let the values of the intermediate nodes be given by n *deterministic* functions, f_i, $i = 1, 2, \ldots, n$, of the values of the causes and of the inhibitors.

$$X_i = f_i(c_i, m_i) \tag{14.10}$$

where we have employed the usual convention that a lower-case symbol (such as c_i) refers to a particular realization of the variable that we denote with the same-letter capital symbol (in this case, C_i). The range of the functions f_i is therefore *TRUE*, *FALSE*. As for the auxiliary variables $\{M\}$ (which we called with some foresight 'inhibitors'), each variable M_i is such that, when *TRUE*, it *inhibits* the corresponding cause, C_i. So, having the inhibitor active ($M_i = TRUE$) ensures that, even if the cause C_i is active, it still has no impact on variable E.

In terms of the deterministic functions f_i introduced above, we can therefore write

$$f_i(c_i, m_i) = TRUE \quad \text{if } c_i = TRUE, m_i = FALSE \tag{14.11}$$

$$= 0 \quad \text{otherwise} \tag{14.12}$$

If we use this interpretation it is immediate to see that these deterministic relationships can be written in probabilistic form as

$$P(X_j = TRUE | C_j = TRUE, M_j = FALSE) = 1 \tag{14.13}$$

$$P(X_j = TRUE | C_j = TRUE, M_j = TRUE) = 0 \tag{14.14}$$

$$P(X_j = TRUE | C_j = FALSE, M_j = TRUE) = 0 \tag{14.15}$$

$$P(X_j = TRUE | C_j = FALSE, M_j = FALSE) = 0 \tag{14.16}$$

This means that for the jth effect to be *TRUE*, its cause C_j certainly has to be *TRUE*. In addition, the associated inhibitor has to be *FALSE*. This probabilistic translation will be used below when we obtain the conditional probabilities $P(E = e | C_1 = c_1, C_2 = c_2, \ldots, C_n = c_n)$ that we are trying to fill in.

From these definitions it is also easy to derive another useful result. Concentrating on one cause, and therefore dropping indices for the moment to lighten notation, let's consider the joint probability $P(X, C, M)$:

$$P(X, C, M) = P(X|C, M)P(C, M)$$

$$= P(X|C, M)P(C)P(M) \tag{14.17}$$

---

[14] To avoid misunderstandings it is essential to understand clearly what this independence entails. We do not mean that the causes are independent. (Whether they are or not depends on the conditional probabilities implied by the net built up to parents in question.) We simply mean that whether cause C_i contributes to the effect, E, is independent of whether there is a contribution from cause C_j.

where the second line follows because of the independence between the cause and its inhibitor. Now that we have the joint probabilities we can calculate any conditional probability we want. In particular, we can calculate $P(X|C)$:

$$P(X|C) = \frac{P(X, C, M) + P\left(X, C, \tilde{M}\right)}{P(C)}$$

$$= \frac{P(X|C, M)P(C)P(M) + P\left(X|C, \tilde{M}\right) P(C)P\left(\tilde{M}\right)}{P(C)}$$

$$= P\left(X|C, \tilde{M}\right) P\left(\tilde{M}\right) = P\left(\tilde{M}\right) \tag{14.18}$$

where the third line follows from Equations (14.13)–(14.16). This tells us that the probability that the jth contribution to the activation of the effect is active ($X_j = T$) given that the cause is *TRUE*, $P(X_j = TRUE|C_j = TRUE)$, is just the probability that the associated inhibitor is *FALSE*:

$$P(X_j = TRUE|C_j = TRUE) = P(M_j = FALSE) \tag{14.19}$$

Intuitively, the auxiliary quantities X_i can therefore be given the interpretation of the impact the ith cause in isolation would have on the effect E.

To complete the causal description of the child–parents relationship in Figures 14.1 and 14.2, we stipulate that the effect variable, E, will be given by a *deterministic* function, $g(\cdot)$, of the intermediate nodes, X_i:

$$e = g(x_1, x_2, \dots, x_n) \tag{14.20}$$

The precise form of the function $g(\cdot)$ depends on the expert's understanding of 'how the world works', i.e., of the relationship between the causes and the effects. For instance, suppose that the expert wanted to assert that the effect E will be *TRUE* only if all the contributory causes, X_i, are *TRUE*. Then the function $g(\cdot)$ (a noisy AND) will be

$$g(x_1, x_2, \dots, x_n) = 1 \quad \text{if } x_1 = x_2 = \dots = x_n = TRUE$$
$$= 0 \quad \text{otherwise} \tag{14.21}$$

If, instead, the expert wanted to state that the effect E will be *TRUE* if at least one of the contributory causes, X_i, is *TRUE*, then the function $g(\cdot)$ (a noisy OR) would be

$$g(x_1, x_2, \dots, x_n) = 0 \quad \text{if } x_1 = x_2 = \dots = x_n = FALSE$$
$$= 1 \quad \text{otherwise} \tag{14.22}$$

Or, again, the expert may want to express her understanding that it takes at least r of the contributory causes to be *TRUE* for the effect to the *TRUE*. This can be expressed as follows (a noisy at-least-r-of-n):

$$g(x_1, x_2, \dots, x_n) = 1 \quad \text{if } \sum_{i=1,n} x_i \geq r$$
$$= 0 \quad \text{otherwise} \tag{14.23}$$

The meaning of the adjective 'noisy' can be clearly seen if we set all the inhibitory variables to be always *FALSE*. In this case, for any i, $c_i = x_i$ and we simply have a deterministic AND, OR, at-least-r-of-n, ... function. For a thorough discussion of the possible functions $g(\cdot)$ that can be handled with this approach, the reader is referred to Jurgelanaite and Lucas (2005, esp. p. 155).

14.5.2 Spelling out the implicit assumptions

A glance at Figure 14.2 may make one fear that we may have simplified the task of providing the conditional probability table for a variable with many parents, but that we have paid a high price in terms of number of nodes. For a number of parents $n = 4$, for instance, the original Bayesian net (including the child) had 5 nodes, but after adding the inhibitors and the auxiliary variables it has 13. However, these nodes are only 'temporary' ones, in the sense that they are only needed in order to build the conditional probability table for the original net using Equations (14.13)–(14.16). Once they have fulfilled their function they can be discarded, and we can revert to the original net.

The structure just described, and whose interpretation is discussed below, is called a Causal Independence Model (which, in turn, is a subclass of Functional Causal Models). Causal independence is a collection of assertions about conditional independence and functional relationships.

The auxiliary net we have built contains several assumptions. Let's spell them out clearly.

Assumption 1. We have assumed, to begin with, that all the inhibitors, M_i, are mutually independent:

$$P(M_k|M_1, M_2, \ldots, M_{k-1}, M_{k+1}, \ldots, M_n) = P(M_k) \qquad (14.24)$$

Assumption 2. We have also assumed that the effect, E, is conditionally independent of the causes and of the inhibitors, given the quantities X_i:

$$P(E|C_i, X_i, M_i) = P(E|X_i) \qquad (14.25)$$

Assumption 3. And finally, given its cause and its inhibitor, we have assumed that each causal contribution X_i is independent of any other causal contribution:

$$P(X_1, X_2, \ldots, X_n|C_1, C_2, \ldots, C_n, M_1, M_2, \ldots, M_n) = \prod_{i=1,n} P(X_i|C_i, M_i)$$

$$(14.26)$$

This is exactly what we meant when we loosely stated that 'causes contribute in an independent manner'.

14.5.3   Obtaining the conditional probabilities

When these assumptions are a reasonable description of reality, then powerful simplifications can be applied, which reduce the number of conditional probability inputs from 2^n to $O(n)$. The reasoning behind this is an extension and generalization of the intuitive considerations we presented in Section 13.6 – intuitive considerations that, not coincidentally, were presented precisely to deal with the case of a child with 'too many' parents.

The general strategy is

1. to start from the joint probability, $P(E = e, C_1 = c_1, \ldots, C_n = c_n, X_1 = x_1, \ldots, X_n = x_n)$;
2. to factorize it using the chain rule into a conditional probability times a joint probability of a combination of *TRUE* and *FALSE* for the causes, C_i:

$$P(E = e, C_1 = c_1, \ldots, C_n = c_n, X_1 = x_1, \ldots, X_n = x_n)$$
$$= P(E = e | C_1 = c_1, \ldots, C_n = c_n, X_1 = x_1, \ldots, X_n = x_n)$$
$$\times P(C_1 = c_1, \ldots, C_n = c_n, X_1 = x_1, \ldots, X_n = x_n) \qquad (14.27)$$

3. to factorize the joint probability $P(C_1 = c_1, \ldots, C_n = c_n, X_1 = x_1, \ldots, X_n = x_n)$ as

$$P(C_1 = c_1, \ldots, C_n = c_n, X_1 = x_1, \ldots, X_n = x_n)$$
$$= P(X_1 = x_1, \ldots, X_n = x_n | C_1 = c_1, \ldots, C_n = c_n)$$
$$\times P(C_1 = c_1, \ldots, C_n = c_n)$$

4. to make use of the independence assumptions highlighted above to simplify the factorizing conditional probability, $P(X_1 = x_1, \ldots, X_n = x_n | C_1 = c_1, \ldots, C_n = c_n)$;
5. to sum over all the possible combination of *TRUE* and *FALSE* for the variables X_i for which the deterministic function $g(\cdot)$ has non-zero value to obtain the joint probability $P(E = e, C_1 = c_1, \ldots, C_n = c_n)$;
6. to divide by the joint probability $P(C_1 = c_1, \ldots, C_n = c_n)$ in order to obtain the desired conditional probability $P(E = e | C_1 = c_1, \ldots, C_n = c_n)$.

The gory details are presented in Appendix 14.B. The crucial steps to remember are the following

Relationship 1:

$$P(X_j = TRUE | C_j = TRUE, M_j = FALSE) = 1 \qquad (14.28)$$
$$P(X_j = TRUE | C_j = TRUE, M_j = TRUE) = 0 \qquad (14.29)$$
$$P(X_j = TRUE | C_j = FALSE, M_j = TRUE) = 0 \qquad (14.30)$$
$$P(X_j = TRUE | C_j = FALSE, M_j = FALSE) = 0 \qquad (14.31)$$

Relationship 2:

$$P(X_j = FALSE | C_j = FALSE, M_j = FALSE) = 1 \qquad (14.32)$$

$$P(X_j = FALSE | C_j = FALSE, M_j = TRUE) = 1 \qquad (14.33)$$

Relationship 3:

$$P(X_j = TRUE | C_j = TRUE) = P(M_j = FALSE) \qquad (14.34)$$

All the rest is plain, if rather tedious, sailing.

14.5.4 A few important cases

Different specifications of the logical function $g(\cdot)$ give different expressions for the conditional probabilities. However, in all cases we obtain the same result: when causal independence applies, we can reduce the task of assigning 2^n conditional probabilities to the much more manageable task of assigning n conditional probabilities. This can make an enormous difference, not just in the elicitation phase, but also in focusing the attention in the sensitivity analysis phase on the conditional probabilities that 'really matter'.

As for the specific form of the conditional probabilities, define first $P(M_i) \equiv 1 - \pi_i$. Call $\mathcal{D}$ the subset of $(X_1, X_2, \ldots, X_n)$ that makes the logical function $g(\mathcal{D}) = TRUE$ (i.e., assume the value 1). Then application of the strategy outlined above with the sum in step 5 carried out over the elements in the set $\mathcal{D}$ gives the following.

Noisy OR   For n causes, consider the $2^n = J$ combinations of *TRUE* and *FALSE* for the causes. Denote by $\{C\}_j$, $j = 1, 2, \ldots, J$, the jth combination of *TRUE* and *FALSE* causes. Define $\mathcal{E}_j$ to be the set made up of the indices of the causes which are *TRUE* in the jth combination of causes.

In the case of a noisy OR, the effect is *TRUE* if at least one of the causes is active. Then

$$g(X_1, X_2, \ldots, X_n) = OR(X_1, X_2, \ldots, X_n) \qquad (14.35)$$

and we can write (using shorthand notation):

$$P(e | \{C\}_j) = 1 - \prod_{i \in \mathcal{E}_j} P(M_i) \equiv 1 - \prod_{i \in \mathcal{E}_j} (1 - \pi_i) \qquad (14.36)$$

where the product is over those causes which are *TRUE*.

Noisy AND   If all the causes must be activated for the effect to be *TRUE* we are in the case of the noisy AND. In this case we have

$$P(e | C_1, C_2, \ldots, C_n) = \prod_{i:1,n} \pi_i \qquad (14.37)$$

Other cases (or, of snakes and serums)   For other cases see Jurgelenaite and Lucas (2005, pp. 155–156) (for the exclusive OR and the bi-implication) or Zagorecki and Druzdzel (2002, Sect. 6) (for the noisy average).

To see how the exclusive noisy OR may come in handy, consider the following example. Suppose that, if John is bitten by the dangerous ExOr snake, he will die with 90% probability. (Death happens because the blood is thickened by the venom.) If he is given the serum (which thins the blood) after the snake bite, then his survival probability is 80%. However, if he is given the serum without a snake bite, he will die with probability of 60%. The interplay between the causes is now far more complex than in the case of the inclusive noisy OR or the noisy AND.

Moving from snakes to the economic sphere, a similar type of dependence could occur in a situation like this: consider a tightening of the Fed rates in an economic environment when the inflationary outlook is uncertain. The tightening may well be beneficial to the economy if inflationary pressure is indeed building up, but it would be detrimental to the economy if inappropriately applied (because, say, the inflation reading was a 'blip', and the economy was actually sluggish).

To present another case where a subtler relationship than a noisy OR or a noisy AND may be justified, think of the following financial scenario. The Fed is reluctantly considering a further round of quantitative easing: let's call it QE*n*. We are looking at a node associated with the S&P 500, with two parents: the GDP number and the non-farm-payroll number. Now, a bad reading for GDP growth would be negative for the S&P. So would a bad employment number. But a bad GDP *and* a bad employment number could increase the probability of an equity rally, because they could push the Fed into a new round of quantitative easing. For how to handle a type of dependence like this, see Jurgelenaite and Lucas (2005, pp. 155–156).

These more 'exotic' dependencies are interesting, but relatively rare, and therefore we do not pursue this topic in detail, and just point the reader in the direction of the references above. By far the most common case encountered in practice is the noisy OR.

14.5.5   Where do the probabilities of the inhibitors being active come from?
When we use inhibitors in the noisy OR, we are in the situation where, if a single 'pure' cause were present, the effect would certainly be activated. As we observe that this is not always the case, we introduce the 'fiction' of an inhibitor. See Pearl (1986, esp. pp. 242, 270) for a discussion of the importance and pervasiveness of this mental construct.

As the expressions above indicate, the heart of the parameter specification for casual independence lies in the ability to assign the probability that the effect may not be activated even if a single cause may be active (while the other causes are inactive). This is naturally linked to the probability of the inhibitor being in the state *TRUE*.

When the probabilities are assigned from empirical data, this often brings in the topic of counterfactuals (see, e.g., in this respect Weisberg (2010) and Angrist and Pischke (2009)). When the probabilities are assigned subjectively, structural models (or glorified rules of thumb) come to the fore.

14.5.6 A simple example

Consider the canonical alarm example (see, e.g., Pearl 1986), in which the alarm can be activated either by a burglar or by an earthquake. Let $A = TRUE$ (or just A) denote the alarm being activated, and C_1 and C_2 the burglar and earthquake causes, respectively. Suppose that we have directly assigned (perhaps on the basis of repeated reliability tests of the alarm) the following conditional probabilities

$$P(A|C_1, C_2) = 0.90$$
$$P(A|C_1, \tilde{C}_2) = 0.80$$
$$P(A|\tilde{C}_1, C_2) = 0.70$$
$$P(A|\tilde{C}_1, \tilde{C}_2) = 0.05 \tag{14.38}$$

Given their 'exogenous' and 'objective' nature, these conditional probabilities need not reflect casual independence. They just are what they are. We want to see what we would obtain if we *imposed* causal independence. Since the alarm can be activated either by a burglar or by an earthquake, and since both possible causes may fail to produce the effect, doing so is at least reasonable. In particular, the situation seems to be a promising candidate for handling by means of a noisy (inclusive) OR, and by invoking causal independence. What would we obtain for the conditional probabilities if we did that?

To answer the question, note that the quantity $P(A|C_1, \tilde{C}_2)$ gives the probability of the effect given that only the burglar cause is active. Similar considerations apply to $P(A|\tilde{C}_1, C_2)$. Let us then write

$$P(X_i|C_i) = P(\tilde{M}_i) \equiv \pi_i, \quad i = 1, 2$$

Since we have access to the reliability studies of the alarm mentioned above, we have the two doubly conditioned probabilities $P(A|C_1, \tilde{C}_2) = 0.80$ and $P(A|\tilde{C}_1, C_2) = 0.70$, i.e., the probability of the alarm being activated if only one cause is active. However, we have no access to the doubly conditioned probability $P(A|C_1, C_2)$. Not knowing how to assign it, we decide to invoke causal independence.

We are going to obtain from first principles the equations required for the noisy OR in this simple case.

We want to calculate $P(A|C_1, C_2)$. This is given by

$$P(A|C_1, C_2) = \frac{\sum_{x,m} P(A, C_1, C_2, X_1, X_2, M_1, M_2)}{P(C_1, C_2)}$$

Let's therefore begin by calculating the numerator, $P(A, C_1, C_2, X_1, X_2, M_1, M_2)$:

$$P(A, C_1, C_2, X_1, X_2, M_1, M_2)$$
$$= P(A|C_1, C_2, X_1, X_2, M_1, M_2)P(X_1, X_2, M_1, M_2, C_1, C_2)$$
$$= P(A|X_1, X_2)P(X_1, X_2, M_1, M_2, C_1, C_2)$$
$$= P(A|X_1, X_2)P(X_1, X_2|M_1, M_2, C_1, C_2)P(M_1, M_2, C_1, C_2)$$
$$= P(A|X_1, X_2)P(X_1, X_2|M_1, M_2, C_1, C_2)P(C_1, C_2)P(M_1)P(M_2)$$
$$= P(A|X_1, X_2)P(X_1|M_1, C_1)P(X_2|M_2, C_2)P(C_1, C_2)P(M_1)P(M_2)$$
$$= g(X_1, X_2)P(X_1|M_1, C_1)P(X_2|M_2, C_2)P(C_1, C_2)P(M_1)P(M_2) \quad (14.39)$$

where, in the last line, the $g(\cdot)$ function represents the OR operator.

Then we have

$$P(A|C_1, C_2) = \frac{\sum_{x,m} P(A, C_1, C_2, X_1, X_2, M_1, M_2)}{P(C_1, C_2)}$$

$$= \frac{\sum_{x,m} g(X_1, X_2)P(X_1|M_1, C_1)P(X_2|M_2, C_2)P(C_1, C_2)P(M_1)P(M_2)}{P(C_1, C_2)}$$

$$\times \sum_{x,m} g(X_1, X_2)P(X_1|M_1, C_1)P(X_2|M_2, C_2)P(M_1)P(M_2) \quad (14.40)$$

In order to calculate the required sums it is useful to make use of the following aide memoir:

$$P(X_i|M_i, C_i)P(M_i) = 0 \quad (14.41)$$
$$P(\tilde{X}_i|M_i, C_i)P(M_i) = P(M_i) \quad (14.42)$$
$$P(X_i|\tilde{M}_i, C_i)P(\tilde{M}_i) = P(C_i)P(\tilde{M}_i) \quad (14.43)$$
$$P(\tilde{X}_i|\tilde{M}_i, C_i)P(\tilde{M}_i) = [1 - P(C_i)]P(\tilde{M}_i) \quad (14.44)$$

where

- the first relationship holds because, if the inhibitor is *TRUE*, the auxiliary variable is always *FALSE*;
- the second relationship holds because if the inhibitor M_i is *TRUE*, X_i is always *FALSE*, irrespective of the logical value of the cause;
- the third relationship holds because if the inhibitor is not active, then X_i will be *TRUE* if its associated cause, C_i, is *TRUE*;
- the fourth relationship holds because if the inhibitor is not active, then X_i will be *FALSE* if its associated cause, C_i, is *FALSE*.

Then we can build Table 14.1.

We note that there are just five non-zero terms (the 7th, 10th, 11th, 12th and 15th). Consider the case where both causes are *TRUE*. If we set $C_1 = C_2 = TRUE$ the terms

Table 14.1 *Auxiliary table used for the calculations in the text*

$g(X_1, X_2)$	$P(X_1\|M_1, C_1)P(M_1)$	$P(X_2\|M_2, C_2)P(M_2)$	X_1	M_1	X_2	M_2
1	0	0	T	T	T	T
1	$P(M_1)$	0	F	T	T	T
1	$P(C_1)P(\tilde{M}_1)$	0	T	F	T	T
1	$[1 - P(C_1)]P(\tilde{M}_1)$	0	F	F	T	T
1	0	$P(M_2)$	T	T	F	T
0	$P(M_1)$	$P(M_2)$	F	T	F	T
1	$P(C_1)P(\tilde{M}_1)$	$P(M_2)$	T	F	F	T
0	$[1 - P(C_1)]P(\tilde{M}_1)$	$P(M_2)$	F	F	F	T
1	0	$P(C_2)P(\tilde{M}_2)$	T	T	T	F
1	$P(M_1)$	$P(C_2)P(\tilde{M}_2)$	F	T	T	F
1	$P(C_1)P(\tilde{M}_1)$	$P(C_2)P(\tilde{M}_2)$	T	F	T	F
1	$[1 - P(C_1)]P(\tilde{M}_1)$	$P(C_2)P(\tilde{M}_2)$	F	F	T	F
1	0	$[1 - P(C_2)]P(\tilde{M}_2)$	T	T	F	F
0	$P(M_1)$	$[1 - P(C_2)]P(\tilde{M}_2)$	F	T	F	F
1	$P(C_1)P(\tilde{M}_1)$	$[1 - P(C_2)]P(\tilde{M}_2)$	T	F	F	F
0	$[1 - P(C_1)]P(\tilde{M}_1)$	$[1 - P(C_2)]P(\tilde{M}_2)$	F	F	F	F

$[1 - P(C_i)]P(\tilde{M}_i)$, $i = 1, 2$, are zero. Then we are left with three terms:

$$P(C_1)P(\tilde{M}_1)P(M_2) = P(\tilde{M}_1)P(M_2) = [1 - P(M_1)]P(M_2) \quad (14.45)$$

$$P(C_2)P(\tilde{M}_2)P(M_1) = P(\tilde{M}_2)P(M_1) = [1 - P(M_2)]P(M_1) \quad (14.46)$$

$$P(C_1)P(\tilde{M}_1)P(C_2)P(\tilde{M}_2) = [1 - P(M_1)][1 - P(M_2)] \quad (14.47)$$

After adding the three terms we obtain the relationship

$$P(A|C_1, C_2) = 1 - \prod_{i=1,2} P(M_i) = 1 - \prod_{i=1,2}(1 - \pi_i) \quad (14.48)$$

as required.

Application of Equation (14.48) to this simple case then gives

$$P(A|C_1, C_2) = 1 - [1 - \pi_1][1 - \pi_2] = 0.94 \quad (14.49)$$

$$P(A|C_1, \tilde{C}_2) = 1 - [1 - \pi_1] = 0.80 \quad (14.50)$$

$$P(A|\tilde{C}_1, C_2) = 1 - [1 - \pi_2] = 0.70 \quad (14.51)$$

$$P(A|\tilde{C}_1, \tilde{C}_2) = 0 \quad (14.52)$$

When we compare the conditional probabilities obtained invoking causal indepen-dence with the ones that were observed in the real world, the only difference can be in the probability of the alarm being activated given that both the burglar and the earthquake event happened. In this simple example, of course, this is no coincidence.

If we had had more causes, and only had access to the singly conditioned probabilities $P(A|\widetilde{C}_1, \ldots, \widetilde{C}_{j-1}, C_j, , \widetilde{C}_{j+1}, \ldots, \widetilde{C}_n)$, then all the higher-order conditioned probabilities could in general be different. From 'reality' (to which we had no access), the right answer was $P(A|C_1, C_2) = 0.90$; invoking causal independence we obtained $P(A|C_1, C_2) = 0.94$.

What conclusions can we draw from this difference? In this stylized case, the conclusion is that in the real world the two causes are not exactly causally independent, and that the degree of causal dependence was such as to decrease the probability of the alarm being activated when both causes were *TRUE*.

This is all well and good, but in a real-life application, of course, we do not have the luxury of comparing the highly conditioned probabilities obtained invoking causal independence with the 'correct answer'. (If we could, we would not have embarked on this tortuous journey in the first place.)

What we *can* do however, is to ask ourselves whether, on the basis of our expert knowledge and the structural models at our disposal, we can say that the independence conditions that lie at the heart of the approach are closely approximated. If they were *exactly* satisfied, then, of course, causal independence could be used in a normative manner, by telling us what the high-order conditioned probabilities *must* be like, and any other assignment would be logically wrong.

14.5.7 Leak causes

In this section we comment on the other probability for which invoking causal independence as introduced above will, in general, give a different answer: the probability of neither cause being active. We obtained from the casual independence condition $P(A|\widetilde{C}_1, \widetilde{C}_2) = 0$, but the 'true' conditional probability was $P(A|\widetilde{C}_1, \widetilde{C}_2) = 0.05$. This is a direct consequence of the fact that the noisy-OR condition requires at least one of the direct causes to be active for the effect to have a non-zero probability of being true. But, in general, there could be other causes at play – causes that, for the sake of parsimony we have not included in our Bayesian net, but that could activate the alarm. Henrion (1988) shows that this problem can be fixed in the case of the noisy OR by introducing the idea of a 'leak cause' or 'background probability', π_0.[15] When this background probability is introduced, the conditional probabilities are replaced by

$$P(A|C_1 = c_1, C_2 = c_2, \ldots, C_n = c_n) = 1 - (1 - \pi_0) \prod_{k \in \mathcal{E}_k} \frac{1 - \pi_k}{1 - \pi_0} \qquad (14.53)$$

14.5.8 Extensions

The treatment above only scratches the surface of causal independence. There are many more special sets of assumptions that give rise to different net configurations and, often,

---

[15] See Henrion (1988, p. 136).

to more efficient computation. These more specific forms of causal independence go under the names of Amechanistic Causal Independence (see, e.g., Heckerman and Breese 1994), Decomposable Causal Independence (see, e.g., Heckerman and Breese 1994) and Temporal Causal Independence (Heckerman (1993). However, the price to pay for the more efficient and cleverer algorithms is that the conditions of applicability are correspondingly reduced.

For related treatments, the reader can see Jurgelanaite and Lucas (2005) who deal in detail with the functions we have referred to as $f(\cdot)$ and $g(\cdot)$ above. In our treatment we assumed that the effect could only be generated, if at all, by one of the specified causes. Jensen and Nielsen (2007) deal with the case of a background cause in their treatment of noisy functional dependence (another name for causal independence) (see their Section 3.3.2).

Appendix 14.A

In this appendix we show how to derive the Maximum-Entropy distributions associated with two simple cases of knowledge about the distribution, namely knowledge about its range or knowledge about its expectation. The point of the derivations is to show the general procedure, and to suggest how this procedure can be extended to other situations (e.g., knowledge about the expectation and variance of the distribution).

14.A.1   *Knowledge about the range*

The simplest type of information that the expert may have is simply that the values of a random variable should be between, say, a and b. She therefore considers probability densities which are non-zero only over the interval $[a, b]$. She wants to maximize entropy, $H(p)$,

$$H(p) = -\int_a^b p(x)\ln[p(x)]dx \qquad (14.54)$$

subject to the conditions

$$p(x) > 0 \qquad (14.55)$$

$$\int_a^b p(x)dx = 1 \qquad (14.56)$$

We note that $H(p)$ is a functional, i.e., it is a mapping from a set of functions to the real numbers. The tools required in order to carry out the constrained maximization of a functional are functional derivatives and Lagrange multipliers. More specifically, the objective function, $J(p)$, becomes

$$J(p; \lambda_0) = -\int_a^b p(x)\ln[p(x)]dx + \lambda_0\left(\int_a^b p(x)dx - 1\right) \qquad (14.57)$$

We drop from the notation the parametric dependence on the Lagrange multiplier, and we carry out a functional differentiation with respect to $p(x)$ to obtain

$$\frac{\partial}{\partial p(x)} J(p) = -(\ln[p(x)] + 1) + \lambda_0 \qquad (14.58)$$

Setting to 0 the derivative with respect to $p(x)$, and solving for $p(x)$ gives

$$\frac{\partial}{\partial p(x)} J(p) = 0 \Longrightarrow p(x) = \exp[\lambda_0 + 1] \qquad (14.59)$$

And, of course, setting to zero the derivative with respect to λ_0 simply recovers the constraint,

$$\frac{\partial}{\partial \lambda_0} J(p) = 0 \Longrightarrow \int_a^b p(x) dx = 1 \qquad (14.60)$$

as it should.

Substituting the probability density from Equation (14.59) in the constraint equation (14.60) gives

$$\int_a^b \exp[\lambda_0 + 1] dx = 1 \Longrightarrow \lambda_0 = \ln\left[\frac{1}{(b-a)}\right] - 1$$

and therefore

$$p(x) = \exp[\lambda_0 + 1] = \exp\left[\ln\frac{1}{(b-a)}\right] = \frac{1}{(b-a)}$$

So, as we could have probably guessed without doing any calculations, the least prejudicial probability density compatible with the minimal knowledge about the non-zero domain of the random variable is the density that uniformly 'spreads' the probability over the interval:

$$p(x) = \frac{1}{(b-a)} \qquad \text{for } a \leq x \leq b$$
$$= 0 \qquad \text{otherwise}$$

Verifying that the solution found is neither a minimum nor an inflection point is straightforward, and simply entails taking the second (functional) derivatives with respect to $p(x)$.

14.A.2 Knowledge about the expectation
Suppose that the expert knows that the possible values of the random variable at play can only assume non-negative values and also knows the value of its finite mean, say, μ. Then, the normalization condition for the density function now reads:

$$\int_0^\infty p(x) dx = 1$$

To this we must add the condition about the expectation:

$$\int_0^\infty xp(x)dx = \mu \tag{14.61}$$

This gives rise to the following objective function, parametrized by two Lagrange multipliers:

$$J(p; \lambda_0, \lambda_1) = -\int_0^\infty p(x)\ln[p(x)]dx + \lambda_0 \left(\int_0^\infty p(x)dx - 1\right)$$

$$+ \lambda_1 \left(\int_0^\infty xp(x)dx - \mu\right) \tag{14.62}$$

The functional derivative with respect to $p(x)$ now gives

$$\frac{\partial}{\partial p(x)} J(p) = \frac{\partial}{\partial p(x)} \left[-\int_0^\infty p(x)\ln[p(x)]dx + \lambda_0 \left(\int_0^\infty p(x)dx - 1\right) \right.$$

$$\left. + \lambda_1 \left(\int_0^\infty xp(x)dx - \mu\right) \right] = -(\ln[p(x)] + 1) + \lambda_0 + \lambda_1 x$$

Setting this to zero gives

$$\frac{\partial}{\partial p(x)} J(p) = 0 \implies \ln[p(x)] + 1 = \lambda_0 + \lambda_1 x$$

Solving for $p(x)$ gives

$$\frac{\partial}{\partial p(x)} J(p) = 0 \implies \ln[p(x)] = \lambda_0 + \lambda_1 x - 1 \implies p(x) = \exp(\lambda_0 - 1 + \lambda_1 x)$$

$$\tag{14.63}$$

We now make use of the two constraints to obtain

$$\int_0^\infty p(x)dx = 1 \implies \int_0^\infty \exp(\lambda_0 - 1 + \lambda_1 x)dx = 1$$

$$\implies \int_0^\infty \exp(\lambda_1 x)dx = \frac{1}{\exp(\lambda_0 - 1)} \tag{14.64}$$

and

$$\int_0^\infty xp(x)dx = \mu \implies \int_0^\infty \exp(\lambda_0 - 1 + \lambda_1 x)xdx = \mu$$

$$\implies \frac{\mu}{\exp(\lambda_0 - 1)} = \int_0^\infty \exp(\lambda_1 x)xdx \tag{14.65}$$

This gives

$$\frac{\int_0^\infty \exp(\lambda_1 x)xdx}{\int_0^\infty \exp(\lambda_1 x)dx} = \mu \tag{14.66}$$

Evaluating the integrals, solving for λ_1, and then for λ_0 gives the exponential distribution:

$$p(x) = \frac{1}{\mu} \exp \left[-\frac{x}{\mu} \right] \tag{14.67}$$

14.A.3 Knowledge about the expectation and the variance

Following exactly the same steps outlined above it is easy, if somewhat tedious, to show that the Maximum-Entropy distribution arising if we know only the expectation and the variance of a distribution is the Gaussian.

Appendix 14.B

Our goal is to obtain the conditional probabilities $P(E = e | C_1 = c_1, \ldots, C_n = c_n)$. Let's begin with the joint probability, $P(E = e, C_1 = c_1, \ldots, C_n = c_n, X_1 = x_1, \ldots, X_n = x_n, M_1 = m_1, \ldots, M_n = m_n)$, which can be written as

$$P(E = e, C_1 = c_1, \ldots, C_n = c_n, X_1 = x_1, \ldots, X_n = x_n, M_1 = m_1, \ldots, M_n = m_n)$$

$$= P(E = e | C_1 = c_1, \ldots, C_n = c_n, X_1 = x_1, \ldots, X_n = x_n, M_1 = m_1, \ldots, M_n = m_n)$$

$$\times P(X_1 = x_1, \ldots, X_n = x_n, M_1 = m_1, \ldots, M_n = m_n, C_1 = c_1, \ldots, C_n = c_n)$$

$$\tag{14.68}$$

Given our assumptions and the structure of the augmented net, the event E is conditionally independent of both the causes C_i and the inhibitors, M_i, given the 'stand-alone contributions', X_i. So the first term (the conditional probability) on the right-hand side of Equation (14.68) becomes:

$$P(E = e | C_1 = c_1, \ldots, C_n = c_n, X_1 = x_1, X_n = x_n, M_1 = m_1, \ldots, M_n = m_n)$$

$$= P(E = e | X_1 = x_1, \ldots, X_n = x_n) \tag{14.69}$$

As for second term on the right-hand side of Equation (14.68), i.e., the probability $P(X_1 = x_1, \ldots, X_n = x_n, M_1 = m_1, \ldots, M_n = m_n, C_1 = c_1, \ldots, C_n = c_n)$, we can decompose it as follows

$$P(X_1 = x_1, \ldots, X_n = x_n, M_1 = m_1, \ldots, M_n = m_n, C_1 = c_1, \ldots, C_n = c_n)$$

$$= P(X_1 = x_1, \ldots, X_n = x_n | M_1 = m_1, \ldots, M_n = m_n, C_1 = c_1, \ldots, C_n = c_n)$$

$$\times P(M_1 = m_1, \ldots, M_n = m_n, C_1 = c_1, \ldots, C_n = c_n)$$

$$= P(X_1 = x_1, \ldots, X_n = x_n | M_1 = m_1, \ldots, M_n = m_n, C_1 = c_1, \ldots, C_n = c_n)$$

$$\times P(C_1 = c_1, \ldots, C_n = c_n) \prod_{j=1,n} P(M_j = m_j) \tag{14.70}$$

where to obtain the last line we have used independence between the cause variables C_i and the inhibitors, M_i, and between all the inhibitors.

Moving to the term $P(X_1 = x_1, \ldots, X_n = x_n | M_1 = m_1, \ldots, M_n = m_n, C_1 = c_1, \ldots, C_n = c_n)$, we invoke the independence of each contribution, X_i, given its cause and inhibitor to obtain

$$P(X_1 = x_1, \ldots, X_n = x_n | M_1 = m_1, \ldots, M_n = m_n, C_1 = c_1, \ldots, C_n = c_n)$$
$$= \prod_{j=1,n} P(X_j = x_j | M_j = m_j, C_j = c_j) \tag{14.71}$$

We can therefore write:

$$P(X_1 = x_1, \ldots, X_n = x_n, M_1 = m_1, \ldots, M_n = m_n, C_1 = c_1, \ldots, C_n = c_n)$$
$$= \left[\prod_{j=1,n} P(X_j = x_j | M_j = m_j, C_j = c_j) P(M_j = m_j) \right]$$
$$\times P(C_1 = c_1, \ldots, C_n = c_n) \tag{14.72}$$

Now, the quantities $P(E = e | X_1 = x_1, X_n = x_n)$ are just the result of the application of the deterministic function $g(\cdot)$ to the various combinations of contributory causes, X_i. Taking some liberties with notation, we can write

$$P(E = e | X_1 = x_1, \ldots, X_n = x_n) = g(X_1 = x_1, \ldots, X_n = x_n) \tag{14.73}$$

As for the quantities $P(X_j = x_j | M_j = m_j, C_j = c_j)$, these are given by the deterministic relationships (14.11) (or, equivalently, (14.13) to (14.16)):

$$P(X_j = x_j | M_j = m_j, C_j = c_j) = h_j(X_j = x_j, M_j = m_j, C_j = c_j) \tag{14.74}$$

with

$$h_j(X_j = x_j, M_j = m_j, C_j = c_j) = f_j(M_j = m_j, C_j = c_j) \quad \text{if } x_j = TRUE \tag{14.75}$$

$$h_j(X_j = x_j, M_j = m_j, C_j = c_j) = 1 - f_j(M_j = m_j, C_j = c_j) \quad \text{if } x_j = FALSE \tag{14.76}$$

Putting together the pieces obtained so far we therefore obtain for the joint probability $P(E = e, C_1 = c_1, \ldots, C_n = c_n, X_1 = x_1, \ldots, X_n = x_n, M_1 = m_1, \ldots, M_n = m_n)$:

$$P(E = e, C_1 = c_1, \ldots, C_n = c_n, X_1 = x_1, \ldots, X_n = x_n, M_1 = m_1, \ldots, M_n = m_n)$$
$$= g(X_1 = x_1, \ldots, X_n = x_n)[h_j(X_j = x_j, M_j = m_j, C_j = c_j) P(M_j = m_j)]$$
$$\times P(C_1 = c_1, \ldots, C_n = c_n)$$

From this joint probability let's marginalize (sum over) the variables X_i and M_i, to give for $P(E = e, C_1 = c_1, \ldots, C_n = c_n)$:

$$P(E = e, C_1 = c_1, \ldots, C_n = c_n) = \sum_{\substack{x=T,F \\ m=T,F}} g(X_1 = x_1, \ldots, X_n = x_n)$$

$$\times \left[\prod_{j=1,n} h_j(X_j = x_j, M_j = m_j, C_j = c_j) \right]$$

$$\times P(C_1 = c_1, \ldots, C_n = c_n)$$

However, we also know that

$$P(E = e, C_1 = c_1, \ldots, C_n = c_n)$$
$$= P(E = e|C_1 = c_1, \ldots, C_n = c_n)P(C_1 = c_1, \ldots, C_n = c_n) \quad (14.77)$$

Therefore, after remembering that

$$e = g(x_1, x_2, \ldots x_n) \quad (14.78)$$

that

$$P(X_j = TRUE|C_j = TRUE, M_j = FALSE) = 1 \quad (14.79)$$

$$P(X_j = TRUE|C_j = TRUE, M_j = TRUE) = 0 \quad (14.80)$$

$$P(X_j = TRUE|C_j = FALSE, M_j = TRUE) = 0 \quad (14.81)$$

$$P(X_j = TRUE|C_j = FALSE, M_j = FALSE) = 0 \quad (14.82)$$

and after cancelling terms $P(C_1 = c_1, \ldots, C_n = c_n)$, we finally obtain

$$P(E = e|C_1 = c_1, \ldots, C_n = c_n)$$
$$= \sum_{\substack{x=T,F \\ m_j=T,F}} P(E = e|X_1 = x_1, X_2 = x_2, \ldots, X_n = x_n)$$

$$\times \prod_{j=1,n} P(X_j = x_j|C_j = c_j, M_j = m_j)P(M_j = m_j) \quad (14.83)$$

$$= \sum_{\substack{x=T,F \\ m_j=T,F}} g(X_1 = x_1, \ldots, X_n = x_n)$$

$$\times \left[\prod_{j=1,n} h_j(X_j = x_j, M_j = m_j, C_j = c_j)P(M_j = m_j) \right] \quad (14.84)$$

Looking at Equation (14.84) one can see that, to compute the desired conditional probabilities, the expert has to provide the marginal probabilities for the inhibitory variables M_i, $P(M_j = m_j)$. This is where the subjective understanding and domain knowledge of the expert comes in: given the interpretation suggested above, for each parent i the expert has to assign for $P(M_i)$ the probability that the cause is true, but, for some reason, it does not exert its effect on the event E, $(P(M_i) = P(X_j = FALSE|C_j = TRUE) = P(M_j = TRUE))$; or, equivalently, she has to assign for $P(\tilde{M}_i)$ the probability that the cause is true but it does not exert its contribution to the effect, E. Very often this can be a relatively easy task. When it is, the cognitive savings afforded by the construction just presented are substantial.

15 Additional more advanced topics

In this chapter we look at a number of additional tools that can help in dealing with large or complex Bayesian nets. Again, we are only scratching the surface of a vast topic, and we are guided in our selective choice by our expectations of the problems the typical asset manager is likely to encounter.

15.1 Efficient computation

In this section we assume that we have assigned (at least tentatively) all the required conditional probabilities to define the Bayesian net, and that, using the Master Equation, we can therefore obtain the joint probabilities for all the possible values of the nodes. Once we have reached the final leaves and we are about to embark on the optimization we are typically interested only in the joint probabilities of the market risk factors (i.e., the variables associated with the leaves themselves). This requires 'integrating out' a large number of variables. Doing so by 'brute force' is inefficient. We therefore present a method for variable elimination from Murphy (2001) (a brief tutorial that we warmly recommend, and which we follow closely in the next subsection).

We note in passing that repeated marginalization of variables is also required when we calculate conditional probabilities other than those in the Master Equation. We may want to do so in order to check the reasonableness of the Bayesian net during its construction. See, for instance, the discussion in Chapter 16. The same need to calculate non-canonical conditional probabilities can arise when we do Maximum-Entropy optimization, or when we calculate the sensitivity of outputs to uncertain inputs. For all these applications an algorithm, such as the one presented below, to perform the required sums efficiently can be useful.

15.1.1 Pushing sums in

Consider the problem of obtaining the marginal distribution, $P(X_4)$, of variable X_4, given the joint distribution, $p(X_1, X_2, X_3, X_4)$, of variables X_1, X_2, X_3 and X_4. The

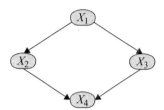

Figure 15.1 The Bayesian net discussed in the text to illustrate the technique of 'pushing the sums in'.

brute-force approach would be to perform the following sums

$$P(X_4 = x_4) = \sum_{x_1 x_2 x_3} p(X_1 = x_1, X_2 = x_2, X_3 = x_3, X_4 = x_4) \tag{15.1}$$

However, if we have built a Bayesian net, we have implicitly specified conditional independencies that can be exploited when factorizing the joint probabilities. Consider for instance the simple net shown in Figure 15.1.

For this net we can write

$$P(X_4 = x_4) = \sum_{x_1 x_2 x_3} P(X_1 = x_1)P(X_2 = x_2|X_1 = x_1)P(X_3 = x_3|X_1 = x_1)$$

$$\times P(X_4 = x_4|X_2 = x_2, X_3 = x_3)$$

$$= \sum_{x_1} P(X_1 = x_1) \sum_{x_2 x_3} P(X_2 = x_2|X_1 = x_1)P(X_3 = x_3|X_1 = x_1)$$

$$\times P(X_4 = x_4|X_2 = x_2, X_3 = x_3) \tag{15.2}$$

This can be re-written as

$$P(X_4 = x_4) = \sum_{x_1} P(X_1 = x_1) \sum_{x_2} P(X_2 = x_2|X_1 = x_1)Term_1(x_1, x_4, x_2)$$

with

$$Term_1(x_1, x_4, x_2) = \sum_{x_3} P(X_3 = x_3|X_1 = x_1)P(X_4 = x_4|X_2 = x_2, X_3 = x_3) \tag{15.3}$$

We can continue this way, by writing

$$P(X_4 = x_4) = \sum_{x_1} P(X_1 = x_1)Term_2(x_1, x_4) \tag{15.4}$$

with

$$Term_2(x_1, x_4) = \sum_{x_2} P(X_2 = x_2|X_1 = x_1)Term_1(x_1, x_4, x_2) \tag{15.5}$$

A glance at the procedure explains why the technique is called 'pushing the sums in': we keep in the 'outer loop(s)' the root variable(s) for which only the marginal(s) are required, and we work our way in (and down the tree). In detail, the magic of pushing the sums in works as follows.

- The second line of Equation (15.2) requires 4 multiplications, the results of which are added 2^3 times. This gives 32 operations. In general we also have to compute $P(\widetilde{X}_4)$, but this is easy because, for Boolean variables, $P(\widetilde{X}_4) = 1 - P(X_4)$. So, in total we require 33 operations.
- By splitting the problem using the techniques of pushing the sums in we have
  - 2 operations for Equation (15.5): one multiplication and one addition;
  - 2 operations for Equation (15.4);
  - $2 \times 4 = 8$ operations for the RHS of Equation (15.2);
  - one operation for $P(\widetilde{X}_4) = 1 - P(X_4)$.

  In total we therefore have 13 operations, instead of the 33 required for the brute-force approach.

As usual, the advantage may not appear overwhelming for such a small-size example, but it quickly becomes substantial for large nets.

There are deep links between this simple technique and more advanced algorithms, such as the Fast Fourier Transform (with which we are reasonably familiar), and the Viterbi decoding method (with which our familiarity is passing at best). Therefore, in keeping with Leopardi's quote that opens this chapter, we refer the interested reader to McEliece and Aji (2000), and Kschischang *et al.* (2001).

15.2 Size constraints: Monte Carlo

It can happen that a scenario requires too many nodes for our rather brute-force techniques to be up to the task. As usual, when it comes to sampling from a high-dimensional distribution, Monte-Carlo techniques can almost invariably be of great help. We do not claim that, *in the case of Bayesian nets*, Monte-Carlo sampling is the most efficient, or perhaps even a particularly efficient, technique to overcome the dimensionality curse. However, it is extremely easy (indeed, almost trivial) to implement, and can provide a nice intermediate tool to use when brute-force use of the Master Equation becomes impractical, but the complexity of the problem does not warrant the use of the really heavy-duty (and relatively complex) weaponry developed to deal with hundreds or thousands of variables – usually in diagnostic applications.[1]

To illustrate the idea behind using Monte-Carlo simulations for Bayesian nets we can refer to the net in Figure 15.2. For such a simple net, of course, we do not need Monte-Carlo sampling at all. However, we keep the example simple for ease of presentation.

We are going to carry out a number, N_{sim}, of 'simulations'. Let's start from the first. We begin, as usual, from the root. Since the root has no parents, its conditional probability table is just made up of its marginal probability. Let's call this $P(A)$. We

---

[1] For a thoughtful discussion of some aspects of Monte-Carlo techniques tailored to the Bayesian-net applications at hand we refer the reader to Coca (2011).

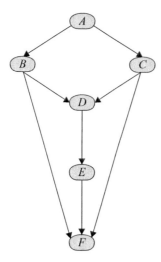

Figure 15.2 The Bayesian net used to discuss the Monte-Carlo application discussed in the text.

now draw a random number, u_A, from the [0 1] uniform distribution: $u_A \sim \mathcal{U}(0, 1)$. If $u_A > P(A)$, we say that in the first simulation variable A was TRUE. If not, then we say that it was FALSE. For the sake of concreteness, let's assume that, in the first simulation, $A = FALSE$.

We now move to node B, which has one parent, and two non-trivial entries in its conditional probability table ($P(B|A)$ and $P(B|\widetilde{A})$). Since in the first simulation we have obtained $A = FALSE$, the entry of the conditional probability table of relevance for node B is $P(B|\widetilde{A})$. Again, we are going to draw a random number, $u_{B|\widetilde{A}}$, from the [0 1] uniform distribution: $u_{B|\widetilde{A}} \sim \mathcal{U}(0, 1)$. If $u_{B|\widetilde{A}} > P(B|\widetilde{A})$, we say that in the first simulation variable B was TRUE.

We proceed exactly in the same way for node C. Let's assume that we obtained $B = TRUE$ and $C = FALSE$.

We are still in the first simulation, and we can move to node D, which has two parents (one TRUE, B, and one FALSE, C), and a non-trivial ('concise') conditional probability table made up of $P(D|BC)$, $P(D|\widetilde{B}C)$, $P(D|B\widetilde{C})$ and $P(D|\widetilde{B}\widetilde{C})$. Therefore the entry of interest in this simulation is $P(D|B, \widetilde{C})$. We now draw a random number, $u_{D|B,\widetilde{C}}$, from the [0 1] uniform distribution: $u_{D|B,\widetilde{C}} \sim \mathcal{U}(0, 1)$. If $u_{D|B,\widetilde{C}} > P(D|B, \widetilde{C})$, we say that in the first simulation variable D was TRUE.

It is easy to see how we can follow exactly the same procedure all the way to the final leaf. When we have done so, we have finished the first simulation. The outcome of the simulation is an ordered sequence of *TRUE* and *FALSE* assignments for all the variables in the net. Each sequence is, of course, a joint event. We store this sequence in memory, and move to the second simulation.

We repeat the same procedure N_{sim} times.

Once we have produced N_{sim} simulations, we count how many times each of the various combinations of *TRUE* and *FALSE* (i.e., each joint event) has been produced.

For event i, $i = 1, 2, \ldots, 2^N$ (with N equal to the number of nodes), call n_i the number of times this event has been produced during the course of the N_{sim} simulations. Then the probability, p_i, of joint event event i will be approximated as the occurrence frequency, f_i:

$$p_i \approx f_i \equiv \frac{n_i}{N_{sim}} \tag{15.6}$$

15.2.1   Obvious improvements

The brute-force procedure highlighted above will converge to the correct solution (the joint probabilities) in the limit as N_{sim} tends to infinity. It can be woefully inefficient, however, if naively implemented. Consider in fact the (very common) case where the root of the tree is a very-low-probability event (we are, after all, talking about tail events). In this case only a very small fraction of the simulations will 'activate' this node (which is just the one we are interested in), and convergence will take forever.

There is a simple fix to this problem. One runs two simulations, one conditioned on $Root = TRUE$ and the other on $Root = FALSE$. Proceeding as above, with obvious notation one then calculates n_i^{TRUE} and n_i^{FALSE}, from which one obtains f_i^{TRUE} and f_i^{FALSE}:

$$f_i^{TRUE} = \frac{n_i^{TRUE}}{N_{sim}^{TRUE}}$$

$$f_i^{FALSE} = \frac{n_i^{FALSE}}{N_{sim}^{FALSE}} \tag{15.7}$$

Then, if we call $P(Root)$ the marginal probability of the root event being TRUE, the joint probabilities are approximated as

$$p_i \approx P(Root) f_i^{TRUE} + (1 - P(Root)) f_i^{FALSE}$$

$$= P(Root) \frac{n_i^{TRUE}}{N_{sim}^{TRUE}} + (1 - P(Root)) \frac{n_i^{FALSE}}{N_{sim}^{FALSE}} \tag{15.8}$$

15.2.2   More advanced improvements: adapting the Weighted Monte-Carlo Method

A more advanced (yet still very simple) method to improve the accuracy of the naive Monte-Carlo estimates of the joint probabilities borrows from a simple observation originally presented in Avellaneda et al. (1997), Avellaneda (1998), Avellaneda et al. (2000). The idea (which goes under the name of the Weighted Monte-Carlo Method) is as follows.

Typically, one obtains an estimate, x_{est}, of a quantity, say, x, using a naive Monte-Carlo procedure by averaging over the realizations of x obtained in the course of the simulation by assigning an identical weight to each realization:

$$x_{est} = \frac{1}{N_{sim}} \sum_{i=1,N_{sim}} x(\omega_i) \tag{15.9}$$

where ω_i denotes the ith Monte-Carlo path. Trivially, this can be re-written as

$$x_{est} = \sum_{i=1,N_{sim}} \pi_i x(\omega_i) \tag{15.10}$$

with $\pi_i = \frac{1}{N_{sim}}$, $i = 1, 2, \ldots, N_{sim}$. Now, suppose that we happen to know exactly the values, $y^1, y^2, \ldots, y^m$, of m quantities, and that these quantities are in some sense 'closely related' to the quantity we want to simulate. We can always obtain m estimates for these quantities as

$$y_{est}^k = \sum_{i=1,N_{sim}} \pi_i y^k(\omega_i) \quad k = 1, 2, \ldots, m \tag{15.11}$$

and, of course, in general

$$y_{est}^k \neq y^k \quad k = 1, 2, \ldots, m \tag{15.12}$$

We can also find new weights, λ_i, $i = 1, 2, \ldots, N_{sim}$, such that

$$y_{est}^k = \sum_{i=1,N_{sim}} \lambda_i y^k(\omega_i) = y^k \quad k = 1, 2, \ldots, m \tag{15.13}$$

Intuitively, to the extent that the known quantities $y^1, y^2, \ldots, y^m$ are 'closely related' to the unknown quantity we are interested in (i.e., x) one can expect that the estimate x_{est} obtained as

$$x_{est} = \sum_{i=1,N_{sim}} \lambda_i x(\omega_i) \tag{15.14}$$

should be closer to its true value than the naive estimate. However, since in general $m \ll N_{sim}$, there is an infinity of weights, λ_i, such that the m equalities in Equation (15.13) are exactly satisfied – and, of course, some of these solutions can be quite 'pathological'. The idea then is to find *the* set of weights that satisfies exactly the relationships in Equation (15.13) and that, at the same time, minimize the distance between $\{\lambda\}$ and $\{\pi\}$. As Avellaneda and his coauthors convincingly argue, cross-entropy could be one such (quasi)-distance, with attractive properties. The intuition is to alter the weights $\pi_i = \frac{1}{N_{sim}}$ as little as possible, while at the same time obtaining an exact estimate for the control variables. Since we know that, asymptotically, the weights $\pi_i = \frac{1}{N_{sim}}$ would be the correct ones, they constitute a reasonable anchor solution.

How can we apply this idea to our Bayesian nets? What we want to estimate, of course, are the joint probabilities $\{p\}$. Now, we do know exactly a large number of 'closely related' quantities, namely the input master probabilities that populate the conditional probability tables. Some (say, m) of these will be our 'control variates',

$\{cp\}$.[2] The estimates of these conditional probabilities, cp_{est}^k, are a function of the estimated joint probabilities, $\{p_{est}\}$:

$$cp_{est}^k = f(p_{est}) \neq cp^k \quad k = 1, 2, \ldots, m \tag{15.15}$$

In keeping with Avellaneda's idea, we are going to determine new joint probabilities, $\{p_{new}\}$, in such a way that Equations (15.15) are exactly satisfied,

$$cp_{est}^k = f(p_{new}) = cp^k \quad k = 1, 2, \ldots, m \tag{15.16}$$

and that the new joint probabilities are as close as possible to the naive Monte-Carlo estimates:

$$\min d[p_{new}, p_{est}] \tag{15.17}$$

where $d|\cdot|$ is a distance functional of our choice. Again, using cross-entropy as a (quasi)-distance is attractive for a number of information-theoretical reasons (see, e.g., Ash 1965, 1990; Cover and Thomas 2006).[3]

We must remember than we are at liberty to 'deform' the original probabilities, $\{p_{est}\}$, but we must retain their normalization. The easiest way to handle this constraint is to choose one of the joint probabilities (that we are going to label as p_{2^n}) and solve for it as

$$p_{2^n} = 1 - \sum_{k=1, 2^n - 1} p_k \tag{15.18}$$

If we choose for probability p_{2^n} the largest of the original set of joint probabilities, we can rest virtually assured that, for reasonable deformations of the set $\{p_{est}\}$, the constraint-satisfying probability p_{2^n} will be non-negative. Of course, the linear constraint $\sum_k p_k = 1$ can in general be directly implemented in the minimization $\min\{p_{new} \in C\}d[p_{new}, p_{est}]$, where the set C is made up of a number of linear constraints, of which the normalization requirement could be one.

15.3   Size constraints: joining nets

So far we have implicitly assumed that we have only one major event at the root of our tree. It can be that, at a particular point in time, more than one major event will attract our attention as potential candidates for tree roots. Let's assume, for simplicity, that we are dealing with two root events, and that they are independent (if they were not, we should insert in the net their common parent).

---

[2] We can be guided in choosing the most effective control variates by the sensitivity results presented in Section 31.2.1.

[3] And, in our case, as long as we have assigned conditional probabilities between 0 and 1 – as we always will – the solution *will* exist. Once again, this is the beauty and power of our workhorse, the No-Constraints Theorem.

Now, two situations present themselves.

1. In the first case the two sub-trees originating from the two distinct roots only combine at the terminal leaves (which, we recall, contain the market risk factors of relevance for our portfolio). Nothing changes in the treatment presented so far, and we 'simply' have to deal with two computational issues: (i) the number of nodes in the overall net may be rather large, and we may therefore have to resort to Monte-Carlo techniques; (ii) the terminal leaves are likely to have a large number of parents, and therefore we may have to employ the causal-independence tools introduced above.
2. In the second, and by far more common, case the sub-trees originating from the two roots will meet for some transmission-mechanism node before the terminal leaves. We are faced again with two computational problems: (i) The first is the large number of parents for the transmission-channel node where the recombination occurs. Again, the causal-independence techniques introduced above can come in handy. (ii) The second problem is again the large total number of nodes in the combined sub-trees. Here we *can* do something computationally useful by recalling the concept of conditional independence and d-separation. If we can identify in the combined sub-trees a set of nodes that d-separate the common transmission nodes from the 'upstream' nodes in either sub-tree, these can be simply cut off, after the marginal probabilities in the new 'midstream' roots have been calculated.

So, bringing together the computational techniques introduced in this chapter, relatively complex and sufficiently realistic situations can be handled.

16 A real-life example: building a realistic Bayesian net

In preparing for battle I have always found that plans are useless, but planning is indispensable.
General Dwight D Eisenhower, 34th president of US 1953–1961 (1890–1969)[1]

16.1 The purpose of this chapter

In this chapter we present a step-by-step construction of the Bayesian net associated with a reasonably realistic scenario. This is the scenario for which in Chapters 26–29 we will obtain and analyse in detail the allocation results, and for which we will carry out a detailed sensitivity analysis.

Rather than presenting a doctored and sanitized 'authorized version', we go through all the steps of the construction of the net, including the false starts, the errors and the hard choices that any real-life implementation inevitably entails. For this reason in this chapter elegance of presentation is not our main concern, and we prefer to show the construction in a warts-and-all manner. As the quote that opens this chapter alludes to, we find the effort put into the preparation phase of a Bayesian net invaluable, and the clarity of thought it stimulates useful, even if, much as General Eisenhower's battle plans, the events in our scenario will not ultimately unfold as we tried to model.

16.2 Step-by-step construction in a realistic case

16.2.1 Roots, leaves and transmission channels

Let us start from the following stress scenario, provisionally mapped onto the Bayesian net depicted in Figure 16.1.

The perspective is that of a UK asset (or risk) manager whose portfolio is exposed to UK Government bonds (Gilts), UK equities and UK corporate bonds. We assume that the event that may trigger significant changes in the value of her portfolio is not UK-based. For the sake of concreteness, we choose as the stress event in question a highly indebted European sovereign nearing default on its Euro-denominated debt.

---

[1] The quote is reported in *Six Crises* (1962) by Richard Nixon, and it is currently on display on the wall of the Eisenhower Hall at the USMA at Westpoint, VA.

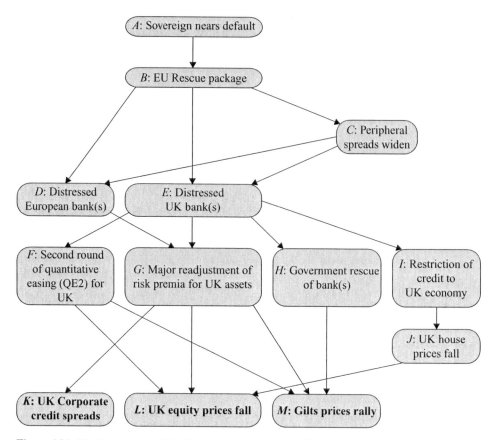

Figure 16.1 The first version of the Bayesian net associated with the scenario described in the text.

As explained in Chapter 12, our general strategy is to try to formulate the most 'direct' and plausible route (i.e., to identify the most direct and plausible transmission channels) to connect the event in question with the large positions in the portfolio. To help the intuition, recall the courageous analogy we offered in Chapter 12 with the path-integral formulation in physics: the two fixed points, i.e., the starting point (the macro scenario) and the arrival point (the events directly affecting the focus portfolio), must be reached via the 'least action' path.

In the case we are analysing, this means that the simplest (highest probability) links must be established between a European-based event (the near-default of a sovereign) and the UK-based portfolio described above. Needless to say, there is no guarantee that a simpler route may not exist, or that a route considered too 'complex' (and therefore excluded from the analysis) may not ultimately be the one that will occur in reality.

One reasonably direct way to connect the event and the portfolio could be the following.

- As we said, the stress event (the root of our tree) is a highly indebted European sovereign nearing default on its Euro-denominated debt.
- As default is neared, the EU may or may not approve a rescue package (over and above enacting what it has already announced it would do).
- This decision by the EU affects three events:
  - the widening of the credit spreads of other peripheral, but less vulnerable, European countries;
  - the possible distress of one or more European[2] banks, either because of deposit flight, or because of large positions in the trading or credit book in the debt of the weak country;
  - the possible distress of one or more UK banks, most likely because of large positions in the trading or credit book in the debt of the weak country.
- The distress in the European banking sector feeds into the readjustment of risk premia for all assets, and in particular for UK assets.
- The distress of UK banks has the same effect, but also has an impact on:
  - the likelihood of the Bank of England engaging in a further round of quantitative easing;
  - the likelihood of the government being forced to carry out a bail-out of one or more UK banks;
  - the expected amount of credit advanced by the UK banking sector to the UK economy.
- We assume that a restriction of credit to the UK economy would have a knock-on effect on the UK housing market, and would create a negative 'wealth effect' among UK investors.
- After all these transmission channels have been specified, we reach the portfolios held by the UK-based asset manager (i.e., the leaves of the tree):
  - Gilts prices, which are affected by the likelihood of further quantitative easing, by the fiscal condition of the UK government after another bank bail-out, and by the flight to quality away from risky assets;
  - UK corporate spreads, which are mainly affected by the readjustment of risk premia for UK assets;
  - equity prices, which are affected by the same readjustment of risk premia, by quantitative easing and (via the wealth effect) by the decline in house prices.

16.2.2 A first attempt

These causal links are tentatively translated in the Bayesian net shown in Figure 16.1.

Prima facie, the net seems plausible and effective in linking in a parsimonious and credible manner the chosen macro event to the specific portfolio. It also appears to reflect correctly our understanding of the relationships between the various variables. For instance, the node related to the enactment or otherwise of a further round of

---

[2] In keeping with British usage, we take the term 'European' to mean 'continental European' (non-UK) countries.

quantitative easing by the Bank of England is motivated by the presence in the portfolio
of Gilts (which would presumably benefit under quantitative easing). Similarly, the
weakening in the UK property market has been introduced because the expert believes
in a direct and strong relationship between the 'wealth effect' linked to the level of
house prices and equity prices. Similar considerations apply to the other nodes and to
the chosen connections (the 'arrows', or directed edges). At first blush, in short, the
construction does not appear unnecessarily complex, nor is it apparent that anything too
obvious has been left out. Let's construct the net one step at a time, however, in order
to understand if the plausible graph we have drawn truly reflects our understanding of
the situation.

To keep the discussion simple, in this chapter we are going to assume each variable
to be Boolean. The extension to multi-valued variables is conceptually straightforward.

We are going to make use of the Master Equation,

$$p(e_1, e_2, e_3, \ldots, e_n) = \prod_{j=1,n} P(E_j = e_j | \text{Parents } \{E_j\}) \qquad (16.1)$$

in order to build the joint probabilities of all the events. A bit of book-keeping quickly
shows that we are faced with the task of providing one marginal and 42 conditional
probabilities, in order to produce $2^{13} - 1 = 8192 - 1 = 8191$ joint probabilities. Of
the conditional probabilities, $7 \times 2 = 14$ will be singly conditioned, $4 \times 3 = 12$ will be
doubly conditioned, and $8 \times 2 = 16$ trebly conditioned. We shall see if it is reasonable
to assign as many, and as complex, conditional probabilities when we construct the net.

16.2.3   Quantifying the horizon and the magnitude of the 'stress events'

Speaking of probabilities, even in a subjective sense, requires the specification of the
time horizon, and of the magnitude of the stress events (for instance, when we say 'A
fall in the FTSE' do we have in mind a 3% or a 10% fall? Over a day, a week, or three
months?). Even if the example presented in this chapter is somewhat stylized, some
quantification of the magnitude of the events is necessary for the discussion to make
sense.

We therefore start by assuming a quarterly horizon. As for the magnitude or severity
of the events, we specify the following:

- By 'being near to default' we mean that the market concludes that the peripheral
  European country perceived as most vulnerable will be unable to refinance its debt.
- A 'rescue package' is a new measure by the EU or the International Monetary Fund
  (IMF) that, at least temporarily, ensures orderly refinancing of the short-term debt.
- By 'distress of a UK or European bank' we mean a deterioration of its perceived
  liquidity and/or solvency sufficiently severe to cause its Credit Default Swap (CDS)
  spreads to widen to 500 basis points (bp) or more.
- By 'quantitative easing by the Bank of England' we mean a new, unplanned round
  of quantitative easing of a magnitude similar or greater to the first one.

- By 'readjustment of the risk premia for UK assets' we mean an increase in Overnight Indexed Swap (OIS)/London Interbank Offered Rate (LIBOR) spread by 60 bp or more and/or an increase of the VIX to a level of 30 or more.
- By 'government intervention to rescue a UK bank' ('bank bail-out') we mean any measure involving expenditure of taxpayers' money to ensure the survival of the UK bank under distress. We will assume the magnitude of the taxpayers' rescue to be of the order of several tens of billions of dollars.
- By 'fall in house prices' we mean that over the next quarter the consensus about the path of house prices over the next few years points to a decline of 20% to 40%.
- By 'restriction of credit to the UK economy' we mean a reduction by 20% or more of the amount of credit extended by banks to the UK corporate or private sector.
- By 'widening in credit spreads' we mean an increase in the investment-grade corporate bond index IBOXX by 200 bp or more over the quarter.
- By 'fall in equity prices' we mean a decline of the FTSE 250 index over the quarter by 20%–40%.
- By 'rally of Gilts' we mean a tightening in the 10-year yield curve by 50 bp or more.

An important observation is in order here. When we assign probabilities, events like 'A fall in the S&P by 22%' do not have a well-defined probability – technically speaking, if we regard the magnitude of the fall as a real number, it is an event of measure zero. More practically, if the S&P were to fall by 22.001%, surely we would not want to say that the event did not happen. Therefore, when it comes to assigning probabilities we must always specify an interval. When we do asset allocation, or, for that matter, risk management, however, we need a precise loss. This can be accommodated by specifying first the probabilities for events like 'Modest Fall', 'Severe Fall', 'no change', etc., where each event is characterized by a range ('no change' for instance, could mean 'changes between plus or minus 3%'). Once this is done, we can 'collapse' the possible outcomes within the range in a variety of ways: for instance, we can associate a Dirac-δ distribution centred around, say, -20% to the losses for the event 'Severe Fall', which might have been probabilistically characterized by the range, say, 'a loss of 15% or more'; or we can stipulate that if the event 'Severe Fall' is *TRUE*, then we draw from a Gaussian distribution (or, say, a displaced lognormal distribution), with mean -20% and an appropriate variance. The important point here is that we need both a range (to assign meaningful probabilities), and a mapping from the event to precise losses (to carry out asset allocation or for risk management applications).

The reader may ask why we assigned probabilities for events like 'A fall in the S&P between 20% and 40%'. This is because the probability mass between 40% and $+\infty$ is negligible, and, for any realistic portfolio, the probability of losses should decline much more rapidly than their magnitude, or any reasonable decrease in utility.

Finally, we are ultimately interested in the impact of these events on our portfolio. We must therefore specify its exact composition. We assume, for simplicity, that it is made up of

Table 16.1 *The joint probabilities*
for the variables A and B

A	B	$p(AB)$
1	1	0.0250
0	1	0.0095
1	0	0.0250
0	0	0.9405

- a long position with notional equivalent of £400 million in the FTSE 250 index;
- a long (short protection) position in the IBOXX index with notional equivalent of £400 million;
- a long positions in 10-year Gilts with a notional of £200 million.

With these definitions in mind, we at least know what probabilities the conditional probability tables refer to, and we can begin the construction of the net.

16.2.4   The construction

The root – sovereign crisis   We start from the root, node A ('Sovereign nears default'). As this node has no parents, only a marginal probability, $P(A)$, has to be assigned. We set, perhaps on the basis of CDS information, $P(A) = 0.05$. (Recall that this is the probability of default over the next quarter.) Obviously, the probability of no default, $P(\tilde{A})$, is $P(\tilde{A}) = 1 - P(A) = 0.95$.

The rescue package   We now move to node B ('A rescue package is put in place'). To fill in the associated conditional probability table, we have to provide two conditional probabilities: $P(B|A)$ and $P(B|\tilde{A})$. If the European country does not approach a crisis, we assume that the likelihood of an expected rescuer package is very remote. We therefore set $P(B|\tilde{A}) = 0.01$. If a crisis does materialize, we assume that there is, say, a 50–50 chance that an extraordinary package will be put in place. Therefore $P(B|A) = 0.5$. This automatically gives $P(\tilde{B}|\tilde{A}) = 0.99$ and $P(\tilde{B}|A) = 0.5$.

This allows us to build the joint probability out to this stage as follows:

$$p(ab) = P(A)P(B|A) \tag{16.2}$$

$$p(\tilde{a}b) = P(\tilde{A})P(B|A) \tag{16.3}$$

$$p(a\tilde{b}) = P(A)P(\tilde{B}|A) \tag{16.4}$$

$$p(\tilde{a}\tilde{b}) = P(\tilde{A})P(\tilde{B}|\tilde{A}) \tag{16.5}$$

The numerical values obtained for the table are shown in Table 16.1.

As a by-product of the table we can immediately calculate $P(B)$ (the probability that a rescue package will be forthcoming) and we obtain $P(B) = 0.035$.

Table 16.2 *The joint probabilities*
for the variables A, B and C

A	B	C	$p(ABC)$
1	1	1	0.005
0	1	1	0.002
1	0	1	0.025
0	0	1	0.931
1	1	0	0.020
0	1	0	0.008
1	0	0	0.000
0	0	0	0.009

We can pause to see if everything makes sense so far. First of all, we are implying from the construction that the probability of an extraordinary rescue package by the EU is low, and lower than the probability of a near-default. This makes sense: for the rescue package to be forthcoming the sovereign must get into serious trouble first (an event to which we have assigned a 5% probability), and then the EU must decide to intervene (we said that there was a 50–50 chance of this happening.)

We are also saying that the most likely joint event is that nothing happens (at least over the chosen horizon): $p(\tilde{a}\tilde{b}) = 0.9405$. Since we have posited $P(A) = 0.05$ this also makes sense.

Finally, we are saying that the most *un*likely joint event is that no sovereign crisis materializes for the most vulnerable sovereign, and yet the EU passes an emergency measure: $p(\tilde{a}b) = 0.0095$. Given the structure of our scenario, this also seems plausible.

Credit spreads of peripheral countries widen   As all these sanity checks have been successfully passed, we can move to the next step, i.e., the building of the conditional probability table for node C ('Credit spreads of peripheral countries widen').

We have assumed one parent for node C, so we are saying at this stage that knowing whether the rescue package has occurred or not is all we need to know (looking 'upstream') to ascertain the likelihood of C. We want to cater for the possibility that, even if the EU does put forth an emergency rescue plan, there is still a non-negligible probability that the peripheral credit spreads may widen. Let's then assign, say, $P(C|B) = 0.20$. But if the EU is not forthcoming with its rescue package (and a crisis is unfolding), we can be almost sure that the peripheral spreads will widen. We therefore set $P(C|\tilde{B}) = 0.99$. Using the Master Equation, and proceeding as for Equations (16.2)–(16.5), we therefore build the following joint probability table (Table 16.2). Does this table, and the derived information we can obtain from it, make intuitive sense?

The most likely event in Table 16.2 is (by far) event $p(\tilde{a},\tilde{b},c)$, i.e., the event that no sovereign state nears default, the EU (quite logically) does not pass an emergency package, but the peripheral spreads still widen dramatically: $p(\widetilde{a},\widetilde{b},c) = 0.931$. Surely, this is not what we were trying to express with our net. Where did we go wrong?

A moment's reflection shows where our 'mistake' was: our assignment of the widening of the credit spreads given no approval of the EU rescue package did not distinguish whether the sovereign crisis had occurred or not. But this is clearly not plausible: if no package has been passed because no crisis has materialized for the most vulnerable country, there is no reason to believe that the less vulnerable countries will come under stress. We have assumed in our net that the variable B screens variable C from variable A. However, the conditional independence embedded in the net does not reflect what happens in reality.

We stress that this is the most common 'mistake' in building a Bayesian net: the net builder gets so carried away with the scenario she is constructing that the probabilities attaching to what happens if nothing much happens are neglected. In our case, we focused on the crisis having happened (despite the fact that this is a very-low-probability event), and therefore we quickly concluded that the absence of an EU rescue package must be very bad news for the spreads of the peripheral countries. We fell prey, in short, to 'crisis tunnel vision'.

We must therefore redraw our Bayesian net to take into account the possibility that the EU help may not have been forthcoming for the very simple reason that nothing bad had happened 'upstream'. The new net is shown in Figure 16.2.

The first three nodes revisited   As node C (the widening of credit spreads) now has two parents, a richer conditional probability table must be provided. Let's consider its various elements in turn:

- $P(C|AB)$. Here we are trying to assign the probability of peripheral spreads widening given that the crisis has materialized ($A = TRUE$), and the EU has come up with a rescue package ($B = TRUE$). This is the probability we had in mind when we assigned $P(C|B) = 0.20$, so we keep $P(C|AB) = 0.20$.
- $P(C|\widetilde{A}B)$. This is the probability of the spread of peripheral countries widening, given that a sovereign has not come close to crisis, but the EU has nonetheless announced an extra rescue fund. An extra safety net will make the widening very remote, and we therefore set $P(C|\widetilde{A}B) = 0.01$. This automatically implies that the probability, $P(\widetilde{C}|\widetilde{A}B)$, of no spread widening given no crisis ($\widetilde{A}$), and yet an EU rescue package ($B = TRUE$), is very high: $P(\widetilde{C}|\widetilde{A}B) = 0.99$. Are we happy with this implication? Isn't this combination of the two parent events (no crisis and yet a rescue package) extremely unlikely? How do we end up with such a high conditional probability? Note that we must distinguish carefully between the likelihood of the events we are conditioning on (in this case, a rescue package with no crisis) and the conditional probability we are trying to assign given that the event (however unlikely) has materialized. In general, the probability of the conditioning events may be very low, but we must always picture the situation where they have nonetheless occurred. Therefore the joint event ($\widetilde{A}$, B) may well have a very low probability (and

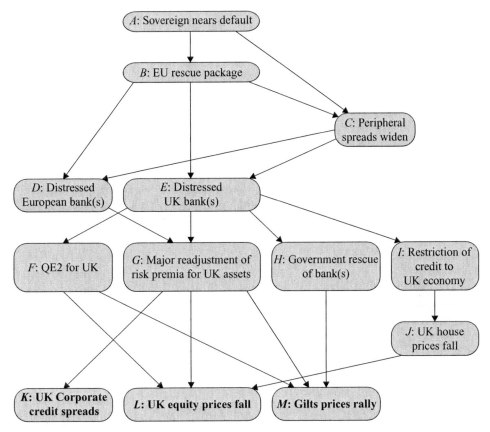

Figure 16.2 First revision of the original Bayesian net shown in Figure 16.1.

we already know that it does from the joint probability table constructed for variables A and B: $p(\widetilde{A}, B) = 0.0095$); however, given that this event has after all occurred, then we are confident to say that spreads will not widen.

We must be careful here. Assigning these 'awkward' conditional probabilities (i.e., conditional probabilities conditioned on the occurrence of very unlikely combinations of events) runs against our cognitive grain. This makes our subjective task difficult. Luckily, we should not agonize too much over these assignments. If the events we condition on are truly so remote, it matters little which conditional probability we assign: after all, the associated joint probability will have the form $P(A|RareEvent)P(RareEvent)$. So, if $P(RareEvent)$ is a number much smaller than 1, it does not really matter if we multiply this very small number by any number of order 1.

- $P(C|A\widetilde{B})$. This is the probability of the spread of peripheral countries widening, given that the most vulnerable sovereign is under severe stress, but no rescue package has been passed. This is probably what we 'truly meant' when we set $P(C|\widetilde{B}) = 0.99$. We therefore set $P(C|A\widetilde{B}) = 0.99$.

Table 16.3 *The revised joint probability*
table for the first three variables

A	B	C	p(ABC)
1	1	1	0.005
0	1	1	0.000
1	0	1	0.025
0	0	1	0.047
1	1	0	0.020
0	1	0	0.009
1	0	0	0.000
0	0	0	0.893

- $P(C|\widetilde{A}\widetilde{B})$. This is the probability of the spread of peripheral countries widening, given that there has been no crisis for the most vulnerable sovereign and no rescue package. There could be some plausible reasons for this widening, but the event seems of rather low probability. We can tentatively set $P(C|\widetilde{A}\widetilde{B}) = 0.05$, but this would be a good candidate for sensitivity testing once the Bayesian net has been completed.

The new joint probability table is given in Table 16.3.

Let's proceed to our sanity checks. First of all, we can now check that, as our intuition suggested, $p(\widetilde{A}, \widetilde{B}, C)$ is no longer the most likely event, as $p(\widetilde{A}, \widetilde{B}, C)$ has moved from 0.931 to 0.047. Indeed, it was the previous high value for this joint probability (0.931) that had drawn our attention to the inadequacy of our original construction of the net, and it is therefore reassuring that our 'fix' appears to have done the job.

Next, direct calculation of the marginal probability of the spread of a peripheral country widening is $P(C) = 0.077$. This is higher than our assumed probability of distress for the most vulnerable country. Are we happy with this? Mathematically, this stems from our assignment of $P(C|\widetilde{A}\widetilde{B}) = 0.05$ to the event of a widening of peripheral spreads with no sovereign crisis and no rescue package. Economically, we are saying that there could be as many reasons for the peripheral spreads to widen 'by themselves' as for a sovereign crisis of the most vulnerable state to materialize. (Recall that we assigned $P(A) = 0.05$.) If this is not what we meant, we may want to revise our assignment of $P(C|\widetilde{A}\widetilde{B})$ to a significantly smaller value, say, $P(C|\widetilde{A}\widetilde{B}) = P(A)/4 = 0.0125$. For the moment, we will retain the $P(C|\widetilde{A}\widetilde{B}) = 0.05$.

Let's continue with our sanity checks. We can now compute $P(C|A)$, i.e., the conditional probability of a peripheral spread widening given that the sovereign crisis has occurred. When we do this, we get $P(C|A) = 0.595$, higher than the probability of the EU organizing a rescue package, $P(B|A)$, that we had set at 50%. This is indirectly linked to our assumption that, if the sovereign crisis happens, spreads can still widen even if the rescue package is approved.

Finally, our most unlikely joint event is that a sovereign crisis occurs, no rescue package is approved, yet spreads do not widen: $p(A, \widetilde{B}, \widetilde{C}) = 0.0003$. This is just what we expect.

We can now move to new nodes.

Distress in European or UK banks   As the construction of the conditional probability table for node C has made us better and wiser persons, we can immediately see that, for the very same reasons discussed above, we have to introduce a directed arrow (a link) between event A and events D and E (distress in European or UK banks, respectively). However, both these children now have three parents, and their conditional probability table requires the specification of eight conditional probabilities. This is likely to stretch our cognitive abilities. Can we simplify the problem, while retaining the 'spirit' of the scenario we want to run?

Given the composition of the portfolio under consideration, perhaps the scenario we are most worried about is a sovereign debt crisis *without* a rescue package by the EU. It would be nice to be able to explore the more nuanced combinations arising from the four possible combinations of these elementary events (i.e., sovereign crisis = *TRUE* or *FALSE* and rescue package = *TRUE* or *FALSE*). However, we may gain more in cognitive simplicity than we lose in precision of scenario definition by creating a simpler tree. This simpler tree is achieved by collapsing the variables A and B (the sovereign crisis and the EU rescue package, respectively) into one, with the following three possible values: (i) we have no sovereign crisis (and therefore no EU rescue package is forthcoming; (ii) we do have a sovereign crisis and no EU rescue package is forthcoming, or (iii) we have a sovereign crisis and a EU rescue package is put together.

This is shown in Figure 16.3.

Doing so reduces the number of parents for the third-generation children from 3 to 2 (but increases the number of conditional probabilities per parent).

But we can do better. We had concluded that if a crisis materialized and no rescue package was put forth, the widening of the peripheral spreads was almost certain. We also said that the probability of credit spreads widening was rather low. If this is the case, we lose little additional information by collapsing the original three events into a single two-valued event, that now reads 'Sovereign nears default with no rescue package and widening of peripheral spreads'. (As this is quite a mouthful, we will call this from now on 'Sovereign crisis', but it is important to keep in mind exactly how the crisis has been defined.)

It is very important to stress that we have made a big simplification here. Implicitly we are saying that we are not 'worried about' the occurrence of a sovereign crisis as long as the rescue package is put together. As a consequence of this highly debatable choice we are only explicitly considering two states of the world:

[the crisis happens, there is no rescue package and spreads widen]
and
[the negation of the above].

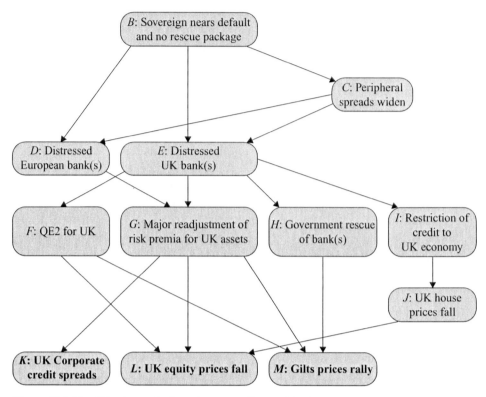

Figure 16.3 Simplification of the Bayesian net as discussed in the text.

We have, in a sense, 'folded' the probability of the event *There is a crisis, but there is a rescue package, and hence spreads do not widen* into the probability of the event *There is no crisis and hence spreads do not widen*. In a realistic application this is not normally a choice we would like to make, and we would much prefer to specify three values for the node in question. We will make the choice in this chapter purely for expositional purposes, and to keep the presentation uncluttered by non-essential complications.

Having swallowed hook line and sinker this assumption, we can at least check from the joint probability table that the probability of one of the events we are effectively setting to zero ($P(A, \widetilde{B}, \widetilde{C}) = 0.003$) would indeed have been negligible in the original, fuller net – indeed, it was the smallest joint probability we had estimated. We note in passing that also the conditional probability of a peripheral spread widening given no crisis is low ($P(C|\widetilde{A}) = 0.047$). We therefore 'prune' the Bayesian net as in Figure 16.4.

We now have to assign $P(B|A)$ and $P(C|A)$, i.e. the probability of distress in one or more European (B) or UK (C) banks, given the sovereign crisis, A. We assign $P(B|A) = 0.20$ and $P(C|A) = 0.15$, assuming, perhaps somewhat optimistically, that UK banks may be more insulated from a European crisis than European ones. We also set the probabilities of distress for a European or a UK bank, $P(B|\widetilde{A})$ and $P(C|\widetilde{A})$,

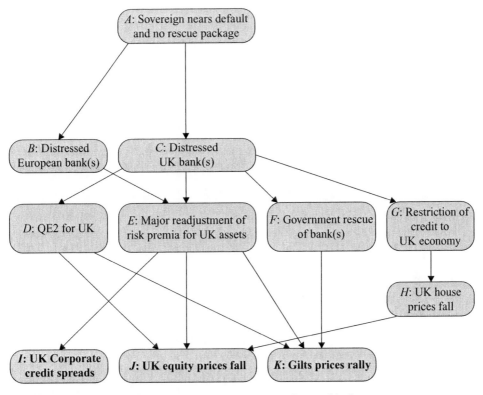

Figure 16.4 A further simplification of the Bayesian net as discussed in the text.

respectively, to a similarly very low value: $P(B|\tilde{A}) = P(C|\tilde{A}) = 0.01$. We imply by doing so that no other major disasters are on the horizon.

Let's continue the analysis. From the way the net has been constructed, the

[probability of distress in a UK bank given that
the sovereign crisis has materialized
and a European bank is in distress]
is equal to the
[probability of distress in a UK bank given the sovereign crisis]:

$$P(C|AB) = P(C|A) = 0.15$$

This means that we have built into the net conditional independence between B and C (the distress of the European bank and of the UK bank). But, surely, knowing that a European bank is in distress tells us something about the likelihood of a UK bank being in trouble, *especially since we have assumed that non-European-sovereign-related dangers were minimal*. And, indeed, this conditional independence makes the conditional probabilities of a European bank being in distress given the state

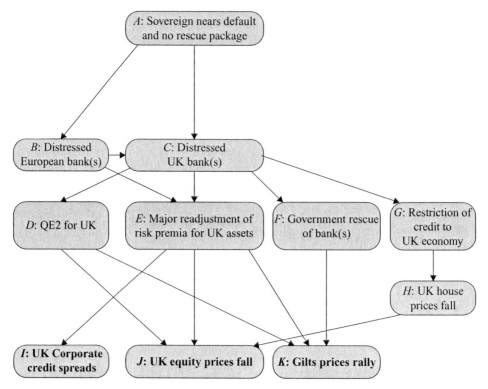

Figure 16.5 Evolution of the Bayesian net, as discussed in the text. Note the arrow that has been added to link nodes B and C.

of distress of a British bank, and vice versa, implausibly low: $P(B|C) = 0.063$ and $P(C|B) = 0.057$. What has gone wrong? And how can we fix the problem?

One way would be to insert a dependence from B to C and from C to B. Doing so, however, would make our net cyclical. Unfortunately, as we mentioned in Chapter 7, the tools for handling cyclical nets are more complex, and go beyond the techniques presented in this book. Another possibility is the following. Since our focus is on a UK portfolio, it seems more important to capture the dependence from B to C than vice versa. We therefore 'complicate' the net as shown in Figure 16.5.

The conditional probability table for node C now becomes:

$$P(C|AB) = 0.400 \tag{16.6}$$

$$P(C|\tilde{A}B) = 0.050 \tag{16.7}$$

$$P(C|A\tilde{B}) = 0.150 \tag{16.8}$$

$$P(C|\tilde{A}\tilde{B}) = 0.005 \tag{16.9}$$

The resulting new joint probability table is shown in Table 16.4.

Table 16.4 *The new joint probabilities for the variables A, B and C*

A	B	C	p(ABC)
1	1	1	0.0020
0	1	1	0.0005
1	0	1	0.0030
0	0	1	0.0048
1	1	0	0.0030
0	1	0	0.0093
1	0	0	0.0170
0	0	0	0.9604

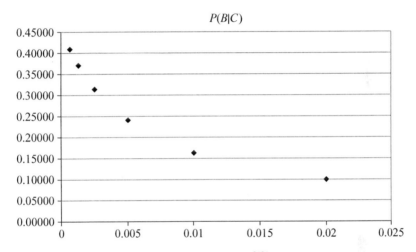

Figure 16.6 Possible values of $P(B|C)$ as a function of $P(C|\widetilde{A}\widetilde{B})$.

From this table we can calculate several important quantities, to check whether the net we have built so far effectively translates into numbers our intuition. For instance, let's consider the conditional probabilities $P(B|C)$ and $P(C|B)$, whose smallness in the previous net had prompted our modification. Now they have the values $P(B|C) = 0.241$ and $P(C|B) = 0.169$, more in line with our intuition.

One of the input doubly conditioned probabilities that most strongly affect the singly conditioned probability, $P(B|C)$, is the doubly conditioned probability $P(C|\widetilde{A}\widetilde{B})$, i.e., the probability of UK bank distress given no European bank crisis and no sovereign stress. This is shown in Figure 16.6, which presents the derived value of $P(B|C)$ as a function of $P(C|\widetilde{A}\widetilde{B})$.

Therefore, if the expert has a clearer perception of the conditional probability $P(B|C)$ than of $P(C|\widetilde{A}\widetilde{B})$, she can gain assistance in assigning the 'difficult' quantity, $P(C|\widetilde{A}\widetilde{B})$, by observing how it affects the 'easy' quantity, $P(B|C)$. This is an example of a recurrent theme in the building of moderately complex Bayesian nets: by calculating and critically examining at each step of the net construction what the 'difficult' conditional probabilities required as inputs to the Master Equation imply, the expert can guide her judgement.

Major readjustment of risk premia of UK assets   Let's continue with the building of the net by adding node E ('Major readjustment of risk premia of UK assets'). As the node has two parents (node B – distress for a European bank – and node C – distress for a UK bank), we have to supply four conditional probabilities. These we assign as follows:

$$p(E|CB) = 0.95$$

$$p(E|\widetilde{C}B) = 0.80$$

$$P(E|C\widetilde{B}) = 0.70$$

$$P(E|\widetilde{C}\widetilde{B}) = 0.05 \qquad (16.10)$$

What we are saying is that if both a UK and a European bank run into serious trouble, then a major readjustment of risk premia for UK assets is almost certain; that the distress of either a UK or a European bank is highly likely to cause a readjustment of risk premia; that the distress of a UK bank would be likely to have a slightly greater effect than the distress of a European bank; and that if neither a European nor a UK bank find themselves in trouble the probability of a premia readjustment is low.

As sanity checks we calculate the marginal probability for event E ('Major readjustment of risk premia of UK assets') and a few conditional probabilities of the readjustment of the risk premia:

$$P(E) = 0.066$$

$$P(E|C) = 0.836$$

$$P(E|B) = 0.742$$

$$P(E|A) = 0.290 \qquad (16.11)$$

The high conditional probabilities of risk premia readjustment given the distress of either a European or a UK bank make perfect sense. Also the fact that troubles for a UK bank would affect UK risk premia more than troubles for a European bank passes our sanity check.

The question mark raised by the results above is the surprisingly low probability of risk premia readjustment given that a sovereign crisis with no rescue (event A) occurred in the first place: $P(E|A) = 0.290$. The question here is whether we believe that the transmission channel from

[sovereign crisis with no rescue package]

to

[UK risk premia readjustment]

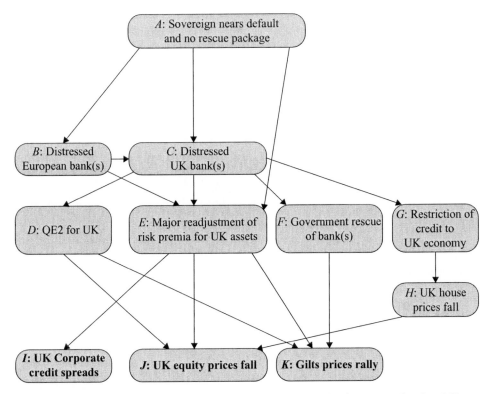

Figure 16.7 Evolution of the Bayesian net. Note the added connection between nodes A and E.

is only via the possible distress of (European or UK) banks; or whether we think that the source cause (A) can affect the effect we are looking at (E) also via a channel not necessarily mediated by a bank (UK or European) ending up in trouble.

We stress here two of the commonest mistakes in building Bayesian nets: the first is the excessive belief that an outcome (in this case, the widening risk premia) can only be due to the precise transmission channels we have put in our net; the second is the related, but distinct, underestimation of the existence of other background causes.

Now, if, after examining the net built out to this point, we believe that the possibility of a background cause for the readjustment of risk premia merits our attention, we must insert a direct connection between A and E, as shown in Figure 16.7.

Doing so, of course, requires a more complex conditional probability table for node E. Let's see how we can reasonably assign its entries.

Let's begin from the conditioning sets in which the event A (sovereign crisis with no rescue) has happened. We then have to consider four possibilities: either, both or none of the bank events (B and C) have occurred:

$$\{P(E|ABC), P(E|A\widetilde{B}C), P(E|AB\widetilde{C}), P(E|A\widetilde{B}\widetilde{C})\} \qquad (16.12)$$

When assigning these four conditional probabilities, we make use of the reasoning presented in Section 13.6. We could also make use of the formal tools available when causal independence applies (see Section 14.5), but, since we are only dealing with three parents, this is probably an overkill.

So, let's start from the easiest conditional probability to assign. Plausibly, conditioning on the state of the world where all the stress events have occurred should give rise to the highest conditional probability of a major readjustment for the risk premia of UK assets. So

$$P(E|ABC) > \max\{P(E|A\widetilde{B}C), P(E|AB\widetilde{C}), P(E|A\widetilde{B}\widetilde{C})\} \qquad (16.13)$$

Following the same line of reasoning, conditioning on the occurrence of A but on the occurrence of neither B nor C should give rise to the lowest of the four probabilities (16.12). So:

$$P(E|A\widetilde{B}\widetilde{C}) < \min\{P(E|ABC), P(E|A\widetilde{B}C), P(E|AB\widetilde{C})\}$$

Finally, when we condition on the banking system of one and only one country going into distress, the impact on the UK risk premia should be higher if it is a UK bank to get into trouble. Therefore

$$P(E|A\widetilde{B}C) > P(E|AB\widetilde{C})$$

This allows us to create the following ranking of the first four conditional probabilities that we have to assign:

$$P(E|ABC) > P(E|A\widetilde{B}C) > P(E|AB\widetilde{C}) > P(E|A\widetilde{B}\widetilde{C})$$

Can we venture a guess for the two extreme points? Let's try.

$$P(E|ABC) = 0.99$$

$$P(E|A\widetilde{B}\widetilde{C}) = 0.60$$

Then we can propose

$$P(E|A\widetilde{B}C) = 0.90$$

and

$$P(E|AB\widetilde{C}) = 0.75$$

Let's now move to the conditioning sets where the prime cause (A) has not occurred:

$$\{P(E|\widetilde{A}BC), P(E|\widetilde{A}\widetilde{B}C), P(E|\widetilde{A}B\widetilde{C}), P(E|\widetilde{A}\widetilde{B}\widetilde{C})\} \qquad (16.14)$$

The first observation is that the probability of occurrence of some of the elements of this conditioning sets is rather low – see, for instance $P(E|\widetilde{A}BC)$: we are looking here at those situations where there has been no sovereign crisis, yet both the UK and the European banking sectors have fallen into trouble. However, we must disregard this 'baseline frequency' when we try to estimate the conditional probabilities: the conditioning events may be extremely unlikely, but we are placing ourselves in those states of the world where they have jointly occurred, and we are looking at what this would do to the conditioned event. This can be cognitively awkward, because some of the combinations may be rather 'unnatural' or counterintuitive. As mentioned above, however, we can be somewhat more cavalier in our assignments here: exactly because the conjunctions of conditional events are so 'unnatural' their joint probabilities will be very low (if we have built our net well.). Therefore the conditional probabilities we are going to choose will multiply very low joint probabilities, and they will have a correspondingly low impact on the final solution.

Note that we qualified the previous statement with the sentence 'if we have built our net well'. Before proceeding, let's therefore check that the net we have built so far does indeed reflect the intuition that a situation of joint distress for UK and European banks without a sovereign crisis should be a very low probability event. We can do so by calculating $P(\widetilde{A}BC)$. Direct computation gives $P(\widetilde{A}BC) = 0.0005$, perfectly in line with our intuition.

With the previous caveat in mind, and the sanity check under the belt, we can move to the conditional probabilities that still need assigning.

First of all, we can certainly say that the lowest conditional probability should be associated with adjustment of the UK risk premia if no sovereign default and no (European or UK) bank distress has happened. We can suggest that this conditional probability, $P(E|\widetilde{A}\widetilde{B}\widetilde{C})$, should be very low, say

$$P(E|\widetilde{A}\widetilde{B}\widetilde{C}) = 0.025$$

Conversely, the highest conditional probability in the set (16.14) should be $P(E|\widetilde{A}BC)$. If we can have a good stab at these two values we would have set the two end points in the range for set (16.14), and we would be in a good position, because, following the same reasoning as above, we can suggest the ranking

$$P(E|\widetilde{A}BC) > P(E|\widetilde{A}\widetilde{B}C) > P(E|\widetilde{A}B\widetilde{C}) > P(E|\widetilde{A}\widetilde{B}\widetilde{C})$$

Now, if, for whatever reason both the UK and the European banks were distressed even without a sovereign crisis, this would certainly (and strongly!) affect the risk premia of UK assets, as these are barometers of general risk appetite, not specifically of sovereign health. So, $P(E|\widetilde{A}BC)$ should be very high. Do we think that a readjustment of UK risk premia would be more likely if

- a sovereign crisis happened ($A = TRUE$), but neither banking sector ran into trouble ($B = FALSE$, $C = FALSE$);

or if

- a sovereign crisis did not happen ($A = FALSE$), but both banking sectors ran into trouble ($B = TRUE$, $C = TRUE$)?

If we believe the latter, then we should set $P(E|\widetilde{A}BC) > P(E|A\widetilde{B}\widetilde{C})$. Since we already set $P(E|A\widetilde{B}\widetilde{C}) = 0.60$, then we should require

$$P(E|\widetilde{A}BC) > 0.60$$

A plausible choice could be $P(E|\widetilde{A}BC) = 0.90$. This is the same value we assigned for $P(E|A\widetilde{B}C)$. Are we comfortable with saying $P(E|\widetilde{A}BC) = P(E|A\widetilde{B}C)$? What we are implying is that, given the state of distress of the UK banking sector, the sovereign crisis and the European banking system distress play a similar role in affecting the readjustment of the UK risk premia. We can decide whether we are comfortable with this implication of our construction.

We only have two conditional probabilities left, $P(E|\widetilde{A}\widetilde{B}C) > P(E|\widetilde{A}B\widetilde{C})$, to be chosen in the range

$$0.90 > P(E|\widetilde{A}\widetilde{B}C) > P(E|\widetilde{A}B\widetilde{C}) > 0.025$$

We can propose

$$P(E|\widetilde{A}\widetilde{B}C) = 0.80$$

and

$$P(E|\widetilde{A}B\widetilde{C}) = 0.50$$

where the last entry has been chosen to reflect the view that $P(E|\widetilde{A}B\widetilde{C}) < P(E|A\widetilde{B}\widetilde{C})$.

By building this more complex net, have we fixed the problem we set out to solve in the first place, i.e., have we managed to produce a more believable conditional probability for the UK risk premia readjustment, given the occurrence of the sovereign crisis, $P(E|A)$? A direct calculation shows that the new Bayesian net now gives $P(E|A) = 0.685$, to be compared with $P(E|A) = 0.29$ obtained with the previous net. Reassuringly, the quantity we were focusing on has moved in the right direction, and by a significant amount.

Note that we have obtained the result that we were looking for (a non-negligible value for $P(E|A)$) at the expense of complicating the net by adding an extra parent for node E – and, as we know, adding parents is never something to be undertaken lightly. Could we have achieved the same result by tinkering with the original net? Recall that in the net in Figure 16.5 we had set a very low value for the conditional probability of a UK risk premia readjustment given that neither banking sector had gone under stress, $P(E|\widetilde{C}\widetilde{B}) = 0.05$. Could we have more simply translated the possibility of different (but unspecified!) transmission channels by setting this probability to a higher value, say $P(E|\widetilde{C}\widetilde{B}) = 0.5$?

Had we done so, then $P(E|A)$ would indeed have increased significantly (from $P(E|A) = 0.29$ to $P(E|A) = 0.596$); however, the marginal (unconditional) probability of event E (the risk premia readjustment) would have changed dramatically (from $P(E) = 0.066$ to $P(E) = 0.506$), *and, arguably, beyond what is plausible given the scenario we are examining.* Another sign of trouble would have been the probability associated with the event 'nothing happens'. With the complex net we get

$P(\widetilde{A}\widetilde{B}\widetilde{C}\widetilde{D}\widetilde{E}) = 0.843$, but with the simpler net with the ad-hoc adjustment the value for the same quantity is $P(\widetilde{A}\widetilde{B}\widetilde{C}\widetilde{D}\widetilde{E}) = 0.432$, an implausibly low value. This also points to the fact that the 'complication' we introduced cannot be avoided.

This observation highlights the importance of looking comprehensively at *all* the implications for which we have a robust intuition, and to beware of ad-hoc fixes. Pruning and simplifying is useful and often beneficial, but only as long as it retains the correct 'story' underpinning the chosen scenario.

Let's conduct a few more sanity checks for the net we have built so far. The lowest probability event is $P(\widetilde{A}BC\widetilde{D}\widetilde{E}) = 0.00001$. This corresponds to the following joint event:

- there has not been a sovereign crisis;
- yet both the UK and the European banks have managed to get into serious trouble;
- however, the Bank of England has refused to engage in a second round of quantitative easing;
- and the UK risk premia have remained broadly unaffected.

The scenario is so far fetched that it is difficult to comment whether it should definitely qualify as the lowest-probability one, but it is certainly a strong candidate.

What about the highest probability joint event? Reassuringly it is the 'nothing happens' event, with a probability, as we saw, of $P(\widetilde{A}\widetilde{B}\widetilde{C}\widetilde{D}\widetilde{E}) = 0.843$. What about the next most likely event? It is the probability that nothing happens, apart from quantitative easing from Bank of England: $P(\widetilde{A}\widetilde{B}\widetilde{C}D\widetilde{E}) = 0.093$. This is almost directly related to the relatively high value that we assigned to the probability of quantitative easing given no UK banking crisis ($P(D|\widetilde{C}) = 0.10$). What we are saying here is that there is a non-negligible probability of quantitative easing for reasons other than a sovereign-crisis-induced UK distress. If we thought that this probability is too high, it is easy to adjust downward the conditional probability, $P(D|\widetilde{C})$, with little effect on the net built so far. (Changing this probability, however, *will* have an effect on portions of the net we have not built yet, i.e., on the prices of Gilts and of UK equities. We will have to check the sensitivity of the results on $P(D|\widetilde{C})$ at later stage.)

We can move the last transmission channels in the net.

Nodes G and H　The construction of the net for nodes G and H and the assignment of the attending conditional probabilities are straightforward, and do not pose particular problems. The following values were chosen in the construction:

$$P(G|C) = 0.90$$
$$P(G|\widetilde{C}) = 0.10$$
$$P(H|G) = 0.75$$
$$P(H|\widetilde{G}) = 0.10$$

The thinking behind these assignments is that a situation of distress for a UK bank is highly likely to bring about a restriction of credit to UK consumers and investors (hence

$P(G|C) = 0.90$); that, without the distress, the restriction of credit may nonetheless occur with non-negligible probability, perhaps simply as a consequence of the desire of households to rebuild their balance sheet (hence $P(G|\widetilde{C}) = 0.10$); that, given a restriction in the supply of credit, UK house prices are likely to suffer a substantial fall (hence $P(H|G) = 0.75$); and that such a fall in price is far less likely, but may well still happen, even without the restriction in credit supply ($P(H|\widetilde{G}) = 0.10$).

Examining, for our sanity checks, the unconditional marginal probabilities of G and H (i.e., of the restriction in the supply of credit and of the falling house prices) we find

$$P(G) = 0.108$$

and

$$P(H) = 0.170$$

two *a priori* unexceptionable numbers.

We may want to ask ourselves why the probability of a fall in house prices turned out to be considerably higher than the probability of a restriction in the supply of credit, given that the only channel of transmission (within the net) to the house price fall is via the credit crunch. Looking at the conditional probability tables we have supplied we can see that the answer lies in the relatively high probability of an 'exogenous' house price fall (we provided $P(H|\widetilde{G}) = 0.10$). Indeed, the conditional probabilities of a house price fall conditioned on the sovereign crisis happening or not happening, $P(H, A)$ and $P(H, \widetilde{A})$, are

$$P(H|A) = 0.269$$

and

$$P(H|\widetilde{A}) = 0.1678$$

respectively. But, without a sovereign crisis, what can account for the house price fall over and above the 'exogenous' probability ($P(H|\widetilde{G}) = 0.10$)? The other, non-sovereign-related, possible source of distress that converges into node G (the restriction of credit) is the distress of a UK bank, or, indirectly, the distress of a European bank. If we felt that these communication channels are too strong (i.e., that $P(H|\widetilde{A}) = 0.1678$ is too high compared with $P(H|\widetilde{G}) = 0.10$), then we should weaken the links between nodes B (the European bank distress) and C (the UK bank distress) and/or C and G (the credit crunch). Indeed, the strength of the transmission channel between the UK bank distress and the house price fall is confirmed by

$$P(H|C) = 0.685$$

This prompts, however, another observation: we have assigned a high probability of a fall in house prices given a credit crunch ($P(H|G) = 0.75$) and a very high probability of restriction of credit given the distress of UK bank(s) ($P(G|C) = 0.90$). However, note that

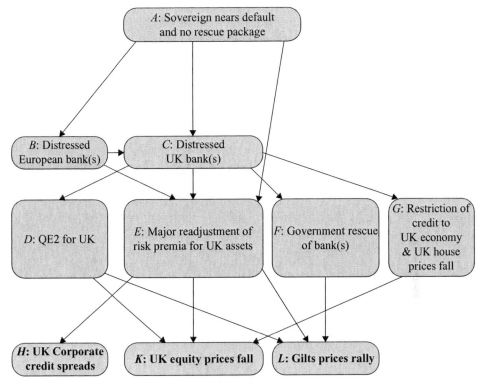

Figure 16.8 The simplification of the Bayesian net discussed in the text.

[the conditional probability of a fall in house prices
given the distress of UK bank(s)]
is approximately equal to the product of
[the probability of house price fall given credit crunch]
times
[the probability of credit crunch fall given the distress of UK bank(s)]:

$$P(H|C) = 0.685 \approx P(H|G) \times P(G|C) = 0.675 \qquad (16.15)$$

This suggest that with little loss of information we can collapse nodes G and H into a single node (which we can call 'There occurs a restriction in the supply of credit and house prices fall'). The reasonableness of this choice is after all consistent with our assignment of $P(H|\tilde{C}) = 0.10$: as this number is reduced the difference between $P(H|C)$ and $P(H|G) \times P(G|C)$ becomes smaller and smaller (e.g., for $P(H|\tilde{C}) = 0.05$ the difference becomes as small as 0.0050). We therefore simplify the net as shown in Figure 16.8.

The conditional probability table for the new G node now looks like this:

$$P(G|C) = 0.80 \tag{16.16}$$

$$P(G|\widetilde{C}) = 0.10 \tag{16.17}$$

The net we have built implies that there is an unconditional probability of 0.107 $(P(G) = 0.107)$ of having a restriction of credit to the UK economy, and that this probability rises to 0.240 if we condition on the occurrence of the sovereign crisis $(P(G|A) = 0.240)$. If we condition on the sovereign crisis not happening, we get $P(G|\widetilde{A}) = 0.101$. Of course, $P(G)$ must be a weighted average of $P(G|A)$ and $P(G|\widetilde{A})$, since

$$P(G) = P(G|A)P(A) + P(G|\widetilde{A})P(\widetilde{A}) \tag{16.18}$$

The closeness of $P(G|\widetilde{A}) = 0.101$ and $P(G) = 0.107$ is reflected in the low assumed probability of a sovereign crisis $(P(A) = 0.025)$.

The leaves   We have finally reached the nodes in the net directly associated with the assets in the portfolio made up of UK corporate bonds, UK equities and Gilts. Let's start from the 'easiest', node H, associated with a severe widening in UK corporate bond spreads. The parent of this note is event E, the marked readjustment in risk premia for UK assets. We start by assigning the following conditional probabilities:

$$P(H|E) = 0.800 \tag{16.19}$$

$$P(H|\widetilde{E}) = 0.100 \tag{16.20}$$

This gives

$$P(H) = 0.135 \tag{16.21}$$

$$P(H|A) = 0.580 \tag{16.22}$$

$$P(H|\widetilde{A}) = 0.124 \tag{16.23}$$

$$P(H|C) = 0.709 \tag{16.24}$$

The most noteworthy feature is the high conditional probability of a widening of UK spreads given the distress of a UK bank, $P(H|C) = 0.709$, compared with the probability of a spread widening conditioned on its direct parent, the readjustment in risk premia, $P(H|E) = 0.800$. This can be understood in terms of the assumed strong links between nodes C and E, as shown by $P(E|C) = 0.871$.

Consider next the relatively high conditional probability of the credit spreads widening given a restriction of credit to the UK economy, $P(H|G) = 0.174$. This high value may be surprising because we have not posited any direct link between the credit restriction and the credit spreads. The information, however, flows 'backwards' (in the diagnostic direction) and then 'forwards' (in the causal direction): knowledge that the credit to the UK economy has been restricted increases (more then seven-fold) our assessment of the probability that a UK bank may have been under distress

($P(C|G) = 0.0769$ compared with $P(C) = 0.0103$); information then flows from the distress in a UK bank to the spreads via the readjustment in the UK risk premia.

Let's move to the last two leaves, K and L, the equity price fall and the *rise* in Gilt prices.[3] Let's start from the latter, the more interesting of the two.

Three nodes (D, the extra round of quantitative easing by Bank of England, E, the widening of the risk premia, and F, the Government rescue of a UK bank), affect the prices of Gilts. Quantitative easing is likely to increase the prices of Gilts. As long of the finances of the UK government are perceived to be sound, the flight to quality following the widening of the risk premia should have a beneficial effect on the prices of Gilts. However, if the government had had to extend a rescuing hand to a UK bank, its finances could be under severe strain, and it could be seen as being more part of the problem than part of the solution. Therefore, if event F (the government bail-out) is true, the 'safe haven' effect could disappear, and the impact on prices could be negative. Therefore a plausible conditional probability table for node L could be profitably built by considering first those states of the world where the bank bail-out has not taken place ($\widetilde{F}$):

$$P(L|\widetilde{F}DE) = 0.80 \tag{16.25}$$

$$P(L|\widetilde{F}\widetilde{D}E) = 0.30 \tag{16.26}$$

$$P(L|\widetilde{F}D\widetilde{E}) = 0.75 \tag{16.27}$$

$$P(L|\widetilde{F}\widetilde{D}\widetilde{E}) = 0.10 \tag{16.28}$$

We can then move to the situation when the government bail-out of a bank has taken place (F). It is plausible to suggest the following:

$$P(L|FDE) = 0.100 \tag{16.29}$$

$$P(L|F\widetilde{D}E) = 0.050 \tag{16.30}$$

$$P(L|FD\widetilde{E}) = 0.075 \tag{16.31}$$

$$P(L|F\widetilde{D}\widetilde{E}) = 0.010 \tag{16.32}$$

The information we have provided implies that:

- the unconditional probability of a rally in UK Gilts is $P(L) = 0.174$;
- the conditional probability of a Gilt rally given the sovereign crisis is $P(L|A) = 0.285$;
- if we condition on the sovereign crisis not occurring, on the other hand, we have a conditional probability of a Gilt rally, $P(L|\widetilde{A})$, of $P(L|\widetilde{A}) = 0.171$.

None of these results offends our intuition.

We can finally move to the last node, K, the fall in equity prices. Of the three parents (D, E and G), only a second round of quantitative easing (event D) could have a

---

[3] There is no node I, to avoid possible confusion between the upper-case letter I and the indicator function or the numeral 1.

positive effect on the prices of equities, but a more muted one than the effect on Gilts (as, presumably, the Bank of England purchases would not be of equities). We can therefore suggest the following table:

$$P(K|\tilde{D}EG) = 0.90$$

$$P(K|\tilde{D}\tilde{E}G) = 0.35$$

$$P(K|\tilde{D}E\tilde{G}) = 0.70$$

$$P(K|\tilde{D}\tilde{E}\tilde{G}) = 0.05$$

and

$$P(K|DEG) = 0.800$$

$$P(K|D\tilde{E}G) = 0.250$$

$$P(K|DE\tilde{G}) = 0.600$$

$$P(K|D\tilde{E}\tilde{G}) = 0.025$$

This gives us a unconditional probability of a fall in equity prices, $P(K) = 0.109$, and a conditional probability of an equity fall (of the size we have posited) given a sovereign crisis of $P(K|A) = 0.535$.

Unassigned conditional probabilities   To gain confidence in the soundness of the construction, we can check what the conditional probabilities we have assigned imply about conditional probabilities we have not assigned, but about which we may have a reasonably strong intuition. For instance, we expect that, given a government bank bail-out (event F), the probability of a widening in the UK risk premia (event E) should be rather high. Indeed, direct computation gives us $P(E|F) = 0.770$.

Conversely, we do not expect the probability of a bank bail-out given that risk premia have widened (an effect that can happen for a multiplicity of causes) to be nearly as high. Again, this is reflected in our net, which gives us $P(F|E) = 0.126$.

What about the probability of quantitative easing (event D) given a widening of risk premia (event E), $P(D|E)$, or given a bank bail-out, $P(D|F)$? Conditioning on the widening of risk premia gives us $P(D|E) = 0.207$, and on the bail-out $P(D|F) = 0.617$. What gives rise to this marked disparity? The most direct cause for this large difference in probabilities stems from the assigned conditional probabilities of quantitative easing (event D) and a bank bail-out (event F) given the distress of a UK bank (event C): $P(D|C) = 0.70$ and $P(F|C) = 0.60$. Are we really so confident that, in a situation of distress for a UK bank, the Bank of England would embark on a further round of quantitative easing? If not, and we reverse the assignments ($P(D|C) = 0.60$ and $P(F|C) = 0.70$), we already obtain $P(D|E) = 0.189$, and for the bail-out we get $P(D|F) = 0.540$. Lowering $P(D|C)$ further (say, $P(D|C) = 0.40$) gives $P(D|F) = 0.363$ and $P(D|E) = 0.154$. To obtain $P(D|E) = P(D|F)$, we must

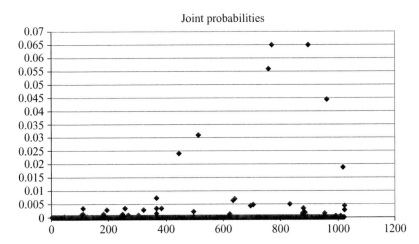

Figure 16.9 A plot of the 1203 joint probabilities (i.e., the 1024 probabilities excluding the probability that nothing happened) obtained with the Bayesian net in Figure 16.8.

set $P(D|C) = 0.10$. This is clearly an important part of our net, where sensitivity analysis is surely warranted. For future analysis we set $P(D|C) = 0.30$ and $P(F|C) = 0.70$.

16.3   Analysis of the joint distribution

We are now in a position to analyse the joint probability distribution.[4] A plot of the 1023 joint probabilities (i.e., the 1024 probabilities excluding the probability that nothing happened) gives what is shown in Figure 16.9.

One can readily see that there are only 10 joint events with a probability greater than 0.005. (Three events have a probability just below this arbitrary cut-off, at 0.004925.) It pays to identify them and see if they are associated with the events that we would consider to be of highest likelihood. Unfortunately, they are all relatively 'uninteresting', because they are associated with event A (the sovereign default) not happening. Let's try to focus, therefore, on the highest-probability events associated with the occurrence of the sovereign crisis. These are shown, after sorting, in Figure 16.10.

The highest is $P(A, \widetilde{B}, \widetilde{C}, \widetilde{D}, \widetilde{E}, \widetilde{F}, \widetilde{G}, \widetilde{H}, \widetilde{K}, \widetilde{L}) = 0.00423$, i.e., the probability that the sovereign crisis occurs, but neither a UK nor a European bank goes under distress; that there is no bank rescue, no readjustment of risk premia, no quantitative easing and no restriction of credit to the UK economy; and no rise in Gilt price or fall in equities or in corporate bond prices. Are we happy with this result?

To answer this question, let's go back to the joint probabilities, and calculate the conditional probability of *no* readjustment in the risk premia given that the sovereign

---

[4] In this section we carry out the analysis of the joint distribution of all the possible events (root(s), transmission channels and leaf-associated market risk factors). It is often easier, but less instructive, to work with the compacted distribution (see Section 22.1), obtained by 'integrating out' (summing over) all the non-leaf (and, hence, all the non-market-risk-factor) probabilities.

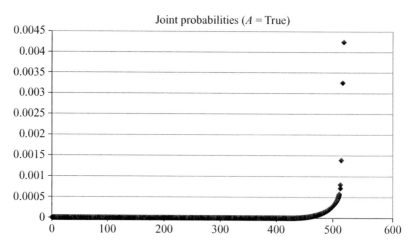

Figure 16.10 The highest-probability events – sorted in order of increasing magnitude – associated with the Bayesian net in Figure 16.8.

crisis has happened, i.e., $P(\widetilde{E}|A)$. (Recall that we already calculated $P(E|A) = 0.685$.) We obtain $P(\widetilde{E}|A) = 0.315$. This value is probably implausibly high. Let's look at the conditional probabilities we have provided for the table for node E (the readjustment in risk premia) that most directly affect $P(\widetilde{E}|A)$. These will be those conditional probabilities for which $A = TRUE$ and $E = FALSE$. From the net we constructed we read off

$$P(\widetilde{E}|ABC) = 0.01 \tag{16.33}$$

$$P(\widetilde{E}|A\widetilde{B}C) = 0.10 \tag{16.34}$$

$$P(\widetilde{E}|AB\widetilde{C}) = 0.25 \tag{16.35}$$

$$P(\widetilde{E}|A\widetilde{B}\widetilde{C}) = 0.40 \tag{16.36}$$

(Recall that events B and C were the distress of a European and a UK bank, respectively.)

Let's focus on the last entry. The conditional probability $P(\widetilde{E}|A\widetilde{B}\widetilde{C}) = 0.40$ was obtained as $P(\widetilde{E}|A\widetilde{B}\widetilde{C}) = 1 - P(E|A\widetilde{B}\widetilde{C})$. The value assigned to $P(E|A\widetilde{B}\widetilde{C})$ was 0.60. If we increase this conditional probability to, say, $P(E|A\widetilde{B}\widetilde{C}) = 0.80$ we obtain $P(\widetilde{E}|A) = 0.179$. Raising $P(E|AB\widetilde{C})$ to 0.85 from 0.75 has a limited effect on $P(\widetilde{E}|A)$, which moves from 0.179 to 0.167. Similarly moving $P(E|A\widetilde{B}C)$ from 0.90 to 0.95 only marginally lowers $P(\widetilde{E}|A)$ (from 0.179 to 0.173). We therefore conclude that the most effective way to translate our intuition into the conditional probability table for node E is to raise $P(E|A\widetilde{B}\widetilde{C})$. We choose $P(E|A\widetilde{B}\widetilde{C}) = 0.85$, which gives $P(\widetilde{E}|A) = 0.139$. This says that, if a sovereign crisis occurs, even if neither a European nor a UK bank goes into trouble, the probability of no major readjustment in UK risk premia is still relatively low.

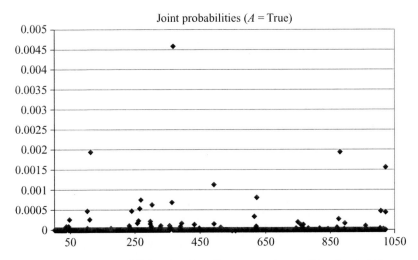

Figure 16.11 Plot of the joint probabilities after the adjustment to the conditional probability, $P(E|A\widetilde{B}\widetilde{C})$, as described in the text.

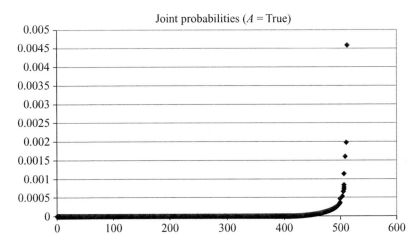

Figure 16.12 Same as Figure 16.11, after sorting.

As a result of the adjustment we made to $P(E|A\widetilde{B}\widetilde{C})$, the joint probability that gave rise to our original concern, $P(A, \widetilde{B}, \widetilde{C}, \widetilde{D}, \widetilde{E}, \widetilde{F}, \widetilde{G}, \widetilde{H}, \widetilde{K}, \widetilde{L})$, is reduced by a factor of almost 3 (it goes from 0.00423 to 0.00159).

With the adjusted joint probabilities, we can carry out along the same lines the sorting and the attending plausibility analysis that led to this revision. The new plot of the joint probabilities is shown in Figures 16.11 and 16.12.

The joint events associated with a probability greater than 0.001 are events 367, 879, 111, 1023 and 495, with a probability for event 367 ($p(367) = 0.0046$) more than twice as large as the second largest probability ($p(879) = 0.00196$). We therefore look more closely at this event.

Event 367 is $P(A, \widetilde{B}, \widetilde{C}, \widetilde{D}, E, \widetilde{F}, \widetilde{G}, H, K, \widetilde{L})$. This corresponds to

- the occurrence of the sovereign crisis,
- no distress by a UK or European bank,
- no quantitative easing by Bank of England,
- a major readjustment in risk premia for UK assets,
- no bank bail-out and no major house price fall,
- widening in credit spreads,
- a fall in equity prices, but
- no rally in Gilts.

This joint scenario looks eminently sensible as a relatively high-probability one given that the sovereign default has occurred.

Let's look at the second-largest event, i.e., event 879. This corresponds to $P(A, \widetilde{B}, \widetilde{C}, \widetilde{D}, E, \widetilde{F}, \widetilde{G}, H, \widetilde{K}, \widetilde{L})$. This event is identical to the previous one, with the only difference that in this scenario the fall in equity prices does not occur.

Finally, the third-largest probability event is event 111 ($p(111) = 0.00196$): $P(A, \widetilde{B}, \widetilde{C}, \widetilde{D}, E, \widetilde{F}, \widetilde{G}, H, K, L)$. Again, there is a sovereign crisis, but no distress by a UK or European bank, no quantitative easing by Bank of England, a major readjustment in risk premia for UK assets, no bank bail-out and no major house price fall. The difference with respect to scenarios 367 and 879 is that now the equity market falls, the credit spreads widen, *and the Gilts rally*. This last event occurs without quantitative easing by the Bank of England. Does this make sense?

Let's calculate the probability of a rally in Gilts (event L) given quantitative easing (event D), $P(L|D)$, and given no quantitative easing, $P(L|\widetilde{D})$. We get $P(L|D) = 0.738$ and $P(L|\widetilde{D}) = 0.109$. We see that, indeed, we have implied by our net a significant probability of a Gilt rally even without quantitative easing. To understand where this comes from, let's look at the entries to the conditional probability table for node L (rally in Gilts) associated with no quantitative easing (node D). We have assigned

$$P(L|\widetilde{D}FE) = 0.05$$

$$P(L|\widetilde{D}F\widetilde{E}) = 0.01$$

$$P(L|\widetilde{D}\widetilde{F}E) = 0.30$$

$$P(L|\widetilde{D}\widetilde{F}\widetilde{E}) = 0.10$$

Now, recall that event F was a bank bail-out, and event E a widening of risk premia. The reasoning underlying these assignments is that a sovereign crisis would be beneficial for safe assets in countries not directly affected by a Euro crisis. Also the occurrence of a widening of risk premia would encourage a flight to quality, which would be beneficial to Gilts. However, if a bank bail-out had taken place, the finances of the UK government would come under question, and the likelihood of a rally in Gilts would be greatly reduced. This is sensible, and confirms that the relatively high probability for $P(L|\widetilde{D})$ ($P(L|\widetilde{D}) = 0.109$) arrives for the right reasons and not 'by accident'.

We could, of course, continue the analysis along these lines by examining more and more joint and conditional probabilities. However, the returns from our efforts are, after a while, rapidly diminishing, especially if we are guided in our analysis by the indications provided in Section 28.2.1 about which conditional probabilities matter most. We therefore do not pursue the analysis further and leave to the enthusiastic reader the pleasure of further investigations.

16.4   Using Maximum Entropy to fill in incomplete tables

In Section 14.2 we suggested one possible way to use the principle of Maximum Entropy in order to fill in the conditional probability tables. Let's see what this procedure yields when we apply it to one of the most complex nodes, node K (the fall in equity prices). With the conditional probabilities provided in the sections above the entropy turns out to be $H_{exp} = 2.850389$. This will be our reference value. Let's then suggest the following bounds for the conditional probabilities:

Conditional probability	Assigned value	Lower bound	Upper bound
$P(K\|DEG)$	0.800	0.65	0.95
$P(K\|D\tilde{E}G)$	0.250	0.15	0.40
$P(K\|DE\tilde{G})$	0.600	0.45	0.75
$P(K\|D\tilde{E}\tilde{G})$	0.025	0.01	0.05
$P(K\|\tilde{D}EG)$	0.900	0.75	0.98
$P(K\|\tilde{D}\tilde{E}G)$	0.350	0.25	0.50
$P(K\|\tilde{D}E\tilde{G})$	0.700	0.55	0.85
$P(K\|\tilde{D}\tilde{E}\tilde{G})$	0.050	0.02	0.075

Optimizing over the eight angles θ_j, $j = 1, 2, \ldots, 8$ as described in Section 14.2 gives

Conditional probability	Max-Entropy value	Lower bound	Upper bound
$P(K\|DEG)$	0.65	0.65	0.95
$P(K\|D\tilde{E}G)$	0.4	0.15	0.40
$P(K\|DE\tilde{G})$	0.500	0.45	0.75
$P(K\|D\tilde{E}\tilde{G})$	0.05	0.01	0.05
$P(K\|\tilde{D}EG)$	0.75	0.75	0.98
$P(K\|\tilde{D}\tilde{E}G)$	0.500	0.25	0.50
$P(K\|\tilde{D}E\tilde{G})$	0.550	0.55	0.85
$P(K\|\tilde{D}\tilde{E}\tilde{G})$	0.075	0.02	0.075

The entropy, H_{ME}, obtained after maximizing over the values of the conditional probabilities within the assigned range turns out to be $H_{ME} = 2.950597$. This is greater than our reference value, $H_{exp} = 2.850389$.

We note in passing that, for this particular node (which is a leaf), no numerical search was actually needed, because, *in the case of a leaf*, it is easy to show that

- the Maximum-Entropy solution is attained when all the 'free' conditional probabilities are set to 0.5;
- when the bounds are biting (i.e., they do not bracket the value 0.5), then the Maximum-Entropy solution will be attained as close to 0.5 as the bounds allow.

This would not be necessarily the case if the node were not a leaf, and we have therefore described how to proceed in the general case.

Note also that, in this case, almost all the bounds we have assigned are 'biting'. Therefore (with one exception) the Maximum-Entropy solution actually settles either on an upper or a lower bound. This is not very satisfactory, but, in general, this will not be the case for non-leaf nodes.

Do we like the Maximum-Entropy solution better or worse than the original solution? Of the by-product probabilities that we monitored, the only ones that changed were $P(K)$ and $P(K|A)$: the Maximum-Entropy solution increased the unconditional probability from $P(K) = 0.1097$ to $P(K) = 0.1382$ and decreased the conditional probability, $P(K|A)$, from $P(K|A) = 0.5355$ to $P(K|A) = 0.4484$. Neither change is significant. As a consequence, in the rest of the analysis we continue to use the conditional probability tables that we have supplied using our expert judgement.

16.5   Determining the P&L distribution

With the joint distribution for the events obtained above we can obtain the profit and loss (P&L) distribution by adding all the probabilities corresponding to a given profit or loss. Given the moves in market variables we have posited, the individual profits or loss have been estimated as follows.

- Loss from FTSE: $-20\% \times$ £400 mill. $= -$£80 mill.
- Loss from corporate spread: $-0.02 \times$ £400 mill. $\times 3.75 = -$£30 mill. (a duration of 3.75 has been assumed)
- Gain from Gilts: £200 mill. $\times 0.0050 \times 8 = +$£8 mill. (a duration of 3.75 has been assumed)

The various combinations of profits and losses give rise to $2^3 = 8$ distinct values: $-110, -102, -80, -72, -30, -22, 0,$ and 8. The associated profit-and-loss distribution is shown in Figure 16.13.

We see that the P&L event with the highest probability (approximately 65%) corresponds to $P\&L = 0$. There is probability of about 1/8 of actually making a modest profit (these are the states of the world where there is a Gilt rally, but no major fall in equity prices or widening of corporate spreads). So, in almost 80% of the case the portfolio fares well. There is, however, a probability of approximately 10% of incurring a loss at least as large as £80 million (an 8% decline in value of the portfolio). If this loss were deemed unacceptable, the composition of the portfolio would have to be changed. The expected P&L is $-$£11 million.

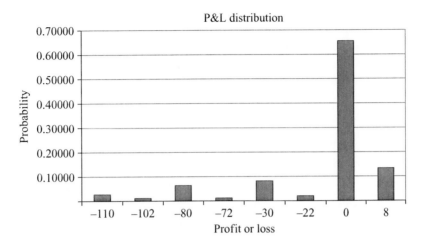

Figure 16.13 The profit-and-loss distribution resulting from the Bayesian net in Figure 16.8, and from the assumed stress gains and losses.

16.6 Sensitivity analysis

In our example we have assumed the profits and losses to be known with certainty. Therefore the uncertainty is only in the values attached to the individual conditional probabilities used to construct the conditional probability tables. We translate our uncertainty about the true values of the conditional probabilities by imposing that each entry, cp_j, should be given by

$$cp_j(u) = L_j + (U_j - L_j)u$$

with $u \sim U(0, 1)$. As we discussed in Section 13.3, a better choice could be a truncated continuous distribution with expected value equal to the value assigned by the expert, and variance related to the degree of uncertainty in the entry. For the sake of simplicity, we do not pursue this route in this chapter.

As a guiding principle, we want to 'stress' our assumptions about conditional probabilities, but we don't want the bounds so large as to invalidate the financial 'story' that we have built around our net. For very low probabilities (say, of the order of 0.01), we stress the input by setting the bounds roughly at half or double the assigned value. For very high probabilities (say, 0.95), the bounds are set close to the probability of 1 (say, 0.9 to 0.99). For medium probabilities (of the order of, say, 0.50) the bounds are set 10–15% above and below the expert-assigned value. The results are shown in Figure 16.14 below.

It is clear that, while there is obvious variability (as there should be), 'large' and 'small' joint probabilities remain 'large' and 'small', and that, by and large, the ordering of most joint probabilities remains unchanged. The results therefore appear sensibly robust. These observations are quantified in Table 16.5, which displays the expected value and the standard deviation of the individual probabilities, and the expectation and standard deviation of the profit or loss from the portfolio. Note, in particular, that,

Table 16.5 *The expected value and the standard deviation of the individual probabilities, and (top row) the expectation and standard deviation of the profit or loss from the portfolio (in million $)*

	Average	StDev
E[P&L]	−12.856	2.346283
p(−110)	0.0316	0.0072
p(−102)	0.0112	0.0031
p(−80)	0.0687	0.0133
p(−72)	0.0106	0.0028
p(−30)	0.0817	0.0225
p(−22)	0.0137	0.0035
p(0)	0.6854	0.0368
p(8)	0.0970	0.0281

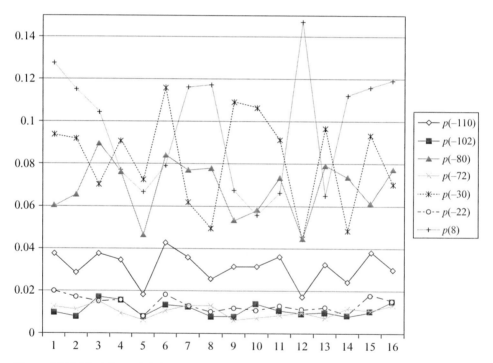

Figure 16.14 The joint probabilities associated with significant joint events as a function of the random draw (x-axis, 16 realizations) of the conditional probabilities within the assigned bounds.

despite the rather wide bounds for the conditional probabilities, the standard deviation of the portfolio profit and loss is of only £2.34 million, for stand-alone losses that can be as large as $80 million. The 'economic significance' of our uncertainty does not seem to be large.

We will have a lot more to say about sensitivity analysis in the later parts of the book. (In Section 28.2.1, in particular, we will show how to focus on those conditional probabilities that 'matter most'.) For the moment, we trust that we have at least given a taste of how sensitivity analysis can be carried out, and of the information it yields.

Part VI

Dealing with normal-times returns

In this part of the book we present the techniques required to identify the body of the return distribution and to describe it via a parametric family of marginals and copulae.

It is important to make an important observation at this point. As we state repeatedly in the book, we hold two related, but logically distinct, sets of beliefs: the first is that information about the 'next crisis' is often best gleaned from a forward-looking, causal-model-inspired analysis. The consequences of, say, a possible break-up of the Euro should be examined, we believe, on its own specific terms, not as an instantiation of a generic 'past crisis'. We also believe that little information of relevance to the crisis at hand is contained in the analysis of past crises. We are less emphatic about this point. If the reader believed that, by culling all of the past outliers out of the return distribution, she would be throwing away useful 'crisis information', she could dispense with the culling part of the procedure we recommend, and simply renormalize the joint distribution in such a way to accommodate for the new crisis. So, if the probability of the current crisis not happening obtained via the Bayesian net were, say, 90%, one could renormalize the *full* past distribution (certainly informative about *past* crises) to 0.9, and 'splice' on top the new tail contributions. This is not the procedure we prefer, but it is a perfectly feasible, and logically defensible, one.

If the reader would like to carry out the culling of past crises that we recommend, suitable statistical techniques must be employed to do so effectively. In this chapter we briefly review the culling methodologies we have found useful. We do not put ourselves forward as experts in this area, and we are heavy users of, but not original contributors to, these techniques. Nevertheless, for two related reasons we did not want to leave the reader with generic pointers to the copious literature on the subject of removal of outliers: first, because we would like our treatment to be self-contained; second, because we want to empower the reader to apply in practice, if she so wants, the full methodology – soup to nuts – that we present in this book.

So, the references are there, for those readers who would like to gain a deeper understanding of the techniques we present. But the impatient reader should be able to glean enough detailed information from our (at times unabashedly recipe-like) treatment of the statistical identification topics, to move confidently to the implementation phase.

17 Identification of the body of the distribution

17.1 What is 'normality'? Conditional and unconditional interpretation

One of the central ideas behind our approach is to treat separately and differently the 'normal' and the exceptional parts of the return distribution. The idea seems natural enough and, at least in principle, well defined. However, defining what we mean by the 'normal' part of the distribution is not quite as straightforward as it may at first glance appear. In order to illustrate where the problems lie, we are going to use in this chapter much longer time series than those we employ in the part of the book devoted to asset allocation. In particular, in this chapter we are going to use as our data set 3360×4 daily returns, covering the period February 1997 to June 2010 for three asset classes: Government Bonds, Investment-Grade Credit Bonds, and Equities (called asset class *Bond*, *Credit* and *Equity*, respectively, in the following). More precisely, the following indices were used:

1. for *Bond* the BarCap US Treasury Index;
2. for *Credit* the BarCap US Credit Index;
3. for *Equity* the S&P 500.[1]

   To understand where our problem lies, let us look at Figures 17.1–17.4, which display two pairs of time series. Each pair displays the rolling pairwise correlation between the same two asset classes, in one case using the whole data set, in the other just the 'normal' portion of the data.[2] The time series we look at are *Bonds*, *Credit* and *Equities*. In the discussion presented in this section, we are going to assume that, using one of the methods explained later in the chapter, we have found a way to cull the exceptional returns (the 'outliers') from the joint distribution of returns. So, we can look at the correlation between changes in *Bonds* and in *Credit* and between changes in *Bonds* and in *Equities*, both using the whole data set, and the 'normal' data only.

   Let's look first at the correlation between changes in *Bonds* and in *Credit*. As we shall see, if all our asset pairs behaved this way, our life would be much easier.

---

[1] Elsewhere in the book we occasionally use the asset class *Mortgage*, which was proxied by the BarCap US MBS Index.

[2] The correlations were calculated using the daily time series with a rolling window of 40 data points.

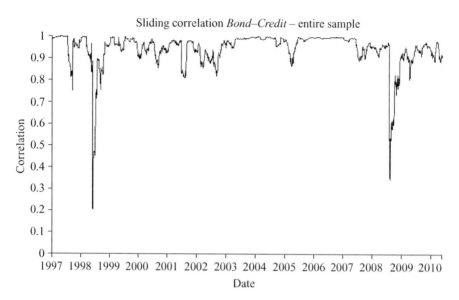

Figure 17.1 The rolling correlation between changes in the time series *Bonds* and *Credit* before culling the outliers.

Looking at Figure 17.1, we immediately notice that most of the time the running correlation is very high (close to 100%), but that occasionally it drops significantly (in one case as low as 20%). We also notice, however, that, after these sudden and relatively brief dips, the correlation reverts to its 'original' and very high levels of almost 100%.[3]

We can understand what is happening very easily by looking at Figure 17.2. It displays the same rolling correlation after the excited periods (the 'outliers') have been culled using one of the techniques described in this chapter. We stress that the culling exercise was carried out 'without peeking' (i.e., without any knowledge about the behaviour of the rolling correlation shown in Figure 17.1).

Even without carrying out any formal statistical analysis,[4] what is happening jumps out at us. The sudden drops in the correlation between these two asset classes are associated with (we are tempted to say 'are caused by') the onset of an excited period.[5] When 'normal' market conditions prevail again, we are back to the original (i.e., pre-crisis) levels of correlation. Most important for our discussion, this high level

---

[3] If anything, the drops are in reality even more sudden than the figure suggests, because we are using for the estimation of the correlation a naive rolling window methodology, that, by its nature, is either noisy or poorly suited to producing a responsive point estimate of the correlation. For a responsive estimation of correlation that makes use of the full data set, see Engle (2009).

[4] But we did, just in case: a simple Fisher transform test strongly rejects the null hypothesis that the correlations in the two periods come from the same population.

[5] By the way, this simple observation should pour some cold water on the facile statement that, in conditions of market distress, 'all correlations tend to ±1'. What we would like to have is an understanding of what is driving these changes in correlation, not some magic rule of thumb. We need, in short, a (possibly crude and imperfect) structural model capable of explaining why some correlations increase, but some, as we clearly see here, dramatically *de*crease. This is where Bayesian nets can provide valuable help.

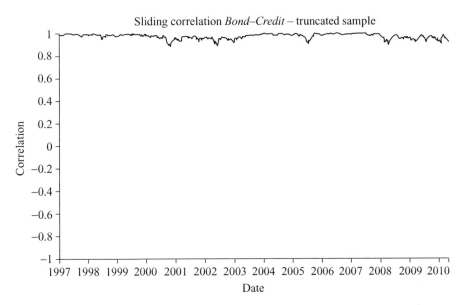

Figure 17.2 The rolling correlation between changes in the time series *Bonds* and *Credit* after culling the outliers. We stress that the removal of the outliers was carried out without reference to the rolling correlation. Therefore the culling of the original time series 'naturally' removed most of the variations in the correlation. In 'normal times' the correlation is stable and very close to a constant.

of correlation appears to be a persistent market feature, whose occurrence mainly depends on the market not being in an excited state. In other words, as long as markets are in a 'normal' state, we seem to have identified a *conditional* feature of the running correlation, where the conditioning is simply on the world being in a normal state. We stress that when we assert it makes sense to condition simply on the state being 'normal', without any further specification of what constitutes 'normality', we are strictly referring to this pair of assets.

The explanation for the behaviour of the correlation just described seems to be simple and convincing: if all time series behaved this way we could truly state that most of the time the degree of correlation between returns in different asset classes is a stable quantity, which is only briefly disturbed by the onset of crisis. If this were always the case, using as long a (culled!) time series as possible would be the best strategy to extract information about this time-stationary phenomenon.

Let's look, however, at the next pair of figures, Figures 17.3 and 17.4, which show the rolling correlation between changes in *Equities* and *Bonds* before and after the removal of the outliers.

The behaviour is now completely different, both when we look at the full data set and when we consider the culled one. Starting from the full data set, we fail to notice any stable level to which the rolling correlation reverts after sudden and brief changes. Instead, we appear to have periods during which the rolling correlation moves in wide but well-defined ranges around certain levels (about 0.5, for instance, for the first three

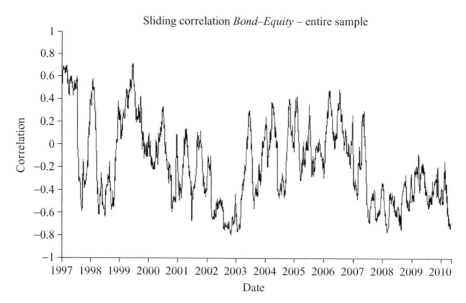

Figure 17.3 The rolling correlation between changes in the time series *Bonds* and *Equities* before culling the outliers.

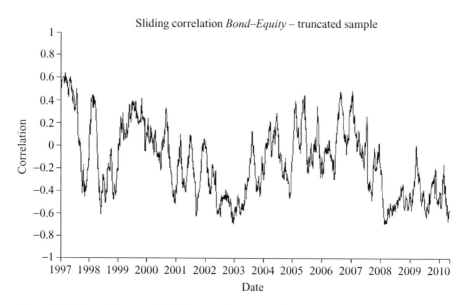

Figure 17.4 The rolling correlation between changes in the time series *Bonds* and *Equities* after culling the outliers. Note how in this case the removal of the outliers only brings about a minor 'stabilization' of the rolling correlation.

years in our time series); and we have long 'trending' periods (again lasting several years), during which the rolling correlation declines from over 0.60 to −0.80, climbs back up around zero, and then quickly drops to negative values again.[6]

More strikingly, culling the excited data does not change this picture substantially. Yes, if we run statistical tests, we can show that the culled rolling correlation is somewhat more stable. However, looking at Figure 17.4 it is clear that removing the excited periods does not make the underlying correlation in any way self-similar (i.e., time-independent). Even if we are in 'normal' times, the level of correlation between changes in *Equities* and *Bonds* fundamentally depends on when the measurement is taken. Just conditioning on the world being in a 'normal' state is no longer sufficient to pin down the correlation between *Equity* and *Bond*. Therefore, purely conditioning on our being in a non-excited state would hardly help us in our prediction. As for an *unconditional* estimate of the correlation over the whole non-excited data set, this may well be interesting from a descriptive point of view, but, if we are interested in what the correlation will be like '*tomorrow*', it would have very poor predictive power. Clearly, just conditioning on our being in a 'normal' state is not enough to get a decent prediction. How does this fit with our overall philosophy?

Let's remind ourselves of our objective: ultimately, we want to get the best possible prediction of the codependence between changes in different asset classes over the next investment horizon. We will have to make this prediction either in a normal or in an excited state. Let's begin from estimates made in the 'normal' state.

17.2 Estimates in the 'normal' state

When we have to make a prediction in 'normal' times, it is natural for us to look at similarly 'normal' past historical periods. We do *not* state, however, that volatilities and codependencies (or, more generally, the moments of the joint distributions of returns) are time-invariant in non-excited conditions. Rather, we make the weaker statement that, in normal market conditions, the marginals and copulae can be described by the same *family* of functions. So, for instance, we may be able to establish that in 'normal' times the marginal distribution for the *Equity* returns are satisfactorily described by a Student-t distribution. We do not assert, however, that the same parameters for the Student-t distribution (the location parameter, μ, the dispersion parameter, λ, and the number, ν, of degrees of freedom) will always describe the normal-times distribution. Rather, we prefer to employ a fast-reacting estimation technique that can 'calibrate' the free parameters of the family of distributions we have chosen to the current ('normal') market conditions.

---

[6] For an early account of the changes in correlation between these two asset classes, see Campbell and Ammer (1993). For a discussion of the economic determinants of this changing correlation which takes into account more recent behaviour, see Anderssona, Krylovab and Vahamaa (2008). For a discussion of estimation issues see de Goeji and Marquering (2004) and Engle (2009), who compares moving averages and various types of dynamic conditional correlation models. At the qualitative level of the present discussion all these estimation methods are roughly equivalent.

We can do the same for the codependence structure. When we are in normal market conditions, we may want to state that a particular copula (say, a Gaussian copula) does, in 'normal' market conditions, a good job of describing the co-movements between the returns in the various asset classes. However, we may then calibrate the parameters of the copula to the specific market conditions in which we find ourselves today. As Figures 17.3 and 17.4 clearly show, doing so can dramatically change our conditionally normal estimates.

If we look at the problem in this light, the name of the game is how to estimate the conditional quantities that pin down the 'free parameters' of our family of distributions or copulae in an accurate and responsive manner. There are at least two distinct approaches to doing so. When it comes to 'responsive' estimates of volatilities, the main candidates are GARCH-family methods,[7] and high-frequency ('realized volatility') techniques.[8]

As usual, we are between a rock and a hard place: if we use lots of data, our statistical estimator becomes more precise (if the data are drawn from the same distribution); if we use very recent data sampled at daily or longer intervals, we greatly increase the probability that these data may be relevant to the current market conditions, but we degrade the quality of the statistical estimator (simply because we have few data points). When available, the use of high-frequency data is very appealing, because it allows us to use *plenty* of *relevant* data. Five-minute sampling, for instance, gives us hundreds of data points for a single day. With 200 data points, the uncertainty in a correlation estimation is between 5% and 10%.

Such abundance does come at a price, however. The shorter the sampling interval (and, hence, the more plentiful the data), the greater the microstructural source of noise. 'Microstructural noise' is a blanket term that covers a variety of sins – from non-synchronicity of prices for correlation estimates, to bid-offer bounce. A variety of techniques then exist to filter the signal from the noise. The literature has grown enormously in recent years. For a good survey, we refer the interested reader to Lopez de Prado (2011) and references therein.

In our work we tend to use eclectically both the realized-variance approach with high-frequency data (when available) and GARCH models. (When it comes to estimating correlations, the so-called 'anticipating-correlation' techniques pioneered by Engle (2009) are the counterpart of the traditional GARCH techniques for estimating volatilities.) Academic studies (Doust and Chien 2008) appear to suggest that predictions based on the so-called realized (co-)variance approach tend to be superior to GARCH-family predictions. We caution, however, against simplistic 'horse races', as there is no such thing as *the best* GARCH model, or *the best* filtering technique.

---

[7] The literature on GARCH techniques is vast. A few benchmark or introductory papers are the following: Engle (1982), Bollerslev (1986), Engle (1995, 2001, 2002). For a perspective that relates to risk estimation see Engle (2004). For a simple how-to guide to Maximum-Likelihood Estimation of GARCH-(1,1) processes, see, e.g., Reider (2009).

[8] See, e.g., Bollerslev and Zhou (2002), Andersen *et al.* (2001a, b, 2003), Barndorff-Nielsen and Shepard (2001).

We stress again that, in the treatment of normal-times distributions, we are simply committing ourselves to the same *family* of marginals and copulae. This still allows great flexibility to describe time-varying phenomena by using time-varying parameters, at least as long as the degree of variation is such that our 'basis functions' can cope with the change in behaviour. One should distinguish carefully here between the ability to estimate the changes in parameters in a sufficiently responsive manner, and the intrinsic ability of the chosen family of marginals and copulae to describe the behaviour explored over time. So, for instance, the dramatic variation in correlation (between 0.60 and −0.80) between *Equity* and *Bonds* alluded to earlier in this chapter does not, *per se*, indicate that a simple Gaussian copula with time-dependent parameters cannot be up to the task of accounting for the observed dependence.

17.3   Estimates in an excited state

So much for the treatment of conditional estimates when the estimate itself is made in normal market conditions. But what are we to do when we already are in an excited state (and we are contemplating both the possibility of further excitation ahead, which we will try to capture with the Bayesian-net part of our procedure, and of reversion to a possibly 'new normal' state)?

Of course, the whole approach we present in this book is based on the idea that *we*, the asset managers, are going to provide an important forward-looking component to the joint distribution of returns by means of our Bayesian-net construction. However, even if we are in an excited state today, we do not suggest for a moment that we can subjectively prescribe, as it were, 'by hand' a full description of the excited world over the next rebalancing period. Exactly because *we already are* in an excited state, exceptional events over and above those that we are keen to describe with our Bayesian net must have occurred already. These already-occurred events will leave the market 'reeling', i.e., in a state of uncertainty and turmoil. So, we must ask ourselves the following question. Suppose that we were to carry out the procedures described in this book during, say, the week after the default of Lehman. Suppose also that we wanted to describe the then-current joint distribution of market risk factors distinct from the extra source of turmoil that we were going to model using our Bayesian net. How would we have liked to model this pre-existing joint distribution?

Here the validity of the assumption that it is enough to 'stretch' (by, say, adapting its variance) a marginal distribution while retaining the same functional form used in 'normal' times becomes much more debatable, and more difficult to validate empirically. The same applies, in spades, to the choice of our family of copulae.

Starting from the marginals, one may be tempted to estimate the family of return distributions that prevails when the market is excited. Even leaving aside our reservations about the universality of 'signatures' (see the discussion in Chapter 4), the statistical task is formidable. Recall that most studies of fat-tailed distributions use the whole data set, not just the excited points. A number of mechanisms can then be invoked to generate these leptokurtic *overall* distributions. For instance, one of the many ways to obtain these fat-tailed distributions is to posit Hidden-Markov-Chain-type models for the process of the volatility.[9] This approach can be very effective and convincing. However, in financial applications the assumption is typically made that, *in each state*, the return is drawn from a Gaussian distribution with a state-dependent variance and mean. No justification, other than tractability, is usually given for such a choice of basis functions.

And, of course, when it comes to the choice of the family of copulae that should be used to describe codependencies in periods of turmoil, the problems just multiply. In our experience with Markov-chain modelling, *once the assumption is made that the basis functions are Gaussians*, a different number of states is found for different historical periods, and periods of turmoil typically exhibit a higher number of states. A possible explanation of these observations is that the Markov-chain technique requires a higher number of basis functions simply to account for the increased leptokurtosis of the emission distribution during excited periods. One can argue, in other words, that in periods of turmoil there aren't truly more numerous emission distributions, but that the emission distributions become more 'excited' (leptokurtic, negative-skewed, etc.). This suggests that there is a trade-off between the leptokurtosis of the basis functions and the number of identified states. With an inappropriate choice of basis functions, the Markov-chain algorithm is 'tricked' into believing there are many states when the emission distribution becomes more leptokurtic. Unfortunately, we can measure the (time-varying) degree of leptokurtosis of the overall distribution, but not that of the basis functions.

All of this long and somewhat hand-waving discussion (see, however, a more precise treatment in Doust and Chien (2008)) simply indicates that choosing the right *type* of distribution in an excited state (let alone its correct parametrization) is a formidable task.

Pragmatically, we therefore make use again of Occam's razor, and postulate that the *same* type of distribution or copula describes both the normal and the excited states. We then make use of all the timely and responsive information we can meaningfully extract to calibrate the member of the distribution or copula function to the current market conditions (normal or excited as they may be).

In general – i.e., irrespective of whether we are in an excited or in a 'business-as-usual' state of the world – we recommend going back as far as the last visible structural change, which can be estimated using a number of parametric or non-parametric techniques, and confining the estimation of the variances and of the codependence structure to this (possibly rather limited) data set. Since with this ruthless culling we are likely to throw away a lot of data, the estimates we have to work with may be very noisy, but the old adage that it is better to be approximately right than precisely wrong springs to mind again.

---

[9] Some of the early work in Hidden Markov Models was by Baum *et al.* (1970). For a good tutorial on Hidden Markov Models, see Section II.A (p. 259) of Rabiner (1989).

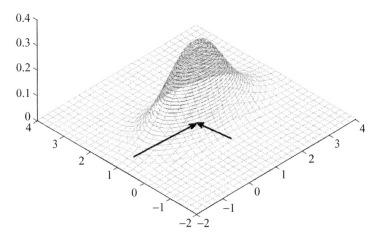

Figure 17.5 The distance from the centre of a distribution of two points on an equiprobability contour (as shown by the length of the two arrows) does not provide a useful identification of outliers. Zero correlation was assumed between the two variables.

17.4   Identifying 'distant points': the Mahalanobis distance

We assume in what follows that the spirit of the recommendations we have made in the opening sections of this chapter have been accepted. We are therefore now faced with the task of identifying the overall structure of the body of the joint distribution of interest. By 'overall structure' we mean that we want to understand which classes of marginals and copulae are good candidates for describing the normal-times distributions. We will then leave to a separate, and later, stage the specification of the particular set of parameters that uniquely identify a member of the class (of marginals or of copulae) and carry out the conditioning to the current state of the world.

In this first stage of our recommended procedure we are therefore going to work with all the data at our disposal, and our task is to remove those data points (where 'point' means 'vector') that are associated with past crises.

Given a panel of n vectors of dimension p, identifying the body of a distribution is tantamount to finding a set of $m < n$ vectors which are in some sense 'too distant' from the body of the distribution. In this context, one of the most appealing measures of distance is the Mahalanobis measure. In order to gain an intuitive understanding of the Mahalanobis distance (and related measures) consider the problem of identifying the outliers of a sample drawn from a bivariate distribution. In some way to be made more precise, it could be tempting to proceed as follows: first we could locate the centre of the distribution; we could then measure the distance of each point from this centre; finally we could label as outliers those points whose distance is greater than a certain threshold.

A moment's thought shows that there would be serious problems with this naive procedure. Suppose that the two variables at hand have very different variances. Then the naive distance from the centre would not be a good measure of how distant a point

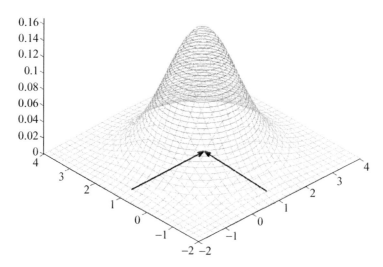

Figure 17.6 In the case of zero correlation between two variables, after normalizing by the standard deviation the distance from the centre does help in identifying outliers: the arrows now have the same length.

is from the centre, as shown in Figure 17.5 in the case of zero correlation: the down arrow is much longer than the horizontal arrow, but the volume element around the starting point of the first arrow has a higher probability than the volume element around the starting point of the second arrow.[10]

The first obvious fix to this problem is to normalize the distances from the centre by the standard deviations of the two variables. This was indeed the approach taken by Mahalanobis in his original (Mahalanobis 1927) paper on the statistical characteristics of – of all things – human skulls. Now, as Figure 17.6 shows in the case of zero correlation between the two variables, after normalization equal arrow lengths do correspond to equal probabilities. However, this is no longer true if the correlation is non-zero, as Figure 17.7 shows.

In order to retain a notion of 'distance from the centre' that reflects our intuition about the likelihood of an event we have to take into account also the information about the correlation between the two variables, as Mahalanobis did in a later paper (Mahalanobis 1936).

More precisely, let's generalize the approach to the case of n variables (see Kritzman and Li (2010) for a simple discussion with financial applications), by defining a $1 \times n$ vector y of observations (in our case returns), the $1 \times n$ vector μ of their averages and an $[n \times n]$ covariance matrix, Σ.

---

[10] What we mean here, of course, is that the probability associated with the volume element centred around the starting point of the first arrow is greater than the probability associated with the volume element centred around the starting point of the second. As this is quite a mouthful, here and subsequently we use the same shorthand expressions.

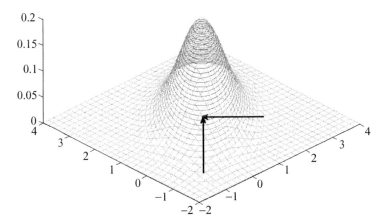

Figure 17.7 Even after normalizing by the standard deviations, in the case of non-zero correlation two arrows of identical length originating from the centre can reach points on different equiprobability contours.

Then the Mahalanobis distance, d_M, can be defined as

$$d_M = \sqrt{(y - \mu)\Sigma^{-1}(y - \mu)^T} \qquad (17.1)$$

We can interpret this distance by observing that it reduces to the usual Euclidean norm[11] of the distance vector $(y - \mu)$ when the covariance matrix Σ is the unit matrix (or, more generally, diagonal). As we saw above, this corresponds to lack of correlation between the variables. When the matrix Σ is not diagonal, we can interpret d_M as the distance in the metric induced by the 'metric tensor' Σ.[12]

Using this distance, we can now verify that two points on the same equiprobability line (such as the points $\{-0.9, -1\}$ and, say, $\{0.2, -0.965\}$) have the same Mahalanobis distance for the bivariate Gaussian distribution characterized by $\mu_1 = 1, \mu_2 = 1, \sigma_1 = 1, \sigma_2 = 0.5$ and $\rho = 0.4$, despite having very different distances from the centre.

The important point about the Mahalanobis measure is that it captures not only the magnitude of the assets' returns, but also the interactions between them. The focus is on the full *vector* of returns, not on the individual returns, however exceptional these may be. If we take a large Mahalanobis distance as an indication of exceptionality, we may classify a vector of returns as exceptional even if the magnitudes of the individual returns are very ordinary, as long as their relative movements are in unusual 'directions' (with respect to what is implied by the covariance matrix). Since the focus of our analysis is precisely on co-movement of returns (and in breakdowns in diversification), this is exactly the type of approach we need.

---

[11] Given an n-dimensional Euclidean space $\mathbb{R}^n$, the Euclidean norm, $||x||$, of a vector, x, with components x_i, $i = 1, 2, \ldots, n$, captures the familiar notion of Pythagorean distance: $||x|| = \sqrt{\sum_{i=1,n} x_i^2}$.

[12] In this 'curved space' minimum-distance lines (geodesics) cease to be 'straight lines' – readers familiar with general relativity may find this analogy useful. Otherwise we leave it at that.

17.5   Problems with the Mahalanobis distance

Appealing as it is, using the Mahalanobis distance is not without its problems. If the data come from a multivariate Gaussian distribution, the Mahalanobis distances follow a χ_p^2 distribution. It would be intuitive to define the body of data as the locus of points such that

$$L = \left\{ y : d_M(y) \leq \chi_p^2(\alpha) \right\} \tag{17.2}$$

where α represents a pre-determined confidence level. This approach, however, has a fundamental problem. The covariance matrix Σ and the means μ in Equation (17.1) are both estimated from the sample. The presence of outliers can inflate heavily these estimates. As a consequence, if we made use of Equations (17.1) and (17.2) using the full data set we could miss some potential outliers, which would camouflage as 'normal' points. This problem is called the 'masking effect'.

There is a degree of circularity to the problem: in order to calculate the robust Mahalanobis distance we need the location vector, μ, and the dispersion matrix, Σ, calculated using the non-outliers. But to determine the outliers, we need the Mahalanobis distance.

To overcome this problem, two related measures have been introduced, the Minimum Volume Ellipsoid (MVE) and the Minimum Covariance Determinant (MCD). (We explain in Section 17.8 how they are connected.) For both measures, in order to be able to calculate a Mahalanobis distance, we need to define a suitable and self-consistent location vector and dispersion matrix. Lest the reader gets distracted by the definitions and algorithms it is important to keep in mind that what lies at the heart of these outlier-culling techniques is simply the identification of where the body of the distribution is (the location vector), and of how dispersed the body is around this location vector (the dispersion matrix).

Historically, the Minimum-Volume-Ellipsoid method was preferred, because of the computational burden associated with the Minimum-Covariance method. However, as we mention in Section 17.6, the introduction of the FAST-MCD algorithm has recently renewed interest in the Minimum-Covariance method. See, e.g., Rousseeuw and Van Driessen (1999).

17.6   The Minimum-Volume-Ellipsoid method

Let us start with the Minimum-Volume-Ellipsoid method. The Minimum Volume Ellipsoid is one of the techniques used in robust estimation of the location and shape of a multivariate distribution. As Poston et al. (1997, p. 302) clearly state: '[t]he problem of robust estimation of multivariate location and shape is: given a set of p-dimensional observations, find an estimate of location and shape that is resistant to outliers or contaminated data'.

The Minimum Volume Ellipsoid of a given data set is determined by a subset of m points subject to the constraint that the ellipsoid that covers the points has minimum volume among all ellipsoids constructed using m points. (Cook, Hawkins and Weisberg 1993; Rousseeuw 1987; Woodruff and Rocke 1993).[13]

This informal definition clearly shows that there are two parts to the problem: the identification of the m optimal points; and the calculation of the volume of the ellipsoid. If approached in a brute-force manner, the first problem is combinatorial in nature and, even for a moderately high number of observations, it is effectively unfeasible. Approximate solutions to the search problem must therefore be found.

These approximate solutions can be either random or deterministic. See Woodruff and Rocke (1993) for a review of random methods (such as simulated annealing, genetic algorithms, etc.). Poston *et al.* (1997) among others propose a deterministic method.[14]

17.6.1 Definition

The Minimum-Volume-Ellipsoid method to identify outliers was introduced by Rousseeuw and Leroy (1987), Rousseeuw and Van Aelst (2010) and Rousseeuw and Van Driessen (1999). Following their treatment, let N be the number of observation vectors in our data sample, let p be the number of components in each vector, and let h be a number such that

$$\left[\frac{N}{2} + 1\right] \leq h \leq N \tag{17.3}$$

(The symbol $[x]$ indicates the integer part of x.) Let the notation $\#\{i; A\}$ denote the number of points in a set enjoying property A. We can define the location estimator, m, and the dispersion matrix, Σ, of the Minimum Volume Ellipsoid as follows.

DEFINITION 9 *Given an integer h as in Equation (17.3) and a strictly positive constant c^2, the Minimum-Volume-Ellipsoid location estimator m and scatter estimator Σ minimize the determinant of Σ subject to*

$$\{\#i; (y - m)\Sigma^{-1}(y - m)^{\mathrm{T}} \leq c^2\} = h \tag{17.4}$$

where m belongs to $\mathbb{R}^p$ and Σ belongs to the class of positive definite symmetric matrices of rank p, $PDS(p)$.

17.6.2 The intuition

The definition above makes reference to the minimization of the determinant of Σ, subject to a constraint: Woodruff and Rocke that the number, i, of points whose Mahalanobis distance $((y - m)\Sigma^{-1}(y - m)^{\mathrm{T}})$ is smaller than c^2 should be equal to h.

To get an intuitive understanding of why minimizing the magnitude of this determinant is related to the identification of the most tightly clustered points, consider for

---

[13] Poston *et al.* (1997, p. 301). See also Woodruff and Rocke (1994).
[14] Deterministic methods present the computational advantage of repeatability without having to use the same seed for a random search process.

a moment the bivariate case. Suppose we consider h points out of N. We can choose $U = \binom{N}{h}$ combinations of h points. Let $u = 1, 2, \ldots, U$ be one of these combinations. For each u, we can form a covariance matrix, $\mathbf{\Sigma}(u)$:

$$\mathbf{\Sigma}(u) = \begin{bmatrix} \sigma_1^2(u) & \sigma_1(u)\sigma_2(u)\rho(u) \\ \sigma_1(u)\sigma_2(u)\rho(u) & \sigma_2^2(u) \end{bmatrix} \tag{17.5}$$

where we have explicitly shown the dependence of $\sigma_1(u)$, $\sigma_2(u)$ and $\rho(u)$ on the particular combination, u, that we have chosen. The determinant, $\det(u)$, of the matrix $\mathbf{\Sigma}(u)$ is given by

$$\det(u) = \sigma_1^2(u)\sigma_2^2(u) - \sigma_1^2(u)\sigma_2^2(u)\rho^2(u) \tag{17.6}$$

and, of course, is also a function of the combination, u. So, according to the definition above, we want to look over all the combinations of points for which the determinant of $\mathbf{\Sigma}(u)$ is smallest. But why would we want to do so?

To understand the motivation, consider a special covariance matrix, $\mathbf{\Sigma}$, for which $\sigma_1 = \sigma_2 = \sigma$. For this matrix the expression for the determinant simplifies to

$$\det(u)^1 = \sigma^4(1 - \rho^2) \tag{17.7}$$

This shows that in this case the determinant will be minimized when ρ approaches 1, i.e., *when the points are clumped most closely together*. Therefore, one can easily see that, at least in this simple case, the covariance matrix with the smallest determinant will be associated with the set of most closely packed points.

Given these most closely packed points, the location estimator, m, and the dispersion estimator, $\mathbf{\Sigma}$, are vectors and positive definite matrices, respectively, such that their induced Mahalanobis distance is smaller than or equal to a predetermined quantity, c^2. Therefore the Minimum Volume Ellipsoid is an estimator of the centre and the scatter of the h points that are the most concentrated in a given data set.

As for the constant c, it can be chosen according to different criteria. One of the possible criteria leads to the choice of c as a consistent estimator of the covariance matrix for data coming from a multivariate normal distribution, i.e.,

$$c = \sqrt{\chi_p^2(\alpha)} \tag{17.8}$$

where $\alpha = h/n$, but there is nothing fundamental behind this choice.

17.6.3 Detailed description
In this subsection we present the shortcut to calculate the Minimum Volume Ellipsoid proposed in Meucci (2009), which is in turn based on the methods presented in Poston *et al.* (1997) and Titterington (1975). It consists of three distinct routines (that we imaginatively call A, B and C below) combined together. More precisely, Routine A is Titterington's (1975) algorithm to find the Minimum Volume Ellipsoid given h points.

Routine B is Peston's algorithm to cull outliers. Routine C presents Meucci's (2009) suggestion to cull outliers.

Routine A – Calculation of the smallest ellipsoid that contains h elements
- Step 1: Given a set of h elements define the initial weights as follows:

$$w_n = \frac{1}{h}, \quad n = 1, 2, \ldots, h \tag{17.9}$$

- Step 2: Compute the location parameter m and scatter Σ according to

$$m = \frac{1}{\sum\limits_{n=1}^{h} w_n} \sum_{n=1}^{h} w_n y_n \tag{17.10}$$

$$\Sigma = \sum_{n=1}^{h} w_n (y - m)(y - m)^{\mathrm{T}}$$

- Step 3: Calculate the squared Mahalanobis distance:

$$d_{M,n}^2 = (y_n - m)\Sigma^{-1}(y_n - m)^{\mathrm{T}}, \quad n = 1, 2, \ldots, h \tag{17.11}$$

- Step 4: For every n for which $d_{M,n}^2 > 1$ change the respective weight to:

$$w_n \longrightarrow w_n d_{M,n}^2 \tag{17.12}$$

- Step 5: If there is no value of n for which the transformation (17.12) has to be carried out, stop and define the volume of the ellipsoid as:

$$V = \gamma_p \sqrt{|\Sigma|} \tag{17.13}$$

where γ_p is the volume of the unit sphere in p dimensions:

$$\gamma_p = \frac{\pi^{p/2}}{\Gamma\left(\frac{p}{2} + 1\right)} \tag{17.14}$$

and $\Gamma(\cdot)$ is the Gamma function; otherwise go to Step 2.

Routine B – Removal of the farthest outlier
- Step 1: Define the $N \times p$ matrix U,

$$U = \begin{bmatrix} y_1 - \overline{m} \\ y_2 - \overline{m} \\ \vdots \\ y_n - \overline{m} \end{bmatrix} \tag{17.15}$$

where $\overline{m}$ is the vector of sample means of the data.

- Step 2: Construct the $n \times n$ information matrix,[15] $\boldsymbol{B}$:

$$\boldsymbol{B} = \boldsymbol{U}(\boldsymbol{U}^{\mathsf{T}}\boldsymbol{U})^{-1}\boldsymbol{U}^{\mathsf{T}} \qquad (17.16)$$

- Step 3: Denote by λ_n the nth element of the diagonal of the information matrix:

$$\lambda_n = (\boldsymbol{B})_{nn} \qquad (17.17)$$

and remove the observation with the highest value of λ_n. This by definition is the observation that changes most the determinant of the sample covariance matrix.

Routine C – Truncation

- Step 1: Start with the entire data set.
- Step 2: Calculate the sample covariance matrix $\boldsymbol{\Sigma}$.
- Step 3: Use Routine A to find the location and scatter parameters of the ellipsoid of minimum volume, ε.
- Step 4: Find the farthest outlier with Routine B and remove it from the data.
- Step 5: If the number of data points left equals $h = 0.75 \times N$ stop the algorithm. Otherwise go to Step 2.

The idea behind this procedure is that by plotting quantities associated with the ellipsoid of minimum volume, ε, and with its covariance matrix, $\boldsymbol{\Sigma}$, as a function of the points left in the data set the boundary between the outliers and the body can be located where these values start to show abrupt changes. As we show below, other important quantities can also be monitored during the truncation and their stabilization can also be used to infer a boundary between the body of the distribution and the cloud of outliers.

17.6.4   An example and discussion of results

An example of this procedure is shown in Figures 17.8 to 17.13. Let's define first the variation, $\Delta(i)$, of a quantity, q, as

$$\Delta(i) = \frac{q(i+1) - q(i)}{q(i)}$$

where $q(i)$ is the value of the quantity estimated on the data set if i observations are removed. Figure 17.8 then shows the volume of the ellipsoid as a function of numbers of observations removed from the data set, and Figure 17.9 displays the changes in the volume of the Minimum Volume Ellipsoid as more and more points are removed.

---

[15] Information matrices naturally arise from traditional regression analysis. Following Poston *et al.* (1997), consider the case when $y = x\beta + \epsilon$, where, as usual, y is an n-dimensional vector of responses, x is an $n \times p$ matrix of known inputs and ϵ is the noise in the measurements, with $\mathbb{E}[\epsilon] = 0$ and $\boldsymbol{\Sigma} = \mathbb{E}[\epsilon\epsilon^{\mathsf{T}}]$. The information matrix, $\boldsymbol{IM}$, is then given by $\boldsymbol{IM} = x^{\mathsf{T}}x$. The information matrix is real and symmetric, and therefore can always be orthogonalized, yielding positive eigenvalues, $\lambda_i, i = 1, 2, \ldots, p$. The determinant of the information matrix, $\det(\boldsymbol{IM})$, is then given by $\det(\boldsymbol{IM}) = \prod_{j=1}^{p} \lambda_j$. This shows that 'the eigenvalues are also a measure of the information and indicate the contribution of a data point to the determinant of the information matrix' (Poston *et al.* 1997, p. 304).

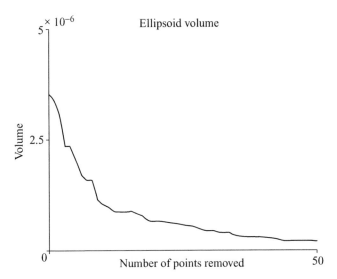

Figure 17.8 The volume of the ellipsoid as a function of the number of points removed.

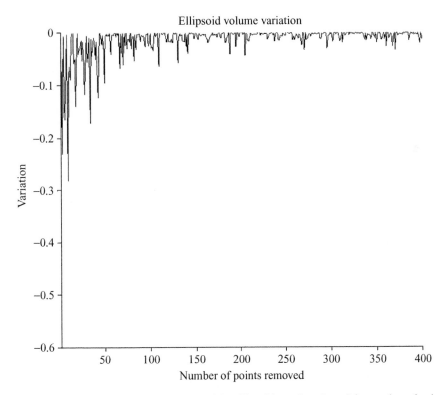

Figure 17.9 The changes in the volume of the ellipsoid as a function of the number of points removed.

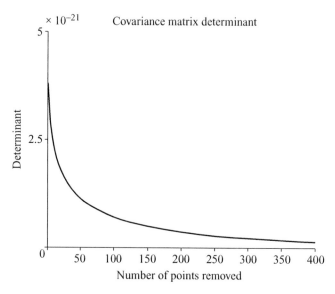

Figure 17.10 The determinant of the covariance matrix as a function of the number of points removed.

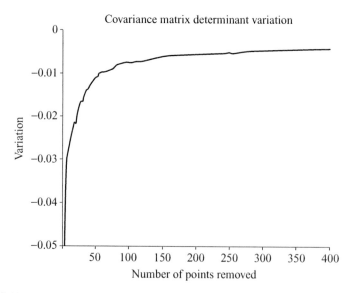

Figure 17.11 The changes in the determinant of the covariance matrix as a function of the number of points removed.

Figures 17.10 and 17.12 display the determinant of the covariance and correlation matrices, respectively, also as function of number of removed observations, and Figures 17.11 and 17.13 show the variations in the same quantities.

When the first outliers are removed note how abruptly the volume and the determinant change. As more and more outliers are removed, both the volume of Minimum Volume

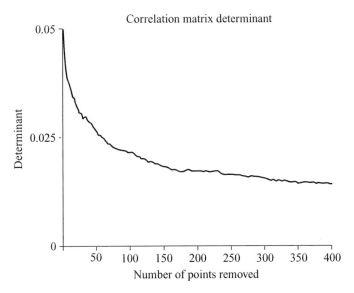

Figure 17.12 The determinant of the correlation matrix as a function of the number of points removed.

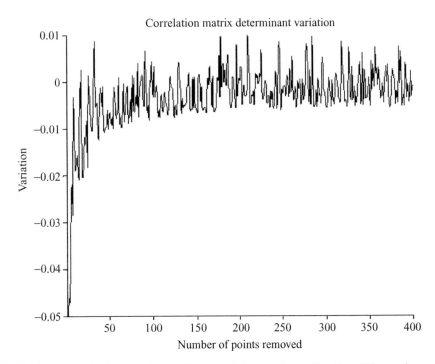

Figure 17.13 The changes in the determinant of the correlation matrix as a function of the number of points removed.

Ellipsoid and the determinant of the covariance matrix begin to stabilize. Monitoring the changes in these two quantities as a function of the residual number of points in the sample can suggest how many points should be culled.

There is no hard-and-fast rule as to whether monitoring changes in the determinant of the correlation or the covariance matrix is 'better'. Looking at Figures 17.11 and 17.13, for instance, shows that the determinant of the covariance matrix changes more smoothly, because of the reduction in variance as outliers are culled. The determinant of the correlation matrix is, on the other hand, much more 'spiky', and is more sensitive to the removal of the individual outlier. Since the method is ultimately subjective, we have found that visual inspection of *all* the sources of information at one's disposal can provide a more reliable and robust picture of what constitutes the body of the distribution. The determinant of the correlation matrix, in particular, by pointing to specific points or sets of points, is useful for case-by-case inspection.[16]

It is apparent from these figures that, for the data set described in the introductory section, excluding 100 to 200 points (3% to 5% of the whole data set) renders the covariance and correlation structure much more stable. Figure 17.14 shows that this is indeed the case by displaying the individual elements of the correlation matrix among the *Bond, Credit, Mortgage* and *Equity* time series as a function of the number of points removed. Note that removing more and more points does not appreciably stabilize the correlation between *Equity* and the other time series in the same way as the correlation between *Bond, Credit* and *Mortgage* does. Figure 17.15 displays this feature very vividly. This is due to the inherently non-stationary nature of the dependence between changes in equity prices and changes in the other asset classes. See the discussion in Section 17.1. This observation underlines how important it is to look at a variety of indicators in order to assess the body of a distribution.

Figure 17.16 then displays the stabilization of the four eigenvalues of the correlation matrix as more and more points are removed.

For the specific case examined in this study we chose to classify the first 160 truncated points as outliers and the rest as the 'body'. Reassuringly, we found that the results of our analyses did not change significantly for reasonable changes (say, between 125 and 200) around this value. Figure 17.17 shows the body (black points) and the outliers (grey points) for the *Equity, Bond* and *Credit* returns. Figure 17.18 shows the robust Mahalanobis distances (defined in Section 17.7) after the removal of the outliers. This figure should be compared and contrasted with Figure 17.21. Note how the 'spikes' have been successfully removed.

Finally, influence plots between selected asset classes are shown in Figures 17.19 and 17.20. (The influence contour lines show by how much the correlation coefficient varies if we remove a single point sitting on that line. Influence plots are described in Denev (2011).) Some outliers may appear as not particularly influential on a two-dimensional

---

[16] We note in passing that the FAST-MCD method can be used in the same fashion. Once the robust distances are determined for the whole dataset, one can start by removing the point with the largest distance, then the second largest point and so on and monitor some key quantities, such as the covariance matrix determinant, until they stabilize.

Correlations

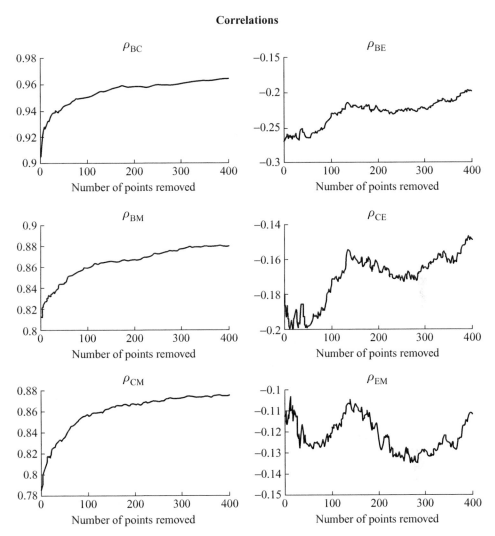

Figure 17.14 The individual elements ρ_{ij}; $i, j = $ *Bond, Credit, Mortgage, Equity,* of the correlation matrix as a function of the number of points removed.

graph but we must remember that the truncation was carried out in a four-dimensional space, where they are influential. The important thing to note is that *most of the outliers contribute to a decrease in the correlation.*

We note in closing this section that Bouchaud and Potters (2000) find that, by excluding the smallest frequency eigenvalues from the orthogonalization of an empirical correlation matrix obtained from S&P returns, the resulting efficient frontier becomes much more stable as a function of the temporal subsection of data used (e.g., first half versus second half). They also find that the purged correlation matrices become much more stable over time. They point out that, even if an investor availed herself of the

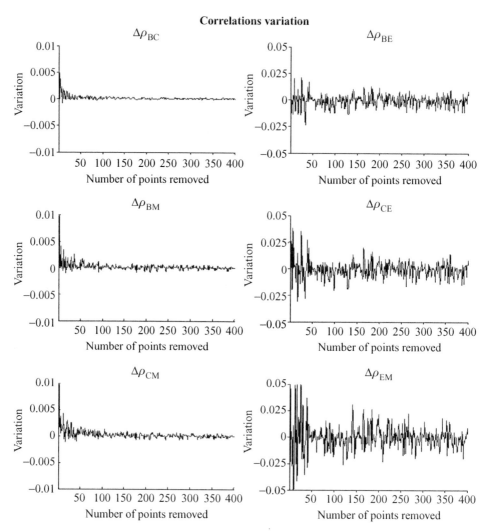

Figure 17.15 Variation of the individual elements ρ_{ij}; i, j = Bond, Credit, Mortgage, Equity, of the correlation matrix as a function of the number of points removed.

knowledge of the realized returns, investing according to a Markowitz prescription using all the eigenvectors of the correlation matrix would result in much riskier *ex post* portfolios than if the investment had been made using a small number of stable eigenvalues. Bouchaud and Potters offer two possible explanations: either the smallest eigenvalues are simply picking up noise, and this statistical noise (in an otherwise stationary phenomenon) is responsible for the low performance of the full-eigenvalue portfolio; or 'there is a genuine time dependence in the structure of the meaningful correlations' (Bouchaud and Potters 200, p. 120). The analysis in this chapter, and, in particular, the difference in behaviour between *Credit*, *Bond* and *Mortgage* on the

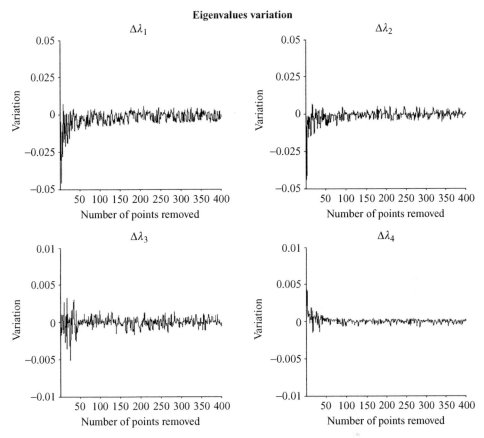

Figure 17.16 Changes in the four eigenvalues of the correlation matrix as a function of the number of points removed.

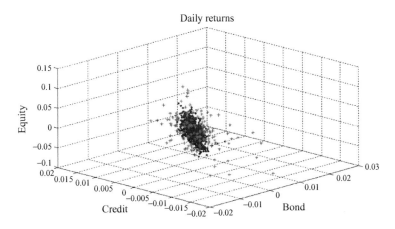

Figure 17.17 The body (black points) and the outliers (grey points) for the *Equity*, *Bond* and *Credit* returns.

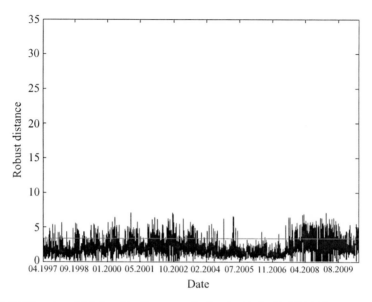

Figure 17.18 The robust Mahalanobis distances calculated with the FAST-MCD approach as a function of the observation date in the data set. The body of the data was identified by culling all the points above a threshold. The grey horizontal line corresponds to $\chi_4^2(0.975) = 3.34$, and the parameter h was set to $0.75 \times N$.

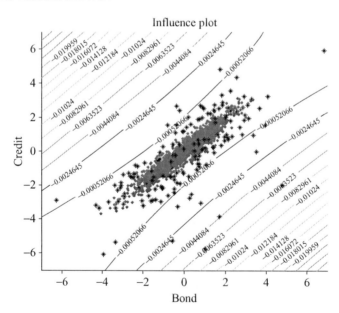

Figure 17.19 The influence plot for *Credit* and *Bond*. The influence contour lines show by how much the correlation coefficient varies if we remove a single point sitting on that line. The grey squares represent the outliers eliminated by the truncation algorithm. Some outliers may appear as not particularly influential on a two-dimensional graph but we must remember that the truncation was carried out in a four-dimensional space, where they are influential. *Note that most of the outliers contribute to a decrease in the correlation.*

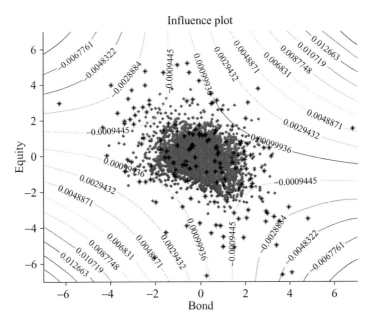

Figure 17.20 The influence plot for *Equity* and *Bond*.

one hand and *Equity* on the other, suggests that the second explanation, based on lack of time homogeneity and the idiosyncratic nature of the exceptional returns, is more convincing.

17.7   The Minimum-Covariance-Determinant method

Despite the fact that in our study we have mainly used the Minimum-Volume-Ellipsoid method, we should mention that a different method to identify the location estimator and the scatter estimation, i.e., the Minimum-Covariance-Determinant method, has recently attracted some interest. See again Rousseeuw and Van Driessen (1999). Also with this method, the main effort is devoted to finding the location and dispersion vector and matrix, respectively, that characterize the body of the distribution. More precisely, we can give the following definition.

DEFINITION 10   *Given an integer h as in Equation (17.3), the location estimator $\tilde{m}$ in the Minimum-Covariance-Determinant method is the average of h points, and the scatter estimator is covariance matrix $\tilde{\Sigma}$ of the same h points with the smallest determinant subject to the following condition:*

$$\{\#i\,;(\boldsymbol{y}-\boldsymbol{m})\Sigma^{-1}(\boldsymbol{y}-\boldsymbol{m})^{\mathrm{T}}\} = h \tag{17.18}$$

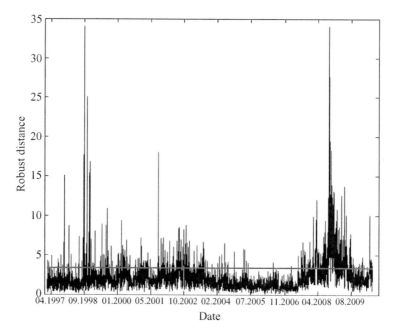

Figure 17.21 The robust Mahalanobis distances calculated with the FAST-MCD approach as a function of the observation date in the data set. The grey line corresponds to $\chi_4^2(0.975) = 3.34$. The parameter h was set to $0.75 \times N$. Some of the major crises in the period covered in our data set (the Russian crisis, the dot.com crisis and the recent subprime debacle) are clearly visible. For instance, the two peaks on the rightmost part of the figure correspond to the dates immediately after Lehman's default: 15 and 17 September 2008; the highest peak in the middle of the graph is the reopening of the stock exchange after 9/11; and the highest peak on the left is the 31 August 1998, a few days after Russia defaulted on its debt.

Once the location and dispersion estimators are found, they can be used in Equation (17.1) to calculate the robust Mahalanobis distances and to label as outliers observations whose robust distance exceeds a given threshold.

This is conceptually neat. However, given h points in the p-dimensional space finding the Minimum Volume Ellipsoid or Minimum Covariance Determinant means sweeping through $\binom{N}{h}$ possible combinations. Even for small data sets it soon becomes impossible to apply a brute-force approach and one has to make use of approximate computational methods.

Luckily, new methods have recently been introduced to simplify the combinatorial problem. One such popular method to find the Minimum Covariance Determinant is the FAST-MCD method, described for instance, in Rousseeuw and Van Driessen (1999). As an illustration of the application of this method, we show in Figure 17.21 the robust Mahalanobis distances calculated with the FAST-MCD approach as a function of the observation date in the data set. The grey line corresponds to $\chi_4^2(0.975) = 3.34$. The parameter h was set to $0.75 \times N$ (this is also the value suggested in Rousseeuw and Van Driessen (1999)).

Looking at Figure 17.21, some of the major crises in the period covered in our data set (the Russian crisis, the dot-com crisis and the recent subprime debacle) are clearly visible, as they show up as concentrations of large values of the robust distance. More precisely, the two peaks on the rightmost part of the figure correspond to the dates immediately after Lehman's default: 15 and 17 September 2008; the highest peak in the middle of the graph is the reopening of the stock exchange after 9/11; and the highest peak on the left is the 31 August 1998, a few days after Russia defaulted on its debt.

We do not pursue in greater detail the description of this method, because in our work we used the related ellipsoid method, which we have described in detail above.

17.8   Some remarks about the MVE, MCD and related methods

It is important to contrast the 'brute-force' estimation of the Minimum Volume Ellipsoid (or the Minimum Covariance Determinant) on the one hand, and the approximate method described in Routines A, B and C above.

Starting with the former, the Minimum Volume Ellipsoid of $h = \xi \times N$ points out of N, where ξ is a fraction, is defined as the volume of those h points that are the most concentrated. So, if we are given a set of 100 points and we choose $\xi = 0.75$, we have to play with all the different combinations of 75 points out of those 100 until we find those that have the containing ellipsoid with the minimum possible volume. That ellipsoid is the Minimum Volume Ellipsoid for the given parameter h.

The original authors (Rousseeuw *et al.*) first fix ξ, let's say $\xi = 0.75$, and then find the most concentrated set of points for the corresponding value of h. Finding those points means finding the dispersion matrix, Σ, and the location vector, m, in Equation (17.4). With this information, obtained for the h most concentrated points (for $\xi = 0.75$), one can then calculate the Mahalanobis distance for all the points in the data set.

The reasoning behind the Minimum-Covariance-Determinant method is the same, but Equation (17.18) is used instead. The numerical search for the Minimum Covariance Determinant is fast thanks to the FAST-MCD method. The search for the Minimum Volume Ellipsoid is slower but, nevertheless, there are some numerical techniques which render it faster than the brute-force search.

Once the Mahalanobis distances are calculated in this way for all the points – either with the Minimum-Volume-Ellipsoid metric in Equation (17.4) or with the Minimum-Covariance-Determinant metric in Equation (17.18) – they can be ordered and a procedure can be employed to eliminate one by one the most distant points and to monitor variation in some key quantities.

In our study we have not followed this brute-force procedure, but a related one inspired by the suggestions in Meucci (2009). He recommends calculating the Minimum Volume Ellipsoid for all the N data points, then calculating it for $N - 1$ data points, then for $N - 2$, and so on. The calculation is therefore carried out not just for the $h = 0.75 \times N$ most concentrated points. This raises the question of how the Minimum Volume Ellipsoid can be found for $N - 1$, $N - 2$, etc. data points. The answer is presented in Routines A, B and C above: first we calculate with Routine A the Minimum Volume Ellipsoid for N points.[17] With Routine B we then eliminate the farthest outlier and thus get $N - 1$ points. The $N - 1$ points thus obtained are those that are contained by the Minimum Volume Ellipsoid. In other words, if, instead of removing the farthest outlier, we removed another point at random, we would still have $N - 1$ points, but the ellipsoid that contains these points would have a bigger volume than the one calculated on the $N - 1$ points obtained by removing the farthest outlier. By definition it would not be the Minimum Volume Ellipsoid. So, if we want to find the Minimum Volume Ellipsoid of $N - 1$ points out of N, we have two possibilities:

1. Play with all the possible $N - 1$ points out of N until we get to the $N - 1$ points with the smallest volume of the containing ellipsoid.
2. Start from N points, remove the farthest outlier, calculate the ellipsoid volume for the remaining ones; we can then be reasonably confident that this is the ellipsoid with the minimum volume, i.e. the Minimum Volume Ellipsoid.

Procedure 2 is, of course, faster and simpler than procedure 1 (which, if implemented naively, is combinatorial), but it is not guaranteed to yield the true minimum volume ellipsoid. In our studies we have used the second procedure, but we have checked that, for the data we have been using, the two approaches give qualitatively very similar results.

Finally, Routine C makes use of routines A and B as described in detail in Section 17.6.3 above.

The final outcome of the procedures presented in this chapter is the identification of the body of the distribution. The next chapters deal with the decomposition of this joint distribution into marginals and copulae.

---

[17] This procedure, as Poston *et al.* (1997) admits, may sometimes be sub-optimal, but is in general effective.

18 Constructing the marginals

18.1 The purpose of this chapter

Once the 'normal' portion of the data has been identified as suggested in Chapter 14, we have two tasks ahead: the first is the modelling of the underlying univariate distributions; the second is the choice of how to conjoin them using a suitable copula. In this chapter we look at standard approaches to fitting the univariate distributions. In Chapter 19 we describe how they can be conjoined.

When it comes to modelling the univariate distributions, one can follow a parametric or a non-parametric approach (i.e., one can use the empirical cumulative distributions). There are pros and cons to both methods. We prefer a parametric method because it lends itself more easily to exploring the sensitivity of the results to the input parameters of the marginal distributions. See also the discussion in Section 17.1 regarding our 'scaling' approach in normal and excited conditions – an approach that naturally lends itself to a parametric formulation of the problem.

Once the choice has been made to pursue a parametric approach, a suitable distribution must be selected to fit the empirical distribution of 'normal' returns obtained for each individual risk factor. The task is made easy by the fact that we only have to fit the body of the empirical distributions; as a consequence, relatively 'tame' distributions may describe the data well. The need to use power law distributions, more or less truncated Levy flights, and other very-fat-tailed distributions arises when one tries to fit at the same time the body and the tails of the empirical distribution. From a practical perspective, restricting the family of parametric distributions to the elliptical family can facilitate the numerical burden for later computations, but the advantage is not crucial.

It must be stressed that, depending on the risk factor and the sampling interval, a Gaussian distribution may or may not be adequate even to describe the body – i.e., the 'normal' part – of the distribution. Indeed, we find that, for daily returns, even the body of most distributions obtained from the empirical time series is not well described by a Gaussian distribution. See Connor, Goldberg and Korajczyk (2010). This should not be cause for concern, because deviations from a Gaussian distribution can arise for reasons that have nothing to do with turbulent market periods. For instance, the presence of stochastic volatility gives rise to distributions with higher leptokurtosis than a Gaussian one. Therefore, we may well find a non-Gaussian body of a distribution, but this need not imply that our data set contains 'exceptional' returns. In any case, with our data we find that, for monthly and quarterly returns, the Gaussian assumption becomes more acceptable. Also on this point, see Connor, Goldberg and Korajczyk (2010) for a discussion of empirical findings.

18.2   The univariate fitting procedure

A simple strategy to choose a suitable parametric univariate distribution can be carried out along the following lines. Let's define the empirical cumulative distribution by:

$$F_n(x) = \frac{1}{n} \sum_{i=1}^{n} \mathbf{1}_{X_i \leq x} \tag{18.1}$$

where, as usual, $\mathbf{1}_{X_i \leq x}$ is the indicator function, equal to 1 if the condition $X_i \leq x$ is true and to 0 otherwise. Let's then consider the Kolmogorov–Smirnov (KS) distance, D_n^{KS}, defined as

$$D_n^{KS} = \sup_x |F_n(x) - F^*(x)|$$

where $F^*(x)$ is the hypothesized distribution with parameters estimated from the sample. Since the parameters are not known but estimated, the Kolmogorov–Smirnov test cannot be applied directly, at least by using the commonly tabulated critical points. We can, however, use Monte Carlo simulations[1] in order to find the distribution of D_n^{KS} and hence the confidence levels.

We find that a Student-t distribution provides an adequate fit for our data set for daily returns. As an example, Figures 18.1 and 18.2 present the unidimensional fit in the form of a histogram and a quantile–quantile plot for the asset class *Equity* using the Gaussian and the Student-t distributions.

18.2.1   *Other possible approaches*
We note that, in general, Student-t distributions can capture heavy tails, but still constrain the returns to be symmetrical about their mean. If capturing the skew were deemed important, one could resort to the multivariate skewed Student-t distribution described in Bauwens and Laurent (2005), which allows each marginal distribution to have its own asymmetry parameter. In this setting, however, every marginal has the same degree of kurtosis. If specifying a different skew and a different kurtosis for each marginal were deemed important, one could make use of the approach described in Jondeau and Rockinger (2008). See also Jondeau, Poon and Rokinger (2007) for a

---

[1] For the case of Kolmogorov–Smirnov S test in case of unknown mean and variance for the normal distribution, see Lilliefors (1967). The method to infer a distribution for the distance D will be described in detail in Section 19.2 in the context of copula fitting.

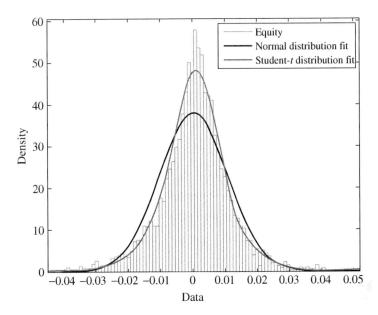

Figure 18.1 The fit to the S&P daily returns obtained using a Gaussian and a Student-t distribution.

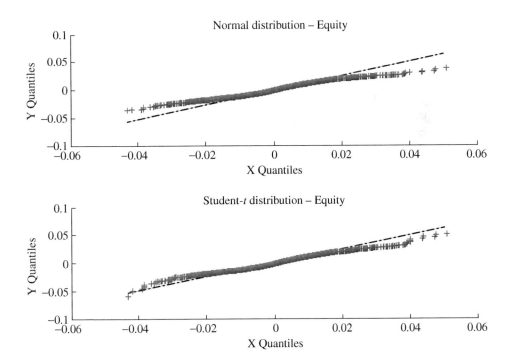

Figure 18.2 The quantile–quantile plot for the two fits in Figure 18.1.

discussion of these generalized multivariate Student-t distributions, and the discussion in Garcia-Alvarez and Luger (2011).

For reasons that will become apparent in the later parts of this book, we do not pursue these avenues.

18.3   Estimating the vector of expected returns

Irrespective of whether we use a parametric or a non-parametric approach, implicitly or explicitly we will always have to provide an estimate of the vector of expected returns. We stress that the expected returns of relevance in this part of the exercise are those that pertain to normal market conditions. Given n asset classes, this corresponds to the vector μ:

$$\mu = \begin{bmatrix} \mu_1 \\ \mu_2 \\ \vdots \\ \mu_n \end{bmatrix} \tag{18.2}$$

Methodologically, it is not obvious that relying on the historical culled data is the best approach to estimate the vector of returns. Indeed we look in detail in Chapter 21 at several model-based ways to either ascertain the relative ranking of the returns for the various assets, or perhaps even pin down exactly their values. A mixed approach is also possible, and often appealing. For instance, we could choose the vector of returns whose rankings are consistent with a normative model (such as CAPM) under the constraint of being as close as possible to the statistically estimated values. (See Ni *et al.* (2011) in this respect.) As mentioned, we touch on these approaches in Chapter 29, and for the moment we assume that we are simply engaging in a statistical estimation of the vector of returns, μ.

A naive estimation approach suggests that the sample averages should provide the best (unbiased) estimate of the unknown expected returns. As early as the 1950s, Stein (1956) showed that this is, in general, not the case. He showed that, under very general conditions, naive sample means are not admissible estimators for a multivariate population,[2] and suggested an estimation technique to provide a better estimate. Although no Bayesian interpretation was provided in the original paper, the procedure is readily understandable in Bayesian terms: the 'experimental evidence' (i.e., the data) is mixed with a prior distribution to obtain a posterior distribution for the unknown parameters (the 'true' expectations). The weaker the evidence (e.g., the fewer the reliable data points) the closer the estimation will be to the prior. The remarkable result is that, in general, the expectation of the posterior distributions of the parameters, μ_i, will not

---

[2] We remind the reader that an estimator is admissible if no other estimator is uniformly better for a given loss function. See Michaud and Michaud (2008).

be the same as the corresponding sample average. This is simply a reflection of the 'shrinking' effect of the prior.[3]

This naturally raises the question: where does the prior come from? When it comes to the stand-alone estimation of the means,[4] James and Stein (1961) recommend that a plausible uninformative prior should be that all the returns are the same. Under this assumption, given a vector of sample averages, x_i,

$$\begin{bmatrix} x_1 \\ x_2 \\ \vdots \\ x_n \end{bmatrix} \tag{18.3}$$

the Stein estimator for the expectation of the population, $\widehat{\mu}_i$, is given by

$$\widehat{\mu}_i = \overline{x} + c_i(\overline{x}_i - \overline{x}) \tag{18.4}$$

with

$$c_i = \max \left\{ 0, 1 - \frac{(k-3)\sigma_i^2}{\sum_i (\overline{x}_i - \overline{x})^2} \right\} \tag{18.5}$$

where k is the number of assets (as long as $k \geq 3$),[5] $\overline{x}_i$ is the sample average for asset i, $\overline{x}$ is the global sample mean, and σ_i^2 is the variance of asset i.[6]

This is plausible, but not consistent with most accepted asset-pricing theories, such as the CAPM, according to which the expected return should be proportional via the coefficient β to the market return. If one did not want to link the results too strongly to a particular pricing model (such as the CAPM or a factor model), one could simply impose that all the expected returns should be proportional to their volatility. The proportionality constant could be obtained using a simple regression. For a more sophisticated, but more theory-laden, approach see Ni *et al.* (2011) and the discussion in Chapter 21.

---

[3] It is interesting to note that, as we live in a Bayesian age, we are readily inclined to recast results obtained using non-Bayesian approaches in Bayesian language. As we already mentioned, the word 'Bayes' does not appear in Black and Litterman's original paper, and the prior/posterior interpretation of their results is a latter-day reconstruction – so much so, that different 'interpreters' differ in identifying the subjective return views or the market-implied returns as the prior. In the case of Stein, contemporary readers also promptly coat his results with a thin Bayesian veneer. However, Stein, a 'frequency-based theorist, ... studiously avoided discussing [his results'] relationships with Bayes' (McGrayne, 2011, p. 130). When published, his shrinkage results were quickly seized upon with delight by contemporary Bayesians, but 'Stein ... continued to regard Bayes' philosophical framework as a "negative" and subjective priors as "completely inappropriate"' (p. 131, quote in the citation from Efron (1977) and Mcgrayne interview (2011)).

[4] For a joint estimation of means and covariances, see Frost and Savarino (1986). For a Stein estimation of the sample covariance matrix, see Ledoit (1994, 1997).

[5] The dominance of the Stein estimator in terms of mean-squared error over the least-squares estimator is only guaranteed for $k > 2$. See Stein (1956).

[6] The original work by Stein (1956) required the variance to be known. James and Stein (1961) then showed that the same result holds when the variance has to be estimated from the sample data.

It is clear enough how to apply these shrinkage methods if one chooses to use an empirical distribution. But what should one do if one wanted to use a parametric approach? The simplest solution in this case is to make use of a two-stage procedure. First, the Stein or related estimation is carried out on the empirical data to determine μ. The vector μ thus estimated will, in general, be different from the vector of sample means. As a second step, the empirical data can be adjusted (for instance, by adding or removing the difference between the sample-means vector and μ).[7] The parametric estimate can then be carried out using the 'doctored' input data.

18.3.1   What shrinkage fixes (and what it does not fix)

Shrinkage techniques are very useful, specially when dealing with the estimation of the first moment of the distribution of returns. It must be stressed, however, that they are ideally designed in order to deal with the effect of statistical noise, and that their application to the case of heteroskedasticity is more problematic. That is, the assumption is that the underlying distributions of returns are constant over time, and that our sample estimate is only contaminated by statistical noise due to the finite size of our sample. Since we are dealing with the 'normal' part of the distribution this is not such a bad choice. However, as we have seen in Section 17.1, even in 'normal' periods the parameters of the underlying distribution may well change over time. When this is the case, it is not clear how much an uninformative shrinkage approach can help.

When statistical noise is not the main reason why our sample estimate may not be representative of the next-period distribution, one should try to estimate a possibly-time-varying vector of first moments. Doing so in full generality, however, is very complex, and the success of the enterprise will crucially depend on the interplay between the frequency of data collection (and hence the amount of data available) and the typical time scales of change.

The task is somewhat simplified if one assumes that the first moment can move, but only in a restricted manner. For instance, one can make the assumption that the underlying time series was generated by an n-state Markov chain, where in different states the observed realizations were drawn from different distributions (see, e.g., Rebonato and Chien 2009). The approach is appealing, but not without problems: first one must assume a parametric form for the distributions in the different states; for tractability the Gaussian assumption is typically made. Second, one must estimate how many states there are: i.e., one must determine the n in the n-state Markov chain – this is not too difficult, but obviously depends on the chosen parametric form for the 'base' distributions. And then, of course, the third step is the estimation of the parameters themselves. This is typically carried out using Markov-Chain–Monte-Carlo techniques. Conceptually these are not particularly complicated, but can quickly become computationally very intensive. See, e.g., Gamerman and Lopes (2006), or Lancaster (2004) for a clear didactic description of the technique.

---

[7] This simple adjustment is not universal, but gives an idea of the type of doctoring needed.

As this brief sketch suggests, the estimation problem is non-trivial. The important point is that, *especially when it comes to the estimates of the first moment*, a naive reliance on the sample average can easily produce nonsensical results: think, for instance, of the estimated drift of technology stocks using data collected in the run-up to 2001. In similar situations even very simple and crude techniques, such as the non-informative Stein shrinkage approach, can bring about significant improvements.

19 Choosing and fitting the copula

19.1 The purpose of this chapter

The procedure described in Chapter 18 produces univariate marginal distributions for each risk factor. These marginals may well display fatter tails than Gaussians, but nonetheless refer to non-extreme market conditions. The next step to characterize the normal-times joint distribution is to conjoin them using a copula. We are going to choose a copula that provides an acceptable fit to the data. We are aware that estimating the marginal distributions first, and then the copula, is statistically sub-optimal, as a joint maximum-likelihood would in general give a different solution. We justify our two-step approach by pointing to the computational advantages and the conceptually 'neat' decomposition afforded by this standard decomposition of the estimation problem. As we shall see, this two-step procedure will also greatly facilitate the construction of the spliced distribution – see Chapter 20, Section 20.5 in particular.

If for each risk factor the normal-times portion of the data can be satisfactorily described by a Gaussian distribution and if all the risk factors can be joined by a Gaussian copula, we shall see that important computational savings can be achieved (because a simple closed-form expression can be obtained in some cases by linking the distribution of portfolio returns and the weights of the individual sub-portfolios). If this is not the case, the procedure described in the following can still be applied, but the final numerical search becomes somewhat more burdensome. Conceptually, however, nothing changes.

19.2 Methods to choose a copula

Broadly speaking, there are three methods to estimate the parameters of a copula from data (see, e.g., Cherubini and Luciano 2004):

1. Exact Maximum-Likelihood Method: this is a one-step method that estimates jointly the parameters of the marginals and those of the copula. As mentioned above, this is statistically the most efficient method, but it is computationally very onerous.

2. Inference-from-Marginals Method: this is a two-step procedure whereby the marginals are fitted first, and then the copula. This is the method that has been used in this study.
3. Canonical Maximum-Likelihood Method: this estimates directly the parameters of the copula without fitting the marginals, as the empirical marginals are used instead. We do not pursue this avenue because we prefer to model the marginals parametrically, rather than using the empirical distributions.

In this study two types of copulae were tested for goodness of fit: the Student-t and the Gaussian. To see which copula gives a better description of the data we ran a log-likelihood test. The Student-t copula showed a higher likelihood for our daily data (6990 versus 6620 for the Gaussian copula). However, the likelihood in itself is a relative, not an absolute, measure of how good a fit is, and it does not give p-values on the basis of which we could reject a hypothesis. We therefore present below some shortcut methods that allow a fast computation of the goodness of fit.

Goodness-of-fit measures for copulas are well described in Hauksson *et al.* (2001). The computational complexity of these methods is much higher than those used to assess the goodness of fit of one-dimensional (marginal) distributions. The starting point is the construction of the empirical copula, $C_n(\boldsymbol{u})$:

$$C_n(\boldsymbol{u}) = \frac{1}{n} \sum_{i=1}^{n} \mathbf{1}(U_{i1} \leq u_1, U_{i2} \leq u_2, \ldots, U_{id} \leq u_d) \tag{19.1}$$

$$\boldsymbol{u} = (u_1, u_2, \ldots, u_d) \in [0, 1]^d \tag{19.2}$$

where d is the dimensionality of the problem (the number of variables), $\mathbf{1}(\cdot)$ denotes the indicator function, and n is the number of d-dimensional observation vectors.

The second step is to use a kind of Kolmogorov–Smirnov or Anderson–Darling test for the distance between this copula and a hypothesized copula. However, the empirical copula may become very hard to estimate especially for the data studied in this work – in the application we discuss in the following we have four assets, with as many as 3200[1] observation data points for each asset. Apart from the computational demands, the storage of information is another issue.[2]

Malevergne and Sornette (2001) propose another, much faster, method to tackle this problem for the special but important case of a Gaussian copula. They show that under the hypothesis H_0 that the dependence between random variables can be described by a Gaussian copula, the variable z^2, defined as

$$z^2 = \sum_{i,j}^{1,p} \Phi^{-1}(F_i(x_i))(\rho^{-1})_{ij} \Phi^{-1}(F_j(x_j)) \tag{19.3}$$

---

[1] This is the number of data points left after truncation (which entails the removal of 160 observations).
[2] Some methods exist to optimize the calculation time and to store the information more efficiently by using some properties of the empirical copula. A solution is proposed in Strelen and Nassy (2007) which comes with an accompanying MATLAB program *pwlCopula* freely available on the Internet.

follows a χ^2 distribution with p degrees of freedom. In Equation (19.3) $\Phi^{-1}(\cdot)$ is the inverse cumulative standardized normal distribution, F_i is the cumulative marginal distribution function for the ith asset, p is the number of assets, and the matrix ρ is defined as

$$\rho = \mathrm{Cov}\left[\Phi^{-1}(F_i(x_i)), \Phi^{-1}(F_j(x_j))\right] \qquad (19.4)$$

Malevergne and Sornette (2003) then propose four distance measures:

$$\text{Kolmogorov–Smirnov: } d_1 = \max_z \left|F_{z^2}(z^2) - F_{\chi^2}(z^2)\right|$$

$$\text{Average Kolmogorov–Smirnov: } d_2 = \int \left|F_{z^2}(z^2) - F_{\chi^2}(z^2)\right| dF_{\chi^2}(z^2)$$

$$\text{Anderson–Darling: } d_3 = \max_z \frac{\left|F_{z^2}(z^2) - F_{\chi^2}(z^2)\right|}{\sqrt{F_{\chi^2}(z^2)\left[1 - F_{\chi^2}(z^2)\right]}}$$

$$\text{Average Anderson–Darling: } d_4 = \int \frac{\left|F_{z^2}(z^2) - F_{\chi^2}(z^2)\right|}{\sqrt{F_{\chi^2}(z^2)\left[1 - F_{\chi^2}(z^2)\right]}} dF_{\chi^2}(z^2)$$

All these distances can be computed numerically with little effort, as they are just differences between cumulative distributions. For instance, for the distance d_1 one can directly calculate the empirical $F_{z^2}(z^2)$, subtract it from the theoretical $F_{\chi^2}(z^2)$ and take the maximum value of the difference.

The Kolmogorov–Smirnov distances are more sensitive to deviations in the bulk of the distributions, while the Anderson–Darling statistics are more sensitive to the tails. Note that, unlike what is normally found for commonly used statistics, for all these measures the absolute value appears in the numerator instead of squares. The advantage is that the resulting distances are less sensitive to outliers. The disadvantage is that standard statistical tests (ω-test and Ω-test) cannot be used. However this disadvantage is more theoretical than practical, as the covariance matrix is not known, but must be estimated from data, and in any case the exact parameters needed in the derivation of such statistics ω and Ω are not known. A bootstrap method can be used as in Efron and Tibshirani (1986) to obtain critical values to test the hypothesis that the tested copula is a good fit.

19.3   The covariance matrix and shrinkage

For the applications discussed in Chapter 21, the vector, $\boldsymbol{\sigma}$, of standard deviations, and, more generally, the covariance matrix, play an important role. As far as its estimation is concerned, shrinkage techniques similar to those presented in Chapter 18 can play an important role. See, e.g., Ledoit (1994, 1997). However, when it comes to the estimation of the second moments of a distribution, the degree of confidence in the results is generally much greater than for the first moment. For instance, Pantaleo *et al.* (2011) point out that

...the determination of expected returns is the role of the economist and of the portfolio manager, who are asked to generate or select valuable private information, while estimation of the covariance matrix is the task of the quantitative analyst...[3] As a consequence, one can often do significantly better than simply 'shrinking' the sample data to an uninformative prior. For this reason the use of purely statistical techniques is better justified in the case of the estimation of covariance matrix than of the vector of returns.

Indeed, Pantaleo *et al.* (2011) carried out an empirical investigation of which of nine covariance estimators performed best in the case of stock returns. Their criterion of 'performance' was the *ex-post* behaviour of Markowitz-optimized portfolios. We refer the interested reader to the original reference (Pantaleo *et al.* 2011) for details of the nine estimators and for their relative performances. For the purpose of our discussion, it is enough to point out that they found that no estimator was the undisputed winner, and that their relative performances depended on the nature of the problem. They identified three important variables in assessing the relative effectiveness of the various estimators, namely: (i) the ratio of data points, T, to the number, n, of assets;[4] (ii) whether short-selling was allowed or not; and (iii) the precise metric used to asses performance. Their conclusions was that, when short-selling was allowed, several estimation methods performed significantly better than the naive sample estimate (especially when the ratio T/n was close to 1 – a case of limited interest to us). However, if all the weights were constrained to be positive, it turned out to be almost impossible to improve upon the performance of portfolios constructed using the naive covariance estimation technique. However, some of the more sophisticated estimators gave rise to significantly more diversified portfolios – a 'robustness' feature that could be considered desirable in itself, and which we discuss in the later parts of this book.

We note in closing that, when high-frequency data are available, exciting new techniques have recently been proposed to estimate the first and second moments of distributions of returns. Given the importance of the topic, and the potential effectiveness of the estimation techniques based on high-frequency data, we refer the reader to (Anderson *et al.* 2001).

19.4   The procedure followed in this work

In the present work we followed the procedure described below (see Malevergne and Sornette (2003).)

19.4.1   The algorithm for Gaussian copula
1. Given the original time series, we first generated the Gaussian variables $\widehat{y} = \Phi^{-1}(F_i(x_i))$.

---

[3] See also Ledoit and Wolf (2003) in this respect.
[4] In the study by Pantaleo *et al.* (2011) the number of assets was the number of stocks in an equity portfolio. In our applications we are almost invariably going to use many fewer variables (associated with asset classes) than the number used in typical stock-portfolio applications.

2. We estimated the covariance matrix $\widehat{\rho}$ of the Gaussian variables $\widehat{y}$. Using this covariance matrix, we computed the variable z^2 in Equation (19.3).
3. We then measured the distance (using any of the four proposed distance measures above) of its estimated distribution from the χ^2 distribution.
4. Given this covariance matrix $\widehat{\rho}$, we generated numerically a panel of $N \times p$-dimensional random vectors drawn from a 4-variate Gaussian distribution with the same covariance matrix $\widehat{\rho}$. The length N of the simulated time series was chosen to be equal to the length (3200) of our actual data series, and p (the number of asset classes) was 4.
5. For the panel of Gaussian vectors synthetically generated with covariance matrix $\widehat{\rho}$ as in point 4 above, we estimated its sample covariance matrix $\widetilde{\rho}$.
6. Using the $N \times p$-dimensional vectors of the synthetic Gaussian time series, we associated the corresponding realization of the random variable z^2; let's call this $\widetilde{z}^2$.
7. We constructed the empirical distribution for the variable $\widetilde{z}^2$ and measured the distance between this distribution and the χ^2-distribution with $p = 4$ degrees of freedom.
8. By repeating many (say, 10 000) times the steps 4 to 7, we obtained an accurate estimate of the cumulative distribution of distances between the distribution of the synthetic Gaussian variables and the theoretical χ^2 distribution.
9. Finally, the distance obtained at step 2 for the true variables was transformed into a significance level by using the synthetically determined distribution of distances between the distribution of the synthetic Gaussian variables and the theoretical χ^2-distribution.

19.4.2   The algorithm for Student-t copula

The procedure can be extended to a Student-t copula as shown in Kole *et al.* (2007). They show that if H_0 is the hypothesis that the dependence structure comes from a Student-t copula with correlation matrix ρ and v degrees of freedom then the variable z^2, defined as

$$z^2 = \frac{\left[\Psi^{-1}(F_i(x_i; v))(\rho^{-1})_{ij} \Psi^{-1}(F_j(x_j; v)) \right]}{p} \tag{19.5}$$

is distributed according to an F-distribution with degrees of freedom p and v. In Equation (19.5) $\Psi^{-1}(F_i(x_i; v))$ is the inverse of the cumulative standard Student-t distribution with v degrees of freedom.

The same steps as in the case of Gaussian copula with obvious modifications can then be applied to this variable and a distribution of the four goodness-of-fit distances can be estimated.

19.5   Results

When we applied the techniques described above to our data set for the Gaussian and the Student-t copulae we obtained the results shown in Table 19.1 for the four distances (two Kolmogorov–Smirnov and two Anderson–Darling) described above.

Table 19.1 *The p-values representing the probability of error if H_0 is rejected for the entire data set. H_0 is the null hypothesis that the empirical multivariate distribution comes from the type of copula in the top row. The four rows correspond to the four different distances (two Kolmogorov–Smirnov and two Anderson–Darling) described in the text. d_1 = Kolmogorov–Smirnov, d_2 = Average Kolmogorov–Smirnov, d_3 = Anderson–Darling, d_4 = Average Anderson–Darling*

	p-values for Gaussian copula	p-values for Student-t copula
d_1	$< 10^{-3}$	$< 10^{-3}$
d_2	$< 10^{-3}$	0.002
d_3	$< 10^{-3}$	0.007
d_4	$< 10^{-3}$	0.197

Table 19.2 *Same as Table 19.1 for the first data subset*

	p-values for Gaussian copula	p-values for Student-t copula
d_1	0.018	0.104
d_2	0.012	0.244
d_3	0.032	0.087
d_4	0.002	0.392

Table 19.3 *Same as Table 19.1 for the second data subset*

	p-values for Gaussian copula	p-values for Student-t copula
d_1	0.046	0.344
d_2	0.053	0.642
d_3	0.044	0.082
d_4	0.006	0.708

We see that, although the Student-t copula shows a better fit (as shown by the higher p-values,[5] neither of the copulae provides a particularly good fit, as indicated from the three out of four p-values, at least if we choose a threshold value of 1% or higher. To understand the origin of this poor fit, we split the last 10 years of the data set into five equal parts and run the fit (univariate and copula) separately on each subset, after applying the truncation methods described in Chapter 17.[6]

The results of the fit are shown in Tables 19.2–19.6. For each subset the null hypothesis can no longer be rejected at the conventional acceptance level of 1%. The Student-t copula now also shows a much better absolute fit for each subset.

---

[5] This is also confirmed by log-likelihood of the Student-t copula, which for our data is 6990 while that of the Gaussian copula is 6620.

[6] Recall that 5% of the data points were truncated.

Table 19.4 *Same as Table 19.1 for the third data subset*

	Gaussian copula	p-values for Student-*t* copula
d_1	$< 10^{-3}$	0.098
d_2	$< 10^{-3}$	0.456
d_3	$< 10^{-3}$	0.156
d_4	$< 10^{-3}$	0.462

Table 19.5 *Same as Table 19.1 for the fourth data subset*

	p-values for Gaussian copula	p-values for Student-*t* copula
d_1	$< 10^{-3}$	0.042
d_2	$< 10^{-3}$	0.514
d_3	$< 10^{-3}$	0.032
d_4	$< 10^{-3}$	0.692

Table 19.6 *Same as Table 19.1 for the fifth data subset*

	p-values for Gaussian copula	p-values for Student-*t* copula
d_1	0.084	0.252
d_2	0.138	0.273
d_3	0.052	0.062
d_4	0.128	0.328

We display in Figures 19.1 and 19.2 the cumulative distributions of the four distances relating to the last subset for the two copulae. Once we know the values of the four distances, let's say for the last subset, we can read from the figures what percentage of the simulated copulae are below that distance. This is just a graphical way to obtain the p-value. We note that some distances, such as the Anderson–Darling,

$$d_3 = \max_z \frac{|F_{z^2}\left(z^2\right) - F_{\chi^2}(z^2)|}{\sqrt{F_{\chi^2}(z^2)\left[1 - F_{\chi^2}(z^2)\right]}} \tag{19.6}$$

display a much more peaked density (corresponding to a much steeper cumulative distribution). As the two figures suggest, this is a feature of the distance measure.

In Figures 19.3 and 19.4 we then show scatter plots between pairs of assets (*Bond* and *Mortgage* for Figure 19.3 and *Bond* and *Equity* for Figure 19.4) for the five subsets. Apart from the visually obvious differences in the scatter plots between the two pairs, careful inspection also reveals, for each pair, different correlations in different time sections. This clearly indicates a changing underlying structure for the codependence.

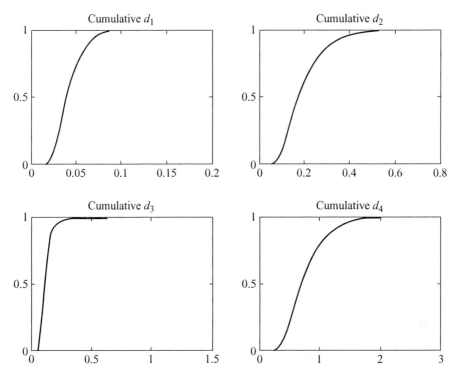

Figure 19.1 Gaussian copula. Cumulative distributions of the four distances used to assess the goodness of fit of the copula for the last subset: d_1 = Kolmogorov–Smirnov, d_2 = Average Kolmogorov–Smirnov, d_3 = Anderson–Darling, d_4 = Average Anderson–Darling.

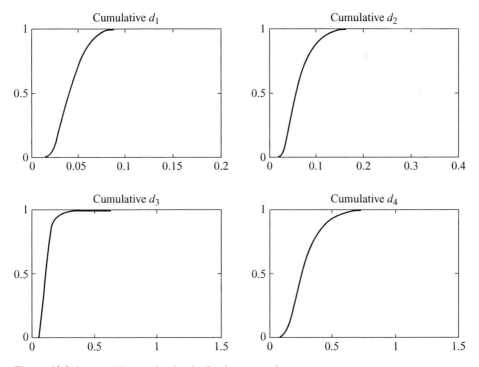

Figure 19.2 Same as Figure 19.1 for the Student-t copula.

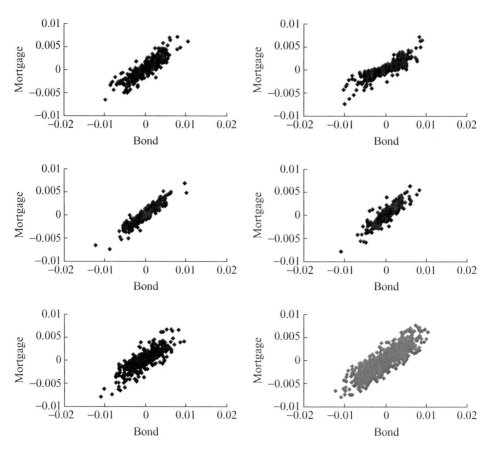

Figure 19.3 Scatter plot between *Bond* and *Mortgage* for the five different subsets. In the bottom-right corner the scatter plot on the entire data set is shown. The correlations are 88.1%, 87.1%, 93.1%, 91.3%, 81.6% for the five subsets, and 86.5% for the full data set.

As additional confirmation, we present in Figure 19.5 the correlation coefficient between *Bond* and *Equity* calculated using a sliding window of 250 data points. The time-varying nature of this correlation (discussed in Section 18.1) leads the goodness-of-fit tests over the whole sample to reject both elliptical copulae even with 1% threshold.

The effect on copulae of changing correlations is examined in Remillard *et al.* (2010). By introducing the concept of dynamic copula Remillard *et al.* show that for the correlation between Can\$/US\$ exchange rate and oil prices (NYMEX oil futures) the Gaussian copula provides a good fit (high *p*-value) if the sample is split into sub-samples. This is not the case if the entire sample is taken into account. They attribute this to the time dependence of correlation.

Another line of research is that of Dias and Embrechts (2004), who try to model the change of dependence structure by assigning a time dependence to the parameters of

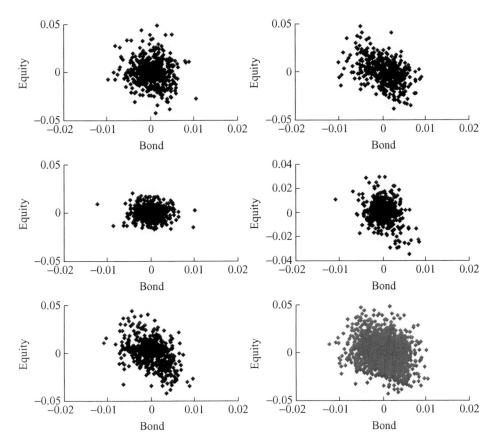

Figure 19.4 Same as Figure 19.3 for *Bond* and *Equity*. The correlations are −13.1%, −43.2%, −2.9%, −29.6%, −43.5% for the five subsets, and −22.2% for the full data set.

the chosen copula. We do not pursue this route here. Finally, we note that Busetti and Harvey (2011) offer a test to check against the hypothesis that the copula is changing over time.

The discussion above points to the importance of taking the time dependence of codependencies into account when modelling returns, especially when the projection horizon is relatively short. When we are interested in how asset classes will co-move over the next portfolio rebalancing horizon, using marginals and copulae relevant to the present market conditions is extremely important. Doing so when the estimates are carried out in normal market conditions is relatively easy. More difficult is the task faced by the portfolio manager when she is operating in conditions of market turmoil. We refer the reader to Section 18.3 for a discussion of this point.

Once the marginals have been conjoined using the copula of choice, the modelling of the normal-times portion of the joint distribution is complete. As an example, in Figure 19.6 we show the scatter plot of data points generated following the procedure

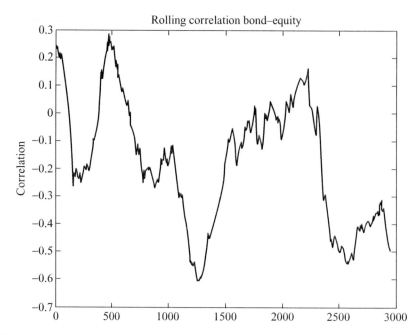

Figure 19.5 The correlation coefficient between *Bond* and *Equity* calculated using a sliding window of 250 data points.

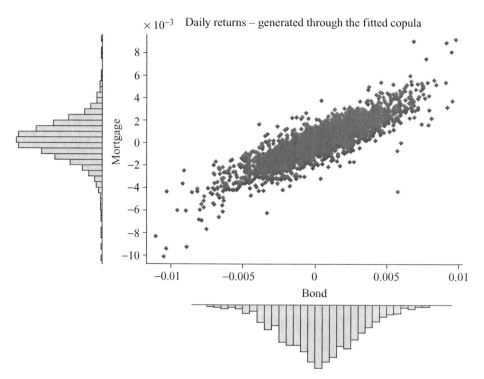

Figure 19.6 Scatter plot of the random numbers generated with the fitted copula (and mapped inversely from [0, 1] to the real axis with the help of the fitted marginals) for asset classes *Bond* and *Mortgage*.

described above through the fitted Student-t copula for one particular pair of assets, *Bonds* and *Mortgage*.

We close this chapter by noting that some useful information about the choice of marginals and copula can be gleaned by looking at the symmetry, or lack thereof, of the return distribution.

Part VII

Working with the full distribution

In this part of the book we deal with the problem of creating a 'good' joint distribution of risk factors that takes into account ('knows about') the exceptional events which have informed the construction of our Bayesian net.

Building a 'good' distribution entails two different things.

First, we must make sure that we combine ('splice together') the normal-times and excited distributions in an effective manner. As we shall see, there is no unique, 'right' way to do so, as any choice will depend on how we think that normal and exeptional regimes interact. (If this statement is somewhat cryptic now, it will become clear in Section 20.5.)

Second, a good spliced joint distribution will have to respect some fundamental, if somewhat stylized, relationships between risk and return. In Chapter 21 we shall therefore employ in a normative manner a simple asset-pricing model such as the CAPM in order to guide us in the construction of the spliced distribution. In doing so, we do not subscribe to the view that a model such as the CAPM is 'right' (whatever that means), but that it is 'reasonable' (whatever *that* means).

20 Splicing the normal and exceptional distributions

20.1 Purpose of the chapter

In the previous chapters we have obtained the joint distribution of changes in market risk factors that applies to the 'normal' times. As a next step, we want to obtain the joint probabilities of the changes in market risk factors derived from the events described by our Bayesian net. We are a small step away from this, and we will show how to do it in the next section.

Once this is done, the task at hand will be to conjoin these two distributions into an overall ('spliced') joint distribution of changes in market risk factors. And once this spliced distribution is available, given a set of weights (asset allocations) we will be able to create the full joint distribution of portfolio returns. As the distribution of portfolio returns will be a function of the assigned weights, in the next step (Chapter 24) we shall vary these weights so as to optimize some target function – typically, our chosen utility function.

Before embarking on this project, however, the preliminary step alluded to in the opening paragraph must be undertaken: we must turn the joint distribution of events produced by the Bayesian nets into a joint distribution of changes in market risk factors. This is accomplished in the next section.

20.2 Reducing the joint probability distribution

In the Bayesian nets we have built so far, only some of the nodes are directly associated with changes in market risk factors events. For instance, a node such as 'Greece defaults' is not directly linked to a change in a market risk factor, while a node such as 'Credit spreads of Spain widen by 200 basis points' is. Now, speaking of events associated with changes in market risk factors is quite a mouthful. With transparent, if inelegant, terminology, we shall therefore refer to events associated with changes in market risk factors as *return-related events*, and to events associated with the transmission channels as *non-return-related events*.

A crucial step in the asset-allocation procedure will be what we call the mapping, i.e., the association of a monetary return (a change in the value of the portfolio) with changes in the market risk factors. See in this respect our discussion in Chapter 12. Of course, we will only be able to carry out this mapping for return-related events. Therefore, the joint probabilities of exceptional changes in portfolio values ('money returns') will have to be obtained from the return-related events only. The non-return-related events are, of course, extremely important, because they construct the 'story' of the scenario or stress event and they provide the causal connections (the transmission channels) that 'hold together' the net. However, once they have been specified, and they have fulfilled their function of transmission channels, in order to construct the distribution of exceptional returns they can be discarded as pieces of scaffolding.

The first step is therefore to create a *reduced* joint probability table, i.e., a set of probabilities relating only to the joint realizations of changes in market risk factors. The notation here can quickly become cumbersome. For simplicity of exposition, we shall therefore consider the case of four events, A, B, C and D, of which B and D are return-related events (leaves).

Then we can write for the joint probability of the particular combination of return-related events $B = \tilde{b}$, $D = \tilde{d}$:

$$P(B = \tilde{b}, D = \tilde{d}) = \sum_{a \in \mathcal{A}, c \in \mathcal{C}} \mathbf{1}_{a,\tilde{b},c,\tilde{d}} P(A = a, B = \tilde{b}, C = c, D = \tilde{d}) \qquad (20.1)$$

where $\mathcal{A}$ and $\mathcal{C}$ denote the possible ranges of values for the variables A and C, respectively, and $\mathbf{1}_{a,\tilde{b},c,\tilde{d}}$ denotes the indicator function, which assumes the value of 1 if the variables have the appropriate logical values in its arguments, and 0 otherwise.

More generally, if we have N events, n return-related events, E_k^{rr}, $k = 1, 2, \ldots, n$, and $m = N - n$ non-return-related events, E_k^{nrr}, $k = 1, 2, \ldots, m = N - n$, we can write for the joint probability of a particular combination of return-related events, say, $E_1^{rr} = \tilde{e}_1^{rr}$, $E_2^{rr} = \tilde{e}_2^{rr}, \ldots, E_n^{rr} = \tilde{e}_n^{rr}$,

$$P\left(E_1^{rr} = \tilde{e}_1^{rr}, E_2^{rr} = \tilde{e}_2^{rr}, \ldots, E_n^{rr} = \tilde{e}_n^{rr}\right)$$

$$= \sum_{e_1^{nrr} \in \mathcal{E}_1^{nrr}, \ldots, e_m^{nrr} \in \mathcal{E}_m^{nrr}} \mathbf{1}_{e_1^{nrr}, \ldots, e_m^{nrr}, \tilde{e}_1^{rr}, \ldots, \tilde{e}_n^{rr}}$$

$$\times P\left(E_1^{nrr} = e_1^{nrr}, \ldots, E_m^{nrr} = e_m^{nrr}, E_1^{rr} = \tilde{e}_1^{rr}, \ldots, E_n^{rr} = \tilde{e}_n^{rr}\right) \qquad (20.2)$$

This, by the way, is what we meant when we warned that the notation can get a bit messy. This is the key equation of this section, in that it shows how to carry out the required marginalization of the non-return-related probabilities. Of course, there are more efficient ways to carry out the computation: see, in this respect, the discussion in Section 15.1. Since, however, this marginalization only needs doing once, a brute-force approach is almost certainly adequate for the task.

In the rest of this chapter we will always assume that this marginalization has been carried out, i.e., that we are working directly with the joint distribution of return-related events. We shall call this distribution the *reduced joint distribution*.

20.3 Defining the utility-maximization problem

The distribution we have described above is the distribution of changes in market risk factors associated with the exceptional events. Recall that a market risk factor is a quantity – say, an interest rate – that determines, or contributes to determine, the value of an asset – say, a bond. We must combine this distribution with the distribution of market risk factors obtained from the normal body of the distribution, to derive from these two components the 'spliced' distribution of returns. Once this joint distribution is available we can move to the utility-maximization part of the problem.

In keeping with the notation introduced in Chapter 3, let the n assets be denoted by $x_1, x_2, \ldots, x_n$.[1] Let there be N market risk factors, $\xi_i, i = 1, 2, \ldots, N$. Our goal is to obtain, via statistical analysis and by means of the Bayesian net we have already determined, the joint distribution of the changes, $\Delta\xi_i$, in these market risk factors over a time interval Δt. Let us call this joint distribution $\varphi(\Delta\xi_1, \Delta\xi_2, \ldots, \Delta\xi_N)$.

In general, we write for the return from the jth asset

$$R_j = R_j(\Delta\xi_1, \Delta\xi_2, \ldots, \Delta\xi_N) \qquad (20.3)$$

With this notation we allow the return, R_j, from asset j to depend on the changes in *all* the market risk factors. This is fine, if we want to keep our notation as general as possible. But this will virtually never be the case in practice. Most commonly, the change in the value of one asset (say, a bond) will depend on the change of one factor (say, the level of rates). Sometimes the dependence may be more complex: for instance, the change in value of the bond may depend on the change in level and slope of the yield curve; or perhaps the jth asset could be a call option, whose change in value depends on changes in the price of the underlying and in the volatility (i.e., on changes in market risk factors, say, $\Delta\xi_r$ and $\Delta\xi_s$). But a more realistic notation would be

$$R_j = R_j(\Delta\xi_1, \Delta\xi_2, \ldots, \Delta\xi_{n_j}) \qquad (20.4)$$

with

$$n_j \ll N \qquad (20.5)$$

The important message is that the reader should not get discouraged by the 'heaviness' of the full mapping (20.3), and keep in mind that real-life situations tend to be far simpler than suggested by Equation (20.3).

Let Π be a portfolio made up of n assets,[2] each with weight w_i:

$$\Pi = \sum_{i=1,n} w_i x_i \qquad (20.6)$$

The portfolio return, R_Π, over the chosen time interval Δt is given by

$$R_\Pi = \sum_{i=1,n} w_i R_i(\Delta\xi_1, \Delta\xi_2, \ldots, \Delta\xi_N) = \sum_{i=1,n} w_i R_i(\Delta\xi) \qquad (20.7)$$

[1] With a slight abuse of notation we shall denote by x_i both the ith asset and its value.
[2] Also in this case, the symbol Π will denote both the portfolio and its value.

The expectation of the change in value of the portfolio, i.e., the expected return from the portfolio over the time interval Δt, $E[R_\Pi]$, is given by

$$E[R_\Pi] = \int \cdots \int \sum_{i=1,n} w_i R_i(\Delta\xi)\varphi(\Delta\xi)d^N(\Delta\xi) \qquad (20.8)$$

As for the variance of the change in the value of the portfolio, this is given by

$$\text{Var}[R_\Pi] = E[(R_\Pi)^2] - (E[R_\Pi])^2$$

$$= \int \cdots \int \sum_{i=1,n} \{w_i R_i(\Delta\xi) - E[R_\Pi]\}^2 \varphi(\Delta\xi)d^N(\Delta\xi) \qquad (20.9)$$

Expectation and variance of a portfolio are intrinsically interesting, and, of course, constitute the building blocks of mean-variance optimization. In our approach we present first a more general utility-maximization strategy, rather than a mean-variance optimization. We shall see, however, that the expectation and variance of the portfolio will play a very important role, not only when we apply some of the approximations we present in Chapter 25, but also in the asset allocation proper (see Chapter 29, Section 29.4 in particular).

20.4   Expected utility maximization

Let us write down, at lest formally, the expected-utility-maximization problem. We say 'formally' because we have not yet provided an explicit expression for the spliced joint distribution of market risk factors, $\varphi(\Delta\xi)$. However, it is useful to get an idea of where we are heading.

Let W_{t_0} be the initial wealth of the investor invested in the portfolio Π at time t_0. Then after a time interval Δt the wealth of the investor who holds portfolio Π will be given by

$$W_{t_0+\Delta t} = W_{t_0}(1 + R_\Pi)$$

Let the utility function of the investor be denoted by $U(W)$. Then the utility at time $t_0 + \Delta t$ is given by

$$U(W_{t_0+\Delta t}) = U(W_{t_0}(1 + R_{\Pi_i})) = U\left(W_{t_0}\left[1 + \sum_{i=1,n} w_i R_i(\Delta\xi)\right]\right) \qquad (20.10)$$

and the expected utility at time $t_0 + \Delta t$ is given by

$$E[U(W_{t_0+\Delta t})] = E[U(W_{t_0}(1 + R_{\Pi_i}))] = E\left[U\left(W_{t_0}\left[1 + \sum_{i=1,n} w_i R_i(\Delta\xi)\right]\right)\right]$$

$$= \int \cdots \int U\left(W_{t_0}\left[1 + \sum_{i=1,n} w_i R_i(\Delta\xi)\right]\right)\varphi(\Delta\xi)d^N(\Delta\xi) \qquad (20.11)$$

This expression gives the expected utility as a function of the portfolio weights for a fixed 'background' joint spliced distribution. Equation (20.11) is the quantity that we want to maximize by varying the allocations to the various assets (the weights). We stress that in this optimization procedure the joint spliced distribution, $\varphi(\Delta\xi_1, \Delta\xi_2, \ldots, \Delta\xi_N)$, which will be obtained by combining the 'normal' and exceptional contributions to the distribution, will not change, as only the weights will be varied. This is why we referred to it as the 'background' joint spliced distribution. So, even if the procedure presented in the next section may seem somewhat convoluted, it will only have to be carried out once.

To turn the 'formal' expression (20.11) into a quantity we can actually work with, we have to find a concrete formulation for the spliced joint density function. How to deal with the 'normal' part is easy enough to understand.[3] But what are we to do for the exceptional component of the return distribution? And how are we to combine the two components? We turn to these questions in the next sections.

20.5   Constructing the joint spliced distribution

To answer the questions presented at the end of the previous section, we place ourselves in the following setting.

20.5.1   The setting

We assume that we have built the Bayesian net in such a way that its leaves contain events linked to realizations of the changes in the market risk factors that affect the portfolio of interest. All leaves will therefore contain return-related events, as there would be no point in having a non-return-related event as a leaf 'leading nowhere'. To be concrete, the kth leaf may be associated with a statement like: 'The return over the next period from the S&P will be drawn from an excited distribution, $\psi_k^{exc}(\Delta\xi_1, \Delta\xi_2, \ldots, \Delta\xi_N)$, for the market risk factor(s) associated with that leaf'. If the statement is *TRUE*, then the return will be drawn from the chosen excited distribution.[4] To see what happens if it is *FALSE*, we need to handle the situation with some care, as explained below.

Let N_{leaf} be the number of leaves in the Bayesian nets. Let $p_0, p_1, p_2, \ldots, p_{2^{N_{\text{leaf}}}-1}$ be the (reduced) joint probabilities of occurrence of the different combinations of return-related events associated with the leaves. These are just the reduced joint probabilities that we have obtained in the first section of this chapter. Let the 0th event (i.e., the event associated with probability p_0) be the 'nothing-happens' event.

The investor enters a lottery with Nature. First, with probability p_0 the returns from her (the investor's, that is, not Nature's) portfolio are drawn from the 'normal-times'

---

[3] See, however, the discussion in Section 18.1.

[4] One must be careful when assigning the variance of return(s) in the excited state. This variance should reflect our uncertainty in the central value of excited returns, *not* the variance of returns in the excited state.

In particular, if we assign a very high value to the quantity $(\sigma_{exc}^{S\&P})^2$, we may end up with a positive draw even if our expectation is very negative. This is unlikely to be what we meant.

joint distribution, $\psi_0(\Delta\xi_1, \Delta\xi_2, \ldots, \Delta\xi_N)$. The distribution $\psi_0(\Delta\xi_1, \Delta\xi_2, \ldots, \Delta\xi_N)$ (which pertains to the 'nothing-happens' event) is estimated in our approach using the statistical techniques described in Part IV. It is the joint distribution of changes in the market risk factors under current 'normal' market conditions.

Next, let's move to any other joint event, which we label as event i, which occurs with probability p_i. For this joint event, a number, n_{exc}^i, of market risk factors are in the excited state, and a number, n_{norm}^i, are in the normal state.[5] Of course

$$n_{exc}^i + n_{norm}^i = N \tag{20.12}$$

The superscript 'i' indicates that these are the numbers of excited and non-excited nodes in the joint event of the reduced distribution that we have labelled with the index i. Since we are dealing with the reduced distribution, the excited and non-excited nodes will all correspond to excited and non-excited market risk factors. Let's consider the various component distributions in stages.

20.5.2   Building block 1: The excited-events distribution

Recall that $\psi_k^{exc}(\Delta\xi_1, \Delta\xi_2, \ldots, \Delta\xi_N)$ is the distribution of the changes in the market risk factors if the kth leaf is activated (*TRUE*). We have used a very general notation, by allowing in principle the dependence of the excited distribution associated with the kth leaf on all the market risk factors. However, in practice, for any given leaf each distribution $\psi_k^{exc}(\Delta\xi_1, \Delta\xi_2, \ldots, \Delta\xi_N)$ will have very low dimensionality – indeed, very often there will be a single market risk factor associated with a given leaf, and therefore $\psi_k^{exc}(\Delta\xi_1, \Delta\xi_2, \ldots, \Delta\xi_N) = \psi_k^{exc}(\Delta\xi_k)$.

For instance, for the case of a node associated with a movement in the S&P index, the associated statement that could be *TRUE* or *FALSE* could be something like: 'If the exceptional event occurs, the return for the S&P index will be drawn from a normal distribution with mean of -20% and a variance of $(5\%)^2$.' In this case only one market risk factor will be non-zero (let's call it $\Delta\xi_{S\&P}$) and the distribution the expert has to assign is one-dimensional, say, $\Delta\xi_{S\&P} \sim \mathcal{N}(-.20, 0.05^2)$.

To be more specific, we can stipulate that each 'building block' excited-event distribution, $\psi_k^{exc}(\Delta\xi_1, \Delta\xi_2, \ldots, \Delta\xi_N)$, should be of the type

$$\psi_k^{exc}(\Delta\xi_1, \Delta\xi_2, \ldots, \Delta\xi_N) = \mathcal{N}\left(\mu_{exc}^k, \Sigma_{exc}^k\right) \tag{20.13}$$

where $\mathcal{N}(\mu_{exc}^k, \Sigma_{exc}^k)$ denotes the Gaussian distribution, and, for the reasons discussed above, in most cases the covariance matrix Σ_{exc}^k will be just a number.

So, associated with each leaf in an activated state we now have a concrete excited distribution, $\psi_k^{exc}(\Delta\xi_1, \Delta\xi_2, \ldots, \Delta\xi_N)$. These are the first building blocks from which we are going to build the spliced joint distribution.

---

[5] For the 'nothing-happens' event, of course, $n_{exc}^i = 0$ and $n_{norm}^i = N$.

20.5.3   Building block 2: The 'compacted' normal-times distribution for the ith event

For the ith joint event we now have to create a 'compacted' normal-market distribution, $\psi_{\text{comp}}^{0(i)}$, of market risk factors, which is in theory obtainable by integrating the frequentist distribution $\psi_0(\Delta\xi_1, \Delta\xi_2, \ldots, \Delta\xi_N)$ over all the excited variables.[6] We need a compacted normal-times distribution because in the ith joint event only a subset of the market risk factors associated with the terminal leaves will be in the normal state, and therefore we have to exclude from the normal-times distribution those variables which are in the excited state. After a renumbering of the variables whereby we put the non-excited variables first, we can write

$$\psi_{\text{comp}}^{0(i)} \left(\Delta\xi_1, \Delta\xi_2, \ldots, \Delta\xi_{n_{\text{norm}}^i} \right)$$

$$= \int \cdots \int \psi_0(\Delta\xi_1, \Delta\xi_2, \ldots, \Delta\xi_N) d\left(\Delta\xi_{n_{\text{norm}}+1}\right) \ldots d\left(\Delta\xi_{n_{\text{exc}}^i}\right) \qquad (20.14)$$

This 'normal-times' compacted distribution for joint event i is the second building block in our construction.

20.5.4   ith event: the combined distribution

Let's now look at how to combine the normal-times part and the exceptional part of the distribution for the same joint event – say, the ith event.

Recall that associated with the joint event i we have n_{exc}^i excited distributions $\psi_k^{\text{exc}}(\Delta\xi_1, \Delta\xi_2, \ldots, \Delta\xi_N)$, $k = 1, 2, \ldots, n_{\text{exc}}^i$, and one compacted normal-times distribution. To obtain the combined distribution for joint event i, we can follow (at least) two different routes, each with its strengths and weaknesses. It is important to understand the choices we make very carefully, and we discuss these alternatives in the following.

Procedure 1   With the first procedure we create the combined (normal plus excited) distribution associated with joint event i, $\varphi_i(\Delta\xi_1, \Delta\xi_2, \ldots, \Delta\xi_N)$, as follows:

$$\varphi_i(\Delta\xi_1, \Delta\xi_2, \ldots, \Delta\xi_N)$$

$$= \psi_{\text{comp}}^0 \left(\Delta\xi_1, \Delta\xi_2, \ldots, \Delta\xi_{n_{\text{norm}}^i} \right) \prod_{k=1,n_{\text{exc}}^i} \psi_k^{\text{exc}}(\Delta\xi_1, \Delta\xi_2, \ldots, \Delta\xi_N) \qquad (20.15)$$

Let's look at Equation (20.15) in some detail.

Consider the normal-times compacted component distribution, ψ_{comp}^0, first. This is the component we derived above in the discussion leading to Equation (20.15). Recall that, as we have pointed out, to obtain it we only have to conjoin the marginals of the n_{norm}^i variables which are in a non-excited state for the joint event i.

---

[6] We say 'in theory' because in practice our task is simplified by the way we have built the normal-times joint distribution in the first place, i.e., by constructing marginals and conjoining them using the chosen copula. So, in reality we will simply have to conjoin the n_{norm}^i marginal distributions for the market risk factors that are not in the excited state for joint event i.

With Equation (20.15) we then make two distinct assumptions (whose validity we discuss below):

1. that each excited distribution, $\psi_k^{exc}(\Delta\xi_1, \Delta\xi_2, \ldots, \Delta\xi_N)$, is independent of the 'compacted' normal-market distribution, $\psi_{comp}^0(\Delta\xi_1, \Delta\xi_2, \ldots, \Delta\xi_{n_{norm}^i})$;
2. that the particular draw of the jth excited leaf is independent of the draw of the kth excited leaf.

As we discuss below, we are *not* assuming that the jth and the kth excited events are independent – they are clearly not, as they are linked by the chains of dependencies embedded in the Bayesian net. We are simply saying that, *given that they are both excited*, the specific draws will be independent.

How reasonable are the two assumptions above? What do they actually entail? As these assumptions have an important bearing on the codependence of the market risk factor returns in the joint distribution we have to look at them in some detail. There are three types of dependence to consider:

- the dependence between non-excited risk factors;
- the dependence between excited risk factors;
- the dependence between excited and non-excited risk factors.

Let's look at these in turn.

Dependence between non-excited risk factors The first implication of the assumptions we have made is that, *for those risk factors which are not in an excited state, the same dependence applies in the ith joint event and in the 'normal' times*: this is because for the normal-times part of the compacted distribution we are still using (after integrating out the excited degrees of freedom) the 'normal' statistical distribution.

Is this reasonable? To answer the question, consider the case where, for a particular joint event, only one leaf is in the excited state. In this case there is probably some idiosyncratic reason for the associated factor, *and that factor alone*, to be excited. Hopefully the idiosyncratic nature of this excitation has been well captured in the way we have built our Bayesian net.

Suppose, however, that, for another joint event, most of the leaves are in the excited state. Then it is probably not as palatable to assume that the dependence among the non-excited risk factors should be the same as in the normal state. However, we do not give a literal interpretation to the term 'normal times', as we allow for any statistical estimation of the market co-movements that have already been observed in the market. As we discussed, this estimation can be a quickly responsive one (perhaps based on high-frequency data, on GARCH modelling, or on anticipating correlations). With this qualification, this first assumption is therefore more reasonable than it may prima facie appear.

Dependence between excited risk factors Let's look at the second type of dependencies, those between the excited events. From Equation (20.15) we are implying that the draws from the excited risk factor are independent. This is literally true, but we have to be careful about what this means. What we are saying is simply that, given that we made, say, a 'high' draw from the excited distribution for risk factor k, this will have no bearing on the magnitude of the draw we make for *excited* factor j. It is essential to point out, however, that also the factor j is drawn from an excited distribution. If both factors j and k are excited in the ith joint event, we are *not* saying that the excitation of factor j has no influence (is independent of) factor k being excited. The event codependence between excited risk factors is fully reflected in the structure and in the conditional probability tables of our Bayesian net. To the extent that the standard deviations of the excited distributions are not very large compared with the expectation component this assumption also appears not too unrealistic.

In the limit, there is nothing stopping the expert from assigning a Dirac-δ for the excited distribution of the risk factor. If this were the choice of the expert, the issue of the correlation between the magnitudes of the draws in the excited states would disappear altogether. We do not recommend pursuing this route, because both in an expected-utility-maximization framework and when matching moments of joint distributions it is conceptually consistent to treat on the same footing *all* sources of uncertainty, including therefore the one coming from our ignorance of the precise realization of the stress event. However, we stress that the assumption of independence between excited risk factors is far less restrictive than it may at first glance appear.

Dependence between excited and non-excited risk factors Finally, let's consider the dependence between normal and excited returns. Here we have enforced independence again, and doing so is somewhat more problematic – but, we believe, not unduly so. Consider in fact two market risk factors: let one be associated with a fall in the S&P and the other with a fall in the FTSE. Suppose that, in the joint event i, the FTSE factor happens to be excited but the S&P factor is in the normal state. Suppose also that the root event was a major terrorist attack. Then we may feel that a fall in the FTSE should definitely be strongly correlated with a fall in the S&P. This is not reflected in the joint distribution associated to event i.

This is true, but, if we have constructed our Bayesian net well, *the joint probability associated with event i (an event that corresponds to a terrorist-attack-induced fall in the FTSE but not in the S&P) will be extremely low*. For a well-built Bayesian net, this low joint probability will flow naturally from the conditional probabilities that we have assigned to reflect our expert understanding.

In sum: we think that Procedure 1, as quantitatively expressed by Equation (20.15) presents a reasonable way to build the overall joint distribution of market risk factors.

Many alternative procedures are, of course, possible. We discuss a second approach below.

Procedure 2 In the second procedure we do not have to build a compacted normal-times distribution at all. To see how to proceed, recall that we built the normal distribution by constructing marginals first, and then conjoining through our chosen copula. For each joint event i we can first simply record which market risk factors are in the excited state. For these risk factors we then substitute the excited distribution, $\psi_k^{\text{exc}}(\Delta\xi_1, \Delta\xi_2, \ldots, \Delta\xi_N)$, to the normal distribution that has been estimated using frequentist techniques. The new set of marginals is then conjoined using the same copula determined for the normal distribution.

What does this procedure imply about the three sets of dependencies outlined above?

For the non-excited factors the dependence remains of course the same. The same comments as above apply.

Let's now consider the dependence between the excited factors. The draws from the distributions for the excited factors are now not independent, but are linked by the same type of dependence established in normal times. This is probably (but not necessarily!) more palatable than the assumption of independence. But we must recall again that we are talking about a second-order effect, at least to the extent that the standard deviation is much smaller than the expectation of the excited distribution.

Finally, let's look at the dependence between the normal and the excited factors. Here, by construction, we are forced to have exactly the same dependence as in the normal state. Despite the different joint probabilities assigned by the set $\{p_i\}$, in all the joint states the dependence between all the variables (as expressed by the copula) remains exactly the same. The 'power' of the causal dependence induced by the Bayesian net is therefore greatly diluted.

For this reason, despite the minor advantage afforded by the second procedure when it comes to representing the dependence between the magnitude of the draws for the excited factors, we find the first procedure to be overall more appealing, and more consonant with our way of thinking about what happens to codependencies during periods of excitation.

20.5.5 The full spliced distribution

If we are happy with Equation (20.15), the total joint distribution, $\varphi(\Delta\xi_1, \Delta\xi_2, \ldots, \Delta\xi_N)$, in terms of which the utility-maximization problem above was expressed, can finally be written as

$$\varphi(\Delta\xi_1, \Delta\xi_2, \ldots, \Delta\xi_N) = \sum_{i=0,2^{N_{\text{leaf}}}-1} p_i \varphi_i(\Delta\xi_1, \Delta\xi_2, \ldots, \Delta\xi_N) \qquad (20.16)$$

In words:

- the total joint spliced distribution, $\varphi(\Delta\xi_1, \Delta\xi_2, \ldots, \Delta\xi_N)$, is obtained as a linear combination of basis functions, $\varphi_i(\Delta\xi_1, \Delta\xi_2, \ldots, \Delta\xi_N)$;
- there are as many basis functions as joint events in the reduced distribution (20.2) – i.e., $2^{N_{\text{leaf}}}$;
- the weights, p_i, in the linear combinations are the probabilities of each joint event;
- the basis functions $\varphi_i(\Delta\xi_1, \Delta\xi_2, \ldots, \Delta\xi_N)$ are constructed as the product of the compacted normal-times distribution, $\psi_{\text{comp}}^0(\Delta\xi_1, \Delta\xi_2, \ldots, \Delta\xi_{n_{\text{norm}}^i})$, (see

Equation (20.15)) and the product of the excited distributions associated with the leaves in the excited state in event i, $\prod_{k=1,n_{exc}^i} \psi_k^{exc}(\Delta\xi_1, \Delta\xi_2, \ldots, \Delta\xi_N)$;

- for the 0th joint event (the 'nothing-happens' event) associated with the weight p_i, the basis function $\varphi_0(\Delta\xi_1, \Delta\xi_2, \ldots, \Delta\xi_N)$ is degenerate, as the product $\prod_{k=1,n_{exc}^i}$ is empty, and the basis function itself is simply the normal-times joint distribution estimated using the statistical techniques described in Part VI.

With the assumptions we made above about the excited distribution of the market risk factors if the kth leaf is activated, $\psi_k^{exc}(\Delta\xi_1, \Delta\xi_2, \ldots, \Delta\xi_N)$ (we have proposed the Gaussian assumption, but the approach can be extended to any distribution the portfolio manager may feel comfortable with), the spliced joint distribution, $\varphi(\Delta\xi_1, \Delta\xi_2, \ldots, \Delta\xi_N)$, is fully specified and is given by Equation (20.16).

As we have seen, the nothing-happens probability, p_0, plays a specially important role in our treatment, as it is associated with the normal-times distribution, and is likely to be the largest weight in the linear combination $\varphi = \sum p_i\varphi_i$. For this reason this quantity deserves special attention, and, as we discuss below, can be used as a 'free parameter' to express our degree of confidence in the quantitative information conveyed by the Bayesian net. We therefore turn to this topic in the last part of this chapter. Before that, however, we want to show in a simple concrete case how the procedure described above works in practice.

20.6 A worked example

Consider a Bayesian net with three terminal leaves, L_1, L_2 and L_3, each one with two possible states, an excited one and a normal one. The reasoning still goes through if the leaves have more than two states as long as we can associate a normal state to each leaf.

For simplicity, we assume that each leaf is associated with one market risk factor, ξ (say, the S&P 500, the 10-year Treasury yield, etc).

For each leaf i, if it is in the excited state we draw the realization of the associated change in the market risk factor ($\Delta\xi_i$) from an excited distribution, $\psi_i^{exc}(\Delta\xi_i) = \mathcal{N}_{exc}(\mu_i^{exc}, \sigma_i^{exc})$, $i = 1, 2, 3$. What happens when a leaf is in the normal state is explained below.

Our goal is to obtain the full joint spliced distribution, $\varphi(\Delta\xi_1, \Delta\xi_2, \Delta\xi_3)$, of the market risk factors associated with the three leaves. This is the joint distribution that takes account of the normal and of the excited states.

Following the terminology and the procedure described in Section 20.1 we show in Table 20.1 the resulting reduced joint probability table. In this table we call p_0 the probability that 'nothing happens', i.e., that all the leaves are in the non-excited state.

Let us denote the 'normal-times' joint distribution of the market risk factors by $\psi_0(\Delta\xi)$. This is the joint distribution that we have determined from culled historical data by fitting each marginal to our parametric distribution of choice, and by fitting the Gaussian copula.

Table 20.1 *The reduced joint probability table associated with the three terminal leaves*

Leaf 1	Leaf 2	Leaf 3	Joint probability
$L_1 = \text{norm}$	$L_2 = \text{norm}$	$L_3 = \text{norm}$	p_0
$L_1 = \text{exc}$	$L_2 = \text{norm}$	$L_3 = \text{norm}$	p_1
$L_1 = \text{norm}$	$L_2 = \text{exc}$	$L_3 = \text{norm}$	p_2
$L_1 = \text{exc}$	$L_2 = \text{exc}$	$L_3 = \text{norm}$	p_3
$L_1 = \text{norm}$	$L_2 = \text{norm}$	$L_3 = \text{exc}$	p_4
$L_1 = \text{exc}$	$L_2 = \text{norm}$	$L_3 = \text{exc}$	p_5
$L_1 = \text{norm}$	$L_2 = \text{exc}$	$L_3 = \text{exc}$	p_6
$L_1 = \text{exc}$	$L_2 = \text{exc}$	$L_3 = \text{exc}$	p_7

Clearly, if we are in state 0 (nothing happens, first row, probability p_0), then the *full* joint probability of the market risk factor returns is just $\psi_0(\Delta\xi)$ (because none of the leaves is excited).

Let us move to the second row, i.e., the one associated with probability p_1.

Here we have two leaves (L_2 and L_3) in a normal state, and the other leaf (L_1) in its excited state. As discussed above, we denote the number of excited leaves in the ith state by n^i_{exc} and the number of normal leaves in the ith state by n^i_{norm}. Clearly, for any i,

$$n^i_{\text{norm}} + n^i_{\text{exc}} = 3 \tag{20.17}$$

For this state $n^1_{\text{exc}} = 1$ and $n^1_{\text{norm}} = 2$.

As a next step we are going to obtain the compacted joint distribution associated with the ith state, $\psi^i_{\text{comp}}(\Delta\xi_2, \Delta\xi_3)$. This is done by integrating the full normal-times distribution, $\psi_0(\Delta\xi)$, over the excited variables. For the state associated with p_1, this means integrating $\psi_0(\Delta\xi)$ over the first market risk factor (because only L_1 is in an excited state):

$$\psi^1_{\text{comp}}(\Delta\xi_2, \Delta\xi_3) = \int \psi_0(\Delta\xi_1, \Delta\xi_2, \Delta\xi_3) d(\Delta\xi_1) \tag{20.18}$$

We repeat this compacting procedure for $N - 2 = 6$ states. ($N - 2$ because we need no compacting if all or none of the leaves are in the excited states.) So we obtain the following compacted distributions

$$
\begin{aligned}
&\text{State 0} \quad \psi_0(\Delta\xi_1, \Delta\xi_2, \Delta\xi_3) \\
&\text{State 1} \quad \psi^1_{\text{comp}}(\Delta\xi_2, \Delta\xi_3) \\
&\text{State 2} \quad \psi^2_{\text{comp}}(\Delta\xi_1, \Delta\xi_3) \\
&\text{State 3} \quad \psi^3_{\text{comp}}(\Delta\xi_3) \\
&\text{State 4} \quad \psi^4_{\text{comp}}(\Delta\xi_1, \Delta\xi_2) \\
&\text{State 5} \quad \psi^5_{\text{comp}}(\Delta\xi_2) \\
&\text{State 6} \quad \psi^6_{\text{comp}}(\Delta\xi_1) \\
&\text{State 7} \quad -
\end{aligned}
\tag{20.19}
$$

We stress that, in practice, we do not need to carry out the marginalizations, because we already have the normal-state distribution in the form of marginals and copulae.

Now, for the generic ith state we recall that $\varphi_i(\Delta\xi)$ is given by

$$\varphi_i(\Delta\xi_1, \Delta\xi_2, \Delta\xi_3) = \psi^i_{\text{comp}}(\Delta\xi_{\text{norm}}) \prod_{k=1,n^i_{\text{exc}}} \psi^{\text{exc}}_k(\Delta\xi_{\text{exc}}) \tag{20.20}$$

We then obtain the full spliced joint distribution, $\varphi(\Delta\xi_1, \Delta\xi_2, \Delta\xi_3)$, as

$$\varphi(\Delta\xi_1, \Delta\xi_2, \Delta\xi_3) = \sum_{i=0,7} p_i \varphi_i(\Delta\xi_1, \Delta\xi_2, \Delta\xi_3) \tag{20.21}$$

Of course, everything rests on Equation (20.20). Let's revisit in this simple and transparent case whether it is reasonable, and what it implies.

First of all, it implies that the particular draw in excited state k is independent of the particular draw in excited state j. Again, this does not mean that leaves j and k are independent! Their dependence is fully encoded in the Bayesian net 'upstream' of the three leaves, and is reflected in the joint probabilities $\{p_i\}$. The independence we are talking about is to do with the particular realizations of the excited draws.

To see clearly what we are doing, suppose that node j is the FTSE and node k is the S&P 500. From experience we know that, if one of the two indices were to experience a large fall, the other would be very likely to display a large fall as well. The two leaves are therefore certainly highly correlated, and, if we have constructed our Bayesian net properly, this dependence should already have been built in. But what about the particular 'bad' draws? Suppose that we have stipulated

$$\mu^{\text{exc}}_j = -25\%, \quad \sigma^{\text{exc}}_j = 5\% \tag{20.22}$$

$$\mu^{\text{exc}}_k = -35\%, \quad \sigma^{\text{exc}}_k = 5\% \tag{20.23}$$

We are saying that about 90% of the draws for the S&P will be between -35% and -15%, and that that about 90% of the draws for the FTSE will be between -45% and -25%. In those states when both leaves are excited, we will certainly draw a strongly negative return both for the S&P 500 and for the FTSE. In this sense the two leaves *are* strongly correlated. What we are also saying that if the S&P draws a relatively benign draw (say, -18%) this will not affect the severity of the negative FTSE draw. Note that, if we assigned for the excited distributions Dirac-δs – as one often does in assigning 'stressed outcomes' – then this issue of independence of draws would not even arise.

Next we are implying with Equation (20.20) that knowledge that leaf, say, k, is excited, does not change the joint distribution of the non-excited leaves. This is more questionable, but not totally unreasonable, as discussed in the previous sections. It also makes our life much easier.

Finally, those variables which are not in an excited state retain the full dependence coming from their marginals and their (portion of) the Gaussian copula.

20.7   Uncertainty in the normalization factor: a Maximum-Entropy approach

20.7.1   Introducing the normalization factor

The Bayesian procedure that we have described in the previous chapters provides one and only one value for the probability mass of the 'normal' part of the distribution: this is exactly equal to the probability, p_0, obtained from our Bayesian net that none of the joint stress events will occur. If we had full faith in our Bayesian procedure, then, for our chosen utility function, there will be one and only one optimal allocation among the portfolio assets, and this optimal allocation would be a function of p_0.

Given the approximate and subjective nature of the inputs, however, such a 'fundamentalist' belief in the output of the Bayesian analysis is probably unwarranted. As we shall see in the following chapters, this is the reason why we like to present graphically our allocation results as a function of the probability of the nothing-happens event, p_0, or, as we shall see, of a suitably defined normalization factor, k.

This normalization factor is defined as follows. Let's rewrite the full distribution of the market risk factors as follows:

$$\varphi(\Delta\xi_1, \Delta\xi_n, \ldots, \Delta\xi_n)$$

$$= (1-k)\varphi_0(\Delta\xi_1, \Delta\xi_n, \ldots, \Delta\xi_n) + \frac{k}{1-p_0}\sum_{i>0} p_i\varphi_i(\Delta\xi_1, \Delta\xi_n, \ldots, \Delta\xi_n)$$

Of course, if $k = 1 - p_0$ we are back exactly to the same description as above (see Equation (20.16)). However, we now allow for the possibility that the probability of the nothing-happens event may be different from that determined by our Bayesian net.

Admittedly, there is uncertainty about *all* the joint probabilities determined using the Bayesian net. So, why focus our attention on the nothing-happens probability, p_0? A facile answer is that this is the largest probability by far. A more insightful answer would point to the fact that the probability p_0 is directly linked to (1 minus) the marginal probability of the root of our Bayesian net, i.e., to the probability of the stress event(s) that we have placed at the origin(s) of our net. This, in general, will be the (very-difficult-to-estimate) stand-alone probability of a rare event. Now, we have based our Bayesian-net construction on the causal nature of the dependence between the variables. Our assumption throughout this book has been that, if we have a causal model of reality in our minds, assigning conditional probabilities is a difficult, but not hopeless, task.[7]

---

[7] This may sound surprising: how can assigning a probability of something conditioned on a rare event be easier than assigning the marginal probability of the same rare event? It is indeed more difficult if we use a purely association-based, frequentist approach, where all of our information about the conditional event comes from empirical observation. But it can be much easier if we have a structural model that links the cause(s) (however rare) to the effect(s). Consider, for instance, the following example, discussed in greater detail in Rebonato (2010a). I might not know with any degree of precision the probability of ending up in hospital today; and I may not know any more precisely the probability of being hit by a car today. However, given the causal link between the two events, I can easily venture that the probability of my being taken to hospital *given that I have been hit by a car* is somewhere between, say, 60% and 90%. Note that the reverse conditional probability, i.e., the probability of having been hit by a car given that I have ended up in hospital, is much more difficult to ascertain, because I am no longer working in the causal direction.

Our focusing on the uncertainty in the probability p_0 is therefore motivated by our belief that assigning *marginal* non-frequentist probabilities of rare events is more difficult than assigning subjective (but causally inspired) conditional probabilities.

So, being skeptical and pragmatic people, when it comes to determining the optimal asset allocation from 'spliced' distributions we do not recommend using a ruler, placing it perpendicularly to the x-axis in correspondence to the Bayesian-net-determined probability that nothing happens, p_0, and reading the optimal allocation by looking at where our transparent ruler intersects the smooth allocation curves. We feel that a more nuanced approach, that takes into account the uncertainty we have in the probability p_0, is arguably more reasonable. If the reader accepts our reasoning, we propose in what follows a way to embed this uncertainty in our procedure in a coherent manner.

20.7.2 Introducing uncertainty in the normalization factor

We may not have a clear intuitive perception of what precise value the normalization factor should have, but nonetheless we often have a strong and clear intuition about the range of values it may (or may not) reasonably assume. Can we make this intuition more precise? As Maximum Entropy is a concept dear to our hearts, this is the angle from which we try to answer (in the affirmative) the questions above.

As usual, applying the Maximum-Entropy principle means in our case maximizing the entropy, $H(g)$, defined as

$$H(g) = -\int g(k) \ln[g(k)] \, dk \qquad (20.24)$$

where g is the imperfectly known distribution of k. Since this distribution is imperfectly known, the Maximum-Entropy way of attacking a problem begins by asking what we know about the phenomenon under study. In our case, what can we reasonably say about k? Here are three plausible and useful starting points.

1. The factor k is defined in the interval $[0, 1]$.
2. Its mode is given by $1 - p_0$.
3. Our degree of confidence about its true value can be expressed by a variance Ω^2.

The second *desideratum* reflects our belief that the most likely value for k should be around the Bayesian-net-derived value $1 - p_0$. If we did not hold this belief it would mean that we believe that there is something wrong (rather, something *biased*) in the Bayesian net we have built. If this is how we felt, then the more constructive approach would be to go back to the net and refine it according to our understanding.

The three beliefs above may not amount to much, but they already allow us to draw on some well-known Maximum-Entropy-related results. To begin with, as Dowson and Wrag (1973) show, if we know that a distribution has a support in the finite interval $[a, b]$ and we know its first two moments, $\mu_1 = E[k]$, $\mu_2 = \mu_2(E[k])$, then the Maximum-Entropy (i.e., the least 'arbitrary' or 'presumptive') distribution is[8]

---

[8] See Appendix 20.B for a more general treatment.

1. the truncated exponential if $\mu_2(E[k]) = \mu_{2,\text{te}}(E[k])$;
2. the truncated Gaussian if $\mu_2(E[k]) < \mu_{2,\text{te}}(E[k])$;
3. the U-shaped distribution if $\mu_2(E[k]) > \mu_{2,\text{te}}(E[k])$.

where $\mu_{2,\text{te}}(E[k])$ is the second moment of the truncated exponential distribution. Appendix 20.B gives an expression for the first two moments of truncated exponential and truncated Gaussian distributions. In practice, however, when the mode has values as small as those typically found in a stress-testing context, Denev (2011) shows that the three conditions above can be approximated as follows:

1. $\mu_2(E[k]) = \mu_{2,\text{te}}(E[k]) \Longrightarrow E[k] = \Omega$;
2. $\mu_2(E[k]) < \mu_{2,\text{te}}(E[k]) \Longrightarrow E[k] < \Omega$;
3. $\mu_2(E[k]) > \mu_{2,\text{te}}(E[k]) \Longrightarrow$ if $E[k] > \Omega$.

Which of these three possibilities looks more reasonable? For the first, we certainly have no *a priori* reason to believe that the expected value of the normalization factor, k, should be exactly equal to our uncertainty about its value. Furthermore, to the extent that we are dealing with 'stress' events, we should be reasonably confident that the probability of nothing happening, p_0, should be 'rather high'. Or, looking at the matter from a similar angle, it would not make a lot of sense to assign an uncertainty greater than the expected value of p_0 (which should typically be in the 0.80–0.95 range). Therefore we are in case 2 (the truncated Gaussian, for which mode, median and mean value coincide if the truncation in 'symmetric'). We can call this truncated Gaussian $g_{\text{tG}}(k; \Omega^2)$.

Using a truncated Gaussian distribution to express our uncertainty about the normalization factor, k, makes good intuitive sense if our uncertainty, Ω^2, is not only smaller, but *significantly* smaller, than our expected value, μ, for k. If this is not the case, then the probability that the normalization factor, k, should lie in the immediate neighbourhood of 0 is non-negligible. We are effectively saying that we do not really believe that, after all, any of the root stress events will materialize. This raises the question as to why we embarked on the Bayesian-net project in the first place.

The opposite problem is that, unless our uncertainty is rather large, we cannot give significant probability to 'reasonably large' values of k. What about increasing our degree of uncertainty, Ω^2? If we do so 'too much', then the least-informative distribution becomes the U-shaped, which does not make great intuitive sense for the problem at hand. Can we do better?

Let's try to enrich our information set, i.e., let's try to inject more information about what we believe we know about k. We can require for instance the following.

1. The factor k should be defined in the interval $[0, b]$, with $b \leq 1$. We refine, that is, the condition on the support of k.
2. Its mode m should be given by p_0.
3. Our degree of confidence about its true value can be expressed by a variance Ω^2.
4. The distribution function should vanish at the boundaries of its support: $g(k = 0) = g(k = b) = 0$.

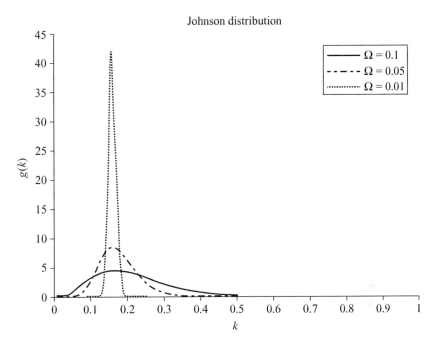

Figure 20.1 The Johnson distribution for different values of the variance Ω^2 for $m = 0.16$.

If we are ready to subscribe to these intuitively rather appealing conditions, then Goodman (1987) proves that the associated Maximum-Entropy distribution is given by the modified lognormal (Johnson) distribution, given by:

$$g^J(k) = \frac{b}{\sqrt{2\pi}\sigma k(b-k)} \exp\left[-\frac{1}{2}\left(\frac{\ln\left(\frac{k}{b-k}\right) - \mu}{\sigma}\right)^2\right] \tag{20.25}$$

and shown in Figure 20.1.

To clarify the procedure: the user provides two parameters, the mode m and Ω. With these two parameters she can calculate the two parameters μ and σ to input in the expression for the Johnson distributions, which, just as the Gaussian and the lognormal, is also fully characterized by its first two moments. The main drawback of the Johnson distribution is that it does not lend itself to as intuitive and immediate an appreciation as the symmetrical Gaussian distribution does. The (square root of the) variance is easily imagined in the case of a bell curve as the width of the distribution, but it is more difficult to make this identification in the case of an asymmetrical distribution such as the Johnson.

Now, Chebishev theorem states that, for *any* distribution, given a random variable X with finite expected value, μ, and non-zero variance, Ω^2, and for any real number $h > 0$,

$$\Pr(|X - \mu| \geq h\Omega) \leq \frac{1}{h^2} \tag{20.26}$$

In our case this tells us that the probability, $G^J(1 - \widehat{h})$, of a draw more than three standard deviations away from the mean, i.e., of a draw exceeding the value $\widehat{h}$, given by

$$\widehat{h} = \mu + 3\Omega \tag{20.27}$$

must be smaller than approximately 10%:

$$G^J(1 - \widehat{h}) \leq 0.1 \tag{20.28}$$

By taking the first derivative of Equation (20.25) and setting it to zero at the modal value we can then obtain a useful relation between the parameters μ and σ[9] (see Appendix 20.A), which for $b = 1$ reads:

$$\sigma^2 = \frac{\ln\left(\frac{m}{1-m}\right) - \mu}{2m - 1} \tag{20.29}$$

In Equation (20.29) m is the mode, and it is assumed to be known at the outset. We still have one free parameter left, which we can find numerically by availing ourselves of the knowledge of the variance Ω^2 – the other given input of the problem together with the mode.

The portfolio manager may want to experiment with the Johnson distribution, or remain closer to shore, and employ a truncated Gaussian distribution. In either case she will have assigned a distribution to the possible values of the all-important normalization factor, k. We shall show in the following chapters (see Chapter 27 and Sections 27.2 and 27.3 in particular) how this information can be made use of in the optimization phase of our procedure.

Appendix 20.A

The Johnson distribution was first introduced in Johnson (1949). Johnson noticed that a bounded random variable x could be turned into a normal variable by the transformation

$$z = \gamma + \delta \ln \frac{k - \xi}{\xi + \lambda - k} = h(k) \tag{20.30}$$

where z is a standardized normal variable (i.e., $z \sim \mathcal{N}(0; 1)$) and ξ, λ, γ and δ are parameters with the following domains:

$$\xi \leq k \leq \xi + \lambda \tag{20.31}$$

$$-\infty < \gamma < \infty \tag{20.32}$$

$$\lambda > 0 \tag{20.33}$$

$$\xi \geq 0 \tag{20.34}$$

$$\delta > 0 \tag{20.35}$$

---

[9] The parameters μ and σ do not coincide with mean and variance. See Parresol (2003) for a detailed analytical derivation of the moments of the Johnson distribution. These moments, unfortunately, do not have a simple form.

The Johnson SB distribution, which is the distribution of k, can be deduced from:[10]

$$f(k) = \mathcal{N}(h(k)) \left| \frac{dh(k)}{dk} \right| \qquad (20.36)$$

The parameters have the following interpretation:

- ξ is a location factor;
- λ is a scale factor;
- γ and δ determine the shape.

In our case we want the variable k to vary within $[0, b]$ and so we can set $\xi = 0$ and $\lambda = b$. By substituting then

$$\delta = \frac{1}{\sigma} \qquad (20.37)$$

and

$$\gamma = -\frac{\mu}{\sigma} \qquad (20.38)$$

we obtain the expression (20.25):

$$g(k) = \frac{b}{\sqrt{2\pi}\sigma k(b-k)} \exp\left[-\frac{1}{2}\left(\frac{\ln\left(\frac{k}{b-k}\right) - \mu}{\sigma} \right)^2 \right] \qquad 0 \le k \le b \qquad (20.39)$$

If we expand Equation (20.39) we find that

$$\lim_{k \to 0} k^{-n} g(k) = \lim_{k \to b}(b - k)^{-n} g(k) = 0 \qquad (20.40)$$

for any value of n. The distribution of k therefore has 'high contact' at both ends of its range of variation. By taking the first derivative of $g(k)$ and equating it to zero we therefore obtain:

$$2k - b = \left(\ln \frac{k}{b-k} - \mu \right) \frac{b}{\sigma^2} \qquad (20.41)$$

If we call m the value of k corresponding to its mode, we find the useful expression for σ with $b = 1$ reported without proof in Equation (20.29):

$$\sigma^2 = \frac{\ln\left(\frac{m}{1-m}\right) - \mu}{2m - 1} \qquad (20.42)$$

Appendix 20.B

In this appendix we provide without proof the expressions for, and the first two moments of, the truncated exponential and truncated normal distributions. For a derivation see Olive (2008).[11]

---

[10] See also Parresol (2003).   [11] See the chapter 'Truncated distributions'.

20.B.1 *Truncated exponential*

The probability density, $f(x)$, of a truncated exponential distribution is given by

$$f(x) = \frac{\frac{\exp(-x/m)}{m}}{1 - \exp(-b/m)} \tag{20.43}$$

with $x \in (0, b]$. If we write

$$b = lm \tag{20.44}$$

the first two moments become

$$E[X] = m \left[\frac{1 - (l+1)\exp[-l]}{1 - \exp[-l]} \right] \tag{20.45}$$

and

$$E[X^2] = 2m^2 \left[\frac{1 - \frac{1}{2}(l^2 + 2l + 2)\exp[-l]}{1 - \exp[-l]} \right] \tag{20.46}$$

When l is large

$$E[X] \approx m \tag{20.47}$$

$$E[X^2] \approx 2m^2 \tag{20.48}$$

and therefore

$$\text{Var}[X] = m^2 \tag{20.49}$$

20.B.2 *Truncated Gaussian*

Let $\mathcal{N}(x; m, \sigma^2)$ be a Gaussian density with mean m and variance σ^2, and let $\Phi(x; m, \sigma^2)$ be the associated cumulative density.

For a Gaussian distribution the mean and the mode coincide. This is no longer necessarily the case for a truncated Gaussian distribution if the support $[a, b]$ is not symmetrically positioned around the mean of the non-truncated distribution. So, in general, the density, $f(x)$, of a truncated Gaussian distribution with mode mo is given by

$$f(x) = \frac{\mathcal{N}(x; mo, \sigma^2)}{\Phi\left(\frac{b-mo}{\sigma}\right) - \Phi\left(\frac{a-mo}{\sigma}\right)} I_{[a,b]}(x) \tag{20.50}$$

where $I_{[a,b]}$ is the indicator function over the interval $[a, b]$.

The first and second moments are then given by

$$E[X] = mo + \frac{\mathcal{N}\left(\frac{a-mo}{\sigma}\right) - \mathcal{N}\left(\frac{b-mo}{\sigma}\right)}{\Phi\left(\frac{b-mo}{\sigma}\right) - \Phi\left(\frac{a-mo}{\sigma}\right)}\sigma \tag{20.51}$$

$$E[X^2] = \sigma^2\left[1 + \frac{\frac{a-mo}{\sigma}\mathcal{N}\left(\frac{a-mo}{\sigma}\right) - \frac{b-mo}{\sigma}\mathcal{N}\left(\frac{b-mo}{\sigma}\right)}{\Phi\left(\frac{b-mo}{\sigma}\right) - \Phi\left(\frac{a-mo}{\sigma}\right)} - \left(\frac{\mathcal{N}\left(\frac{a-mo}{\sigma}\right) - \mathcal{N}\left(\frac{b-mo}{\sigma}\right)}{\Phi\left(\frac{b-mo}{\sigma}\right) - \Phi\left(\frac{a-mo}{\sigma}\right)}\right)^2\right] \tag{20.52}$$

21 The links with CAPM and private valuations

21.1 Plan of the chapter

This chapter naturally splits into two parts, which address related but different concerns.

In the first part we look at the assignment of the expected returns obtainable from the spliced distribution of the various risk factors. Assigning this input is delicate and affects greatly the optimal allocation, as we discuss in Chapter 28. We provide a 'model-assisted' answer to this problem. We say 'model-assisted' instead of 'model-based', because the expected returns implied by our subjective views will be guided, but not dictated, by an asset-pricing model.

The model we use is the CAPM. We choose to work with it not because we believe that it is a normatively 'perfect' model, but because that it can provide a useful sanity check that our return expectations are at least consistent (say, in terms of ranking) and that they reflect a plausible trade-off between return and risk (with risk understood as variance and covariance).

The treatment in the first part of the chapter almost completely disregards information from market prices. What we are trying to achieve is a degree of model-guided internal self-consistency.

Observed market prices come to the fore in the second part of the chapter (Sections 21.6–21.9). Here we assume that the consistency checks in the first part of the chapter have been carried out to our satisfaction, and we try to ascertain whether, *given our views*, a security is 'cheap' or 'dear'. To carry out this analysis we must decompose and treat separately different possible causes of discrepancy between our 'private' valuation and the market's: 'our' prices may differ from those observed in the market because we have a different impatience, a different degree of aversion to risk, or different expectations from the representative investor. We are mainly interested in the third possible source of pricing differences (i.e., differences in expectations), and we propose a way to distill this quantity.

21.2 Expected returns: a normative approach

As we mentioned in the introductory section, one of the most delicate tasks in quantitative asset management is the assignment of the expected returns for the various assets.

This is the most difficult input to estimate statistically, yet the one that typically affects results (allocations) most strongly. (See in this respect the discussion in Chapter 8 and in Section 28.3 in particular.)

Our Bayesian-net-based approach is not immune from these problems – if anything, our task is even more daunting than the usual one, because we have to assign the first moments both for the normal and for the excited states. (Of course, the two will be combined to form the first moments from our spliced marginal distribution.)

Given the importance and the difficulty of the task, any structure we can impose on the problem and any information we can extract from our understanding of 'how the world works' is invaluable. Asset pricing models are exactly one way to formalize and give structure to this understanding, and the CAPM, for all its shortcomings, is a simple and intuitive asset-pricing model.

If we accept that the CAPM model is an imperfect but reasonable description of reality, there is value in obtaining the CAPM asset returns consistent with our spliced distribution. More precisely, given our subjective views about the scenario at hand, we can ask what the returns *should* look like if we lived in a CAPM world.

Now, we are well aware that in the last two decades the CAPM has come under a lot of criticism for its lack of empirical cross-sectional explanatory power. We nonetheless want to take a closer look at what the CAPM normatively implies for two reasons, which we briefly discuss in the next section.

21.3 Why CAPM?

Recent studies (Levy and Roll 2010, Ni *et al.* 2011) suggest that news of the death of CAPM may have been greatly exaggerated. These studies acknowledge all the well-known weaknesses of practical implementations of the CAPM. For our applications, the most important criticism is that the optimal portfolio weights are very sensitive to return expectations, which in turn are very difficult to determine (see, e.g., Siegel and Woodgate 2007). And also the estimation of the covariance matrix is 'a delicate statistical challenge that requires sophisticated methods' (Ni *et al.* 2011).

However, Levy and Roll (2010) have reverse-engineered the usual approach to the CAPM modelling by positing that the market portfolio should be mean-variance efficient (i.e., should be the efficient tangent Markowitz portfolio; see Figure 7.1), and then asking by how much the returns and the covariances have to be tinkered with, *while remaining as close as possible to the corresponding sample-determined quantities*, to obtain this result. As Ni *et al.* (2011) point out, the answer is that 'only minor adjustments of the inputs parameters are needed, *well within the statistical uncertainty*'.[1]

These findings are encouraging, and the approach (with its emphasis on minimizing the 'distance' from some anchor solution, and with its conceptual similarities with the Doust approach to the Black–Litterman model) is very close to our way of thinking.

---

[1] Emphasis added.

We refer readers to these recent studies for a closer look at these results. What is of relevance for our purposes is that these studies suggest that a simple and intuitive asset-pricing model (the CAPM) can provide us with a reasonable and robust source of guidance.

We mentioned a second reason why we think that making reference to the CAPM makes sense. Whatever its descriptive power, we are mainly going to use the CAPM in a *relative* manner, i.e., as a tool to ensure the overall plausibility of the implicit statements we make about the relative size of the first moments of the marginal return distributions. Recall that our task is particularly difficult, because these first moments will be a result of:

- the expectation we assign to the 'normal-times' distribution;
- the precise centring of the stressed distributions (the means of the excited and non-excited Gaussian distribution we assign to the leaves);
- the details of the Bayesian net;
- the precise value we choose for the 'normalization factor', k.

Given the subtle interplay of all these quantities, we want to make sure that the return expectations that come out of our complex procedure are broadly consistent with a reasonable way of ranking expected returns, *assuming that our views about the future are correct*. The CAPM provides one such reasonable way to rank returns.

We point out in closing this justificatory digression that our approach is similar to what has been successfully advocated by Levy and Roll (2010): we want to tinker with a difficult-to-estimate and difficult-to-assign set of quantities (the expected returns) in order to obtain results in line with a plausible view of the world.

21.4   Is there an alternative to the CAPM?

There is, of course, nothing magical about the CAPM approach, and the reader can carry out this self-consistency exercise using any other asset-pricing model with which she might feel more comfortable.

There is one approach, however, that stands out for its appeal and for being conceptually rather different from the CAPM, from the Arbitrage Pricing Theory (APT) model (Ross 1976) and from the various Factor Models (Connor and Korajczyk 2010): the No-Too-Good-Deal approach by Cochrane and Saa-Requejo (1999).

The idea is something intermediate between a fully specified model and pure no-arbitrage bounds (which typically tend to be too loose to be of much use). In this view of the world, the investor is supposed to 'snatch up' portfolios ('deals') with a Sharpe Ratio that is too attractive. Therefore portfolios with too-attractive Sharpe Ratios are unlikely to exist.

Now, recall that the Sharpe Ratio is directly linked to the variance of the stochastic discount factor (see, e.g., Cochrane 2001). This observation gives the authors the opportunity to handle the problem of finding no-too-good deals by using a conceptually simple linear optimization problem, where constraints are placed on the positivity of the stochastic discount factor (this is the familiar no-arbitrage condition), and on its volatility (this is linked to the Sharpe Ratio, and where the 'no-too-good-deal' bit comes in).

A full discussion of the approach would entail a long detour, but the conceptual approach is very appealing and the interested reader is referred to Cochrane and Saa-Requejo (1999) and Cochrane (2001) for details.

In the following we shall assume for the sake of simplicity that the normative asset-pricing model of choice is the CAPM, but the no-too-good-deal approach deserves in this context careful attention.

21.5   Using the CAPM for consistency checks

So, we start with that we normatively believe in the CAPM ('this is how asset *should* be priced'), and we want to see what this implies about expected returns given the views embedded in our spliced distribution. In the following the shall make use of the 'market portfolio'. In this section we are going to proxy it by the S&P 500 index. We are well aware that this is far from satisfactory (see, e.g., the discussion in Bandourian and Winkelmann (2003)), and indeed, as we discuss in Chapter 29, we use a different (composite) proxy for the market portfolio when we carry out our explicit calculations. In this chapter we identify the market portfolio as the S&P 500 index purely for the sake of simplicity.

In keeping with CAPM notation, let's denote the return for asset i obtained using our spliced distribution by R_i^{BN}, and by $E[R_i^{BN}] = \mu_i^{BN}$ the expected return for asset i obtained by marginalizing (integrating over) the spliced distribution of the non-market-risk-factor-related variables (see Section 20.4). Note that, to keep notation light, we use the superscript BN (obviously inspired by the initials of the words *Bayesian Nets*) to denote the returns from our full spliced distribution, but we stress that these are the returns from the *full* (subjective-plus-statistical) spliced distribution, not just the Bayesian-net contribution.

In a CAPM world these expected returns would be given by

$$E\left[R_i^{BN,CAPM}\right] = r + \beta_i^{BN}(E[R_{MKT}] - r) \tag{21.1}$$

with

$$\beta_i^{BN} = \frac{\text{Cov}\left(R_i^{BN}, R_{MKT}\right)}{\text{Var}(R_{MKT})} \tag{21.2}$$

In terms of excess returns, this can be written more compactly as

$$E\left[\overline{R}_i^{BN,CAPM}\right] = \beta_i^{BN} E[\overline{R}_{MKT}] \tag{21.3}$$

where $\overline{R}$ (appropriately superscripted) denotes *excess* return.

Let's look at Equation (21.2). To evaluate the 'CAPM-beta' for asset i we need its covariance with the market (excess) return, $\text{Cov}(R_i^{BN}, R_{MKT})$, and the variance of the market (excess) return, $\text{Var}(R_{\text{MKT}})$. And then, to get the expected return for asset i, of course we need the expected return for the market portfolio, $E[R_{\text{MKT}}]$. How can we get these terms?

We can proceed as follows. We can treat the S&P 500 as one of our market risk factors, for which we construct from historical data a normal-times marginal distribution that we conjoin with the other marginal distributions using a normal-times copula. Then we associate the S&P 500 market risk factor to one of the terminal leaves. This terminal node will be connected to as many transmission channels as required. With the normal-times marginal distribution, with the normal-times copula and with the Bayesian net we can create the full spliced distribution of all the risk factors, including the S&P 500 (the market portfolio). Once this distribution is available we can do several things.

First, given our spliced distribution, we can calculate the expectation of the market excess return, *according to our views* ($E[\overline{R}_{\text{MKT}}^{\text{BN}}]$). This will give us the last term on the right-hand side of Equation (21.3), which we now rewrite as

$$E\left[\overline{R}_i^{\text{BN,CAPM}}\right] = \beta_i^{\text{BN}} E\left[\overline{R}_{\text{MKT}}^{\text{BN}}\right] \tag{21.4}$$

(i.e., with $E[\overline{R}_{\text{MKT}}^{\text{BN}}]$ instead of $E[\overline{R}_{\text{MKT}}]$) to stress that this is our estimate of the market return.

Second, since we have the full spliced distribution, we can also calculate, by evaluating the appropriate covariances and the required variance, the term β_i^{BN}, also 'according to our view of the world'.

Once we have calculated these quantities, we have all the terms we need to evaluate the CAPM expected excess returns for each asset, $E[\overline{R}_i^{\text{BN,CAPM}}]$, consistent with our views about covariances, and about the expected return from the market portfolio and with a normative interpretation of the CAPM.

We can now ask the question whether the expected excess returns from our spliced distributions, $E[R_i^{\text{BN}}]$ happen to coincide with the expected excess returns obtained from the CAPM, and from the covariances, variances and market-portfolio returns obtained using our spliced distribution, $E[\overline{R}_i^{\text{BN,CAPM}}]$. So, we can then test if it is indeed the case that:

$$E\left[\overline{R}_i^{\text{BN,CAPM}}\right] =? = E\left[R_i^{\text{BN}}\right] \tag{21.5}$$

What information can we extract from this comparison? As we said in the opening paragraphs of this chapter, our philosophy is that, even if we do not fully 'believe in' the CAPM, we believe that it nonetheless contains more than a grain of truth about relative asset returns. If this is the case, we can question whether the inputs of our subjective distribution are reasonable by performing the comparisons in Equation (21.5). The set of comparisons in Equation (21.5) can therefore give us a way to refine, or correct, one of the most difficult inputs to our procedure: the 'all-in' expected return for each asset.

The comparison can be carried by placing different degrees of trust in the CAPM. For instance, as an 'entry-level' test, we can ask ourselves whether our spliced distribution produces at least the same ranking of excess expected returns as it would if the CAPM held exactly.

At a more quantitative level, we could easily extend the approach in Levy and Roll (2010) and Ni *et al.* (2011), by finding the overall distribution that is CAPM-compatible (either exactly or in a ranking sense) and is at the same time closest to the subjective spliced input distribution that we have assigned. We could achieve this by playing with the normalization factor, k, with the first moment of the 'normal-times' distribution, with the location of the stressed-returns distributions, or with our Bayesian net.

Of course, we do not have to achieve an exact identity for each of the equations in expression (21.5). Perhaps we do not 'truly' believe in the CAPM, and we think that higher moments should be 'priced in' in a way that the CAPM approach does not know about. In any case, the comparison is very worthwhile making.

We stress that so far we have not made any comparisons with market-related quantities, and we have just confined ourselves to checking the *internal* consistency of our 'brave new world', given a normative view of how assets should be priced. In the next sections we begin to explore how our views compare with the market's.

21.6 Comparison of market-implied and subjectively assigned second and higher moments

As a first step towards comparing our views about and the market's, we can project from the fully spliced distribution the subjective full marginal (normal plus excited times) distributions (we can do this by marginalization – i.e., by integrating out the other market risk factors) for all the market risk factors. When this information is available, we can then compare the marginal distribution for asset i (which may be, but need not be, the S&P 500) thus obtained with the market-implied marginal distribution that we can extract from the option markets. (Rebonato and Cardoso (2004) suggest a simple and effective way to do this.)

In carrying out these comparisons, we cannot say anything about the first moment, because the option-extracted distribution will refer to the risk-neutral measure. However, this measure is not only equivalent to the objective (real-world) measure (an extremely weak requirement), but is simply related to it by a set of drift transformations (Girsanov's theorem). So, we can, at least in theory, compare what we say about, say, variance, skewness and kurtosis, and what the market implies. This is interesting in itself.

Why did we qualify our encouraging statement above with the words 'at least in theory'? In order to understand to what extent we can 'trust' the simple comparison above, let's place ourselves in the simplest and cleanest possible conceivable setting. Let's assume, that is, that options are priced in an efficient and frictionless market according to the Black(-and-Scholes) formula, and that asset prices follow a geometric Brownian motion.

If this were exactly true, the volatility in the objective and in the pricing measures would perfectly coincide, and a direct comparison between the second moment implied by our views and that obtained from the risk-neutral option-implied distribution would be possible.

This is true in a Black-and-Scholes world. We know, however, that, if hedging is not perfect and costless (as it is not, for instance, in the case of jumps and transaction costs, respectively), and arbitrage is not riskless,[2] then the net demand and supply for options can alter (widen, skew, etc.) the risk-neutral distribution. Indeed, one of the most common explanations for the existence of a skew in the equity option markets points to the desire by asset managers to buy downward-jump protection for their equity exposure.

When this is the case, the comparison between our subjective higher-order moments (which are expressed in the objective measure) and the corresponding market-implied quantities do not directly tell us something between differences in 'views'. The market-implied higher moments would in fact contain both the market's views and a risk premium component (e.g., a 'volatility risk premium'), where the relevant risk premia act as as many 'wedges' between the actuarial views and the market-implied views.[3]

In this more realistic case the analysis becomes considerably more complex, but is also potentially more interesting. If we believe in our views, in fact, by looking at these distributional features we can get a glimpse of the relevant market risk premia, and express a view as to whether the compensation for bearing these sources of risk over and above the corresponding actuarial risks is attractive or not (given, say, our risk appetite, and our institutional constraints).

We leave it at that, but, again, even a simple qualitative comparison between the available higher moments obtained from option-implied distributions and from our spliced distribution can be very informative and thought provoking.

21.7   Comparison with market expected returns

In order to carry out a more direct comparison between our views of the world and what the market believes about expected returns we need a stronger medicine. We present a simplified line of attack in this section, and a more self-consistent and informative approach later in this chapter (Section 21.8 in particular).

So, to begin with we are going to look at those market risk factors for which liquid option markets exist, and for the moment we make the bold joint assumptions that

---

[2] For a general discussion of the limits to arbitrage see, e.g., Shleifer and Summers (1990) and Shleifer (2000).
[3] For the estimation of bond risk premia, the literature is huge. We refer the reader to Cochrane and Piazzesi (2005, 2008), Hellerstein (2011), Cieslak and Povala (2010) and Radwanski (2010) for recent studies. For the estimation of the volatility risk premium in equities, see, e.g., Jiang and Tian (2005). For the volatility risk premium in currency options, see, e.g., Low and Zhang (2005), and references therein.

(i) the market believes in the CAPM;
(ii) it uses the full historical data (including past stress events) in order to calculate the
    correlation between the S&P index and the other risk factors.

If we are happy to make these joint assumptions, then using the option-implied
density for the S&P (*and, if available, also for the other market risk factors*[4]) we can
calculate the betas:

$$\beta_i^{\text{MKT}} = \frac{\text{Cov}\left(R_i^{\text{MKT}}, R_{\text{MKT}}\right)}{\text{Var}(R_{\text{MKT}})} \tag{21.6}$$

We can plug this quantity into the CAPM pricing equation, to obtain

$$E\left[\overline{R}_i^{\text{MKT,CAPM}}\right] = \beta_i^{\text{MKT}} E[\overline{R}_{\text{MKT}}] \tag{21.7}$$

We stress that the quantity $E[\overline{R}_i^{\text{MKT,CAPM}}]$ represents the market expectation of the first
moment under the assumption that the market believes in the CAPM and calculates
the quantities required for its 'calibration' using the full (i.e., non-culled) statistical
distribution.

Now we have three sets of quantities that we can compare:

$$E\left[\overline{R}_i^{\text{MKT,CAPM}}\right], \tag{21.8}$$

which we have just defined,

$$E\left[\overline{R}_i^{\text{BN}}\right], \tag{21.9}$$

the expected return for asset i according to our views, and

$$E\left[\overline{R}_i^{\text{BN,CAPM}}\right], \tag{21.10}$$

the expected return for asset i according to our views in a CAPM world.

We have now introduced a first element of external comparison. Since in obtain-
ing the terms $E[\overline{R}_i^{\text{MKT,CAPM}}]$ and $E[\overline{R}_i^{\text{BN,CAPM}}]$ we have used the CAPM to estimate the returns of the various assets, the differences between the 'market-implied'
CAPM-based expected excess returns, $E[\overline{R}_i^{\text{MKT,CAPM}}]$, and the subjective-views, but
still CAPM-based, expected excess returns $E[\overline{R}_i^{\text{BN,CAPM}}]$, can only stem from differences in our subjective views about returns.

We provide in what follows a more comprehensive, and more satisfactory, comparison of the market prices and of our subjective valuation,[5] but, before doing that, a
simple example can clarify the reasoning so far.

---

[4] If we do not have option-implied information for the ith asset, we are going to make again the assumption that
the market uses the full historical data (normal + excited times) to estimate the marginal distributions.
[5] The Achilles' heel of this simplified approach, is, of course, the assumption that the market uses the full past
historical sample to estimate the correlations between risk factors.

Table 21.1 *The payoffs and the associated probabilities, π_i^j, for each asset i in each state j for the example discussed in the text*

Market portfolio			
Ass1_0	100		
Ass1_Up	114	**0.55**	PrAss1_Up
Ass1_Down	90	**0.4**	PrAss1_Down
Ass1_Stress	80	0.05	PrAss1_Stress
Aggressive asset			
Ass2_0	100		
Ass2_Up	130	**0.55**	PrAss2_Up
Ass2_Down	80	**0.4**	PrAss2_Down
Ass2_Stress	60	0.05	PrAss2_Stress
Defensive asset			
Ass3_0	100		
Ass3_Up	108	**0.55**	PrAss3_Up
Ass3_Down	92	**0.4**	PrAss3_Down
Ass3_Stress	110	0.05	PrAss3_Stress

21.8   A worked example

In order to show exactly how the ideas above can be used in practice, we present a stylized example that displays the essential elements of what we are trying to capture.

We consider a universe with three assets:

1. Asset 1 (the market portfolio);
2. Asset 2 (an 'aggressive' asset that does on average better than the market portfolio in normal market conditions, displays greater volatility in normal times, has large losses during stress events, and whose returns are positively correlated with the returns of the market portfolio);
3. Asset 3 (a 'defensive' asset that does on average worse than the market portfolio in normal market conditions, displays lower volatility in normal times, has large *gains* during stress events, and whose returns are negatively correlated with the returns of the market portfolio).

For simplicity, we assume that at time t_0 all assets have the price of 100: $P_i(t_0) = 100$, for $i = 1, 2, 3$.

We also assume that three possible states can prevail at time t_1: an *Up*, a *Down* and a *Stress* state, which are common to, and fully span the uncertainty of, the three assets. The payoff from asset i in state j at time t_1 is denoted by $P_i^j(t_1)$.

All the payoffs, and the associated probabilities, π_i^j, are displayed in Table 21.1. We assume that the probabilities for the *Up* and *Down* states were obtained from our statistical analysis of the body of the distribution, and that the *Stress* probability was obtained from our Bayesian net.

Table 21.2 *The correlations between the three assets in our example*

	Asset 1	Asset 2	Asset 3
Asset 1	1	0.6	−0.4
Asset 2	0.6	1	−0.6
Asset 3	−0.4	−0.6	1

Table 21.3 *The expected returns and the standard deviations in the subjective measure obtained using the statistical analysis of the body of the distribution and the Bayesian net*

	$E[R_i^{BN}]$	StDev$[R_i^{BN}]$
Asset 1 (Market portfolio)	2.70%	12.67%
Asset 2 (Aggressive asset)	6.50%	26.32%
Asset 3 (Defensive asset)	1.70%	7.93%

For a given asset, $\hat{i}$, the three probabilities, $\pi_{\hat{i}}^j$, $j = Up, Down, Stress$, constitute its marginal distribution. These marginal distributions are conjoined, using the Gaussian copula shown in Table 21.2, to produce the spliced distribution.[6]

The expected returns and the standard deviations in the subjective measure implied by the spliced distribution are given in Table 21.3.

We can now ask ourselves what the expected returns should be, *given our views*, if the asset were priced according to the CAPM. To answer this question, we first calculate the coefficients β_i^{BN} for each asset as

$$\beta_i^{BN} = \frac{\text{Cov}\left(R_i^{BN}, R_{MKT}\right)}{\text{Var}(R_{MKT})} \tag{21.11}$$

For comparison we estimate these coefficients for the correlation matrix we have assigned (we call this the 'Full Correlation' case), and also for the two limiting cases of perfect and zero correlation ($\rho_{ij} = 1 \ \forall i, j$ and $\rho_{ij} = \delta_{ij}, i, j = 1, 2, 3$, respectively).

Finally, we assign the risk-free rate, r:

$$r = 2.00\% \tag{21.12}$$

We are now in a position to calculate the expected returns in a CAPM world:

$$E\left[R_i^{BN,CAPM}\right] = r + \beta_i^{BN}(E[R_{MKT}] - r) \tag{21.13}$$

---

[6] In this stylized example we assume for the sake of simplicity that the same codependence structure applies both in the normal and in the excited states. In our real applications the conjoining of the marginals via the Gaussian copula only applies to the normal states.

Table 21.4 *The betas for the three assets given our subjective distribution. Note that the third asset has a negative beta. This is always the case for any asset with a negative correlation with the market portfolio. Since the CAPM pricing equation is* $E[R_i^{BN,CAPM}] = r + \beta_i^{BN}(E[R_{MKT}] - r)$ *this will always imply an expected return lower than the riskless rate (which we set to 2% in our example)*

	$\beta_i, \rho = $ Full	$\beta_i, \rho = 0$	$\beta_i, \rho = 1$
Asset 1	1.000	1.000	1.000
Asset 2	1.246	0.000	2.077
Asset 3	−0.250	0.000	0.626

Table 21.5 *The expected returns from our subjective distribution, $E[R_i^{BN}]$, and the expected returns that would obtain, given the views we have expressed, through the spliced distribution, if the CAPM held exactly, for three possible correlation matrices: the one we truly assigned ($\rho = $ Full), and the limiting cases of independence and of zero correlation, respectively. Note how the negative beta for the defensive asset produces a return lower than the riskless rate*

	$E[R_i^{BN}]$	$E[R_i^{BN,CAPM}, \rho = $ Full$]$	$E[R_i^{BN,CAPM}, \rho = 0]$	$E[R_i^{BN,CAPM}, \rho = 1]$
Asset 1	2.70%	2.70%	2.70%	2.70%
Asset 2	6.50%	2.87%	2.00%	3.45%
Asset 3	1.70%	1.82%	2.00%	2.44%

and compare them with the expected returns from our subjective distribution, $E[R_i^{BN}]$. We can do this for the three correlation assumptions above. The results are shown in Table 21.4, and those for the expected returns in Table 21.5.

A few observations are in order. First of all, since the CAPM provides a relative valuation with respect to the market portfolio, the market portfolio itself is, of course, always fairly priced by construction:

$$E\left[R_{MKT}^{BN,CAPM}\right] = r + \beta_i^{BN}(E[R_{MKT}] - r)$$

$$= r + \frac{Cov\left(R_{MKT}^{BN}, R_{MKT}\right)}{Var\left(R_{MKT}^{BN}\right)} (E[R_{MKT}] - r) = E[R_{MKT}] \qquad (21.14)$$

The next observation is that the returns from the three assets implied by our spliced distribution display a ranking consistent with the CAPM, at least as long as the correlation between the assets is not zero.

Finally we note that the expected return for the defensive asset is lower than the return from the riskless asset. This is an inescapable consequence of the CAPM whenever an

Table 21.6 *Same as Table 21.5, but obtained by raising the probabilities π_i^{Stress} from 5% to 10%, and by reducing by 2.5% the probabilities in the normal Up and Down states*

	$E\left[R_i^{\text{BN}}\right]$	$E\left[R_i^{\text{BN,CAPM}}, \rho = Full\right]$	$E\left[R_i^{\text{BN,CAPM}}, \rho = 0\right]$	$E\left[R_i^{\text{BN,CAPM}}, \rho = 1\right]$
Asset 1	1.60%	1.60%	1.60%	1.60%
Asset 2	4.25%	1.50%	2.00%	1.17%
Asset 3	2.20%	2.10%	2.00%	1.76%

asset has a negative correlation with the market portfolio (just recall that the coefficient β_i can be written as $\beta_i = \frac{\sigma_i}{\sigma_{\text{mkt}}}\rho_{i,\text{mkt}}$). The conclusion is both logical (in a CAPM world) and not very plausible. The problem can be serious if one chooses an equity index as a proxy for the market portfolio, and then looks at the CAPM expected returns from long-dated bonds. To the extent that these have displayed in the last twenty years or so a negative correlation with equities, this creates a problem, as the negative correlation must inescapably give rise to a negative excess return.[7]

At a more quantitative level, one immediately observes that in our world the 'aggressive' asset appears far too attractive, and the defensive one a bit unattractive, with respect to a CAPM world *that shares the same return views as ours*. Let's focus on the most glaring discrepancy, i.e., $E[R_2^{\text{BN}}] = 6.50\%$ against $E[R_2^{\text{BN,CAPM}}, \rho = Full] = 2.87\%$. Looking at the coefficients β_i^{BN} calculated using the polar opposite assumptions about correlation, and at the CAPM-compatible expected returns that these imply $(E[R_2^{\text{BN,CAPM}}, \rho = 0] = 2.00\%$ and $E[R_2^{\text{BN,CAPM}}, \rho = 1] = 3.45\%)$, we clearly see that a substantially closer alignment between $E[R_2^{\text{BN}}]$ and $E[R_2^{\text{BN,CAPM}}]$ is not going to come from tinkering with the correlation matrix. What else could bring down then the 'excessive' expected return that the aggressive asset earns in our world?

We could assume that our asset will do even worse in the distressed state. However, we are already assigned a 40% fall in this state of the world. As the probability of distress is low, in order to obtain a substantial reduction we would need a negative return in state *Stress* that would be implausibly negative. We could play with the normalization factor, k, which, in this stylized example is directly linked to the probability of occurrence of the distressed state. What if we raised this probability from 5% to 10%?

If we do this by reducing by an equal amount (i.e., by 2.5%) the probabilities in the normal *Up* and *Down* states for all the assets (this is the effect of playing with the normalization factor, k), what we obtain still does not work very well. Let's look in fact at the new return table, Table 21.6.

What is happening now is that the market portfolio has a return lower than the riskless rate. And as for the problem we were trying to fix, i.e., the too-good-to-be-true

---

[7] There are two ways out of this impasse: either one redefines the market portfolio to include at least a debt component (see, e.g., Doeswijk, Lam and Swinkels 2011); or one looks at longer time horizons, over which the correlation between equities and long-dated bonds is not necessarily negative.

return for the aggressive asset, yes, its return as implied by our spliced distribution has decreased, but so has the CAPM-implied return. We are no better off.

This clearly shows that, if we want to bring the return output implied from our spliced distribution more in line with the CAPM prescription, we must tinker directly with the marginal distribution for the aggressive asset. If we do not, we are effectively saying that the distributional features of the return of the asset under scrutiny obtained from our subjective views are such that the CAPM is a totally inappropriate tool to look at asset returns. Again, it would be very interesting and profitable to analyse this example through the prism of Cochrane's no-too-good-deal approach (see Section 21.3).

It is just as important to stress what this part of the analysis does *not* tell us. The discrepancy we observe does not imply anything about how plausible or outrageous our views about the world are *with respect to the market*. It only tells us how plausible or outrageous they are with respect to a normative view of how the market should behave.

We therefore move to a more direct market comparison in the next section.

21.9   Private valuation: linking market prices and subjective prices

From now on we shall assume that our expected returns have been 'scrubbed' as described in the previous section by using as 'anchor' the normative asset-pricing model of our choice (we have chosen to use the CAPM for this purpose, but, as we made clear, nothing hangs on this).

We highlighted in Section 21.6 the limitations of the simplified comparison of the market and subjective inputs presented there. Our goal in this section is to obtain a more satisfactory 'private valuation' for security i, i.e., to obtain what we think security i should be worth given our subjective views about its joint distribution with all the other securities in the market. In practice, this will boil down to determining its joint distribution with the market return, but for the moment we leave the treatment general. If our private valuation is lower than the market price, we should buy the security; if it is higher, we should try to short it. Of course, in practice our 'trade' will depend on how strong the 'signal' is, but let's leave this important consideration to one side for the moment.

It all sounds simple (and fundamentally it is), but the interplay between market prices, equilibrium prices and subjective prices is somewhat subtle, and it pays to look at these quantities in some detail.

Consider a two-period setting (which is ideally suited to our modelling).[8] Following Cochrane (2001), we assume that we have a two-period, time- and state-separable utility function, $U(c)$, of the form

$$U(c_t, c_{t+1}) = U(c_t) + \beta E_t \left[U(c_{t+1}) \right] \tag{21.15}$$

---

[8] We make this assumption for the sake of simplicity, but the treatment below does not require a two-period economy.

where c_t denotes consumption at time t, β (the subjective discount factor) captures impatience, and the expectation is taken at time t in an appropriate measure.

Whose utility function are we talking about? And what does 'in the appropriate measure' mean? As Cochrane (200, p. 37) makes clear, for Equation (21.15) to apply we do not have to assume representative investors or complete markets, as the equation can be understood to apply to each individual investor (with β in this case representing *her* impatience, $U(c)$ *her* utility function and the expectation taken under *her* subjective measure).

Given *any* investor (possibly the representative investor), the time-t value of security i according to this investor is given by the fundamental pricing equation:

$$P_t^i = E_t \left[m_{t+1} x_{t+1}^i \right] \tag{21.16}$$

with m_{t+1} the stochastic discount factor, and x_{t+1} the payoff at time $t + 1$. We stress that this may be a non-equilibrium price. As is well known (Cochrane 2001), the stochastic discount factor is given by

$$m_{t+1} = \beta \frac{U'(c_{t+1})}{U'(c_t)} \tag{21.17}$$

where $U'(c_t)$ represents the derivative (with respect to consumption) of the utility function at consumption level c_t.[9]

Note that, *if we assume that we all agree on the measure under which the expectation has to be taken* (i.e., if we all agree on how expectations should be formed), Equation (21.16) neatly factorizes the quantity under the expectation operator into two parts: one that depends only on the specific security we are looking at (x_{t+1}^i); and one that depends only on the preferences and impatience of the investor (m_{t+1}). Given our approach, the homogeneity of expectations is for us too big a pill to swallow. If we find it indigestible, then we must remember that also the expectation operator becomes investor-specific.

Now, *if* the prices P_t^i in Equation (21.16) are the observed market prices, *if* we make some assumptions about the structure of the stochastic discount factor as a function of market observables, *and if we assume that all investors agree on the joint distribution of asset payoffs*, then we can in theory 'impute the parameters' of ('calibrate') the market-implied stochastic discount factor. We can interpret this as the stochastic discount factor of a 'representative investor'. This is clearly difficult, but, for the moment, let's leave these practical difficulties to one side.

In which way could a 'private valuation' be different? Of course, the individual investor could have a different degree of impatience, or a different utility function. However, she may also hold different beliefs about the joint distribution of the asset

---

[9] The stochastic discount factor is given by the product of time impatience (β) and the ratio of the marginal utilities of consumption at times $t + 1$ and t. It is a *stochastic* discount factor because the investor does not know her consumption, c_{t+1}, at time $t + 1$, which enters the (derivative of the) deterministic utility function.
  For a sketch of the derivation, see Appendix 7.B.

payoffs. This possibility is somewhat 'frowned upon' in a lot of rational-expectation-based analyses – so much so, that *the* distribution with respect to which the expectation is taken in Equation (21.16) is called the 'objective' measure.

What about us? With Shefrin (2008), we heartily entertain the possibility that our subjective views may differ from the market's. This, however, leaves us with a lot of degrees of freedom in order to link prices today with 'our' stochastic discount factor via 'our' expectation operator: we would have to assign both our utility function and degree of impatience (the investor-specific part of the stochastic discount factor), and our subjective distribution for the payoff.

To simplify our task we will therefore follow a mixed approach: we are going to assume that we share the market impatience and utility function, but we entertain the possibility that our joint distribution may be different from the market's. Therefore, given our subjective views about the payoff distribution, we proceed to work out what the price of security i should be assuming that we have the same impatience and risk aversion as the market.

Following Cochrane's notation, we denote this private valuation by v_i. Such a valuation could be 'private' either because of the investor-specific term $\beta \frac{U'(c_{t+1})}{U'(c_t)}$, or because we have different expectations from the market's. To highlight that we are interested in the latter possible source of difference, we emphasize the private nature of the expectation by writing

$$P_t^{i,\mathrm{BN}} = E_t^{\mathrm{BN}}\left[m_{t+1}x_{t+1}^i\right] \tag{21.18}$$

where the superscript BN indicates that the relevant quantity refers to our subjective spliced distribution (BN stands for Bayesian net, but, as explained in Section 21.4, what we are using is really the full distribution, built from the Bayesian-net and the statistically determined distribution). This can be expanded as

$$P_t^{i,\mathrm{BN}} = E_t^{\mathrm{BN}}\left[\beta \frac{U'(c_{t+1})}{U'(c_t)} x_{t+1}^i\right] \tag{21.19}$$

Note that we have not appended any subjective superscripts to the investor-specific part of the stochastic discount factor, because of the joint assumption of common impatience and risk aversion. If we did not make this assumption, when we came to comparing private valuations with market prices we would no longer be able to tell whether we think that a security is, say, cheap, because we are less impatient or more risk averse than the representative investor, or because we hold different views about the return. What we are trying to do is to tell whether a security is cheap or dear *even if we share the same impatience and risk aversion as the market.*

To hammer the point home, we therefore choose to answer first the following question: if we shared the same impatience and risk aversion as the representative investor, but we had potentially different views about the joint distribution of returns, what would our private valuation for security i be?

We stress that we said 'potentially different'. We have our views, but we do not know if the market shares them. If it does, then, given our assumptions about common impatience and risk aversion, our private valuation will coincide with the market's.

21.9.1 *Distilling the market's impatience and risk aversion*

To accomplish this task, we must first deal with the 'market-implied' impatience and risk aversion. To make clear that we value a security with our views, but sharing the market's impatience and risk aversion, we write

$$P_t^{i,\text{BN}} = E_t^{\text{BN}} \left[\left(\beta^{\text{ri}} \frac{U'^{\text{ri}}(c_{t+1})}{U'^{\text{ri}}(c_t)} \right) x_{t+1}^i \right] \tag{21.20}$$

where the superscript ri stands for representative investor.

Equation (21.20) is still too general to make much progress. We are therefore going to assume that, according to the market, only expectations and (co)-variances matter for valuation, and that the market is therefore consistent with a CAPM-like model. If that is the case then we know (see, e.g., Cochrane 2001) that

$$m_{t+1} = a_t - b_t G R_{t+1}^{\text{MKT}} \tag{21.21}$$

where $G R_{t+1}^{\text{MKT}}$ is the gross market return, and a_t and b_t are two positive quantities to be 'calibrated'.[10] (We sketch in Appendix 21.A how this equation comes about.)[11] Via the coefficients a_t and b_t we are trying to get into the head of the representative investor, in order to distil her risk aversion and impatience. Once the quantities a_t and b_t have been estimated, we will be able to write our private valuation as

$$P_t^{i,\text{BN}} = E_t^{\text{BN}} \left[\left(a_t - b_t G R_{t+1}^{\text{MKT}} \right) x_{t+1}^i \right] \tag{21.22}$$

So, we start again from the fundamental pricing equation[12]

$$P_t^{i,\text{ri}} = E_t^{\text{ri}} \left[m_{t+1}^{\text{ri}} P_{t+1}^i \right] = E_t^{\text{ri}} \left[\left(a_t^{\text{ri}} - b_t^{\text{ri}} G R_{t+1}^{\text{MKT}} \right) P_{t+1}^i \right] \tag{21.23}$$

Dividing through by $P_t^{i,\text{ri}}$ we obtain

$$1 = E_t^{\text{ri}} \left[\left(a_t^{\text{ri}} - b_t^{\text{ri}} G R_{t+1}^{\text{MKT}} \right) G R_{t+1}^i \right] \tag{21.24}$$

We now use Equation (21.24) for two special cases: to value the market portfolio itself; and to value the riskless security. In the first case we get

$$1 = E_t^{\text{ri}} \left[\left(a_t^{\text{ri}} - b_t^{\text{ri}} G R_{t+1}^{\text{MKT}} \right) G R_{t+1}^{\text{MKT}} \right] \tag{21.25}$$

---

[10] The negative sign in Equation (21.21) comes from the positivity of the two 'coefficients'. See below.

[11] The gross market return in Equation (21.21) is, of course, the gross market return according to the market. That is, even if we are trying to work out our private valuation based on our subjective views, if we want to distil the quantities a_t and b_t, we still have to use in Equation (21.21) the representative investor's views about the market return.

[12] We do not really need to write $P_t^{i,\text{ri}}$, as these are just the observable market prices, and they are what they are. However, we prefer to overload the notation to be totally clear.

and in the second

$$1 = E_t^{\text{ri}} \left[\left(a_t^{\text{ri}} - b_t^{\text{ri}} G R_{t+1}^{\text{MKT}} \right) G R_f \right] \tag{21.26}$$

(where $G R_f$ denotes the gross riskless return). Of course, everybody agrees on the riskless return (and therefore no superscripts need to clutter the symbol $G R_f$), and it is a non-stochastic quantity. After some rearrangements we get

$$a_t^{\text{ri}} = \frac{1}{G R_f} + b_t^{\text{ri}} E_t^{\text{ri}} \left[G R_{t+1}^{\text{MKT}} \right] \tag{21.27}$$

$$b_t^{\text{ri}} = \frac{E_t^{\text{ri}} \left[G R_{t+1}^{\text{MKT}} \right] - G R_f}{G R_f \text{Var}^{\text{ri}} \left[G R_{t+1}^{\text{MKT}} \right]} \tag{21.28}$$

where the superscript 'ri' appended to the operator Var indicates that the variance has been calculated using the distribution of the representative investor.

Where are we going to get the quantities $E_t^{\text{ri}} \left[G R_{t+1}^{\text{MKT}} \right]$ and $\text{Var}^{\text{ri}} \left[G R_{t+1}^{\text{MKT}} \right]$? For the variance, if we are happy to identify the market portfolio with the S&P index, and to make some assumptions about the measure invariance of the volatility,[13] we can extract it from the prices of traded S&P options. What about the market-implied gross expected return from the market portfolio? Distressingly, 'the market, God and the econometrician'[14] all appear to know with certainty this quantity (and much more, since they know the full joint distribution!), but nobody seems to be able to tell us.

Pragmatically, a long-term estimation of the returns from the global equity and debt markets should not be too wide of the mark. Of course, the correct estimation would have to be a conditional expectation, but, since we have to guess what the representative investor thinks, we prefer to assume a rather uninformative prior.

More encouragingly, as long as we calibrate our subjective expected return for the various securities to the CAPM (as suggested in the first part of this chapter), and as long as we look at the *relative* valuation of one security with respect to another, we can hope for some degree of first-order cancellation of errors.

21.9.2 *Obtaining our private valuation*

Be that as it may, we can assume that we have distilled the quantities a_t and b_t, which reflect the market's risk aversion and impatience. We can therefore finally go back to obtaining an expression for our private valuation, $P_t^{i,\text{BN}}$:

$$P_t^{i,\text{BN}} = E_t^{\text{BN}} \left[m_t^{\text{ri}} x_{t+1}^i \right] = E_t^{\text{BN}} \left[m_t^{\text{ri}} \right] E_t^{\text{BN}} \left[x_{t+1}^i \right] + \text{Cov}^{\text{BN}} \left(m_t^{\text{ri}}, x_{t+1}^i \right) \tag{21.29}$$

Now

$$E_t^{\text{BN}} \left[m_t^{\text{ri}} \right] = \frac{1}{G R_f} \tag{21.30}$$

---

[13] See the discussion in Section 21.6 above.

[14] We refer with this quote to the 'communism of models' in neoclassical economics, whereby 'all agents inside the model, the econometrician and God all share the same model' (interview with Thomas Sargent quoted in Frydman and Goldman (2007)).

and therefore

$$P_t^{i,\text{BN}} = \frac{E_t^{\text{BN}}\left[x_{t+1}^i\right]}{GR_f} + \text{Cov}^{\text{BN}}\left(m_t^{\text{ri}}, x_{t+1}^i\right) \tag{21.31}$$

We divide as usual by the observable market price of asset i, $P_t^{i,\text{ri}}$, to obtain:

$$\frac{P_t^{i,\text{BN}}}{P_t^{i,\text{ri}}} = \frac{E_t^{\text{BN}}\left[GR_{t+1}^i\right]}{GR_f} + \text{Cov}^{\text{BN}}\left(m_t^{\text{ri}}, GR_{t+1}^i\right)$$

$$= \frac{E_t^{\text{BN}}\left[GR_{t+1}^i\right]}{GR_f} + \text{Cov}^{\text{BN}}\left[\left(a_t^{\text{ri}} - b_t^{\text{ri}} GR_{t+1}^{\text{MKT}}\right), GR_{t+1}^i\right] \tag{21.32}$$

Now, once they have been calibrated, the quantities a_t^{ri} and b_t^{ri} are just 'numbers' and they have no stochastic component. Therefore

$$\frac{P_t^{i,\text{BN}}}{P_t^{i,\text{ri}}} = \frac{E_t^{\text{BN}}\left[GR_{t+1}^i\right]}{GR_f} + \text{Cov}^{\text{BN}}\left[\left(a_t^{\text{ri}} - b_t^{\text{ri}} GR_{t+1}^{\text{MKT}}\right), GR_{t+1}^i\right]$$

$$= \frac{E_t^{\text{BN}}\left[GR_{t+1}^i\right]}{GR_f} - b_t^{\text{ri}} \text{Cov}^{\text{BN}}\left[GR_{t+1}^{\text{MKT}}, GR_{t+1}^i\right] \tag{21.33}$$

and finally

$$P_t^{i,\text{BN}} = P_t^{i,\text{ri}}\left(\frac{E_t^{\text{BN}}\left[GR_{t+1}^i\right]}{GR_f} - b_t^{\text{ri}} \text{Cov}^{\text{BN}}\left[GR_{t+1}^{\text{MKT}}, GR_{t+1}^i\right]\right) \tag{21.34}$$

This is the equation we were looking for. It tells us that our private valuation differs from the market price by the term in round brackets. This term can be readily calculated using the spliced distribution that we have built.

21.9.3 Sanity checks

Does the equation make intuitive sense? As a first sanity check, we can ask the question: 'What would be the private valuation for the market portfolio (which, in order to avoid confusion, we now denote by ^{MPort})?' The derivation in Appendix 21.B gives

$$\frac{P_t^{\text{MPort,BN}}}{P_t^{\text{MPort,ri}}} = E_t^{\text{BN}}\left[\left\{\frac{GR_{t+1}^{\text{MPort}}}{GR_f}\right\}\right]$$

$$+ b_t^{\text{ri}}\left(E_t^{\text{BN}}\left[GR_{t+1}^{\text{MPort}}\right]E_t^{\text{ri}}\left[GR_{t+1}^{\text{MPort}}\right] - E_t^{\text{BN}}\left[\left(GR_{t+1}^{\text{MPort}}\right)^2\right]\right) \tag{21.35}$$

To see whether this expression makes sense, we can look at what would happen if we also shared the same views as the market's, $E_t^{\text{ri}}\left[\cdot\right] = E_t^{\text{BN}}\left[\cdot\right]$. If that were the case we would get

$$
\frac{P_t^{\mathrm{MPort,BN}}}{P_t^{\mathrm{MPort,ri}}} = E_t^{\mathrm{ri}} \left[\left\{ \frac{GR_{t+1}^{\mathrm{MPort}}}{GR_f} \right\} \right] + b_t^{\mathrm{ri}} \left(\left(E_t^{\mathrm{ri}} [GR_{t+1}^{\mathrm{MPort}}] \right)^2 - E_t^{\mathrm{ri}} \left[(GR_{t+1}^{\mathrm{MPort}})^2 \right] \right)
$$

$$
= E_t^{\mathrm{ri}} \left[\left\{ \frac{GR_{t+1}^{\mathrm{MPort}}}{GR_f} \right\} \right] - b_t^{\mathrm{ri}} \mathrm{Var}^{\mathrm{ri}} [GR_{t+1}^{\mathrm{MPort}}] \tag{21.36}
$$

where the last equality follows because, of course,

$$
E_t^{\mathrm{ri}} \left[(GR_{t+1}^{\mathrm{MPort}})^2 \right] - \left(E_t^{\mathrm{ri}} [GR_{t+1}^{\mathrm{MPort}}] \right)^2 = \mathrm{Var}^{\mathrm{ri}} [GR_{t+1}^{\mathrm{MPort}}]
$$

If now we substitute the expression for b_t^{ri},

$$
b_t^{\mathrm{ri}} = \frac{E_t^{\mathrm{ri}} [GR_{t+1}^{\mathrm{MPort}}] - GR_f}{GR_f \mathrm{Var}^{\mathrm{ri}} [GR_{t+1}^{\mathrm{MPort}}]} \tag{21.37}
$$

we finally get

$$
\frac{P_t^{\mathrm{MPort,BN}}}{P_t^{\mathrm{MPort,ri}}} = \frac{1}{1+R_f} \left[E_t^{\mathrm{ri}} [GR_{t+1}^{\mathrm{MPort}}] - E_t^{\mathrm{ri}} [GR_{t+1}^{\mathrm{MPort}}] \right] + 1 \tag{21.38}
$$

$$
\implies P_t^{\mathrm{Mport,BN}} = P_t^{\mathrm{Mport,ri}} \tag{21.39}
$$

This is just what we would expect: since we are using the market impatience and risk aversion, if we also share the market's views we must recover for the market portfolio (and for any other asset) the same price as the market's.

This sanity check is not particularly powerful, and simply shows that we have not introduced logical errors in the derivation. However, as sanity checks go, it is at least reassuring.

21.10   Conclusions

To sum up: in the latter part of this chapter we have provided a way to make a quantitative comparison between market prices, given our subjective views (which may or may not coincide with the market's), and assuming that we have the same degree of impatience and risk aversion as the market. More precisely, we obtained that our private valuation differs from the market price by the term in square brackets in Equation (21.34). This term can be readily calculated using the full spliced distribution. By employing a pricing model (the CAPM) in a normative manner, we can tell not only whether a given asset is cheap or dear, but also by how much. This was the goal of this chapter. We direct the reader to Appendix I for a related link with the Black–Litterman approach. We do not explicitly pursue the Black–Litterman route in the rest of the book.

Appendix 21.A: Derivation of $m_{t+1} = a + bc_{t+1} = a - bGR^{\text{MKT}}$

The setting is a two-period economy, with consumption, c, at times t and $t + 1$. We want to show that in a CAPM with quadratic utility functions, the stochastic discount factor, m_{t+1}, can be proxied by[15]

$$m_{t+1} = a - bGR^{\text{MKT}} \qquad (21.40)$$

We make four assumptions.

Assumption 1: Separable quadratic utility function (with c^* the 'bliss point', i.e., the consumption level above which the quadratic utility begins to decrease):

$$u(c_t, c_{t+1}) = -(c_t - c^*)^2 - \beta E[(c_{t+1} - c^*)^2] \qquad (21.41)$$

Assumption 2: The representative investor believes in the CAPM.
Assumption 3: There is no endowment in period 2.
Assumption 4: Time-t endowment is given by y_t.

Then

$$m_{t+1} = \beta \frac{u'(c_{t+1})}{u'(c_t)} = \beta \frac{c_{t+1} - c^*}{c_t - c^*} \qquad (21.42)$$

Recall that c_t and c^* are known quantities at time t. Then

$$m_{t+1} = a + bc_{t+1} \qquad (21.43)$$

with

$$a = -\beta \left[\frac{c^*}{c_t - c^*} \right] \qquad (21.44)$$

$$b = \beta \left[\frac{1}{c_t - c^*} \right] \qquad (21.45)$$

So, the stochastic discount factor is linear in the time-$t+1$ consumption.

Now we make use of the assumption that the representative investor believes in CAPM. Then at time t she will invest in the market portfolio with the observed market capitalization. So, her consumption at time $t + 1$, c_{t+1}, is given by

$$c_{t+1} = GR^{\text{MKT}} (y_t - c_t) \qquad (21.46)$$

The quantity $(y_t - c_t)$ is just how much the representative investor decided not to consume at time t and to invest. This investment has grown to $GR^{\text{MKT}}(y_t - c_t)$, a random quantity, and this is what the representative investor consumes at time $t + 1$.
Then

$$m_{t+1} = \beta \frac{c^*}{c^* - c_t} - \beta \frac{y_t - c_t}{c^* - c_t} GR^{\text{MKT}} = a - bGR^{\text{MKT}} \qquad (21.47)$$

---

[15] We say 'proxied' because the derivation strictly gives $m_{t+1} = a - bc_{t+1}$.

This is the stochastic discount factor of a quadratic-utility-function representative investor who believes in the CAPM. We have used the CAPM to extract a behavioural feature of the representative investor, namely her intertemporal marginal rate of substitution.

We do not necessarily believe in the specific representative-investor version of the CAPM – because we have different expectations, and because we have a different rate of intertemporal marginal rate of substitution. Therefore, if we were the market, we would come up with a different market portfolio. If the representative had our impatience, risk aversion and expectations, the market portfolio would have different weights. But this is a counterfactual.

Appendix 21.B: Private valuation for the market portfolio

We want to know what the private valuation for the market portfolio (which, in order to avoid confusion, we now denote by ^{MPort}) would be, given the setting in Section 21.8.2. We write

$$P_t^{\text{MPort,BN}} = E_t^{\text{BN}} \left[\left(a_t^{\text{ri}} - b_t^{\text{ri}} G R_{t+1}^{\text{MKT}} \right) x_{t+1}^{\text{MPort}} \right] \tag{21.48}$$

where x_{t+1}^{MPort} is the time $t+1$ payoff from the market portfolio. Let us divide by $P_t^{\text{MPort,ri}}$, which is an observable price today. We get

$$\frac{P_t^{\text{MPort,BN}}}{P_t^{\text{MPort,ri}}} = E_t^{\text{BN}} \left[\left(a_t^{\text{ri}} - b_t^{\text{ri}} G R_{t+1}^{\text{MKT}} \right) \frac{x_{t+1}^{\text{MPort}}}{P_t^{\text{MPort,ri}}} \right] \tag{21.49}$$

$$= E_t^{\text{BN}} \left[\left(a_t^{\text{ri}} - b_t^{\text{ri}} G R_{t+1}^{\text{MKT}} \right) G R_{t+1}^{\text{MPort}} \right] \tag{21.50}$$

Let us expand the term $\left(a_t^{\text{ri}} - b_t^{\text{ri}} G R_{t+1}^{\text{MKT}} \right) G R_{t+1}^{\text{MPort}}$ using the expression for a_t^{ri}:

$$\left(a_t^{\text{ri}} - b_t^{\text{ri}} G R_{t+1}^{\text{MKT}} \right) G R_{t+1}^{\text{MPort}}$$

$$= \left(\frac{1}{G R_f} + b_t^{\text{ri}} E_t^{\text{ri}} \left[G R_{t+1}^{\text{MPort}} \right] - b_t^{\text{ri}} G R_{t+1}^{\text{MPort}} \right) G R_{t+1}^{\text{MPort}}$$

$$= \left(\frac{1}{G R_f} + b_t^{\text{ri}} \left(E_t^{\text{ri}} \left[G R_{t+1}^{\text{MPort}} \right] - G R_{t+1}^{\text{Mport}} \right) \right) G R_{t+1}^{\text{Mport}}$$

$$= G R_{t+1}^{\text{MPort}} \left\{ \frac{1}{G R_f} + b_t^{\text{ri}} \left[E_t^{\text{ri}} \left[G R_{t+1}^{\text{MPort}} \right] - G R_{t+1}^{\text{MPort}} \right] \right\} \tag{21.51}$$

Let's put this back into Equation (21.49) to obtain:

$$\frac{P_t^{\text{MPort,BN}}}{P_t^{\text{MPort,ri}}} = E_t^{\text{BN}} \left[\left(a_t^{\text{ri}} - b_t^{\text{ri}} G R_{t+1}^{\text{MKT}} \right) G R_{t+1}^{\text{MKT}} \right]$$

$$= E_t^{\text{BN}} \left[G R_{t+1}^{\text{Mport}} \left\{ \frac{1}{G R_f} + b_t^{\text{ri}} \left[E_t^{\text{ri}} \left[G R_{t+1}^{\text{MKT}} \right] - G R_{t+1}^{\text{MKT}} \right] \right\} \right] \tag{21.52}$$

This breaks down into two parts:

$$\frac{P_t^{\text{MPort,BN}}}{P_t^{\text{MPort,ri}}} = E_t^{\text{BN}}\left[\left\{\frac{GR_{t+1}^{\text{MPort}}}{GR_f}\right\}\right] + b_t^{\text{ri}} E_t^{\text{BN}}\left[GR_{t+1}^{\text{MPort}}\left\{E_t^{\text{ri}}\left[GR_{t+1}^{\text{MPort}}\right] - GR_{t+1}^{\text{MPort}}\right\}\right]$$

$$(21.53)$$

Now

$$E_t^{\text{BN}}\left[E_t^{\text{ri}}\left[GR_{t+1}^{\text{MPort}}\right]\right] = E_t^{\text{ri}}\left[GR_{t+1}^{\text{MPort}}\right] \tag{21.54}$$

so

$$E_t^{\text{BN}}\left[GR_{t+1}^{\text{MPort}}\left\{E_t^{\text{ri}}\left[GR_{t+1}^{\text{MPort}}\right] - GR_{t+1}^{\text{MPort}}\right\}\right]$$
$$= E_t^{\text{BN}}\left[GR_{t+1}^{\text{MPort}}\left\{E_t^{\text{ri}}\left[GR_{t+1}^{\text{MPort}}\right]\right\}\right] - E_t^{\text{BN}}\left[GR_{t+1}^{\text{MPort}} GR_{t+1}^{\text{MPort}}\right]$$
$$= E_t^{\text{ri}}\left[GR_{t+1}^{\text{MPort}}\right] E_t^{\text{BN}}\left[GR_{t+1}^{\text{MPort}}\right] - E_t^{\text{BN}}\left[\left(GR_{t+1}^{\text{MPort}}\right)^2\right] \tag{21.55}$$

and finally

$$\frac{P_t^{\text{MPort,BN}}}{P_t^{\text{MPort,ri}}}$$

$$= E_t^{\text{BN}}\left[\left\{\frac{GR_{t+1}^{\text{MPort}}}{GR_f}\right\}\right] + b_t^{\text{ri}}\left(E_t^{\text{BN}}\left[GR_{t+1}^{\text{MPort}}\right] E_t^{\text{ri}}\left[GR_{t+1}^{\text{MPort}}\right] - E_t^{\text{BN}}\left[\left(GR_{t+1}^{\text{MPort}}\right)^2\right]\right)$$

$$(21.56)$$

Part VIII

A framework for choice

Engaging in an exercise of asset allocation means making choices between future expected consumption and the risks attending to each possible consumption pattern. We all like to consume more; but, for a given level of total consumption, most of us prefer to avoid feast and famine, and to smooth out our consumption pattern.

Implicitly or explicitly we all look at the properties of assets in this light: knowing the expected return from an asset and its 'risk' is not enough: we also want to know whether the asset is expected to perform well in hard times; or whether it will generate losses just in those states of the world when the performance of the *rest* of our portfolio is forcing a diet of bread and thin soup on us.

Making these trade-offs without a clear framework (by 'the seat of our pants', as Markowitz says in the quote reported in the Introduction; see Section 1.2) is very difficult. Utility theory and choice theory provide a logically coherent conceptual crutch in helping us in the task.

We are well aware of the problems with utility theory – indeed, to the extent that these problems are relevant to our project, we devote a substantial portion of this part of the book to their discussion. However, we believe that it is safer to use judiciously a logically coherent optimization programme than to listen to the sirens calls of ad-hoc allocation recipes. It is for this reason that we propose in the rest of the book an approach that modifies, but rests heavily on, the framework for choice afforded by utility theory.

22 Applying expected utility

22.1 The purpose of this chapter

Chapter 24 will show how to obtain an optimal allocation across the asset classes over which the portfolio manager has a mandate to invest. The result of the optimization will, of course, depend on her choice of utility function. We therefore discuss this important topic in the present chapter. We also make an important distinction between 'proper' and what we call 'reduced-form' utility functions. The latter should be used with care, but can prove useful in practical applications.

In the next chapter we discuss some alternatives to traditional expected utility maximization (either in its 'proper' or in its reduced form). Some of these extensions come from 'within the theory' (such as the family of Epstein–Zinn recursive utilities), and some from 'outside', such as some forms of Robust-Decision-Making theory. We briefly discuss these topics not because we want to wade into the deep waters of the utility debate – tempting and interesting as doing so might be. Rather we touch on some alternative choice strategies because we find that *for our purposes* the results provided by 'straight' utility maximization display some very undesirable features: *in primis*, the instability of the optimal allocation weights to small changes in the expected returns. (This feature, as we shall see, is intimately linked to the way utility functions have to be 'calibrated'.[1]) This instability of the allocation weights is a worrisome feature of virtually any asset-allocation technique based on the maximization of expected utility reasonably calibrated to *risk* aversion. One of the recurrent themes of this book is how to contain and exorcise this instability.

So, in this chapter we present expected utility optimization with a 'properly' calibrated utility function as a high-pedigree and valuable technique – and many readers may choose to stop their analysis at the end of this well-trodden path. In the next chapter we discuss what some of its shortcomings are, and whether there are some effective ways to overcome them.

---

[1] These problems have nothing to do with the Bayesian-net technology that we have introduced in this book. If anything, we had hoped that our approach could have helped to tame the instability problem. Unfortunately, it turned out that this was not the case.

22.2   Utility of what?

Modern economic analysis eschews any hedonistic interpretation of utility as 'plea-sure'. The cornerstone of modern expected discount utility theory is the representation theory, at the heart of which lies a powerful 'as if'. The representation theorem in essence states that, if the preferences of an individual obey certain axioms and the indi-vidual is consistent in making choices, then the observed choices could be represented *as if* she were maximizing an expected utility function. See, e.g., Binmore (2009), Kreps (1988).

The second most salient feature of modern choice theory under uncertainty is how the preferences are discovered. Without going into too deep a discussion, the prevailing view is that of 'revealed preferences', whereby the act of choosing reveals the preference of the individual. So, in this account of preferences an agent does not follow a certain course of action because doing so increases her utility. Rather, we say that a course of action must have increased her utility, because we observe the agent freely choosing it.

Both these features make the theory terse and elegant – if slightly otherworldly. When we use the concept of utility in practice, however, it is almost impossible to stifle the pleasure-interpretation of utility. And, of course, whenever we embark on mean-variance optimization, we justify the procedure by positing that the investor 'likes' returns, and 'dislikes' risk (understood as variance).

All of this is to say that, if we want to make use of utility theory in its modern formulation, answering the question *Utility of what?* is not easy, and perhaps does not even make sense. However, if we set about an optimization programme, we must know what we are going to maximize. The answer given by modern economists is that the utility of an individual is (observed to be) increased by consumption – which, of course, includes such intangibles as leisure time. 'Proper' utility functions therefore maximize (lifetime, discounted) consumption, and maximizing instrumental quantities that are not plausible proxies for consumption is viewed with suspicion, if not with outright disdain (Cochrane (2001) dubs these ad-hoc utility functions 'vacuous').

Nonetheless, the need to input in the optimization engine something tangible and easily measurable justifies the widespread use of proxies for consumption. The mon-etary wealth of an investor is one such proxy. To increase tractability, in the context of portfolio investing the further assumption is often made that all the wealth of the individual comes from her investments – not, say, from the salary she draws from her employer.[2]

So, applications of utility theory that are practical in nature, but still remain firmly in the narrow furrow of the orthodox theory, typically posit an initial wealth (an endowment) that can be either consumed or invested at time t_0 in a portfolio of market instruments for future consumption.

Life is then made much easier if we decide to deal with a two-period economy. If we stipulate that all consumption will occur by time t_1, after normalizing the investable

---

[2] This is one of the assumptions often made in the derivations of the CAPM, but there is nothing special about this particular model in its link of consumption with wealth, and of wealth with wealth produced by investments.

wealth to unity without loss of generality,[3] the approach then maximizes the expected utility $E[U(\cdot)]$ of returns from this investment portfolio, $R_\Pi = (1 + \boldsymbol{w}^{\mathsf{T}}\boldsymbol{R})$ where $\boldsymbol{w}$ denotes the allocation weights to the various investment opportunities (assets), and $\boldsymbol{R}$ their returns:

$$\max E^{\mathbb{P}}\left[U(1 + \boldsymbol{w}^{\mathsf{T}}\boldsymbol{R})\right] \tag{22.1}$$

where the superscript $\mathbb{P}$ emphasizes that the expectation is taken in the objective measure.

This is the approach that we shall follow, at least as a benchmark, in most of our work. We also allow, however, for more ad-hoc optimizations, and for different 'versions' of utility maximization. We explain when it might be justifiable to do this at the end of the next chapter, and in the closing chapter of the book.

22.3   Analytical representation and stylized implied-behaviour

Now that we know how to answer (or duck) the question 'utility of what?', we can begin to look at the desirable properties of a time-separable utility function.

Let's start from rather uncontroversial properties of this class of utility functions. Two obvious requirements are that the utility function chosen for the analysis should belong to $\mathcal{U}_2$, the class of non-decreasing functions of wealth, with negative second derivatives, i.e., for any $U(\cdot) \in \mathcal{U}_2$,[4]

$$\frac{dU}{dW} = U' \geq 0 \tag{22.2}$$

$$\frac{d^2U}{dW^2} = U'' < 0 \tag{22.3}$$

The first condition reflects the fact that we prefer more to less; and the second that, as Cochrane (2001) says, the last bite is never quite as satisfactory as the first: for the same absolute increase in wealth our utility increases less and less the wealthier we are. Note that this second property (the decreasing marginal utility of wealth) is directly related to risk aversion. A moment's reflection suggests that this is an uneasy marriage that is bound to beget awkward children. (Much) more about this later.

Preferring more to less is a rather obvious feature of a desirable utility function. But what about risk aversion? Following Arrow (1965) and Pratt (1964), the class of useful utility function can be grouped by considering the relative and absolute risk-aversion measures, $R_R(W)$ and $R_A(W)$, respectively, defined as

$$R_R(W) = -W\frac{U''(W)}{U'(W)} \tag{22.4}$$

$$R_A(W) = -\frac{U''(W)}{U'(W)} \tag{22.5}$$

---

[3] This, of course, will entail a rescaling of any non-linear utility function.
[4] For a thorough treatment of utility functions see Gollier and Brunak (2001).

Functions $U(\cdot) \in \mathcal{U}_2$, such that

$$\frac{\partial R_A(W)}{\partial W} < 0 \tag{22.6}$$

$$\frac{\partial R_A(W)}{\partial W} = 0 \tag{22.7}$$

$$\frac{\partial R_A(W)}{\partial W} > 0 \tag{22.8}$$

or

$$\frac{\partial R_R(W)}{\partial W} < 0 \tag{22.9}$$

$$\frac{\partial R_R(W)}{\partial W} = 0 \tag{22.10}$$

$$\frac{\partial R_R(W)}{\partial W} > 0 \tag{22.11}$$

belong to the class of

- Decreasing Absolute Risk Aversion (DARA),
- Constant Absolute Risk Aversion (CARA),
- Increasing Absolute Risk Aversion (IARA),
- Decreasing Relative Risk Aversion (DRRA),
- Constant Relative Risk Aversion (CRRA),
- Increasing Relative Risk Aversion (IRRA),

respectively, where the terms 'increasing' and 'decreasing' must be understood with reference to consumption, or its chosen proxy.

Utility functions in the DARA class imply that investors are willing to invest (and risk) more of their money (in absolute $ terms) as their wealth increases. This seems a reasonable modelling assumption: presumably Bill Gates and Warren Buffet would enter a $10 000 bet with a lighter heart than the authors of this book. The same assumption, however, no longer looks necessarily as palatable if we look at behaviour when wealth decreases. Yes, sometimes investors are observed to become more cautious after incurring large losses. But 'rolling the dice' when a desired target looks less and less attainable is another commonly observed behavioural response (especially when the investment decision are carried out by agents with a convex payoff function). The issue is complex and subtle, and brings in both questions of alignment of the interest of principals and agents (notice how we surreptitiously introduced the term 'target') and questions of whether optimizing always makes more sense than 'satisficing'. We do not pursue this important line of discussion, but refer the reader to Hansen and Sargent (2008) and Simon (1957).

CRRA utility functions (which require that investors put at risk a constant *fraction* of their wealth as their wealth changes) are a special case of DARA functions. They constitute a special case because they give a precise specification of how much more money an investor is ready to put at risk as her wealth increases. So, with obvious notation,

$$\mathcal{U}_2^{\text{CRRA}} \subset \mathcal{U}_2^{\text{DARA}} \tag{22.12}$$

The power and the logarithmic utility functions make up the class of the Constant Relative Risk Aversion (CRRA) utility function.

The exponential utility function implies constant (absolute) risk aversion with respect to wealth and is therefore of the CARA type. As Infanger (2006) points out, these two classes are part of, and together exhaust, the class of Hyperbolic Absolute Risk Aversion (HARA) functions:

$$\mathcal{U}_2^{\text{HARA}} = \mathcal{U}_2^{\text{CRRA}} \cup \mathcal{U}_2^{\text{CARA}} \tag{22.13}$$

defined by the differential equation

$$-\frac{U''(W)}{U'(W)} = a + bW \tag{22.14}$$

HARA utility functions account for a variety of risk-aversion patterns. If the HARA class is still deemed to be too restrictive, one can resort to one-switch utility functions. See, e.g., Bell (1988): with this class of functions, an investor is allowed to prefer lottery A over lottery B below a certain level of wealth, W^*, and to reverse her preference above W^*. As Infanger (2006) points out, one-switch utility functions include and exhaust the following types:

- quadratic: $U(W) = cW^2 + bW + a$;
- double exponential (sumex): $U(W) = a \exp[bW] + c \exp[dW]$;
- linear plus exponential: $U(W) = aW + b \exp[cW]$; and
- linear times exponential: $U(W) = (a + bW) \exp[cW]$.

For a discussion of more 'exotic' utility functions, see Infanger (2006, Section 4).

22.4   The 'rationality' of utility theory

Utility theory is usually presented as *the* rational way of choosing. We do not disagree, even if we prefer the word 'consistent'. (See, however, the discussion of the rationality of utility theory in Section 7.5 of Rebonato (2012).) However, it must be stressed that rationality or, for that matter, consistency, *by themselves* do not give rise to a recognizable utility function. The von-Neumann–Morgenstern postulates that define rational choice are perfectly consistent, for instance, with a risk-neutral or a risk-seeking set of preferences, or with a utility function *decreasing* with consumption. There is no 'rational' reason why individuals should be risk averse. Nor is preferring less to more intrinsically 'irrational'. And some philosophers (see, e.g., Persson 2008) contend that there is nothing 'rational' in preferring consumption now to the same consumption tomorrow, or in a year's time. Risk aversion, impatience and preference for more rather than less are just recurrent behavioural features frequently observed in the primate *Homo Sapiens* (and, even more frequently, in *Homo Economicus*).

All of this is simply to point out that, unless a utility function is 'calibrated' to some aspect of observed behaviour, it remains an amorphous vessel. We cannot create our preferences simply by using the bootstraps of rationality. To be of relevance, utility theory must, in this sense, be behavioural.

This matters for us greatly in practice. If we accept that utility functions must be calibrated to observed behaviour to be empirically relevant, we should regard with suspicion attempts to use the 'free parameters' of a utility function (say, its degree of risk aversion) in order to make a model behave properly (say, to make an asset allocation model display more stability) if the degree of risk aversion this calibration 'implies' runs counter to what we observe in human behaviour. Furthermore, if we observe that certain recurrent behavioural features remain unexplained by the traditional formulation of rational choice theory, we should not dismiss these observations and insist that the chooser should 'choose differently'. As long as the unexplained choices do not bring about logical inconsistencies, we should look with interest at ways to broaden traditional choice theory (while retaining its logical and rational structure). More about this in the last sections of this chapter, when we deal with ambiguity aversion.

22.5   Empirical evidence

In the light of the considerations above, what can one empirically say about the way investors actually choose under conditions of uncertainty?

There is a large body of (by and large not-very-recent) literature on the topic. The reader is referred, for instance, to Levy, Levy and Solomon (2000, esp. Ch. 3, p. 45) for a succinct review of theoretical and empirical results, and to the references quoted in this work for a more detailed analysis. In a nutshell, on the basis of empirical evidence it is reasonable to assume that investors' behaviour is not too dissimilar from what is predicted by the DARA, and possibly a CRRA, utility functions: absolute risk aversion (i.e., aversion to a fixed $ loss) should decrease with wealth. However, investors do not appear to be willing to put at risk exactly the same fraction of wealth as their wealth increases. So, 'CARA [functions are] seen as possibly too conservative for large levels of wealth and CRRA seen as possibly too aggressive for large levels of wealth' (Infanger 2006, p. 211). Markowitz (1994) argues that the exponential utility function may be too conservative, and Friend and Blume (1975) suggest that assuming a constant relative risk aversion may be a reasonable first-order approximation to investors' behaviour, but Faig and Shum (2002) present data to show that a *decreasing* relative risk aversion may provide a more appropriate model.

Levy, Levy and Solomon (2000, Theorem 3.1, p. 62) prove that the only functions satisfying the DARA and CRRA properties are the power utility functions, i.e., utility functions of the form

$$U(W) = \frac{W^{1-\alpha} - 1}{1 - \alpha} \tag{22.15}$$

which 'nest' the logarithmic utility function[5]

$$U(W) = \ln(W) \tag{22.16}$$

as the limit as the coefficient α tends to 1:

$$\ln(W) = \lim_{\alpha \to 1} \frac{W^{1-\alpha} - 1}{1 - \alpha} \tag{22.17}$$

By direct calculation it is then easy to derive that the exponent α is equal to the coefficient of relative risk aversion, $R_R(W)$:

$$\alpha = R_R(W) \tag{22.18}$$

This identification allows an estimation (via experiment or empirical observation) of a reasonable range of values for the exponent. The references quoted in Levy, Levy and Solomon (2000) point to a range for α between 0.6 and 2.

It is important to keep in mind this result when we discuss ways to stabilize the asset allocation produced by expected-utility maximization. One such way, as we shall see, is to increase the coefficient of risk aversion by almost one order of magnitude. This will indeed stabilize the solution, but the utility function thus calibrated seems to have now become rather untethered from its behavioural moorings.

Finally, there is an unresolved long-standing debate between the views of Latane (1959), Hakansson (1971) and Markowitz (1976) on the one hand, and Merton and Samuelson (1974) on the other. The former 'school' maintains that, at least for very-long-term investors, the logarithmic utility function should be preferred. Merton and Samuelson show, however, that for a power utility function (of which the logarithmic utility constitutes a special case) the asset-allocation problem for each investment period can be solved independently (i.e., the power utility function is 'myopic'). If this is the case the long-term and the one-period investor should employ at time t_0 ('today') exactly the same strategy.

In sum: given the theoretical, observational and experimental considerations above, when in our work we follow a traditional utility-maximization approach, we will use power utility functions with coefficients of relative risk aversion between 0.6 and 1.4 (thus bracketing symmetrically the logarithmic case). For reasons we shall discuss in Chapters 28 and 29, we shall also explore much higher values for the coefficient of risk aversion.

The use of a 'myopic' class of utility functions enormously simplifies our task, as a complex multi-period problem of dynamic optimization is reduced to a much more tractable one-period problem, without losing the validity of the results for more realistic applications. We stress, however, that our choice of utility function is only provided as a familiar reference benchmark. We have a lot of sympathy with the approach suggested

---

[5] We note in passing that Sinn (2002) makes the interesting observation that 'expected utility maximization with logarithmic utility is a dominant process in the biological selection process in the sense that a population following any other preference for decision-making will, with a probability that approaches certainty, disappear relative to the population following this preference as time goes to infinity'.

by Infanger (2006),[6] who recommends modelling directly the degree and nature of risk aversion and obtaining the associated utility function 'by integration'.

We close this section by stressing that we have only considered so far calibration of the utility function to *risk* aversion. We shall see in the last sections of this chapter how the issue becomes considerably richer when we bring *ambiguity* aversion into play.

22.6   Reduced-form utility functions

We are well aware that utility functions (probably of their perceived black-box nature) tend to have few friends among practitioners; and even among academics, albeit for different reasons, they are often harshly criticized. Speaking with asset managers we have often heard the statement: 'I don't really care much for utility maximization. I much prefer a mean-variance approach.' We are puzzled by this statement, because infact the asset manager who holds this view would have obtained exactly the results she derives from the mean-variance approach by using a particular utility function, and one – the quadratic – of the most problematic!

As for us, we are well aware of the criticisms that have been levelled from different quarters at the expected-utility-maximization framework (criticisms, by the way, rarely articulated by practitioners). However, we feel that 'traditional' expected utility theory can provide at the vary least a logically coherent benchmark against which the outputs of more ad-hoc or theoretically shaky approaches can be assessed.

Our preferences or prejudices, however, are neither here nor there when it comes to the adoption of a methodology to determine the allocation across different assets of the wealth in a given portfolio. If practitioners, wisely or unwisely, do not want to hear the 'U' word, we would be tilting at windmills if we tried to impose this choice at all costs.

Having said this, we find that even staunch utility-bashing practitioners are more sympathetic to the idea that *some* quantity should be maximized (typically an ingenious function that combines attractive features – such as returns and positive skewness – and negative attributes – such as variance, negative skewness and excess kurtosis – of a distribution), probably subject to some constraints (e.g., losses greater than X are unacceptable, no allocation should be greater than $Y\%$, etc).

For all their ad-hockery, these maximizations of rather arbitrary target functions should not be dismissed too quickly, because, after all, asset and portfolio managers are agents and not ultimate investors. If the agent gets fired if her loss is greater than X, it is not unreasonable for her to introduce this element in *her* utility function, and hence in *her* decision-making.

This poses problems for a naive utility-maximization programme: even if the portfolio managers were, as individuals, perfect utility maximizers, their 'optimal' investment actions can only be properly analysed by adding to the expected maximization tools the added complication of the analysis of the underlying agency/principal relationship with the ultimate providers of capital – the investors. The full modelling of these

---

[6] See Section 5, A General Approach to Modelling Utility.

relationships (for instance, how well the agency arrangements in place – incentives, penalties, etc – achieve a good alignment of the interests of the principal with those of the agent) can quickly become very complex – and perhaps intractable. We therefore believe that there is value in reduced-form utility (or penalty) functions that reflect in a summary manner the complexity of this web of interactions.

So, an asset manager who is given the mandate of producing outperformance relative to a well-defined index may introduce large deviations from the index as a component of her penalty function. Or, a pension-fund manager whose trustees would consider a loss greater than a certain amount 'unacceptable' may introduce an 'unacceptability region' in her target function. Similarly, changes in wealth with reference to some level may be particularly important in the case of a hedge fund manager (think, for instance, of high and low watermarks). In this case, expressing the utility as a function of *changes* in wealth can therefore be appealing, irrespective of whether the 'true' utility function of the individual investor is indeed a function of wealth or, as proposed by Kahneman and Tversky (1979), of *changes in* wealth. And so on.

22.7   Imposing exogenous constraints

Before leaving this chapter it is important to mention the issue of exogenous constraints. As Herold and Maurer (2006) point out,

[i]n investment practice MV [mean variance] analysis is performed – if at all – only after including a variety of weights constraints. Some constraints must be taken into account due to legal consideration (e.g., short-selling restrictions). But in their internal guidelines asset managers usually impose an extensive set of additional constraints. By construction, constraints enforce diversification, which in turn is expected to improve out-of-sample performance . . .[7]

Now, exogenous external constraints are usually looked upon with suspicion in academic circles. As Herold and Maurer (2006) suggest, however, they can be given a more sympathetic interpretation. Of course, if one lived in a perfect mean-variance world, and one knew perfectly the model parameters (the expected returns and the covariance matrix), placing restrictions on the weights could only mean misspecifying the model, and should always give rise to sub-optimal allocations. However, given our imperfect knowledge of the input parameters, and the imperfection of any one asset-pricing model, it is observed in practice that 'the constrained [Mean-Variance Portfolio] often performs better than its unconstrained counterpart. Jagannathal and Ma (2003) conduct an out-of-sample study to investigate which of both effects – misspecfication by imposing "wrong constraints" or estimation error is predominant. They come to the conclusion that the impact of estimation errors is the more important one and hence, restrictions are justified' (Herold and Maurer 2006, p. 140).

It must be stressed that the point made here is far stronger than the simple assertion that one source of error dominates the other. The implication is that well-designed constraints can to some extent *remedy* the shortcomings arising from estimation error.

---

[7] Page 139. It should be noted that exogenous constraints can, but need not, increase diversification.

The question then naturally arises of what we mean by 'well-designed'. One systematic view to look at this topic is by recognizing that mathematically any (linear) constraint gives rise to a Lagrangian function to be optimized with an associated Lagrange multiplier. Once the optimization has been carried out, one obtains optimal weights consistent with the constraints and Lagrange multipliers, which will be different from zero for binding constraints. (See, in this respect, Grinold and Easton (1998) and Jagannathan and Ma (2003).)

As Herold and Mauer (2006) point out, the Lagrange multipliers used with the original input variables (expected returns and covariance matrix) imply a new set of input variables (new expected returns and a new covariance matrix) in an unconstrained problem which would yield the same weights as the original constrained problem. Any set of constraints can therefore be seen as an implicit modification of the input expected returns and covariances. Indeed, Doust's (2008) Geometric Allocation approach, discussed in Sections 8.4 and 9.3, specifies one such mapping from a set of weights to the expected returns that would generate these weights in an unconstrained Markowitz optimization:[8]

$$\boldsymbol{\mu}_w = \frac{1}{\lambda} \boldsymbol{\Sigma} \boldsymbol{w} \qquad (22.19)$$

One can then assess the nature of the exogenous constraints by examining the reasonableness of the inputs they imply – in this case, the expected returns.

More generally, as discussed above, exogenous constraints tend to enforce greater diversification than the unconstrained mean-variance solution would afford. This is likely to be translated into covariance elements of larger magnitude. As we discuss later, these can in turn be interpreted as a larger degree of risk aversion. We refer the reader to Herold and Mauer (2006), Grinold and Easton (1998) and Jagannathan and Ma (2003) for a more thorough discussion of these interesting and important points. We also invite the reader to re-read the sections (8.4 and 9.3) of this book dedicated to the Doust Geometric approach, which looks at the interplay between sets of 'desirable' allocations and the associated sets of expected returns.

In sum: we will first present in the concluding chapters our results by using a 'standard' class of (CRRA) utility functions, without any exogenous constraints. Our approach, however, can be used just as effectively by maximizing any sensible 'homemade', user-defined target function, and by imposing any set of 'well-designed' constraints (where 'well-designed' should be understood in the sense alluded to above).

Over and above these pragmatic considerations, there may be additional, and more fundamental, reasons for departing from traditional expected utility maximization. We touch upon this important topic in the next chapter.

---

[8] Doust's (2008) approach takes the covariance matrix as a given and imputes the expected returns associated with a given set of weights. There are, of course, different alternatives, similar in spirit, but different in detail.

23 Utility theory: problems and remedies

23.1 The purpose of this chapter

The taxonomy presented in the previous chapter, and our vague nods to reduced-form utility functions, provide scant guidance for the practical choice and calibration of a utility function. We find that, in order to provide practical solutions, the best way is to understand where the 'real' problems are, and how these can be tackled. Somewhat paradoxically, this pragmatic interest naturally pushes us in this chapter towards a deeper analysis of the theoretical problems and limitations of 'standard' utility theory, and of the remedies that have been proposed to fix it. This detour into some foundational aspects of utility theory should be seen as a form of *reculer pour mieux avancer*.

23.2 'Inside- and outside-the-theory' objections

The literature on the paradoxical results that 'traditional' expected-utility theory can produce is vast and we do not intend to deal with this body of work in a systematic manner.

Some of these objections have been raised from 'within the theoretical fold', in the sense that they have prompted attempts to improve and fix the theory, rather than reject it. Other lines of criticism have called for the outright abandonment of the concept of utility theory (famously, if unkindly, referred to by Rabin and Thaler (2001) as Monty Python's 'dead parrot').[1] We discuss briefly those critiques that have a direct bearing on our study. We deal first with 'inside-the-theory' objections in Sections 23.2

---

[1] 'In a classic sketch from the television show *Monty Python's Flying Circus*, a customer attempts to return a parrot (a "Norwegian Blue") he bought from a pet shop earlier in the day, complaining the parrot was dead when he bought it. The sketch consists of a series of more and more surreal claims by the shopkeeper that the parrot is still alive–that it is merely resting, that it is shagged out after a long squawk, that it prefers resting on its back, and that it is pining for the fjords of Norway. To prove the parrot is dead, the customer takes it out of the cage and starts beating it against the countertop. The shopkeeper repeatedly tries to distract the angry customer from the fact that the parrot is dead by pointing out the parrot's "beautiful plumage." The customer responds that "the plumage don't enter into it," and proceeds to list numerous different ways of saying that the parrot is dead, the most famous of which is the declaration: "This is an ex-parrot."

We feel much like the customer in the pet shop, beating away at a dead parrot' (Rabin and Thaler 2001, p. 230).

to 23.5, and then with outright rejections in Section 23.7.[2] We stress that this distinction is somewhat arbitrary, as it focuses more on the intention (or perhaps the 'agenda') of the person raising the criticism, than on objective features of the critique. The reason why we choose to make this distinction is that (for a number of reasons articulated subseqently) we prefer to handle the problems we encounter in our applications by modifying the 'standard theory' (and its mean-variance incarnation) as little as possible. In so doing, we openly admit that we have an 'agenda' ourselves: namely, producing the simplest, most intuitive and most practical asset-allocation methodology, compatible with solid theoretical foundations, and with the desiderata (such as weight stability) that we consider essential. So, let us start from some classic within-the-theory critiques of standard utility theory, and let's see what bearing they have on the topic at hand.

Three of the main problems linked with traditional, time-separable utility functions refer to the link between substitution, risk aversion and temporal behaviour of consumption (see, e.g., Epstein and Zin 1989, 1991); to the problem of achieving a simultaneous calibration of a utility function to risk aversion 'in the small' and 'in the large'; and to the aversion to ambiguity (defined later) which is not accounted for by utility theory. The three problems are quite distinct.

The first two objections point as the source of the difficulty to the many tasks the curvature of the utility function has to fulfil. More specifically, the first problem has its root in the uneasy coincidence of the coefficient of relative risk aversion and the (inverse of) the intertemporal elasticity of substitution for consumption. This is a good place to start.

23.3   The two roles of the curvature of the utility function

To understand the nature of the problem, we can begin with Ramsey's theorem, which states that, along an optimal growth path, the discount rate for consumption equals the productivity of capital. This theorem was then translated (see Cass 1965; Koopmans 1965) into 'Ramsey's equation':

$$r = \delta + \eta g \tag{23.1}$$

which relates the discount rate for consumption, r, to the (perfectly known) rate of growth per capita, g, to the rate of pure time preference, δ, *and to the elasticity of the marginal utility of consumption*, η. For a sketch of the derivation of Ramsey's equation in the certainty case, one can start from the fundamental equation of asset pricing (see, e.g., Cochrane 2001):

$$p = E(m x_{i+1}) \tag{23.2}$$

---

[2] We hasten to add that we classify Rabin's (2001) problems of calibrating a utility function in the small and in the large as a 'within-the-theory' problem, even if Rabin used this example to justify his claim that utility theory should be abandoned.

where p_i is the time-i price of an asset of time-$i + 1$ stochastic payoff x_{i+1}, and m is the stochastic discount factor:

$$m = \exp(-\delta)\frac{U'(W_{i+1})}{U'(W_i)} \tag{23.3}$$

Recall that the riskless gross return, R_f, is given by

$$R_f = \frac{1}{E(m)} \tag{23.4}$$

If we take the power utility function we have introduced in the previous chapter, and we rewrite it as a function of consumption, c,

$$U(c) = \frac{c^{1-\eta} - 1}{1 - \eta} \tag{23.5}$$

we can see that

$$E(m) = \exp(-\delta)E\left[\frac{U'(c_{i+1})}{U'(c_i)}\right] = \exp(-\delta)E\left[\left(\frac{c_{i+1}}{c_i}\right)^{-\eta}\right] \tag{23.6}$$

and

$$R_f = \frac{1}{E(m)} = \exp(\delta)\left(\frac{c_{i+1}}{c_i}\right)^{\eta} \tag{23.7}$$

(The expectation operator disappears because the growth in consumption, $\frac{c_{i+1}}{c_i} = \exp(g)$, is assumed to be known and we are moving along an optimal path.)

Taking logs, and recalling that, for small $R_f - 1$, $\ln(R_f) \approx r_f$, we obtain the Ramsey equation:

$$r = \delta + \eta g \tag{23.8}$$

which says that the discount factor, r, is given by the sum of a time-preference component, δ, and a term related to the trade-off between present and future consumption – more precisely, to the product of the rate of growth, g, and the elasticity of the marginal utility of consumption, η. This gives us a first interpretation for this latter quantity.

But we can look at the quantity η from a different perspective. Let us, in fact, calculate the coefficient of relative risk aversion, $R_R(W) = -c\frac{U''(c)}{U'(c)}$, using the same power utility function. We have:

$$U'(c) = c^{-\eta} \tag{23.9}$$

$$U''(c) = -\eta c^{-\eta - 1} \tag{23.10}$$

$$R_R(c) = c\frac{\eta c^{-\eta - 1}}{c^{-\eta}} = \eta \tag{23.11}$$

which suggests a second 'meaning' for the quantity η as the coefficient of risk aversion. So, both the elasticity of the marginal utility of consumption and the coefficient of relative risk aversion are given by η.

The derivations are simple enough, but the result is startling: it would be an extraordinary coincidence if the same number (η) were to describe our degree of risk aversion to a bet today, and how we would trade off present and future consumption to avoid feast and famine. As Ackerman, Stanton and Bueno (2012) point out,

these two interpretations of η may appear parallel to each other – larger η means greater aversion to lower consumption in both cases – [but] they are actually on a collision course. Expressing more aversion to ... risk via a larger η ... implies a higher discount rate and greater disinterest in the future .... Economists are thus apparently condemned to choose between a low discount rate, reflecting heightened concern for future generations but a very low level of current risk aversion (as in Cline (1992); Stern (2006)), or a high discount rate, reflecting more aversion to current risks at the expense of greater indifference to future generations (as in Norhdaus and many others). There is no natural way to model a combination of strong risk aversion and strong future orientation.

Actually there *are* ways to get out of this impasse. One such escape route is afforded by a class of (Epstein–Zin) utility functions which allow us to break this uneasy alliance. This can be done by relinquishing the time-separable framework, and by positing that preferences should be defined recursively over current consumption (which is known) and a certainty equivalent, CE, of tomorrow's utility:

$$U_t = F(c_t, CE(U_{t+1})) \tag{23.12}$$

$$CE(U_{t+1}) = G^{-1}(E_t[G(U_{t+1})]) \tag{23.13}$$

with F and G increasing and concave functions (Epstein and Zin 1991).

We do not pursue this avenue here (incidentally, the recursive nature of the problem greatly increases its complexity), but, lest the reader may be tempted to think that the subject is arcane and remote from real-life application, we hasten to point out that it has direct relevance for many extremely important and pressing policy problems. Much of the serious current economic debate and disagreement about the costs and benefits of abatement measures against global warming, for instance, stems exactly from the 'double life' of η discussed above. See, e.g., Ackerman, Stanton and Bueno (2012), Nordhaus (2007, 2008), Stern (2008) and Dasgupta (2008).

This topic is, of course, extremely relevant to investment problems over secular horizons and the relevance of the techniques alluded to above comes to the fore when dynamic optimizations over very long periods are carried out – let's call it the strategic aspect of, say, a pension fund investment policy. We deal mainly deal in this book with the tactical ('cyclical') dimension of portfolio allocation and therefore we do not deal with Epstein–Zin recursive utility functions. However, we think the topic is important for long-horizon investment strategies, and refer the interested reader to Ackerman, Stanton and Bueno (2012).

23.4   Risk aversion 'in the small' and 'in the large'

What *is* of great relevance to the topic of this book is another risk-aversion-related 'problem with utility theory', i.e., how to account for risk aversion in the small and in the large. The nature of this problem is clearly highlighted in a well-known paper by Rabin and Thaler (2001), a paper that raises important questions about the uses and interpretation of the concept of utility for asset allocation.[3] The argument goes as follows.

Suppose that we have calibrated our utility function[4] to the choices of an individual (*any* utility function, as long as it displays *some* degree risk aversion – the beauty of the argument lies in the fact that it does not depend on the details of any specific utility function). Now, suppose that the utility function has been calibrated to account for the observation that a subject (let's call him Johnny) turns down a 50–50 bet of losing $10 against winning $11. Then it can be proven (see Rabin and Thaler 2001) as a matter of mathematical certainty that *Johnny will turn down bets of losing $100, no matter how high the upside risk.* As Rabin and Thaler say, this statement 'is true for all preferences consistent with Johnny being a risk averse utility maximizer who turns down a 50–50 lose $10/win $11 bet'. In particular, Johnny will turn down a 50–50 bet to lose $100 and win $2.5 billion (or $25 billion, or $2.5 trillion).

This does not tell us that traditional expected utility optimization is logically 'wrong'; it simply tells us that its treatment of risk aversion produces results that are far removed from the way human beings are observed to make choices. Once again, the heart of the problem is to be found in the risk-aversion coefficient – more specifically in the degree of convexity required to account for a plausible choice such as turning down a 50–50 bet of losing $10 against winning $11. In Rabin and Thaler's words 'Johnny's risk aversion over small bets means ... that his marginal utility for wealth diminishes incredibly rapidly.'

One may object that we have calibrated the utility function over too-small a bet ($10 loss – $11 win), or that Johnny was not representative of how a real investor would behave – arguably he was too chicken-livered if he turned down an advantageous 50–50 bet where the maximum downside was $10. This objection does not hold. Rabin and Thaler show that similarly improbable results follow even if Johnny turns down bets for more substantial sums like 'lose $1000/win $1100'.

What is at the root of this apparently paradoxical result? Ultimately, expected utility maximization implies that risk attitudes are derived only from changes in marginal utility that affect lifetime wealth.[5] According to the theory, people *should therefore be almost risk neutral* about gains and losses that do not alter significantly their lifetime wealth.[6] And indeed, as we shall discuss in Chapter 29,[7] once 'properly calibrated', log or power utility functions look very close to linear even over relatively large changes in wealth. As we shall see, this is directly relevant for our discussion, because quasi-linearity implies quasi-risk-neutrality, and we will identify in the following this quasi-risk-neutrality as the main culprit for the weight-allocation instability.

---

[3] For a discussion of the paper see, e.g., Rubinstein (2002) and references therein.
[4] We must specify here we are not dealing with Epstein–Zip utility.
[5] See, however, Rubinstein's (objection on this point, and the difficulties (hyperbolic discounting, multiple selves, money pumps), that this introduces.
[6] See Rabin and Thaler (2001, p. 222) on this point.   [7] See the discussion in Section 32.1 in particular.

The same article by Rabin and Thaler (2001) also reports the following discussion, which we think is worthwhile reporting in full:

Expected utility theory's presumption that attitudes towards moderate-scale and large-scale risks derive from the same utility-of-wealth function relates to a widely discussed implication of the theory: that people have approximately the same risk attitude towards an aggregation of independent, identical gambles as towards each of the independent gambles. This observation was introduced in a famous article by Paul Samuelson (1963), who reports that he once offered a colleague a bet in which he could flip a coin and either gain $200 or lose $100. The colleague declined the bet, but announced his willingness to accept 100 such bets together. Samuelson showed that this pair of choices was inconsistent with expected utility theory, which implies that if (for some range of wealth levels) a person turns down a particular gamble, then the person should also turn down an offer to play many of those gambles.

Now, the predicament of the portfolio manager is in between the single-bet and the 100-bet case: she will often manage the wealth of investors (pension funds, insurance companies, etc.) with very long horizons (she will 'toss the coin' many times), but she also will be 'benchmarked' against her peers after almost every single 'bet'. This creates a tension that we avoid confronting head-on when we model choice, as we often do, using a myopic utility function such as the logarithmic one. The problem, however, does not go away, and, in practical applications, is an acute one.

23.5   Aversion to ambiguity

One of the most attractive features of the Bayesian approach is its recognition of the legitimacy of a plurality of (coherently constrained) responses to data. Any approach to scientific inference which seeks to legitimize an answer in response to complex uncertainty is, for me, a parody of a would-be rational learning process. A F Smith[8]

We alluded at the beginning of this chapter that a third problem has a direct bearing on our work. To understand the nature of the problem, a good place to start is the Ellsberg paradox (Ellsberg 1961), which we will rephrase as follows.

Suppose that you are promised one million dollars if you draw a red ball from either of two opaque urns. You are told that each urn contains only red and blue balls. You are also told that urn A contains a 50–50 ratio of red and blue balls. You have no information whatsoever about the relative frequencies of red and blue balls in urn B. Without performing any calculation, from which urn would you prefer to draw?

Almost invariably, respondents prefer drawing from urn A, for which the ratio of red-to-blue balls is known. As Gilboa and Schmeidler (1989) point out, 'it is easy to see that there is no probability measure supporting these preferences through expected utility maximization', as the chooser should be indifferent between the two urns. In particular, the expectation, the variance and all the higher moments of the wealth distribution resulting from choosing either urn can be shown to be exactly the same.

---

[8] Smith (1984), quoted in Poirier (1995, p. xii), emphasis in the original.

The explanation (which is truly a description rather than a true explanation) of this 'paradox' points to the fact that human beings appear to be averse not just to risk (which, for simplicity, we could equate with variance of returns), but also to *ambiguity*, i.e., to types of uncertainty which have no bearing on the moments of the wealth distribution.[9]

Now, recall that we stressed that, for all its logical terseness and cogency, expected utility is an 'empty vessel' unless it is complemented by a set of 'robust and recurrent' behavioural inputs (such as preference of more to less, or aversion to risk). The Ellsberg paradox suggests that ambiguity aversion is another instance of a 'robust and recurrent' behavioural response in choice settings. If we accept that it is, it would be nice to account for this feature in a framework of similar logical tightness to the expected utility model. We will touch briefly in what follows on how this can be done. The more relevant question at this stage, however, is whether aversion to ambiguity figures prominently in our project.

As it happens, it does. Recall the emphasis we place on the stability of the allocation weights to small changes in the inputs. There are, of course, practical reasons (such as reduction of transaction costs) for wanting stable weights. But there is a deeper motivation. If two nearby portfolios have almost identical expected utilities (and their certainty equivalents is therefore economically almost indistinguishable), but the associated portfolio weights are radically different, we are in a situation similar to the chooser in the Ellsberg paradox: we would very much prefer to draw from an 'urn' with stable weights, but we are continually asked to draw from 'urns' whose compositions we do not *ex ante* know. We therefore suffer from 'ambiguity aversion'.

Let's look at the problem more precisely. We start from the uncertainty in the estimation of the expected returns and covariances that constitute the inputs to a mean-variance optimization problem. As Garlappi, Uppal and Wang (2006, p. 42) point out

> [t]he standard method ... to deal with estimation error is to use a Bayesian approach, where the unknown parameters are treated as random variables. A Bayesian decision-maker combines a pre-specified prior over the parameters with observation from the data to construct a predictive distribution[10] of returns. Bayesian optimal portfolios then maximize expected utility, where the expectation is taken with respect to the predictive distribution.
>
> The Bayesian decision-maker, however, is assumed to have only a single prior .... Given the difficulty in estimating moments of assets returns, the sensitivity of the portfolio weights to a particular prior, and the substantial evidence from experiments that agents are not neutral to ambiguity, it is important to consider investors with multiple priors who are averse to this ambiguity and hence desire robust portfolio rules that work well for a set of possible models ...

The topic of multiple priors goes back a long way, at least to Hurwicz (1951), who deals with the situation where an agent is 'too ignorant to have unique 'Bayesian' prior, but 'not quite as ignorant' as to apply Wald's decision rule with respect to all

---

[9] We give a more precise definition of ambiguity in the following.

[10] The predictive distribution is the posterior distribution after marginalization (i.e., after integrating out) the uncertainty metaparameters.

priors'.[11] The important observation for our discussion is that ambiguity aversion can be accommodated in the theoretical fold of classical decision-making by modifying some of the axioms of 'classic' utility theory (e.g., the independence axiom is weakened) and introducing a new one.[12] Ambiguity aversion therefore can be built upon a set of axioms which are behaviourally as well founded as, or better founded than, the classical axioms,[13] and which allow the same degree of logical rigour as the standard theory.

We will not pursue the computational high-road prescribed by utility maximization under aversion to risk and ambiguity, and we just give a sketch of the theory in Section 23.6.2. *However, we justify our striving for stable asset allocations in the light of aversion to ambiguity.* And, as we discuss later in this chapter, we extract one important result from the ambiguity aversion literature, namely that, under the usual 'suitable conditions', the aversion-ambiguity-aware solution can be interpreted as the solution to a standard (risk-aversion) utility maximization, but with a different (higher) coefficient of risk aversion.

We therefore propose a shortcut to the full max–min utility optimization problem that dealing with ambiguity would entail. The short cut boils down to using an 'effective' coefficient of *risk* aversion that incorporates ambiguity aversion. As for the calibration of this coefficient, we take our dislike for the weight instability as a symptom of our aversion to ambiguity and therefore suggest that we should be directly guided in setting the effective coefficient *by the width of the distribution of allocation weights.* We should stop 'regularizing' our problem, in other words, when we find the allocation 'stable enough'. There is no 'scientific' answer to the question of what 'stable enough' means – just as there is no scientific answer to the question of how risk averse one 'should be'.

All of this will become clearer in Section 23.6.2, and in the final chapter of this book when we put our suggestion to work.

23.6   Dealing with uncertainty: the Bayesian route

Introducing ambiguity aversion is, of course, not the only way to deal with uncertainty in model specification. Another very natural way – a way which is firmly within the fold of classic expected-utility maximization – is to make use of a Bayesian approach. It is important to deal with this topic before moving to 'outside-theory' objections and remedies. We start, however, with a short, but, as we shall see, very pertinent, digression.

23.6.1   *Another effective coefficient of risk aversion*
Consider a standard quadratic utility function of the form

$$U = w^{\mathrm{T}}\mu - \frac{1}{2}\lambda w^{\mathrm{T}}\Sigma w \tag{23.14}$$

---

[11] Gilboa and Schmeielder (1989, p. 142.)   [12] *Ibid*, p. 144.
[13] Hedging, for instance, is better accounted for by the C-independence axiom than by the stronger and traditional independence axiom.

Write the covariance matrix as

$$\Sigma = \sigma bb^{\mathrm{T}}\sigma^{\mathrm{T}} \tag{23.15}$$

with the correlation matrix, ρ, given by

$$bb^{\mathrm{T}} = \rho \tag{23.16}$$

and with the diagonal matrix σ given by

$$\sigma = \mathrm{diag}[\sigma_1, \sigma_2, \ldots, \sigma_n] \tag{23.17}$$

Then

$$U = w^{\mathrm{T}}\mu - \frac{1}{2}\lambda w^{\mathrm{T}}(\sigma bb^{\mathrm{T}}\sigma^{\mathrm{T}})w \tag{23.18}$$

Now suppose, for simplicity, that our uncertainty increases for all assets uniformly by a factor κ, $\kappa > 0$:

$$\sigma' = \kappa\sigma$$

Then the new utility becomes

$$U = w^{\mathrm{T}}\mu - \frac{1}{2}\lambda\kappa^2 w^{\mathrm{T}}(\sigma bb^{\mathrm{T}}\sigma^{\mathrm{T}})w \tag{23.19}$$

This shows that increasing our uncertainty by a factor of κ is equivalent to increasing our risk aversion by a factor of κ^2: the new problem (with high uncertainty) can be recast in terms of the old (low-uncertainty) problem by modifying the degree of risk aversion:

$$\lambda \Longrightarrow \lambda' = \lambda\kappa^2 \tag{23.20}$$

So, if for some reason we doubled our uncertainty about the asset returns, the coefficient of risk aversion would equivalently move from a behaviourally plausible value of, say, 1.5, to a value of 6.

Recall now that in this setting the sensitivity of the optimal allocation weights to the expected returns is given by

$$\frac{\partial w_i^*}{\partial\mu_j} = \frac{1}{\lambda}\Sigma_{ij}^{-1} \tag{23.21}$$

As this equation shows (and as we will discuss at greater length below), increasing risk aversion reduces the sensitivity of the optional allocation weights to the difficult-to-estimate expected returns and therefore stabilizes the allocations. And we will show in Chapter 29 that an exponent greater than 5 and less than 10 is roughly what is required to give rise to acceptably stable and diversified solutions. If we could justify such a coefficient of risk aversion, we would, in other words, have gone a long way towards solving the weight-instability problem.

Now, we have already given a preview of the result that accounting for ambiguity aversion can be accommodated by using an effective coefficient of risk aversion. But the analysis sketched above suggests that perhaps increasing our uncertainty using a Bayesian framework can achieve the same result. More precisely, this second 'effective' coefficient of risk aversion could be interpreted, as the derivation above shows, as a reflection of the greater degree of uncertainty brought about by a Bayesian analysis. This would give us an alternative, or perhaps a complementary, way towards justifying using a coefficient of risk aversion higher than what we would behaviourally observe in settings with perfect knowledge of the parameters of the governing statistical model and no aversion to ambiguity.

As we shall see, matters are not quite so simple, but it is important to explore the promises and the limitations of this route.

23.6.2   *Modelling uncertainty using the Bayesian approach*

The idea is simple. The three-step tango of Bayesian modelling (which moves from the prior, through the likelihood function, to the posterior) takes the following interpretation in the mean-variance allocation context. See Avramov and Zhou (2010) for a clear recent review.

First we have our priors, expressed as probability distributions for the parameters, $\{\theta = \mu, \Sigma\}$, that characterize the problem at hand. These priors can be either uninformative (diffuse) or informative. When the priors are uninformative, the modeller has no *a priori* knowledge of where these model parameters should lie, and derives all of her information from the data. She acknowledges, however, that she only has access to statistically noisy estimates for the parameters, and therefore wants to take into account the uncertainty due to this noise when performing the simulation. In the case of uninformative priors it is customary to assume that returns are identically and independently distributed.

When the priors are informative, the modeller has two choices: either she injects subjective expert domain knowledge into the problem – information that could have the form of an asset-pricing model, of subjective views (see the Black–Litterman approach), or of predictions of asset returns; or she requires that the statistical estimate should be 'shrunk' towards some stable and uninformative benchmark cases – the Stein estimators that we briefly discussed in Sections 18.1 and 29.2 belong to this class.

It is important to stress that when priors are uninformative the first moment of the posterior distribution does not change, but its variance increases; in the case of informative priors also the location of the first moment changes, and it becomes a 'blend' of the subjective input and of what is suggested by the likelihood function. Even when the first moments do not change, however, the optimal allocation will change, because the variance will have increased.

The second ingredient of the Bayesian approach is the likelihood function which, as usual, describes what Avramov and Zhou (2010, p. 26) call 'the laws of motion governing the evolution of asset prices returns, asset pricing factors, and forecasting variables'.

Combination of the prior and the likelihood function gives the posterior distribution. Once this has been obtained, the model parameters are integrated out, leaving the predictive distribution. The asset allocation is then obtained by carrying out the maximization of the expected utility over the predictive distribution (See, e.g., Zellner and Chetty 1965).

The procedure is conceptually clear enough. But how effective is it in bringing about an increase in our uncertainty, and hence, indirectly, in stabilizing the allocation solution? To answer the question, let us focus on the case where our uncertainty stems only from statistical noise. Denote by m and V the parameters of the distributions describing our uncertainty about returns and covariances, and, to focus on the essence of the problem, let's assume that (i) our prior is diffuse; (ii) the asset returns are identically and independently distributed; and (iii) they are joint normally distributed. Under these assumptions, Avramov and Zhou (2010, p. 29) show that the posterior distribution for the parameters, ψ, is given by

$$\psi(m, V) = \psi(m|V)\psi(V) \tag{23.22}$$

with

$$\psi(m|V) \propto |V|^{-\frac{1}{2}} \exp\left\{-\frac{1}{2}\text{tr}[N(\mu - \widehat{\mu})(\mu - \widehat{\mu})^T V^{-1}]\right\} \tag{23.23}$$

$$\psi(V) \propto |V|^{-\frac{1}{2}} \exp\left\{-\frac{1}{2}tr[V^{-1}(N\widehat{V})]\right\} \tag{23.24}$$

where $\widehat{\mu}$ and $\widehat{V}$ are the sample estimates for the returns and the covariance matrix, respectively, and N is the number of observations, $v = N + n$, with n equal to the number of assets.

Then (see, e.g., Avramov and Zhou 2010, p. 29) the optimal allocation weights obtained by maximizing the usual mean-variance quadratic utility over the predictive distribution are given by

$$w^*_{\text{Bayes/Diffuse}} = \frac{1}{\lambda}\left(\frac{N - n - 2}{N + 1}\right)\widehat{V}^{-1}\widehat{\mu} \tag{23.25}$$

One can immediately note that the solution is exactly the same as the traditional Markowitz solution (often referred to in the Bayesian literature as the 'plug-in' solution, because one can simply 'plug in' the naive sample estimates) times a correction factor.

The presence of the correction factor is, at the same time, both encouraging and disappointing. It is encouraging because it could be 'absorbed' into an equivalent (and greater) coefficient of risk aversion, λ',

$$\lambda' = \lambda\left(\frac{N + 1}{N - n - 2}\right) \tag{23.26}$$

It is 'disappointing' because, when the number of assets is much smaller than the number of observations, the multiplicative factor is very close to 1, and the correction is therefore limited. If our uncertainty is only due to statistical noise, embedding it into our allocation process via the Bayesian machinery will make very little difference: the Bayesian mountain will have given birth to a Markowitz-like mouse.

Clearly, if we have *informative* priors, the results are different. However, as we have seen, the main effect will be to change the first moment of the predictive distribution. This may well be important, but does not address (let alone solve) the instability problem; that requires an increase in the second moment – an increase that, as shown in Section 23.6.1, can give a higher effective coefficient of risk aversion and hence, ultimately, more stable weights.

So, if we are looking for ways to justify a substantially higher coefficient of risk aversion, the Bayesian-uncertainty route does not offer the help we needed. What about looking again at ambiguity aversion?

23.6.3   Taking ambiguity aversion into account

We can try to account for this important aspect of choice behaviour following the approach by Garlappi, Uppal and Wang (2006, p. 1):

In contrast to the Bayesian approach to estimation error, where is only a single prior and the investor is neutral to uncertainty,[14] we allow for multiple priors and aversion to uncertainty. ... The multi-prior approach has several attractive features: One, just like the Bayesian model, it is firmly grounded in decision theory; ... Two, in several economic interesting cases ... the multi-prior model can be simplified to a mean-variance model, but where the expected return is adjusted to reflect the investor's uncertainty about its estimate.

More precisely, the standard mean-variance optimization problem is modified in two respects: (i) an additional constraint is imposed on the expected returns by requiring that they should lie within a certain confidence interval of the statistically estimated value; (ii) the agent carries out not only a standard utility *maximization* over portfolio weights, but also a minimization over the possible expected returns (and hence over the 'models') compatible with the constraints expressed in (i).

In order to explain the role played by the confidence interval mentioned above, the authors point out that 'when confidence interval is large [..], then the investor relies less on the estimated mean, and hence, reduces the weight invested in that asset. When this interval is tight, the minimization is constrained more tightly, and hence, the portfolio weight is closer to the standard weight that one would get from a model that neglects estimation error' (p. 3).

The starting point is the traditional maximization problem,

$$\max_{w} \left\{ w^{\mathsf{T}} \mu - \frac{\lambda}{2} w^{\mathsf{T}} \Sigma w \right\} \qquad (23.27)$$

with optimal solution

$$w^* = \frac{1}{\lambda} \Sigma^{-1} \mu \qquad (23.28)$$

[14] In this context 'uncertainty' is what we refer to as 'ambiguity'.

where all the symbols have the usual meaning. The additional optimization introduced by Garlappi, Uppal and Wang (2006) to account for ambiguity aversion requires the investor to minimize over expected returns, and the problem becomes

$$\max_{w} \min_{\mu} \left\{ w^{\mathrm{T}}\mu - \frac{\lambda}{2}w^{\mathrm{T}}\Sigma w \right\} \tag{23.29}$$

subject to

$$f(\mu, \widehat{\mu}, \Sigma) \leq \eta \tag{23.30}$$

where, as usual, $\widehat{\mu}$ denotes the vector of estimated expected returns, η is a coefficient that describes aversion to ambiguity (more about this later) and $f(\cdot)$ is a vector-valued function to the field of real numbers.

Max–min problems can be computationally burdensome to compute. However, Garlappi, Uppal and Wang (2006) show that the optimization can be recast in terms of a simple maximization over a transformed objective function. If the uncertainty is estimated asset-by-asset they prove that the problem becomes

$$\max_{w} \left\{ w^{\mathrm{T}}(\widehat{\mu} - \Delta\mu) - \frac{\lambda}{2}w^{\mathrm{T}}\Sigma w \right\} \tag{23.31}$$

with

$$\Delta\mu_i = \mathrm{sign}(w_i)\frac{\sigma_i}{\sqrt{N}}\sqrt{\eta_i} \tag{23.32}$$

So, in the optimization problem the expected returns are modified from their statistically estimated value ($\widehat{\mu}_i$) by the term $\mathrm{sign}(w_i)\frac{\sigma_i}{\sqrt{N}}\sqrt{\eta_i}$, which reduces them if the allocation weight is positive, and increases them if negative.

When the uncertainty about expected returns is estimated jointly for all the assets, Garlappi, Uppal and Wang (2006) then show that the optimal weights, w^*, are given by

$$w^* = \frac{1}{\lambda}\left(\frac{1}{1+\xi}\right)\Sigma^{-1}\widehat{\mu} \tag{23.33}$$

with

$$\xi = \frac{\sqrt{\varepsilon}}{\lambda\sigma_{\mathrm{P}}^*} \tag{23.34}$$

$$\varepsilon = \eta\frac{(N-1)n}{N(N-n)} \tag{23.35}$$

where σ_{P}^* denotes the variance of the optimal portfolio.

It is easy to see the effect of the ambiguity-aversion coefficient, η: as it goes to zero, ε goes to zero, ξ goes to zero, the ratio $\frac{1}{1+\xi}$ tends to 1, and the solution goes to the Markowitz solution,

$$w^* = \frac{1}{\lambda}\Sigma^{-1}\widehat{\mu} \tag{23.36}$$

At the opposite extreme, as the ambiguity aversion coefficient, η, approaches infinity, so do ε and ξ, the ratio $\frac{1}{1+\xi}$ tends to zero, and the portfolio tends towards the minimum-variance portfolio. (Recall that returns are essentially irrelevant in determining the minimum-variance portfolio.)

For any intermediate value of η, we note that, once again, the optimal solution can be interpreted as the outcome of a traditional optimization, carried out with an 'effective' degree of risk aversion, λ':

$$\lambda' = \lambda(1 + \xi) \tag{23.37}$$

This is exactly the result we were looking for, because we saw in Section 23.6.1 that an increased (effective) coefficient of risk aversion has the effect of reducing the sensitivity of the weights to the expected returns, (see Equation (23.21)) and, hence, to stabilize the allocation solution.

What about the calibration of this effective coefficient of risk aversion? As we mentioned above, we propose to solve the thorny calibration issue *by varying the coefficient(s) until the distribution of allocation weights becomes sufficiently localized.* This, incidentally, constitutes an appealing alternative to the exogenous specification of weights constraints discussed in the closing section of the previous chapter.[15]

We note in closing this section that very similar results are obtained when one is faced with a dynamic portfolio and consumption problem. Indeed, Maenhout (2001) shows that the classic Merton solution to this problem for a power utility function is simply modified in the presence of ambiguity aversion by deriving a new 'effective' coefficient of risk aversion. More precisely, given a power utility function with risk-aversion coefficient, γ,

$$U(c) = \frac{c^{1-\gamma}}{1-\gamma} \quad \gamma \neq 1 \tag{23.38}$$

the optimal portfolio and consumption rules in the presence of ambiguity aversion are given by

$$c^* = \frac{a}{1 - \exp[-a\tau]} W_t \tag{23.39}$$

$$\alpha^* = \frac{1}{\gamma + \theta} \frac{\mu - r}{\sigma^2} \quad \theta > 0 \tag{23.40}$$

---

[15] Admittedly, this heuristic suggestion may seem topsy-turvy, because ambiguity aversion is about aversion to uncertainty in the *input* parameters (whilst, broadly speaking, we can characterize Robust Decision-Making as being about aversion to uncertainty in the *outputs*); see Section 26.7. When we are averse to ambiguity we don't like to draw from an urn with an unknown distribution of red and blue balls even if *ex ante* the distribution of outcomes is the same. Our dislike is about our epistemic state, even if the outcome is *ex-ante* indistinguishable. However, if we are happy to make the *Ansatz* that a 'reasonable' degree of ambiguity aversion should produce 'acceptably' stable distribution of weights, then we can reverse engineer the effective coefficient of risk aversion from our dislike about outputs.

where W_t denotes wealth at time t, α^* is the optimal fraction of wealth invested in the risky asset, a is a constant defined in Maenhout (2001, below Eqn (26)), and all the other symbols have the standard meaning.[16]

The important thing to notice for our purposes is that also in the dynamic allocation case the difference from the standard Merton solution in the optimal fraction of risky asset is simply the replacement $\gamma \longrightarrow \gamma + \theta > \gamma$: *once again, the effect of introducing ambiguity aversion is to model the investor as if she were only risk averse, but had a higher coefficient of risk aversion:*

> The portfolio weight is the standard Merton solution, where the usual risk aversion adjustment γ is replaced by $\gamma + \theta > \gamma$. Robustness amounts therefore to an increase in risk aversion .... The consumption rule has the same structure as Merton solution.[17]

23.7   Robust Decision-Making

We dealt in the previous section with the criticisms that have been levelled at traditional utility theory from within its normative fold. There is one approach that straddles the within-the-theory/outside-the-theory divide: Robust Decision-Making. We look briefly at what it offers, because, in some of its incarnations, it promises to deal with the allocation instability problems that we shall discuss at length in Chapter 28.

Robust Decision-Making is not one single technique, but a set of methods and tools designed to assist the decision-making process in conditions of deep uncertainty. The idea, if not the name, of 'deep uncertainty' goes back to the early 1920s with the work by Keynes (1921) and Knight (1921), who stressed the existence of uncertainty *about* uncertainty, and the impossibility of capturing via any single probability distribution 'imprecision and ambiguity in human knowledge' (Lempert and Collins 2007).[18] This should be contrasted with the expected-utility-maximization framework, which 'views risk as characterized by a single probability distribution over future states of the world, *estimated prior to any choice of actions*' (Lempert and Collins 2007, p. 1010, our emphasis). As the field of Robust Decision-Making is relatively new, we take the definition of Robust Optimization given by Bertsimas and Thiele (2006) as a useful reference point:

> [Robust Optimization] present[s] a mathematical framework that is well-suited to the limited information available in real-life problems and captures the decision-maker's attitude towards uncertainty; the proposed approach builds upon recent developments in robust and data-driven optimization. In robust optimization, random variables are modeled as uncertain parameters belonging to a convex uncertainty set *and the decision-maker protects the system against the worst case within that set.*[19]

More generally, Robust Decision-Making objects to the use of point estimates of probabilities, and, in some of its incarnations, claims to offer 'richer' description of risk aversion than what is afforded by the utility formalism.

---

[16] See Maenhout (2001, p. 18 and App. A) for a derivation.   [17] *Ibid.*, p. 19.
[18] In this respect, see also Ellsberg's (1961) classic work on ambiguity, revisited in Ellsberg (2001).
[19] Bertsimas and Thiele (2006, our emphasis).

Decisional contexts where the Robust Decision-Making framework may make useful contributions are characterized, *inter alia*, (i) by the coexistence of multiple plausible views of the future, (ii) by a strong dependence of the outputs to small variations in these views and (iii) by the importance of the robustness of the chosen solution.

All these features are present in spades in asset-allocation problems: the expected returns are extremely difficult to pinpoint with any precision, and knowledgeable 'experts' can hold substantially different views (see, e.g., Shefrin 2008); small changes in expected returns can affect very strongly the allocation results; lack of stability of the allocations as a consequence of small changes in the difficult-to-estimate expected returns inflicts high transaction costs and, what is more, destroys the confidence of the portfolio manager in the robustness – nay, credibility – of the suggested course of action. So, given our concerns about the stability of allocations, Robust Decision-Making should definitely be considered in our work.

Even the sketchiest account of Robust Decision-Making, however, would not do justice to the topic if one failed to distinguish between at least three different strands to Robust Decision-Making in general, and to Robust Optimization in particular.

In the 'high-road' approach the utility framework is retained, and so are the traditional axioms of choice theory, and it is simply the uncertainty faced by the decision-maker that becomes 'deeper'. The utility-maximizing agent, for instance, may be uncertain about the true model describing reality. This strand tends to lead to the formulation of minimax problems (see, e.g., Section 23.6.3), and often the robust solutions have the same form as those obtained under condition of model certainty, but some crucial parameter is replaced by an 'effective' one (see, e.g., Hansen and Sargent 2008). Indeed, our favourite asset-allocation technique, described in detail in the last chapters of the book, can be recast in a traditional mean-variance language, but with an 'effective' (and higher) coefficient of risk aversion, which takes into account aversion to ambiguity as well. In this sense, we are robust decision-makers ourselves. So, in our definition, Bayesian techniques used in the context of utility maximization (as in Section 23.6.1), or the results that derive from the ambiguity-aversion axiomatization are part of the high-road Robust Decision-Making techniques.

The second strand of Robust Decision-Making is more radical, in that it rejects *tout court* the optimization conceptual framework, and follows instead the 'satisficing' and bounded-rationality approach described, for example, in Simon (1956, 1957) and Gigerenzer (2002). In a nutshell, these researchers point out that the heuristics employed to reach decisions without making use of full-blown expected utility maximization are not only informationally and computationally much cheaper – something that one would expect; in a variety of important settings, they can also produce as good or 'better' results, where 'better' is often understood in an adaptive sense. We do not know whether the authors would agree with our taxonomy, but the $1/n$ allocations (suggested, e.g., by de Miguel, Garlappi and Uppal (2009), and discussed in a very insightful article by Lee (2011, p. 14)) or the risk-parity portfolio by Qian (2005) (which allocates the portfolio variance equally across the portfolio components) can be looked at as instances of simple heuristics that can perform as well as, if not better, than naive optimization. We find this line of thought very interesting, but we do not pursue in this book this route of investigation.[20]

There is then a third strand to Robust Decision-Making, represented by those researchers who employ a set of techniques that still remain in the broad computational framework of traditional utility-maximization (or who, at least, borrow from it concepts such as efficient frontiers), but who eschew a 'deep'[21] axiomatization of the choice process. This strand directly offers instead a number of ad-hoc and *a priori* prescriptions as to what an agent should optimize over. Examples of this approach are the various mean-VaR (Value-at-Risk), mean-CVaR optimization techniques (see, e.g., Boudt, Carl and Peterson (2013) for a recent treatment that emphasizes diversification and sensitivity to model parameters), or Michaud's resampling.

Regarding the second and third strands, the 'impatience' shown for traditional optimization techniques is understandable:[22] it is certainly true that in matters financial we do not know 'objective' probabilities with any degree of certainty. In particular, we do not know expected returns precisely, and, as we have seen, these affect the allocations greatly. However, there is nothing in conventional decision theory and in the expected-utility-maximization framework that requires perfect knowledge of the probabilities attaching to different events, or of the model parameters. If we can state how uncertain we are about these quantities, we should be able to translate this 'second-order uncertainty' into a Bayesian framework, by introducing the appropriate meta-parameters.[23] After introducing in a Bayesian way the uncertainty in the input parameters into account, the expected utility formalism should know about all the uncertainty 'that is out there'. So, our first question is: why exactly can a Bayesian approach not address the 'uncertainty-about-uncertainty' objection? And if we are averse to ambiguity, why doesn't the approach outlined above provide a useful answer?

More generally, if one adds to one's optimization procedure extra ad-hoc robust constraints (such as constraints on Value-at-Risk, on the conditional expected loss, on the maximum acceptable loss, etc.), the results may well end up being more 'robust'. However, the question naturally arises: 'If these aspects of risk truly describe so much better our responses to choice under uncertainty, and do not introduce logical inconsistencies, why couldn't these behavioural responses be "baked into" a better utility function to begin with?'

---

[20] See, however, Gigerenzer (2002), Gigerenzer and Brighton (2009), Gigerenzer and Edwards (2003), Gigergrenzer and Hoffrage (1995), Gigergrenzer and Selten (2002a), and Rebonato (2012) for a discussion of bounded rationality and of the rationality of *Homo Economicus*.

[21] We remind the reader that we define an axiomatic system of the choice process to be 'deep' when it reaches all the way down to the way elementary decisions are made (Can an agent rank any two lotteries? Is the choice between lottery *A* and lottery *B* influenced by the introduction of an unrelated lottery *C*? etc.) A 'shallow' axiomatization would be one, for instance, that directly posited as a primitive axiom that agents 'dislike' distribution with large negative third moments.

[22] Indeed, some authors make a virtue of employing heuristic shortcuts. For instance, speaking of the global minimum-variance portfolio, Lee (2011) claims that it is 'potentailly more applicable *because of its heuristic nature*, economic intuition, and the financial interpretation that ties its concepts to economic losses' (emphasis added).

[23] We remind the reader that meta-parameters are parameters that describe our knowledge (or lack thereof) about the the 'proper' model parameters.

We are therefore rather reluctant to abandon a logically consistent construct (with – admittedly – some deeply rooted problems and paradoxes attaching to it) for a conceptual framework whose 'deep' logical coherence is still to be proved, and where inconsistencies and paradoxes may lurk just as numerous.

It is true, we have argued that there are some deep problems in the way expected utility theory deals with risk aversion 'in the small' and 'in the large'. However, these problems at least arise out of a logically very solid theory, girded by 'deep' axioms – axioms that, as axioms in economics go, are amongst the more plausible and appealing. Also, very bright minds have been dissecting expected-utility theory for half a century. It is not surprising that, as a result of these concerted efforts, wrinkles (or cracks) may have appeared. But why should we expect that the ad-hoc patching one introduces with many of the third-strand Robust-Decision-Theory constraints, underpinned by equally generous helpings of intuition, hard-nosed pragmatism and hope, might not hide more serious problems?

So, for instance, making use of Mean-Value-at-Risk or Mean-Conditional-Expected-Shortfall optimization is often touted as a 'solution' to the allocation instability problem. Let's leave to one side the nettlesome problem of how we choose the percentile of interest, and of why the investor should care about *that* particular percentile. The fact remains that, under some relatively mild distributional assumptions,[24] a VaR or CVaR optimization gives exactly the same results as would be obtained using a mean-variance optimization, *but with a larger coefficient of risk aversion*. In these cases, why don't we simply change the coefficient of risk aversion? And, if we found such a coefficient of risk aversion behaviourally unpalatable, why do we prefer the suggestions of a VaR-based allocation system that produces exactly the same answers?

In sum: we cannot do justice in a few paragraphs to what is an interesting, and still developing, field of research. We simply caution against embracing with enthusiasm some intuitively appealing alternatives to expected utility maximization. We are all in favour to subjecting the latter to serious scrutiny and to the barrage of criticism to which it has been exposed. However, we think that the same standards of rigour and critical analysis should be used for the new kids on the optimization block. In particular, we are suspicious of 'shallow' axiomatizations, which start from where a good theory should arguably lead to.

---

[24] We simply require the joint distributions of returns to be elliptical, not Gaussian.

Part IX

Numerical implementation

In this part of the book we present the numerical techniques needed to turn the ideas presented so far into an efficient allocation algorithm. In particular, first we show how to solve efficiently the full optimization problem. Then, in Chapter 25, we show that two approximations are both surprisingly effective and capable of recasting the full optimization problem into a much simpler and more familiar mean-variance framework.

The surprising effectiveness of these approximations will also give us additional insight on the stability problem (which we first touched upon in Chapter 8). We shall expand on this insight in the final parts of the book.

24 Optimizing the expected utility over the weights

24.1 The purpose of this chapter

The purpose of this chapter is to show how to combine the information from the spliced joint distribution of changes in market risk factors (made up of the 'body' and of the excited components) with the chosen utility function to obtain a *coherent* allocation to the various sub-portfolios in the presence of (i.e., taking into due account) stress events. The adjective 'coherent' stresses that the allocation has been arrived at by taking into account in a consistent manner the investor's preferences over the outcomes associated with both normal and exceptional market conditions. In our methodology, 'protection trades' (such as, say, purchasing out-of-the-money puts or buying CDS protection) are not attached as an *ex post* afterthought to an optimization previously carried out assuming a stable investing universe. Rather, they are an integral and, again, *coherent* part of the process.

The emphasis of this chapter is computational. In this respect, it is arguably less 'exciting' than the conceptual and methodological parts of the book. However, there is little point in developing interesting ideas unless they can be implemented effectively. From this perspective this apparently mundane chapter is therefore one of the most important of the book.

We also present in this chapter a method to explore the sensitivity of the outputs to one important component of the Bayesian-net construction, i.e., the probability mass associated with the 'nothing happens' event. This quantity is, at the same time, very important in our approach and very difficult to estimate with great precision. In keeping with our skeptical philosophy it is only natural, then, that we should look in detail at the sensitivity of our results to it. This is undertaken in the later sections of this chapter.

24.2 Utility maximization – the set-up

Given the discussion in the previous chapters, we will assume in the following:

- that we have determined from the full spliced distribution a reduced distribution, $\varphi(\Delta \boldsymbol{\xi})$, of changes in market risk factors (see Section 20.1);

- that we know how to map these changes in market risk factors to changes in the value of our portfolio;
- that we have settled for a utility function (in reduced-form or otherwise) of our liking.

Our goal is then to vary the elements of the vector of weights, w, until the objective function (the end-of-period utility of the final wealth) is maximized. How can we carry out this optimization in an efficient manner?

Let's refresh our memory about the various components of the object function, the expected utility, $E[U]$:

$$E[U] = \int U(W_{t_0}[1 + w^T r(\Delta\xi)])\varphi(\Delta\xi)d(\Delta\xi)$$

$$= \int U(W_{t_0}[1 + w^T r(\Delta\xi)]) \sum_{i=0,M} p_i\varphi_i(\Delta\xi)d(\Delta\xi) \qquad (24.1)$$

$$w^* = \arg\max_{w\in\Theta}[E(U)] \qquad (24.2)$$

Here $M = 2^{N_{leaf}} - 1$, N_{leaf} is the number of leaves in the Bayesian net, W_{t_0} is the initial wealth, $\Delta\xi$ denotes the vector whose components $\Delta\xi_1, \Delta\xi_2, \ldots, \Delta\xi_N$ are the changes in the market risk factors, $\varphi(\Delta\xi)$ denotes their joint probability density, which has been expressed as a linear combination of $M + 1$ 'basis functions', $\varphi_i(\Delta\xi)$, with weights p_i,

$$\varphi(\Delta\xi_1, \Delta\xi_n, \ldots, \Delta\xi_n) = \sum_{i=0,M} p_i\varphi_i(\Delta\xi_1, \Delta\xi_n, \ldots, \Delta\xi_N) \qquad (24.3)$$

and Θ represents the set of constraints, such as short-selling, budget constraints, maximum allocations to each asset class, etc. Finally, the weights, p_i, are the joint probabilities of the reduced distribution.

As for the basis functions, φ_i, recall from Chapter 20 that $\psi^0_{comp}(\Delta\xi_1, \Delta\xi_2, \ldots, \Delta\xi_{n^i_{norm}})$ is the compacted distribution obtained as in Section 20.5 by integrating out the non-excited distribution over all the variables that are excited in the ith joint event. Each basis function is then given by

$$\varphi_i(\Delta\xi_1, \Delta\xi_n, \ldots, \Delta\xi_N)$$
$$= \psi^0_{comp}(\Delta\xi_1, \Delta\xi_2, \ldots, \Delta\xi_{n^i_{norm}}) \prod_{k=1,n^i_{exc}} \psi^{exc}_k(\Delta\xi_1, \Delta\xi_2, \ldots, \Delta\xi_N) \quad (24.4)$$

where the product is over the number of excited states, n^i_{exc}, in joint event i. Recall also that we made the assumption that each basis distribution, $\psi^{exc}_k(\Delta\xi_1, \Delta\xi_2, \ldots, \Delta\xi_N)$, should be of the type

$$\psi^{exc}_k(\Delta\xi_1, \Delta\xi_2, \ldots, \Delta\xi_N) = \mathcal{N}\left(\mu^k_{exc}, \Sigma^k_{exc}\right) \qquad (24.5)$$

where, in most cases, for $i \neq 0$, the covariance matrix Σ^k_{exc} will just be a number, expressing our uncertainty about the first moment of *the* market risk factor associated with the kth leaf. This fully specifies the distribution we are going to use to calculate the expectation.[1]

As for the constraints, the budget constraint

$$\boldsymbol{w}^\mathrm{T}\mathbf{1}^M = 1 \tag{24.6}$$

is the simplest one, and can be handled very easily. The positivity constraint requires more careful treatment, as discussed below.

For a logarithmic or power utility function finding the solution requires numerical optimization in general. This is, of course, computationally somewhat demanding, but, given the relatively small number of asset classes and the attending low dimensionality of the compacted distribution, does not pose a prohibitive burden on the whole procedure.

However, if one expands the power utility function to second order, significant computational savings can be achieved in a number of interesting cases, which are treated in the following sections. In particular, if we approximate the distribution of risk factors by a Gaussian *with the correct total variance*, we will show that a Monte-Carlo-based optimization is not required: if the returns are jointly Gaussian the problem can be solved (sometimes analytically, but otherwise by numerical quadrature) by evaluating a one-dimensional integral.

More radically, we will show in Chapter 25 that in most realistic applications very little information is lost if the problem is 'skilfully' recast in a traditional mean-variance framework. But let's not get ahead of ourselves, and let's look first at the brute-force solution that can be applied in the general case.

24.3 The general case

The procedure followed in the general case to carry out the optimization in Equations (24.1) and (24.2) works as follows.[2]

Let M be the number of terminal Bayesian-net leaves – each associated, in general, with one or more market risk factors; let N be the number of risk factors affecting the portfolios in the M leaves of the Bayesian net, X be the number of assets in the portfolio and N_{sim} be the number of scenarios that will be sampled. For the sake of simplicity we shall assume that there is one and only one market risk factor associated with each terminal leaf. Therefore $N = M$. We will also assume that each risk factor will affect the value of exactly one asset. So, $N = M = X$. These choices keep the notation lighter, and the extension to the general case does not present any conceptual difficulties. The algorithm to obtain the optimal allocation can then be described as follows.

---

[1] We note in passing that, if the normal-state distribution is Guassian, then the reduced distribution, φ, is just a linear combination of Gaussians, with weights p_i. This can greatly simplify the computation.

[2] We assume in the following that the marginals and the copula have been fitted to generate a distribution of returns over the same horizon as the investment period.

1. We start with an initial guess for the weights, $\boldsymbol{w}^*$, where the vector $\boldsymbol{w}^*$ has N components.
2. We go in turn over all the joint states i, $i = 0, 1, 2, \ldots, 2^N - 1$, of the compacted joint distribution (i.e., the distribution obtained from the Bayesian net from which the probabilities associated with the transmission channels have been integrated out). For each joint state, i,
   - we make n_{norm}^i independent draws from $[0, 1]^D$;
   - we conjoin these independent draws using the chosen copula – if the chosen copula is Gaussian this can be done using a Choleski-like procedure. This will give us $u_1, u_2, \ldots, u_D$ *dependent* random numbers;
   - we apply the inverse transformation of the marginal distribution, $F_i(\Delta\xi_i^{\text{norm}})$, for the ith non-excited variable, to obtain $\Delta\xi_i^{\text{norm}} = F^{-1}(u_i)$;
   - we make n_{exc}^i draws, one for each leaf that is activated, from the excited distribution of the associated market risk factor in the excited state, $\mathcal{N}(\mu_{\text{exc}}^1, \Sigma_{\text{exc}}^1)$, $\mathcal{N}(\mu_{\text{exc}}^2, \Sigma_{\text{exc}}^2), \ldots, \mathcal{N}(\mu_{\text{exc}}^N, \Sigma_{\text{exc}}^N)$: $\Delta\xi_{1,i}^{\text{exc}}, \Delta\xi_{2,i}^{\text{exc}}, \ldots, \Delta\xi_{n_{\text{exc}}^i,i}^{\text{exc}}$;
   - these normal-times and excited-time draws, $\{\Delta\xi^{\text{norm}(i)}, \Delta\xi^{\text{exc}(i)}\}$ collectively constitute one scenario, say, the lth scenario, for the ith state as $\{\Delta\xi^{\text{norm}(i)}, \Delta\xi^{\text{exc}(i)}\}_{i,l}$;
3. We repeat this procedure for N_{sim} scenarios, each associated with the ith joint state:
   $\{\Delta\xi^{\text{norm}(i)}, \Delta\xi^{\text{exc}(i)}\}_{i,1}, \{\Delta\xi^{\text{norm}(i)}, \Delta\xi^{\text{exc}(i)}\}_{i,2}, \ldots, \{\Delta\xi^{\text{norm}(i)}, \Delta\xi^{\text{exc}(i)}\}_{i,N_{\text{sim}}}$.
4. Let the vector $\boldsymbol{R}_{i,l}$

$$\boldsymbol{R}_{i,l} = \boldsymbol{R}_{i,l}(\{\Delta\xi^{\text{norm}(i)}, \Delta\xi^{\text{exc}(i)}\}_{i,l}) \tag{24.7}$$

be the result of the mapping from the combination of market risk changes associated to the lth scenario for the ith joint state to the change in value of the portfolio associated with a unit holding in the asset affected by the mth risk factor. Given our assumptions, $N = M = X$, this vector has as many components, $R_{i,l}^m$, $m = 1, 2, \ldots, M$, as there are terminal leaves, M (and, given our simplifying assumptions, market risk factors and assets).
5. The portfolio return associated with the lth scenario and the ith joint state, $r_{i,l}^{\Pi}$, is given by

$$R_{i,l}^{\Pi} = \sum_{m=1,M} w_m^* R_{i,l}^m \tag{24.8}$$

6. Given the weights chosen in step 1 and given the change in value of the portfolio associated with the ith joint state in scenario l, we can obtain the corresponding utility:

$$U_{i,l} = U_{i,l}(1 + R_{i,l}^{\Pi}) \tag{24.9}$$

7. We can now calculate the expected utility for scenario l, $E[U^l]$, as

$$E[U^l] = \sum_{i=0,2^M-1} p_i U_{i,l} = \sum_{i=0,2^M-1} p_i \left(\sum_{m=1,M} U\left(1 + R_{i,l}^{\Pi}\right) \right) \tag{24.10}$$

where the expectation is taken over the 2^M compacted joint probabilities.

8. We repeat the procedure for N_{sim} scenarios.
9. We can then calculate the expected utility, $E[U(\boldsymbol{w}^*)]$, associated with the initial guess for the weights, $\boldsymbol{w}^*$, as

$$E[U(\boldsymbol{w}^*)] = \frac{1}{N_{\text{sim}}} \sum_{l=1,N_{\text{sim}}} E[U^l]$$

10. We can now feed the expected utility into the chosen optimization engine. The search for the maximum expected utility can be achieved using standard techniques (such as conjugate gradients). As we show below, positivity constraints can be efficiently handled using the hypersphere technique in Rebonato and Jaeckel (1999), which allows unconstrained optimization over 'angles', ϑ. See the discussion below.

The procedure as described above may seem rather forbidding. However, it is in practice much simpler than it seems, for the reasons listed below.

REMARK 1 *In step 2 above, fourth bullet point, when we draw the excited factors we can draw independently from each marginal, as the draws should be independent.*

REMARK 2 *Since we work with a compacted distribution, the number of variables is typically rather small. Therefore the joint probabilities which are summed over in the outer sum in Equation (24.10) are not the $2^{N_{\text{nodes}}}$ joint probabilities obtained from the Bayesian net (which could be of order $O(10^3)$ or $O(10^4)$), but the joint probabilities of the compacted distribution (which will typically be of order $O(10^1)$ or $O(10^2)$).*

REMARK 3 *Since the optimization is over the weights, $\boldsymbol{w}$, the samples from the distribution of returns in market risk factors have to be generated only once. For a given net and for a given set of market risk factors associated with the terminal leaves, we can produce all these samples as best we can once and for all and store them in memory. These samples will then act as the fixed background to the optimization.*

REMARK 4 *Consider a particular disjoint event, i, in scenario l. For this event there will be n_{norm}^i changes in market risk factors in the non-excited state. As these factors are in general not independent we must draw from their joint compacted distribution. These joint distributions of non-excited risk factors will be made up of different numbers and different combinations of variables for each disjoint event, i. In general, in the ith state a number of excited risk factors dependent on the state will have to be integrated out. However, as we pointed out in Chapters 18 and 19, in order to obtain the joint distribution of the non-excited states it is not necessary to obtain the full joint distribution first, and then integrate (marginalize) over the excited variables. This would be messy and wasteful, because for each joint event one has a different combination and a different number of variables to integrate over. This laborious step can be circumvented, because our decomposition of the joint distribution of 'normal'* *market returns in terms of marginals and pairwise copulae allows us to sample directly from the distribution of any combination of non-excited risk factors.*

REMARK 5 *Consider all the disjoint events associated with a scenario, l. Thanks to our assumptions, the draws in excited states from the $\mathcal{N}(\mu_{exc}^k, \Sigma_{exc}^k)$ distributions are all independent. Therefore, we can make these draws once and for all, and then use them to create the required products in whichever combination we please. We do not need to carry out a joint draw for the variables in the excited states associated with different leaves.[3]*

REMARK 6 *Since we are conjoining via the chosen copula exactly as many draws from the marginal distributions as required in the ith state, also the draws from the copula can be carried out once and for all.*

24.3.1 Enforcing the budget and non-negativity constraints

Remaining with the general case, one very common constraint is to require that all the weights should be non-negative (no short-sale constraint). In the realistic case when the number of assets for which the optimal weights must be positive is no greater than approximately 10 or 20, a simple transformation of variables allows the optimization to remain unconstrained. The intuition is very simple: consider the trigonometric relationship

$$\sin^2 \theta + \cos^2 \theta = 1 \tag{24.11}$$

which holds true for any angle θ. If two quantities, say w_1 and w_2, are set equal to the squares of the sine and cosine terms above,

$$w_1 = \sin^2 \theta$$

$$w_2 = \cos^2 \theta$$

the (budget) constraint on the sum of the weights, $w^T 1 = 1$ is automatically satisfied. The generalization to M variables is then immediate: we simply have to use as optimization variables the $(M - 1)$ angles that define the surface of an $(M - 1)$-dimensional hypersphere[4] of unit radius:

$$e_k = \cos \theta_k \prod_{j=1}^{k-1} \sin \theta_j \quad k = 1, 2, \ldots, M - 1$$

$$e_k = \prod_{j=1}^{k-1} \sin \theta_j \quad k = M$$

---

[3] However, we occasionally may have to carry out a draw from a low-dimensional distribution of excited risk factors if a leaf has more than one market risk factor associated with it.

[4] Mathematicians (and relativists) define such a surface as an S^{k-1} sphere, where k is the number of the dimensions of the space in which the surface is embedded, and $k - 1$ the number of *intrinsic* coordinates necessary to specify a point on the surface. So, the perimeter of a circle is an S^1 sphere, and the surface of a three-dimensional sphere an S^2 sphere. We do not use this terminology.

The optimization is then achieved

- by starting from an initial inspired guess for the angles, $\{\theta\}$ (or, failing that, from random variates drawn from the uniform $\mathcal{U}[0, 2\pi]$ distribution);
- by obtaining the weights as $w_i = e_i^2$. Note that this choice automatically ensures both the non-negativity of the weights and the budget constraints;
- by maximizing the utility *in an unconstrained manner* over the angles.

Appendix 25.A provides an alternative formulation taken from Doust and Chien (2008) for the weights which can be numerically more efficient, and which can allow the portfolio manager to work with a higher number of variables.

24.3.2 *Enforcing the concentration constraints*

Suppose then that the portfolio manager has concentration constraints, of the type

$$0 < K_k^{\text{lower}} \le w_k \le K_k^{\text{upper}} < 1 \qquad (24.12)$$

The utility optimization can still be carried out as above in an unconstrained manner over 'angles' with a minor modification:

$$w_k = K_k^{\text{lower}} + \left(K_k^{\text{upper}} - K_k^{\text{lower}}\right) e_k^2 \qquad (24.13)$$

Note, however, that by proceeding in this manner the budget constraint is lost, unless we have the same upper and lower concentration constraints for all the asset classes: $K_k^{\text{upper}} = K^{\text{upper}}$ and $K_k^{\text{lower}} = K^{\text{lower}}$, in which case summing over the weights in Equation (24.13) gives

$$\sum_{k=1,l} w_k = l * K^{\text{lower}} + (K^{\text{upper}} - K^{\text{lower}}) \qquad (24.14)$$

As

$$\sum_{k=1,l} w_k = 1 \qquad (24.15)$$

one immediately obtains

$$K^{\text{upper}} = 1 - (l - 1)K^{\text{lower}} \qquad (24.16)$$

24.4 Optimal allocation with k determined via Maximum Entropy

We saw in Section 20.6 that we can determine a Maximum-Entropy distribution for the normalization factor k. If we follow this approach – i.e., we think of the probability of nothing happening as a distribution and not a number – how would the optimal allocations to the various asset classes change?

In the case of a fixed k, we have found that the optimal allocation (i.e., the optimal values for the weights w) is obtained by maximizing (under the desired constraints) the expectation of the utility:

$$E[U] = \int U(W_{t_0}[1 + \boldsymbol{w}^\mathsf{T}\boldsymbol{r}(\Delta\boldsymbol{\xi})])\varphi(\Delta\boldsymbol{\xi})d(\Delta\boldsymbol{\xi})$$

$$= \int U(W_{t_0}[1 + \boldsymbol{w}^\mathsf{T}\boldsymbol{r}(\Delta\boldsymbol{\xi})]) \sum_{i=0,M} p_i\varphi_i(\Delta\boldsymbol{\xi})d(\Delta\boldsymbol{\xi}) \qquad (24.17)$$

$$\boldsymbol{w}^* = \arg\max_{w \in \Theta}[E(U)]$$

If k is not a known value, but follows a distribution $g(k; \Omega)$ (where Ω is a parameter giving the level of confidence in the true value of k) the optimization that must now be carried out is the following. Recall first that

$$\varphi(\Delta\boldsymbol{\xi}; k) = (1 - k)\varphi_0(\Delta\boldsymbol{\xi}) + \frac{k}{1 - p_0} \sum_{i>0} p_i\varphi_i(\Delta\boldsymbol{\xi})d(\Delta\boldsymbol{\xi}) \qquad (24.18)$$

Then

$$E_g(U) = \int_0^1 g(k; \Omega) \left[\int U(W_{t_0}[1 + \boldsymbol{w}^\mathsf{T}\boldsymbol{r}(\Delta\boldsymbol{\xi})])\varphi(\Delta\boldsymbol{\xi}; k)d(\Delta\boldsymbol{\xi})\right] dk \qquad (24.19)$$

Dropping the arguments to lighten notation we get

$$\int_0^1 g(k; \Omega) \left[\int U(W_{t_0}[1 + \boldsymbol{w}^\mathsf{T}\boldsymbol{r}]) \left((1 - k)\varphi_0 + \frac{k}{1 - p_0} \sum_{i>0} p_i\varphi_i\right) d(\Delta\boldsymbol{\xi})\right] dk$$

$$(24.20)$$

$$\boldsymbol{w}_f^* = \arg\max_{w \in \Theta}\{E_f(U)\} \qquad (24.21)$$

We note in passing that a tempting approach would be to obtain an optimal weight allocation that takes into account the uncertainty over the normalization factored, say, $\overline{\boldsymbol{w}}_g$, by averaging over the distribution $g(k; \Omega)$ the k-dependent optimal allocations, $\overline{\boldsymbol{w}}(k)$:

$$\overline{\boldsymbol{w}}_g = \int_0^1 \overline{\boldsymbol{w}}(k)g(k)dk \qquad (24.22)$$

This approach, intuitively appealing as it may be, is not correct in the context of a utility maximization framework. Michaud (1989) follows a similar procedure when he recommends averaging (via resampling) over the parameters of the distribution of returns. When he does so, however, mean-variance is taken as an *a priori* allocation criterion of (presumably) self-evident appeal, and is not derived within the context of an expected-utility-maximization approach. If we work in an expected-utility-maximization framework, the expectation must be taken over all the sources of uncertainty at the same time – which is just what Equation (24.20) does. The difference, as usual, lies in the difference between averages of expectations and expectations of averages.

Going back to the correct optimization (Equation (24.20)), carrying out the integration with respect to k is straightforward. As the density $g(k; \Omega)$ normalizes to 1 we obtain:

$$E_g(U) = \int U(W_{t_0}[1 + \mathbf{w}^\mathsf{T}\mathbf{r}]) \left((1 - \mu_k)\varphi_0 + \frac{\mu_k}{1 - p_0} \sum_{i>0} p_i\varphi_i \right) d(\Delta\xi) \quad (24.23)$$

with

$$\mu_k = \int_0^1 kg(k; \Omega)dk \quad (24.24)$$

The conclusion is therefore that, after we make the replacement $k \to \mu_k$, the solution of (24.20) is given by the optimal allocation evaluated at one particular point, the average value of k.

This particularly simple solution only comes about because of the very special dependence (linear) of the distribution on the parameter k. If the uncertainty had been in a distributional parameter that affects non-linearly the distribution (say, in the mean or the variance), the result would not be so simple. We mentioned in Section 20.7 that the Johnson distribution can be an appealing functional choice to describe the uncertainty about the factor k. If this choice is made, we note in closing that for the Johnson distribution mode and median do not coincide, so the allocation solution at the average point is different from the solution at the mode.

25 Approximations

25.1 The purpose of this chapter

The results presented in the previous chapter provide a general, if rather brute-force, solution to the optimization problem which has been set up throughout the book. If some approximations are made, the optimization and the sensitivity analysis described in Chapter 28 can be carried out very efficiently. In particular, we intend to show in this chapter:

1. how to calculate the weights if we are happy to expand the chosen power utility function to second order;
2. how to calculate the weights if we are happy to match the first two moments of the true spliced distribution and the first two moments of a multivariate Gaussian;
3. how to deduce at trivial computational cost the optimal allocation weights once the optimization has been carried out for one particular value of the normalization constant, k.

These approximations are useful in their own rights. However, they also give us the tools to explore deeper questions, namely, why second-order expansions turn out to be so effective. Once we understand why this is the case, it will become apparent that a much simpler approach than the full expected-utility optimization can produce results which are almost as accurate, and far more intuitive, than the 'full' solution.

We present the theory behind these approximations in the remainder of the chapter, and we discuss how well they work in the next chapter.

25.2 Utility maximization – the Gaussian case

We have normality. I repeat, we have normality. Anything you still can't cope with is therefore your own problem. Douglas Adams, The Hitchhiker's Guide to the Galaxy

The procedure presented in the previous section provides a general solution to the expected-utility-maximization problem. This solution can be rather laborious, especially if it has to be repeated several times in the early stages of fine-tuning of the construction of a Bayesian net. Can we obtain a simpler, approximate, but still accurate, solution?

As mentioned above, this can be achieved by attacking the problem from two distinct angles:

1. first, we can use, instead of the true joint spliced distribution obtained as shown in Chapter 20, a multivariate Gaussian distribution with the same first and second moments;
2. second, we can expand to second order the chosen power utility function.

In principle, it seems as if we have four possible 'permutations': we could work with the full spliced distribution or the moment-matched associated multivariate Gaussian distribution; and/or we could work with the full utility function, or with the utility function expanded to second order. A moment's reflection shows, however, that if we choose to work with the second-order expansion of the utility function we obtain exactly the same results as if we use the full spliced distribution, or the second-order matched multivariate Gaussian distribution. Therefore, if we can show – as we will in the following – that working with a second-order expansion of the utility function entails little loss of accuracy,[1] a powerful shortcut beacons: we could work without any further loss of accuracy with the moment-matched multivariate Gaussian distribution, and turn the multi-dimensional Monte-Carlo optimization described in the previous chapter into a much simpler unidimensional maximization. This is, of course, due to the fact that, when the returns are Gaussian, the portfolio expected return and variance, $\mathbb{E}[R_\Pi]$ and $\text{Var}[R_\Pi]$, are simply given by

$$\mathbb{E}[R_\Pi] = \sum_i w_i \mathbb{E}[R_i] \qquad (25.1)$$

and

$$\text{Var}[R_\Pi] = \sum_{i,j} w_i w_j \sigma_i \sigma_j \rho_{ij} \qquad (25.2)$$

All of this will become clearer subsequently, but our strategy is now the following: first we obtain the first two moments of the spliced distribution (to which the moments of the multivariate Gaussian will be matched); then we match the moments of the two distributions;[2] finally (and this we do in the following chapters) we explain why doing so can be justified.

25.3 Matching the moments of the true and Gaussian distributions

As explained above, as a first step we would like to use instead of the true distribution, $\varphi(\Delta\xi_1, \Delta\xi_n, \ldots, \Delta\xi_N)$, a multivariate Gaussian with the same first two moments. To

---

[1] At least over realistic changes in wealth.   [2] See Sections 25.3.1 to 25.3.3.

do this we must calculate the moments of the true distribution. To lighten notation, when no ambiguity can arise, we write

$$\varphi(\Delta\xi_1, \Delta\xi_n, \ldots, \Delta\xi_N) = \varphi(\Delta\xi)$$

To refresh our memory, recall again that the total joint distribution, $\varphi(\Delta\xi)$, can be written as

$$\varphi(\Delta\xi) = \sum_{i=0,2^{N_{\text{leaf}}}-1} p_i \varphi_i(\Delta\xi) \tag{25.3}$$

where the distribution associated with joint event i is given by:

$$\varphi_i(\Delta\xi) = \psi_{\text{comp}}^0 \left(\Delta\xi_1, \Delta\xi_2, \ldots, \Delta\xi_{n_{\text{norm}}^i}\right) \prod_{k=1,n_{\text{exc}}^i} \psi_k^{\text{exc}}(\Delta\xi) \tag{25.4}$$

where ψ_{comp}^0 is the 'compacted' distribution, obtained as in Section 22.4.3. We also remind the reader that we made the assumption that each basis distribution, $\psi_k^{\text{exc}}(\Delta\xi)$, should be of the type

$$\psi_k^{\text{exc}}(\Delta\xi) = \mathcal{N}\left(\mu_{\text{exc}}^k, \Sigma_{\text{exc}}^k\right)$$

where, in most cases, for $i \neq 0$, the covariance matrix Σ_{exc}^k will just be a number, expressing our uncertainty about the precise realization of the draw(s) for the variable(s) associated with the kth leaf if this leaf is in the excited state.

Now, we have set up our Bayesian net in such a way that all price-sensitive events (changes in market risk factors) are associated with leaves – and, incidentally, all leaves are associated with price-sensitive events: if they were not, there would have been no reason for building the tree out to those leaves.

As for the price-sensitive events, we have stipulated that we are only going to consider those changes in market risk factors that affect the portfolio under consideration. See in this regard the discussion in Chapter 13, and Sections 13.2 and 13.5 in particular. Given this set-up, one leaf can have more than one risk factor associated with it, but no two leaves are associated with the same risk factor.

To keep our notation simple we denote the event associated to leaf j by E_j and the probability of it being true by $P(E_j)$ (without any special symbol to remind ourselves that we are dealing with a leaf-event), but we should keep this in mind in the rest of this subsection. Finally, recall that the event variance, $\text{Var}_s(E_j)$ of variable E_j is given by[3]

$$\text{Var}_s(E_j) = P(E_j)(1 - P(E_j)) \tag{25.5}$$

We now have all the ingredients required for the evaluation of the first and second moments of the full spliced distribution. We do so for the case when Boolean variables are associated with the leaves. The extension to multivalued variables is conceptually straightforward, but the expressions become more cumbersome.

---

[3] See Rebonato (2010a) for a simple derivation.

25.3.1 First moment

The evaluation of the first 'total' moment of the change in the market risk factor, $\Delta\xi_j$, is straightforward. Define $E_T[\cdot]$ the 'total' expectation operator (i.e., the expectation over the full – normal plus excited – distribution), $E_{norm}[\cdot]$ the normal-times expectation operator and $E_{exc}[\cdot]$ the expectation operator in the excited state. By the discussion above, the market risk factor $\Delta\xi_j$ is associated with one and only one node – the node with event E_j. We therefore have for the first moment

$$E_T[\Delta\xi_j] = \left(1 - k + \frac{k}{1-p_0}(1 - P(E_j) - p_0)\right) E_{norm}[\Delta\xi_j]$$

$$+ \frac{k}{1-p_0}P(E_j)E_{exc}[\Delta\xi_j] \tag{25.6}$$

This expression reduces to:

$$E_T[\Delta\xi_j] = (1 - P(E_j))E_{norm}[\Delta\xi_j] + P(E_j)E_{exc}[\Delta\xi_j] \tag{25.7}$$

at the point $k = 1 - p_0$.

25.3.2 Second moments: variance

To calculate the second 'total' moment of $\Delta\xi_j$ we must evaluate

$$Var_T(\Delta\xi_j) = E_T\left[\Delta\xi_j^2\right] - (E_T[\Delta\xi_j])^2$$

We begin with the first term, i.e., the 'total' expectation of $\Delta\xi_j^2$, $E_T[\Delta\xi_j^2]$:

$$E_T\left[\Delta\xi_j^2\right] = \left(1 - k + \frac{k}{1-p_0}(1 - P(E_j) - p_0)\right) E_{norm}\left[\xi_j^2\right]$$

$$+ \frac{k}{1-p_0}P(E_j)E_{exc}\left[\xi_j^2\right]$$

Now, we define the following quantities:

$$P'(E_j) = k - \frac{k}{1-p_0}(1 - P(E_j) - p_0)$$

$$P''(E_j) = \frac{k}{1-p_0}P(E_j)$$

and[4] by adding and subtracting the terms $(1 - P'(E_j))^2 E_{norm}[\xi_j^2]$ and $P''(E_j)^2 E_{exc}[\xi_j^2]$ we rewrite the expression for the variance as:

$$Var_T[\Delta\xi_j] = (1 - P'(E_j))^2 Var_{norm}[\Delta\xi_j] + Var_s[\widetilde{E}_j']E_{norm}\left[\Delta\xi_j^2\right]$$

$$+ Var_s[E_j'']E_{exc}\left[\xi_j^2\right] + P''(E_j)^2 Var_{exc}[\xi_j]$$

$$- 2(1 - P'(E_j))P''(E_j)E_{norm}[\Delta\xi_j]E_{exc}[\Delta\xi_j] \tag{25.8}$$

[4] One can easily verify that $P' = P''$ at $k = 1 - p_0$. The P' and P'' are not necessarily probabilities.

where again $\mathrm{Var}_{\mathrm{norm}}$ indicates the normal-times variance, $\mathrm{Var}_s(E_j)$ is the event variance of E_j, and

$$\mathrm{Var}_s[E'] = P'(E)(1 - P'(E)) \tag{25.9}$$

A similar expression holds for $\mathrm{Var}_s[E'']$. At $k = 1 - p_0$ this expression reduces to:

$$\mathrm{Var}_T[\Delta\xi_j] = (1 - P(E_j))^2\mathrm{Var}_{\mathrm{norm}}[\Delta\xi_j] + \mathrm{Var}_s[\tilde{E}_j]E_{\mathrm{norm}}\left[\Delta\xi_j^2\right]$$

$$+ \mathrm{Var}_s[E_j]E_{\mathrm{exc}}\left[\xi_j^2\right] + P(E_j)^2\mathrm{Var}_{\mathrm{exc}}[\xi_j]$$

$$- 2(1 - P(E_j))P(E_j)E_{\mathrm{norm}}[\Delta\xi_j]E_{\mathrm{exc}}[\Delta\xi_j] \tag{25.10}$$

25.3.3   Second moments: covariance

For the covariance we need to evaluate the joint expectation of $\Delta\xi_j$ and $\Delta\xi_i$, with $j \neq i$:

$$E_T[\Delta\xi_i\Delta\xi_j] = \left(1 - k + \frac{k}{1 - p_0}(P(\tilde{E}_i, \tilde{E}_j) - p_0)\right) E_{\mathrm{norm}}[\Delta\xi_i\Delta\xi_j]$$

$$+ \frac{k}{1 - p_0}P(\tilde{E}_i, E_j)E_{\mathrm{norm}}[\Delta\xi_i]E_{\mathrm{exc}}[\Delta\xi_j]$$

$$+ \frac{k}{1 - p_0}P(\tilde{E}_j, E_i)E_{\mathrm{norm}}[\Delta\xi_j]E_{\mathrm{exc}}[\Delta\xi_i]$$

$$+ \frac{k}{1 - p_0}P(E_i, E_j)E_{\mathrm{exc}}[\Delta\xi_i]E_{\mathrm{exc}}[\Delta\xi_j] \tag{25.11}$$

After some substitutions and manipulations we obtain:

$$\mathrm{Cov}_T(\Delta\xi_i, \Delta\xi_j) = P'(\tilde{E}_i, \tilde{E}_j)E_{\mathrm{norm}}[\Delta\xi_i\Delta\xi_j]$$

$$+ P''(\tilde{E}_i, E_j)E_{\mathrm{norm}}[\Delta\xi_i]E_{\mathrm{exc}}[\Delta\xi_j]$$

$$+ P''(\tilde{E}_j, E_i)E_{\mathrm{norm}}[\Delta\xi_j]E_{\mathrm{exc}}[\Delta\xi_i]$$

$$+ P''(E_i, E_j)E_{\mathrm{exc}}[\Delta\xi_i]E_{\mathrm{exc}}[\Delta\xi_j]$$

$$- (1 - P'(E_i))(1 - P'(E_j))E_{\mathrm{norm}}[\Delta\xi_i]E_{\mathrm{norm}}[\Delta\xi_j]$$

$$- P''(E_i)P''(E_j)E_{\mathrm{exc}}[\Delta\xi_i]E_{\mathrm{exc}}[\Delta\xi_j]$$

$$- (1 - P'(E_i))P''(E_j)E_{\mathrm{norm}}[\Delta\xi_i]E_{\mathrm{exc}}[\Delta\xi_j]$$

$$- (1 - P'(E_j))P''(E_i)E_{\mathrm{norm}}[\Delta\xi_j]E_{\mathrm{exc}}[\Delta\xi_i] \tag{25.12}$$

where again

$$P'(E_j) = k - \frac{k}{1 - p_0}(1 - P(E_j) - p_0)$$

$$P''(E_j) = \frac{k}{1 - p_0}P(E_j)$$

and

$$P'(E_i, E_j) = k - \frac{k}{1 - p_0}(1 - P(E_i, E_j) - p_0)$$

$$P''(E_i, E_j) = \frac{k}{1 - p_0}P(E_i, E_j)$$

with obvious modifications where the events E_i and/or E_j are replaced by their negations. The expression can be simplified at the point $k = 1 - p_0$. By adding and subtracting $P(\widetilde{E}_i)P(\widetilde{E}_j)E_{\text{norm}}[\Delta\xi_i\Delta\xi_j]$ we finally get to:

$$\begin{aligned}
\text{Cov}_T[\Delta\xi_i, \Delta\xi_j] = {} & P(\widetilde{E}_i)P(\widetilde{E}_j)\text{Cov}_{\text{norm}}[\Delta\xi_i, \Delta\xi_j] \\
& + \text{Cov}_s[\widetilde{E}_i, \widetilde{E}_j]E_{\text{norm}}[\Delta\xi_i\Delta\xi_j] \\
& + \text{Cov}_s[E_i, E_j]E_{\text{exc}}[\Delta\xi_i]E_{\text{exc}}[\Delta\xi_j] \\
& + \text{Cov}_s[\widetilde{E}_i, E_j]E_{\text{norm}}[\Delta\xi_i]E_{\text{exc}}[\Delta\xi_j] \\
& + \text{Cov}_s[E_i, \widetilde{E}_j]E_{\text{norm}}[\Delta\xi_j]E_{\text{exc}}[\Delta\xi_i] \qquad (25.13)
\end{aligned}$$

It is important to stress that this result is valid only for $i \neq j$. (For the case $i = j$ see expression (25.10).) Indeed, it is the independence between the excited distributions that allows the split of the last term in Equation (25.11).

Equations (25.6), (25.8) and (25.12) achieve our goal: they provide us with the first and second moments of the full 'true' distribution of market risk factors, and they tell us how to associate to the full spliced 'true' distribution a unique multivariate Gaussian distribution. We shall denote this multivariate Gaussian distribution by $\mathcal{N}(\Delta\xi; \Delta\xi_T, \Sigma_T)$, or $\mathcal{N}(\Delta\xi)$ for brevity when it is not essential to highlight the mean and covariance of the distribution.

We will discuss in the next chapter the surprising effectiveness of this approximation.

25.4 Efficient optimization for different values of k

We now move to a different type of approximation altogether. We assume that, either using the full non-linear optimization, or the approximate methods described above, we have obtained a set of optimal allocation weights for a particular value of k (linked, as we know, to the probability of the nothing-happens event). We now ask ourselves whether we can accurately deduce the optimal weights that would apply to different values of k, without having to redo *ex novo* the optimization for each k value.

This would be in practice very useful, because in order to perform the sensitivity analysis described in Chapter 26 we would like to carry out the optimization over the weights for several values of the relative mass of the 'normal' and 'excited' distribution. What we mean by this is the following: our Bayesian net may have assigned a probability of, say, 90% to the 'nothing-happens' event. This means that the body of the normal-times distribution will integrate up to 0.90. We may want to look at the stability of our allocation weights when these relative masses change over a reasonable range – i.e., when the normalization factor k is varied.

Repeating our numerical search for each new value of the normalization factor could easily turn a relatively simple numerical task into a rather burdensome one. We therefore present in this section a very fast, yet surprisingly accurate, approximate algorithm to infer optimal allocations for different values of k without resorting to a full Monte-Carlo simulation once the optimal allocation for one k has been obtained.

Let's write the joint probability of returns in the market risk factors in the following form:

$$\varphi(\Delta\xi) = (1 - k)\varphi_0(\Delta\xi) + \frac{k}{1 - p_0} \sum_{i>0} p_i\varphi_i(\Delta\xi)$$

What we have done is to take out of the summation the term $\varphi_0(\Delta\xi) = \psi_0(\Delta\xi)$, i.e., the distribution associated with the non-excited state of the world, and to write its weight as $1 - k$. The reason for doing this is that, if we set

$$k = 1 - p_0$$

we are, of course, back to the general formalism explored above. However, if we allow $k \neq 1 - p_0$, we will be able to explore how the results vary as a function of the relative weight of the normal and excited states. See in this respect the discussion in Section 20.6.

We want to obtain the optimal weights for an arbitrary value of k, given the optimal weights already obtained for a reference normalization value, $\tilde{k}$. We proceed in two steps.

25.4.1   Part I: Normal-times optimization
Let's first consider the optimization with respect to the normal-times distribution. Again, to lighten notation, we set the initial wealth to unity: $W_{t_0} = 1$.[5] In this case, the problem reduces to optimizing

$$E_{\text{norm}}[U] = \int U(1 + w^{\mathsf{T}}r(\Delta\xi))\psi_0(\Delta\xi)d(\Delta\xi) \tag{25.14}$$

where again $E_{\text{norm}}[\cdot]$ denotes the expectation operator in normal times, and we may want to add the constraints

$$\sum w_i = 1 \quad \text{(budget constraint)} \tag{25.15}$$

$$w_i \geq 0 \quad \text{(no-short-selling constraint)} \tag{25.16}$$

---

[5] As before, this requires a rescaling of any non-linear utility function.

Let's start by considering the problem without the no-short-selling constraint. Lagrange multipliers can be used to find a stationary point. By defining the Lagrangian function, Λ, as

$$\Lambda = E_{\text{norm}}[U] - \lambda \left(\sum w_i - 1 \right) \tag{25.17}$$

the following equations must be satisfied (necessary conditions):

$$\frac{\partial \Lambda}{\partial w_j} = 0, \ \frac{\partial \Lambda}{\partial \lambda} = 0 \tag{25.18}$$

or

$$\int \frac{\partial U(1 + w^{\mathsf{T}} r(\Delta \xi))}{\partial w_j} \psi_0(\Delta \xi) d(\Delta \xi) - \lambda = 0 \tag{25.19}$$

$$\sum w_i - 1 = 0 \tag{25.20}$$

(with the last equation being simply a restatement of the budget constraint).

Before proceeding, we want to derive a simple relationship that will be of use later on. Denote by $\overline{w}$ the optimal normal-times solution (we stress that the point $\overline{w}$ is only stationary with respect to the normal-times operator, $E_{\text{norm}}[\cdot]$). Then from the stationarity condition we have at the normal-times stationary point $\overline{w}$:

$$\int \frac{\partial U(1 + \overline{w}^{\mathsf{T}} r(\Delta \xi))}{\partial w_j} \psi_0(\Delta \xi) d(\Delta \xi)$$

$$= \int \frac{\partial U(1 + \overline{w}^{\mathsf{T}} r(\Delta \xi))}{\partial w_l} \psi_0(\Delta \xi) d(\Delta \xi), \quad \text{for any } j, l \tag{25.21}$$

25.4.2   *Part II: From normal times to full optimization*

Suppose then that we have already found the solution, $\overline{w}$, of the 'normal' part of the problem, and that we want to calculate the shift in weights $\overline{w} + \delta w$ that optimize the full problem (24.1), i.e., we want to optimize the weights with respect to the full (normal-plus-excited-times) operator, $E_{\mathsf{T}}[\cdot]$. To do so, we can expand the utility function around $\overline{w}$:

$$U(\overline{w} + \delta w) = U(\overline{w}) + J(\overline{w})\delta w + \frac{1}{2}\delta w^{\mathsf{T}} H \delta w \tag{25.22}$$

where J is the Jacobian matrix, which is a vector (the gradient) for the scalar-valued utility function of elements $J_j(\overline{w})$ and H is the square matrix of second-order partial derivatives of the utility function (the Hessian matrix) of elements $H_{lj}(\overline{w})$. We stress that the Jacobian and the Hessian contain derivatives of the utility with respect to the weights.

Again Lagrange multipliers can be used to find the maximum. If we define the Lagrangian as

$$\Lambda = E[U] - \lambda \left(\sum w_i - 1 \right) \tag{25.23}$$

the following equations must be satisfied at each stationary point:

$$\frac{\partial \Lambda}{\partial w_j} = 0, \quad \frac{\partial \Lambda}{\partial \lambda} = 0 \tag{25.24}$$

or

$$(1 - k) \int \frac{\partial U(1 + \boldsymbol{w}^{\mathrm{T}} \boldsymbol{r}(\Delta \boldsymbol{\xi}))}{\partial w_j} \varphi_0(\Delta \boldsymbol{\xi}) d(\Delta \boldsymbol{\xi})$$

$$+ \frac{k}{1 - p_0} \sum_{i>0} p_i \int \frac{\partial U(1 + \boldsymbol{w}^{\mathrm{T}} \boldsymbol{r}(\Delta \boldsymbol{\xi}))}{\partial w_j} \varphi_i(\Delta \boldsymbol{\xi}) d(\Delta \boldsymbol{\xi}) - \lambda = 0 \tag{25.25}$$

$$\sum w_i - 1 = 0 \tag{25.26}$$

We stress that Equation (25.25) differs from Equation (25.19) because we are now integrating over the full spliced distribution, not just the normal-times density.

Now, if we take the derivative with respect to the generic weight w_j of the expansion of the utility function we obtain

$$\frac{\partial U(1 + \overline{\boldsymbol{w}}^{\mathrm{T}} \boldsymbol{r}(\Delta \boldsymbol{\xi}))}{\partial w_j} = J_j(\overline{\boldsymbol{w}}) + \sum_i \delta w_i H_{ij}(\overline{\boldsymbol{w}}) \tag{25.27}$$

Substituting the expansion of the utility function around $\overline{\boldsymbol{w}}$ in Equation (25.25) we can therefore restate the first condition, $\frac{\partial \Lambda}{\partial w_j} = 0$, as:

$$\frac{\partial \Lambda}{\partial w_j} = \int J_j(\overline{\boldsymbol{w}}) \left[(1 - k_0) \varphi_0(\Delta \boldsymbol{\xi}) + \frac{k}{1 - p_0} \sum_{i>0} p_i \varphi_i(\Delta \boldsymbol{\xi}) \right] d(\Delta \boldsymbol{\xi})$$

$$+ \sum_l \delta w_l \left[\int H_{lj}(\overline{\boldsymbol{w}}_j) \left((1 - k_0) \varphi_0(\Delta \boldsymbol{\xi}) + \frac{k}{1 - p_0} \sum_{i>0} p_i \varphi_i(\Delta \boldsymbol{\xi}) \right) d(\Delta \boldsymbol{\xi}) \right] - \lambda = 0$$

$$\tag{25.28}$$

As for the second condition, $\frac{\partial \Lambda}{\partial \lambda} = 0$, it simply becomes

$$\frac{\partial \Lambda}{\partial \lambda} = - \sum_i \delta w_i = 0 \tag{25.29}$$

Therefore Equations (25.28) and (25.29) become a system of linear equations in the shifts $\delta \boldsymbol{w}$, with coefficients given by the value of the Hessian element H_{lj} averaged over the full (normal plus excited) distribution.

To lighten notation, define

$$h(\boldsymbol{\Delta\xi}, k) = (1 - k)\varphi_0(\boldsymbol{\Delta\xi}) + \frac{k}{1 - p_0} \sum_{i>0} p_i\varphi_i(\boldsymbol{\Delta\xi}) \tag{25.30}$$

Then in the first conditions we have integrals of the type

$$\int H_{lj}(\overline{\boldsymbol{w}})h(\boldsymbol{\Delta\xi})d\,\boldsymbol{\Delta\xi} \tag{25.31}$$

and

$$\int J_j(\overline{\boldsymbol{w}})h(\boldsymbol{\Delta\xi})d\,\boldsymbol{\Delta\xi} \tag{25.32}$$

These integral can be easily performed, once and for all, by means of simple Monte-Carlo techniques.

Once the integrals have been calculated, they are just coefficients. The associated system of equations can be solved with traditional linear algebra methods using a bordered Hessian.[6] The coefficients of the Lagrange multiplier are all -1, except for the equation $\sum \delta w_i = 0$, where it does not appear, and therefore its coefficient is zero. So, if we define the total bordered Hessian matrix as:

$$H_{\mathrm{T}} = \begin{bmatrix} \int H_{11}(\overline{\boldsymbol{w}})h(\boldsymbol{\Delta\xi})d\,\boldsymbol{\Delta\xi} & \int H_{12}(\overline{\boldsymbol{w}})h(\boldsymbol{\Delta\xi})d\,\boldsymbol{\Delta\xi} & \dots & -1 \\ \int H_{21}(\overline{\boldsymbol{w}})h(\boldsymbol{\Delta\xi})\boldsymbol{\Delta\xi} & \int H_{22}(\overline{\boldsymbol{w}})h(\boldsymbol{\Delta\xi})\boldsymbol{\Delta\xi} & \dots & -1 \\ \dots & \dots & \dots & \dots \\ -1 & -1 & \dots & 0 \end{bmatrix} \tag{25.33}$$

with $h(\boldsymbol{\Delta\xi}; k)$ as in Equation (25.30), we can express the solution as

$$\delta w_j = \frac{\det H_j}{\det H_{\mathrm{T}}} \tag{25.34}$$

where H_j is the total bordered Hessian matrix in which in the jth column the vector of coefficients is given by the Jacobian instead of the Hessian:

$$H_j = \begin{bmatrix} \int H_{11}(\overline{\boldsymbol{w}})h(\boldsymbol{\Delta\xi})d\,\boldsymbol{\Delta\xi} & \dots & -\int J_1(\overline{\boldsymbol{w}})h(\boldsymbol{\Delta\xi})d\,\boldsymbol{\Delta\xi} & \dots & -1 \\ \int H_{21}(\overline{\boldsymbol{w}})h(\boldsymbol{\Delta\xi})\boldsymbol{\Delta\xi} & \dots & -\int J_2(\overline{\boldsymbol{w}})h(\boldsymbol{\Delta\xi})\boldsymbol{\Delta\xi} & \dots & -1 \\ \dots & \dots & \dots & \dots & \dots \\ -1 & \dots & 0 & \dots & 0 \end{bmatrix} \tag{25.35}$$

---

[6] Bordered Hessians arise naturally in constrained optimizations, i.e., in problems when there is an extra equation for the Lagrange multiplier, λ. In our case, in the system of linear equations in the δws we have the Lagrange multiplier, λ, which is also unknown. The coefficients -1 in the bordered Hessian are associated with the unknown Lagrange multiplier, λ. See, e.g., Luenberger (2003).

We stress that these matrices are calculated at the 'normal-times' equilibrium point $\overline{w}$, and that they parametrically depend linearly on the normalization coefficient, k, because of the embedded dependence on k in the term $h(\Delta\xi) = h(\Delta\xi; k)$. Therefore, once these matrices have been calculated for one value of k, the value of each of their elements is immediately obtainable for any other value of k.

Finally, we note in the passing that in the case $k = 0$ the column containing the Jacobian is composed of identical elements because of Equation (25.21) we derived in Section 25.4.1:

$$\int \frac{\partial U(1 + \overline{w}^{\mathrm{T}} r(\Delta\xi))}{\partial w_j} \psi_0(\Delta\xi) d(\Delta\xi)$$

$$= \int \frac{\partial U(1 + \overline{w}^{\mathrm{T}} r(\Delta\xi))}{\partial w_l} \psi_0(\Delta\xi) d(\Delta\xi), \quad \text{for any } j, l$$

Since a matrix with two rows proportional to each other has a zero determinant, we recover that the shift δw_j of the weight w_j from the $k = 0$ allocation is trivially zero.

Equation (25.34) gives us the tool we were looking for to avoid re-optimizing over the weights for every different value of the normalization factor, k. Indeed, we can first compute the optimized solution for, say, $k = 0$. During this first optimization the elements of the matrices H_{T} and H_j can be evaluated and stored in memory at virtually no extra cost. Once they have been calculated and stored, they can then be reused to infer the shifts, δw, in the weights from the anchor solution (typically, the nothing-happens solution), $\overline{w}$, for any value of k using Equation (25.34).

25.4.3 Positivity constraints
If we introduce short selling constraints in the form $w_i > 0$ the equality (25.21) is in general no longer valid. However, one can still utilize the expansion of $U(w)$ around $\overline{w}$ and maximize the following expression over the weights for each k:

$$\int [U(\overline{w}) + J(\overline{w})\delta w] \left[(1 - k)\varphi_0(\Delta\xi) + \frac{k}{1 - p_0} \sum_{i>0} p_i \varphi_i(\Delta\xi) \right] d(\Delta\xi)$$

$$+ \frac{1}{2} \int [\delta w^{\mathrm{T}} H \delta w] \left[(1 - k)\varphi_0(\Delta\xi) + \frac{k}{1 - p_0} \sum_{i>0} p_i \varphi_i(\Delta\xi) \right] d(\Delta\xi) \quad (25.36)$$

For the numerical search one can resort to techniques which include inequality constraints such as the Kuhn–Tucker optimization. The function *fmincon* in MATLAB, which accepts inequality constraints, can be also used and the above expression is easily optimized over w.

If we also wanted to save the time for the initial Monte-Carlo simulation we could resort to the Taylor expansion of the utility around the final wealth value $1 + \mathbf{w}^\mathsf{T} r(\Delta \boldsymbol{\xi})$ and again make use of a fast numerical recipe. This procedure is described in Jondeau and Rockinger (2006).

We point out in closing this section that the method in this section makes use of a different expansion than the total-moments approximation discussed in the last sections of this chapter: in that case we were treating as expansion variables the changes in the market risk factors $(\Delta \boldsymbol{\xi})$; in the present case, the weights, $\mathbf{w}$. Moreover, the approximation in this section does not make any assumption (e.g., Gaussian assumption) about the distribution of the market risk factors. The weight expansion may fail if the allocations are unconstrained (i.e., if the weights, $\mathbf{w}$, can be positive or negative), as the solution can be pushed very far away from the reference point. However, it is unlikely that positivity constraints are not imposed in practice. When the weights are constrained to lie in [0 1] the weights expansion is generally very accurate, as shown in the next chapter.

Appendix 25.A

Various problems involve a constrained maximization or minimization over quantities whose squares must sum to 1.[7] Denoting by p_i these n squared quantities, this means that the constraints to be satisfied are

$$\sum_{i=1}^n p_i = 1, \quad p_i \geqslant 0 \text{ for all } i. \tag{25.37}$$

Without loss of generality we can think of the squared quantities as probabilities. One way to satisfy these conditions automatically (see Section 6.2.3) is to use internal variables θ_j $(j = 1, \ldots, n-1)$ where

$$p_i = p_i(\theta_j) = \begin{cases} \cos^2 \theta_1 & i = 1 \\ \sin^2 \theta_1 \cos^2 \theta_2 & i = 2 \\ \sin^2 \theta_1 \sin^2 \theta_2 \cos^2 \theta_3 & i = 3 \\ \vdots & \\ \sin^2 \theta_1 \ldots \sin^2 \theta_{n-2} \cos^2 \theta_{n-1} & i = n-1 \\ \sin^2 \theta_1 \ldots \sin^2 \theta_{n-2} \sin^2 \theta_{n-1} & i = n \end{cases} \tag{25.38}$$

and where $0 \leqslant \theta_j < \pi/2$.

However, assuming that numerical methods are being used to solve the problem at hand, Doust and Chien (2008) point out that Equation (25.38) is sub-optimal because

---

[7] The following is taken from Doust and Chien (2008) with thanks.

a uniform probability distribution for each θ_i implies $E(p_i) \sim 2^{-i}$ which is highly non-uniform.

A better transformation of variables is the following:

$$n = 2 \begin{cases} p_1 = \cos^2 \theta_1 \\ p_2 = \sin^2 \theta_1 \end{cases}$$

$$n = 3 \begin{cases} p_1 = \cos^2 \theta_1 \cos^2 \theta_2 \\ p_2 = \sin^2 \theta_1 \\ p_3 = \cos^2 \theta_1 \sin^2 \theta_2 \end{cases}$$

$$n = 4 \begin{cases} p_1 = \cos^2 \theta_1 \cos^2 \theta_2 \\ p_2 = \sin^2 \theta_1 \cos^2 \theta_3 \\ p_3 = \cos^2 \theta_1 \sin^2 \theta_2 \\ p_4 = \sin^2 \theta_1 \sin^2 \theta_3 \end{cases}$$

$$n = 5 \begin{cases} p_1 = \cos^2 \theta_1 \cos^2 \theta_2 \cos^2 \theta_4 \\ p_2 = \sin^2 \theta_1 \cos^2 \theta_3 \\ p_3 = \cos^2 \theta_1 \sin^2 \theta_2 \\ p_4 = \sin^2 \theta_1 \sin^2 \theta_3 \\ p_5 = \cos^2 \theta_1 \cos^2 \theta_2 \sin^2 \theta_4 \end{cases} \tag{25.39}$$

$$n = 6 \begin{cases} p_1 = \cos^2 \theta_1 \cos^2 \theta_2 \cos^2 \theta_4 \\ p_2 = \sin^2 \theta_1 \cos^2 \theta_3 \cos^2 \theta_5 \\ p_3 = \cos^2 \theta_1 \sin^2 \theta_2 \\ p_4 = \sin^2 \theta_1 \sin^2 \theta_3 \\ p_5 = \cos^2 \theta_1 \cos^2 \theta_2 \sin^2 \theta_4 \\ p_6 = \sin^2 \theta_1 \cos^2 \theta_3 \sin^2 \theta_5 \end{cases}$$

and so on.

Although it is hard to write down a closed-form formula for this algorithm, the rule to generate the formulae is easy to specify. To generate the formulae for $n = m$ given the formulae for $n = m - 1$, work down the formulae for $n = m - 1$ starting at p_1 and locate the first p_i with fewer sin / cos terms than p_1. Then multiply this p_i by $\cos^2 \theta_{m-1}$ and define p_m by using the original p_i but multiplied by $\sin^2 \theta_{m-1}$. If $m - 1$ is a power of 2 then all the p_i have the same number of terms, so modify p_1 to create p_m.

For (25.39), if the θ_i are uniformly distributed then $E(p_i)$ just depends on how many sin / cos terms the formula for p_i contains. If n is such that $2^{m-1} < n \leqslant 2^m$, all p_i will have either $m - 1$ or m sin / cos terms and $E(p_i) = 2^{-m-1}$ or 2^{-m} accordingly. Furthermore if $n = 2^m$ then $E(p_i) = 2^{-m}$ for all i and in these special cases the distribution will be uniform across the p_i.

For both (25.38) and (25.39) the derivatives $\frac{\partial p_i}{\partial \theta_j}$ are easy to calculate if needed. Again this is more easily specified by a rule rather than a formula as follows

$$\frac{\partial p_i}{\partial \theta_j} = \begin{cases} \dfrac{2p_i}{\tan(\theta_j)} & \text{if } p_i \text{ contains a term in } \sin^2 \theta_j \\ -2p_i \tan(\theta_j) & \text{if } p_i \text{ contains a term in } \cos^2 \theta_j \\ 0 & \text{otherwise} \end{cases} \tag{25.40}$$

Note that (25.37) guarantees that

$$\sum_i \frac{\partial p_i}{\partial \theta_j} = 0 \tag{25.41}$$

Part X

Analysis of portfolio allocation

In Parts I to IX we have presented the tools required to build a coherent asset allocation in the presence of stress events. In the last part of the book we look in detail at the allocations obtained using this procedure from three different perspectives.

In Chapter 26 we obtain the optimal allocations for a simple but realistic problem; we discuss the properties of the solution; and, what is most important, we try to understand the intuition behind the results.

In Chapter 27 we explore how well the many approximate numerical techniques that we have described in the previous chapters actually work. As we shall see, the answer is that they are surprisingly effective, and that they can therefore greatly reduce the computational burden of the optimization.

In Chapter 28 – one of the most important of the book – we look at the sensitivity of the results to the unavoidable uncertainty in the inputs. We shall discover that the allocations are very sensitive to the precise values of the expected returns. We hasten to stress that the high sensitivity of the results to the expected returns is not brought about by the Bayesian-net methodology – if anything, the latter goes some way towards stabilizing the results. But, as we shall see, there is something rather deep about asset allocation in general, and this lack of stability in particular, that these results will bring to light.

Finally, Chapter 29 draws on the results of Chapters 27 and 28 and on the discussion of ambiguity aversion (see Section 23.5) to present our final recommendations.

26 The full allocation procedure: a case study

In order to show how the procedure introduced in the previous chapters works in practice, we now present in some detail the asset allocation produced by the Bayesian net we have discussed in Chapter 16. We have chosen not to deal with a stylized example because we wanted to show the technique at work in a realistic case.

26.1 The scenario and the associated Bayesian net

We refer the reader to the detailed description of the scenario and of the associated Bayesian net provided in Chapter 16. For ease of reference we show again the net in Figure 26.1, with some modifications that we explain below.

We have placed ourselves in the shoes of a US$ asset manager who is responsible for a portfolio of UK assets, but who converts all gains and losses into US$.

We have also added a leaf to the net, associated with the 'market portfolio', M. This is required because we want to carry out the CAPM-related sanity checks described in Chapter 21 (see Section 21.5 in particular). For the sake of simplicity, the node associated with the market portfolio is assumed to depend directly on the outcome of the Sovereign Crisis (node A), and on whether either a UK or a European bank enters a state of distress (nodes B and C). We associated with the realization $M = TRUE$ the state of the world 'The market portfolio suffers a significant fall.' We quantify the magnitude of this fall below.

We assigned the following conditional probabilities to the new leaf node:

$$P(M|ABC) = 0.99$$
$$P(M|A\widetilde{B}C) = 0.90$$
$$P(M|AB\widetilde{C}) = 0.95$$
$$P(M|A\widetilde{B}\widetilde{C}) = 0.80$$
$$P(M|\widetilde{A}BC) = 0.70$$
$$P(M|\widetilde{A}\widetilde{B}C) = 0.60$$
$$P(M|\widetilde{A}B\widetilde{C}) = 0.80$$
$$P(M|\widetilde{A}\widetilde{B}\widetilde{C}) = 0.04 \tag{26.1}$$

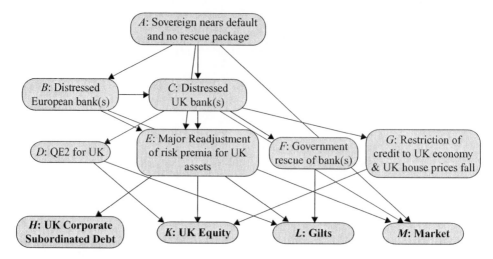

Figure 26.1 The Bayesian net used in this section. It is an adaptation of the Bayesian net developed in Chapter 16, with the addition of an additional *Market* node, which proxies the market portfolio. The *Market* node is required to carry out the CAPM ranking described in Chapter 21. See the text for a discussion.

The joint probability table after the non-market-risk-factor variables were integrated out (marginalized) is shown in Table 26.1. Table 26.2 shows the same quantity after integrating out the market portfolio.

Finally, from direct calculation the marginal probabilities associated with the four terminal leaves turned out to be as follows:

$$P(Credit) = 0.142$$
$$P(Equity) = 0.143$$
$$P(Bond) = 0.087$$
$$P(Market) = 0.069 \tag{26.2}$$

26.2   Data description

We looked at the following four indices as proxies for the asset classes of interest:

- the FTSE 100 Total Return index (*Equity*);
- the IBoxx GBP Corporate Subordinated Debt Total Return Index (*Credit*);
- the FTSE Government Securities UK Gilts Total Return Index (*Bond*);
- a portfolio made up of 60% of the JP Morgan Global Bonds Total Return Index and 40% of the S&P 1200 Global Total Return Index, chosen as a proxy for the market portfolio (*Market*).[1]

---

[1] For current review of market portfolio construction, see, e.g., Doeswijk, Lam and Swinkels (2011). See also, e.g., Bandourian and Winklemann (2003, esp. p. 91) for a discussion of the evolution of the proxies for the market portfolio, and for the recent choices. We find reassurance in the arguments by Rosenberg (1981) and Stambaugh (1982) that different but reasonable specifications of market portfolios have relatively modest impacts on CAPM-based asset allocations.

Table 26.1 *Joint probabilities of the market-risk-factor variables*

Credit	Equity	Bond	Market	Joint probability
0	0	0	0	0.6856
0	0	0	1	0.0336
0	0	1	0	0.0357
0	1	0	0	0.0853
1	0	0	0	0.0789
0	0	1	1	0.0030
0	1	0	1	0.0050
0	1	1	0	0.0077
1	0	0	1	0.0057
1	0	1	0	0.0096
1	1	0	0	0.0149
0	1	1	1	0.0027
1	0	1	1	0.0052
1	1	0	1	0.0039
1	1	1	0	0.0136
1	1	1	1	0.0098

Table 26.2 *Joint probabilities of the market-risk-factor variables, after integrating out the variable* Market

Credit	Equity	Bond	Joint probability
0	0	0	0.7192
0	0	1	0.0387
0	1	0	0.0903
1	0	0	0.0846
0	1	1	0.0104
1	0	1	0.0148
1	1	0	0.0188
1	1	1	0.0233

In order to estimate the parameters describing the body of the joint distribution we could have used a long data set, stretching back many years; or a more recent, and hence presumably more relevant, portion of it. In keeping with the philosophy presented in the previous chapters, we opted for a relatively small and recent subset of the available data. The reason for doing so is that we believe that different periods display different 'normal features' (for instance, different degrees of correlation between equities and bonds), and that, even for the body of the distribution, it is therefore important to capture its time-varying features. Our hope is that, after culling, the parameters that describe the joint distribution of the risk factors over this relatively short sample period will be reasonably representative of the next investment horizon.

Table 26.3 *The gains or losses associated with the terminal leaves*

Asset class	Stress loss/gain
Credit	−18%
Equity	−23%
Bond	+5%
Market	−18%

Choosing a 'homogeneous' period is, of course, far from easy, and a lot of subjective judgement is involved. The occurrence of a crisis often ushers in a different regime,[2] with different, relatively stable, relationships between the asset classes. But this is not always the case. The Greenspan years, for instance, have seen many crises (from the bursting of dot.com bubble, to September 11th, to the defaults of Russia and the Long-Term Capital Management (LTCM) debacle); yet the underlying philosophy of using monetary tools to counter unexpected negative shocks, or to 'mop up' the debris of the bursting of a bubble remained fundamentally unchanged. So, if one takes out the individual crisis, one can hope that the relationships between asset classes in the normal periods *of the Greenspan years* may be relatively stable. (Of course, one can do better than hoping, and a battery of statistical tests can be deployed to test the validity of the hypothesis.)

The post-Lehman-crisis years, however, have arguably been *qualitatively* different from the Great Moderation of the Greenspan era: short-term rates, by approaching zero, have dulled the efficacy of traditional monetary tools; both deflation and inflation have begun to be perceived as real dangers; 'unconventional' monetary techniques, such as quantitative easing, have come to the fore; and the long-forgotten dynamics of depression economics appear to have resurfaced. And, of course, the loss in confidence in the creditworthiness of erstwhile rock-solid government debt has given a totally new complexion to the investment landscape.[3]

So, we have chosen the post-Lehman years as representative of the 'new normal' and, in order to obtain conditional rather than long-term estimates, we have made use of the last 756 data points (out of the available 1473), covering the period May 2009 to May 2012. These 756 data points should reflect the post-crisis environment, and should contain information about normal-times behaviour during the unsettled sovereign-crisis period the scenario in question focuses on. These data points constitute what we refer to in the following as the 'full sample'.

The losses or gains associated with the final leaves were as in Table 26.3.

---

[2] Here we use the word 'regime' in a colloquial and rather loose sense, without implying that we are referring to the precise 'regime shifts' discussed in Chapter 4.

[3] For a discussion of the radical change in macroeconomic thinking regarding the proper role of central banks, and the types of interventions they can most profitably engage in, see, e.g., Blanchard *et al.* (2012, Chs 1, 2 and 4).

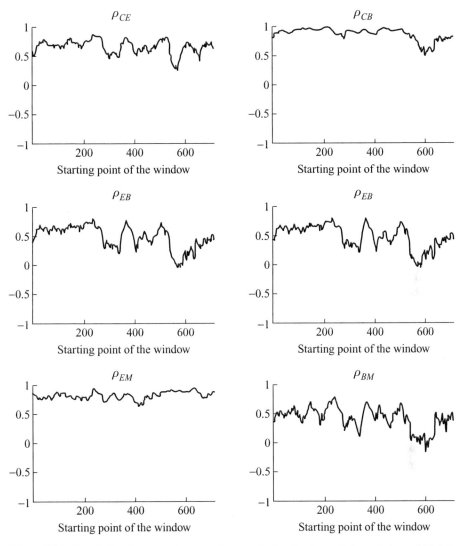

Figure 26.2 Correlations between the asset classes calculated using a sliding window of 40 data points on the full sample (i.e., before culling).

26.3 Analysing the body of the distribution

26.3.1 *Correlations and volatilities before culling*
Figures 26.2 and 26.3, respectively, display the correlations between, and the volatilities of, the four asset classes using the full sample. We obtained them using a simple-minded 40-day rolling window. As we are interested in the qualitative behaviour of these quantities, this crude estimate is adequate for our purpose.

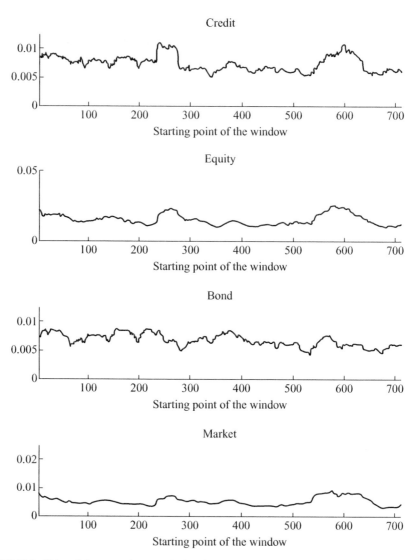

Figure 26.3 Volatilities of the asset classes calculated using a sliding window of 40 data points on the full sample.

We note that the correlation between *Equity* and *Bond* is strong, positive and stable during the first year (at a level of approximately 50%), and then fluctuates in a pronounced manner in the last two-thirds of the sample, dipping at times below zero and averaging around 25%. This should be contrasted with the correlation between *Equity* and *Credit*, which, despite similarly located fluctuations, remains far more stable (and positive) throughout the whole sample. This despite the fact that the correlation between *Bond* and *Credit* is very high and stable, averaging around 80% and never dipping below 50%. This suggests that whatever factor *Bond* and *Credit* do *not* have in common is responsible for the very different degrees of correlation with *Equity*.

Not surprisingly the correlation between *Market* on the one hand, and *Equity* and *Bond* on the other, is overall strong and positive (after all, *Market* is made up of bonds and equities, albeit of non-exactly-overlapping currencies). However, the correlation is far higher and more stable between *Market* and *Equity* than between *Market* and *Bond*, despite the greater weight to *Bond* in the index. This is, of course, due to the greater volatility of *Equity*. See below.

Moving to volatilities, Figure 26.3 highlights that *Equity*, *Credit* and *Bond* display decreasing degrees of volatility in that order (note the different scale for the y-axis for *Equity*). We also note synchronized spikes of volatility for *Credit* and *Equity*, both at the beginning of the second year of data, and in the middle of the last year. As noted above, this points to a common factor affecting *Credit* and *Equity*.

26.3.2   Truncation

After choosing our reference period, we proceeded with the removal of the 'outliers'. There have been bouts of great volatility in the period under study, associated with the European-sovereigns-related recurring crises which have punctuated the period in question. These bouts of volatility will, of course, be picked out by the culling techniques described in Chapter 17. Whether this culling will remove 'structurally' different patches – i.e., time periods with significantly different relationships between asset classes – or will simply take out more volatile, but otherwise similar, sub-periods can only be ascertained after the operation. An examination of the original and post-culling correlation matrix is, in this respect, very useful. We discuss this in what follows.

Figure 26.4 displays the behaviour of the ellipsoid volume, of the determinant of the correlation matrix, of the determinant of the covariance matrix, of the changes in ellipsoid volume, of the changes in the determinant of the correlation matrix and of the changes in the determinant of the covariance matrix as more and more points are removed.

Using the techniques described in Chapter 18, we decided to remove 10% of the data points. We discuss below the effect of this culling.

26.3.3   Correlations and volatilities after culling

We show in Figures 26.5 and 26.6 the correlation among and the volatilities of the four asset classes, respectively.

We note that the correlations, unsurprisingly, appear more stable – note, in particular the correlation between *Credit* and *Bond* in the last 150 data points. However, by and large, there is no fundamental change: those correlations that were stable before the culling remain stable after the culling (even more so); those that were fluctuating

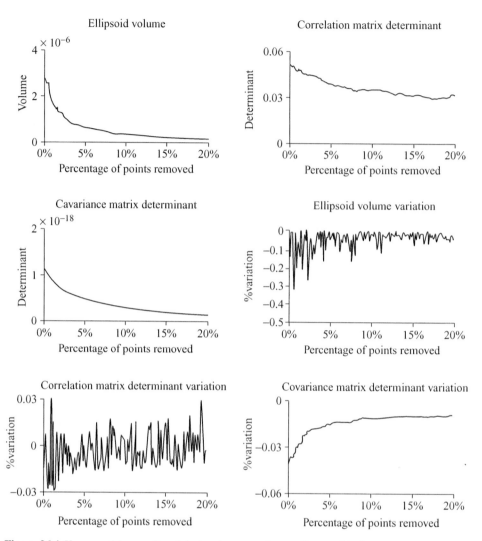

Figure 26.4 Key quantities monitored during the truncation, as discussed in the text. See picture labels for a description.

only display a minor degree of stabilization. Therefore, *for the particular period under observation*, the culling procedure does not bring about substantially different codependence patterns before and after the operation. We stress, however, that this need not be the case. We show, for instance, in Figures 26.7 and 26.8 similar graphs obtained over a longer period. In this case we removed a smaller fraction (a bit more than 5%) than the fraction culled in the present exercise. Yet note how in this case the culling almost perfectly removes the localized sharp drops in correlation between *Credit* and *Bond*, and stabilizes the correlation at a very high level.

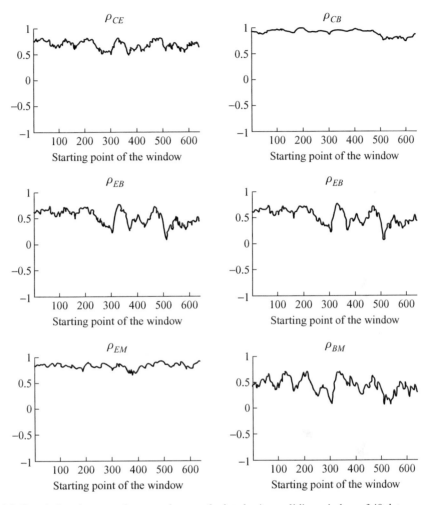

Figure 26.5 Correlations between the asset classes calculated using a sliding window of 40 data points after the culling.

The point to stress here is that the effectiveness of the culling procedure in stabilizing the correlation structure can only be ascertained on a case-by-case basis after the analysis.

Coming back to our data, and focusing now on volatility, it comes as no surprise that its overall level is significantly reduced after the culling.[4] See Table 26.4, which shows the individual elements of the correlation matrix before and after the culling (the number in parentheses refers to the post-culling correlation). What is more interesting

---

[4] This is plausible, but not automatic. We are using Mahalanobis distance – hence, low-volatility but different-correlation points may be culled.

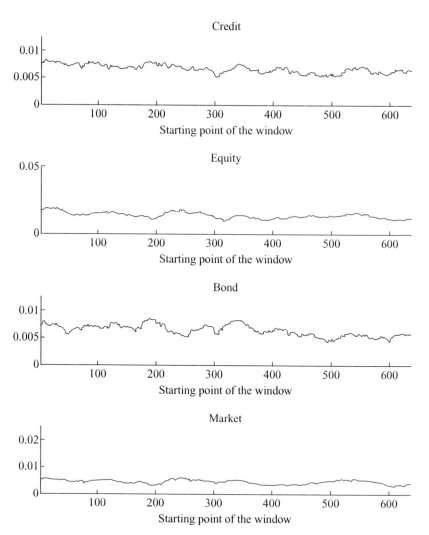

Figure 26.6 Volatilities of the asset classes calculated using a sliding window of 40 data points after culling.

is that the culling reduces the volatility clustering clearly visible in the full data set, especially for *Credit* and *Equity*. Compare in this respect Figures 26.3 and 26.6.

Table 26.4 *The individual elements of the correlation matrix before and after the culling (the number in parentheses refers to the post-culling correlation)*

	Credit	Equity	Bond	Market
Credit	1	0.645 (0.674)	0.833 (0.890)	0.551 (0.556)
Equity	0.644 (0.674)	1	0.429 (0.507)	0.831 (0.813)
Bond	0.833 (0.890)	0.429 (0.507)	1	0.370 (0.414)
Market	0.551 (0.556)	0.831 (0.813)	0.370 (0.414)	1

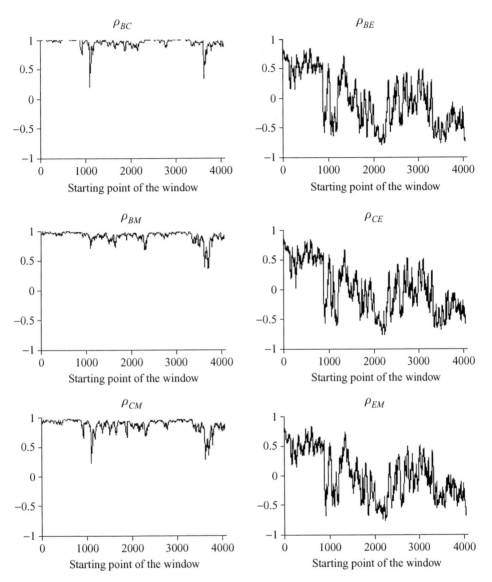

Figure 26.7 Correlations between the four asset classes calculated in a sliding window of 40 data points on a long sample (no culling).

After the culling the volatilities for the four asset classes are as shown in Table 26.5.

We note that *Equity* is by far the most volatile asset class, and *Market* has a lower volatility than either *Bond* or *Equity*, thanks to the diversification benefit it enjoys. This points to a very low, or possibly even negative, correlation between *Bond* and *Equity* in the period in question.

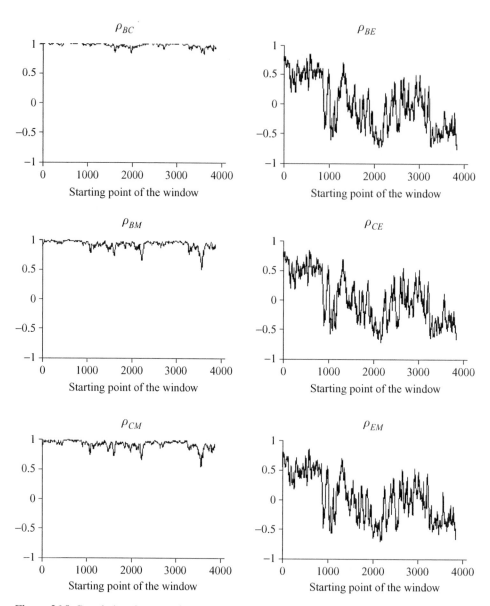

Figure 26.8 Correlations between the four asset classes calculated in a sliding window of 40 data points on a long sample after culling.

26.4   Fitting the body of the joint distribution

As described in Part VI, we carried out a separate fit to the marginals and to the copulae.[5] An example of the fits is provided in Figure 26.9 for the *Market* returns, which displays both the Gaussian and the Student-*t* distribution best fits.

[5] The fits were carried out on daily returns. The tables later in this chapter refer to annualized quantities.

Table 26.5 *The volatilities for the four asset classes after the culling*

	Volatility
Credit	10.8%
Equity	22.3%
Bond	10.1%
Market	7.4%

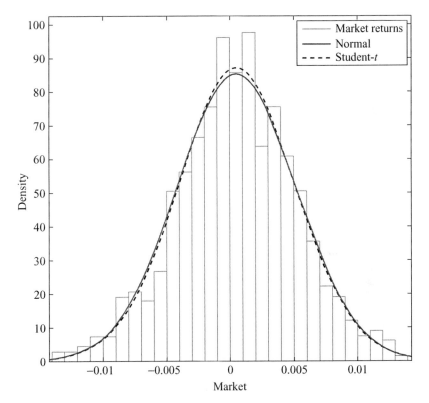

Figure 26.9 An example of the fits for the *Market* returns, which displays both the Gaussian and the Student-t distribution best fits.

As one can see, after the culling there is very little to choose between the two distributions, even for the asset class (*Market*) for which there is the greatest difference in p-values. The p-test for the marginals are reported in Table 26.6.

We note that only for the *Market* asset class does the Student-t distribution yield a significant improvement over the Gaussian distribution. We stress that this is not always the case.

Table 26.6 *The p-test for the marginals of the four asset classes for the Gaussian and the Student-t distributions. We find an appreciable difference only for Market*

	p-values (Gaussian)	p-values (Student-t)
Bond	0.71	0.72
Credit	0.95	0.96
Equity	0.93	0.94
Market	0.79	0.91

As for the expected returns, we pointed out in the preceding chapters that it would be foolhardy to estimate these from the limited data set we have chosen to work with. An important subjective element,[6] in the spirit of the Black–Litterman approach, is therefore essential. In the next section we are therefore going to make use of the CAPM to guide us in this difficult task, as explained in Chapter 21.

26.5   CAPM and the total moments

Our goal is to check whether the spliced distribution we have obtained is compatible with the CAPM view of the world. If it is not, we may want to adjust it. A possible way to do so would be the following.

Recall that we want to calculate the CAPM return, μ_i, from asset i:

$$\mu_i = r_f + (r_M - r_f)\beta_i \tag{26.3}$$

First of all we need a value for the riskless rate, r_f. In our case study we have chosen

$$r_f = 0.25\% \tag{26.4}$$

Next we have to estimate the beta coefficients β_i. To do so we use the spliced distribution that we have already been obtained:

$$\beta_i = \rho_{i,M}\frac{\sigma_i}{\sigma_M} \tag{26.5}$$

The total standard deviations for the four asset classes obtained for the original (i.e., pre-CAPM processing) full spliced distribution are reported in Table 26.7. The corresponding values for the body of the distribution are shown in parentheses.

Table 26.8 shows the individual elements of the correlation matrix for the total distribution. For comparison we also show (in parentheses) the same correlation elements for the body of the distribution after the culling.

---

[6] This subjective input will, of course, take estimates of long-term returns into account.

Table 26.7 *The standard deviations for the four asset classes from the total (spliced) distribution. The corresponding values for the body of the distribution are shown in parentheses*

	Standard deviation
Credit	12.94% (10.8%)
Equity	23.27% (22.3%)
Bond	9.74%(10.1%)
Market	9.23% (7.4%)

Table 26.8 *The correlation matrix for the total distribution and (in parentheses) the same quantity after the culling. Note the significant reduction brought about by the culling*

$$
\begin{bmatrix}
 & \text{Credit} & \text{Equity} & \text{Bond} & \text{Market} \\
\text{Credit} & 1 & 0.459(0.674) & 0.610(0.890) & 0.371(0.556) \\
\text{Equity} & 0.459(0.674) & 1 & 0.392(0.507) & 0.540(0.813) \\
\text{Bond} & 0.610(0.890) & 0.392(0.507) & 1 & 0.286(0.414) \\
\text{Market} & 0.371(0.556) & 0.540(0.813) & 0.286(0.414) & 1
\end{bmatrix}
$$

Unless we have been inordinately lucky (or prescient), when we calculate the returns using Equation (26.3), we will find that the first moments from our spliced distribution are not precisely CAPM-compatible. We can either decide that the differences are small and that we can live with them. Or we can judge that we should enforce a better agreement. If we choose the latter option, how should we 'fix' our spliced distribution?

A naive and tempting way would be the following: we could assign the expected returns that we think appropriate, say, in normal market conditions. If we do so, the probability of the stressed event is fixed by the Bayesian net we have built (or, more precisely, it will lie within a range, determined by our confidence in the conditional probability inputs to the net). It would therefore seem that, if we want the total first moment for a given asset exactly to match the CAPM return, we have a single degree of freedom, i.e., the return for that asset in the stressed state. Unfortunately, life is not that simple, because the covariance term that enters the coefficient β_i is a function both of the normal and of the excited expected returns. Therefore, as we change the normal, or, for that matter, the excited return, the β_i also changes.

The correct solution is given by the intersection of two surfaces, one given by Equation (25.7) (reproduced below for ease of reference as Equation (26.6)):

$$
E_T[\Delta \xi_j] = \mu_j = (1 - P(E_j))E_{\text{norm}}[\Delta \xi_j] + P(E_j)E_{\text{exc}}[\Delta \xi_j] \tag{26.6}
$$

and the other by Equation (26.3):

$$
\mu_j = r_f + (r_M - r_f)\beta_j \tag{26.7}
$$

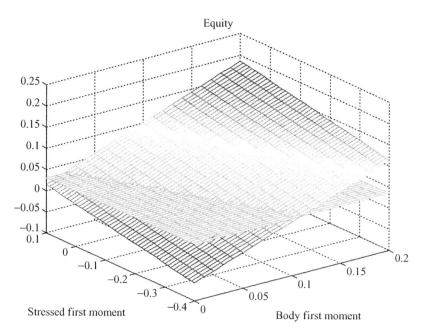

Figure 26.10 The CAPM procedure described in the text to read on the intersection line the possible values of $E_{exc}[\Delta\xi_j]$. If $E_{norm}[\Delta\xi_j]$ is fixed, then a single value for $E_{exc}[\Delta\xi_j]$ is obtained.

The two surfaces and their intersection are shown in Figure 26.10. One surface is clearly exactly a plane; the other looks like a plane over the display range, but it is not exactly so. If we fix $E_{norm}[\Delta\xi_j]$, we can read on the intersection line the value of $E_{exc}[\Delta\xi_j]$.[7]

When we do this, the betas we obtain using the total spliced distribution are displayed in Table 26.9.

Table 26.9 *The betas obtained using the spliced distribution as described in the text*

Asset	β
Credit	0.52
Equity	1.36
Bond	0.30
Market	1.00

(26.8)

The normal-times, stressed and total returns obtained from the spliced distribution are shown alongside the CAPM-implied returns in Table 26.10.

---

[7] Of course, we also have to fix $E_{norm}[\Delta\xi_{MKT}]$ and $E_{exc}[\Delta\xi_{MKT}]$.

Table 26.10 *The normal-times, stressed and total returns obtained from spliced distribution (first three columns), shown alongside the CAPM-implied returns. Note that, despite* Market *being made up of an equity and bond component, its expected return is not equal to the weighted average of the* Bond *and* Equity *returns. This is because the* Bond *and* Equity *asset class in our case study refer to the UK market, and are threfore a subset of the global bond and equity portfolio. In a period of Euro-centred stress, US assets may be expected to perform better than Euro-denominated – or, for that matter, sterling-denominated – assets, hence the higher total expected return for* Market

Asset	μ_i(normal)	μ_i(stressed)	μ_i(total)	μ_i(CAPM)
Credit	5.50%	−18.00%	2.17%	2.17%
Equity	9.00%	−23.00%	4.43%	4.43%
Bond	1.50%	+5.00%	1.81%	1.81%
Market	5.00%	−18.00%	3.42%	3.42%

We have therefore gained some confidence that, if our implied views about covariances are correct, the returns we have assigned are compatible with a reasonable asset-pricing model. Before proceeding with the optimization, however, we want to discuss more carefully how the betas, which play such an important role in our construction, have been determined.

26.5.1   Are we using the right betas?

It is important to pause and understand clearly what we have done. The betas we have obtained for the various assets are a function of the spliced distribution, made up of a normal-times (body) component and a Bayesian-net component. This spliced distribution refers to a relatively short horizon, of the order of 3–12 months. However, these betas affect, via Equation (26.3), the prices of possibly very-long-maturity assets (or, as in the case of equities, of assets of infinite maturity). One may question whether it is reasonable to use the spliced distribution, which may reflect very unique and transitory situations, to infer betas that will in turn dictate returns of instruments of much longer maturity. We believe it is. We can see why this is the case as follows.

When we assign returns – even returns that will apply over a short period of time – given *today's* prices we are effectively saying what *future prices* (i.e., prices at the end of the investment horizon) will be. These future prices are future discounted expectations of cash flows. If we claim that we know these short-horizon returns, the values of these future discounted expectations (the future prices) are uniquely determined. And if we require that these future prices should be compatible with the CAPM, then we should indeed apply Equation (26.3) using the betas implied from the spliced distribution.

The slightly subtle point is that, if we *really* thought that the stress event of concern should have only a transitory effect on the future prices because the expectations of long-term cash flows (extending perhaps to infinity) will not be affected, then we should not have assigned, say, such a large stressed fall to the equity index. If we *do* assign a 20% for the fall of the FTSE index, for instance, we are not saying that the dividend cash flows *over the next period* will be 20% lower than expected. We are saying that, if the stress event we focus on materializes, the market will revise its long-term expectations and reprice *the infinite stream of dividend cash flows* in such a radical way that the price of the FTSE in, say, three months' time will be 20% lower than it is today.[8]

26.6   The optimal-allocation results

26.6.1   *Results for logarithmic utility function*

We have now gathered all the information needed to carry out our asset allocation. We present and discuss in this and in the following sections the results obtained using a full Monte-Carlo simulation as described in Chapter 24. We show in the following chapters that (at least in the absence of strongly non-liner payoffs) the much-simpler-to-perform Gaussian approximation discussed in Chapter 25 provides almost identical results. From the practical point of view this is extremely useful. However, we prefer to keep the numerical and computational issues distinct from the conceptual ones. We therefore deal in this chapter with the results obtained using the high road of the full expected utility maximization, rather than the many shortcuts that we will be using in practice (effective as these may be).

The allocations thus obtained for the case of the logarithmic utility function are shown in Figure 26.11.

In order to understand the figure, recall that the probability of the occurrence of the nothing-happens event has a particular importance in our analysis. If the probability of the stressed events is 0, the allocation will in fact be wholly driven by the body of the distribution, and the results will be identical to those obtained using traditional expected utility maximization (or, in the first two-moment approximation, identical to the Markowitz solution).

As we have explained in Chapter 24, we can treat the probability of the 'nothing-happens' event as a degree of freedom that controls how much weight should be assigned to the body of the distribution. When we do so, in Figure 26.11 we show on the far right the allocations that would obtain if the probability of the 'nothing-happens' event were 100%.[9] (This corresponds to our normalization factor $1 - k$ having a value of 1.) The allocation in this case goes almost totally to equities. Looking at Table 26.10 this is hardly surprising: we are looking at the allocation that would prevail if it were impossible for the stress event of concern to materialize. In this case the very high expected return for equities in the normal case (9.00%) dictates that virtually all of our eggs should go in the *Equity* basket.

---

[8] We are, of course, sidestepping here the issue of possible market overreaction to financial news and events. A landmark paper on overreaction ('excessive volatility') is Shiller (1981) – about overreaction in equity markets. See also Shiller (1979) for a related discussion in the area of interest rates, and, more generally on the topic, Shiller (1989, 2000).

[9] We carried out 1 000 000 runs for each value of $1 - k$.

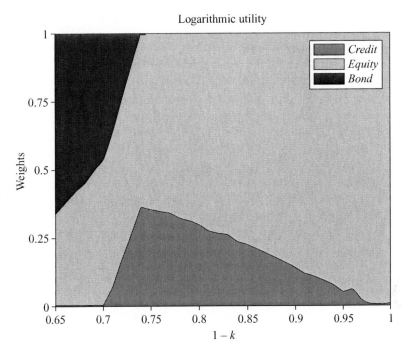

Figure 26.11 Allocations as a function of the probability of 'normal' state $(1 - k)$, displayed on the *x*-axis, for a logarithmic utility.

As the probability of the focus stress event increases (i.e., as we move to the left in the graph) the allocation to *Credit* gradually picks up, as this asset class fares considerably better than *Equity* in the stress case. Recall that *Bond* actually posts a positive expected return in the stress scenario of focus. Yet, even when the probabilities of the nothing-happens event become as small as approximately 73%, the allocation to *Bond* remains effectively zero: for all the diversification that *Bond* could provide, return considerations still dominate the allocation.

It is when the possibility of the stress event becomes really significant that safety-first considerations kick in. The most noteworthy effect, however, is that the increase in allocation to *Bond* occurs at the expense of the allocation to the *Credit* asset class, not of the much riskier *Equity* asset class. It is *Credit* that now gets penalized for its lower expected return with respect to *Equities*. This is interesting. What happens is that the allocation engine sees the protection afforded by the defensive asset *Bond* (which performs relatively well in a situation of distress) as an opportunity to 're-leverage up' the *Equity* allocation.

26.6.2 Sensitivity to different degrees of risk aversion
Figures 26.12 and 26.13 display the allocations that result from the use of power utility functions that bracket the logarithmic one in risk aversion (recall that the logarithmic

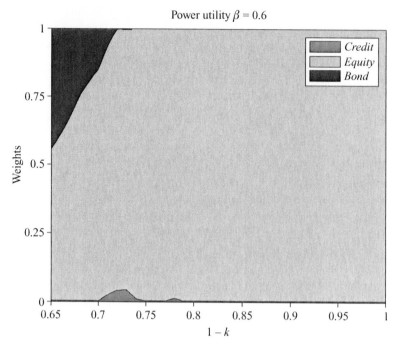

Figure 26.12 Same as Figure 26.11 for a power utility function with an exponent $\beta = 0.6$, corresponding to less risk aversion than in the logarithmic-utility case.

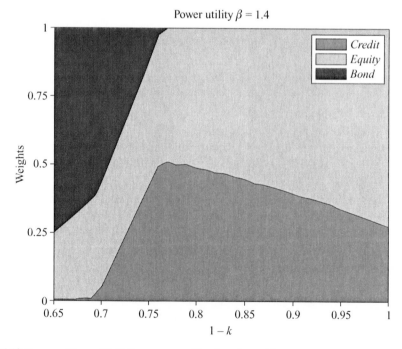

Figure 26.13 Same as Figure 26.11 for a power utility function with an exponent $\beta = 1.4$, corresponding to greater risk aversion than in the logarithmic-utility case.

utility function obtains as a limiting case for the exponent in the power utility function going to 1).

Some features of the differences in allocation as the degree of risk aversion changes are easy to understand. For instance, as the exponent decreases to 0.6 (less risk aversion), the utility function becomes less concave, returns 'matter' more (with respect to risk) and the allocation to *Equities* increases. Conversely, as the degree of risk aversion increases (i.e., as the exponent becomes 1.4), the allocation to *Equities* is reduced.

What is less obvious is why in the high-risk-aversion case *Credit* becomes a contender – indeed, in the $\beta = 1.4$ case even for $k = 0$ (i.e., even if we are certain that 'nothing will happen') the allocation to *Credit* is above 25%. It then progressively increases up to a maximum of approximately 50%, to decay then to zero for $k = 30\%$. The reader should compare this allocations with the one illustrated in Figure 26.11 (obtained with a logarithmic utility function), which displays zero allocation to *Credit* in correspondence to the nothing-happens event (i.e., for $k = 0$).

To understand this behaviour, one must recall that the greatest benefit from *Bond* comes from how well it pays out in a situation of distress. Otherwise, in 'normal times' its expected return is the lowest of the three asset classes. So, to the far right of the graph (which corresponds to low or zero probability of the stress event), the benefit from *Bond* is not felt. This was, of course, also true in the case of the logarithmic utility function. In that case, however, a lower degree of risk aversion was making the high return from *Equities* highly desirable. With a risk aversion exponent of 1.4 the same return is less attractive with respect to the risk that it entails. So, to the right of the graph *Credit* is left as a viable alternative almost by exclusion: *Equities* are too risky, and the *Bond* asset class does not display its crisis-resilience properties yet.

26.6.3 Conclusions

In sum: we have shown that the allocation results produced by the Bayesian-net technology introduced in the first parts of the book are highly intuitive, and do give rise, even for as few as three asset classes, to interesting allocation suggestions. For the logarithmic utility function, for instance, the analysis suggests that, if we become increasingly worried about the stress event we are considering, we should cut down drastically on our exposure on *Credit*, in favour of the safe *Bond* asset class, but only reduce slowly the *Equity* allocation.

We also discussed the 'logic' behind the polarization between *Equity* and *Bond* at the expenses of *Credit* to the left of the graph (i.e., for high probabilities of the stress event occurring): the very good diversification and return properties of *Bond* in crisis situations suggest a releveraging strategy in favour of *Equity*. Needless to say, the robustness of this strategy hinges on the desired diversification afforded by *Bond* actually being forthcoming when needed most. The portfolio manager may want to reflect carefully on this feature.

We also understood the interplay between our assessment of the probability of the stress event occurring and the degree of risk aversion, and how and when this combination can give rise to a meaningful allocation to *Credit*.

At this stage we can therefore at least say that the results are interesting, informative and intuitive. Above all, they invite and facilitate a critical understanding of the allocations, rather than a passive acceptance of the output of a black box.

26.7   The road ahead

Encouraging as these results are, we still have a lot of work to do, both from the methodological and from the implementation point of view.

Starting from the methodological perspective, to gain confidence that the allocations can be used reliably we must see how stable the allocations are to our many subjective inputs. We give great importance to the stability of the allocations, and, as we shall see, achieving this is not always easy.

As for the implementation considerations, if applied in a brute-force manner the procedure presented in this chapter is computationally rather expensive. We have suggested in the previous chapters several shortcuts and numerical techniques that could make our life much easier, by reducing dramatically the computational burden and the complexity of the implementation. We still have to explore whether these approximations live up to their promise. We turn to this topic in the next chapter, but we can already reassure the reader that we have not wasted her time in the previous chapters, because, indeed, the approximations will work remarkably well. Most importantly, an understanding of *why* they work so well will help us make our final case in Chapter 29, where we argue that (at least for assets with almost-linear payoffs) the problem can be profitably recast in a simple and traditional mean-variance framework.

27 Numerical analysis

In this chapter we review in detail the quality of the various numerical approximations we have introduced in Part IV of the book. As we shall see, the good news is that they tend to be surprisingly successful, and can therefore greatly lighten the computational burden of the optimization. They will also suggest an approach to asset allocation using Bayesian nets which is not only computationally lighter, but also intuitively more appealing.

We begin by looking at the quality of the mean-variance approximation.

27.1   How good is the mean-variance approximation?

In this section we are trying to ascertain how accurate the mean-variance Gaussian approximation presented in Sections 25.2 and 25.3 actually is, once the moments of the full distribution obtained by the Bayesian net are matched.

The answer is apparent from Figure 27.2, which shows the allocations as a function of $(1 - k)$ obtained using the Gaussian approximation. This figure can be compared with the allocations obtained using the full Monte-Carlo optimization and the logarithmic utility function, shown again in Figure 27.1 for ease of comparison.

The similarity between the two sets of optimal weights is remarkable, and is shown even more clearly in Figure 27.3, which displays the allocations as a function of $(1 - k)$ for the the three methods. Again, it is apparent that the Gaussian approximation, once the moments are matched, is extremely accurate.

These results give a strong indication of where the Bayesian-net technology, and, more generally, the inclusion of tail events in portfolio optimization make a difference, and of whether inclusion of these low-probability events is important in determining the optimal allocation. As we shall see, the answer is that the inclusion of low-probability tail events is indeed *very* important, but mainly because of their effect on the second moment of the portfolio distribution of returns, not necessarily because of their contribution to its skewness, or kurtosis.[1] These results give the first indication that the fine

---

[1] Of course, everybody agrees that *ex post* tail events are extremely important. The question addressed in this section is whether, given their low probability, they can make a difference to the before-the-event allocation: as we shall show, they do.

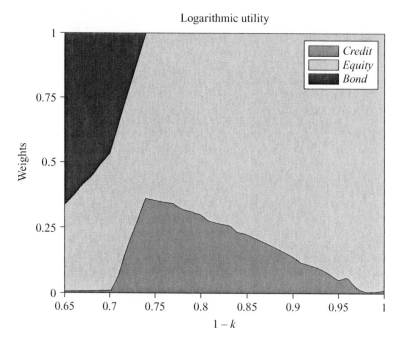

Figure 27.1 Allocations as a function of the probability of 'normal' state $(1 - k)$ for a logarithmic utility and using full Monte-Carlo simulation.

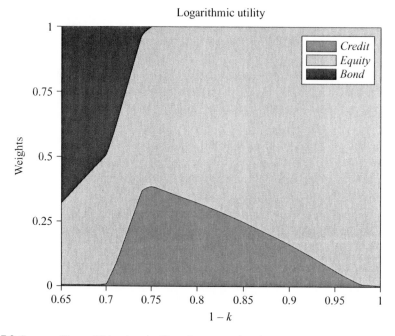

Figure 27.2 Same as Figure 27.1 using the Gaussian approximation.

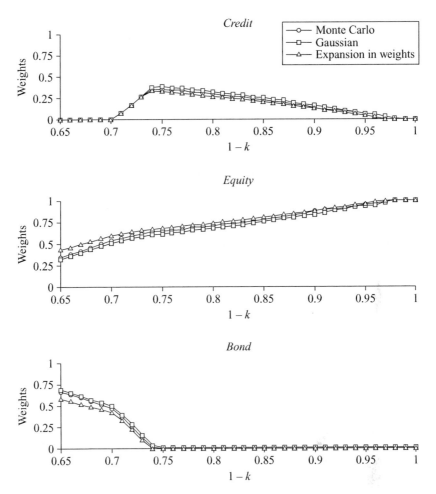

Figure 27.3 Comparison of the allocations with the three different methods: full Monte Carlo, Gaussian approximation, expansion in weights as a function of the probability of 'normal' state $(1 - k)$.

details of the utility function matter relatively little, as long as the first two moments of the distribution and the degree of risk aversion are matched. Of course, adding fatter tails to the body of the distribution does make some difference. This difference, however, comes about not so much because we are introducing skewness and kurtosis (which will be picked up by non-quadratic utility functions, but will be missed by the second-order expansion we presented above); rather, the difference in allocations comes about because the stress events that we introduce will increase the variance of the full spliced distribution – an increased variance that *will* be picked up by the simple quadratic utility function that we are effectively using.

These results suggest that the well-established – and extremely simple – analytical tools developed over several decades in connection with mean-variance optimization (efficient frontiers, tangent portfolios, minimum-variance portfolios, Sharpe Ratios, etc.) can be effectively re-employed in a Bayesian-net context, once the total second moments are correctly accounted for.

To avoid misunderstandings, we stress again that we are *not* saying that the real returns are well approximated by a Gaussian distribution. This statement would not even be true for the body of the distribution, as discussed in Chapter 18. Certainly it is even farther from the truth after we add the contributions from the Bayesian-net construction. What we *are* asserting is that, once the first two moments of this much more complex distribution have been estimated, the allocations obtained by the maximization of a logarithmic utility function are virtually indistinguishable from what would have been obtained if the first-two-moments-matched distribution had been Gaussian. We will discuss the implications of this result in the next chapter.

27.2   Using the weight expansion for the k dependence

Recall from our previous discussion that, when the Bayesian net reflects a situation where we want to take into account the effect of a very 'large' but very rare event, the probability, p_0, of the 'nothing-happens' event will tend to be very large. When nothing indeed happens, then the allocation produced by our technology is exactly the same as what would be produced by a conventional utility maximization over the 'normal-times' distribution. We also explained that, even if the net produces a unique value for the nothing-happens probability p_0, it can be wise to treat this quantity as a distribution, in order to explore the sensitivity of our results to the construction of the net. We therefore introduced in Section 20.6 a variable 'normalization factor', k, that specifies the probability mass concentrated in the normal-times distribution. We recommended exploring the sensitivity of the allocation results as the 'normalization factor', k, changes over a reasonable range. Doing so 'brute-force', however, can be computationally demanding.

In Section 25.2 we showed that the recalculation of the weights for different values of the normalization factor, k, can be avoided by using an expansion in the weights. Thanks to this approximation, the optimization only has to be carried out once, and all the other allocations can be (approximately) obtained at very little computational cost. For instance, consider the graphs shown in Sections 26.6.1 and 26.6.2. Obtaining one such graph by repeating the optimization for each value of k requires approximately 60 minutes on a desktop computer using an AMD Phenom Triple-Core 2.1 GHz processor. With the approximation described in Section 25.2 the total required time is that of the first simulation for $k = 0$, i.e., approximately 2 minutes, plus five additional seconds to infer the rest of the graph. So, the computational savings are substantial. But is the approximation accurate?

To answer this question, Figure 27.4 shows the allocations produced using the expansion-in-weights approximation when the utility function used for the maximization is logarithmic.

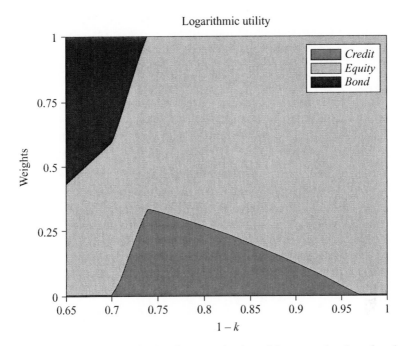

Figure 27.4 The allocations produced using the expansion-in-weights approximation when the utility function used for the maximization is logarithmic.

As the figure shows, the approximation remains remarkably accurate for values of k at least as large as $k = 0.75$.

In order to have an idea about the 'economic cost' of this approximation we have searched for each k for a constant c that would make the investor indifferent between the two optimizations:

$$E[U(1 + w^*_{opt}r + c)] = E[U(1 + w_{opt}r)] \qquad (27.1)$$

where w^*_{opt} are the optimal weights obtained with the approximated utility function, w_{opt} are optimal weights obtained as a solution to the full problem and c is the opportunity cost. In Table 27.1 we can see the value of the opportunity cost c multiplied by 10^3 for several values of the normalization factor.

As the table shows, the economic cost of using the approximation under study is negligible, and we can therefore conclude that the approximation is very effective. The expansion-in-weights approximation for the k-dependent allocations is therefore another useful tool in the Bayesian-net technology. The approximation is actually *so* accurate that it pays to understand a bit better where such precision comes from.

27.2.1 *Gaining intuition*

Looking at Figure 27.3, the question naturally arises as to why a simple second-order expansion such as the one described in Chapter 25 can be so accurate over such a wide

Table 27.1 *Opportunity cost, c, of the weight-expansion approximation for the logarithmic utility as a function of* $1 - k$

$(1-k)\%$	$c \times 10^3$	$(1-k)\%$	$c \times 10^3$
100	0	87	−0.4096
99	+0.1844	86	−0.2184
98	−0.2451	85	−0.0497
97	−0.6969	84	−0.0744
96	−0.4004	83	−0.5565
95	−0.5113	82	−0.1409
94	−0.5979	81	+0.0171
93	−0.5850	80	−0.2868
92	−0.3806	79	−0.3183
91	−0.0425	78	−0.0069
90	−0.1880	77	−0.3370
89	−0.2899	76	−0.2424
88	−0.1197	75	−0.0487

range of values of k as the one explored in the analysis. In order to gain some intuition as to why Equation (25.22) works so well, we plot in Figure 27.5 the logarithmic utility associated with returns from three asset classes, i.e., we plot the quantity

$$U(w_1, w_2) = \ln[1 + w_1 r_1 + w_2 r_2 + (1 - w_1 - w_2)r_3] \qquad (27.2)$$

for two sets of returns, r_i, as w_1 and w_2 vary. The third asset allocation is of course given by

$$w_3 = 1 - w_1 - w_2$$

For illustrative purposes we do not impose a short-selling constraint, and therefore we do not require that $w_3 > 0$. If these constraints were imposed, the results would simply be a subset of Figure 27.5.

From this diagram we can see that the utility as a function *of the weights* is almost a plane and, therefore, even drastic changes in the allocations can be satisfactorily accounted for by a second-order expansion.

As we shall see, the almost-linearity of a reasonably calibrated utility function with respect to a number of key variables will play an important role when we discuss in more detail the stability of the allocation. See Chapter 28.

27.3 Optimal allocation with uncertain k via Maximum Entropy: results

As explained in Section 24.4, another way to deal with the uncertainty in the value of the normalization factor, k, – and, in a way, the theoretically 'cleanest' way – is to introduce this uncertainty in the optimization itself. We present in this section the allocation weights that we obtain when we do so, as a function of the degree of

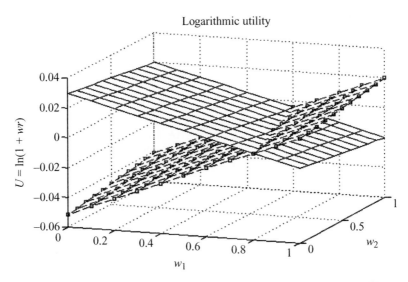

Figure 27.5 Logarithmic utility (z-axis) for two sets of expected returns as a function of the allocations to three assets. The first set expected returns (square makers) are $\boldsymbol{u} = \{1\%; -4\%; -5\%\}$; the second expected returns (no markers) are $\boldsymbol{u} = \{-1\%; 2\%; 3\%\}$. The allocations to assets 1 and 2, w_1 and w_2, respectively, are shown on the x- and y-axis. The third asset allocation is given by $w_3 = 1 - w_1 - w_2$.

confidence in the precise value of k. This discussion will also constitute a useful prelude to the sensitivity analysis carried out in the next chapter.

The net has produced a single value for the probability, p_0, of the nothing-happens event. However, as non-dogmatic users of Bayesian nets, we entertain the possibility that this probability may range over a set of values and we therefore want to treat it as a 'normalization factor', as explained in Section 24.4. Let us then denote by $g(k)$ the distribution of possible values for the normalization factor k. We require that the expectation (or, if different, the mode) of $g(k)$ will be located where suggested by the net. Its variance then describes our uncertainty around this value.

The allocations obtained by choosing for $g(k)$ a truncated Gaussian with mode equal to 0.2808, or a Johnson distribution with $b = 1$, are plotted in Figures 27.6 and 27.7 for different values of the confidence parameter, Ω.

We recall that, if the distribution $g(k)$ were a Dirac-δ centred at the Bayesian-net-produced value, we would exactly obtain the allocation which can be read from Figure 27.1 in correspondence with the value $k = 0.28$: we find a bit more than 50% of the portfolio allocated to *Equity*, about 27% to *Bond*, and less than 20% to *Credit*. We then plot how these allocations change moving from left to right as the uncertainty in the normalization factor, k, increases. As long as this uncertainty increases modestly, we see that in the case of the truncated Gaussian distribution the allocation remains broadly stable until the confidence parameters exceeds 0.10. Above this value, the most dramatic change is not so much the decrease in the allocation to *Equity*, but

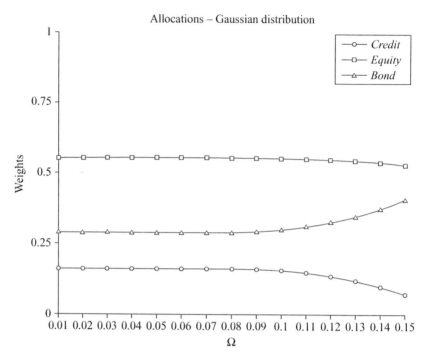

Figure 27.6 Allocations as a function of the confidence parameter Ω in the case of truncated Gaussian distribution with mode equal to 0.2808.

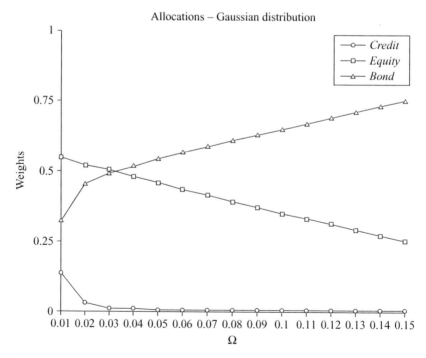

Figure 27.7 Same as Figure 27.6 for the Johnson distribution with $b = 1$.

the progressive shift from *Credit* to *Bond*. Indeed, for an uncertainty $\Omega = 0.15$, the allocation to *Credit* has all but disappeared.[2]

We recover here the same behaviour observed in the case of the expected-utility optimization as the normalization factor is k increased from right to left. We stress, however, that we are looking at two different phenomena: in the discussion in Chapter 26, we were looking at the change in allocations as the value of k, *assumed to be perfectly known*, steadily increased from 0 to about 30%. Now we are observing the effects on the allocations of our uncertainty around a fixed value of k. Our uncertainty produces both increases and decreases in the normalization factor. The interesting observation is that this degree of uncertainty brings about the same result as increasing outright the mass in the distressed state: as the normalization factor must be calculated at the average value of $g(k)$, this value becomes bigger and bigger – and it does so much faster for the Johnson distribution. For a given value of uncertainty, one can therefore almost speak of a certainty-equivalent value for the normalization factor, k_{eq} – a certainty-equivalent value that would be substantially higher than the single value determined by the net.[3]

The same message is conveyed, with greater strength, by Figure 27.7, obtained by using the Johnson distribution to describe our uncertainty about the 'true' value of k. Here the allocation to *Credit* falls very quickly to zero, even for very modest values of the uncertainty, and the allocation to *Bond* rises almost linearly at the expense of *Equity*.[4] We stress again that we are observing here non-linearity effects, because the uncertainty in the distribution $g(k)$ brings about two-sided variations in the normalization factor. The reason why the effect is so much stronger in the case of the Johnson distribution with respect to the truncated Gaussian distribution is due to its pronounced asymmetry, which quickly becomes more marked as the uncertainty increases. After all, starting as it does from a relatively small value, the mass in the stressed state cannot become smaller than zero, but has plenty of 'room to increase'.

This discussion is the perfect introduction to the topic of the sensitivity of the allocations to the uncertainty in all of our inputs (not just in the normalization factor). This is the extremely important topic that we address in the next chapter.

---

[2] An explanation for this behaviour can be found in Section 29.6.

[3] We note in passing that this is a recurrent feature of Robust Optimization: the introduction of uncertainty about the model parameters often retains the same structure as the certain-parameter solution, but replaces the uncertain parameter(s) with 'effective' ones. These often correspond, in the certain-parameter setting, to a situation of greater risk aversion. See, e.g., Hansen and Sargent (2008) or Garlappi, Uppal and Wang (2006).

[4] Also in this case, we explain this behaviour in Section 29.6.

28 Stability analysis

28.1 General considerations

The analysis of the sensitivity of the allocation weights to the uncertain inputs is closely linked to the issue of the (lack of) stability of the allocations – a stability issue with which portfolio managers are very familiar. This instability is one of the greatest drawbacks of Markowitz-like solutions. The allocations produced by the Black–Litterman model are somewhat more stable, but, for reasons that we discuss below, not always significantly so. Are the allocations produced by the Bayesian-net technology more stable, or are they plagued by the same instability problems?

Now, as we began using the Bayesian-net technology, we did not know for sure whether the allocations produced by the procedure described in this book would be greatly affected by small changes in the marginal (root) probabilities, in the conditional probabilities, in the expected returns, in the stressed sampling distributions that we associate with the leaves, etc. We *did* know, however, that, unless we could find a satisfactory solution to the stability problem, the usefulness of any asset-allocation approach, including the Bayesian-net approach of which we are so fond, was going to be limited.

With an eye to this stability issue, we can begin the discussion by making two general observations.

The first is that we do not expect Bayesian nets *in themselves* to be responsible for any additional instability over and above what is already produced by the Markowitz-like optimization. If anything, we explain later why they should have a modest stabilizing effect. Whether this stabilizing effect is strong enough to 'solve' the stability problem is an empirical issue that we explore in this chapter.

The second observation has to do with the desirability or otherwise to embed our Bayesian-net approach in a Black–Litterman framework. (It is in order to keep this route open that we have made the links between our approach and the Black–Litterman model explicit in Appendix I.) Why would we want to establish this link? Because one of the ways to 'regularize' the Markowitz results is to 'nest them' into the Black–Litterman model, of which the former results can be seen as a special case.

This route is still open to us when we use Bayesian nets, as we always have the option of a Black–Litterman-like anchoring towards the market-portfolio allocation as a fall-back to achieve stability. See the discussion in Appendix I. However, this is not an option we are very fond of. Yes, the asset allocation does become more stable as we tilt towards the market portfolio. However, we achieve this stabilization by effectively negating the views expressed by the asset manager – as the reader will recall, the stability is achieved by increasing the degree of uncertainty in the manager's subjective views about the returns, and tilting the solution towards the market 'prior'. The greater the lack of confidence in the views, the more the portfolio achieves its stability by tilting towards the market portfolio. More fundamentally, we argue in what follows that, *if the Black–Litterman is used purely as a regularization device*, it misdiagnoses the cause of the instability, and therefore 'sedates' the patient rather than curing it. We explain in the last sections of this chapter where we believe the true problem to lie, and what the possible solutions (or patches) may be.

If the portfolio manager remains unconvinced by our argument and still wants to embed our approach in a Black–Litterman framework in order to increase the stability of the solutions, another practical problem comes to the fore. What does it mean in practice 'to tilt the solution towards the market portfolio'? A common proxy for the market portfolio is a broad equity index, such as, say, the S&P 500. Does this mean that a weak-convictions portfolio manager with a mandate to invest in, say, fixed income or FX strategies should invest a large fraction of her portfolio in the S&P 500 if she felt uncertain about her views? This is hardly a realistic recommendation and, even if she had the mandate to do so, this supposedly 'non-committal' strategy would introduce very large P&L volatility (tracking error) to her portfolio.

In this case, a more realistic and pragmatically useful definition of the market portfolio could perhaps be the portfolio against which the manager is benchmarked. Absence of views, or lack of conviction, would then naturally translate into an allocation tilted towards the benchmark. However, it is not straightforward to recast the Black–Litterman approach in terms of an arbitrary benchmark portfolio.

And what about an absolute-return manager, for whom an explicit benchmark is by definition absent? In this case, the manager often tries to achieve the best possible absolute return under the 'soft' constraint of not exceeding the volatility of some reference asset class – often, the volatility of a broad equity index. In this case the market portfolio could arguably be the reference asset(s) whose volatility the manager is expected not to exceed. This approach could then be combined with a judicious choice for what we called in Section 22.5 a 'reduced-form' utility function. This approach is attractive, but the fact remains, however, that in a Black–Litterman world stable solutions are mainly associated with weak views.

With these general considerations in the back of our minds we can begin the stability analysis proper, by looking at the sensitivity of the outputs

- to uncertainty in the conditional probabilities;
- to uncertainty in the first moments of the return distribution, arising both from uncertainty in the stressed returns and in the first moments of the body of the distribution;
- when the degree of risk aversion becomes 'very large'.

28.2   Stability with respect to uncertainty in the conditional probability tables

We begin this part of the analysis by exploring how stable the results are to uncertainty in the input conditional probabilities.

As a guiding principle, we wanted to 'stress' our assumptions about conditional probabilities without the bounds becoming so large as to invalidate the financial 'story' that we have built around our net. We can do so in two ways. First, we can impose that each entry, cp_j, should be between a lower and an upper bound, L_j and U_j, and given by

$$cp_j(u) = L_j + (U_j - L_j)u$$

with $u \sim U(0, 1)$.[1] This is very simple, and can be appropriate if the portfolio manager has a passably clear idea of the reasonable values that a given marginal or conditional probability can assume. However, this approach does not lend itself easily to specifying the upper and lower bounds for a large number of probabilities, especially when the probabilities can be very small or very close to 1.

In order to find a systematic and consistent way to stress these probabilities we have therefore followed the procedure suggested in Pradhan *et al.* (1995). More precisely, we first changed each probability, p, according to the transformation T:

$$T(p) = \log_{10}\left[\frac{p}{1-p}\right] \tag{28.1}$$

Then we added Gaussian noise $e = \mathcal{N}(0, s^2)$, and transformed back according to

$$p_{\text{noise}} = T^{-1}[T(p) + e] \tag{28.2}$$

Figures 28.1 and 28.2 show the range of values (plus or minus three standard deviations) attained for each possible value of the input probability.

Unless otherwise stated, this is the procedure that we have followed in the rest of the empirical analysis.

28.2.1   Analytical expressions for the sensitivities

It is, of course, difficult to make general statements about the sensitivity of the allocations to small changes in the conditional probabilities, as the stability of the solution depends on the specific features of the Bayesian net used to describe a given problem. In order to identify the most salient sensitivities of a given net we therefore proceed as follows.

We place ourselves in a mean-variance setting. We are therefore going to use the total first and second moments obtained from the spliced distribution (see Section 25.3). Given a Bayesian net with number of nodes n_{nodes}, let

---

[1] A better choice could be a truncated continuous distribution with expected value equal to the value assigned by the expert, and variance related to the degree of uncertainty in the entry. We do not pursue this route.

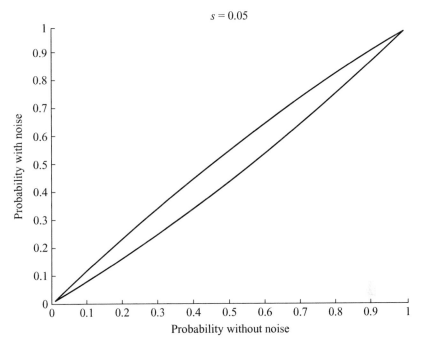

Figure 28.1 Region of variability (+/−3 standard deviations) of the perturbed probabilities for $s = 0.05$.

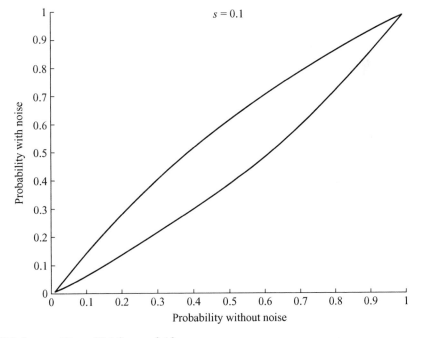

Figure 28.2 Same as Figure 28.1 for $s = 0.10$.

- p_i be the ith joint probability;[2]
- cp_j^i be the jth conditional probability that affects p_i in the Master Equation;
- μ_k be the expected return from asset k obtained from the Bayesian net;
- w_r be the allocation weight assigned to asset r by the maximization of a quadratic utility function with risk aversion λ and covariance matrix $\boldsymbol{\Sigma}$;
- n be the number of assets in the terminal leaves;
- n_{jp} be the number of joint probabilities in the Bayesian net.

In order to find the sensitivity of the allocation weights to the subjectively assigned conditional probabilities, we are going to focus on the impact that changes in the conditional probabilities have on the allocation weights via the changes they generate in the expected returns. (We explain in the next section why expected returns are particularly important.) There are similar effects due to the changes they induce in the second moment. However, we assume that the uncertainty in the estimation of expected returns is much larger than the uncertainty in the estimation of the second moments. In any case, if the portfolio manager so wished, the analysis we present in this section can be extended without difficulty to the second moment as well.

We then have

$$\frac{\partial w_r}{\partial cp_j^i} = \sum_{i=1,n_{\text{jp}}} \frac{\partial w_r}{\partial p_i} \frac{\partial p_i}{\partial cp_j^i} \tag{28.3}$$

$$\frac{\partial w_r}{\partial p_i} = \sum_{k=1,n} \frac{\partial w_r}{\partial \mu_k} \frac{\partial \mu_k}{\partial p_i} \tag{28.4}$$

and therefore

$$\frac{\partial w_r}{\partial cp_j^i} = \sum_{i=1,n_{\text{jp}}} \sum_{k=1,n} \frac{\partial w_r}{\partial \mu_k} \frac{\partial \mu_k}{\partial p_i} \frac{\partial p_i}{\partial cp_j^i} \tag{28.5}$$

Given a quadratic utility function, the optimal weights (no constraints) are given by

$$w = \frac{1}{\lambda} \boldsymbol{\Sigma}^{-1} \mu \tag{28.6}$$

and therefore, as we saw in Chapter 8,

$$\frac{\partial w}{\partial \mu} = \frac{1}{\lambda} \boldsymbol{\Sigma}^{-1} \tag{28.7}$$

or, in components,

$$\frac{\partial w_r}{\partial \mu_k} = \frac{1}{\lambda} S_{rk} \tag{28.8}$$

with

$$S \equiv \boldsymbol{\Sigma}^{-1} \tag{28.9}$$

---

[2] Strictly speaking, we should be dealing with the reduced joint probabilities here. See Section 22.1. Since these are just sums of 'raw' joint probabilities, we keep the notation simpler by just referring to 'joint probabilities' without further qualification.

So we have

$$\frac{\partial w_r}{\partial cp^i_j} = \frac{1}{\lambda} \sum_{i=1,n_{jp}} \sum_{k=1,n} S_{rk} \frac{\partial \mu_k}{\partial p_i} \frac{\partial p_i}{\partial cp^i_j} \tag{28.10}$$

The quantity $\frac{\partial \mu_k}{\partial p_i}$ can be calculated from the expression for the first 'total moment'. Let in fact the full spliced distribution be given by

$$\varphi(\Delta\xi_1, \Delta\xi_n, \ldots, \Delta\xi_n) = \sum_{t=0,M} p_t \varphi_t (\Delta\xi_1, \Delta\xi_n, \ldots, \Delta\xi_N) \tag{28.11}$$

with

$$\varphi_t(\Delta\xi_1, \Delta\xi_n, \ldots, \Delta\xi_N)$$
$$= \psi^0_{comp}\left(\Delta\xi_1, \Delta\xi_2, \ldots, \Delta\xi_{n'_{norm}}\right) \prod_{k=1,n'_{exc}} \psi^{exc}_k(\Delta\xi_1, \Delta\xi_2, \ldots, \Delta\xi_N) \tag{28.12}$$

As we showed in Section 25.3, the first total moment, μ_k, for factor k is then given by

$$\mu_k = \int \sum_{t=0,M} p_t \varphi_t (\Delta\xi_1, \Delta\xi_k, \ldots, \Delta\xi_N) \Delta\xi_k d(\Delta\xi) \tag{28.13}$$

Then

$$\frac{\partial \mu_k}{\partial p_i} = \frac{\partial}{\partial p_i} \int \sum_{t=0,M} p_t \varphi_t (\Delta\xi_1, \Delta\xi_k, \ldots, \Delta\xi_N) \Delta\xi_k d(\Delta\xi)$$
$$= \int \varphi_i(\Delta\xi_1, \Delta\xi_k, \ldots, \Delta\xi_N) \Delta\xi_k d(\Delta\xi) \equiv J_{ki} \tag{28.14}$$

and

$$\frac{\partial w_r}{\partial cp^i_j} = \frac{1}{\lambda} \sum_{i=1,n_{jp}} \sum_{k=1,n} S_{rk} \frac{\partial \mu_k}{\partial p_i} \frac{\partial p_i}{\partial cp^i_j} = \frac{1}{\lambda} \sum_{i=1,n_{jp}} \sum_{k=1,n} S_{rk} J_{ki} \frac{\partial p_i}{\partial cp^i_j} \tag{28.15}$$

This leaves the quantity $\frac{\partial p_i}{\partial cp^i_j}$ to evaluate. Consider the Master Equation:

$$p_i = \prod_{p=1,n_{nodes}} cp(e_p | PA_p) \tag{28.16}$$

where, as usual, PA_p denote the parents of the pth event, e_p. Then

$$\frac{\partial p_i}{\partial cp^i_j} = \frac{p_i}{cp^i_j} \tag{28.17}$$

and finally

$$\frac{\partial w_r}{\partial cp^i_j} = \frac{1}{\lambda} \sum_{i=1,n_{jp}} \sum_{k=1,n} S_{rk} J_{ik} \frac{p_i}{cp^i_j} \tag{28.18}$$

The (subtle) beauty of this expression is that the sensitivity can be (approximately) evaluated even if the joint probabilities have been obtained numerically (say, using Monte Carlo).

If the joint probabilities have been obtained numerically, they are probably too many to be enumerated one by one. In this case, we just have to sort the joint probabilities obtained numerically. Then the sum $\sum_{i=1,n_{jp}}$ can be restricted to an index $\widehat{n}$ such that $p_i \leq \varepsilon$, for $i \geq \widehat{n}$:

$$\frac{\partial w_r}{\partial cp_j^i} = \frac{1}{\lambda} \sum_{i=1,\widehat{n}} \sum_{k=1,n} S_{rk} J_k \frac{p_i}{cp_j^i} \qquad (28.19)$$

These expressions (and, if one so wished, the similar, but algebraically more tedious, expressions that can be obtained by looking at the sensitivities mediated by changes in the total second moment) can immediately give the portfolio manager very useful indications as to which conditional probabilities truly matter in the building of the net. We shall see in what follows how this information can be put to use.

28.2.2 Empirical results

With these considerations in the back of our minds we can look at Figures 28.3 and 28.4, which display the allocations obtained with a logarithmic utility function by varying the conditional probabilities as described above with an uncertainty parameter, s, equal to 0.05 and 0.1, respectively. In this part of the test we have made no attempts to retain the CAPM ranking that we ensured would prevail for the unperturbed case.

Not surprisingly, the greater the uncertainty (the greater the shock to the conditional probabilities), the wider the dispersion of allocations. For both degrees of uncertainty, the message about *Equity* is clear: the allocation to this asset class should be substantial. When it comes to the allocations to *Credit* and *Bond*, however, the range of allocations becomes very wide. As *Equity* takes on average a share of about 50%, the weights assigned to the other asset classes have to be in the left half of the allocation spectrum. Apart from this we can say little more than that the *Credit* allocation is more shifted towards the 0, and the allocation to *Bond* towards 0.5. If we were looking for stability in the allocations, these first results are not encouraging.

As mentioned above, these results were obtained without preserving the CAPM ranking. Would greater stability be achieved if we required that only those perturbations of the conditional probabilities would be accepted that retained the correct CAPM ranking?[3] We explore this possibility in Figures 28.5 and 28.6. As one can observe, the qualitative features of the allocations are unfortunately not changed by imposing that the CAPM ranking should be preserved.

---

[3] We stress that, in the present context, in looking at the effect of enforcing a CAPM-consistent ranking, we are not necessarily endorsing CAPM as a normatively valid asset-pricing model. We are just exploring the effect that imposing such a ranking might have on the dispersion of weights.

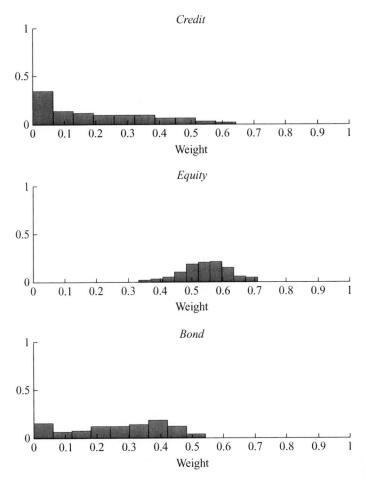

Figure 28.3 Histograms of the distribution of the allocations as the conditional probabilities are perturbed with $s = 0.05$ in 2000 simulations.

So, *for the degree of risk aversion implied by a logarithmic utility function*, we can conclude that the allocation results display a noticeable dependence on reasonable variations in the subjective conditional probabilities.

When we dig deeper, we often find that the sensitivity of the allocations to changes in conditional probabilities tends to be mediated by the induced changes in expected returns that the variations in probabilities induce. We therefore move to the analysis of the changes in allocations caused by our uncertainty in the expected returns.

28.3   Stability with respect to uncertainty in expected returns

In our approach, the expected returns from each asset class are a function of the first moment of the marginal normal-times distribution for that asset class, and, for a given net, of the stressed returns for the leaves that affect the same asset class. So, in order

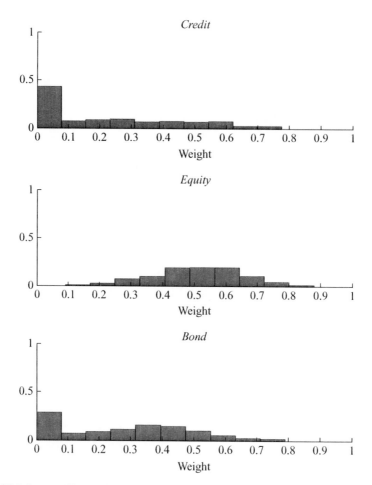

Figure 28.4 Same as Figure 28.3 for $s = 0.10$.

to explore the sensitivity of the allocation results to changes in expected returns, we assign changes in the total returns (the first moments of the distributions obtained by marginalizing the spliced distribution) by altering both the first moments of the distributions in the normal states and the stressed returns, i.e., the first moments of the excited distributions, $\mathcal{N}(\mu_{\text{exc}}, \Sigma_{\text{exc}})$, from which we are going to draw if the associated terminal leaf is excited.

We begin the analysis by looking at the sensitivity to changes in the first moments of the stressed distribution in order to focus on the original part (the Bayesian-net part) of our procedure, and because of the almost exclusively subjective nature of this input.

28.3.1   *Sensitivity to stressed returns*

In order to carry out the sensitivity analysis we proceed as follows. Recall that,when we built the basis function, we stated that in the excited state we would draw the

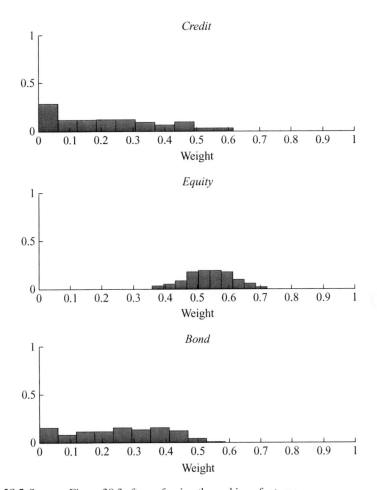

Figure 28.5 Same as Figure 28.3 after enforcing the ranking of returns.

returns from a Gaussian distribution $\mathcal{N}(\mu_{\text{exc}}, \Omega_{\text{exc}})$. In the limit when $\Omega_{\text{exc}} \to 0$, these distributions become Dirac-δ functions. (Indeed, we take this limit for simplicity of exposition in Chapter 16 and in the last chapters of the book.) In the sensitivity analysis presented in this section we perturb the parameter μ_{exc}, by saying that μ_{exc} is now drawn from a distribution $\mathcal{N}(m_{\text{exc}}, S_{\text{exc}})$, where m_{exc} and S_{exc} are now meta-parameters. Once we make a draw from this distribution, the spliced distribution of returns becomes fixed, and we can calculate the allocation weights. We then make another draw, recalculate the allocation weights, and so on.

Also for this part of the analysis we looked at two different cases: in the first, we allowed the random draws for the excited returns to produce the total expected return that could subvert the CAPM ranking for the different asset classes. In the second we only accepted the ranking-preserving draws. For both these cases, we ran 2000 simulations and obtained the distribution for various quantities discussed below. In

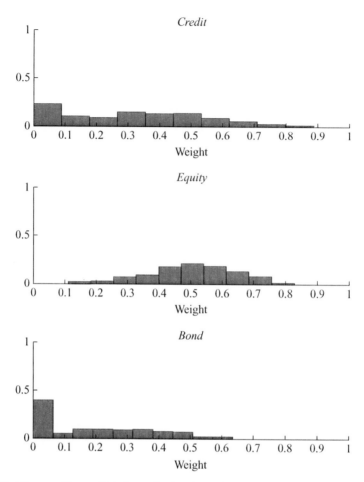

Figure 28.6 Same as Figure 28.4 after enforcing the ranking of returns.

these calculations we used the value, p_0, for the 'nothing-happens' event produced by the unperturbed Bayesian net, and assumed a logarithmic utility function. The results are presented in Figures 28.7 and 28.8.

To put these results in perspective, in Table 28.1 we show how big a change in *total* expected return is produced by a change of 10% in the excited return (by which we mean that a, say, −5% return becomes a −5.5% return, not a −15% return).

For the discussion in the following analysis it is important to stress that these changes are rather small (at most little more than half a percentage point) on the scale of reasonable uncertainty in estimating expected returns. We stress that we are therefore exploring the effects of small – and, in real life, unavoidable – perturbations around the inputs we have prescribed, not the effects of a 'completely different world'.

Despite the relatively modest perturbation in the vector of expected returns brought about by a reasonable (and, arguably, 'optimistic') degree of uncertainty in expected

Table 28.1 *The change in total expected return for each asset class obtained by increasing by* 10% *the excited return from its originally assigned value for different values of the normalization constant k*

k	Equity	Credit	Bond
0.05	−0.0012	−0.0009	0.0003
0.10	−0.0023	−0.0018	0.0005
0.15	−0.0035	−0.0027	0.0008
0.20	−0.0046	−0.0036	0.0010
0.25	−0.0058	−0.0045	0.0013
0.30	−0.0069	−0.0054	0.0015

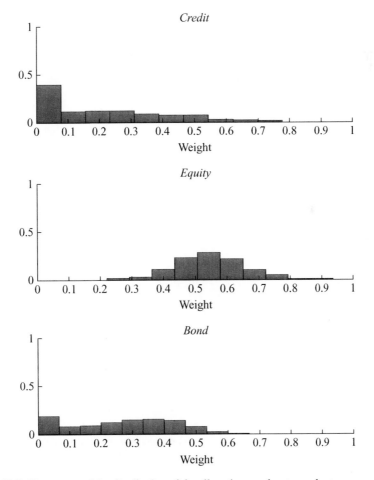

Figure 28.7 Histograms of the distribution of the allocations as the stressed returns are perturbed in 2000 simulations without enforcing CAPM ranking.

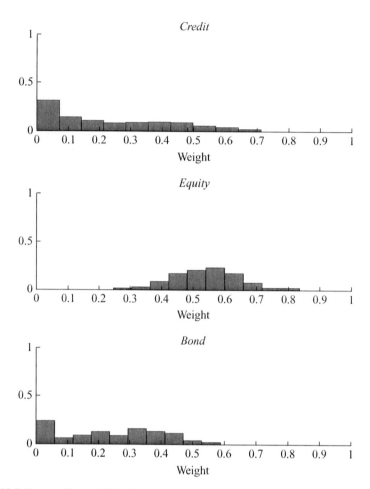

Figure 28.8 Same as Figure 28.7 after enforcing CAPM ranking.

returns, we see that the allocations can vary substantially. The distribution of weights for *Equity* is reasonably localized in the 50–60% range, but even for this asset class allocations as large as 85% and as small as 25% were found over 2000 simulations.

When it comes to *Bond* and *Credit* the distributions of weights are extremely 'diffuse' and we observe again a pronounced instability of the allocations to relatively small changes in the stresses returns. If anything, the distributions of the allocations to *Bond* and *Credit* are even wider, as we find several realization above the 50% mark. (This, of course, means that for these allocations the weight on *Equity* had to be well below 50%.) So, the high degree of variation in weights is not limited to *Credit* and *Bond* (two asset classes that, has we have seen, compete against each other), but extends to *Equity* as well.

Also in this case, imposing that the CAPM ranking of returns should be retained makes little difference. The main effect of imposing the CAPM ranking can be seen for the distribution of allocations to *Equity* – a distribution that is a bit more localized when the CAPM ranking is preserved – and in limiting the right tails of the allocation distributions (extremely polarized allocations become somewhat less likely).

28.4 Effect of combined uncertainty

What ranges of allocation weights do we obtain if we allow for uncertainty both in the conditional probabilities and in the expected returns? The question is interesting because, as uncertainty (and hence variance of returns) increases, the concavity of any risk-aversion-compatible utility function plays a bigger and bigger role. As risk aversion plays an increasingly important role, we may observe greater diversification.

We therefore carried out a weight allocation simulation test by applying to the inputs of our net the changes due to uncertainty both in the expected returns and in the conditional probabilities. (For simplicity we did not distinguish between preservation or otherwise of the CAPM ranking, which, as we discussed above, made little difference.)

Figure 28.9 clearly displays that combining the sources of uncertainty produces ranges of allocations which are not substantially different from what we obtained in the no-ranking case when the conditional probabilities or the expected returns were stressed individually.

We do observe that when the variance of returns becomes very large, the search for extra returns (which, as we discuss below, is at the root of the instability) becomes progressively tempered by safety considerations, but the magnitude of the effect is rather underwhelming.

Of course, similar 'distribution-confining' effects would also be brought about by an increase of risk aversion. We explore this angle in the following sections.

28.5 Stability of the allocations for high degree of risk aversion

In this section we look at the allocations produced with the same degree of uncertainty in expected returns analysed above, but with a much higher degree of risk aversion, as translated by an exponent of 6 in the power utility function (see Figure 28.10).

The allocation results are now qualitatively different, and are different on two accounts: first, the allocation to *Equity* has become much smaller; second, the allocation to the 'defensive' *Bond* asset class now takes the lion's share; and, third, the allocation weights are much more stable to changes in expected returns.

It is easy to understand why the allocations to *Equity* should be significantly reduced: both in the normal and excited states they display a high variance of returns, and this is naturally picked up by the more risk-averse utility function. The distribution of allocations for *Equities* is therefore now centred around the substantially lower value of about 10%.

To understand why such a large fraction of the allocation has been shifted to the unexciting but safe *Bond* asset class, which now commands about 75% of the share

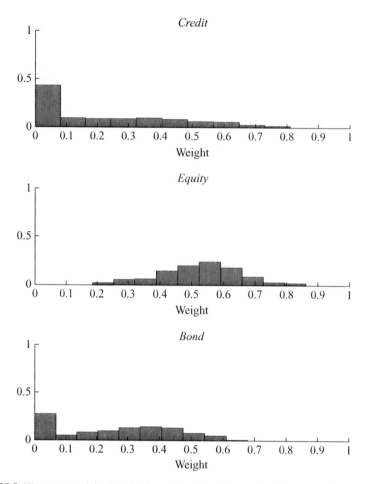

Figure 28.9 Histograms of the distribution of the allocations as both the stressed returns and conditional probabilities ($s = 0.05$) are perturbed.

of the portfolio, recall that *Bond* is the only asset that actually does well (not just less poorly) in situations of distress.

What is most interesting is that the allocations are now far more localized and stable with respect to input uncertainty. We try to understand where this stabilization comes from in the discussion in the next section.

28.6   Where does the instability come from? (again)

The results presented so far in this chapter allow us to draw some important conclusions. Let's collect our thoughts, bringing together some of the conclusions we reached in the previous chapters.

Recall that, when we were looking at the surprising effectiveness of the Gaussian approach, we examined the quality of the mean-variance approximation. As we saw, it

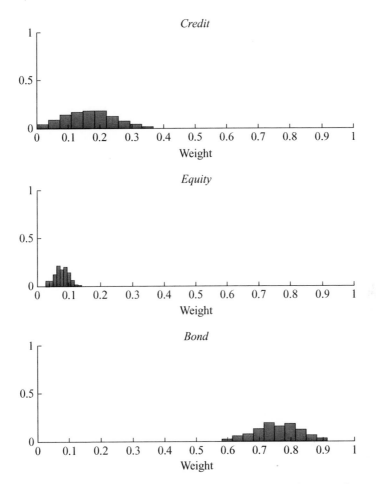

Figure 28.10 Histograms of the distribution of the allocations as both the stressed returns and conditional probabilities (now $s = 0.10$) are perturbed with the risk aversion coefficient, β, increased to $\beta = 6$.

worked remarkably well – by which we mean that, *as long as the expected returns and the covariance structure of the total return distribution were allowed to 'know' about the exceptional returns*, the allocations did not depend greatly, for a given degree of risk aversion, on the details of the utility function.[4] So, we concluded that what matters most is getting the first two moments right, and that, for assets with quasi-linear payoffs, little economic cost is incurred by associating 'risk' with variance.

We also concluded that Bayesian nets can be seen in this respect as devices that know how to increase the portfolio variance in an understandable, logically consistent and financially well-motivated (as opposed to ad-hoc) manner.

---

[4] Of course, we have in mind assets with almost linear payoffs. The presence of out-of-the-money options (tail hedges) would clearly change these considerations.

In this chapter we then moved to the analysis of the stability of the allocations to reasonable changes in the inputs to our model. We saw that the optimal allocations were strongly affected by small changes in the input expected returns. We were surprised by how small these uncertainties in returns could be, and yet produce wide changes in asset allocations. Before running our tests, we thought (or, perhaps, hoped) that the greater variance of the return distribution brought about by the Bayesian-net construction (especially as we varied the normalization factor, k) could 'stabilize' the results by giving more emphasis to the degree of risk aversion. We thought, in other words, that, by bringing to the fore via the Bayesian-net technology clear-and-present-danger scenarios, 'safety-first' considerations and risk aversion would overwhelm the chase for some extra excess return. Usually this turned out not to be the case. By and large, expected returns remained king in determining the allocations.[5] Why is this the case?

Let's go back to basics. We have ascertained that a suitably calibrated mean-variance approach captures very well the essence of the more complex utility-maximization problem. To refresh our intuition, let's go back to the simplest possible setting, i.e., to a Markowitz-like (mean-variance) allocation. In that case we know that the optimal weights, w^*, are given by[6]

$$w^* = \frac{1}{\lambda}\Sigma^{-1}\mu \qquad (28.20)$$

As we showed in Chapter 8, from this it is straightforward to obtain the sensitivity of the weights to the returns, by differentiating with respect to the return vector, μ.[7] One immediately obtains

$$\frac{\partial w^*}{\partial \mu} = \frac{1}{\lambda}\Sigma^{-1} \qquad (28.21)$$

It is clear from this expression that the sensitivity of the weights to the returns is inversely related to the coefficient of risk aversion (λ), and directly related to the magnitude of the inverse of the covariance matrix, Σ^{-1}. Now, the covariance matrix is made up of 'very small' numbers (products of *squares of* volatilities times correlations). Therefore, as we pointed out in Chapter 8, the inverse covariance matrix is made up of 'very large' numbers. As a result, despite the magnitude-reducing effect brought about by dividing by the risk-aversion factor λ, the sensitivities are unavoidably large.

Indeed, Table 28.2 shows the derivatives $\frac{\partial w_i}{\partial \mu_j}$ of the sensitivity for all the asset classes and for different values of the risk aversion coefficient, λ for a reasonable choice of input

---

[5] The statement is of course very sweeping. As discussed in Chapter 8 there are 'knife-edge' situations, associated with assets with very negative correlations, where small changes in volatilities and/or correlations can produce radical changes in allocations. See, for instance, the discussion in Section 8.8 (CAPM2). These tend to be, however, pathological, rather than realistic, cases.

[6] For simplicity we look here at the unconstrained optimization case. Qualitatively similar considerations hold for the more realistic cases of unit sum for the weights ($w^T\mathbf{1} = 1$) or of non-negative holdings.

[7] We are grateful to Dr Vasant Naik for useful discussions of this point.

Table 28.2 *Sensitivity,* $\frac{\partial w_i}{\partial \mu_j}$, *of the allocation weights to changes in expected returns for all the asset classes and for different values of the risk aversion (rounded values)*

$\partial w / \partial \mu$	1	2	6	9
$\partial w(Credit)/\partial \mu(Credit)$	607	303	101	67
$\partial w(Credit)/\partial \mu(Equity)$	−85	−42	−14	−9
$\partial w(Credit)/\partial \mu(Bond)$	−477	−238	−79	−53
$\partial w(Credit)/\partial \mu(Market)$	−18	−9	−3	−2
$\partial w(Equity)/\partial \mu(Credit)$	−85	−42	−14	−9
$\partial w(Equity)/\partial \mu(Equity)$	80	40	13	9
$\partial w(Equity)/\partial \mu(Bond)$	36	18	6	4
$\partial w(Equity)/\partial \mu(Market)$	−144	−72	−24	−16
$\partial w(Bond)/\partial \mu(Credit)$	−477	−238	−79	−53
$\partial w(Bond)/\partial \mu(Equity)$	36	18	6	4
$\partial w(Bond)/\partial \mu(Bond)$	506	253	84	56
$\partial w(Bond)/\partial \mu(Market)$	13	7	2	1
$\partial w(Market)/\partial \mu(Credit)$	−18	−9	−3	−2
$\partial w(Market)/\partial \mu(Equity)$	−144	−72	−24	−16
$\partial w(Market)/\partial \mu(Bond)$	13	7	2	1
$\partial w(Market)/\partial \mu(Market)$	536	268	89	60

parameters. (The covariance matrix was obtained using the normal-times volatility and correlations of the case study examined in this chapter.[8])

With these simple considerations at the back of our mind, we can go back to the results presented in the section about the sensitivity to the coefficient of risk aversion. We now understand, at least mathematically, why a very large coefficient of risk aversion (as translated into an exponent β of 6 for the power utility function) brings about more stable results: we are dividing the very large inverse covariance numbers by a larger factor λ, thereby reducing the sensitivity.

This is indeed *one* way to introduce stability. But have we paid too high a price? The allocation to *Equities* is indeed much more stable, but it is also much smaller. Leaving stability considerations to one side for a moment, which is the 'correct' allocation? 50% or 10%?

In trying to answer this fundamental question we should not forget that the exponent β should be linked to a behavioural feature of investors – i.e., to how they trade off risk against expected return. So, very large values of the exponent β may well stabilize the allocation, but would imply implausibly risk-averse behaviour. And, if stability is all we are looking for, why stop at a β of 6 or 10? Why not use a β of 100 – or of 1000

---

[8] Admittedly, using the normal-times volatilities (smaller than the total-distribution volatilities because of the culling procedure) gives rise to a small covariance element, and large elements for the inverse covariance matrix, thereby exacerbating the problem. Even if we had doubled all the normal-times volatilities, however, we would have only reduced the sensitivity by a factor of 4. The same qualitative results would still apply.

for that matter? As we discuss in the next section, this may well stabilize the results, but not necessarily in a desirable way.

We stress again that the results presented above about the sensitivity of the weights to small changes in expected returns were obtained by placing ourselves in a mean-variance (Markowitz) optimization framework – a framework that, as we discussed in Chapter 7, as been unkindly called an 'error maximization' machine (Scherer 2002).[9] Our allocations, however, were not obtained from mean-variance optimization, but from expected utility maximization, and the utility we used was not quadratic. Yet we seem to have found very similar instability problems. How can this be the case? Aren't leptokurtic distributions coupled with non-quadratic utility functions supposed to capture, and give more importance to, large gains and losses, thereby making the allocation more 'conservative'? Will the same explanation still hold?

We have every reason to believe that it will. Indeed, we have shown in Chapter 27 that, as long as the first two moments of the distribution are correctly captured, the more sophisticated expected-utility-maximization approach gives rise to very similar allocations to the mean-variance approach. We discuss at greater length in the next chapter why this is the case from a different angle. However, we can already give a taste of the explanation. In a nutshell the argument goes as follows.

As shown in Figure 29.1, for reasonably calibrated utility functions the changes in utility associated with large but reasonable changes in wealth turn out to be almost linear. If the utility function is (almost) a linear function of changes in wealth, then the investor is (almost) risk neutral. If she is (almost) risk neutral, she will (almost) only care about maximizing expected returns.

This makes us believe that the explanation we have given for the magnitude of the sensitivity to returns in a simple mean-variance framework can be easily transferred to the more complex non-quadratic-utility-maximization setting, *as long as in both approaches we use an equivalent degree of risk aversion.* We return to this point in the next chapter.

---

[9] See in this respect also Jobson and Korki (1983), Michaud (1989), Best and Grauer (1991), Chopra and Ziemba (1993) and Nawrocki (1996) for a discussion of the problem.

29 How to use Bayesian nets: our recommended approach

29.1 Some preliminary qualitative observations

What lessons can the prudent portfolio manager draw from the sensitivity analysis presented in the previous chapter?

The strong dependence of the recommended allocations on the most-difficult-to-ascertain set of quantities, the expected returns, may, at first blush, appear somewhat dispiriting. Indeed, after running our sensitivity analysis with behaviourally plausible coefficients of *risk* aversion, one can justifiably conclude that it would be foolhardy to rely on even the most careful construction of a Bayesian net to 'read off' with confidence a single set of allocations from a graph such as the one in Figure 26.11: yes, we may well read a precise set of weights today, but small, unavoidable changes in the input expected returns tomorrow (changes which have nothing directly to do with the Bayesian-net method *per se*) could give rise to very different allocations. How can we get around the problem of the instability of the optimal allocations to the various asset classes?

To answer this question, we stress again that the sensitivity of the allocations to small changes in expected returns is not an artifact, or a peculiar feature, of the Bayesian-net approach. The analysis presented in the previous chapter (but see also in this respect Chapter 8) shows that it is an unavoidable feature of all allocation methods based on mean-variance optimization. And, to the extent that reasonably calibrated utility functions give rise to almost-linear variations in utility even with severe-but-reasonable changes in wealth, we argued that switching from mean-variance to full expected-utility optimization is unlikely to give radically different answers. Yes, to some extent, some of this sensitivity of the allocations to the expected returns will be reduced by the ability afforded by the Bayesian nets to 'turn up' the variance of returns if one so wished – but, as we have seen, for logarithmic utility functions, not by much. And we stress again that the similarity of the allocations produced by equivalently calibrated expected-utility maximization already makes us believe that the problem is not limited to a mean-variance setting. Despite the 'bad press' that mean-variance optimization has received, this is not where the stability problem truly lies.

If we want to use Bayesian nets effectively for asset allocations we must therefore find a reasonable solution to the stability problem. It is to this topic that we turn in the next section.

29.2   Ways to tackle the allocation instability

29.2.1   *Optimizing variance for a given return*

Before embarking on the discussion of our preferred stabilization procedure, we must stress that the instability that we intend to exorcise mainly arises when one tries to determine an optimal asset allocation in a utility-maximization framework *given a specified coefficient of risk aversion*. This, however, is not the way asset allocation is normally carried out in investment practice. Very often a target return, or a target variance, is specified in advance and the weights are then determined that minimize variance (or maximize return) given this constraint.

Needless to say, risk aversion has not gone away, but it has been subsumed in the particular mean-variance combination that the optimization will deliver. Indeed, if, in the present investment conditions, an investor were to require an excess return of, say, 9%, there is no doubt that the portfolios able to deliver such stellar returns will have to be extremely risky. A principal investor (as opposed to an agent) who accepted such a risky portfolio would have implicitly specified an extremely high risk tolerance. (Of course, when we deal with principal-agent relationships matters become far more complicated, and whose risk aversion – if anybody's – one is talking about is no longer clear. See in this respect the discussion about 'reduced-form' utility functions in Section 22.5.)

Be that as it may, the fact remains that, if one does not carry out mean-variance optimization for an exogenous degree of risk aversion, but one fixes, say, expected returns, and endogenizes the coefficient of risk aversion, the allocation results tend to be more stable to small changes in the input variables. We do not go into the fine details of why this is the case, but we hand-wavingly suggest that having either expected return or variance fixed acts as an 'anchor' and thus brings about a good degree of stabilization.

So, for the reader who is happy to have a coefficient of risk aversion 'thrust upon her' by a target expected-return requirement, some of our soul searching can be avoided. (We say 'some' because the degree of stabilization depends in subtle, and sometimes unpredictable, ways on the exogenously specified target expected returns.) For those portfolio managers who instead believe that the portfolio allocations should be allocated as a function of their aversion to risk (and, perhaps, to ambiguity), the considerations we present in the rest of the chapter remain fully topical.

If the portfolio manager prefers to take the high road to asset allocation via utility maximization, there are three established ways to deal with the instability of the allocation weights. (See, e.g., the discussion in Meucci (2009).) As we have seen in Chapter 8, one way is to follow a Michaud-like resampling approach (see the discussion in Section 8.3).

The second (theoretically better justified) alternative is a Bayesian approach that directly incorporates uncertainty in the expected returns (and covariances) as an ingredient of the optimization. This we treated in Section 23.6.

The third (closely related) way to deal with instabilities is to embrace the Black–Litterman method, and to apply it in such a way as to tilt the solution towards the market portfolio.[1] None of these alternatives is without problems, but, as we argue below, one is by far the best suited to our goals.

29.2.2 The Black–Litterman stabilization

Let's look at the Black–Litterman way to achieve stability first. The 'prior' implied by the Black–Litterman model can be interpreted to be the views of the portfolio manager, and the 'likelihood function' then becomes related to the views implicitly embedded in the market portfolio – at least if we adopt the interpretation by Satchell and Scowcroft (2000) that we have discussed in Chapter 9.

Now, the allocation produced by this approach can be made extremely stable indeed. This can be simply achieved by tilting the optimal solution more and more towards the market portfolio (which is, in a way, the most stable of portfolios). The price to be paid, however, is not small: to obtain this solution, the portfolio manager, in essence, must say that she has virtually no market views (in which case, of course, her prior plays a close-to-zero role, the likelihood function plays the dominant role in arriving at the posterior, and it makes perfect sense that she should choose an allocation very close to the market portfolio.)

What if the investor were not almost totally agnostic, but had a high-but-not-infinite confidence in her views? As we discussed in Chapter 9, if this is the case the stabilization brought about by the Black–Litterman approach when the investor views are 'robust' turns out to be modest. Yes, the asset allocation instability is somewhat reduced, but it is hardly tamed.

So, in the Black–Litterman approach the portfolio manager's prior must be very diffuse indeed if a stable solution is to be obtained, because, unless the uncertainty in returns is so great as to be almost equivalent to saying that she knows virtually nothing about them, the sensitivity of the allocations to small changes in the returns produced by Bayesian approaches remains large.[2]

29.2.3 The general Bayesian stabilization

One does not have to adopt the specific choice of prior and likelihood function implicit in the Black–Litterman model. More general Bayesian approaches remain wedded to an expected-utility-maximization approach, but embed parameter uncertainty at the very

---

[1] The Black–Litterman approach can be regarded as a particular application of the more general Bayesian approach, in which a special choice for the prior has been assigned.

[2] Admittedly, it is not as large as a mean-variance allocation – and much has been made in the literature of this positive feature – but benchmarking against the stability of allocations produced by mean-variance does not place the bar very high.

start of the procedure – i.e., *before* the optimization is carried out.[3] This will broaden the portfolio variance, and, as the analysis of Sections 8.2 and 23.6.1 suggests, will reduce the sensitivity to changes in expected returns. By extrapolating the discussion presented in Section 23.6, the covariance elements will become larger, and the inverse covariance matrix (directly linked, as we have seen, to the sensitivity) will be correspondingly smaller. This should reduce the emphasis on the chase for extra return, and favour more stable allocations.

Unfortunately, one finds again that, unless the portfolio uncertainty is truly 'deep', and the variance therefore very large indeed, the stabilization produced by incorporating uncertainty about means and returns in the optimization from the very start is modest. (See in this respect the discussion in Section 23.6.) Intuitively, this can also be understood by referring to the simplest mean-variance, unconstrained-weights setting. In this setting the role played by the Bayesian procedure is simply to produce a 'wider' input covariance matrix. For a reasonable degree of uncertainty in the expected returns (i.e., as long as the views are 'informative') the same considerations presented in Chapter 8 about the instability of the coefficients therefore remain valid.

An optimist might retort that perhaps our explanation, which is based on mean-variance optimization, does not transfer to a more general utility-optimization setting. Perhaps the ability of more complex utility functions than the quadratic one to 'feel' higher moments (skewness, kurtosis) can produce more conservative (and hence stable) allocations. As we have seen, this is empirically not the case. But why does the expected-utility-optimization apparatus fail to exorcise the importance of these small differences in expectations beyond what one would have probably guessed – and certainly well beyond the 'economic' significance that we intuitively assign to these small differences? Why is the reduction in instability so small?

Looking at Figure 29.1 tells us at least a good part of the answer: here we have calculated a logarithmic utility function for a portfolio made up of a 50–50 combination of asset 1 and asset 2. On the *x*- and *y*- axes we show the excess returns for the two assets, excess returns that span a range from −7.5% to +7.5% for both assets. For a horizon of a few months this is a wide range indeed. The striking feature of the figure is that *the utility is almost exactly linear over the very wide range of returns* reached over the investment horizon. For such a utility function, as we have shown in Chapter 25, the skewness and leptokurtosis of the returns distribution matter little.

So, strictly speaking, for mean-variance to apply we require either normal returns (and our Bayesian nets certainly produce strongly-non-normal returns), or quadratic utility functions. The logarithmic utility function that constituted our benchmark is certainly not quadratic. However, for wide but reasonable degrees of change in wealth (15% in Figure 29.1) the logarithmic utility function is almost linear. As will be, for that matter, a quadratic utility function calibrated to have the same degree of risk aversion. But an investor whose utility function is almost linear will display almost no degree

---

[3] This should be contrasted with the more ad hoc Michaud's solution (discussed below), where the uncertainty is dealt with by averaging over allocations *after* the optimizations have taken place.

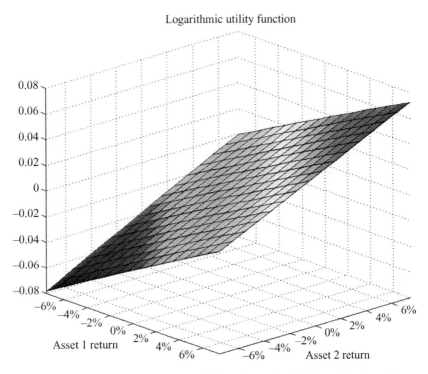

Logarithmic utility function

Figure 29.1 A logarithmic utility function for a portfolio made up of a 50–50 combination of asset 1 and asset 2. On the x- and y-axes we show the excess returns from the two assets.

of risk aversion.[4] She will therefore behave as an almost-risk-neutral investor. As a consequence, she will chase small differences in returns, with little regard for the risks she incurs. Her investment decisions will therefore be little affected even by as large a variance as the one produced by the Bayesian-net construction.

This is one of the reasons why traditional, utility-based optimizations produce allocations as sensitive to small changes in expectations as the ones we have observed.[5] (And, in passing, this is the reason why the Gaussian approximation presented in Section 25.2 worked so well.) Faced with a significant risk, the expected-utility-maximizer sees little reason – when she is as close to a risk-neutral an investor as the one whose utility function is depicted in Figure 29.1 – to throw away the advantage coming from a higher expected return, even if very small.

We have drawn this conclusion with a very common and theoretically appealing[6] utility function, such as the logarithmic one. However, we close this subsection by reminding the reader that investors can be modelled as agents who are not just

---

[4] Recall that the curvature of the utility function is the *only* mechanism available in the standard expected-utility apparatus to give rise to risk aversion.

[5] This, of course, brings in the question of how the utility function has been calibrated. We touch on this important question in the following.

[6] See, e.g., Sinn (2002) for a discussion of the theoretical 'superiority' of the logarithmic utility function.

risk-averse, but also *ambiguity*-averse. When this is the case, their aversion to ambiguity can be translated into an 'effective' increase in their risk aversion. This can change the terms of the discussion radically. We discuss this important point in the next subsection.

29.2.4   *Calibrating the utility function to risk and ambiguity aversion*

An obvious objection to the line of reasoning presented in the previous sub-section springs to mind. We argued that, when it comes to asset allocation, a well-established and theoretically appealing utility function such as the logarithmic one produces a behaviour that is too 'risk-neutral-like'. But what can we mean by this? If we have calibrated our utility function to the observed behaviour of an agent, aren't we assured of the fact that, virtually by construction, her risk aversion has been properly taken into account? How can a utility function be simultaneously calibrated to observed, real-life, *risk-averse* choices, and then imply an almost-risk-neutral behaviour?

At least a good part of the answer lies in the paper by Rabin and Thaler (2001) discussed at some length in Chapter 23 (see Section 23.4 in particular), which shows that if a utility function (*any* utility function) is calibrated to risk aversion 'in the small', then it produces close-to-absurd results 'in the large'.

We may well accept all these points, and we may feel better (or more discouraged) now that we understand more clearly one explanation of where the allocation instability comes from. But, leaving this theoretical thicket behind us, if our pragmatic concern is the stability of the allocations, why don't we just increase the degree of risk aversion? Perhaps we acknowledge that we have to use a short blanket, and that either feet or head will have to remain exposed. We may accept having one part of our risk-aversion body uncovered by the blanket, as long as the important parts (the part linked to the stability of allocations) are properly covered.

This is indeed the route we explored in Section 28.5 when we looked at the allocations obtained with an exponent β of 6, and we showed that we did obtain far more stable results. However, as the mean-variance analysis suggests, *if we believe that investors only care about risk and are ambiguity-neutral*, this is a heavy price to pay: a very large, and behaviourally implausible, degree of risk aversion is needed to obtain a meaningful reduction in the weight sensitivity to the expected returns, and this can have strong implications on the optimal allocations (as the drastic reduction in the weight to *Equity* showed). And, as we asked in Section 28.6, if stability is what we care about, and we are happy about untethering our analysis from the moorings of behavioural plausibility, why stop at 6? Why not choose 100, or 1000? And if we do so, what would happen to the allocation to *Equity*? Increasing risk aversion can be an awkward route to follow for a risk-only sensitive investor.

This is no longer the case, however, if investors are assumed to be averse not just to risk, but to ambiguity as well. And we have shown in Section 23.6.3 that an 'effective' higher degree of risk aversion naturally arises from the ambiguity framework. And, as we saw in the same section, this powerful and simple result arises both in static and in dynamic optimization problems.

This is encouraging. But how large should the ambiguity-aversion coefficient be? Recall that the solution presented in Section 23.6 contained a new parameter, η, that was supposed to account for our aversion to ambiguity. How are we to establish this additional coefficient? We propose the following pragmatic suggestion.

Let us take our 'dislike' for unstable weight allocations as a symptom of our ambiguity aversion. If this is the case, then we should make the ambiguity-aversion-corrected effective coefficient of risk aversion *as large as required to make us feel comfortable with the dispersion of the distribution of allocation weights.*

Is this approach subjective? Of course it is – just as asking which lotteries with actuarially known distributions an agent would choose in order to estimate her degree of *risk* aversion is subjective. In the case both of risk and of ambiguity aversion we are trying to gauge a preference, which is, by definition, subjective. The relevant question is whether the 'symptom' we use to gauge the investor's attitude to ambiguity is reasonably chosen.

If we accept that the indicator we have chosen (our intrinsic[7] dislike for unstable weight allocations) is reasonable, then we can offer a simple operational suggestion: we should increase the (now 'effective') degree of risk aversion up to the point where the allocations become unobjectionably stable.

29.3 The lay of the land

Let's collect our thoughts: we have identified four ways to handle the instability of the asset allocation while remaining within the expected-utility-maximization framework.

1. We can increase the variance of returns. One way to do so is by increasing the uncertainty in the return parameters. But, as discussed, if we remain in a pure *risk*-aversion framework, the increase in uncertainty must be very (and probably implausibly) large to make a meaningful difference to the allocations. In order to obtain reasonable stability, we have to introduce almost-Knightian uncertainty. Effectively we are saying that we have views, but that we are so uncertain about them that 'anything could happen, really'.
2. We can tilt, *à la* Black–Litterman, the solution towards the market portfolio. The price to pay to obtain stability of weights, again, is that we have essentially to negate our views, or to pretend not to have any.
3. We can increase our degree of risk aversion. If we only want to account for aversion to risk, we have to do so, however, far beyond what seems to be behaviourally reasonable. In a purely *risk*-aversion framework, our blanket remains unavoidably short, and choosing to cover with it exclusively the asset-stability part is unsatisfactory.

---

[7] By 'intrinsic' we refer to the fact that our dislike is a primitive, and not just due to, say, increased transaction costs.

4. *We can recognize that investors are averse not only to risk but also to ambiguity.* Aversion to ambiguity, as we have seen, has solid theoretical foundations and can be effectively described in a purely risk-aversion framework by increasing the coefficient of risk aversion. And, as we have discussed many times, increasing the coefficient of risk aversion is one of the most effective mechanisms to reduce the allocation instability (i.e., the high sensitivity of the allocation weights to changes in the expected returns). This is no lucky coincidence. The weight instability is a direct reflection of the coexistence of several parallel 'models' (each one associated with an economically similar vector or expected returns). And aversion to ambiguity means aversion to the coexistence of these plausible parallel models.

There are, of course, other alternatives. If we leave the confines of expected-utility-maximization[8] (possibly implemented in an ambiguity-aversion spirit), we have for instance at our disposal Michaud's resampling, and the panoply of suggestions offered by what we dubbed in Section 23.7 'shallow-axiomatization Robust Decision Making'. Should we be tempted by the siren's calls of these methods?

The idea is appealing, but we are reluctant to embrace it with gusto because of the ad-hockery and theoretical opaqueness of some of the suggestions put forth as a way to make the allocation results more stable, or the portfolio more diversified. What we fear is that intuitively appealing 'recipes' may hide logical problems, or fall short in opaque manners of delivering the improvements they appear to offer.

Are we being too 'purist'? Are we balking at shadows? To explain what we mean, and to give a taste of how a simple and intuitive ad-hoc fix may fail to deliver what it promises, we present in Appendix 29.A a *prima facie* attractive, and certainly intuitively appealing, Michaud-inspired approach to stabilization. We show that, unfortunately, intuition can easily lead us astray. Before doing so, however, we summarize one last time our line of reasoning, lest we (and the reader) lose the logical thread.

29.4   The approach we recommend

What are we to do then? We are not ready to give up on the stability of allocations. When we balance simplicity, transparency and solidity of the theoretical underpinning we ultimately prefer to remain in the well-trodden path of maximization of expected utility, implemented with a high risk-aversion coefficient. This high coefficient of risk aversion should be understood in an 'effective' sense – i.e., as a way to account both for *risk* and for *ambiguity* aversion. We discussed in Section 23.6.2 how this can be justified.

This combination can give us the weight stability we have been looking for, and can be theoretically justified as a simple way to account for investors' aversion to risk and ambiguity.

---

[8] By 'traditional expected-utility-maximization framework' we refer to maximizations of time-separable utility functions over consumptions, or proxies of consumption.

For the applications we have looked at, a power-utility-function exponent β greater than 5 and smaller than 10 seems to do a very good job. The portfolio manager can fine-tune this 'effective' coefficient of risk aversion to the point where she finds acceptable the dispersion on allocation weights given her uncertainty about expected returns. This automatically (if somewhat heuristically) ensures that her aversion to ambiguity is implicitly accounted for.

In sum, after great sound and fury, we have settled on a remarkably simple procedure, which we can summarize as follows.

- Given a scenario of concern, we build a Bayesian net that reflects our subjective views (buttressed by as much statistical information as we think is relevant) about how this scenario may unfold.
- We build a joint distribution for the attending normal-times market risk factors.
- We conjoin the normal-times and the Bayesian-net distribution to obtain the spliced distribution.
- After marginalizing the non-market-risk factors, we calculate the first two 'total' moments of the portfolio returns derived from this spliced and marginalized joint distribution.
- We then obtain the allocation of weights using the traditional (Markowitz-like) mean-variance optimization techniques *with a high coefficient of risk aversion* (which can be naturally interpreted as a nod towards a simplified way to account for ambiguity aversion) and with the portfolio constraints (positivity, budget constraint, etc.) that we deem important.

This procedure is simple, intuitively appealing, familiar to most portfolio managers and computationally very cheap. All our effort is devoted to constructing a 'good' Bayesian net, and a plausible spliced distribution (using CAPM-related suggestions as to what 'plausible' means). Once this is achieved, we translate quickly our problem into familiar mean-variance language, and we make use of all the tools that half a century of practice have carefully honed.

The asset-allocation part of the procedure could be complicated in many ways: we could choose a more 'sophisticated' utility function; we could carry out a full optimization of expected utility; we could deploy some of the computationally-very-intensive stabilization patches that Robust Decision-Making theory suggests. Yes, we could do some, or all, of the above. However, we have found that it is not clear that any of these 'complications' brings about appreciable advantages. What we *have* observed is that they can make the computational burden considerably heavier, and cloud the intuition. Our preferred solution therefore turns out to be computationally very light and 'affordable', and is built on theoretically solid foundations.

Central to our approach is the belief that there is value in incorporating well-thought-out views in the process of portfolio construction. At the heart of the problem then lie two problems: how to ensure that these views are expressed in a logically correct manner; and how to derive asset allocations from these coherent views in a logically consistent manner. We believe that the Bayesian-net technology performs in both respects admirably.

As discussed in Chapters 14 and 15, also the Bayesian-net construction of the procedure could be complicated in several directions (especially when it comes to the elicitation part). We are fond of these techniques, and we find that they can be very useful. We caution, however, the asset manager who has to present her results to an investment committee against overusing these powerful tools, lest the simplicity and the intuitive appeal of the procedure get clouded.

We think that the most appealing feature of the approach we propose is the marriage of the outputs from the Bayesian-net part of the procedure (perhaps just the first two moments of the spliced distribution), with well-established, simple, intuitive and theoretically solid analytical tools (such as mean-variance optimization). We find that this marriage provides a useful way to determine a coherent and stable allocation among asset classes in the presence of tail events. This was the purpose of our book.

Appendix 29.A: The parable of Marko and Micha

A naive way to make use of the information embedded in the distribution of allocation weights in order to make the results more robust could be to calculate the average of the distribution of the allocation weights. Surely, one is tempted to argue, this averaging procedure *must* produce more stable allocations, in the sense that tomorrow's weights should be reasonably similar to today's. We show below that this plausible suggestion is based on a fallacy.[9]

There are two investors, Marko and Micha,[10] who want to optimize (for simplicity without any constraints) their portfolios. Both investors observe a vector of returns, μ_0. For the sake of simplicity we shall assume that they know exactly the covariance matrix, Σ.

The Markowitz mapping from returns to weights is given by

$$\widetilde{w} = \widetilde{w}(\mu_0) \tag{29.1}$$

where the tilde symbol denotes the Markowitz mapping.

Micha believes that returns are stochastic and distributed according to $\mathcal{N}(m_0, S)$. So, according to Micha, the observed return vector is a particular realization of

$$\mu_i = \mu_0 + \Delta\mu_i \tag{29.2}$$

---

[9] We obtain the results in this appendix in the case of an unconstrained optimization. For constrained optimizations the results may be different.

[10] It would be disingenuous to deny that the names Marko and Micha are chosen to remind the reader of Markowitz and Michaud. However, it is only fair to stress that the Micha investor of the parable does not truly act as Michaud recommends and that there is at most a resemblance between what Micha and Michaud would do. The purpose of the parable is simply to show that plausible ways to 'robustize' a portfolio allocation procedure can fail to be effective – even when the suggested procedure seems both intuitively attractive and almost 'guaranteed' to work.

where

$$\Delta\mu_i \propto \mathcal{N}(\mathbf{0}, \mathbf{S}) \tag{29.3}$$

Neither investor knows the true $\mathbf{m}_0$ and therefore sets $\boldsymbol{\mu}_0 = \mathbb{E}[\boldsymbol{\mu}_i] = \mathbf{m}_0$. This is their common starting point.

For Marko, the weights are simply given by

$$\widetilde{\mathbf{w}}_i = \widetilde{\mathbf{w}}_i(\boldsymbol{\mu}_i) \tag{29.4}$$

Marko stops here.

Micha wants to make her results more robust. To achieve this worthy goal, she decides to carry out an average over these weights. Remembering that

$$\frac{\partial \widetilde{\mathbf{w}}}{\partial \boldsymbol{\mu}} = \frac{1}{\lambda} \boldsymbol{\Sigma}^{-1} \tag{29.5}$$

and Taylor expanding, she gets

$$\widetilde{\mathbf{w}}_i = \widetilde{\mathbf{w}}_i(\boldsymbol{\mu}_i) = \widetilde{\mathbf{w}}_i(\boldsymbol{\mu}_0 + \Delta\boldsymbol{\mu}_i) = \widetilde{\mathbf{w}}(\boldsymbol{\mu}_0) + \frac{1}{\lambda}\boldsymbol{\Sigma}^{-1}\Delta\boldsymbol{\mu}_i \tag{29.6}$$

She then calculates the average as

$$\langle \widetilde{\mathbf{w}} \rangle = \frac{1}{n}\sum_{i=1,n} \widetilde{\mathbf{w}}_i = \widetilde{\mathbf{w}}(\boldsymbol{\mu}_0) + \frac{1}{\lambda}\boldsymbol{\Sigma}^{-1}\frac{1}{n}\sum_{i=1,n}\Delta\boldsymbol{\mu}_i = \widetilde{\mathbf{w}}(\boldsymbol{\mu}_0) \tag{29.7}$$

where the last equality follows because of Equation (29.3).

So, the average carried out by Micha still gives her exactly the same allocation as Marko's! Not really what Micha wanted to achieve.

However, Micha knows that she just happens to live in one of many parallel (statistically equivalent) universes. So, she realizes that setting $\boldsymbol{\mu}_0 = \mathbb{E}[\boldsymbol{\mu}_i] = \mathbf{m}_0$ was not really justifiable. She therefore decides that she wants to average 'over universes'. In any of these possible universes that she could have inhabited, Micha would have measured the vector $\boldsymbol{\mu}_i = \boldsymbol{\mu}_0 + \Delta\boldsymbol{\mu}_i$. In each of these possible worlds, following the procedure described above, the parallel Micha would have drawn changes in the return vector, $\Delta\boldsymbol{\mu}_i^k$ (where the superscript k refers to the universe), and would have carried out an average, $\langle \widetilde{\mathbf{w}} \rangle_k$ (where, again, the subscript k signifies that the average has been carried out in the kth universe). Each of these averages is given by

$$\langle \widetilde{\mathbf{w}} \rangle_k = \widetilde{\mathbf{w}}(\boldsymbol{\mu}_k) + \frac{1}{\lambda}\boldsymbol{\Sigma}^{-1}\frac{1}{n}\sum_{i=1,n}\Delta\boldsymbol{\mu}_i^k$$

$$= \left(\widetilde{\mathbf{w}}(\boldsymbol{\mu}_0) + \frac{1}{\lambda}\boldsymbol{\Sigma}^{-1}\Delta\boldsymbol{\mu}_k\right) + \frac{1}{\lambda}\boldsymbol{\Sigma}^{-1}\frac{1}{n}\sum_{i=1,n}\Delta\boldsymbol{\mu}_i^k$$

$$= \widetilde{\mathbf{w}}(\boldsymbol{\mu}_0) + \frac{1}{\lambda}\boldsymbol{\Sigma}^{-1}\Delta\boldsymbol{\mu}_k \tag{29.8}$$

Averaging now over universes, alas, gives

$$\langle\langle\widetilde{\mathbf{w}}\rangle\rangle = \widetilde{\mathbf{w}}(\boldsymbol{\mu}_0) \tag{29.9}$$

Sadly, the allocation Micha comes up with after all this averaging in the one universe she lives in is still identical to the allocation Marko had obtained with one line of code.

And one can easily see that, because of the linearity of the dependence of the weights on the returns, one can carry out averages of averages ... of averages, and she will end up with the same allocation as Marko.

Appendix I
The links with the
Black–Litterman approach

In this appendix we look at how we can reconcile our approach with the Black–Litterman model. Given the subjective nature of both approaches, it is useful to present them using a unified 'language'. In particular, the Black–Litterman approach can be used (admittedly, in a rather reductive manner) as a regularization device to tame the instabilities in allocations from which the Markowitz model notoriously suffers. We show that the Black–Litterman approach can be married to the Bayesian-net construction that we propose, and that also in this marriage it can play a 'regularization' function. In Chapter 29 (see Section 29.2 in particular) we discussed whether this way of achieving a greater stability for the allocation weights is desirable or not.

1 The Black–Litterman 'regularization'

We provided in Chapter 9 what we called a somewhat 'tendentious' presentation of the Black–Litterman approach – where, when we say 'tendentious', we simply mean that we gave a presentation explicitly tailored to highlighting two particular messages out of the many that could be extracted from the approach.

(i) The first 'message' is that, as the Black–Litterman approach naturally incorporates subjective views into its set-up, it is germane in spirit, if not in implementation, to our view of the world. Therefore combining Black–Litterman with Bayesian nets is a natural logical step. We show in the rest of this chapter how this can be done.

(ii) The second characteristic of relevance to us is that the Black–Litterman algorithm has the in-built potential to 'regularize' the Markowitz instabilities. It does so by increasing the manager's uncertainty about her views. As the uncertainty grows, the allocation gravitates more and more towards the market portfolio – which is, by definition, well-behaved. We also highlighted (using Doust's Geometric Variance approach[1]) the interplay between the allocation-weights space and the expected-returns space, and we showed how it is possible to have well-behaved weights while remaining closer than the Black–Litterman to the manager's views. This is

---

[1] See Sections 9.4 and 10.3.

nice and useful, but not essential to this part of the argument, which is simply that the Black–Litterman formalism can be used as a regularization engine. This important strand was covered in Chapters 28 and 29.

In order to show how our approach can be reconciled with Black–Litterman, we follow in the next sections the presentation adopted by Satchell and Scowcroft (2000) to cast the Black–Litterman in a Bayesian form. We will use the following 'configuration' of the Bayesian formula:

$$h(parameters|historical\ data\ or\ market\text{-}implied\ quantities)$$
$$\propto f(historical\ data\ or\ market\text{-}implied\ quantities|parameters)$$
$$\times g(parameters) \tag{A.1}$$

In words, we will try to blend our prior views on certain parameters, expressed by the prior distribution *g(parameters)*, with the market-implied or historical values for the same parameters, in order to obtain the posterior distribution of the parameters, *h(parameters|historical data or market-implied quantities)*. As in all Bayesian analyses, we have to give a concrete representation to the likelihood function and to the prior. This is done in the next sections.

The parameters that enter our Bayesian analysis are returns and covariances.

To keep things simple, let's consider the case where we are estimating these quantities using their historical values – rather than using a mixed statistical/market-implied approach. Perhaps we may want to carry out the estimation using the 'shrinkage' methods discussed in Sections 18.1 and 19.2, but we remain 'agnostic' on this point.

So let's suppose that we have a set of historical observations $\widehat{\mathbf{y}}_1, \widehat{\mathbf{y}}_2, \ldots, \widehat{\mathbf{y}}_n$ on the returns of each asset class. Using these observations we can calculate the averages, the correlation and covariance matrices, and, if we so wish, a lot of additional statistics. We will denote by $\widehat{\boldsymbol{\Omega}}$ the sample covariance matrix (and by $\widehat{\Omega}_{jk}$ the sample covariance element referring to asset classes j and k).

The main question is now: if we have prior views on some of these statistics, e.g., on the mean and covariances, how can we amalgamate them with past data and obtain an updated version through the posterior? This is the essence of Bayesian statistics.

2   The likelihood function

The first step is to calculate the likelihood. Let's denote the prior vector of returns by $\boldsymbol{\mu}$ and the prior covariance matrix by $\boldsymbol{\Omega}$. The joint likelihood is the product of the likelihoods of the individual observations. We will assume that each observation has been drawn from a normal distribution and so will have a normal likelihood:

$$f(\widehat{\mathbf{y}}_1, \widehat{\mathbf{y}}_2, \ldots, \widehat{\mathbf{y}}_n | \boldsymbol{\mu}, \boldsymbol{\Omega}) \propto \prod_{i=1,n} \exp\left[-\frac{(\widehat{\mathbf{y}}_i - \boldsymbol{\mu})'\boldsymbol{\Omega}^{-1}(\widehat{\mathbf{y}}_i - \boldsymbol{\mu})}{2}\right]$$

$$= \exp\left[-\frac{1}{2}\left(\sum_{i=1,n}\widehat{\mathbf{y}}_i'\boldsymbol{\Omega}^{-1}\widehat{\mathbf{y}}_i\right) + n(\boldsymbol{\mu}'\boldsymbol{\Omega}^{-1}\boldsymbol{\mu}) - \sum_{i=1,n}\widehat{\mathbf{y}}_i'(\boldsymbol{\Omega}^{-1}\boldsymbol{\mu}) - \boldsymbol{\mu}'\boldsymbol{\Omega}^{-1}\sum_{i=1,n}\widehat{\mathbf{y}}_i\right]$$

$$\tag{A.2}$$

After defining

$$y_{\text{avg}} = \frac{1}{n} \sum_{i=1,n} \widehat{y}_i \tag{A.3}$$

and rearranging terms, one obtains

$$f(\widehat{y}_1, \widehat{y}_2, \ldots, \widehat{y}_n | \mu, \Omega) \propto \exp\left[-\frac{n}{2}(\mu - y_{\text{avg}})'\Omega^{-1}(\mu - y_{\text{avg}})\right]$$

$$\times \exp\left[-\frac{1}{2}\left(\sum_{i=1,n} \widehat{y}_i'\Omega^{-1}\widehat{y}_i - n y_{\text{avg}}\Omega^{-1} y_{\text{avg}}\right)\right] \tag{A.4}$$

In the first exponential we have the prior average, μ, the prior covariance matrix, Ω, and the sample average, y_{avg}. This term gives us the contribution to the likelihood of the probability of the sample average having been generated by the prior parameters μ and Ω.

Let's shift our attention now to the second term on the right-hand side of Equation (A.4). From the definition of sample covariance element we have

$$\widehat{\Omega}_{jk} = \sum_{i=1,n} \left(\frac{y_{ij} y_{ik}}{n} - y_j^{\text{avg}} y_k^{\text{avg}}\right) \tag{A.5}$$

We can therefore write for the second term in the likelihood function (A.4):

$$\exp\left[-\frac{1}{2}\left(\sum_{i=1,n} \widehat{y}_i'\Omega^{-1}\widehat{y}_i - n y_{\text{avg}}\Omega^{-1} y_{\text{avg}}\right)\right]$$

$$= \exp\left[-\frac{n}{2}\left(\frac{\sum_{i=1,n} \widehat{y}_i'\Omega^{-1}\widehat{y}_i}{n} - y_{\text{avg}}\Omega^{-1} y_{\text{avg}}\right)\right]$$

$$= \exp\left[-\frac{n}{2}\left(\sum_j \sum_k \Omega_{jk}^{-1}\left(\sum_{i=1,n}\left(\frac{y_{ij} y_{ik}}{n} - y_j^{\text{avg}} y_k^{\text{avg}}\right)\right)\right)\right]$$

$$= \exp\left[-\frac{n}{2}\sum_j \sum_k \Omega_{jk}^{-1}\widehat{\Omega}_{jk}\right] \tag{A.6}$$

In sum

$$f(\widehat{y}_1, \widehat{y}_2, \ldots, \widehat{y}_n | \mu, \Omega)$$

$$\propto \frac{1}{\Omega^{\frac{n}{2}}} \exp\left[-\frac{n}{2}\left[(\mu - y_{\text{avg}})'\Omega^{-1}(\mu - y_{\text{avg}}) + \sum_j \sum_k \Omega_{jk}^{-1}\widehat{\Omega}_{jk}\right]\right] \tag{A.7}$$

So far the analysis has been along straightforward Bayesian lines. It is at this point that we make the Black–Litterman assumption, and replace the historical parameters, y_{avg}

and $\widehat{\mathbf{\Omega}}$, with the market-implied ones. (Recall that we include in μ and $\mathbf{\Omega}$ the market portfolio – or, rather, its proxy.)

Now, since we will speak about market-implied forward-looking quantities, we do not have as a parameter the sample size. The problem is solved in the Black–Litterman model by setting the sample size equal to the parameter $1/\tau$, i.e., we imagine that the market-implied parameters are drawn from a sample with size $1/\tau$. In our formulation:

$$f(\widehat{\mathbf{y}}_1, \widehat{\mathbf{y}}_2, \ldots, \widehat{\mathbf{y}}_n | \mu, \mathbf{\Omega})$$

$$\propto \frac{1}{\mathbf{\Omega}^{\frac{1}{2\tau}}} \exp\left[-\frac{1}{2\tau}\left[(\mu - \mathbf{y}_{avg})'\mathbf{\Omega}^{-1}(\mu - \mathbf{y}_{avg}) + \sum_j\sum_k \Omega_{jk}^{-1}\widehat{\Omega}_{jk}\right]\right] \qquad (A.8)$$

We note in passing that the term $(\mu - \mathbf{y}_{avg})'\mathbf{\Omega}^{-1}(\mu - \mathbf{y}_{avg})$ represents, once again, a distance, namely the Mahalanobis distance between the vectors μ and $\mathbf{y}_{avg}$ induced by the metric defined by $\mathbf{\Omega}$.

What about the factor τ? There are two schools of thought about this parameter. (See Walters (2011) for a comparison.) The first school thinks that should be set to a small value around 0.02 (He and Litterman 1999; Black and Litterman 1992; Idzorek 2005). The second school sets it to 1, i.e., eliminates it from the model (Satchell and Scowcroft 2000; Meucci 2009). We refer the reader to the references above and in Section 9.2 for a discussion of the topic. We note, however, the similarity between the interpretation of this parameter and the interpretation of the Bayesian approach to incorporating uncertainty about expected returns in asset allocation, which we discuss at length in Section 9.2.

3   The prior

The second ingredient in the Bayesian recipe is the prior, $g(\mu_{BN}, \mathbf{\Omega}_{BN})$. The prior, in the formulation we have chosen, reflects our subjective views about expected returns and covariances. The expectations and covariances implied by our model, which we will denote by μ_{BN} and $\mathbf{\Omega}_{BN}$, respectively, are affected by the following sources of uncertainty:

1. uncertainty in the probabilities forming the conditional probability tables;
2. uncertainty in the vector of stressed returns;
3. uncertainty in the 'normal' part.

The larger these sources of uncertainty, the less confident we are in the model. If we were absolutely certain about the model and could pin down all the parameters with absolute precision, there would be no need for a Bayesian approach (or, rather, it would be a 'degenerate' Bayesian approach, where the prior would be characterized by as many Dirac-δ distributions as parameters, and the prior would focus in with infinite sharpness on the corresponding portions of the likelihood function), and the concept of amalgamation of prior beliefs with data would not make sense. So, we certainly have to deal with at least *some* sources of uncertainty. Let's consider them in turn.

The last source of uncertainty (item 3) arises if we estimate the 'normal' expectations and variances from a sample of finite size, thus giving rise to noise in the estimation. Let's neglect this 'mundane' source of uncertainty for the moment – but see the discussion in Section 23.5.

As for the second source of uncertainty (item 2), we assume the stressed returns, L_i, are not centred exactly around a fixed value but are only known with a Gaussian uncertainty ϑ_i. Recall that the uncertainties in the stressed returns of the different asset classes are considered independent in our model.

Finally, item 1 above is the one that gives rise to correlation of uncertainty across asset classes. To understand what this means, imagine that we do not know exactly the probabilities of the conditional probability tables but we assign a degree of uncertainty to each of them according to a specific rule. The rule may be the one already suggested in Chapter 13, i.e., choosing a uniform interval around their value determined by the expert. This type of uncertainty creates a correlation between the total drifts and covariances. For example, if we vary, say, $P(E_2|E_1)$ in a given Bayesian net in its uncertainty interval, the total expectations and covariances of all the assets classes may covary together if certain conditions hold (and if they do, they do not covary in a simple manner).

So if we have to express our degree of uncertainty or confidence in the model, we have to take into account all these different contributions. Doing so 'properly' is very difficult. If we want to take a shortcut, we could use the results of the Maximum-Entropy section, i.e., instead of dealing separately with the uncertainty associated with each probability in each node, we could summarize everything in one single number, the normalization factor, k, and its distribution. The variance Σ^2 of the distribution of k then gives directly the degree of confidence.

If we neglect for the moment the uncertainty in the stressed returns (i.e., item 2 in the list above), what will be the uncertainty in the total expectations if we model k as a distribution? Let's write the expression of the total first moment for the change in the jth market risk factor:

$$E_T[\Delta\xi_j]$$
$$= \left[1 - k + \frac{k}{1 - p_0}(1 - P(E_j) - p_0)\right] E_{\text{norm}}[\Delta\xi_j] + \frac{k}{1 - p_0} P(E_j) E_{\text{exc}}[\Delta\xi_j]$$

(A.9)

where $E_T[\cdot]$ and $E_{\text{norm}}[\cdot]$ denote the total and normal-time operators, respectively. As for the expression for the variance of the total first moment due to k one obtains:

$$\text{Var}[E_T[\Delta\xi_j]]$$
$$= \Sigma^2 \left[\left(\frac{1 - P(E_j) - p_0}{1 - p_0} - 1\right) E_{\text{norm}}[\Delta\xi_j] + \frac{1}{1 - p_0} P(E_j) E_{\text{exc}}[\Delta\xi_j]\right]^2$$

(A.10)

The expression for the total variance is more complicated and we will not write it down but the calculations are straightforward. Again, even with this method, which uses a parsimonious uncertainty parameter, we will have uncertainty correlation between the total drifts and variances since they all depend on k^2.

Summarizing, the expression for the prior $g(\boldsymbol{\mu}_{\mathrm{BN}}, \boldsymbol{\Omega}_{\mathrm{BN}})$ in both cases does not in general have a simple form but can be simulated numerically.

4   The posterior

The posterior is given by multiplying the prior and the likelihood. Given the 'unpleasant' form of the likelihood and prior, an analytical expression for the posterior is in general not available. However, Monte-Carlo methods can be used to derive the posterior.

Once we have the posterior, we have a full distribution for the means and covariances given a parsimonious description of the uncertainty associated with our Bayesian net.

References

Ackerman, F, Stanton, E A, Bueno R (2012) Epstein–Zin Utility and DICE: Is Risk Aversion Relevant to Climate Policy?, Working paper, Stockholm Environment Institute – US Centre, Tufts University, March 2012

Addison, P S (1997) Fractals and Chaos, Institute of Physics Publishing, Bristol

Andersen, T G, Bollerslev, T, Diebold, F X, Ebens, H (2001a) The Distribution of Realized Stock Return Volatility, *Journal of Financial Economics*, 61, 43–76

Andersen, T G, Bollerslev, T, Diebold, F X, Labys, P (2001b) The Distribution of Realized Exchange Rate Volatility, *Journal of the American Statistical Association*, 96, 42–55

Andersen, T G, Bollerslev, T, Diebold, F X, Labys, P (2003) Modeling and Forecasting Realized Volatility, *Econometrica*, 712, 579–625

Anderssona, M, Krylovab, E, Vahamaa, S (2008) Why Does the Correlation Between Stock and Bond Returns Vary over Time?, *Applied Financial Economics*, 18, 139–151

Angrist, J D, Pischke, J-S (2009) *Mostly Harmless Econometrics – An Empiricist's Companion*, Princeton University Press, Princeton, NJ, and Oxford, UK

Arrow, K J (1965) The Theory of Risk Aversion. In *Aspects of the Theory of Risk Bearing*, Yrjö Jahnsson Foundation, Helsinki. Reprinted in *Essays in the Theory of Risk Bearing*, Markham, Chicago, IL, 1971, pp. 90–109

Ash, R B (1990 [1965]) *Information Theory*, 1990 Dover, Mineda, NY, republished from 1965 Interscience edition

Avellaneda, M (1998) Minimum-Relative-Entropy calibration of Asset-Pricing Models, *International Journal of Theoretical and Applied Finance*, 1, 447–472

Avellaneda, M, Friedman, C, Holmes, R, Samperi, D (1997) Calibrating Volatility Surfaces via Relative-Entropy Minimization, *Applied Mathematical Finance*, 4, 37–64

Avellaneda, M, Buff, R, Friedman, C, Grandechamp, N, Kruk, L, Newman, J (2000) Weighted Monte Carlo: A New Technique for Calibrating Asset-Pricing Models, *International Journal of Theoretical and Applied Finance*, 4, 91–119

Avnir, D (1998) Is the Geometry of Nature Fractal?, *Science*, 279, 39–40

Avramov, D, Zhou, G (2010) Bayesian Portfolio Analysis, *Annual Review of Financial Eonomics*, 2, 25–47

Bandourian, R, Winkelmann, K (2003) The Market Portfolio. In R Litterman (ed.), *Modern Investment Management*, John Wiley, Chichester

Barber, B, Odean, T (2000) Trading is Hazardous to Your Wealth: The Common Stock Investment Performance of Individual Investors, *Journal of Finance*, 55(2), 773–806

Barndorff-Nielsen, O, Shephard, N (2001) Econometric Analysis of Realized Volatility and Its Use in Estimating Levy Based Non-Gaussian OU Type Stohastic Volatility Models, Working paper, Nuffield College, Oxford University

Baum, L E, Petrie, T, Soules, G, Weiss, N (1970) A Maximization Technique Occurring in the Statis-
   tical Analysis of Probabilistic Functions of Markov Chains, *Annals of Mathematical Statistics*,
   41, 164–196
Bauwens, L, Laurent, S (2005) A New Class of Multivariate Skew Densities, with Application to
   Generalized Autoregressive Conditional Heteroscedasticity Models, *Journal of Business and
   Economic Statistics*, 3, 346–354
Bell, D (1988) One Switch Utility Functions and a Measure of Risk, *Management Science*, 24(12),
   14126–14240
Bertsimas, D, Thiele, A (2006) Robust and Data-driven Optimization: Modern Decision-making under
   Uncertainty. *INFORMS Tutorials in Operations Research: Models, Methods, and Applications
   for Innovative Decision Making*, Informs, Catonsville, MD
Best, M, Grauer, R (1991) On the Sensitivty of Mean-variance Efficient Portfolios to Changes in
   Asset Means: Some Analytical and Computational Results, *Review of Financial Studies*, 4(2),
   314–342
Bevan, A, Winkelmann, K (1998) Using the Black–Litterman Global Asset Allocation Model:
   Three Years of Practical Experience, Working paper, Fixed Income Research, Goldman
   Sachs
Binmore, K (2009) *Rational Decisions*, Princeton University Press, Princeton, NJ
Black, F (2010) *Exploring General Equilibrium*, MIT Press, Cambridge, MA
Black, F, Litterman, R (1990) Asset Allocation: Combining Investors Views with Market Equilibrium,
   Working paper, Fixed Income Research, Goldman Sachs
Black, F, Litterman, R (1991) Global Asset Allocation with Equities, Bonds, and Currencies, Working
   paper, Fixed Income Research, Goldman Sachs
Black, F, Litterman, R (1992) Global Portfolio Optimization, Financial Analysts Journal, September,
   pp. 28–43
Blamont, D, Firoozy, N (2003) Asset Allocation Model, Working paper, Global Markets Research,
   Fixed Income Research, Deutsche Bank
Blanchard, O J, Romer, D, Spence, M, Stigliz J (2012) (eds) *In the Wake of the Crisis – Leading
   Economists Reasses Economic Policy*, MIT Press, Cambridge, MA
Bollerslev, T (1986) Generalized Autoregressive Conditional Heteroskedasticity, *Journal of Econo-
   metrics*, 31(3), 307–327
Bollerslev, T, Zhou, H (2002) Estimating Stochastic Volatility Diffusion Using Conditional Moments
   of Integrated Volatility, *Journal of Econometrcis*, 109, 33–65
Bonabaeu, E, Theraulaz, G (2000) Swarm Smarts, *Scientific American*, 282(3), 72–79
Bouchaud, J-P (2001) Power Laws in Economics and Finance: Some Ideas from Physics, *Quantitative
   Finance*, 1, 105–112
Bouchaud J-P, Cont R (2002) A Langevin Approach to Stock Market Fluctuations and Crashes,
   European Physical Journal B, 6, 543–550
Bouchaud, J-P, Potters, M (2000) *Theory of Financial Risk: From Statistical Physics to Risk Man-
   agement*, Cambridge University Press, Cambridge
Boudt, K, Carl, P, Peterson, B G (2013) Asset Allocation with Conditional Value-At-Risk, *Journal
   of Risk*, 15(3), 39–68
Busetti, F, Harvey, A (2011) When is a Copula Constant? A Test for Changing Relationships, *Journal
   of Financial Econometrics*, 9(1), 106–131
Camilleri, K (2009) *Heisenberg and the Interpretation of Quantum Mechanics*, Cambridge University
   Press, Cambridge
Campbell, J H, Ammer, J (1993) What Moves the Stock and Bond Markets, *Journal of Finance*, 48,
   3–37
Capiello, L, Engle, R, Sheppard, K (2006) Asymmetric Dynamics in the Correlations of Global
   Equity and Bond Returns, *Journal of Financial Econometrics*, 4(4), 537–572

Cass, D (1965) Optimum Growth in an Aggregative Model of Capital Accumulation, *Review of Economic Studies*, 32, 233–240

Caticha, A (2008) Lectures on Probability, Entropy, and Statistical Physics, Working paper, Department of Physics, University of Albany, SUNY, arXiv:0808.0012v1 [physics-data-an], 31 July 2008, available at http://arxiv.org/pdf/0808.0012.pdf (accessed 21 December 2012)

Chackraborti, A, Toke, I M, Patriarca, M, Abergel, F (2011a) Econphysics Review: I. Empirical Facts, *Quantitative Finance*, 11(7), 991–1012

Chakraborti, A, Toke, I M, Patriarca, M, Abergel, F (2011b) Econphysics Review: II. Agent-Based Models, *Quantitative Finance*, 11(7), 1013–1049

Challet, D, Marsili, M, Zhang, Y-C (2005) *Minority Games – Interacting Agents in Financial Markets*, Oxford University Press, Oxford

Chamberlain, G (1983) A Characterization of the Distributions that Imply Mean-Variance Utility Functions, *Journal of Economic Theory*, 29, 185–201

Cherubini, U, Luciano, E (2004) *Copula Methods in Finance*, John Wiley & Sons, Chichester

Chopra, V, Ziemba, W (1993) The Effects of Errors in Means, Variances and Covariances on Optimal Portfolio Choice, *Journal of Portfolio Management*, 19(2), 6–11

Cieslak, A, Povala, P (2010) Understanding Bond Risk Premia, Working paper, University of Lugano and Northwestern University, Kellog School of Management

Clements M P, Hendry, D F (2008) Economic Forecasting in a Changing World, *Capitalism and Society*, 3(2), 1–18

Coca, D (2011) On the Use of Bayesian Networks to Model Stress Events in Banking, Unpublished MSc thesis, Oxford University

Cochrane, J H (2001) *Asset Pricing*, Princeton University Press, Princeton, NJ

Cochrane, J H, Piazzesi, M (2005) Bond Risk Premia, *American Economic Review*, 95(1), 138–160

Cochrane, J H, Piazzesi, M (2008) Decomposing the Yield Curve, Working paper, Graduate School of Business, University of Chicago

Cochrane, J H, Saa-Requejo (1999) Beyond Arbitrage: Good-Deal Asset Bounds in Incomplete Markets, Working paper, Graduate School of Business, University of Chicago

Connor, G, Korajczyk, R A (2010) Factor Models in Portfolio and Asset Pricing Theory. In J B Guerard Jr (ed.), *Handbook of Portfolio Construction*, Springer, New York, pp. 401–418

Connor, G, Goldberg L R, Korajczyk R A (2010) Portfolio Risk Analysis, Princeton University Press, Princeton, NJ

Cook, R D, Hawkins, D M, Weisberg, S (1993) Exact Iterative Computation of the Robust Multivariate Minimum Volume Ellipsoid Estimator, *Statistics & Probability Letters*, 16(3), 213–218

Cover, T M, Thomas, J A (2006) *Elements of Information Theory*, John Wiley, Hoboken, NJ

Dasgupta, P (2008) Discounting Climate Change, *Journal of Risk and Uncertainty*, 37, 141–169

Davidson, P (2009) *John Maynard Keynes*, Palgrave Macmillan, Basingstoke

Davidson, P (2010) Risk and Uncertainty. In R Skidelsky and C W Wigstrom (eds), *The Economic Crisis and the State of Economics*, Palgrave Macmillan, New York

Davis, J K, Sweeney, M J (1999) *Strategic Paradigms 2025: US Security Planning for a New Era*, Institute for Foreign Policy Analysis, Cambridge, Mass

de Goeij, P, Marquering, W (2004) Modelling the Conditional Covariance between Stock and Bond Returns: A Multivariate GARCH Approach, *Journal of Financial Econometrics*, 2, 531–564

de Guillaume, N, Rebonato, N, Pogudin, A (2013) The Nature of the Dependence of Magnitude of Rate Moves on the Rates Levels: A Universal Relationship, *Quantitative Finance*

de Haan, L, Ferreira, A (2006) *Extreme Value Theory – An Introduction*, Springer Verlag, New York

de Miguel, V, Garlappi, L, Uppal, R (2009) Optimal versus Naive Diversification: How Inefficient is the 1/n Portfolio Strategy?, *Review of Financial Studies*, 22(5), 1915–1953

Denev, A (2011) Coherent Asset Allocation and Diversification in the Presence of Stress Events, Unpublished MSc thesis, Oxford University

Denev, A (2013) Credit Portfolio Models in the Presence of Forward-Looking Stress Events, *Journal of Risk Model Validation*, 7(1), 1–38

Dias, A, Embrechts, P (2004) Dynamic Copula Models for Multivariate High Frequency Data in Finance, Manuscript, ETH Zurich

Diebold, F X, and Nason, J A (1990) Nonparametric Exchange Rate Prediction, *Journal of International Economics*, 28, 315–332

Doeswijk R Q, Lam TW, Swinkels, L A P (2011) Strategic Asset allocation: The Global Multi-Asset Market Portfolio 1959–2011, ssrn working paper, available at http://papers.ssrn.com/sol3/papers.cfm?abstract_id=2170275 (accessed 8 January 2013)

Doust, P (2008) Geometric Mean Variance, *Risk*, February, 89–95

Doust, P, Chien, J (2008) Regime Models – How Many States Are There?, Working paper, RBS, Quantitative Research Group

Dowson D C, Wrag A (1973) Maximum-Entropy Distributions having Prescribed First and Second Moments, *IEEE Transactions on Information Theory*, 19(5), 688–693

Easley, D, López de Prado, M, O'Hara, M (2011) The Microstructure of the Flash Crash, *Journal of Portfolio Management*, 37(2), 118–128

Efron, B (1977) Stein's Paradox in Statistics, *Scientific American*, 236, 119–127

Efron, B, Tibshirani, R (1986) Bootstrap Methods for Standard Errors, Confidence Intervals and Other Measures of Statistical Accuracy, *Statistical Science*, 1(1), 54–75

Eichengreen, B (2011) *Exorbitant Privelege*, Oxford Univerity Press, Oxford, UK

El-Erian M A (2010) Looking Ahead, *Journal of Portfolio Management*, 36(2), 4–6

Ellsberg, D (1961) Risk, Ambiguity and the Savage Axioms, *Quarterly Journal of Economics*, 75, 643–669

Ellsberg, D (2001) *Risk, Ambiguity and Decisions*, Garland Publishing, New York

Engle, R F (1982) Autoregressive Conditional Hetroskedasticity with Estimates of the Variance of UK Inflation, *Econometrica*, 50, 987–1008

Engle, R F (1995) Introduction, in *ARCH: Selected Readings*, Advanced Texts in Econometrics, Oxford University Press, Oxford, pp. xi–xviii

Engle, R F (2001) GARCH 101: The Use of ARCH/GARCH models in Applied Econometrics, *Journal of Economic Perspectives*, 15(4), 157–168

Engle, R F (2002) New Frontiers for ARCH Models, *Journal of Applied Econometrics*, 17, 425–446

Engle, R F (2004) Risk and Volatility: Econometric Models and Financial Practice, *Amercian Economic Review*, 94, 405–420

Engle, R F (2009) *Anticipating Correlations – A New Paradigm for Risk Management*, Princeton University Press, Princeton, NJ

Epstein L G, Zin, S E (1991) Substitution, Risk Aversion, and the Temporal Behaviour of Consumption and Asset Returns: An Empirical Analysis, *Journal of Political Economy*, 99(21), 263–279

Faig, M, Shum, P (2002) Portfolio Choice in the Presence of Personal Illiquid Projects, *Journal of Finance*, 57(1), 303–328

Farmer J D, Joshi S (2002) The Price Dynamics of Common Trading Strategies, *Journal of Economic Behavior and Organization* 49, 149–171

Fleming, J, Kirby, C, Ostdiek, B (2003) The Economic Value of Volatility Timing Using 'Realized' Volatility, *Journal of Financial Economics*, 67(3), 473–509

Frydman R, Goldberg, M D (2007) *Imperfect Knowledge Economics: Exchange Rates and Risk*, Princeton University Press, Princeton, NJ

Friend, I, Blume, F (1975) The Demand for Risky Assets, *American Economic Review*, 65(5), 900–922

Frost, P, Savarino J (1986) An Emprical Bayes Approach to Efficient Portfolio Selection, *Journal of Financial and Quantitative Analysis*, 21(3), 293–305

Frydman R, Goldberg M D (2007) *Imperfect Knowledge Economics: Exchange Rates and Risk*, Princeton University Press, Princeton, NJ

Gallegati M, Kee, S, Lux T, Ormerod, P (2006) Worrying Trends in Econophysics, *Physica* A, 370, 1–6

Gamerman, D, Lopes, H F (2006) *Markov Chain Monte Carlo – Stochastic Simulation for Bayesian Inference*, Chapman & Hall Press, Boca Raton, FL

Garcia-Alvarez, L, Luger, R (2011) Dynamic Correlations, Estimation Risk, and Portfolio Management During the Financial Crisis, working paper, available at www.ecb.europa.eu/events/pdf/ conferences/ws_asset/sess1/Garcia-Alvarez-Luger.pdf?b1f03dc4f6a0578b5e79bbb08fa77a28, (acessed 1 September 2012)

Garey, M R, Johnson, D S (1979) *Computers and Intractability: A Guide to the Theory of NP-Completeness*, W H Freeman Publishers, San Francisco

Garlappi, L, Uppal, R, Wang, T (2006) *Portfolio Selection with Parameter and Model Uncertainty: A Mutli-Prior Approach*, Oxford University Press on behalf of The Society of Financial Studies, pp. 42–81

Giffin, A, Caticha, A (2007) Updating Probabilities with Data and Moments, Working paper, Department of Physics, Univerity of Albany, SUNY, arXiv:0708.1593v2 [physics-data-an], available at http://arxiv.org/abs/0708.1593, (accesed 21 December 2012)

Gigerenzer, G (2002) *Reckoning with Risk: Learning to Live with Uncertainty*, Penguin, London (Published in the United States as *Calculated Risks: How to Know when Numbers Deceive You*, Simon & Schuster, New York)

Gigerenzer, G, Brighton, H (2009) Homo Heuristicus: Why Biased Minds Make Better Inferences, *Topics in Cognitive Science*, 1, 107–143

Gigerenzer, G, Edwards, A (2003) Simple Tools for Understanding Risk: From Innumeracy to Insight, *British Medical Journal*, 327, 741–744

Gigerenzer, G, Hoffrage, U (1995) How to Improve Bayesian Reasoning Without Instructions. Frequency Formats, *Psychological Review*, 102, 684–704

Gigerenzer, G, Selten, R (2002a) Rethinking Rationality. In G Gigerenzer and R Selten (eds), *Bounded Rationality – The Adaptive Toolbox*, MIT Press, Cambridge, MA

Gigerenzer, G, Selten R, eds (2002b) Bounded Rationality – The Adaptive Toolbox, MIT Press, Cambridge, Mass, USA

Gilboa, I, Schmeidler, D (1989) Maxmin Expected Utility with Non-Unique Prior, *Journal of Mathematical Economics*, 18, 141–153

Gollier, C, Brunak, S (2001) *The Economics of Risk and Time*, Vol. 1, MIT Press, Cambridge, MA

Goodman, J (1987) A Comment to the Maximum Entropy Principle, *Risk Analysis*, 7(2), 269–272

Gopakrishnan P, Plerou V, Amaral L A N, Meyer M, Stanley H E (1999) Scaling of the Distributions of Fluctuations of Financial Market Indices, *Physical Review* E, 60, 5305–5316

Granger, C W J (1969) Investigating Causal Relations by Econometric Models and Cross-spectral Methods, *Econometrica* 37(3), 424–438

Gregory, P (2005) *Bayesian Logical Analysis for the Physical Sciences*, Cambridge University Press, Cambridge

Grinold, R C, Easton, K K (1998) Attribution of Perfromance and Holding. In J M Mulvey, W T Ziemba (eds), *Worldwide Asset and Liability Modeling*, Cambridge University Press, Cambridge, pp. 87–113

Hakansson, N H (1971) Capital Growth and the Mean-Variance Approach to Portfolio Selection, *Journal of Financial and Quantitative Analysis*, 6(1), 517–557

Haldane, A, Nelson, B (2012) Tails of the Unexpected, Paper presented at The Credit Crisis Five Years On: Unpacking the Crisis, conference held at the University of Edinburgh Business School, 8–9 June 2012

Hansen L P, Sargent, T J (2008) *Robustness*, Princeton University Press, Princeton, NJ, and Oxford

Hauksson, H A, Dacorogna, M, Domenig, T, Muller, U, Samorodnitsky, G (2001) Multivariate Extremes, Aggregation and Risk Estimation, *Quantitative Finance*, 1(1), 79–95

Hawkins, D M (1993) A Feasible Solution Algorithm for the Minimum Volume Ellipsoid. Estimator in Multivariate Data, *Computational Statistics* 8, 95–107

Hayes, M G (2006) *The Economics of Keynes – A New Guide to the General Theory*, Edwar Elgar Publishing, Cheltenham; Northampton, MA

He, G, Litterman, R (1999) The Intuition Behind Black Litterman Model Portfolios, Working paper, Goldman Sachs Quantitative Research Group, available at www.cis.upenn.edu/~mkearns/finread/intuition.pdf (accessed 2 November 2012)

Heckerman, D (1993) Causal Independence for Knowledge Acquisition and Inference. In *Proceedings of the Ninth Conference on Uncertainty in Artificial Intelligence*, Morgan Kaufmann, Seattle, WA, pp. 122–127

Heckerman, D, and Breese, J S (1994) A New Look at Causal Independence. In Proceedings of the Tenth Conference on Uncertainty in Artificial Intelligence, Morgan Kaufmann, Seattle, WA, pp. 286–292

Heckerman, D, Breese, J S (1995) Learning Bayesian Networks: The Combination of Knowledge and Statistical Data, *Machine Learning*, 20, 197–243

Heckerman, D, Breese, J S (1998) Causal Independence for Probability Assessment and Inference Using Bayesian Networks, Microsoft technical report MSR-TR-94-08

Heisenberg, W (1971) *Physics and Beyond*, Harper, New York

Hellerstein, R (2011) Global Bond Risk Premiums, Federal Reserve Bank of New York Staff Reports, Staff Report No 499, June 2011

Hendry, D F (2004) Causality and Exogeneity in Non-Stationary Economic Time Series, in S G Hall, (ed.), *New Directions in Macromodelling: Essays in Honor of J. Michael Finger* (Contributions to Economic Analysis, Volume 269), Emerald Group Bingley, pp. 21–48

Hendry, D F (2005) Unpredictability and the Foundations of Economic Forecasting, Working Paper, Nuffield College, University of Oxford

Hendry, D F (2011) Unpredictability in Economic Analysis, Econometric Modelling and Forecasting, Department of Economics, Oxford University, Discussion Paper No 551, ISNN 1471–0498

Hendry, D F, Mizon, G E (2001) Forecasting in the Presence of Structural Breaks and Policy Regime Shifts, Working Paper, Nuffield College, University of Oxford

Henrion, M (1987) Practical Issues in Constructing a Bayes' Belief Network. In *Proceedings of the Third Annual Conference on Uncertainty in Artificial Intelligence*, Elsevier Science, New York, pp. 132–139

Henrion, M (1988) Propagation of Uncertainty by Probabilistic Logic Sampling in Bayes Networks. In J FLemmer and L N Kanal (eds), *Uncertainty in Artificial Intelligence* Vol. 2, Elsevier, New York, pp. 149–163

Herndon, T, Ash, M, Pollin, R (2013) Does High Public Debt Consistently Stifle Economic Growth? A Critique of Reinhart and Rogoff, Working paper, University of Massachusetts Amherst, availbale at www.peri.umass.edu/fileadmin/pdf/working_papers_301–350/WP322.pdf (accessed 22 April 2013)

Herold, U, Maurer, R (2006) Portfolio Choice and Estimation Risk: A Comparison of Bayesian to Heuristic Approaches (No. 94). Department of Finance, Goethe University Frankfurt am Main

Hoover, K D (2001) *Causality in Macroeconomics*, Cambridge University Press, Cambridge

Hurwicz, L (1951) Aggregation as a Problem in Decision-making under Ignorance or Uncertainty. Cowles Commission Discussion Paper 357S, February

Idzorek, T M (2005) A Step-By-Step Guide to the Black-Litterman Model – Incorporating User-Sepcified Confidence Levels, Working paper, Ibbotson Associates, available at http://corporate.morningstar.com/ib/documents/MethodologyDocuments/IBBAssociates/BlackLitterman.pdf (accessed 2 November 2012)

Infanger, G (2006) Dynamic Asset Allocation Strategies Under a Stochastic Dynamic Programming Approach. In S A Zenios and W T Ziemba (eds), *Handbook of Asset and Liability Management*, Vol. 1, *Theory and Methodology*, North-Holland, Amsterdam, Ch. 5

Jackson, M O (2008) Social and Economic Networks, Princeton University Press, Princeton, NJ, and Oxford

Jagannathan, R, Ma, T (2003) Risk Reduction in Large Portfolios: Why Imposing the Wrong Constraints Helps, *Journal of Finance*, 58, 1651–1683

James, W, Stein, C (1961) Estimation with Quadratic Loss. In *Proceedings of the Fourth Berkeley Symposium on Mathematical Statistics and Probability*, Vol. 2, University of California Press, Berkeley, CA, pp. 361–379

Jaynes, E T (2003) *Probability Theory: The Logic of Science*, Cambridge University Press, Cambridge

Jensen, F V, Nielsen, T D (2007) *Bayesian Nets and Decision Graphs*, 2nd edn, Springer Verlag, Berlin

Jiang, G J, Tian, Y S (2005) The Model-Free Implied Volatility and Its Information Content, *Review of Financial Studies*, 18, 1305–1342

Jobson, J, Korki, K (1983) Statistical Inference in the Two Parameter Portfolio Theory with Mutliple Regression Software, *Journal of Financial and Quantitative Analysis*, 18(2), 189–197

Johnson, N L (1949) Systems of Frequency Curves Generated by Methods of Transalation, *Biometrika*, 36(1/2), 149–176

Jondeau, E, Rockinger, M (2006) Optimal Portfolio Allocation Under Higher Moments, *European Financial Management*, 12(1), 29–55

Jondeau, E, Rockinger, M (2008) The Economic Value of Distributional Timing, University of Lausanne Working Paper

Jondeau, E, Poon, S-H and Rockinger, M (2007) *Financial Modeling Under Non-Gaussian Distributions*, Springer-Verlag, London

Jurgelanaite R, Lucas, P J F (2005) Exploiting Causal Independence in Large Bayesian Networks, *Knowledge-Based Systems*, 18, 153–162

Kadanoff, L P (2000) *Statistical Physics, Dynamics and Renormalization*, World Scientific, Singapore

Kahnman, D, Tversky A (1979) Prospect Theory: An Analysis of Decisions Under Risk, *Econometrica*, 47(2), 263–291

Keller, E F (2005) Revisting 'Scale-Free' Networks, *BioEssays*, 27, 1060–1068

Keynes, J M (1921) *A Treatise on Probability*, MacMillan, London

Kindelberger, C P, Aliber, R Z (2011) Manias, *Panics and Crashes – A History of Financial Crises*, 6th edn, Palgrave Macmillan, Basingstoke

Knight, F H (1921) *Risk, Uncertainty and Profit*, Houghton Mifflin, Boston, MA

Kole, E, Koedijk, K, Verbeek, M (2007) Selecting Copulas for Risk Management, *Journal of Banking & Finance*, 31(8), 2405–2423

Koo, R C (2009) *The Holy Grail of Macroeconomics: Lessons from Japan's Great Recession*, John Wiley, Chichester

Koopmans, T C (1965) On the Concept of Optimal Economic Growth. In *(Study Week on the) Econometric Approach to Development Planning*, North-Holland, Amsterdam, pp. 225–287

Kotz, S, Nadarajaham, S (2000) *Extreme Value Distributions: Theory and Applications*, Imperial College Press, London

Kreps, D M (1988) *Notes on the Theory of Choice*, Westiview Press, Boulder, CO

Kritzman, M, Li, Y (2010) Skulls, Financial Turbulence and Risk Management, *Financial Analyst Journal*, 66(3), 30–41

Kroll, Y, Levy, H, Markowitz, H M (1979) Mean Variance versus Direct Utility Optimization, *Journal of Finance*, 39(1), 47–61

Krugman, P (2012) *Stop This Recession Now*, W W Norton & Co, London and New York

Kschischang, F R, Frey, B J, and Loeliger, H A (2001) Factor Graphs and the Sum-Product Algorithm, *IEEE Transactions on Information Theory*, 47(2), 498–519

Kritzman, M, Li Y (2010) Skulls, Financial Turbulence and Risk Management, *Financial Analyst Journal*, 66(3), 30–41

Lancaster, T (2004) *An Introduction to Modern Bayesian Econometrics*, Blackwell Publishing, Malden, MA and Oxford

Latane, H A (1959) Criteria for Choices Among Risky Ventures, *Journal of Political Economics*, 67(2), 144–155

Ledoit, O (1994) Portfolio Selection: Improved Covariance Matrix Estimation, Working paper, Sloane School of Management

Ledoit, O (1997) Improved Estimation of Covariance Matrix of Stock Returns with an Application to Portfolio Selection, Working paper, Anderson Graduate School of Management at UCLA

Ledoit, O, Wolf, M (2003) Improved Estimation of the Covariance Matrix of Stock Returns with an Application to Portfolio Selection, *Journal of Empirical Finance*, 10, 603–621

Lee, W (2000) *Advanced Theory and Methodology of Tactical Asset Allocation*, John Wiley, New York

Lee, W (2011) Risk-Based Asset Allocation: A New Answer to an Old Question?, *Journal of Portfolio Managament*, 37(4), 11–28

Lempert, R J, Collins, M T (2007) Managing the Risk of Uncertain Threshold Responses: Comparison of Robust, Optimum and Precautionary Approaches, *Risk Analysis*, 27(4), 1009–1026

Levy, H, Markowitz, H M (1979) Approximating Expected Utility by a Function of Mean and Variance, *American Economic Review*, 69, 308–317

Levy, M, Roll, R (2010) The Market Portfolio May Be Effcient After All, *Review of Financial Studies*, 23, 2461–2464

Levy M, Levy H, Solomon, S (2000) *Microscopic Simulation of Financial Markets – From Investor Behavior to Market Phenomena*, Academic Press, San Diego, CA

Lichtenstein, S, Fischhoff, B (1977) Do those Who Know More Also Know More About How Much They Know?, *Organizational Behaviour and Human Decision Processes*, 20, 159–183

Lilliefors, H W (1967) On the Kolmogorov-Smirnov Test for Normality with Mean and Variance Unknown, *Journal of the American Statistical Association*, 62(318), 399–402

Litterman, R (1983) A Random Walk, Markov Model for the Distribution of Time Series, *Journal of Business and Economic Statistics*, 1(2), 169–173

Litterman, R (2003) The Capital Asset Pricing Model. In R Litterman (eds), *Modern Investment Management*, John Wiley, Chichester, Ch. 4

Longin, F, and Solnik, B (1995) Is the Correlation in International Equity Returns Constant: 1960–1990?, *Journal of International Money and Finance* 14, 1, 3–26

Lopez de Prado, M (2011) Advances in High Frequency Strategies, Doctoral Dissertation, Complutense University, Madrid, Spain, available at http://ssrn.com/abstract=2106117

Lorenz, E N (1963) Deterministic Nonperiodic Flow, *Journal of Atmospheric Science*, 20, 130–141

Low, B S, Zhang, S (2005) The Volatility Risk Premium Embedded in Currency Options, *Journal of Financial and Quantitative Analysis*, 40, 803–832

Luenberger, D G (2003) *Linear and Nonlinear Programming*, 2nd edn, Springer Verlag, Heidelberg

Ma, S (2000) *Modern Theory of Critical Phenomena*, Westview Press, Boulder, CO

Mackenzie, D (2008) *An Engine not a Camera – How Financial Models Shape Markets*, Boston, MIT Press, MA

Maenhout, P J (1999) Robust Portfolio Rules, Hedging and Asset Pricing, Working paper, Finance Department, INSEAD, pp. 1–59

Mahalanobis, P C (1927) Analysis of Race-Mixture in Bengal, *Journal of Asiatic Society of Bengal*, 23, 301–333

Mahalanobis, P C (1936) On the Generalized Distance in Statistics, *Proceedings of the National Institute of Sciences of India*, 2(1), 149–155

Malevergne, Y, Sornette, D (2003) Testing the Gaussian Copula Hypothesis for Financial Asset Dependence, *Quantitative Finance*, 3(4), 231–250

Malevergne, Y, Sornette, D (2006) *Extreme Financial Risk – From Dependence to Risk Management*, Springer Verlag, Berlin

Mandelbrot, B (1953) An Informational Theory of the Statistical Structure of Languages. In W Jackson (ed.), Communication Theory, Butterworth, MA, pp. 486–502

Mandelbrot, B (1963) The Variation of Certain Speculative Prices, *Journal of Business*, 36, 394–419

Mandelbrot, B (2001a) Scaling in Financial Prices, I: Tail and Dependence, *Quantitative Finance*, 1, 113–123, Reprinted in D Farmer and J Geanakoplos, *Beyond Efficiency and Equilibrium*, Oxford University Press, Oxford, 2004

Mandelbrot, B (2001b) Scaling in Financial Prices, II: Multifractals and the Star Equilibrium, *Quantitative Finance*, 1, 124–130, Reprinted in D Farmer and J Geanakoplos (eds), *Beyond Efficiency and Equilibrium*, Oxford University Press, Oxford, 2004

Mandelbrot, B (2001c) Scaling in Financial Prices, III: Catroon Brownian Motions in Multifractal Time, *Quantitative Finance*, 1, 427–440

Mandelbrot, B (2001d) Scaling in Financial Prices, IV: Multifractal Concentration, *Quantitative Finance*, 1, 641–649

Mandelbrot, B (2001e) Stochastic Volatility, Power-Laws and Long Memory, *Quantitative Finance*, 1, 558–559

Mandelbrot, B, Hudson, R L (2005) *The (Mis)Behaviour of Markets*, Profile Books, London

Mantegna R N (1991) Lévy walks and Enhanced Diffusion in Milan Stock Exchange, *Physica* A 179, 232–242

Mantegna, R N, Stanley, H E (2000) *Introduction to Econphysics – Correlation and Complexity in Finance*, Cambridge University Press, Cambridge

Manzotti, A, Perez, F J, Quiroz, A J (2002) A Statistic for Testing the Null Hypothesis of Elliptical Symmetry, *Journal of Multivariate Analysis*, 81(2), 274–285

Markowitz, H M (1976) Investment in the Long Run: New Evidence for an Old Rule, *Journal of Finance*, 31(5), 1273–1286

Markowitz, H M (1987) *Mean-Variance Analysis in Portfolio Choice and Capital Markets*, Blackwell, Oxford

Markowitz, H M (1991 [1959]) *Portfolio Selection*, Blackwell, Oxford

Markowitz, H M (1994) The Value of a Blank Check, *Journal of Portfolio Management*, Summer, 82–91

Markowitz, H M (2010) Portfolio Theory: As I Still See It, *Annual Review of Financial Economics*, 2, 1–23

Markowitz, H M, Usmen, N (2003) Resampled Frontiers Versus Diffuse Bayes: An Experiment, *Journal of Investment Management*, 1(4), 9–25

McComb, W D (2004) *Renormalization Methods – A Guide for Beginners*, Oxford University Press, Oxford

McNeil, A J, Frey, R, Embrechts, P (2005) *Quantitative Risk Management: Concepts, Technques, and Tools*, Princeton Unviersity Press, Princeton, NJ

McEliece, R, and Aji, S N (2000) The Generalized Distributive Law, *IEEE Transactions on Information Theory*, 46(2), 325–343

McGrayne, S B (2011) *The Theory That Would Not Die*, Yale University Press, New Haven, CT

Merton, R C (1980) On Estimating the Expected Return on the Market: An Exploratory Investigation, *Journal of Financial Economics*, 8(4), 323–361

Merton, R, Samuelson, P A (1974) Fallacy of the Log-Normal Approximation to Optimal Decision-Making Over Many Periods, *Journal of Financial Economics*, 1(1), 67–94

Meucci, A (2008) Fully Flexible Views, *Risk*, 21, 97–102

Meucci, A (2009) *Risk and Asset Allocation*, Springer Verlag, Berlin

Meucci, A (2010a) Factors on Demand, *Risk*, 23, 84–89

Meucci, A (2010b) Fully Flexible Bayesian Network, available at SSRN: http://ssrn.com/abstract=1721302 (accessed 26 September 2011)

Meucci, A (2010c) Historical Scenarios with Fully Flexible Probabilities, *GARP: Global Association of Risk Professionals*, December, 40–43

Michaud, R (1989) The Markowitz Optimization Enigma: Is Optimized 'Optimal'?, *Financial Analyst Journal*, 45(1), 31–42

Michaud, R O, Michaud, R O (2008) *Efficient Asset Management: A Practical Guide to Stock Portfolio Optimization and Asset Allocation*, Oxford University Press, Oxford

Miller, G A (1957) Some Effects of Intermittent Silence, *American Journal of Psychology*, 70(2), 311–314

Miller J H, Page, S E (2007) *Complex Adaptive Systems – An Introduction to Computational Models of Social Life*, Princeton University Press, Princeton, NJ

Minsky, H P (1975) *John Maynard Keynes*, Columbia University Press, New York

Minsky, H P (1982) The Financial Instability Hypothesis: Capitalistic Processes and the Behaviour of the Economy. In C P Kindelberger and J-P Laffargue (eds), *Financial Crises: Theory, History and Policy*, Cambridge University Press, Cambridge

Mirowski P (1989) *More Heat than Light: Economics as Social Physics*, Cambridge University Press, Cambridge

Mitchell, M (2009) *Complexity – A Guided Tour*, Oxford University Press, Oxford, UK, and New York, USA

Murphy, K P (2001) A Brief Introduction to Graphical Models and Bayesian Networks, available at www.cs.berkeley.edu/~murphyk/Bayes/bayes.html (accessed 26 August, 2011)

Nawrocki, D (1996) Portfolio Analysis with a Large Number of Assets, *Applied Economics*, 28(9), 1191–1198

Nelsen, B R (1993) Some Concepts of Bivariate Symmetry, *Journal of Nonparametric Statistics*, 3(1), 95–101

Ni, X, Malvergne, Y, Sornette D, Woehrmann, P (2011) Robust Reverse Engineering of Cross-Sectional Returns and Improved Porfolio Allocation Performance Using the CAPM, *Journal of Portfolio Management*, 37(4), 76–85

Nordhaus W (2007) The Stern Review on the Economics of Climate Change, *Journal of Economic Literature*, 45, 686–702

Nordhaus W (2008) *A Question of Balance: Weighing the Options on Global Warming Policies*, Yale University Press, New Haven, CT

Oakley, J E (2010) Eliciting Univariate Probability Distributions. In K Bloeker (ed.), *Rethinking Risk Measurement and Reporting*, Vol 1: *Uncertainty, Bayesian Analysis and Expert Judgement*, Incisive Media, London, Ch. 6

Olive, D J (2008) Applied Robust Statisitcs, Preprint M-02-006, available at www.math.siu.edu

Oskamp, S (1965) Overconfidence in Case-Study Judgments, *Journal of Consulting Psychology*, 29, 261–265

Page S, Taborski, M A (2011) The Myth of Diversification: Risk Factors versus Asset Classes, *Journal of Portfolio Management*, 37(4), 3–5

Pais, A (1982) *Subtle Is the Lord. . . – The Science and the Life of Albert Einstein*, Oxford University Press, Oxford

Palczewski, A, Palczewski, J (2010) Stability of Mean-Variance Portfolio Weights, Social Science Research Network paper, SSRN 1553073

Pantaleo, E, Tumminello, M, Lillo, F, Mantegna, R (2011) When Do Improved Covariance Matrix Estimators Enhance Portfolio Optimization? An Empirical Comparative Study of Nine Estimators, *Quantitative Finance*, 11(7), 1067–1080

Parresol, B R (2003) Recovering Parameters of Johnson's SB Distribution, Technical Report, United States Department of Agriculture, Research Paper SRS31

Pearl J (1986) Fusion, Propagation, and Structuring in Belief Networks, *Artificial Intelligence*, 29, 241–288

Pearl, J (2009) *Causality*, 2nd edn, Cambridge University Press, Cambridge

Persson, I (2008) *The Retreat of Reason – A Dilemma in the Philosophy of Life*, Oxford University Press, Oxford

Poirier, D J (1995) *Intermediate Statistics and Econometrics – A Comparative Approach*, MIT Press, Cambridge, MA

Pollin, R, Ash, M (2013) Austerity after Reinhart and Rogoff, *Financial Times*, 17 April, electronic version available at www.ft.com/cms/s/0/9e5107f8-a75c-11e2-9fbe-00144feabdc0.html#axzz2RAkS964q (accessed 22 April 2013)

Poston, W L, Wegman E T, Priebe C E, Solka, J L (1997) A Deterministic Method for Robust Estimation of Multivariate Location and Shape, *Journal of Computational and Graphical Statistics*, 6(13), 300–313

Pratt, J W (1964) Risk Aversion in the Small and in the Large, *Econometrica*, 32(1–2), 122–136

Pulley, L M (1981) A General Mean-Variance Approximation to Expected Utility for Short Holding Periods, *Journal of Financial and Quantitative Analysis*, 16, 361–373

Qian, E (2005) Risk Parity Portfolios: Efficient Portfolios Through True Diversification of Risk, Working Paper, Pangora Asset Management

Rabin, M, Thaler, R H (2001) Anomalies – Risk Aversion, *Journal of Economic Perspectives*, 15(1), 219–232

Rabiner, L R (1989) A Tutorial on Hidden Markov Models and Selected Applications in Speech Recognition, *Proceedings of the IEEE*, 77(2), 257–286

Radwanski, J F (2010) Understanding Bond Risk Premia Uncovered by the Term Structure, Working paper, Vienna Graduate School of Finance (VGSF)

Rebonato, R (2010a) *Coherent Stress Testing – A Bayesian Approach to the Analysis of Financial Stress*, John Wiley, Chichester

Rebonato, R (2010b) A Bayesian Approach to Coherent Stress Testing. In K Bloeker (ed.), *Rethinking Risk Measurement and Reporting*, Vol 1: *Uncertainty, Bayesian Analysis and Expert Judgement*, Incisive Media, London, Ch. 9

Rebonato, R (2010c) A Bayesian Approach to Stress Testing and Scenario Analysis, *Journal of Investment Management*, 8(3) 1–13

Rebonato, R (2012) *Taking Liberties – A Critical Examination of Libertarian Paternalism*, Palgrave MacMillan, London

Rebonato, R, Cardoso, M T (2004) Unconstrained Fitting of Implied Volatility Surfaces Using a Mixture of Normals, *Journal of Risk*, 7(1), 55–65

Rebonato R, Chien J (2009) Evidence for State Transition and Altered Serial Co-dependence in US$ Interest Rates, *Quantitative Finance*, 9(3), 259–278

Rebonato, R, Denev, A (2012) Coherent Asset Allocation and Diversification in the Presence of Stress Events, *Journal of Investment Management*, 10(4), 19–53

Rebonato, R, Gaspari, V (2006) Analysis of Drawdowns and Drawups in the US Interest-Rate Market, *Quantitative Finance*, 6(4) 297–326

Rebonato, R, Jaeckel, P (1999) The Most General Methodology to Create a Valid Correlation Matrix for Risk Management and Option Pricing Purposes, *Journal of Risk*, 2(2), 17–28

Reider R (2009) Volatility Forecasting I: GARCH Models, NYU working paper, available at http://cims.nyu.edu/~almgren/timeseries/Vol_Forecast1.pdf (accessed 14 November 2012)

Reinhart, C M, Rogoff, K S (2009) *This Time Is Different – Eight Centuries of Financial Follies*, Princeton University Press, Princeton, NJ

Reinhart, C M, Rogoff, K S (2012) Sorry, U.S. Recoveries Really Aren't Different, available at www.bloomberg.com/news/print/2012-10-15/sorry-u-s-recoveries-really-aren-t-different.html (accessed 30 November 2012)

Reiss, R-D, Thomas, M (2007) *Statistical Analysis of Extreme Values: With Applications to Insurance, Finance, Hydrology and Other Fields*, Springer Verlag, New York, NY

Remillard, B, Papageorgiou, N A, Soustra F (2010) Dynamic Copulas, Technical Report G-2010-18, Gerad

Rosenberg, B (1981) The Capital Asset Pricing Model and the Market Model, *Journal of Portfolio Management*, 7(2), 5–16

Ross, S A (1976) The Arbitrage Theory of Capital Asset Pricing, *Journal of Economic Theory*, 13(3), 341–360

Rosser, J B (2006) The Nature and Future of Econphyics, Working paper, Department of Economics, J Mason University, Harrisonburg, VA. Reprinted in A Chatterjee and B K Chakrabarty (eds), *Econophysics of Stock and Other Markets*, Springer Verlag, Heidelberg

Rousseeuw, P J, Leroy, A M (1987) *Robust Regression and Outlier Detection*, John Wley, Chichester

Rousseeuw, P J, Van Aelst, S (2010) Minimum Volume Ellipsoid, Wiley Interdisciplinary Reviews, *Computational Statistics*, 1(1), 7182–7201

Rousseeuw, P J, Van Driessen, K (1999) A Fast Algorithm for the Minimum Covariance Determinant Estimator, *Journal of the American Statistical Association*, 41(3), 212–223

Rubinstein, A (2002) Comments on the Risk and Time Preferences in Economics. Working paper, Tel Aviv University, Foerder Institute for Economic Research, Sackler Institute for Economic Studies, 6

Satchell, S, Scowcroft, A (2000) A Demystification of the BlackLitterman Model: Managing Quantitative and Traditional Portfolio Construction, *Journal of Asset Management*, 1(2), 138–150

Scherer, B (2002) Portfolio Resampling: Review and Critique, *Financial Analyst Journal*, 58(6), 98–109

Schumpeter, J A (1939) *Business Cycles: A Theoretical, Historical and Statistical Analysis of the Capitalist Process*, Vol. 1, MacGraw-Hill, New York

Sethna, J P (2006) *Statistical Mechanics: Entropy, Order Parameters and Complexity*, Oxford University Press, Oxford

Shalizi, C (2005) Networks and Netwars, available at www.cscs.unimich.edu/~crshalizi/weblog/347.html

Shefrin, H (2008) *A Behavioural Approach to Asset Pricing*, 2nd edn, Academic Press, San Diego, CA

Shiller, R J (1979) The Volatility of Long-Term Interest Rates and Expectation Models of the Term Structure, *Journal of Political Economy*, 87, 1062–1088

Shiller, R J (1981) Do Stock Prices Move Too Much To Be Justified by Subsequent Movements in Dividens?, *American Economic Review*, 71(3), 421–436

Shiller, R J (1989) *Market Volatility*, MIT Press, Cambridge, MA

Shiller, R J (2000) *Irrational Exuberance*, Princeton University Press, Princeton, NJ

Shleifer A (2000) *Inefficient Markets – An Introduction to Behavioural Finance*, Clarendon Lectures in Economics, Oxford University Press, Oxford

Shleifer A, Summers L H (1990) A Noise Trader Approach to Finance, *Journal of Economic Perpsectives*, 4(2), 19–33

Siegel, J (2004) *Stocks for the Long Run*, 4th edn, McGraw Hill, New York

Siegel, A F, Woodgate, A (2007) Performance of Portfolios Optimized with Estimation Error, *Management Science*, 53(6), 1005–1015

Simon, H, A (1956) Rational Choice and the Structure of Environments, *Psychological Review*, 63, 129–138

Simon, H, A (1957) *Models of Man*, John Wiley, New York

Sinn, H-W (2002) Weber's Law and the Biological Evolution of Risk Preferences: The Selective Dominance of the Logarithmic Utility Function, CESIFO working paper 770, pp. 1–28

Sidelsky, R, Wigstrom, CW, eds (2010) *The Economic Crisis and the State of Economics*, Palgrave Macmillan, London

Smith, A F M (1984) Present Position and Potential Development: Some Personal Views on Bayesian Statistics, *Journal of the Royal Statistical Society*, [A], 147, 245–259

Sornette D (2003) *Why Stock Markets Crash: Critical Events in Complex Financial Systems*, Princeton University Press, Princeton, NJ

Sornette, D (2004) *Critical Phenomena in Natural Sciences: Chaos, Fractals, Selforganization and Disorder: Concepts and Tools*, 2nd edn, Springer, Berlin

Soros, G (2003) *The Alchemy of Finance*, John Wiley, Chichester

Soros, G (2008) *The New Paradigm for Financial Markets – The Credit Crisis of 2008 and What It Means*, Public Affairs, Perseus Books, London

Spiers-Bridge, A, Fidler, F, McBride, M, Flander L, Cumming G, Burgman M (2009) Reducing Overconfidence in the Interval Judgements of Experts, *Risk Analysis*, 1, 1–12

Spirtes, P (1994) Conditional Independnce in Directed Cyclical Graphical Models for Feedback, Working Paper, Carnegie Mellon University, 15213–3890, CMU-PHIL-53

Stambaugh, R F (1982) On the Exclusion of Assets from Tests of the Two-Parameter Model: A Sensitivity Analysis, *Journal of Financial Economics*, 10(3), 237–268

Stein, C (1956) Inadmissibility of the Usual Estimator for the Mean of a Multivariate Distribution. In *Proceedings of the Third Berkeley Symposium on Mathematical Statistics and Probability*, Vol. 1, University of California Press, Berkeley, CA, pp. 197–206

Sterman, J D (1989a) Modelling Managerial Behaviour: Misperceptions of Feedback in a Dynamic Decisin Making Experiment, *Management Science*, 35(3), 321–339

Sterman, J D (1989b) Deterministic Chaos in an Experimental Economic System, *Journal of Economic Behaviour and Organization*, 12, 1–28

Stern, N (2008) The Economics of Climate Change, *American Economic Review*, 98(2), 1–37

Stock, J H, Watson, M W (1996) Evidence on Structural Instability in Macroeconomic Time Series Relations, *Journal of Business and Economic Statistics*, 14, 11–30

Strelen, J C, Nassy, F (2007) Analysis and Generation of Random Vectors with Copulas. In *Proceedings of the 2007 Winter Simulation Conference* (WSC 2007), Washington, DC, pp. 488–496

Tetlock, P E (2005) *Expert Political Judgment*, Princeton University Press, Princeton, NJ

Thomson, J M T, Stewart, H B (1986) *Nonlinear Dynamics and Chaos*, John Wiley, Chichester

Titterington, D M (1975) Optial Design: Some Geomterical Aspects of D-Optimality, *Biometrika*, 62, 311–320

Timmermann, A (2001) Structural Breaks, Incomplete Information and Stock Prices, *Journal of Business & Economic Statistics*, 19(3), 299–314

Tsai, C I, Klayman J, Hastie R (2008) Effects of Amount of Information on Judgment Accuracy and Confidence, *Organizational Behavior and Human Decision Processes*, 107(2), 97–105

Walters, J (2011) The Black–Litterman Model in Detail, available at SSRN: http://ssrn.com/abstract=1314585 (accessed 26 September 2012)

Weisberg, H I (2010) *Bias and Causation – Models and Judgement for Valid Comparisons*, John Wiley, Chichester

Williams, J B (1938) *The Theory of Investment Value*, Harvard University Press, Cambridge, MA

Williamson, J (2005) *Bayesian Nets and Causality: Philosophical and Computational Foundations*, Oxford University Press, Oxford

Wolf, M (2006) Resampling vs Shrinkage for Benchmark Managers, Working paper, Institute for Empirical Research in Economics, Zurich, Switzerland

Woodruff, D L, Rocke, D M (1993) Heuristic Search Algorithms for the Minimum Volume Ellipsoid, *Journal of Computational and Graphical Statistics*, 2, 69–95

Woodruff, D L, Rocke, D M (1994) Computable Robot Estimation of Multivariate Location and Shape in High Dimension Using Compound Estimators, *Journal of American Statistical Association*, 89, 888–896

Zagorecki, A, Druzdzel, M (2006) Probabilitic Independnece of Causal Influences, Working paper, University of Pennsylvania

Zagorecki A, Voortman M, Druzdzel M J (2006) Decomposing Local Probability Distributions in Bayesian Networks for Improved Inference and Parameter Learning. In G Sutcliffe and R Goebel (eds), *Recent Advances in Artificial Intelligence: Proceedings of the Nineteenth International Florida Artificial Intelligence Research Society Conference (FLAIRS-2006)*, AAAI Press, Menlo Park, CA, pp. 860–865

Zellner, A, Chetty, V K (1965) Predcition and Decision Problems in Regression Models from the Bayesian Point of View, *Journal of the Americal Statisitcal Association*, 60, 608–616

Zhang, N L (2008) COMP538: Introduction to Bayesian Networks. Department of Computer Science and Engineering, Hong Kong University of Science and Technology

Zimmermann, H (2011) CAPM: Derivation and Interpretation, Finanzmarkttheorie, Universität Basel, 1–8

Zipf, G K (1932) *Selected Studies on the Principle of Relative Frequency in Language*, Harvard University Press, Cambridge, MA

Index